ReMix reading + composing culture

reading + composing culture

Catherine G. Latterell

PENN STATE ALTOONA

BEDFORD/ST. MARTIN'S

Boston ◆ New York

For Bedford/St. Martin's

Executive Editor: Leasa Burton
Developmental Editor: Ellen Thibault
Production Editor: Arthur B. Johnson
Senior Production Supervisor: Dennis Conroy
Marketing Manager: Karita France dos Santos
Editorial Assistant: Christina Gerogiannis
Production Assistants: Amy Derjue, Kristen Merrill, and Katherine Caruana
Copyeditor: Lisa Wehrle
Text Design: Anna Palchik
Cover Design: Donna Lee Dennison
Cover Art: (Front cover) Photographs of shoes by Pelle Cass; red shoe from the collection of Nina Footwear. (Back cover) Razors © Natasha V/Masterfile; skateboarder © RubberBall; scooter © Index Stock Imagery, Inc.
Composition: Pine Tree Composition, Inc.
Printing and Binding: R.R. Donnelley & Sons Company

President: Joan E. Feinberg
Editorial Director: Denise B. Wydra
Editor in Chief: Karen S. Henry
Director of Marketing: Karen Melton Soeltz
Director of Editing, Design, and Production: Marcia Cohen
Managing Editor: Elizabeth M. Schaaf

Library of Congress Control Number: 2005932489

Manufactured in the United States of America.

0   9   8   7   6
f   e   d   c   b

For information, write: Bedford/St. Martin's, 75 Arlington Street, Boston, MA 02116
(617-399-4000)

ISBN-10: 0–312–43018–3
ISBN-13: 978–0–312–43018–4

Acknowledgments

Diane Ackerman. "We Are All a Part of Nature." From *Parade Magazine*, 2004. Copyright © 2004 by Diane Ackerman. Reprinted by permission of William Morris Agency, LLC on behalf of the author.

Acknowledgments and copyrights are continued at the back of the book on pages 674–78, which constitute an extension of the copyright page. It is a violation of the law to reproduce these selections by any means whatsoever without the written permission of the copyright holder.

To the students who inspired this project.

To my friends and family for their wisdom and good humor.

And, to Stuart for making *my* everyday extraordinary.

About the Author

Catherine G. Latterell is associate professor of English at Penn State Altoona where she teaches first-year composition as well as a range of other rhetoric and writing courses. In addition to composition and cultural studies, her scholarly interests include postcritical pedagogy, literacy studies, and computers and composition. Her published essays consider the intersections of theory and practice in writing programs, writing centers, and composition classrooms. She also co-edited a collection of essays, *The Dissertation and the Discipline: Reinventing Composition Studies* (Boynton Cook, 2002), which examines dissertation writing as a complex site of identity formation for rhetoric and composition professionals.

Preface for Instructors

From Michigan to Texas to Pennsylvania, the students in my composition classes—whatever their differences—have expressed two overlapping attitudes about higher education. First, they have faith in the value of a college education, and second, while they expect school to help advance them in the world, they generally don't expect that process to speak to their everyday lives or to involve them actively. Years of schooling and standardized test-taking have taught them to view learning as memorizing models and regurgitating them in tests and papers. Every semester my students challenge and inspire me to make my composition classroom a dialogic space where they can take active roles in learning—a space where they can not only reflect critically on the cultural forces at work in their lives but also lay claim to their own roles in shaping that culture. That is the commitment grounding this textbook.

ReMix asks students to resee the everyday and consider how their own experiences connect them to larger cultural practices and networks of meaning. Each chapter introduces a familiar concept—identity, community, tradition, romance, entertainment, nature, technology—and poses questions through readings and assignments that help students discover intersections between the personal and social. In the Identity chapter, for example, an excerpt from Lucy Grealy's memoir about living with a facial disfigurement is followed by visuals of tattoos. Together, they challenge students to reexamine the body as a complex site of both personal and social identity. These readings, along with editorial apparatus surrounding them, prompt students to ask questions such as, When it comes to the body, who decides what is "normal"? How does body art represent both personal and cultural markers of identity? By examining such taken-for-granted aspects of everyday life, students can begin to uncover a range of cultural values and assumptions and reflect on how these values and assumptions shape their sense of themselves and the communities they belong to. What's more, this problem-posing approach positions students as having a stake in the work of the classroom, inviting them to ask their own questions and compose their own critical responses.

In *ReMix,* students are the primary investigators of culture. Gone are conventional writing assignments that too often emphasize conforming to an established critic's viewpoint, leaving little room for students' active examination of culture. The readings in *ReMix,* both textual and visual, act as starting points for students' own investigations rather than as sources for "the answers." And the assignments encourage students to observe the world around them more actively and to test the impact of commonly accepted cultural assumptions on everyday life. For instance, in the Nature chapter, students are asked to follow up on Eric Schlosser's essay about the flavor industry by conducting their own investigations of food labels. Another assignment asks them to trace the production of a "natural" food from the produce, dairy, or meat sections of their grocery store in order to get at questions such as, What makes a food natural? And to what extent are natural foods engineered or manufactured? In this way, the organization of chapters, the choice of readings, and the design of assignments work together to go beyond simply "reading" culture.

As participators in—and makers of—culture in their own right, students can take action as cultural critics who speak back to the forces that impact their lives. Even as they compose written and visual projects, they begin to reinterpret, recombine, and reinvent their cultural landscapes. This approach turns the composition classroom into a space where students learn to identify and negotiate among the forces—both personal and cultural—that influence how they live in and understand the world.

FEATURES

A Re-examination of the Familiar
. . . and a Problem-Posing Approach

For most students, everyday concepts—such as identity, community, tradition, romance, entertainment, nature, and technology—seem straightforward enough. But while the term "community" once referred to a neighborhood, does it now also apply to the blogosphere? What impact are bootlegging technologies having on concepts of authorship? How has the popularity of cosmetic surgery and other body enhancements changed attitudes about natural beauty? These are the kinds of questions or problems that *ReMix* poses to students.

ReMix's problem-posing approach brings an active, investigatory dynamic to the study of culture. Students are not treated as passive readers of culture; instead, each chapter challenges students to reexamine familiar, everyday objects and practices so that they can identify, analyze, and respond to how they are connected to larger cultural forces. This approach relies on raising questions and asking students to uncover and develop their own critical responses.

To help students in their investigation, each chapter begins by identifying and unpacking three commonly accepted cultural assumptions about the chapter's theme—for example, "Communities accept us for who we are"—and then threads questions about these assumptions throughout the chapter. This structure offers students a method for analysis—both for working with the wide-ranging readings and materials in the book, and for examining their own ideas about culture.

An Unusual Mix of Readings

As you page through the book's table of contents, you will find texts and images drawn from a variety of popular, professional, and academic sources. These readings include essays and commentaries by a range of writers, from cultural critics and canonical authors to humorists and entertainers. Throughout the book, you'll also find photo essays, comic strips, advertisements, and cultural artifacts from the past and present. Each chapter is anchored with solid academic writing—including David Brooks on urban life, Laura Kipnis on marriage, and Barry Lopez on American geographies—but also mixes in some surprises— such as Jon Stewart on the future and Samuel L. Jackson on race in Hollywood.

ReMix places a special value on the importance of humor as a powerful form of cultural critique. Each chapter contains examples of the comic's or humorist's ability to cut right to important and thought-provoking social problems—from the editors at the *Onion* on technological innovation to Firoozeh Dumas on the immigrant experience in America to Garrison Keillor on family holidays to Sarah Vowell on the meaning of pointless entertainment.

Innovative Assignments That Encourage Critical Thinking

ReMix is built on the concept that fresh thinking and writing springs from students' own active investigations and critiques of culture. In addition to the apparatus that supports each reading, the book offers a number of innovative assignments. The result is writing that is critical, persuasive, often visual, and always based in students' own experiences.

In order to encourage participatory, problem-posing practices, each chapter opens with an **Examining the Everyday** assignment designed to create revelatory moments for students about the intersections between personal identity and culture. They each introduce an ordinary object or practice and ask students to examine it in relation to themselves and to the larger culture. For example, in the Identity chapter, students examine the contents of their own wallets and are asked: What stories could someone piece together about you, based solely on the contents of your wallet?

Following each selection are **Writing about Cultural Practices** assignments that send students out into the world to investigate ideas and assumptions raised in the reading. For instance, in the Community chapter, students research and present the history of a local immigrant community. In the Tradition chapter, they propose a nontraditional memorial to commemorate a person or event, and in the Nature chapter, they analyze cultural assumptions about nature found in fairy tales and children's stories.

Among the book's most distinctive activities are those for **Mixing Words and Images**. Students create collages, photo essays, maps, posters, weblogs, and other documents that mix text and images to make an argument about culture. For example, students are asked to propose a new holiday for their campus or community (Tradition chapter), to design a roadside attraction (Entertainment chapter), and to annotate an everyday object (Technology chapter).

In each chapter, a boxed feature, **Sampling the Old and the New**, presents images of cultural artifacts, past and present. For example, in the Romance chapter, a nineteenth-century valentine is compared to an online dating profile; in the Entertainment chapter, the wholesome Partridge family is juxtaposed with today's most self-promoting, real-life musical family, the Osbournes. Critical questions help students compare cultural phenomena and assumptions, old and new.

Not Your Ordinary Textbook

Inspired by magazine and trade book design, *ReMix* features FOUND **artifacts** (what are the ingredients for McDonald's french fries?), **comic sidebars** (what do David Sedaris and P. Diddy have in common?), and photos that invite analysis, like images of the world's earliest zippers and a cell phone designed for Muslims.

Boldly designed to grab students' attention and fire their imaginations, *ReMix* folds in an appetizing sampling of cultural artifacts (tattoos, product shots, and roadside attractions,) and even a few curiosities, like a postcard featuring a jackalope (the fabled offspring of the jackrabbit and the antelope).

Thought-provoking FOUND documents, woven into the book's margins, add cultural texture to the readings. In the Entertainment chapter, Jennifer L. Pozner's analysis of the portrayal of women in reality TV programming is accompanied by a FOUND document announcing auditions for new MTV reality shows ("Want revenge on someone who has done you wrong?" "Are you the ultimate hook-up artist?").

Sidebars feature social commentary from popular comics. Wondering what you need to know to "make it" in California? George Carlin explains in the Community chapter. How does the holiday season look through the eyes of a Macy's Christmas elf? David Sedaris describes the scene in the Tradition chapter.

Ancillaries That Support Teaching and Learning

Resources for Teaching ReMix: Reading and Composing Culture

ISBN: 0–312–44476–1
Designed for new and experienced instructors alike, this manual supports every selection in the book, offering insightful chapter overviews and suggested responses for the questions in the book. An online version of the instructor's manual is available at bedfordstmartins.com/remix.

An Integrated Companion Site, bedfordstmartins.com/remix

Weblinks throughout the text direct students and instructors to helpful—and free—resources at the book's companion website.

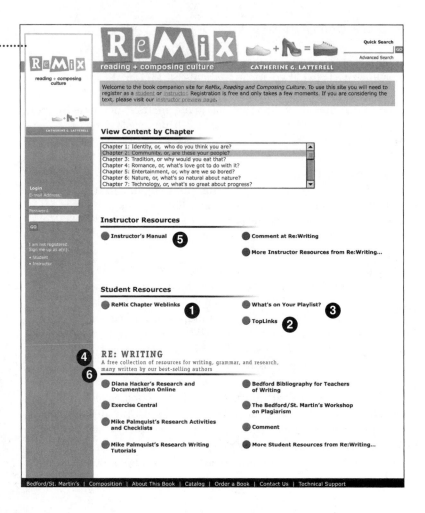

Student resources at the site include:

1 **Weblinks** for each *ReMix* chapter

2 **TopLinks,** a dynamic database of annotated links related to the topics in the book

3 **An online survey: What's on your playlist?** that asks students to share the music they love to write to

4 **Re:Writing,** a free collection of Bedford/St. Martin's most popular online materials for writing, grammar, and research—including Diana Hacker's *Research and*

Documentation Online, with expert and student-friendly advice for finding, evaluating, integrating, and documenting sources; and *Exercise Central,* the largest collection of editing exercises available online offering more than 8,000 items, with instant scoring and feedback

Instructor resources at the site include:

⑤ An online version of the **instructor's manual**

⑥ **Re:Writing**, a comprehensive resource for students and instructors (see above), providing an online gradebook, access to bibliographies and online journals, and much more

Resources for Teaching and Learning Visual Rhetoric, Research, and Argument: i-cite, ix, and i-claim

The following innovative resources are available to package with *ReMix.*

i-cite. Do your students need help working with sources? This new research and documentation CD-ROM brings research to life with animation and four interactive tutorials that explore fundamental concepts about working with sources. Students get concrete practice recognizing, evaluating, incorporating, and citing a wide range of real-life sources from across the disciplines. To order *ReMix* packaged free with i-cite, use ISBN 0–312–45621–2.

ix. Do your students need help working with visuals in their writing? This ground-breaking CD-ROM allows students to analyze and manipulate the elements of visuals, giving them a more thorough understanding of how visual rhetoric works. To order *ReMix* packaged free with ix, use ISBN 0–312–45319–1.

i-claim. Do your students need help writing persuasively? Supporting their arguments? With six tutorials on the fundamental qualities good arguments share, this student-friendly CD-ROM also provides an illustrated glossary that defines 50 key terms from argument theory and classical rhetoric and includes a visual index providing access to more than 70 multimedia arguments. To order *ReMix* packaged free with i-claim, use ISBN 0–312–45320–5.

Acknowledgments

I am deeply grateful to a number of people who supported this project. In the first place, I thank my favorite cultural critics, the students with whom I've been privileged to work. At Bedford/St. Martin's, I am especially grateful to Joan Feinberg for her support and encouragement. Leasa Burton, who invited this project, has been a partner from beginning to end. For her many creative and critical contributions to this project, I say: *Mahalo nui loa*. I thank Denise Wydra, Karen Henry, and Steve Scipione for their ideas early on and their continuing support. Additionally, I am most especially indebted to Anna Palchik for the design.

To the many reviewers who provided valuable feedback at many points, my thanks: Amy Braziller, Red Rocks Community College; Colin Charlton, Purdue University; Shannon Dobranski, Georgia Tech; Laura Gray-Rosendale, Northern Arizona University; Elizabeth Howard, Kent State University; Tobi Jacobi, Colorado State University; Deborah Kirkman, University of Kentucky; Alison Knoblauch, University of New Hampshire; Bob Lundergan, Fullerton College; Matthew Marx, University of Nebraska at Omaha; Kathleen Patterson, Santa Ana College; Mary Piering, Pikes Peak Community College; Jason Snart, College of DuPage; Bryan Stumpf, Highline Community College; William Thelin, University of Akron; Gary Thompson, Saginaw Valley State University; Barbara VanVoorden, University of Missouri at St. Louis; and Laura Scavuzzo Wheeler, Long Beach City College.

It's impossible to express fully my gratitude to those friends and colleagues whose insight and good humor helped guide me. I want to acknowledge Jack Selzer, Cheryl Glenn, and Marie Secor for their sage advice in the planning stages; no first-time author could have asked for better advisors. Additionally, the intellectual, professional, and personal debts I've accumulated over the years to Cindy Selfe, Marilyn Cooper, Johndan Johnson-Eilola, Dennis Lynch, and Anne Wysocki, who all variously advised and inspired this project, run deep. Their footprints are everywhere in these pages. My research assistant Jodie Nicotra listened and counseled, and her detailed comments on early drafts of the Identity, Community, and Romance chapters helped me establish *ReMix*'s unique approach. This project also benefited from the encouragement and help of Bridget Ruetenik, Dinty Moore, Ken Womack, and Rebecca Strzelec and would not have been possible without the support of my home institution, Penn State Altoona.

ReMix simply would not be what it is without the impressive talents and dedication of Ellen Thibault whose efforts exceed her title as developmental editor. Together, Ellen and I forged this book from our collective imagination. I'm also grateful to the editorial assistants—Christina Gerogiannis, Katherine Bouwkamp, Stefanie Wortman, and Maria Halovanic—whose research and detective skills I put to the test. I thank Elizabeth Schaaf for managing the production process and Arthur Johnson for his graceful touch and artist's eye as production editor (and music advisor). Jason Reblando and Sandy Schechter worked tirelessly to clear permissions. I am also grateful for the work of many others at Bedford/St. Martin's but most especially Karita dos Santos, Rachel Falk, Tom Macy, Donna Dennison, Kim Cevoli, Lisa Wehrle, and Ellen Kuhl.

The sonic mix that fed *ReMix*: Van Morrison, the Style Council, the O'Jays, Alicia Keys, Thievery Corporation, Jill Scott, the Kleptones, Angie Stone, the Flaming Lips, Gorillaz, Yo La Tengo, Modest Mouse, the Clash, Green Day, Mos Def, Jeff Buckley, Patty Griffin, Wilco, Sex Pistols, the Replacements, Gillian Welch, David Gray, Ben Harper, Ben Lee, Ben Folds, the Chemical Brothers, DJ DangerMouse, the White Stripes, Earth, Wind, & Fire, Elvis Costello, Kraftwerk, Beastie Boys, Beck, Ryan Adams, Johnny Cash, Nouvelle Vague, Nina Simone, U2, DJ Spooky, Marvin Gaye, Mike Doughty, Moby, and all the mash-up artists.

Finally, I thank my very large and very understanding family who inspire me daily to live fully. And to my soul mate, Stuart Selber, who claims I deserve better, I wish to say you may be right—but, why would a sun-soaked cat leave her patch of floor? This project is dedicated to you.

Brief Contents

Contents

1 Identity

. . . or, who do you think you are?   3

Visuals in the Mix

Birth certificate
[document]

Student identi-kit
[collage]

Mean Girls [poster]

Photobooth pictures
[20 photos]

Bono; Jim Morrison;
Roy Orbison; Elvis
Presley [4 photos]

2 Community
... or, are these your people?   85

Visuals in the Mix

"Running Is a
Community" [poster]

*Mister Rogers'
Neighborhood* [postcard]

"Greetings! from the
Amish country"
[postcard]

"Suburban Sprawl"
[photo]

Friendster homepage
[webscreen]

Sun City, Arizona
[6 photos]

3 Tradition
... or, why would you eat that? 173

4 Romance
. . . or, what's love got to do with it?   261

Visuals in the Mix

"Romantic-Comedy Behavior," *The Onion* [article]

Cupid [diagram]

5   Entertainment
. . . or, why are we so bored?   *359*

Visuals in the Mix

Snoop Dogg's playlist [webscreen]

Marilyn Manson [photo]

Britney Spears [photo]

Ellen DeGeneres [photo]

"Extreme Hair" [vintage cartoon]

Team America creators [photo]

Roadside attractions [6 photos, 1 sign, 2 pamphlets]

"25¢ Matinees: Gallery 10¢" [vintage photo]

Samuel L. Jackson [photo]

Ira Glass [photo]

Howard Stern [photo]

The Partridge Family [photo]; The Osbournes [photo]

6 Nature

... or, what's so natural about nature?   *463*

7 Technology
. . . or, what's so great about progress?   *575*

Visuals in the Mix

"The Hookless Fastener" [1926 ad]

Godzilla [poster]

"The Housewife of 2000," *Popular Mechanics,* 1950 [illustration]

Cell phone for Muslim users [photo]

Society for HandHeld Hushing messages [3 cards]

"Faster, Gentler," Kenmore washers [webscreen]

Pacemaker [x-ray]

ATM receipt [annotated document]

Misbehaving.net [blog]

"Googled" [cartoon]

Astronaut [vintage photo]

Steve Martin [photo]

"Duz Does Everything" [vintage ad]

Introduction for Students

Culture is remix. Knowledge is remix. Politics is remix. Everyone in the life of produc-ing and creating engages in this practice of remix.
  — Lawrence Lessig, "Who Owns Culture?" public lecture, April 7, 2005

We live in a cloud of data, the datacloud, a shifting and only slightly contingently structured information space. In that space, we work with information, rearranging, filtering, breaking down and combining. We are not looking for simplicity, but inter-esting juxtapositions and commentaries. This is the vague shape and erratic trajec-tory of the coming revolution.
  — Johndan Johnson-Eilola, *Datacloud*

What Is Remix?

Radio is filled with the sound of remixes. For example, for her single "Rich Girl," Gwen Stefani remixed a Broadway classic, "If I Were a Rich Man," from the musical *Fiddler on the Roof.* From country music to electronica, remixes are so popular that many artists offer remixes of their songs on their own albums. But remixes aren't found only in music. The marketing of products like Sprite Remixed and home remodeling shows like *Design Remix* on the HGTV cable network illustrate ways that the term has become a modern metaphor for describing revisions, rein-terpretations, new versions, and hybrids.

However, the concept of remix goes beyond these meanings. Lawrence Lessig, an expert on the legal aspects of remix culture, often illustrates the concept using the example of fairy tales. In the early 1800s, the Brothers Grimm collected traditional German folktales like *Hansel and Gretel, Cinderella*, and *Little Red Riding Hood*, and then created their own remixed versions of them. A century later, Walt Disney remixed them again, deem-phasizing the dark and dangerous tone of the Brothers Grimm's tales and making them sweet stories for children. Today, there are dozens of remixes of these tales that have become part of our popular imagination. For instance, when the Oscar-winning movie star Jamie Foxx describes the film *Ray* as a "Cinder-fella story," audiences don't need to be told what that means. The themes and storyline of *Cinderella* are so ingrained in our collec-tive imagination that we use them as references to talk about overcoming unfair odds or to describe what true love should be.

Scott Barbour/Getty Images

*These wristbands include representations of the Lance Armstrong Foundation, LIVE**STRONG**; Oxfam's campaign to end extreme poverty; and Nike's campaign to end racism in sports.*

Throughout this book, the concept of remix is a way of thinking and writing about culture. The objects, ideas, and values that define a culture are fluid, not fixed. They are constantly being reinterpreted, remixed, and applied in new ways. Consider the following example of one object or artifact of everyday American culture. In the summer of 2004, yellow LIVE**STRONG** rubber wristbands were introduced as a fundraiser for the Lance Armstrong Foundation, an advocacy group that funds cancer education and research. The message stamped on these wristbands reflects the personal motto of Lance Armstrong, a cyclist who, after surviving cancer, has won the Tour de France seven times. They became so popular that other nonprofit organizations, both large and small, designed their own versions; by the summer of 2005, brightly colored fashion-oriented wristbands appeared in department stores. These Armstrong-inspired bracelets represent examples of how objects, ideas, and messages often get revised and remixed.

Popular culture is full of messages that have been reinterpreted and reappropriated. Politicians use catchphrases from television commercials and films in their campaigns; suburban kids adopt and adapt urban fashions; advertisers use street slang to sell products. Indeed, culture is not just something hanging on the walls in a museum, nor is culture a static or unchanging story passed down from past generations. Rather, we live in a remix culture in which we are not only the readers and listeners but also the writers and designers—the makers—of culture.

Three guiding principles of *ReMix* are (1) that as a participator in culture, you are already equipped to investigate it; (2) that the things that are closest to us—that we most often take for granted—are most worthy of investigation; and (3) that behind these artifacts of everyday life are collective assumptions that shape and reveal a culture's thinking. These principles position you, the student, as the primary investigator. Throughout this book, your task will be to identify, critique, and respond to the cultural forces and assumptions that affect your everyday life.

As a critic of culture, you will learn to resee—or become more conscious of—how what is "ordinary" gives shape and meaning to day-to-day life. Much as a cultural anthropologist might, you will be studying or "reading" the social world around you. Reading a culture involves paying attention to everyday experiences, routines, and objects at home and work, in the classroom, at play, in online environments, and in other public places. To help you in this process, each chapter begins with an Examining the Everyday activity that focuses your attention on an ordinary object or concept. In the Identity chapter, for example, you will be asked to look closely at the contents of your wallet. What stories could someone piece together about you based on its contents? And in the Tradition chapter, the Examining the Everyday activity will ask you, When it comes to food, what makes a dish "traditional"?

This kind of investigation will help you see the world differently. To start, you will begin to recognize that everyday objects (like wallets and fairy tales) and popular messages (like "live strong") are cultural artifacts. That is, they do not exist in a vacuum. Even ordinary objects and messages like these were created for and are used within cultural settings or contexts, and their value or meaning is tied to these contexts. As you trace the histories and meanings of these artifacts, you'll find yourself noticing more details, becoming more conscious of the assumptions behind them, and marking their impact in your life and on the larger culture.

Investigating Cultural Assumptions

Looking closely at the artifacts of everyday life will reveal a range of cultural assumptions. What are "cultural assumptions"? Assumptions are the popular beliefs and attitudes that people tend to accept as commonsense truths about the world. For example:

Communities accept us for who we are.

True love conquers all.

Entertainment is just for fun.

We call these assumptions "cultural assumptions" because they exist beyond any one individual's personal experiences. Cultural assumptions are beliefs and attitudes that are shared by groups or communities of people.

Why are cultural assumptions important? Why do they matter? Because they shade how we interpret the world around us. As individuals, we do not encounter new experiences as blank slates. Rather, each of us brings his or her own set of assumptions to bear on interpreting and understanding a range of social contexts, artifacts, messages, and more. And these assumptions, while individually held, connect us to larger culturally shared value systems. Consider, for example, how advertisers rely on popular assumptions about beauty, sexuality, family life, and the concept of rugged individualism to attract consumers and sell goods and services. Advertising is a good example for illustrating why cultural assumptions matter because most people readily recognize that ads openly trade on these assumptions in order to sell their products. Advertising slogans such as "Because you're worth it" from L'Oreal and "On the road of life, there are passengers, and there are drivers" from Volkswagen present two such examples. While there are other possible messages behind these slogans, both of them rely on popular assumptions about rugged individualism to catch consumers' attention. Whether or not we agree with particular ads or the assumptions behind them, both are still powerfully present forces in the cultural landscape of everyday life. And neither can be avoided. After all, ads are everywhere: on television, on the radio, on the Internet, in email, on billboards, on cell phones—even on the brand-name clothes people wear. So too, the cultural assumptions that help us interpret the world around us are equally ever-present. This is why they deserve our attention.

Because the effects of culture are so often unconsciously absorbed, *ReMix* makes the everyday the object of your study and investigation. Living, as we do, in a fast-paced society in which we are bombarded continually with media images and messages—where advertising is everywhere, entertainment masquerades as news, and news comes in ever-smaller, quicker sound-bites—it becomes even more necessary that people make space for critically investigating the cultural landscape of everyday life. Throughout this book, the focus of your investigation can be summed up in three questions: What can ordinary artifacts and everyday practices reveal about our culturally shared values or assumptions? How do these assumptions enlighten or benefit us? And, conversely, what do they blind us to?

Reading and Thinking like a Cultural Critic: Four Steps

Cultural critics study everyday texts, images, and objects that may not normally receive your close attention. But what exactly does it mean to work like a cultural critic? The following four steps provide a process you can apply as you work through this book. As heuristics, these steps offer questions and guidelines for you to follow, rather than rigid directions. These steps introduce you to an exploratory approach to studying and writing about culture. To help model each of these steps, the following discussion focuses on an "anti-ad" created by Adbusters (see page xxxvi).

Step 1. Ask questions

The first step in working as a cultural critic is to ask questions. Simply put, as you investigate cultural practices or artifacts like texts or images, you need to pay attention to details that make them up. Ask yourself: Why did the writer or designer choose to use these details? How do the details work together? Questions cue us as to what deserves our attention. Questions prod us to notice patterns in imagery, wording, and human behavior. They also help us see what refuses to be easily categorized and what stands out or most surprises us.

Take a moment to examine the Adbusters "anti-ad" on page xxxvi. In addition to the questions in the annotations accompanying this image, you might ask a few of the following as you approach the image for the first time.

- Which icons, symbols, or text stands out the most as you study this image?
- What might be the significance of portraying Prozac as detergent for the brain?
- How does the image make use of familiar advertising iconography?
- What about the ad catches you by surprise? What might be surprising to other viewers?

Cultural Artifact: Adbusters "Anti-Ad"

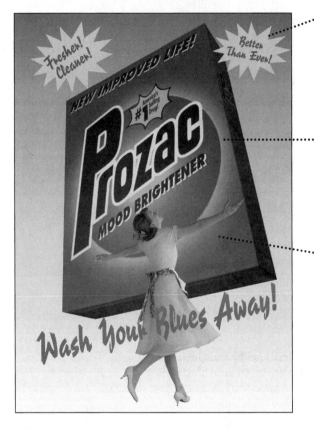

Note the use of familiar icons and ad copy such as #1, "Fresher! Cleaner!" and "Better Than Ever!" How are they being reinterpreted to "sell" an argument?

The Prozac box's classic sunburst design consciously replicates a popular laundry detergent brand. Why choose detergent?

Note how the box looms over the woman. By comparison, she is small, and her pose—arms outstretched, skirt twirling about her, and head tilted back—is joyous and worshipful. What message(s) does the spatial contrast between the woman and the box convey?

Adbusters is a media foundation that critiques consumer culture. It is particularly well known for its "culture jamming" campaigns. Culture jamming is a type of social activism that remixes media images in unexpected ways in order to persuade viewers to shift their perspectives about everyday culture. Notice how the details in this image work together to critique popular assumptions about "the blues."

Asking questions like these will help you develop your initial analysis; however, this is only a starting point. Asking questions and paying close attention to details are on-going methods of analysis. This kind of initial analysis usually leads to *more questions* rather than a set of answers about what something means. For instance, your first questions about the Adbusters image might lead to more-in-depth questions, such as:

- Where might the cultural impulses to be "better" or "improved" come from?
- Who is this anti-ad meant to appeal to?

- What message(s) does the woman's body language convey in this image? What else is important about this figure, for example, the details of her clothing?

These questions will lead you to the next step—identifying cultural assumptions—because they help you see how this image *as well as* your analysis of it are shaped by the social and cultural contexts surrounding it.

Step 2. Identify cultural assumptions

To identify cultural assumptions behind everyday artifacts, habits, or practices, you need to build on your original set of questions and initial analysis. In the case of the Adbusters image, ask yourself, How exactly did I arrive at my initial response to this image? Such questions will push your analysis further by asking you to identify some of the commonly accepted attitudes or beliefs that inform an image or piece of writing.

Whether you agree or disagree with the messages conveyed in the Adbusters anti-ad, it is important to recognize that, as a social commentary, this image asks readers to reflect on some not-uncommon attitudes or assumptions about a range of issues. For instance, when you first looked at the Adbusters ad, you probably immediately noticed the conscious effort made to make the Prozac box look like a popular brand of laundry detergent. Why might Adbusters have chosen to design its anti-ad as it did? What is it about Prozac and American culture that the ad lampoons? What popular attitudes or beliefs does it rely on (or even make fun of)? Here are some possibilities.

- The blues or depression is easy to remove, like removing stains in laundry.
- A "new improved life" can come from the medicine cabinet.
- Being "blue" or feeling down is unhealthy and should be treated with medicine.
- Women, especially housewives, are most in need of treatment for the blues.

No doubt you can uncover several other possible assumptions built into the Adbusters image. What is your take on these assumptions? What do the assumptions built into this anti-ad reveal about contemporary culture? For instance, you might ask: In the current cultural climate, have some personality traits been deemed undesirable? As a culture, have we become bent on cheerfulness or appearing happy? Can you think of examples from your personal experience or from popular culture—in films, on television, in popular music, and so on—in which one or more of these attitudes is expressed or supported? Which of these assumptions would you want to investigate further? As you can see, when you begin to uncover assumptions, things start to get interesting.

Working like a cultural critic in this way requires going beyond studying an artifact (or practice) to unlock "what it means." By asking what an artifact like this image reveals about modern culture, you are, in effect, using these artifacts to "read" and investigate culture.

Step 3. Test assumptions by considering context

Investigating the assumptions that you identify requires working like a cultural anthropologist, testing them against your own observations and experiences, against the observations and experiences of others, and also against other cultural material. Because cultural assumptions are collective and exist beyond any one individual, you cannot rely solely on your personal views to decide whether they are popular or have a broad cultural significance—you will need to go further. For instance, you may not agree with the assumption that the medicine cabinet is an acceptable source for getting a "new improved life." And yet, this assumption or attitude does exist in American culture; in order to investigate it, you will need to trace its broader impact or significance by considering context.

What does it mean to consider context? On one level, context means the *history or background* of an artifact (like an antidepressant) or a practice (like treating depression). In this sense, investigating the context surrounding antidepressants and how they are used requires tracing the circumstances that brought them into being. On another level, context means the *environment or social setting* surrounding an artifact or practice. In this sense, investigating the context of antidepressants and their use means paying attention to how their environment or social setting—including the attitudes of the period from which they emerged—shapes them. Finally, it must be noted that, when testing assumptions, there is rarely only one context or setting worth investigating. For instance, in order to test the assumptions surrounding the Adbusters image, you might investigate a range of related contexts. The following list offers questions that might lead you to learn more about the cultural contexts surrounding the Adbusters image.

- Questions about depression: When, and how, did doctors begin treating people for depression? What are the current treatments?

- Questions about antidepressants in general: How widespread is the use of antidepressants today? Why do people take them? Besides depression, are they prescribed for other medical conditions? How were the first antidepressants perceived by mainstream culture, and how do those views compare with attitudes of today?

- Questions about Prozac: Why did Adbusters target Prozac, among all antidepressants? What is it about the marketing or use of Prozac that might make it especially worthy of investigation and critique? What claims do the manufacturers of Prozac make in actual advertisements?

- Questions about what others have said about Prozac: Beyond Adbusters, how have others studied (and critiqued?) the uses of Prozac or other antidepressants?

These are just a few starting points for investigating the assumptions that give this anti-ad its impact. You could undoubtedly add to this list. To investigate or learn more, you may want to read articles from popular and academic journals that discuss antidepressants, search the Internet for commercial sites and advertisements (past and present) that portray depression or other antidepressant drugs, and interview psychopharmacologists who dispense Prozac and other antidepressants to discover their attitudes. An Eli Lilly ad ("Depression hurts. Prozac can help.") and an excerpt from the article "Personality by Prescription" provide two possible contexts for the Adbusters anti-ad.

In the Eli Lilly ad (p. xl), what messages, for example, are conveyed by the simple use of a black background and storm clouds contrasted with a sun in a clear and bright sky? Some possibilities include:

- Depression can be turned off, like a switch.

- Like changing from rainstorms to sunshine, this pill can effect change in people with depression.

- Depression causes pain to the sufferer and to others around him or her. Depression is a dark cloud that can and should be cleared away.

- Feeling "sunny" and bright is important and desirable.

Additionally, a close look at the excerpt from "Personality by Prescription" (p. xli)—an example of an article from a popular journal that appeared in the 1990s—might uncover some of the following claims:

- Antidepressants have made some positive impacts.

- Antidepressants are problematic and are prescribed irresponsibly.

Cultural Context 1: Concept for an Eli Lilly Advertisement for Prozac

Note the simple, two-sided design. What impact might this stark—almost child-like—design have for readers?

What Western and American assumptions about colors like black are being used to convey the image's broader message?

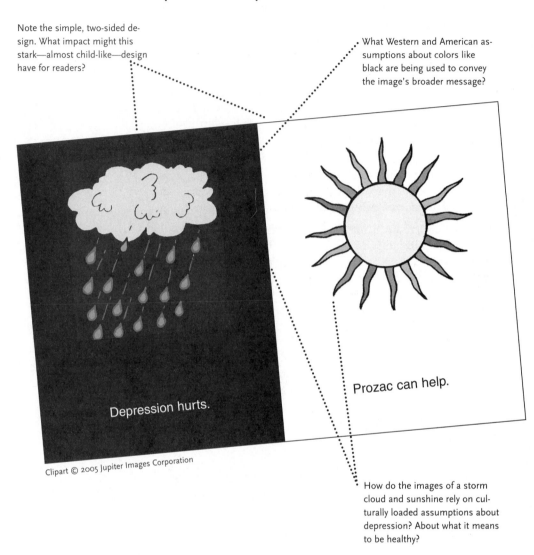

Clipart © 2005 Jupiter Images Corporation

How do the images of a storm cloud and sunshine rely on culturally loaded assumptions about depression? About what it means to be healthy?

A mock-up of the visuals in Eli Lilly's 1997 advertisement for Prozac. Eli Lilly was among the first drug companies to use direct-to-consumer advertising for a prescription drug when it launched a multimillion-dollar Prozac marketing campaign with a two-page ad that appeared in over 20 national magazines. Although the small print in the ad states that Prozac is not a "happy pill," it ends saying, "Chances are someone you know is feeling sunny again because of it." The main impact of the "Depression hurts. Prozac can help." ad was in its design. [Note: This is not a reprint of the original Eli Lilly ad; rather, it is a sketch of the ad's main elements.]

- People taking antidepressants are not properly monitored and may be risking their health.
- Many people who take Prozac are not really depressed.
- People seeking personality "makeovers" are turning to antidepressants.

As you can see with these brief examples, you begin to unlock the significance or meaning of cultural artifacts and practices by investigating what beliefs, attitudes, or assumptions connect them to the social and cultural contexts that surround them. In the case of these two artifacts, at least two possible cultural assumptions can be identified:

Americans are attracted to quick fixes.

Personality traits have become something people treat medically.

Cultural Context 2:
Excerpt from "Personality by Prescription"

This excerpt comes from an article that originally appeared in the magazine Flare *in 1994.*

In the few short years since it first hit the market, Prozac has become a celebrity of the pharmaceutical world. As many as 11 million people worldwide, including 500,000 Canadians, have received prescriptions for these small green-and-yellow capsules. Health professionals have hailed it as a highly effective treatment for clinical depression, causing less severe side effects than the earlier generation of antidepressants. Many now prescribe it for a wide range of conditions besides depression, including obsessive-compulsive disorder, eating disorders, premenstrual syndrome, substance abuse and seasonal affective disorder (SAD). Some, however, worry that Prozac is being dispensed far too casually to relatively healthy individuals. Many who prescribe it aren't even psychiatrists; often, in fact, they're general practitioners who may not be able to properly monitor the effects of the drug on their patients.

Among the most common users of Prozac today are people with the condition known as "dysthymia"—loosely defined as a form of chronic, low-grade depression. Many others who receive the drug may simply be trying to overcome relatively minor personality problems such as low self-esteem. Unlike those suffering from clinical depression, who can end up completely debilitated, these people are capable of going about their normal daily lives without grave distress. Critics would argue that they use Prozac to shed the ordinary burden of human angst—replacing it with the heightened sense of optimism, self-confidence, and clarity of thought that the drug can bring. Which raises a significant ethical question: should anyone really be using a drug like this simply for the purpose of giving oneself a kind of personality makeover?

Notice that the first paragraph begins by listing some positive impacts of antidepressants. How does the point of this paragraph shift by the end?

What claims or support does the writer use to suggest that many people who take Prozac are not really depressed?

The phrase "personality makeover" certainly gets readers' attention. Makeovers have long held positive associations for most people, but how does the writer use "personality makeover" here?

It is possible to name still other cultural assumptions that are shaping or influencing these two artifacts and how we read them or to word these in different ways, yet these are certainly present. Indeed, the Adbusters anti-ad takes aim at these assumptions.

Testing assumptions by considering the cultural contexts surrounding everyday artifacts, practices, and routines allows you to bring into focus how the everyday, which too-often recedes into the background, connects you to culturally shared value systems.

Step 4. Write critically (remix)

As important as investigating or "reading" culture is, it is not the last step. After all, you do not merely stand on the sidelines of life, watching it unfold in front of you. Indeed, we are all active participants in the world around us, and as a result, the ultimate responsibility—and pleasure—of a cultural critic is to speak back to the forces shaping everyday life. As you work with this book, you will encounter opportunities to respond critically in the Writing about Cultural Practices assignments that follow each reading and again in the Connecting to Culture assignments at the end of chapters. Becoming more critically conscious of how cultural assumptions influence how you think and act will inspire you to respond—whether it's to agree, critique, or reinterpret them. Such response is in itself a kind of remixing; it involves reinterpreting, recombining, and reinventing the cultural artifacts and assumptions that exist around you in order to create your own response to them. The next section of this introduction provides some guidelines for the kinds of writing you will undertake in these chapter assignments.

Before providing suggestions for writing critically, let's return a final time to the Adbusters image on page xxxvi. Throughout this introduction, you've analyzed the details in this image and the assumptions behind it, and imagined how you might investigate the cultural contexts surrounding it. However, this anti-ad is also an example of a remix or critical response to specific cultural assumptions about the medicalization of well-being. As a remix, it represents an example of the kinds of Mixing Words and Images projects you will be asked to create in these chapters. The authors of the Adbusters piece could have argued their point in other formats. However, they chose to play on viewers' knowledge of laundry detergent ads by using familiar designs, icons, and ad copy to "sell" their argument about antidepressants and Americans' tendency to seek quick fixes. This anti-ad satirizes the claim that a "new improved life" can come from a pill rather than from within ourselves. It raises questions such as, Should we treat personality "defects," like being blue, by taking a pill? Do we now believe we can buy happiness? In this way, these designers have turned around a set of taken-for-granted assumptions about mental health and consumerism and used them to make their own argument.

Composing with Words and Images

ReMix asks you to analyze and respond to American culture. Your goal will be to identify and investigate cultural assumptions and write about how those assumptions shape our lives. Each chapter focuses your investigative work by presenting cultural artifacts that explore one important everyday concept: identity, community, tradition, romance, entertainment, nature, or technology. The texts and images in these chapters provide the starting points for your cultural critique. Whether you are questioning how gender roles are defined in three dating guides in the Romance chapter, analyzing celebrity worship in popular media by examining celebrity profiles in the Entertainment chapter, or investigating the dark side of community life by studying pro-ana (or pro-anorexia) websites in the Community chapter, *you* will be the primary investigator. Following each reading and again at the end of every chapter, you will encounter these types of critical writing assignments: critical narrative essays, critical analysis essays, and position papers. Additionally, each chapter ends with a Mixing Words and Images assignment that asks you to use a combination of visual images and written text to compose a critical response or position about the chapter themes.

All of these assignments will challenge you to sharpen your own critical perspective toward the attitudes, values, and beliefs that shape modern American culture. This section overviews the three most common types of writing assignments you will encounter in this book and offers advice for getting started.

Critical Narrative Essays

People seem genetically hard-wired to use narratives or stories as a way of making sense of the world. Beyond the many uses of storytelling to entertain us (in music, in film, and on television) or to sell us something (in advertising), *narratives have a critical component*. They are a means of teaching, explaining, connecting, and problem solving. Throughout *ReMix*, you will be asked to write critical narratives, including essays, in which you may

- explore the concept of materialism and the cultural symbolism of objects by describing how a particular object represents members of a social group from your life. (See Community, assignments following "Our Sprawling, Supersize Utopia" by David Brooks, p. 137.)

- delve into the complex relationship people have with the natural world by reflecting on a place—a country road, vacation spot, neighborhood park, or other location—that is particularly important to you or your family. (See Nature, assignments following "The American Geographies" by Barry Lopez, p. 486.)

- examine the trade-offs associated with technological advancement by analyzing a personal tale of frustration with a technological device. (See Technology, assignments following "This Is How We Live" by Ellen DeGeneres, p. 588.)

Critical narrative assignments ask you to connect personal experiences or events to larger cultural contexts. After all, culture is not "out there" somewhere; culture is personal. And, as you noticed in the "Four Steps" (pp. xxxv–xliii), personal observation and experience play important roles as you examine the wide range of cultural forces present in your everyday life. Following are some keys to planning and drafting critical narratives.

- These essays are highly focused, often on a particular personal experience or event from your past. Your past is filled with a range of experiences and events. Deciding which events to describe in a critical narrative essay depends on what questions you are pursuing.

- These types of essays are very descriptive, so you will want to include concrete descriptive details in your writing that paint a vivid picture for readers.

- But critical narratives go beyond simply describing an experience or event. These assignments ask you to narrate a personal story or event in order to explore how it connects you to broader cultural values or assumptions. In this way, critical narrative essays are places for you to reflect on the larger implications or meanings of personal experiences or past events.

- *A Note on Using Visuals:* Consider adding visual elements that support the telling of your narrative by providing readers with who-what-where-when details in a visual format. Choose visuals carefully to ensure that they meaningfully add or extend your narrative. For example, if you were writing about a troublesome technological device (as described in the assignment above) you might include an image of the device, highlighting the most frustrating aspects of the object. To help readers understand the connections between your visuals and your writing, consider writing captions or annotations to the visuals.

Critical Analysis Essays

Generally speaking, "analysis" means breaking something down into its constituent parts in order to understand how these parts work together. For example, in a chemistry lab, you might perform analysis by isolating a particular chemical compound in order to understand its effects. Or, in a marketing class, you might perform analysis by studying how certain demographic or geographic characteristics of a consumer group might affect the overall success of a marketing campaign. However, the critical analysis essay goes beyond explaining how objects (like chemical compounds) or practices (like marketing campaigns) work. The purpose of a critical analysis is to evaluate the impact or significance of an object or practice.

Throughout *ReMix*, you will be asked to analyze a range of cultural artifacts and practices, often using the "Four Steps" outlined in this introduction. Whether you will be analyzing artifacts like tattoos or children's fairy tales or practices like attending a sporting event or celebrating a holiday, the goal of critical analysis is to identify and evaluate the cultural assumptions shaping these artifacts or practices. Often, these tasks will require you to examine the "real-world" contexts within which people use or encounter a particular artifact or practice. For instance, you could be asked to write a critical analysis essay in which you

- analyze how a food you consider to be typically "American" is represented in television or advertising images in order to answer the questions: What is this food's symbolic value? What does this food suggest about American culture? (See Identity, assignments following "The 'F Word'" by Firoozeh Dumas, p. 60.)

- examine the purpose of civic rituals and public spectacles by attending a community event and analyzing how its rituals connect this community to the past as well as reflect attitudes of the present. (See Tradition, end-of-chapter Connecting to Culture assignments, p. 258.)

- examine one or two popular films in order to identify and question the images Hollywood constructs of people of color. (See Entertainment, assignments following "In Character" by Samuel L. Jackson, p. 428.)

Critical analysis essays are not summaries of what others say or simple descriptions based on your observations. This type of writing positions you as a cultural critic conducting your own investigation, often testing the claims offered in the chapter readings. The "Four Steps" section of this introduction will help you plan and write critical analyses; although you'll want to review them again, here is a brief overview.

- Critical analysis assignments begin by asking you to investigate a specific cultural artifact or practice. Typically, the impetus for this writing project will be one of the chapter readings, so one starting point is to ask your own questions about the claims made or questions raised by the author(s). However, the other starting point is to investigate the artifact or practice itself, asking questions about it. (See also "Step 1," p. xxxv.)

- Next, this initial analysis will lead you to identify some of the cultural assumptions connected to this artifact or practice. Again, for many of these assignments, you may use another writer's claims about what values or assumptions are connected to an artifact or practice as a starting point, but this won't preclude you from identifying other cultural assumptions in the course of your own investigation. (See also "Step 2," p. xxxvii.)

- Often, critical analysis essays focus on the third step: testing assumptions by considering context. Considering context means tracing the history of a particular artifact or practice as well as studying the environment(s) or social settings surrounding them. (See also "Step 3," p. xxxviii.)

- Testing assumptions will lead you to write your own analysis. Indeed, as you draft your analysis, you will respond to, critique, or amend the claims made by the authors of readings. (See also "Step 4," p. xlii.)

- *A Note on Using Visuals:* Visual elements allow you to "show" readers your analysis rather than simply "telling" them. Well-chosen images are not merely illustrations— they can be very useful in supporting specific points you make in your essay. As you combine visuals (maps, photos, illustrations, and so on) with your text, be sure to align or cluster visuals and text in meaningful arrangements so that they support and extend your analysis.

Position Papers

Position papers fall under a type of writing called "argument." When you hear the word "argument," you might imagine two people involved in a shouting match or two people who represent opposing viewpoints squaring off on a television news show. But these kinds of arguments represent fights that seldom, if ever, lead to solving problems or coming to a better understanding about complex issues. For our purposes, an argument is defined as a way of connecting to others, not squaring off against them. In these chapters, you will encounter a range of positions on issues in which there are reasonable disagreements among people.

Your task as a cultural critic will be to undertake your own research and develop your own positions on the issues or questions raised throughout this book, and position paper assignments will provide opportunities for you to state your own position on these issues. In position papers, the focus is less on responding to others' claims—as is frequently the case with critical analysis essays—and more on branching out to conduct your own investigation and present your own claims. For instance, you could be asked to write a position paper in which you

- make your own case about the impact of reality television on contemporary American culture and how it has (or hasn't) affected popular assumptions about what's entertaining. (See Entertainment, end-of-chapter Connecting to Culture assignments, p. 460.)

- propose a project for developing more sustainable uses of natural resources at your school. (See Nature, assignments following "Trees for Democracy" by Wangari Maathai, p. 501.)

As you will discover, cultural analysis is rarely clear-cut, and position-taking requires negotiating among several reasonable viewpoints. Such a writing process will demand your full participation.

Additionally, each chapter ends with a special type of position paper assignment called Mixing Words and Images. Perhaps more than other assignments you will encounter in this book, these assignments prompt you to think of yourself not as an observer of culture, but as a *producer* of culture. Each of these assignments calls on you to create a document that combines text and images—collages, photo essays, posters, booklets, and so on—and to write about what you've created. For example, these assignments will ask you to

- create an identi-kit picture of one hyperconscious aspect of your identity in order to offer your "take" on how particular cultural markers construct your identity for others. (See Identity, p. 81.)

- design a local roadside attraction in order to articulate your position about the cultural values revealed in what does (and doesn't) entertain people. (See Entertainment, p. 459.)

- annotate a technological object (cell phone, etc.) to reveal the social, political, and ethical dimensions surrounding its use. (See Technology, p. 671.)

Each Mixing Words and Images assignment puts you in the lead as a cultural investigator. Your task is to go beyond responding critically to the ideas and claims of others by constructing and supporting your own positions.

There are a number of keys to composing both of these kinds of position papers. To begin, review the "Four Steps" (on pp. xxxv–xliii) and consider the following points.

- Position papers are strongest when they provide relevant and persuasive evidence to support your position or main claim. There are at least four types of supporting evidence you might include in your essay: examples, expert testimony, statistics, and published research. To choose the most effective kinds of supporting evidence, seek your instructor's guidance and consider these questions: How relevant is your supporting evidence to the claim or position you are arguing for? How reliable are your sources? How do you account for any gaps or contradictions among your supporting evidence? (See also "Adding Research to the Mix," p. xlix.)

- As you plan and draft your paper, consider what "enabling assumptions" are helping you connect your supporting evidence to your overall position or main claim. Enabling assumptions are commonsense truths (or reasons) that allow cultural critics to connect supporting evidence to their claims in order to persuade their readers. For example, the effectiveness of the Adbusters anti-ad depends on the enabling assumption that people prefer to buy solutions to their problems. This unstated claim (whatever you may think of it) lays the groundwork for Adbusters' larger argument about Prozac. This is how enabling assumptions work. They are the bridges in the architecture of an argument. Although usually unstated, enabling assumptions are the crucial means by which writers use reasoning to connect supporting evidence to their overall claims.

- Also as you draft, consider how you will respond to other possible positions. By their very nature, position-taking essays require you to contextualize your main claim or position within or among other possible positions on the same issue. Even as you work on defining a clear position on a particular issue, you will also be negotiating points of agreement and disagreement with other possible positions.

- *A Note on Using Visuals:* Consider using visual elements as evidence to help support the specific claims you make in your position paper. For example, you might compose some of your supporting evidence visually with photos, graphics, or tables, or even by presenting text in visually interesting ways such as writing interviews in transcript form. If you were writing about the Adbusters anti-ad, your supporting visuals might include a statistical chart on depression and antidepressant use, Eli Lilly's ad for Prozac, ads or promotional materials published by other pharmaceutical companies, or other visuals (for example, web screens or movie stills) that illustrate cultural assumptions about antidepressants. Additionally, if an assignment calls for creating a proposal, you will likely organize your paper using headings and other document design features that will provide visual contrast and clarity for readers.

Adding Research to the Mix

Because you will be actively investigating a range of everyday artifacts and practices, this final section provides an overview for planning and conducting your own research. In many cases throughout *ReMix*, you will conduct field research. There are three common methods of field research that you will encounter: observation, interviews, and surveys or questionnaires. In other cases, you will combine field research with library or Internet research. No matter which form of research you use in your investigation of culture, properly acknowledging the sources of your information (textual *and* visual) is important. The following advice will help you get started on planning and conducting four types of investigative research.

Observing Firsthand

Conducting observations allows you direct access to artifacts or practices in their social contexts. The following questions are designed to help you plan your observations. What questions are you hoping to answer by conducting observations? What do you hope to learn? What location will allow you to answer these questions? Do you need permission to conduct observations? How will you record your observations—with a notebook? Laptop? Camera?

Conducting Observations: When you arrive at your location, find a place to sit that offers a good view but won't put you in anybody's way. Take notes as a cultural anthropologist might. Describe the setting in detail. Draw a map of the layout of the space, noting the arrangement of furniture and important objects. How many people are present? Describe their appearances, actions, and behaviors. Finally, make note of your own reactions or responses to what you are observing.

Conducting Interviews

You may use interviews to collect oral histories, to speak to key participants of a specific event, or to gain the insights of an expert on a particular subject. The following questions will help you plan your interviews. What do you hope to accomplish with this interview? How does this interview relate to your overall investigation? Whom would you like to interview, and why? What factual information do you want to learn from this person? What kinds of questions will you ask to learn this person's opinions or viewpoints? Will the interview take place face-to-face or over email?

Conducting Interviews: Arrange a date and time to conduct the interview. Draft your questions ahead of time. If this is face-to-face, be prepared to take notes—whether by hand, on a laptop, or with a recorder. Record the date, time, and location in your notes. Ask your interviewees for permission to quote them and offer to send them a copy of your research project.

Developing Surveys and Questionnaires

Surveys or questionnaires are similar to interviews except that they allow you to gather responses from a group of people instead of from one or two individuals. Here are some planning questions: What information are you hoping to learn by using a survey or questionnaire? How will you choose the people you wish to survey? What are their profiles? What do you hope to learn from this group? How many people will you survey? What form will your survey or questionnaire take?

Using Surveys/Questionnaires: To write the most effective questions, seek help from your instructor and from the research section of a grammar handbook. Because summarizing and evaluating the responses you receive takes time and because people often dislike being asked to answer more than about 15 questions—especially online—draft your questions carefully and limit the overall number. Consider offering to make the results of your survey available to those who participate.

Using Library and Internet Resources

Library and Internet resources can provide added depth to your own investigation; however, because of the sheer amount of resources available in libraries and on the Internet, you'll need to give yourself plenty of time to find and evaluate sources that actually prove useful to your project. Here are some planning questions: What questions are you hoping to answer by using library or Internet resources? What databases, sections within (or online at) your library, or websites will provide the most relevant and credible information for your project? How up-to-date must these resources be for your project?

Conducting Library or Internet Research: Seek help from your instructor and research librarians to learn the best search methods for using library and Internet resources. Locating and evaluating a particular resource can be time-consuming work and can sometimes require that you retool or revise your original ideas. For these reasons, begin searching for materials as soon as possible in order to allow yourself adequate time to develop your writing fully. Keep track of the bibliographic information for your sources so that you will be able to cite them correctly both in the text of your writing and on a works cited page.

Evaluating and Documenting Sources

For advice on research and documentation, including advice for evaluating sources, go to bedfordstmartins.com/remix and select the online handbook *Diana Hacker's Research and Documentation.*

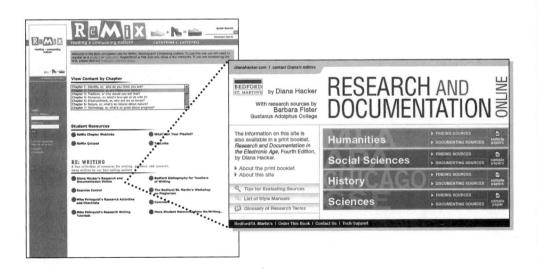

Why the Everyday Matters . . .
A Message from the Author

The goal of *ReMix* is to help you study American culture by identifying and investigating a range of cultural assumptions behind several themes of everyday life. This book's exploratory approach makes *you* the primary investigator of culture. Your task is not merely to reflect on the cultural forces influencing everyday life but also to respond critically to them. The readings and assignments provide starting points for the real work that is *yours*.

Please consider emailing me with your questions and your suggestions. I also hope you will consider sharing your work with me by sending me copies of the projects you produce (my email: clatterell@bedfordstmartins.com). I look forward to hearing from you.

– K.L.

ReMix reading + composing culture

or, who do you think you are?

1 Identity

Examining the Everyday
Identity and Wallets

On August 24, 2003, the *Corpus Christi Caller-Times* newspaper reported the following story. Recently, Casimiro Naranjo III opened his mail to discover that someone had sent him the wallet he lost 46 years earlier when he was a 19-year-old Marine stationed in Okinawa, Japan. Construction workers who were renovating a building on the U.S. base discovered his wallet in a ventilation duct and used the identification cards inside to send it back to him. Everything inside the frayed but still in-

tact brown leather wallet holds special meaning to Naranjo. Among other items, the wallet contained black and white photos of his sister (then 12) and brother (then 17), a pawn shop receipt for his high school class ring (never seen again), a ration card, a military ID card, and a small religious medal that his mother had given him before he left for boot camp. This small token was particularly meaningful to him now, Naranjo explained, because his mother had recently passed away. The only

ON THE WEB
For additional resources for this
assignment, go to Chapter 1,
bedfordstmartins.com/remix

item in the wallet that Naranjo did not remember was a small photo of a young woman. He could not recall who she was or why he had her picture. "How convenient for him to have forgotten," joked his wife.

What do the contents of a wallet reveal about a person's identity? Imagine how your life would be thrown into disorder if you lost your wallet. How would such a loss affect your ability to function normally—at least until you could replace the lost items? In many ways, our wallets and purses represent our identity to the world. For instance, like Naranjo, most of us carry several forms of identification in a wallet or purse: pool or gym memberships, driver's licenses, library cards, ATM cards, video store cards, club membership cards, school IDs, coffee club cards, discount cards, and credit cards. Even wallet-sized photos identify our families and friends.

This is the nature of identification, yet most people do not connect their identification to their sense of identity. After all, what do all of these pocket-sized pieces of plastic and paper really say about us? They identify us to others like bank tellers, librarians, and sales clerks so that we can make transactions. They help to label us to others. However, for Naranjo, each item in his recovered wallet helps construct a portrait of his 19-year-old self. Each item has a story to tell about his identity at that time.

What stories could someone piece together about you based solely on an examination of your wallet and its contents? For this initial assignment, write a one-page profile about yourself using only your wallet or purse and its contents to represent your life. Your profile should answer the following questions.

- Taken separately or together, how do the contents of your wallet construct an image of your identity?

- What assumptions might someone make about your personality, values, or identity based on what you carry in your wallet?

Add a final paragraph that answers this question:

- If all they had to go on is your wallet, what would people miss or be unable to know about you?

Questions about identity can be deeply philosophical, and the act of answering them can require us to think about our beliefs, values, and life goals. Asking "What makes us who we are?" is partly a question about individual beliefs and actions and partly a question about how the people, places, and things in our lives help make us who we are.

If identity provides us with the means of answering the question "Who am I?" it might appear to be a question about personality, but this is only part of the story. Identity is different from personality. Personality describes specific qualities individuals have, such as inherent shyness or sociability, but identity requires some active engagement and choice. For example, we choose to *identify with* a particular identity or group; we choose our friends and we choose how to dress every morning. These kinds of choices lead others to make conclusions about who we are. However, there are some things about ourselves that we cannot choose. For instance, we do not choose our ethnicity or where we were born.

The readings in this chapter explore how people negotiate this terrain between personal choice and larger cultural forces, both of which help shape our identities. They challenge you to reflect on the cultural attitudes and assumptions built into how we think about identity. But before you read these selections, first consider some popular assumptions about identity.

Assumption 1

Identity is what we're born with.

For many people, answering questions about identity begins by listing details that can be found on our birth certificates—name, sex, ethnicity, and family origins. People wishing to research their family histories locate the birth certificates of known family members because these documents provide essential information about the identities of ancestors. As the experts from the PBS television series *Ancestors* explain, birth certificates record a range of vital facts about identity.

They almost always include:	*They may also include:*
name of child	maiden name of mother
sex of child	ages of parents at time of birth
race of child	
date of birth	birthplaces of parents
place of birth	occupations of parents
names of parents	family address
	child's order in family
	name of attending physician or midwife
	exact time of birth
	physical description of child

The importance of birth certificates might suggest that identity is basically fixed and stable from the time of birth. Consider sex and ethnicity, two labels applied at birth that are at the heart of how many people think about identity. Both are generally understood as clear-cut categories from which identity is established. They can act as compass points that ground us as we go through life, giving us a sense of stability, of knowing who we are. But are they so clear cut? Andrew Sullivan, in his essay "The 'He' Hormone" (p. 25), examines how testosterone levels define and even change identities of men and women; and Firoozeh Dumas, in her essay "The 'F Word'" (p. 60), explores the connections between language, ethnic and national identities, and the fluidity of personal identity. Perhaps what birth certificates provide, along with family histories, are markers of identity.

However, the assumption that identity consists merely of what we are "born with" can underemphasize the influences or impact of larger social forces that also affect identity. Consider gender identity, for example. Although it is true in one sense that sex is established at birth, it is important to note that developmental psychologists have concluded that a person's understanding of what it means to be male or female develops through social interaction over time. During preschool years, children begin to discover what gender identity means. They carefully observe who's a boy, who's

CERTIFIED COPY OF BIRTH REGISTER									BRC

State of Minnesota, County of Benton

Recorded in Book __F__ Page __289__ Line __239__ Birth No. _____ Place of Birth (City or Township) St. George Twp.

FULL NAME OF CHILD	Sex	Single Twins Triplets	No. in Order of Birth	No. of Child of this Mother	Legiti-mate	DATE OF BIRTH			
						Month	Day	Year	Hour
Joseph James Latteral	M	D	--	7	yes	Nov.	2	1932	10:45P

FATHER

NAME	Fathers Date of Birth	Birthplace	OCCUPATION
James Latteral	34 yrs of age	Minn.	Farmer

MOTHER

FULL MAIDEN NAME	Mothers Date of Birth	Birthplace	OCCUPATION
Grace Barthelemy	33 yrs of age	Minn.	Housewife

ATTENDING PHYSICIAN, MIDWIFE, PARENT OR OTHER INFORMANT

NAME	ADDRESS	Date of Report
J.F. Schatz	----------------	11-4-32

REGISTRAR

NAME	ADDRESS	Date of Filing
Lester B. Lewis	Foley, MN	11-25-32

STATE OF MINNESOTA)
)ss.
County of __Benton__)

I, __Alice C. Engelmeyer__ County Recorder in and for said County and State, do hereby certify that the forgoing is a full and complete transcript of the entries appearing on record in the Register of Births now remaining in my said office relating to the Birth of said __Joseph James Latteral__ and the whole thereof.

WITNESS my hand and the seal of said office hereto affixed at Foley , Minnesota, this __13th__ day of __May__ A.D., 19 __98__ .

By *Alice C. Engelmeyer* County Recorder _____ Deputy

This birth certificate identifies Joseph James Latterell, whose last name is misspelled, as the "legitimate" seventh child of James Latterell ("Farmer") and Grace Barthelemy ("Housewife"). What assumptions are built into this document?

a girl, how they dress, what they do, and how they are treated. In fact, children's understanding and expectations about gender are largely influenced by what they see and experience. Gender identity is not fixed at birth; rather it is a process that evolves over time.

Similarly, the meaning of ethnic identity and nationality is something worked out within larger social and cultural settings. One illustration is the story of Barack Obama, U.S. senator for Illinois, as told in his memoir, *Dreams from My Father: A Story of Race and Inheritance* (1997). Born in 1961 to a white American mother and a black Kenyan father, Obama was raised in Hawaii by his mother and her parents. His father left the family to attend Harvard University and eventually returned to Kenya, where he worked as a government economist. His mother's second husband was Indonesian, and Obama spent several years of his childhood in Jakarta before returning to the United States to live with his grandparents and follow in his father's footsteps to Harvard, where he earned a law degree. Obama's story suggests that a person's sense of identity is not just the sum of the facts of his or her birth. In his opening remarks at the 2004 Democratic National Convention, Obama said that his parents gave him "an African name, Barack, or 'blessed,' believing that in a tolerant America your name is no barrier to success." He continued, "I stand here today, grateful for the diversity of my heritage, aware that my parents' dreams live on in my two precious daughters. I stand here knowing my story is part of the larger American story." Obama identifies himself in terms of his African heritage and his family, and then goes beyond the facts of his birth by identifying himself within the larger context of American culture.

In reality, the facts of our birth are merely starting points for understanding identity. Larger social and cultural forces also play important roles in shaping our sense of identity—including our ideas about gender and race. As Russell Thornton points out in "What the Census Doesn't Count" (p. 65), it is now widely acknowledged that formally fixed racial categories of identity are, in fact, not so stable. As America becomes increasingly multiethnic, Thornton asks, "Is race really something we can choose, or is it chosen for us?" His essay opens space for examining the dynamic tension between how we see ourselves and how others see us.

As the readings in this chapter illustrate, personal identity cannot be separated from the social contexts we live in. This chapter encourages you to examine how some taken-for-granted aspects of identity, such as gender, ethnicity, and even able-bodiedness, are shaped or influenced by larger cultural forces.

What questions can you ask to uncover the benefits and limitations of the assumption that identity is what we're born with?

- To what extent is our sense of identity predetermined by the facts of our birth?
- To what extent is our sense of identity a negotiation of social and cultural forces?
- In what ways does the concept that identity is what we're born with help us investigate identity? How does this concept of identity hinder or constrain us?

Assumption 2

Identity is shaped by culture.

From this perspective, cultural attitudes and assumptions largely define identity and allow us to label or identify others. People do not live in a vacuum, after all. Instead, we pick up the influences of our surroundings. The student identi-kit picture provided below (see also p. 81) helps illustrate this perspective. To create a self-portrait, this student combined cultural objects that are meaningful to his sense of identity. What this identi-kit picture demonstrates is the extent to which personal identity is connected to our social relationships (our friends, family, and community), to the material objects we choose, and to the various cultural contexts of our lives.

Courtesy of Tom Matisak

This identi-kit was created in response to an assignment that asked students to construct a hyperconscious image of one aspect of their identity. For this student, sports and fitness are important factors in how he sees himself. The baseball, glove, and football also illustrate his connection to communities of teammates. The barbells, weight bench, and superhero costume—a humorous touch—show that this student connects his identity to popular notions of masculinity and strength.

According to this viewpoint, identity is shaped through *acculturation*. Acculturation is the process by which we absorb the practices, attitudes, and beliefs of particular social groups. Culture connects us by providing a shared set of customs, values, ideas, and beliefs. In this chapter, you will examine how the *cultural markers of identity* that we choose—such as the types of cars we drive, the clothes we wear, and the music we listen to—can affect our sense of identity. These markers allow us to label ourselves and others as belonging to a particular social group or as having certain shared interests or values.

Consider, for example, what it means to label someone as "normal." What, after all, is normal? Is normal defined by how you look? How easy your name is to pronounce? Where you shop for clothes? Is it normal to have a pierced tongue and a couple of tattoos? Is normal desirable? Clearly, the label "normal" is loaded with a range of cultural assumptions. Attempting to define "normal" reveals that identity shifts with us as we move in different social settings or contexts. What is viewed as normal on a college campus may not be seen the same way in the workplace or in a social setting. By naming and describing some characteristics that we associate with the term "normal," we can uncover the common assumptions behind the ways that we group ourselves and others.

The concept of "normal" also helps illustrate that our daily lives are saturated with cultural messages about what is valued over what is not. In her essay "Masks," Lucy Grealy addresses the question, "What does it mean to live outside of the social norm?" Grealy, whose face was disfigured by cancer when she was a child, writes of her experience as an adolescent: "I wanted nothing to do with the world of love; I thought wanting love was a weakness to overcome. And besides, I thought to myself, the world of love wanted nothing to do with me." It may be nice to think that our culture accepts everybody for who they are, but, as Grealy's story reminds us, the social and cultural forces that help shape our sense of identity are not neutral. Instead, they operate like a powerful lens through which we make judgments about ourselves and others.

What questions can you ask to uncover the benefits and limitations of the assumption that identity is shaped by culture?

- What count as cultural markers of identity? How do they help others to identify who you are? How accurately do they convey who you are? How do you identify yourself through them?

- How do shared sets of customs, values, attitudes, and beliefs work together to form the cultural contexts of your life? How do they affect your everyday life?

- What are the consequences—both positive and negative—of recognizing that identity is a process of acculturation? In other words, how does your absorption of the culture around you shape who you are and how you live?

Assumption 3

Identity is shaped by personal choices.

Another common assumption about identity is that it is shaped by our personal choices or decisions. According to this viewpoint, to understand identity we must examine the choices we make in our daily lives—choices about our social relationships and anything else we care about. Rather than seeing all matters of identity as determined by larger cultural forces that are beyond our control, this viewpoint recognizes that individuals participate in and make decisions about their identities.

Certainly this assumption is based in truth. After all, we are not simply dupes of Madison Avenue's marketing machines, blindly accepting the trends, fashions, and cultural attitudes that they sell. Rather, we make choices. Consider, for example, the personal choice described by Kathy Wilson in "Dude Looks Like a Lady" (p. 21). For Wilson, her "barely there" hair is inextricably connected to her identity: "I am a black woman whose bald head makes me invisible to some, boyish to others, and beautiful to me." Her short hair boldly signifies to others not only her sense of self, but also her sense of what is beautiful, both of which seem to be at odds with the mostly white, mainstream cultural attitudes she finds herself up against. Wilson's essay supports the idea that personal decisions can be crucial to one's sense of identity, and that personal choices can outweigh the importance of cultural influences and the expectations of others.

"When I grow up, I want to . . ."

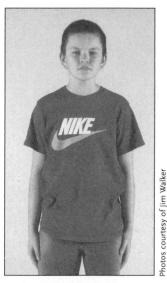

Photos courtesy of Jim Walker

be a lawyer.
Alexander Ugori, 10

be a counselor.
Serina K. Grousby, 10

be a United States Marine.
Shjawn Quinn, 11

When you were 10, what did you want to be when you grew up, and why? Fifth graders at the Peabody School in Cambridge, Massachusetts, were asked this question. When asked why he wants to be a lawyer, Alexander Ugori, 10, responded, "Because I like arguing. And my mom says I'm good at arguing." Shjawn Quinn, 11, said he is inspired by his dad, a former marine, and by what Shjawn believes the military has to offer: "I like that you can serve your country and you can get free houses . . . and I'd like to get to shoot a rifle and a two-barrel shotgun."

What's more, the identity that we convey to others changes according to different social contexts. That is, our individual identities are in constant flux. Recall this chapter's initial assignment, "Identity and Wallets," which includes a list of identification cards. The cards illustrate the idea that identity, unlike identification cards, is not fixed or permanent. While ID cards include a photo and a series of facts (where we live, height, weight, an identification number), the "facts" of our identities are not so fixed. They change and evolve. This is what it means to call identity an open text. ID cards show proof of the ever-evolving nature of identity. The photos in these cards never seem up-to-date, and many of us carry pictures of family and friends that are also out-of-date. Pull out one of these old pictures or IDs and look for details that reveal a now-discarded or changed aspect of your identity.

Another example that illustrates the idea that identity is an open text are the photos and responses of a group of fifth graders who were asked, "What do you want to be when you grow up?" (see the photos on p. 12). How would you have responded to this question when you were 10 years old? Do you still have the same life and career goals, or have they changed? After all, you are not exactly the same person you were when you were ten.

This third assumption suggests that despite the larger cultural contexts in which we live, we shape our identities through the choices we make. According to this view, identity is not fixed, but shifts over time and in different situations.

What questions can you ask to uncover the benefits and limitations of the assumption that identity is a personal choice?

- How does your sense of personal choice help you define your sense of identity?
- How does believing that everything is a matter of personal choice constrain or limit your ability to investigate identity? That is, what does it leave out?

Questioning These Assumptions

The readings and assignments throughout this chapter ask you to examine our cultural assumptions about identity. What makes us who we are? How is identity a negotiation between personal choice and larger cultural forces? On the following page is a menu of this chapter's readings, along with a few more questions to get you thinking about some of the issues this chapter explores.

IN THE MIX

Emily White, **High School's Secret Life**

Emily White is a freelance writer whose work has appeared in *Spin Magazine*, the *New York Times Book Review*, the *Village Voice*, and *L.A. Weekly*. This reading is an excerpt from the first chapter of her book, *Fast Girls: Teenage Tribes and the Myth of the Slut* (2002). In this book, White investigates the impact of social relationships on high school teens. In the following reading, she presents the view that where teens fit into the social pecking order of different groups or cliques in high school affects their sense of identity. To complete her study, White spent a year as an observer in a suburban Seattle, Washington, high school. In this excerpt, she describes this high school's peer groups in detail.

> ▶ Mapping Your Reading
>
> Throughout this reading, White attempts to describe the quality and importance of peer groups among teens in high school. How does White describe these groups, which she calls "tribes"? Underline passages in which she does so. Why does White choose the word "tribe"? What functions do these tribes serve? What is the impact of being in a tribe? Of being left out of a tribe?

Calhoun High is located on the outskirts of Seattle, Washington. A school with a population consisting of mostly working-class white kids, it's located near the freeway. From the Calhoun parking lot, you can hear the traffic, constant as breathing. In 1999, Seattle is a booming new-rich economy, and Calhoun has recently erected a new school building: shiny and modern, with wheelchair ramps and automatic doors, a computer lab with state-of-the-art equipment. The building is so new it seems to have no ghosts. Walls are made of materials such that the moment graffiti is written, it can be washed away.

I spend a series of mornings loitering in the Calhoun cafeteria, observing the tribes of this particular high school. The smell of heat-lamp food, the overhead fluorescent lights, the lunch ladies in their hair nets—all of it brings up my own past in the Washington High cafeteria, where I looked around furtively, trying to find my two friends. Sitting on the sidelines now, I can still feel the adolescent loneliness in my guts.

The cafeteria is high school's proving ground. It's one of the most unavoidable and important thresholds, the place where you find out if you have friends or if you don't. The cafeteria is the place where forms of human sacrifice occur, the merciless rituals of cruelty on which the kids thrive.

Although Calhoun's new building was supposed to be big enough for all of the kids, it seems that more and more of them keep coming out of the woodwork. Because of overcrowding, lunch happens in three shifts: ten-thirty, eleven-fifteen, and noon. Kids who've drawn first lunch often don't seem very hungry—they're wiping the sleep from their eyes and panicking about forgotten homework. They drink coffee, hunched over like harried executives. All the special ed kids are assigned to first lunch. During second lunch, the pace picks up, but the luckiest kids have third lunch, the "fun" lunch.

Each group of kids moves in and out quickly, and in the brief interludes of emptiness, custodians move through with giant brooms. Every time they migrate, the kids leave items behind: backpacks, notebooks, jackets, eyeglasses.

The cafeteria is high school's proving ground. The place where you find out if you have friends or if you don't.

If the cafeteria is the place where kids experience the most prolonged moments of relative freedom, it's also the place where they experience an unobstructed nearness. In these free moments, violence can erupt, and Calhoun has employed an armed cafeteria monitor, a nice guy in a golf shirt with a gun tucked discreetly into his belt.

As the school's ground zero, the cafeteria's tension derives from the way the kids are both in and out of school. It's a de-centered environment, a place where they can make independent choices: sit where they want to sit, whisper to their friends whom they are separated from in class.

Cafeteria life at Calhoun is a game of chance: devastation comes when a kid draws the wrong lunch. One girl tells me about how she used to feel like she had friends, but then all her friends were assigned to third lunch and she was stuck in second by herself. The second-lunch destiny changed her idea of herself as a girl with friends. Now she sees her crowd only after school, and there are many stories she never hears, many plans she is left out of. She tries not to be bitter when she talks to me, but she's clearly troubled that there's no way to cross over into the third-lunch realm now, a realm as distant as the Emerald City.

This girl hovers somewhere on the edge of a tribe; she's not a complete outcast but she isn't popular either. She's arty and bohemian, she possesses a complex prettiness that boys will probably notice later. Although she is clearly in a bind, stuck without her friends, her loneliness is relatively manageable and escapable. Other kids operate on a deeper level of loneliness: an obese girl valiantly ignores the snickers of the boys across the aisle from her as she eats during first lunch; a boy at second lunch has some strange muscle condition that causes him to swat the air, as if he's surrounded by insects.

No matter whether it's first, second, or third lunch, the popular kids always cluster around the same geographical area of the cafeteria: in the front, near the windows. The popular kids sit so close together sometimes they can barely move, smashed into one or two long tables, often remaining on the benches out of sheer will and masterful balance. This is what it means to be part of a crowd: to always have people jammed next to you on the cafeteria bench.

FOUND

from wikipedia.org

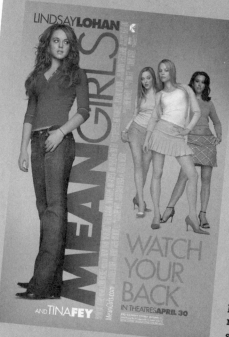

THE COMMON FEATURES OF CLIQUES

A clique is an exclusive social group formed between a few people who share a common interest. Cliques are informal social groups, while formal social groups are known as a society or organization. Cliques are most popularly known in high schools and colleges, and are formed usually by girls. Cliques can be complex and sophisticated, and can vary very much from one to another. However, there are common features which can be looked out for in cliques. Two of them are the Queen bee and the Outcast.

Queen bee

The Queen bee is said to be the member who has "emerged" as the leader of the clique. With the looks, charisma, and the power of manipulation, the queen bee reigns supreme over others and has substantial influence and power on the entire group. Usually envied and looked upon as a role model by her members, the queen bee's actions are closely imitated and followed, even though the actions of the queen bee may not be positive. Individuals that the queen bee dislikes can be targeted and become outcasts; clique members may emulate the queen bee by victimizing the new outcast in order to continue to "fit in."

Outcast

The Outcast is the one targeted by the clique members, facing potentially physical and psychological attacks. The outcast may be humiliated, set up, intimidated and even ostracized. There is little sympathy from witnesses to stand up and defend the outcast, for fear of falling out with the queen bee, being rejected and potentially being the next target. The effect of the damage on an outcast is usually psychological. Being shunned and left out, the outcast may face isolation which can result in depression and psychological trauma; these effects may exhibit later in life in conditions such as anti-social behavior. Outcasts may have difficulty seeking help from an adult, as psychological damage can be hard to prove.

**JANEANE
GAROFALO
. . on Her
Teenage Years**

"I spent the first 20 years of my life attending the school of hard knocks, otherwise known as upper-middle-class suburban New Jersey. I did not have my own phone, and the television in my room was colorless and devoid of cable. Need I even mention the conspicuously absent remote control?

I was also the only kid in the cul-de-sac who was forbidden to use her mother's credit cards. Adding insult to injury, my breasts came in far too pendulous and early. This unwelcome development simultaneously destroyed my posture and the ability to maintain eye contact with the boys in my class. On the heels of those unsightly mammary glands came 'The Curse'—bad skin and fatty tissue. The upside to this aesthetic assault: Your personality is required to pick up the slack and do damage control. The downside: everything else."

—From *Feel This Book*, 1999

At Calhoun, virtually all the popular kids are physically well proportioned; one girl I interview will later describe them as "the kind of kids who get their way because they have perfect hair, perfect teeth, et cetera." Their conformity is remarkable: in haircuts, necklaces, the way they slouch, the way they use their voices. They all imitate one another because the imitation speaks of their power. In this context, conformity is not a cop-out but a way of broadcasting the fact that you aren't a weirdo, that you are speaking in the signs of the chosen ones.

The popular kids at Calhoun dress overwhelmingly in the ubiquitous trendy brand Abercrombie & Fitch. They sport the logo on T-shirts, pants, bags, baseball hats. Calhoun is a school that emphasizes athletics, and Abercrombie & Fitch is a clothing line advertised by soccer-playing boys with perfect tanned bodies and sleek girl models with Grace Kelly class. The mystique of the brand is very East Coast, Kennedy clan, Martha's Vineyard, prep school. In other words, it has nothing to do with the working-class history of Calhoun, where most kids end up going to a local college and never grow up to drink Bloody Marys on Sundays in the Hamptons.

Between the extremes of the popular kids and the loners, there's a vast middle region. The tribes within this region are numerous. A group of overgrown Girl Scouts called the "natural helpers" are neither popular nor outcast; they are girls who are always busy doing charity work, committing an extreme number of good deeds. There are theater kids, who sit near the back of the cavernous space, immersed in the news of the next play, good at acting confident, always an edge of an act about them, always making entrances and exits. There are the computer geniuses, at Calhoun all of them unwashed, disheveled boys; they never seem to look in mirrors or out the window at the natural world. The screens of their computers take their eyes away from everything. A boy carefully pops open his laptop as he devours the cafeteria's fluorescent orange nachos, careful not to drip on his keyboard.

One of the most notable groups in the Calhoun cafeteria appears during third lunch: a gang of boys, huge but not athletic, class clowns, druggies, and rock and rollers. They possess a screaming, ballistic life drive and although they seem to differ in matters of style, their formidable restlessness—their energy of trouble—holds them together. From the moment they enter the cafeteria, the man with the gun hovers around them. Even when I am sitting on the opposite end of the room, I can hear them going wild. Even in my position as an invisible extra to the drama, trying to disappear into the background, I am a little afraid of them, of where their energy might settle, of what might happen if it settles in the wrong place.

This particular week has been designated Multicultural Week. It's a time when kids are encouraged to look up from their lunches and recognize the larger world. Posters advertise, *Celebrate Diversity!* The multiculturalism club is putting on an around-the-world potluck. One day a lone, red-faced girl dances a Scottish jig in the cafeteria, celebrating her heritage, jumping around diligently to a scratchy tape of bagpipes. The spectacle of the girl displaying herself before everyone silences the tribes and lowers the volume of each conversation. For a moment, as she begins her strange dance, there's only a flabbergasted stillness.

> In this context, conformity is a way of broadcasting that you aren't a weirdo.

Some days messengers travel from tribe to tribe, proving that webs can be formed even if they are fragile and fleeting. One day I watch the natural helpers moving from table to table, collecting money for the "penny wars." The idea is that if everyone contributes a penny, all the pennies will be given to the local homeless shelter. In the name of the penny wars, these girls reach out to the other kids in the cafeteria with a slightly condescending smile; with their jars held out, they cross the boundaries of the tribes. It is interesting to watch the rush of this moment, when boundaries are crossed and the lonely kids are being addressed, even if it's only a plea for pennies. The computer geeks look up at the natural helpers as if they are angels. The rowdy boys, the fat girl, the boy swatting the air, the arty girls, the pale orchestra kids, the boy with a T-shirt that says *Porn Star*—they all are amazed that these natural helpers suddenly stand in front of them. "Give a penny for the penny wars!" the helpers say, beaming like saints.

Analyzing the Text

1. White uses words like "tribes" to describe the nature of the social scene among teenagers at this high school. Why does she use these comparisons? And to what effect? Reexamine the essay and find three or four more examples where her language choice highlights a comparison of teens to tribes.

2. Based on her observations at Calhoun High, White suggests that our social relationships help shape our personal identities. Find evidence of this argument in the reading. Look for specific passages in which she supports her claim through her observations.

3. **Interrogating Assumptions.** Would White argue that the identities of the students she describes are shaped more by personal choices or by cultural factors beyond students' control? Or something else?

4. In the high school social scene that White describes, she names the "angels" (the girls she calls "natural helpers") and the "rowdy boys" (the boys who dress and act in wild fashion). How does her act of naming these two ends of the spectrum help her argue that teenage social life is tribal?

5. Do students on college campuses form their own social tribes or groups, or is White describing a situation unique to high schools? To answer this question, observe how students on your campus socialize or form groups. Choose a cafeteria, coffee shop, or eatery that is on or near campus and, on two different days, spend an hour or two at that location. Before beginning this task, your class should develop a list of questions or details that each of you will pay attention to during your observation time. To record your observations, bring a notebook or laptop. Afterwards, organize your notes and observations and write a critical description of the groups you observed. In your essay, follow White's example of naming the types of social groups you observed and of providing concrete details based on your observations to support your claim. (Note: Should you decide that you find no evidence of such groups, then your essay should focus on making and supporting *that* claim, again by providing concrete details based on your observations.) Following are some questions to consider as you write.

   - What is it that holds together each individual student group or "tribe"? White noticed that students who shared similar interests (sports or academics) or who shared a similar social standing (popular kids) formed the core tribes at Calhoun High. What do the details about the social groups you observe tell you about their shared interests or social standing?

   - In what ways do the members of the groups you observe conform to each other? Pay attention to how they interact with one another as well as to their manner of speaking, their style of dress and appearance, and the objects or possessions they carry.

   - Are there members within the groups who in some way choose not to conform? Are there members who appear to identify themselves individually? If so, what evidence supports your observations, and how do such individuals interact with other group members?

   - How does each individual "tribe" relate to other social groups present? In your opinion, is the tribe a healthy and constructive social group? Would you want to be a member of one of these groups? Why or why not?

Kathy Wilson, **Dude Looks Like a Lady**

Award-winning writer Kathy Wilson is a weekly columnist for *Cincinnati CityBeat*. She is a commentator on National Public Radio's *All Things Considered* and has written for *Newsday*. Wilson is also the author of *Your Negro Tour Guide* (2004), from which the following essay is reprinted. As Wilson illustrates in this essay, gender is the first thing we notice about other people. It is perhaps the most prominent marker of identity in our culture, after which follows ethnicity, age, and social status. For proof of gender's importance, consider the lengths to which some parents of newborns go to signal the sex of their child to others, dressing girl babies in pink and putting bows in their hair and dressing boy babies in blue outfits with words like "slugger" embroidered across them. In this humorous yet honest self-portrait, Wilson asks readers to reflect on what makes a woman a woman.

> ▶ **Mapping Your Reading**
>
> "This is about hair, breasts, and identity," claims Wilson at the beginning of her essay. What follows is a narrative about two encounters in which the author's short hair leads people to think she is a man and to question her femininity. Pay attention to the types of identifying labels Wilson uses both to describe herself and to describe the people with whom she interacts. Underline passages where these labels are mentioned. How important are outward markers of gender identity, like hair for women or muscles for men? What do ideas about race have to do with how others see us? To what extent do cultural expectations about gender or race shape your own sense of identity?

There oughta be a name for people like me.

You know, people straddling perception and reality because of interpretation. This is about hair, breasts, and identity.

Let me tell you what it's like walking around as a black woman with barely there hair and 40 Cs. I mostly keep my hair buzzed short not out of any confusion over identity, self-hatred, or penis envy, but because I'm lazy and it's cool looking.

For another reading on gender, see Sullivan, page 25.—EDs.

And I'm cute this way.

Yeah, I've got a pretty, round, brown face and dark eyes. Lest you think this is a singles ad, let me move on.

Let me tell you what it's like walking around as a black woman with barely there hair and 40 Cs.

I had hair—lots of it, in fact. But it's overrated and sometimes a security blanket. I never felt freer than when I first cut my hair off in, I think, 1989. Even when I had hair, I never could relate to those commercials with flaxen-haired white girls throwing their manes around.

My point is, people get so twisted over female presentation and what exactly *is* feminine that my bald head is cause for pause.

People actually stop.

Their physicality changes.

Some stare and, when I attempt eye contact, look away.

Then there's the case of the two white guys—one we'll call Ice Cream Man, the other we'll call Redneck Man.

I'm addicted to those butter cookies at Graeter's, a local ice cream shop pedaling hand-dipped homemade ice cream. One day I was waiting in line with a 50ish, silver-haired matron at the Graeter's in Hyde Park, a toney, posh neighborhood where white people either jog or drive luxury SUVs everywhere.

The clerk—Ice Cream Man—was on the telephone while servicing patrons at the counter.

The lady perused the cases. Hyde Park Man, phone tucked between his ear and shoulder, glanced up at me. "What can I get ya, sir?" he said.

I'm accustomed to but not immune to this kind of hurried assumption.

"Just these," I said, handing over the bag of cookies for purchase.

"Oh . . . uh . . . uh . . . oh, I mean, ma'am. I'm sorry, ma'am." He fell all over himself.

What's best in instances like these is one quick apology.

Either that, or we should all just act like it never happened, like a booger hanging from a friend's nose, an impolite public fart, or the open zipper.

The lady next to me was outraged.

"I cannot *believe* that!" she snorted, her voice hushed like we were at the opera.

"There's no way you could be mistaken for a man. You have such a pretty round face. Those cookies should be free."

I giggled.

I love well-meaning whites.

"Forget the round face," I said, "What about the 40 Cs? How could you *not* see these?"

Unimpressed, she kept her focus on the pastry selection.

Weeks later I was walking into Joseph-Beth, an independent bookstore in a shopping center in Norwood, a working-class white neighborhood bordering Hyde Park.

It was mid-afternoon, so hot I felt delirious.

I thought a skate through the bookstore would inspire me to write.

Plus, I was killing time before returning to the barbershop.

Al, my barber, has an uncanny ability to estimate haircuts to the minute so there's rarely a backlog of uncut heads clogging the waiting area.

You come back, it's your turn.

I couldn't wait to get into the bookstore.

Like an outtake from *Deliverance* appeared a shirtless, raggedy white man driving a raggedy white van.

Yes, it was Redneck Man.

As I walked through the parking lot, we made eye contact.

He slowed down. I slowed down.

Aaaw, I thought. *Bring it on.*

Just as I set foot on the sidewalk to the bookstore, he yelled from his window. "Take your boy-lookin' ass on somewhere!"

His timing was perfect. He'd waited 'til I'd reached a clearing so everyone within earshot could see the bald black bitch he'd caught in his sights.

I felt like I used to in the fourth grade when Robert, son of a Klansman, put pictures of black folks hanging from trees on my desk, trapping me and then smothering me.

I felt ambushed.

I was angry and confused.

How could he just yell out what he thought of me when I'd squelched my classification of him?

I wanted my say.

I turned and walked up the embankment, waiting for him to enter traffic and drive past on the main thoroughfare. Maybe he'd get caught at the light and I could have a word with him.

I remembered a long-ago image of my mother—tall, black, and proud with fists fitted on her waist like an Angela Davis action figure. Throughout my childhood, she was always somewhere setting someone straight. While it was thrilling to watch, it almost always left her drained.

And I caught myself about to disrespect the urban nobility of my mother's sass.

I was 'bout to be a straight nigga.

Then Redneck Man turned the other way. Lucky for both of us.

Laughing at the absurdity of Redneck Man's shout out to my presumed identity, I walked into the bookstore and cooled off. I couldn't shake it so easily, though. I seriously reconsidered cutting my hair again.

Then I stopped myself when I realized I almost let some fool have power over me.

I am a black woman whose bald head makes me invisible to some, boyish to others, and beautiful to me.

It makes me unfettered and unadorned.

Mostly it makes me free.

And without it my name is all woman.

Analyzing the Text

1. Wilson refers to herself as someone who straddles "perception and reality because of interpretation." To what extent is gender identity something that others interpret about us? How do outward markers of female identity like hair affect how you label others?

2. "My point is," Wilson writes, "people get so twisted over female presentation and what exactly *is* feminine that my bald head is cause for pause." What do the two episodes she relates reveal about the ways cultural assumptions shape or affect an individual's gender identity?

3. To what extent is Wilson also making a point about racial markers of identity? How do ideas about race and ethnicity lead people to make interpretations about who we are?

4. How does Wilson use outward cultural markers of identity to label others in her essay? How does her use of these markers impact her argument about the complex nature of identity?

Writing about Cultural Practices

5. Hair is just one example of an outward marker of gender identity in our culture. Other examples include facial hair, jewelry, perfume, and clothing. For this assignment, choose a socially acceptable marker of gender identity and write a descriptive analysis of it. Consider the following questions as you draft.

   - How is this item an outward, or cultural, marker of gender identity?
   - What cultural messages might this item convey? How does this item allow others to interpret someone's gender identity?
   - What makes this item commonly accepted as a marker for one gender? Can you think of situations in which this item would not be acceptable?
   - If you are writing about an item that could be worn by either men or women (like earrings or tattoos), what differentiates what is acceptable for men? Women? Transgendered people?

Andrew Sullivan, **The "He" Hormone**

Born in southern England, Andrew Sullivan studied modern history and modern languages at Oxford University. He went on to complete a master's degree in public administration and a PhD in political science from Harvard University. His essay, "The Politics of Homosexuality," was published in 1993 and hailed by *Nation* magazine as the most influential article of the decade on gay rights. Sullivan has been a contributing writer for the *New York Times Magazine,* a senior editor for the *New Republic,* and maintains a sometimes controversial weblog, andrewsullivan.com. In this essay, originally published in the *New York Times Magazine* in 2000, Sullivan argues that as the popularity of testosterone supplements increases and as researchers study the effects of the male hormone, we will better understand the power of our own biology to affect "every aspect of our society."

Mapping Your Reading

Sullivan contends that testosterone "helps explain . . . why inequalities between men and women remain so frustratingly resilient in public and private life." As you read, pay attention to the supporting evidence Sullivan uses to back up this claim. Use the margins to label or note each new supporting point. To what extent does male and female biology determine the structure of society? Is nature stronger than nurture? How much do testosterone levels have to do with who we are?

It has a slightly golden hue, suspended in an oily substance and injected in a needle about half as thick as a telephone wire. I have never been able to jab it suddenly in my hip muscle, as the doctor told me to. Instead, after swabbing a small patch of my rump down with rubbing alcohol, I push the needle in slowly until all three inches of it are submerged. Then I squeeze the liquid in carefully, as the muscle often spasms to absorb it. My skin sticks a little to the syringe as I pull it out, and then an odd mix of oil and blackish blood usually trickles down my hip.

I am so used to it now that the novelty has worn off. But every now and again the weirdness returns. The chemical I am putting in myself is synthetic testosterone: a substance that has become such a metaphor for manhood that it is

For another reading on gender, see Wilson, page 21.—EDS.

almost possible to forget that it has a physical reality. Twenty years ago, as it surged through my pubescent body, it deepened my voice, grew hair on my face and chest, strengthened my limbs, made me a man. So what, I wonder, is it doing to me now?

There are few things more challenging to the question of what the difference between men and women really is than to see the difference injected into your hip. Men and women differ biologically mainly because men produce 10 to 20 times as much testosterone as most women do, and this chemical, no one seriously disputes, profoundly affects physique, behavior, mood, and self-understanding. To be sure, because human beings are also deeply socialized, the impact of this difference is refracted through the prism of our own history and culture. But biology, it is all too easy to forget, is at the root of this process. As more people use testosterone medically, as more use testosterone-based steroids in sports and recreation and as more research explores the behavioral effects of this chemical, the clearer the power of that biology is. It affects every aspect of our society, from high divorce rates and adolescent male violence to the exploding cults of bodybuilding and professional wrestling. It helps explain, perhaps better than any other single factor, why inequalities between men and women remain so frustratingly resilient in public and private life. This summer, when an easy-to-apply testosterone gel hits the market, and when more people experience the power of this chemical in their own bodies, its social importance, once merely implicit, may get even harder to ignore.

My own encounter with testosterone came about for a simple medical reason. I am HIV-positive, and two years ago, after a period of extreme fatigue and weight loss, I had my testosterone levels checked. It turned out that my body was producing far less testosterone than it should have been at my age. No one quite knows why, but this is common among men with long-term HIV. The usual treatment is regular injection of artificial testosterone, which is when I experienced my first manhood supplement.

Men and women differ mainly because men produce 10 to 20 times as much testosterone as women do.

At that point I weighed around 165 pounds. I now weigh 185 pounds. My collar size went from a 15 to a 17 1/2 in a few months; my chest went from 40 to 44. My appetite in every sense of that word expanded beyond measure. Going from napping two hours a day, I now rarely sleep in the daytime and have enough energy for daily workouts and a hefty work schedule. I can squat more than 400 pounds. Depression, once a regular feature of my life, is now a distant memory. I feel better able to recover from life's curveballs, more persistent, more alive. These are the long-term effects. They are almost as striking as the short-term ones.

Because the testosterone is injected every two weeks, and it quickly leaves the bloodstream, I can actually feel its power on almost a daily basis. Within hours, and at most a day, I feel a deep surge of energy. It is less edgy than a double espresso, but just as powerful. My attention span shortens. In the two or three days after my shot, I find it harder to concentrate on writing and feel the need to exercise more. My wit is quicker, my mind faster, but my judgment is more impulsive. It is not unlike the kind of rush I get before talking in front of a large audience, or going on a first date, or getting on an airplane, but it suffuses me in a less abrupt and more consistent way. In a word, I feel braced. For what? It scarcely seems to matter.

And then after a few days, as the testosterone peaks and starts to decline, the feeling alters a little. I find myself less reserved than usual, and more garrulous. The same energy is there, but it seems less directed toward action than toward interaction, less toward pride than toward lust. The odd thing is that, however much experience I have with it, this lust peak still takes me unawares. It is not like feeling hungry, a feeling you recognize and satiate. It creeps up on you. It is only a few days later that I look back and realize that I spent hours of the recent past socializing in a bar or checking out every potential date who came vaguely over my horizon. You realize more acutely than before that lust is a chemical. It comes; it goes. It waxes; it wanes. You are not helpless in front of it, but you are certainly not fully in control.

Then there's anger. I have always tended to bury or redirect my rage. I once thought this an inescapable part of my personality. It turns out I was wrong. Late last year, mere hours after a T shot, my dog ran off the leash to forage for a chicken bone left in my local park. The more I chased her, the more she ran. By the time I retrieved her, the bone had been consumed, and I gave her a sharp tap on her rear end. "Don't smack your dog!" yelled a burly guy a few yards away. What I found myself yelling back at him is not printable in this magazine, but I have never used that language in public before, let alone bellow it at the top of my voice. He shouted back, and within seconds I was actually closer to hitting him. He backed down and slunk off. I strutted home, chest puffed up, contrite beagle dragged sheepishly behind me. It wasn't until half an hour later that I realized I had been a complete jerk and had nearly gotten into the first public brawl of my life. I vowed to inject my testosterone at night in the future.

That was an extreme example, but other, milder ones come to mind: losing my temper in a petty argument; innumerable traffic confrontations; even the occasional slightly too prickly column or e-mail flameout. No doubt my previous awareness of the mythology of testosterone had subtly primed me for these feelings of irritation and impatience. But when I place them in the larger context of my new testosterone-associated energy, and of what we know about what testosterone tends to do to people, then it seems plausible enough to ascribe some of this increased edginess and self-confidence to that biweekly encounter with a syringe full of manhood.

Testosterone, oddly enough, is a chemical closely related to cholesterol. It was first isolated by a Dutch scientist in 1935 from mice testicles and successfully synthesized by the German biologist Adolf Butenandt. Although testosterone is often thought of as the definition of maleness, both men and women produce it. Men produce it in their testicles; women produce it in their ovaries and adrenal glands. The male body converts some testosterone to estradiol, a female hormone, and the female body has receptors for testosterone, just as the male body does. That's why women who want to change their sex are injected with testosterone and develop male characteristics, like deeper voices, facial hair, and even baldness. The central biological difference between adult men and women, then, is not that men have testosterone and women don't. It's that men produce much, much more of it than women do. An average woman has 40 to 60 nanograms of testosterone in a deciliter of blood plasma. An average man has 300 to 1,000 nanograms per deciliter.

Testosterone's effects start early—really early. At conception, every embryo is female and unless hormonally altered will remain so. You need testosterone to turn a fetus with a Y chromosome into a real boy, to masculinize his brain and body. Men experience a flood of testosterone twice in their lives: in the womb about six weeks after conception and at puberty. The first fetal burst primes the brain and the body, endowing male fetuses with the instinctual knowledge of how to respond to later testosterone surges. The second, more familiar adolescent rush—squeaky voices, facial hair and all—completes the process. Without testosterone, humans would always revert to the default sex, which is female. The Book of Genesis is therefore exactly wrong. It isn't women who are made out of men. It is men who are made out of women. Testosterone, to stretch the metaphor, is Eve's rib.

The effect of testosterone is systemic. It engenders both the brain and the body. Apart from the obvious genital distinction, other differences between men's and women's bodies reflect this: body hair, the ratio of muscle to fat, upper-body strength, and so on. But testosterone leads to behavioral differences as well. Since it is unethical to experiment with human embryos by altering hormonal balances, much of the evidence for this idea is based on research conducted on animals. A Stanford research group, for example, as reported in Deborah Blum's book *Sex on the Brain,* injected newborn female rats with testosterone. Not only did the female rats develop penises from their clitorises, but they also appeared fully aware of how to use them, trying to have sex with other females with merry abandon. Male rats who had their testosterone blocked after birth, on the other hand, saw their penises wither or disappear entirely and presented themselves to the female rats in a passive, receptive way. Other scientists, theorizing that it was testosterone that enabled male zebra finches to sing, injected mute female finches with testosterone. Sure enough, the females sang. Species in which the female is typically more aggressive, like hyenas in female-run clans, show higher levels of testosterone among the females than among the males. Female sea snipes, which impregnate the males, and leave them to stay home and rear the young, have higher testosterone levels than their mates. Typical "male" behavior, in other words, corresponds to testosterone levels, whether exhibited by chromosomal males or females.

Does this apply to humans? The evidence certainly suggests that it does, though much of the "proof" is inferred from accidents. Pregnant women who were injected with progesterone (chemically similar to testosterone) in the 1950s to avoid miscarriage had daughters who later reported markedly tomboyish childhoods. Ditto girls born with a disorder that causes their adrenal glands to produce a hormone like testosterone rather than the more common cortisol. The moving story, chronicled in John Colapinto's book *As Nature Made Him,* of David

Reimer, who as an infant was surgically altered after a botched circumcision to become a girl, suggests how long-lasting the effect of fetal testosterone can be. Despite a ruthless attempt to socialize David as a girl, and to give him the correct hormonal treatment to develop as one, his behavioral and psychological makeup was still ineradicably male. Eventually, with the help of more testosterone, he became a full man again. Female-to-male transsexuals report a similar transformation when injected with testosterone. One, Susan/Drew Seidman, described her experience in the *Village Voice* last November. "My sex-drive went through the roof," Seidman recalled. "I felt like I had to have sex once a day or I would die. . . . I was into porn as a girl, but now I'm *really* into porn." For Seidman, becoming a man was not merely physical. Thanks to testosterone, it was also psychological. "I'm not sure I can tell you what makes a man a man," Seidman averred. "But I know it's not a penis."

The behavioral traits associated with testosterone are largely the cliché-ridden ones you might expect. The Big T correlates with energy, self-confidence, competitiveness, tenacity, strength, and sexual drive.

When you talk to men in testosterone therapy, several themes recur. "People talk about extremes," one man in his late 30s told me. "But that's not what testosterone does for me. It makes me think more clearly. It makes me think more positively. It's my Saint John's Wort." A man in his 20s said: "Usually, I cycle up the hill to my apartment in twelfth gear. In the days after my shot, I ride it easily in sixteenth." A 40-year-old executive who took testosterone for bodybuilding purposes told me: "I walk into a business meeting now and I just exude self-confidence. I know there are lots of other reasons for this, but my company has just exploded since my treatment. I'm on a roll. I feel capable of almost anything."

When you hear comments like these, it's no big surprise that strutting peacocks with their extravagant tails and bright colors are supercharged with testosterone and that mousy little male sparrows aren't. "It turned my life around," another man said. "I felt stronger—and not just in a physical sense. It was a deep sense of being strong, almost spiritually strong." Testosterone's antidepressive power is only marginally understood. It doesn't act in the precise way other antidepressants do, and it probably helps alleviate gloominess primarily by propelling people into greater activity and restlessness, giving them less time to think and reflect. (This may be one reason women tend to suffer more from depression than men.) Like other drugs, T can also lose potency if overused. Men who inject excessive amounts may see their own production collapse and experience shrinkage of their testicles and liver damage.

Individual effects obviously vary, and a person's internal makeup is affected by countless other factors—physical, psychological, and external. But in this complex human engine, testosterone is gasoline. It revs you up. A 1997 study took testosterone samples from 125 men and 128 women and selected the 12 with the lowest levels of testosterone and the 15 with the highest. They gave them beepers, asked them to keep diaries and paged them 20 times over a four-day period to check on their actions, feelings, thoughts, and whereabouts. The differences were striking. High-testosterone people "experienced more arousal and tension than those low in testosterone," according to the study. "They spent more time thinking, especially about concrete problems in the immediate present. They wanted to get things done and felt frustrated when they could not. They mentioned friends more than family or lovers."

Unlike Popeye's spinach, however, testosterone is also, in humans at least, a relatively subtle agent. It is not some kind of on-off switch by which men are constantly turned on and women off. For one thing, we all start out with different base-line levels. Some women may have remarkably high genetic T levels, some men remarkably low, although the male-female differential is so great that no single woman's T level can exceed any single man's, unless she, or he, has some kind of significant hormonal imbalance. For another, and this is where the social and political ramifications get complicated, testosterone is highly susceptible to environment. T levels can rise and fall depending on external circumstances—short term and long term. Testosterone is usually elevated in response to confrontational situations—a street fight, a marital spat, a presidential debate—or in highly charged sexual environments, like a strip bar or a pornographic Web site. It can also be raised permanently in continuously combative environments, like war, although it can also be suddenly lowered by stress.

Because testosterone levels can be measured in saliva as well as in blood, researchers like Alan Booth, Allan Mazur, Richard Udry, and particularly James M. Dabbs, whose book *Heroes, Rogues and Lovers* will be out this fall [2000], have complied quite a database on these variations. A certain amount of caution is advisable in interpreting the results of these studies. There is some doubt about the validity of onetime samples to gauge underlying testosterone levels. And most of the studies of the psychological effects of testosterone take place in culturally saturated environments, so that the difference between cause and effect is often extremely hard to disentangle. Nevertheless, the sheer number and scale of the studies, especially in the last decade or so, and the strong behavioral correlations with high testosterone, suggest some conclusions about the social importance of testosterone that are increasingly hard to gainsay.

Testosterone is clearly correlated in both men and women with psychological dominance, confident physicality, and high self-esteem. In most combative, competitive environments, especially physical ones, the person with the most T wins. Put any two men in a room together and the one with more testosterone will tend to dominate the interaction. Working women have higher levels of testosterone than women who stay at home, and the daughters of working women have higher levels of testosterone than the daughters of housewives. A 1996 study found that in lesbian couples in which one partner assumes the male, or "butch," role and another assumes the female, or "femme," role, the "butch" woman has higher levels of testosterone than the "femme" woman. In naval medical tests, midshipmen have been shown to have higher average levels of testosterone than plebes. Actors tend to have more testosterone than ministers, according to a 1990 study. Among 700 male prison inmates in a 1995 study, those with the highest T levels tended to be those most likely to be in trouble with the prison authorities and to engage

Working women have higher levels of testosterone than women who stay at home.

in unprovoked violence. This is true among women as well as among men, according to a 1997 study of 87 female inmates in a maximum security prison. Although high testosterone levels often correlate with dominance in interpersonal relationships, it does not guarantee more social power. Testosterone levels are higher among blue-collar workers, for example, than among white-collar workers, according to a study of more than 4,000 former military personnel conducted in 1992. A 1998 study found that trial lawyers—with their habituation to combat, conflict, and swagger—have higher levels of T than other lawyers.

The salient question, of course, is, How much of this difference in aggression and dominance is related to environment? Are trial lawyers naturally more testosteroned, and does that lead them into their profession? Or does the experience of the courtroom raise their levels? Do working women have naturally higher T levels, or does the prestige of work and power elevate their testosterone? Because of the limits of researching such a question, it is hard to tell beyond a reasonable doubt. But the social context clearly matters. It is even possible to tell who has won a tennis match not by watching the game, but by monitoring testosterone-filled saliva samples throughout. Testosterone levels rise for both players before the match. The winner of any single game sees his T production rise; the loser sees it fall. The ultimate winner experiences a postgame testosterone surge, while the loser sees a collapse. This is true even for people watching sports matches. A 1998 study found that fans backing the winning side in a college basketball game and a World Cup soccer match saw their testosterone levels rise; fans rooting for the losing teams in both games saw their own T levels fall. There is, it seems, such a thing as vicarious testosterone.

One theory to explain this sensitivity to environment is that testosterone was originally favored in human evolution to enable successful hunting and combat. It kicks in, like adrenaline, in anticipation of combat, mental or physical, and helps you prevail. But a testosterone crash can be a killer too. Toward the end of my two-week cycle, I can almost feel my spirits dragging. In the event of a just-lost battle, as Matt Ridley points out in his book *The Red Queen,* there's a good reason for this to occur. If you lose a contest with prey or a rival, it makes sense not to pick another fight immediately. So your body wisely prompts you to withdraw, filling your brain with depression and self-doubt. But if you have made a successful kill or defeated a treacherous enemy, your hormones goad you into further conquest. And people wonder why professional football players get into postgame sexual escapades and violence. Or why successful businessmen and politicians often push their sexual luck.

Similarly, testosterone levels may respond to more long-term stimuli. Studies have shown that inner-city youths, often exposed to danger in high-crime neighborhoods, may generate higher testosterone levels than unthreatened, secluded suburbanites. And so high T levels may not merely be responses to a violent environment; they may subsequently add to it in what becomes an increasingly violent, sexualized cycle. (It may be no accident that testosterone-soaked ghettos foster both high levels of crime and high levels of illegitimacy.) In the same way, declines in violence and crime may allow T levels to drop among young inner-city males, generating a virtuous trend of further reductions in crime and birth rates. This may help to explain why crime can decline precipitously, rather than drift down slowly, over time. Studies have also shown that men in long-term marriages see their testosterone levels progressively fall and their sex drives subsequently decline. It is as if their wives successfully tame them, reducing their sexual energy to a level where it is more unlikely to seek extramarital outlets. A 1993 study showed that single men tended to have higher levels of testosterone than married men and that men with high levels of testosterone turned out to be more likely to have had a failed marriage. Of course, if you start out with higher T levels, you may be more likely to fail at marriage, stay in the sexual marketplace, see your testosterone increase in response to this, and so on.

None of this means, as the scientists always caution, that testosterone is directly linked to romantic failure or violence. No study has found a simple correlation, for example, between testosterone levels and crime. But there may be a complex correlation. The male-prisoner study, for example, found no general above-normal testosterone levels among inmates. But murderers and armed robbers had higher testosterone levels than mere car thieves and burglars. Why is this not surprising? One of the most remarkable, but least commented on, social statistics available is the sex differential in crime. For decades, arrest rates have shown that an overwhelmingly disproportionate number of arrestees are male.

Murderers and armed robbers had higher testosterone levels than mere car thieves and burglars.

Although the sex differential has narrowed since the chivalrous 1930s, when the male-female arrest ratio was 12 to 1, it remains almost 4 to 1, a close echo of the testosterone differential between men and women. In violent crime, men make up an even bigger proportion. In 1998, 89 percent of murders in the United States, for example, were committed by men. Of course, there's a nature-nurture issue here as well, and the fact that the sex differential in crime has decreased over this century suggests that environment has played a part. Yet despite the enormous social changes of the last century, the differential is still 4 to 1, which suggests that underlying attributes may also have a great deal to do with it.

This, then, is what it comes down to: Testosterone is a facilitator of risk—physical, criminal, personal. Without the influence of testosterone, the cost of these risks might seem to far outweigh the benefits. But with testosterone charging through the brain, caution is thrown to the wind. The influence of testosterone may not always lead to raw physical confrontation. In men with many options it may influence the decision to invest money in a dubious enterprise, jump into an ill-advised sexual affair, or tell an egregiously big whopper. At the time, all these decisions may make some sort of testosteroned sense. The White House, anyone?

The effects of testosterone are not secret; neither is the fact that men have far more of it than women. But why? As we have seen, testosterone is not synonymous with gender; in some species, it is the female who has most of it. The relatively new science of evolutionary psychology offers perhaps the best explanation for why that's not the case in humans. For neo-Darwinians, the aggressive and sexual aspects of testosterone are related to the division of labor among hunter-gatherers in our ancient but formative evolutionary past. This division—men in general hunted, women in general gathered—favored differing levels of testosterone. Women need some testosterone—for self-defense, occasional risk-taking, strength—but not as much as men. Men use it to increase their potential to defeat rivals, respond to physical threats in strange environments, maximize their physical attractiveness, prompt them to spread their genes as widely as possible, and defend their home if necessary.

But the picture, as most good evolutionary psychologists point out, is more complex than this. Men who are excessively testosteroned are not that attractive to most women. Although they have the genes that turn women on—strong jaws and pronounced cheekbones, for example, are correlated with high testosterone—they can also be precisely the unstable, highly sexed creatures that child-bearing, stability-seeking women want to avoid. There are two ways, evolutionary psychologists hazard, that women have successfully squared this particular circle. One is to marry the sweet class nerd and have an affair with the college quarterback: that way you get the good genes, the good sex, and the stable home. The other is to find a man with variable T levels, who can be both stable and nurturing when you want him to be and yet become a muscle-bound, bristly gladiator when the need arises. The latter strategy, as Emma Bovary realized, is sadly more easily said than done.

So over millennia, men with high but variable levels of testosterone were the ones most favored by women and therefore most likely to produce offspring, and eventually us. Most men today are highly testosteroned, but not rigidly so. We don't have to live at all times with the T levels required to face down a woolly mammoth or bed half the village's young women. We can adjust so that our testosterone levels make us more suitable for co-parenting or for simply sticking around our mates when the sexual spark has dimmed. Indeed, one researcher, John Wingfield, has found a suggestive correlation in bird species between adjustable testosterone levels and males that have an active role to play in rearing their young. Male birds with consistently high testosterone levels tend to be worse fathers; males with variable levels are better dads. So there's hope for the new man yet.

From the point of view of men, after all, constantly high testosterone is a real problem, as any 15-year-old boy trying to concentrate on his homework will tell you. I missed one deadline on this article because it came three days after a testosterone shot and I couldn't bring myself to sit still long enough. And from a purely genetic point of view, men don't merely have an interest in impregnating as many women as possible; they also have an interest in seeing that their offspring are brought up successfully and their genes perpetuated. So for the male, the conflict between sex and love is resolved, as it is for the female, by a compromise between the short-term thrill of promiscuity and the long-term rewards of nurturing children. Just as the female does, he optimizes his genetic outcome by a stable marriage and occasional extramarital affairs. He is just more likely to have these affairs than a woman. Testosterone is both cause and effect of this difference.

And the difference is a real one. This is so obvious a point that we some-times miss it. But without that difference, it would be hard to justify separate sports leagues for men and women, just as it would be hard not to suspect judi-cial bias behind the fact that of the 98 people executed last year in the United States, 100 percent came from a group that composes a little less than 50 percent of the population; that is, men. When the discrepancy is racial, we wring our hands. That it is sexual raises no red flags. Similarly, it is not surprising that 55 percent of everyone arrested in 1998 was under the age of 25—the years when male testosterone levels are at their natural peak.

It is also controversial yet undeniable that elevating testosterone levels can be extremely beneficial for physical and mental performance. It depends, of course, on what you're performing in. If your job is to whack home runs, capture criminals, or play the market, then testosterone is a huge advantage. If you're a professional conciliator, office manager, or teacher, it is probably a handicap. Major League Baseball was embarrassed that Mark McGwire's 1998 season home-run record might have been influenced by his use of androstenedione, a legal supplement that helps increase the body's own production of testosterone. But its own study into andro's effects concluded that regular use of it clearly raises T levels and so improves muscle mass and physical strength, without se-rious side effects. Testosterone also accelerates the rate of recovery from physical injury. Does this help make sense of McGwire's achievement? More testosterone obviously didn't give him the skill to hit 70 home runs, but it almost certainly contributed to the physical and mental endurance that helped him do so.

Since most men have at least 10 times as much T as most women, it therefore makes sense not to have coed baseball leagues. Equally, it makes sense that women will be underrepresented in a high-testosterone environment like military combat or construction. When the skills required are more cerebral or more endurance-related, the male-female gap may shrink, or even reverse itself. But otherwise, gen-der inequality in these fields is primarily not a function of sexism, merely of com-mon sense. This is a highly controversial position, but it really shouldn't be. Even more unsettling is the racial gap in testosterone. Several solid studies, published in publications like *Journal of the National Cancer Institute,* show that black men have on average 3 to 19 percent more testosterone than white men. This is some-thing to consider when we're told that black men dominate certain sports because of white racism or economic class rather than black skill. This reality may, of course, feed stereotypes about blacks being physical but not intellectual. But there's no evidence of any trade-off between the two. To say that someone is phys-ically gifted is to say nothing about his mental abilities, as even NFL die-hards have come to realize. Indeed, as Jon Entine points out in his new book, *Taboo,* even the position of quarterback, which requires a deft mix of mental and physical strength and was once predominantly white, has slowly become less white as talent has been rewarded. The percentage of blacks among NFL quarterbacks is now twice the percentage of blacks in the population as a whole.

But fears of natural difference still haunt the debate about gender equality. Many feminists have made tenacious arguments about the lack of any substantive physical or mental differences between men and women as if the political equality of the sexes depended on it. But to rest the equality of women on the physical and psychological equivalence of the sexes is to rest it on sand. In the end, testosterone bites. This year, for example, Toys "R" Us announced it was planning to redesign its toy stores to group products most likely to be bought by the same types of consumers: in marketing jargon, "logical adjacencies." The results? Almost total gender separation. "Girl's World" would feature Easy-Bake Ovens and Barbies; "Boy's World," trucks and action figures. Though Toys "R" Us denied that there was any agenda behind this—its market research showed that gender differences start as young as 2 years old—such a public outcry ensued that the store canceled its plans. Meanwhile, Fox Family Channel is about to introduce two new, separate cable channels for boys and girls, boyzChannel and girlzChannel, to attract advertisers and consumers more efficiently. Fox executives told the *Wall Street Journal* that their move is simply a reflection of what Nielsen-related research tells them about the viewing habits of boys and girls: that, "in general terms, girls are more interested in entertainment that is relationship-oriented," while boys are "more action-oriented." T anyone? After more than two decades of relentless legal, cultural, and ideological attempts to negate sexual difference between boys and girls, the market has turned around and shown that very little, after all, has changed.

Advocates of a purely environmental origin for this difference between the sexes counter that gender socialization begins very early and is picked up by subtle inferences from parental interaction and peer pressure, before being reinforced by the collective culture at large. Most parents observing toddlers choosing their own toys and play patterns can best judge for themselves how true this is. But as Matt Ridley has pointed out, there is also physiological evidence of very early mental differences between the sexes, most of it to the advantage of girls. Ninety-five percent of all hyperactive kids are boys; four times as many boys are dyslexic and learning-disabled as girls. There is a greater distinction between the right and left brain among boys than girls, and worse linguistic skills. In general, boys are better at spatial and abstract tasks, girls at communication. These are generalizations, of course. There are many, many boys who are great linguists and model students, and vice versa. Some boys even prefer, when left to their own devices, to play with dolls as well as trucks. But we are talking of generalities here, and the influence of womb-given testosterone on those generalities is undeniable.

Some of that influence is a handicap. We are so used to associating testosterone with strength, masculinity, and patriarchal violence that it is easy to ignore that it also makes men weaker in some respects than women. It doesn't correlate with economic power: in fact, as we have seen, blue-collar workers have more of it than white-collar workers. It gets men into trouble. For reasons no one seems to understand, testosterone may also be an immune suppressant. High levels of it can correspond, as recent studies have shown, not only with baldness but also with heart disease and a greater susceptibility to infectious diseases. Higher levels of prostate cancer among blacks, some researchers believe, may well be related to blacks' higher testosterone levels. The aggression it can foster and the risks it encourages lead men into situations that often wound or kill them. And higher levels of testosterone-driven promiscuity make men more prone to sexually transmitted diseases. This is one reason that men live shorter lives on average than women. There is something, in other words, tragic about testosterone. It can lead to a certain kind of male glory; it may lead to valor or boldness or impulsive romanticism. But it also presages a uniquely male kind of doom. The cockerel with the brightest comb is often the most attractive and the most testosteroned, but it is also the most vulnerable to parasites. It is as if it has sacrificed quantity of life for intensity of experience, and this trade-off is a deeply male one.

So it is perhaps unsurprising that those professions in which this trade-off is most pronounced—the military, contact sports, hazardous exploration, venture capitalism, politics, gambling—tend to be disproportionately male. Politics is undoubtedly the most controversial because it is such a critical arena for the dispersal of power. But consider for a moment how politics is conducted in our society. It is saturated with combat, ego, conflict, and risk. An entire career can be lost in a single gaffe or an unexpected shift in the national mood. This ego-driven roulette is almost as highly biased toward the testosteroned as wrestling. So it makes some sense that after almost a century of electorates made up by as many women as men, the number of female politicians remains pathetically small in most Western democracies. This may not be endemic to politics; it may have more to do with the way our culture constructs politics. And it is not to say that women are not good at government. Those qualities associated with low testosterone—patience, risk aversion, empathy—can all lead to excellent governance. They are just lousy qualities in the crapshoot of electoral politics.

If you care about sexual equality, this is obviously a challenge, but it need not be as depressing as it sounds. The sports world offers one way out. Men and women do not compete directly against one another; they have separate tournaments and leagues. Their different styles of physical excellence can be appreciated in different ways. At some basic level, of course, men will always be better than women in many of these contests. Men run faster and throw harder. Women could compensate for this by injecting testosterone, but if they took enough to be truly competitive, they would become men, which would somewhat defeat the purpose.

The harder cases are in those areas in which physical strength is important but not always crucial, like military combat or manual labor. And here the compromise is more likely to be access but inequality in numbers. Finance? Business? Here, where the testosterone-driven differences may well be more subtly psychological, and where men may dominate by discrimination rather than merit, is the trickiest arena. Testosterone-induced impatience may lead to poor decision-making, but low-testosterone risk aversion may lead to an inability to seize business opportunities. Perhaps it is safest to say that unequal numbers of men and women in these spheres is not prima facie evidence of sexism. We should do everything we can to ensure equal access, but it is foolish to insist that numerical inequality is always a function of bias rather than biology. This doesn't mean we shouldn't worry about individual cases of injustice; just that we shouldn't be shocked if gender inequality endures. And we should recognize that affirmative action for women (and men) in all arenas is an inherently utopian project.

Then there is the medical option. A modest solution might be to give more women access to testosterone to improve their sex drives, aggression, and risk affinity and to help redress their disadvantages in those areas as compared with men. This is already done for severely depressed women, or women with hormonal imbalances, or those lacking an adequate sex drive, especially after menopause. Why not for women who simply want to rev up their will to power? Its use needs to be carefully monitored because it can also lead to side effects, like greater susceptibility to cancer, but that's what doctors are there for. And since older men also suffer a slow drop-off in T levels, there's no reason they should be cold-shouldered either. If the natural disadvantages of gender should be countered, why not the natural disadvantages of age? In some ways, this is already happening. Among the most common drugs now available through Internet doctors and pharmacies, along with Viagra and Prozac, is testosterone. This summer [2000], with the arrival of AndroGel, the testosterone gel created as a medical treatment for those four to five million men who suffer from low levels of testosterone, recreational demand may soar.

Or try this thought experiment: What if parents committed to gender equity opted to counteract the effect of testosterone on boys in the womb by complementing it with injections of artificial female hormones? That way, structural gender difference could be eradicated from the beginning. Such a policy would lead to "men and women with normal bodies but identical feminine brains," Matt Ridley posits. "War, rape, boxing, car racing, pornography, and hamburgers and beer would soon be distant memories. A feminist paradise would have arrived." Today's conservative cultural critics might also be enraptured. Promiscuity would doubtless decline, fatherhood improve, crime drop, virtue spread. Even gay men might start behaving like lesbians, fleeing the gym and marrying for life. This is a fantasy, of course, but our increasing control and understanding of the scientific origins of our behavior, even of our culture, is fast making those fantasies things we will have to actively choose to forgo.

What our increasing knowledge of testosterone suggests is a core understanding of what it is to be a man, for better and worse.

But fantasies also tell us something. After a feminist century, we may be in need of a new understanding of masculinity. The concepts of manliness, of gentlemanly behavior, of chivalry have been debunked. The New Age bonding of the men's movement has been outlived. What our increasing knowledge of testosterone suggests is a core understanding of what it is to be a man, for better and worse. It is about the ability to risk for good and bad; to act, to strut, to dare, to seize. It is about a kind of energy we often rue but would surely miss. It is about the foolishness that can lead to courage or destruction, the beauty that can be strength or vanity. To imagine a world without it is to see more clearly how our world is inseparable from it and how our current political pieties are too easily threatened by its reality.

And as our economy becomes less physical and more cerebral, as women slowly supplant men in many industries, as income inequalities grow and more highly testosteroned blue-collar men find themselves shunted to one side, we will have to find new ways of channeling what nature has bequeathed us. I don't think it's an accident that in the last decade there has been a growing focus on a muscular male physique in our popular culture, a boom in crass men's magazines, an explosion in violent computer games, or a professional wrestler who has become governor. These are indications of a cultural displacement, of a world in which the power of testosterone is ignored or attacked, with the result that it reemerges in cruder and less social forms. Our main task in the gender wars of the new century may not be how to bring women fully into our society, but how to keep men from seceding from it, how to reroute testosterone for constructive ends, rather than ignore it for political point-making.

For my part, I'll keep injecting the Big T. Apart from how great it makes me feel, I consider it no insult to anyone else's gender to celebrate the uniqueness of one's own. Diversity need not mean the equalization of difference. In fact, true diversity requires the acceptance of difference. A world without the unruly, vulnerable, pioneering force of testosterone would be a fairer and calmer, but far grayer and duller, place. It is certainly somewhere I would never want to live. Perhaps the fact that I write this two days after the injection of another 200 milligrams of testosterone into my bloodstream makes me more likely to settle for this colorful trade-off than others. But it seems to me no disrespect to womanhood to say that I am perfectly happy to be a man, to feel things no woman will ever feel to the degree that I feel them, to experience the world in a way no woman ever has. And to do so without apology or shame.

 ### Analyzing the Text

1. According to Sullivan, how does testosterone affect men? How does it affect women?

2. How, in Sullivan's opinion, does this hormone affect the nature of our culture at large? What sorts of descriptive language does Sullivan use to characterize the nature of modern society? How do you respond to his characterization?

3. Sullivan explains how testosterone was first identified and studied before he explains how it affects people biologically. How does this historical and biological background impact Sullivan's overall argument? Is his research objective? How effectively does he use this research to argue that testosterone explains the dominance of men in our society?

4. How do you respond to Sullivan's characterization of masculinity? Does it fit certain stereotypes of masculine identity?

5. **Connecting to Another Reading.**   To what extent is Kathy Wilson's essay "Dude Looks Like a Lady" a refutation of Sullivan's argument about biological determinism and society?

6. **Interrogating Assumptions.**   How might Sullivan respond to the assumption that identity is "what we're born with" (see p. 5)? Would he agree that identity is established at birth and remains static? Why or why not?

Writing about Cultural Practices

7. For this assignment, you will seek answers to these questions: How does the popular media influence our perceptions about gender identity? What messages do advertising images send us about how men and women should look and behave? What constitutes the "normal" body (male or female) in the advertising world? How are women and men presented in terms of power relationships in advertising? To begin, collect 5 to 10 examples of advertising images that feature men and women. To help focus your analysis, consider choosing images that share a particular focus on either male or female bodies. For example, you might collect images only of men's faces, women's legs, sports stars, middle-aged people, and so on. Alternately, you might choose advertisements that feature men and women in relationship to one another. As you draft your analysis, consider the following questions.

   - How do the details in these images work together to construct a message about gender and body image? Specifically, which characteristics of male or female bodies are considered attractive (positive)? Which are considered unattractive (negative)? How realistic are the body images presented in these advertisements?

   - What are the differences, if any, between how men and women are presented in terms of physical dominance or power? What is the nature of the power being depicted? Notice the models' positions and actions and support your analysis by citing specific details from the images.

   - To what extent does the popular media influence or help establish social norms about gender identity? What assumptions are built into the media's presentation of gender?

Sampling the Old and the New

In the Photobooth: 1927 vs. 2005

1934   2005   c. 1945   c. 1945   date unknown

c. 1950s   1933   1933   c. 1950s   2005

In 1925, a Siberian immigrant, socialist, and traveling photographer named Anatol Josepho had an idea for making "personal photography easily and cheaply available to the masses." He moved to New York City, and, by 1927, his invention, which landed him a fortune in the amount of $1 million, was proclaimed a wild success by the *New York Times*. By 1945, there were more than 30,000 curtained booths—in train stations, at amusement parks, and on busy street corners—where anyone, but especially World War II soldiers and their loved ones, drew the curtains, dropped coins into slots, and took their own portraits privately and affordably. As Babbette Hines writes in her book *Photobooth*, part of what makes these portraits different from others is that the person in the booth is both photographer and subject. "Perhaps it is only in solitude that we are free to decide which face to present to the camera, which story we want to tell." The photos shown here span a period of nearly 80 years. But as Hines writes, "Although different hairstyles and clothing are apparent, there is a timelessness to the pictures, provoking little of the nostalgia that accompanies other photographs. . . . In the photobooth picture, unlike any other portrait or photograph, truth and fiction easily commingle. In a photobooth we choose the moment and the way in which we represent ourselves. We choose our truth."

c. 1945   c. 1945   c. 1945   2005   2005

2005   1927   1927   2005   c. 1940

1. Examine the photographs. Which ones do you find most striking, and why? What do you think the people in these photos are conveying about their identities? Or, in Hines's terms, what "truths" or stories about themselves are they choosing to represent? What leads you to this conclusion?

2. Are you surprised by any of the dates that accompany these photos? Do you agree with Hines that photobooth photos have a kind of timelessness? Why or why not? (Support your answer by comparing one historical photo and one contemporary photo.)

3. What outward cultural markers do you notice in these images? In your opinion, do these markers impact the outward identities of the people in these images? If so, how?

4. As noted on the back of his photo (shown alongside), the young man in the top row, fourth from the right, was killed in battle in World War II. The woman who is third from the right in the second row was among the earliest New Yorkers to take her photo in a photobooth (her comment appears to the left of her photo). Do these facts change your readings of these images?

5. What assumptions about identity do photobooth images reveal? Does the photobooth self-portrait demonstrate that identity is a personal choice? Why or why not?

Lucy Grealy, **Masks**

Born in Dublin, Ireland, Lucy Grealy (1963–2002) moved with her family to Spring Valley, New York, when she was four. At the age of nine, Grealy was diagnosed with Ewing's sarcoma, a lethal form of cancer. She lost nearly half her jaw to the disease, endured three years of chemotherapy, and underwent many operations in the attempt to reconstruct her face. In this reading, taken from her memoir, *Autobiography of a Face* (1994), Grealy tells the story of a different kind of pain— the "deep bottomless grief . . . called ugliness." It is this pain that she calls "the great tragedy of my life. The fact that I had cancer seemed minor in comparison." Her story is a candid account of the alienation, humiliation, and hostility Grealy endured as a result of her deformity. It is also a commentary on the cultural markers of beauty in our society and on what it means to be "normal."

▶ **Mapping Your Reading**

In the following essay, Grealy recalls how she felt when she hid her scarred face behind a mask on Halloween. But what other kinds of masks does Grealy write about? As you read, mark passages in which she addresses masks and their importance. Do masks set us apart? Do they help us to fit in?

H aving missed most of fourth grade and all but a week or so of fifth grade, I finally started to reappear at school sometime in sixth grade during my periodic "vacations" from chemotherapy. I'd mysteriously show up for a week or two weeks or sometimes even three or four, then disappear again for a couple of months.

Most of the sixth-grade class consisted of children I'd grown up with. They were, for the most part, genuinely curious about what had happened to me. They treated me respectfully, if somewhat distantly, though there was a clique of boys who always called me names: "Hey, girl, take off that monster mask—oops, she's not wearing a mask!" This was the height of hilarity in sixth grade, and the boys, for they were always and only boys, practically fell to the ground, besotted with their own wit. Much to their bewilderment and to the shock of my teachers, I retorted by calling out to them, "You stupid dildos."

Derek used to say that word all the time, and I thought it a wonderful insult, though I didn't have a clue as to what a dildo was. After being reprimanded enough times for wielding this powerful insult, I finally asked my brother what it meant: an artificial penis, he informed me. I gave up using the word. I'd known children in the hospital with artificial limbs, and I'd known children with urinary tract problems.

The school year progressed slowly. I felt as if I had been in the sixth grade for years, yet it was only October. Halloween was approaching. Coming from Ireland, we had never thought of it as a big holiday, though Sarah and I usually went out trick-or-treating. For the last couple of years I had been too sick to go out, but this year Halloween fell on a day when I felt quite fine. My mother was the one who came up with the Eskimo idea. I put on a winter coat, made a fish out of paper, which I hung on the end of a stick, and wrapped my face up in a scarf. My hair was growing, and I loved the way the top of the hood rubbed against it. By this time my hat had become part of me; I took it off only at home. Sometimes kids would make fun of me, run past me, knock my hat off, and call me Baldy. I hated this, but I assumed that one day my hair would grow in, and on that day the teasing would end.

We walked around the neighborhood with our pillowcase sacks, running into the other groups of kids and comparing notes: the house three doors down gave whole candy bars, while the house next to that gave only cheap mints. I felt wonderful. It was only as the night wore on and the moon came out and the older kids, the big kids, went on their rounds that I began to realize why I felt so good. No one could see me clearly. No one could see my face.

For the end of October it was a very warm night and I was sweating in my parka, but I didn't care. I felt such freedom: I waltzed up to people effortlessly and boldly, I asked questions and made comments the rest of my troupe were afraid to make. I didn't understand their fear. I hadn't realized just how meek I'd become, how self-conscious I was about my face until now that it was obscured. My sister and her friends never had to worry about their appearance, or so it seemed to me, so why didn't they always feel as bold and as happy as I felt that night?

Our sacks filled up, and eventually it was time to go home. We gleefully poured out our candy on the floor and traded off: because chewing had become difficult, I gave Sarah everything that was too hard for me, while she unselfishly gave me everything soft. I took off my Eskimo parka and went down to my room without my hat. Normally I didn't feel that I had to wear my hat around my family, and I never wore it when I was alone in my room. Yet once I was alone with all my candy, still hot from running around on that unseasonably warm night, I felt compelled to put my hat back on. I didn't know what was wrong. I ate sugar until I was ready to burst, trying hard to ignore everything except what was directly in front of me, what I could touch and taste, the chocolate melting brown beneath my fingernails, the candy so sweet it made my throat hurt.

The following spring, on one of the first warm days, I was playing with an old friend, Teresa, in her neat and ordered back yard when she asked, completely out of the blue, if I was dying. She looked at me casually, as if she'd just asked what I was doing later that day. "The other kids say that you're slowly dying, that you're 'wasting away.'" I looked at her in shock. Dying? Why on earth would anyone think I was dying? "No," I replied, in the tone of voice I'd have used if she'd asked me whether I was the pope, "I'm not dying."

When I got home I planned to ask my mother why Teresa would say such a thing. But just as I was coming through the front door, she was entering from the garage, her arms laden with shopping bags. She took a bright red shirt out of a bag and held it up against my chest. It smelled new and a price tag scratched my neck.

"Turtlenecks are very hard to find in short sleeves, so I bought you several."

I was still a tomboy at heart and cared little about what I wore, just so long as it wasn't a dress. But turtlenecks—why on earth would I want to wear turtlenecks in the spring? I didn't ask this out loud, but my mother must have known what I was thinking. She looked me straight in the eye: "If you wear something that comes up around your neck, it makes the scar less visible."

Genuinely bewildered, I took the bright-colored pile of shirts down to my room. Wouldn't I look even more stupid wearing a turtleneck in the summer? Would they really hide my "scar"? I hadn't taken a good long, objective look at myself since the wig fitting, but that seemed so long ago, almost two years. I remembered feeling upset by it, but I conveniently didn't remember what I'd seen in that mirror, and I hadn't allowed myself a close scrutiny since.

I donned my short-sleeved turtlenecks and finished out the few short months of elementary school. I played with my friend Jan at her wonderful home with its several acres of meadow and, most magnificent of all, a small lake. There was a rowboat we weren't allowed to take out by ourselves, but we did anyway. Rowing it to the far shore, a mere eighth of a mile away, we'd "land" and pretend we'd just discovered a new country. With notebooks in hand, we logged our discoveries, overturning stones and giving false Latin names to the newts and various pieces of slime we found under them.

"If you wear something that comes up around your neck, it makes the scar less visible."

Jan had as complex a relationship to her stuffed and plastic animals as I had to mine, and when I slept over we'd compare our intricate worlds. Sometimes, though not too frequently, Jan wanted to talk about boys, and I'd sit on my sleeping bag with my knees tucked up under my nightgown, listening patiently. I never had much to offer, though I had just developed my very first crush. It was on Omar Sharif.

Late one night I'd stayed up and watched *Dr. Zhivago* on television with my father. Curled up beside him, with my head against his big stomach, I listened to my father's heart, his breathing, and attentively watched the images of a remote world, a world as beautiful as it was deadly and cold. I thought I would have managed very well there, imagined that I would have remained true to my passions had I lived through the Russian Revolution. I, too, would have trudged across all that tundra, letting the ice sheet over me and crackle on my eyebrows. For weeks I pictured the ruined estate where Zhivago wrote his sonnets, aware that the true splendor of the house was inextricably bound to the fact that it was ruined. I didn't understand why this should be so, and I didn't understand why imagining this scene gave me such a deep sense of fulfillment, nor why this fulfillment was mingled with such a sad sense of longing, nor why this longing only added to the beauty of everything else.

Elementary-school graduation day approached. I remembered being in second grade and looking out on a group of sixth-graders preparing for graduation. It had seemed like an unimaginable length of time before I'd get there. But now I was out there mingling in the courtyard, remembering the day when I laid my head down on the desk and announced to the teacher, "I'll never make it." I could even see the classroom window I had gazed out of. So much had happened in four years. I felt so old, and I felt proud of being so old. During the ceremony I was shocked when the vice-principal started speaking about *me*, about how I should receive special attention for my "bravery." I could feel the heat rising in me as he spoke, my face turning red. Here I was, the center of attention, receiving the praise and appreciation I'd been fantasizing about for so many years, and all I could feel was intense, searing embarrassment. I was called up onto the platform. I know everyone was applauding, but I felt it more than heard it. In a daze I accepted the gift Mr. Schultz was presenting me with, a copy of *The Prophet*. I could barely thank him.

Later, alone in my room, I opened the book at random. The verse I read was about love, about how to accept the love of another with dignity. I shut the book after only a page. I wanted nothing to do with the world of love; I thought wanting love was a weakness to be overcome. And besides, I thought to myself, the world of love wanted nothing to do with me.

The summer passed, and junior high school loomed. Jan, Teresa, and Sarah were all very excited at the prospect of being "grown-ups," of attending different classes, of having their own locker. Their excitement was contagious, and the night before the first day of school, I proudly marked my assorted notebooks for my different subjects and secretly scuffed my new shoes to make them look old.

Everyone must have been nervous, but I was sure I was the only one who felt true apprehension. I found myself sidling through the halls I'd been looking forward to, trying to pretend that I didn't notice the other kids, almost all of them strangers from adjoining towns, staring at me. Having seen plenty of teen movies with their promise of intrigue and drama, I had been looking forward to going to the lunchroom. As it happened, I sat down next to a table full of boys.

They pointed openly and laughed, calling out loudly enough for me to hear, "*What* on earth is *that*?" "*That* is the ugliest girl I have *ever* seen." I knew in my heart that their comments had nothing to do with me, that it was all about them appearing tough and cool to their friends. But these boys were older than the ones in grade school, and for the very first time I realized they were passing judgment on my suitability, or lack of it, as a girlfriend. "I bet David wants to go kiss her, don't you, David?" "Yeah, right, then I'll go kiss your mother's asshole." "How'll you know which is which?"

My initial tactic was to pretend I didn't hear them, but this only seemed to spur them on. In the hallways, where I suffered similar attacks of teasing from random attackers, I simply looked down at the floor and walked more quickly, but in the lunchroom I was a sitting duck. The same group took to seeking me out and purposely sitting near me day after day, even when I tried to camouflage myself by sitting in the middle of a group. They grew bolder, and I could hear them plotting to send someone to sit across the table from me. I'd look up from my food and there would be a boy slouching awkwardly in a red plastic chair, innocently asking me my name. Then he'd ask me how I got to be so ugly. At this the group would burst into laughter, and my inquisitor would saunter back, victorious.

After two weeks I broke down and went to my guidance counselor to complain. I thought he would offer to reprimand them, but instead he asked if I'd like to come and eat in the privacy of his office. Surprised, I said yes, and that's what I did for the rest of the year whenever I was attending school. Every day I'd wait for him, the other guidance counselors, and the secretaries to go on their own lunch break. Then I'd walk through the empty outer office and sit down in his private office, closing the door behind me. As I ate the food in my brown paper bag, which crinkled loudly in the silence, I'd look at the drawings his own young children had made. They were taped to the wall near his desk, simplistic drawings in which the sky was a blue line near the top and the grass a green line near the bottom and people were as big as houses. I felt safe and secure in that office, but I also felt lonely, and for the very first time I definitively identified the source of my unhappiness as being ugly. A few weeks later I left school to reenter chemotherapy, and for the very first time I was almost glad to go back to it.

My inner life became ever more macabre. Vietnam was still within recent memory, and pictures of the horrors of Cambodia loomed on every TV screen and in every newspaper. I told myself again and again how good I had it in comparison, what a wonder it was to have food and clothes and a home and no one torturing me. I told myself what fools those boys at school were, what stupid, unaware lives they led. How could they assume their own lives were so important? Didn't they know they could lose everything at any moment, that you couldn't take anything good or worthwhile for granted, because pain and cruelty could and would arrive sooner or later? I bombed and starved and persecuted my own suffering right out of existence.

I had the capacity of imagination to momentarily escape my own pain, and I had the elegance of imagination to teach myself something true regarding the world around me, but I didn't yet have the clarity of imagination to grant myself the complicated and necessary right to suffer. I treated despair in terms of hierarchy: If there was a more important pain in the world, it meant my own was negated. I thought I simply had to accept the fact that I was ugly, and that to feel despair about it was simply wrong.

> I treated despair in terms of hierarchy: If there was a more important pain in the world, it meant my own was negated.

Halloween came round again, and even though I was feeling a bit woozy from an injection I'd had a few days before, I begged my mother to let me go out. I put on a plastic witch mask and went out with Teresa. I walked down the streets suddenly bold and free: No one could see my face. I peered through the oval eye slits and did not see one person staring back at me, ready to make fun of my face. I breathed in the condensing, plastic-tainted air behind the mask and thought that I was breathing in normalcy, that this freedom and ease were what the world consisted of, that other people felt it all the time. How could they not? How could they not feel the joy of walking down the street without the threat of being made fun of? Assuming this was how other people felt all the time, I again named my own face as the thing that kept me apart, as the tangible element of what was wrong with my life and with me.

At home, when I took the mask off, I felt both sad and relieved. Sad because I had felt like a pauper walking for a few brief hours in the clothes of a prince and because I had liked it so much. Relieved because I felt no connection with that kind of happiness: I didn't deserve it and thus I shouldn't want it. It was easier to slip back into my depression and blame my face for everything. . . .

I viewed other people both critically and sympathetically. Why couldn't they just stop complaining so much, just let go and see how good they actually had it? Everyone seemed to be waiting for something to happen that would allow them to move forward, waiting for some shadowy future moment to begin their lives in earnest. Everybody, from my mother to the characters I read about in books (who were as actual and important as real people to me), was always looking at someone else's life and envying it, wishing to occupy it. I wanted them to stop, to see how much they had already, how they had their health and their strength. I imagined how my life would be if I had half their fortune. Then I would catch myself, guilty of exactly the thing I was accusing others of. As clear-headed as I was, sometimes I felt that the only reason for this clarity was to see how hypocritically I lived my own life.

Once, during a week of intensive chemotherapy toward the end of the two and a half years, I was sent to another ward, as 10 was already full when I checked in. My roommate was a girl who'd been run over by an iceboat; the blades had cut her intestines in two, and she'd had to have them sewn back together. She got a lot of attention, lots of calls from concerned relatives and school friends, and I was both a little jealous of her and a little contemptuous because she was taking her accident a bit too seriously for my taste. After all, she'd lived, hadn't she? She'd had one operation and they might do another one the next week, but after that it would be all over, so what was the big fuss about?

▶ **Analyzing the Text**

1. What is the symbolic meaning of a mask? Why does Grealy feel so bold when she wears one on Halloween?

2. According to Grealy's descriptions of her childhood, how did people "read" her disability? In what ways did her deformity become a marker of her identity for the adults and children she encountered? What examples from the essay lead you to your observation?

3. One of Grealy's key memories is being singled out for a special award at her elementary school graduation. She often dreamed of receiving positive attention. When she was acknowledged, though, how did Grealy react?

4. Grealy describes a second Halloween outing in costume: "I was breathing in normalcy." In the midst of her joy, she writes, "I again named my own face as the thing that kept me apart, as the tangible element of what was wrong with my life and with me." How did Grealy's deformity affect her own sense of identity? What details from her essay reveal her feelings?

5. **Interrogating Assumptions.** To what extent does Grealy's essay support the assumption that "identity is shaped by culture" (see p. 9)? What effect do social or cultural norms have on how others see us? On how we see ourselves?

▶ **Writing about Cultural Practices**

6. In "Masks," Grealy recalls how her facial deformity affected how she thought about herself as a child and how others thought about and treated her. Write an analysis of Grealy's perspective in which you discuss the connection between the body and identity and respond to the following questions.

   - How important is physical beauty (or lack of physical beauty) to how we see ourselves? Are our bodies—our abilities and disabilities—inextricably linked to how we think of ourselves? How would Grealy respond to these questions? (Refer to passages from her essay to answer.) Do you agree with her? Why or why not?

   - How important is physical beauty to how others see us? How important is it to be defined as "normal" by others? How do you account for this, culturally speaking?

   - How does Grealy respond to her mistreatment by others who call her ugly? How does she—both as a child and as an adult (through her writing)—protect herself?

   - What attitudes are behind the treatment of people with physical deformities or disabilities as "others"? What social or cultural changes would change these attitudes and improve the experience of people with disabilities?

September 11 Tattoos

The following three images are photographs of tattoos that memorialize the people who died in the September 11, 2001, terrorist attacks in New York and Washington, D.C. One of these photos—the flag tattoo with the silhouette of an airplane—was taken on September 15, 2001, only days after the terrorist attacks. The other two were taken in 2002 and 2003.

▶ Mapping Your Reading

All three of these tattoos are memorials to those who died on September 11, but they are also images of American patriotism. As you examine these images, make notes in the margins about how these tattoos use patriotic symbols. What other messages do the tattoos convey? Why do you think people commemorate events or people through body art? Is such commemoration effective? Why or why not?

"A woman displays a tattoo she had applied to her arm featuring the Stars and Stripes with the black outline of a jumbo jet and a yellow rose at the tenth annual Inkslingers Ball featuring tattoo art in Hollywood, September 15, 2001." [original caption, Reuters, September 15, 2001]

© Reuters/CORBIS

49

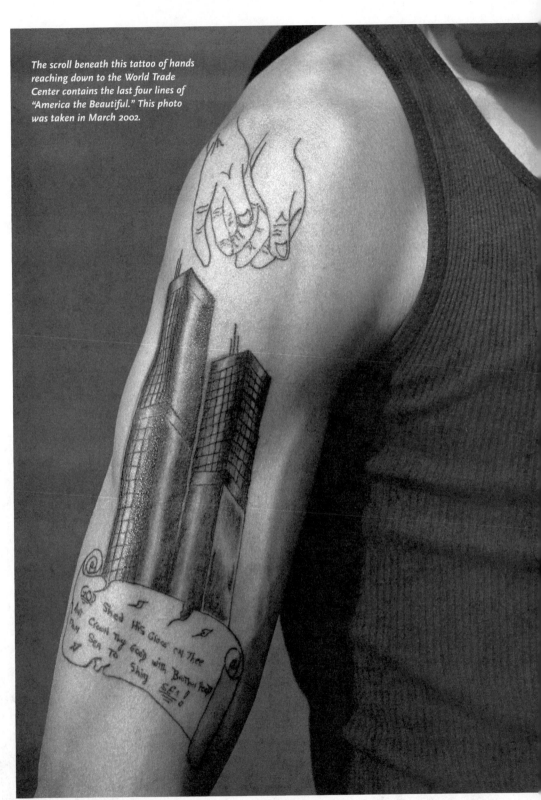

The scroll beneath this tattoo of hands reaching down to the World Trade Center contains the last four lines of "America the Beautiful." This photo was taken in March 2002.

THE LORD IS MY SHEPHERD—
AMERICA IS MY COUNTRY!!

SEPT. 11ᵀᴴ 2001
WILL NEVER FORGET
BROTHERS AND SISTERS

"A construction worker with a September 11 tattoo listens to a speech at a rally in support of American troops near the site of the World Trade Center in New York on April 10, 2003. About 25,000 workers clad in hard hats, blue jeans, and work-men's boots gathered near the site where many of them dug relentlessly through rubble after the September 11 attacks." [original caption, Reuters, April 10, 2003]

Analyzing the Text

1. List all the symbols you notice in these tattoos. What are the meanings behind these symbols?

2. How did these individuals combine different symbols to create their own themes in their tattoos? What message is each tattoo-wearer communicating?

3. Reexamine the third photograph (the one of the construction worker) and answer this question: What does this man's body-text say to you? In other words, how do you read the image of the man in this photograph? To answer this, pay attention to his entire image—his clothes, his hat, everything about him—including his tattoo.

4. Tattoos can convey messages that make a statement about a person's identity. How would you analyze the symbols and themes of the tattoos shown in these photographs? Are tattoos or other forms of body art effective ways to convey to others who we are? Why or why not?

Writing about Cultural Practices

5. Patriotism is just one common theme of tattoo art. Create your own photo essay in which you examine a different tattoo theme, one that makes a statement about people and contemporary American life. To do this, collect images of tattoos or other body art that share a similar theme. Write a descriptive essay in which you use your examples to explain the common theme and describe its importance within popular culture. As you write, consider the following questions.

   - What theme unifies your visual examples of tattoos? Why do you think this theme appeals to people?

   - What symbols, images, or colors commonly appear in tattoos of this theme? What meanings do these details convey?

   - What messages or attitudes do the tattoos convey about the people wearing them? Explain what leads you to your conclusions.

Gloria Anzaldúa, **How to Tame a Wild Tongue**

Gloria Anzaldúa (1942–2004) was a poet, writer, cultural theorist, and Chicana feminist who was born in south Texas to a Mexican immigrant family. Anzaldúa is most notably recognized for her books *Borderlands/La Frontera: The New Mestiza* (1987), from which "How to Tame a Wild Tongue" is taken, and *This Bridge Called My Back* (1981). One of the first openly lesbian Chicana writers, she worked to redefine minority identities through both her writing and her teaching at San Francisco State University; Oakes College at the University of California, Santa Cruz; and Norwich University.

 Mapping Your Reading

"If you want to be American, speak 'American,'" said a teacher to a young Gloria Anzaldúa. In the following essay, the author traces her linguistic experience as a Chicana and her resistance to attempts made by others to "tame" her "wild tongue." "Ethnic identity," she writes, "is twin skin to linguistic identity—I am my language." As you read this piece, consider this idea. Are we our languages? What does language represent about us within our culture? Who would want to tame another person's "wild tongue," and why?

W e're going to have to control your tongue," the dentist says, pulling out all the metal from my mouth. Silver bits plop and tinkle into the basin. My mouth is a motherlode.

The dentist is cleaning out my roots. I get a whiff of the stench when I gasp. "I can't cap that tooth yet, you're still draining," he says.

"We're going to have to do something about your tongue," I hear the anger rising in his voice. My tongue keeps pushing out the wads of cotton, pushing back the drills, the long thin needles. "I've never seen anything as strong or as stubborn," he says. And I think how do you tame a wild tongue, train it to be quiet, how do you bridle and saddle it? How do you make it lie down?

"Who is to say that robbing a people of its language is less violent than war?"
—RAY GWYN SMITH[1]

---

[1]Ray Gwyn Smith, *Moorland Is Cold Country,* unpublished book.

For another reading on language, see Dumas, page 60.—EDS.

I remember being caught speaking Spanish at recess—that was good for three licks on the knuckles with a sharp ruler. I remember being sent to the corner of the classroom for "talking back" to the Anglo teacher when all I was trying to do was tell her how to pronounce my name. "If you want to be American, speak 'American.' If you don't like it, go back to Mexico where you belong."

"I want you to speak English. *Pa' hallar buen trabajo tienes que saber hablar el inglés bien. Qué vale toda tu educatión si todavía hablas inglés con un* 'accent,'" my mother would say, mortified that I spoke English like a Mexican. At Pan American University, I, and all Chicano students, were required to take two speech classes. Their purpose: to get rid of our accents.

> All Chicano students were required to take two speech classes. Their purpose: to get rid of our accents.

Attacks on one's form of expression with the intent to censor are a violation of the First Amendment. *El Anglo con cara de inocente nos arrancó la lengua.* Wild tongues can't be tamed, they can only be cut out.

Overcoming the Tradition of Silence

> *Ahogadas, escupimos el oscuro.*
> *Peleando con nuestra propia sombra*
> *el silencio nos sepulta.*

En boca cerrada no entran moscas. "Flies don't enter a closed mouth" is a saying I kept hearing when I was a child. *Ser habladora* was to be a gossip and a liar, to talk too much. *Muchachitas bien criadas,* well-bred girls don't answer back. *Es una falta de respeto* to talk back to one's mother or father. I remember one of the sins I'd recite to the priest in the confession box the few times I went to confession: talking back to my mother, *hablar pa' 'tras, repelar. Hocicona, repelona, chismosa,* having a big mouth, questioning, carrying tales are all signs of being *mal criada.* In my culture they are all words that are derogatory if applied to women—I've never heard them applied to men.

The first time I heard two women, a Puerto Rican and a Cuban, say the word *"nosotras,"* I was shocked. I had not known the word existed. Chicanas use *nosotros* whether we're male or female. We are robbed of our female being by the masculine plural. Language is a male discourse.

> And our tongues have become
> dry   the wilderness has
> dried out our tongues   and
> we have forgotten speech.
> — IRENA KLEPFISZ[2]

---

[2]Irena Klepfisz, "*Di rayze aheym*/The Journey Home," in *The Tribe of Dina: A Jewish Women's Anthology,* Melanie Kaye/Kantrowitz and Irena Klepfisz, eds. (Montpelier, VT: Sinister Wisdom Books, 1986), 49.

Even our own people, other Spanish speakers *nos quieren poner candados en la boca*. They would hold us back with their bag of *reglas de academia*.

Oyé como ladra: El lenguaje de la frontera

> *Quien tiene boca se equivoca.*
> —MEXICAN SAYING

"*Pocho*, cultural traitor, you're speaking the oppressor's language by speaking English, you're ruining the Spanish language," I have been accused by various Latinos and Latinas. Chicano Spanish is considered by the purist and by most Latinos deficient, a mutilation of Spanish.

But Chicano Spanish is a border tongue which developed naturally. Change, *evolución, enriquecimiento de palabras nuevas por invención o adopción* have created variants of Chicano Spanish, *un nuevo lenguaje. Un lenguaje que corresponde a un modo de vivir.* Chicano Spanish is not incorrect, it is a living language.

For people who are neither Spanish nor live in a country in which Spanish is the first language; for a people who live in a country in which English is the reigning tongue but who are not Anglo; for a people who cannot entirely identify with either standard (formal, Castillian) Spanish or standard English, what recourse is left to them but to create their own language? A language which they can connect their identity to, one capable of communicating the realities and values true to themselves—a language with terms that are neither *español ni inglés,* but both. We speak a patois, a forked tongue, a variation of two languages.

Chicano Spanish sprang out of the Chicanos' need to identify ourselves as a distinct people. We needed a language with which we could communicate with ourselves, a secret language. For some of us, language is a homeland closer than the Southwest—for many Chicanos today live in the Midwest and the East. And because we are a complex, heterogeneous people, we speak many languages. Some of the languages we speak are:

1. Standard English
2. Working class and slang English
3. Standard Spanish
4. Standard Mexican Spanish
5. North Mexican Spanish dialect
6. Chicano Spanish (Texas, New Mexico, Arizona, and California have regional variations)
7. Tex-Mex
8. *Pachuco* (called *caló*)

My "home" tongues are the languages I speak with my sister and brothers, with my friends. They are the last five listed, with 6 and 7 being closest to my heart. From school, the media, and job situations, I've picked up standard and working class English. From Mamagrande Locha and from reading Spanish and Mexican literature, I've picked up Standard Spanish and Standard Mexican Spanish. From *los recién llegados*, Mexican immigrants, and *braceros,* I learned the North Mexican dialect. With Mexicans I'll try to speak either Standard Mexican

Spanish or the North Mexican dialect. From my parents and Chicanos living in the Valley, I picked up Chicano Texas Spanish, and I speak it with my mom, younger brother (who married a Mexican and who rarely mixes Spanish with English), aunts, and older relatives.

With Chicanas from *Nuevo México* or *Arizona* I will speak Chicano Spanish a little, but often they don't understand what I'm saying. With most California Chicanas I speak entirely in English (unless I forget). When I first moved to San Francisco, I'd rattle off something in Spanish, unintentionally embarrassing them. Often it is only with another Chicana *tejana* that I can talk freely.

Words distorted by English are known as anglicisms or *pochismos*. The *pocho* is an anglicized Mexican or American of Mexican origin who speaks Spanish with an accent characteristic of North Americans and who distorts and reconstructs the language according to the influence of English.[3] Tex-Mex, or Spanglish, comes most naturally to me. I may switch back and forth from English to Spanish in the same sentence or in the same word. With my sister and my brother Nune and with Chicano *tejano* contemporaries I speak in Tex-Mex.

From kids and people my own age I picked up *Pachuco*. *Pachuco* (the language of the zoot suiters) is a language of rebellion, both against Standard Spanish and Standard English. It is a secret language. Adults of the culture and outsiders cannot understand it. It is made up of slang words from both English and Spanish. *Ruca* means girl or woman, *vato* means guy or dude, *chale* means no, *simón* means yes, *churro* is sure, talk is *periquiar*, *pigionear* means petting, *que gacho* means how nerdy, *ponte águila* means watch out, death is called *la pelona*. Through lack of practice and not having others who can speak it, I've lost most of the *Pachuco* tongue.

Chicano Spanish

Chicanos, after 250 years of Spanish/Anglo colonization, have developed significant differences in the Spanish we speak. We collapse two adjacent vowels into a single syllable and sometimes shift the stress in certain words such as *maíz/maiz, cohete/cuete*. We leave out certain consonants when they appear between vowels: *lado/lao, mojado/majao*. Chicanos from South Texas pronounce *f* as *j* as in *jue (fue)*. Chicanos use "archaisms," words that are no longer in the Spanish language, words that have been evolved out. We say *semos, truje, haiga, ansina,* and *naiden.* We retain the "archaic" *j*, as in *jalar,* that derives from an earlier *h* (the French *halar* or the Germanic *halon* which was lost to standard Spanish in the sixteenth century), but which is still found in several regional dialects such as the one spoken in South Texas. (Due to geography, Chicanos from the Valley of South Texas were cut off linguistically from other Spanish speakers. We tend to use words that the Spaniards brought over from Medieval Spain. The majority of the Spanish colonizers in Mexico and the Southwest came from Extremadura—

---

[3]R. C. Ortega, *Dialectología Del Barrio,* trans. Hortencia S. Alwan (Los Angeles, CA: R. C. Ortega Publisher & Bookseller, 1977), 132.

Hernán Cortés was one of them—and Andalucía. Andalucians pronounce *ll* like a *y*, and their *d*'s tend to be absorbed by adjacent vowels: *tirado* becomes *tirao*. They brought *el lenguaje popular, dialectos y regionalismos.*[4])

Chicanos and other Spanish speakers also shift *ll* to *y* and *z* to *s*.[5] We leave out initial syllables, saying *tar* for *estar*, *toy* for *estoy*, *hora* for *ahora* (*cubanos* and *puertorriqueños* also leave out initial letters of some words). We also leave out the final syllable such as *pa* for *para*. The intervocalic *y*, the *ll* as in *tortilla, ella, botella*, gets replaced by *tortia* or *tortiya, ea, botea*. We add an additional syllable at the beginning of certain words: *atocar* for *tocar*, *agastar* for *gastar*. Sometimes we'll say *lavaste las vacijas*, other times *lavates* (substituting the *ates* verb endings for the *aste*).

> **Repeated attacks on our native tongue diminish our sense of self.**

We use anglicisms, words borrowed from English: *bola* from ball, *carpeta* from carpet, *máchina de lavar* (instead of *lavadora*) from washing machine. Tex-Mex argot, created by adding a Spanish sound at the beginning or end of an English word such as *cookiar* for cook, *watchar* for watch, *parkiar* for park, and *rapiar* for rape, is the result of the pressures on Spanish speakers to adapt to English.

We don't use the word *vosotros/as* or its accompanying verb form. We don't say *claro* (to mean yes), *imagínate*, or *me emociona*, unless we picked up Spanish from Latinas, out of a book, or in a classroom. Other Spanish-speaking groups are going through the same, or similar, development in their Spanish.

Linguistic Terrorism

> *Deslenguadas. Somos los del español deficiente.* We are your linistic nightmare, your linguistic aberration, your linguistic *mestisaje*, the subject of your *burla*. Because we speak with tongues of fire we are culturally crucified. Racially, culturally and linguistically *somos huérfanos*—we speak an orphan tongue.

Chicanas who grew up speaking Chicano Spanish have internalized the belief that we speak poor Spanish. It is illegitimate, a bastard language. And because we internalize how our language has been used against us by the dominant culture, we use our language differences against each other.

Chicana feminists often skirt around each other with suspicion and hesitation. For the longest time I couldn't figure it out. Then it dawned on me. To be close to another Chicana is like looking into the mirror. We are afraid of what we'll see there. *Pena.* Shame. Low estimation of self. In childhood we are told that our language is wrong. Repeated attacks on our native tongue diminish our sense of self. The attacks continue throughout our lives.

---

[4]Eduardo Hernández-Chávez, Andrew D. Cohen, and Anthony F. Beltramo, *El Lenguaje de los Chicanos: Regional and Social Characteristics of Language Used by Mexican Americans* (Arlington, VA: Center for Applied Linguistics, 1975), 39.

[5]Hernández-Chávez, xvii.

Chicanas feel uncomfortable talking in Spanish to Latinas, afraid of their censure. Their language was not outlawed in their countries. They had a whole lifetime of being immersed in their native tongue; generations, centuries in which Spanish was a first language, taught in school, heard on radio and TV, and read in the newspaper.

If a person, Chicana or Latina, has a low estimation of my native tongue, she also has a low estimation of me. Often with *mexicanas y latinas* we'll speak English as a neutral language. Even among Chicanas we tend to speak English at parties or conferences. Yet, at the same time, we're afraid the others will think we're *agringadas* because we don't speak Chicano Spanish. We oppress each other trying to out-Chicano each other, vying to be the "real" Chicanas, to speak like Chicanos. There is no one Chicano language just as there is no one Chicano experience. A monolingual Chicana whose first language is English or Spanish is just as much a Chicana as one who speaks several variants of Spanish. A Chicana from Michigan or Chicago or Detroit is just as much a Chicana as one from the southwest. Chicano Spanish is as diverse linguistically as it is regionally.

By the end of this century, Spanish speakers will comprise the biggest minority group in the U.S., a country where students in high schools and colleges are encouraged to take French classes because French is considered more "cultured." But for a language to remain alive it must be used.[6] By the end of this century English, and not Spanish, will be the mother tongue of most Chicanos and Latinos.

So, if you want to really hurt me, talk badly about my language. Ethnic identity is twin skin to linguistic identity—I am my language. Until I can take pride in my language, I cannot take pride in myself. Until I can accept as legitimate Chicano Texas Spanish, Tex-Mex, and all the other languages I speak, I cannot accept the legitimacy of myself. Until I am free to write bilingually and to switch codes without having always to translate, while I still have to speak English or Spanish when I would rather speak Spanglish, and as long as I have to accommodate the English speakers rather than having them accommodate me, my tongue will be illegitimate.

I will no longer be made to feel ashamed of existing. I will have my voice: Indian, Spanish, white. I will have my serpent's tongue—my woman's voice, my sexual voice, my poet's voice. I will overcome the tradition of silence.

My fingers
move sly against your palm
Like women everywhere, we speak in code. . . .
—MELANIE KAYE/KANTROWITZ[7]

---

[6]Irena Klepfisz, "Secular Jewish Identity: Yidishkayt in America," in *The Tribe of Dina*, Kaye/Kantrowitz and Klepfisz, eds., 43.

[7]Melanie Kaye/Kantrowitz, "Sign," in *We Speak in Code: Poems and Other Writings* (Pittsburgh, PA: Motheroot Publications, Inc., 1980), 85.

▶ Analyzing the Text

1. Anzaldúa writes, "Wild tongues can't be tamed, they can only be cut out." What does she mean?

2. The essay includes many Spanish phrases, some of which are translated and some of which are not. Why do you think Anzaldúa chooses not to translate all of the phrases? What effect does this create in the essay?

3. "Chicano Spanish is not incorrect, it is a living language," writes Anzaldúa. According to the author, how and why did Chicano Spanish come into being? What does the evolution of the language have to do with national borders? What does it have to do with social pressures? With the culture and language that dominates American society?

4. Anzaldúa equates language with identity and argues that her language will be "illegitimate" as long as she is made to "accommodate" others, specifically English speakers. Do you relate to this argument? Have you ever had to accommodate others through your linguistic choices? Or through your consciousness of an accent? If so, what effect, if any, did this have on your sense of identity?

5. **Interrogating Assumptions.** How would you apply the assumption that identity is shaped by culture to Anzaldúa's argument about language (see p. 9)? And would Anzaldúa embrace the concept of acculturation (see p. 10)? Why or why not?

▶ Writing about Cultural Practices

6. Anzaldúa writes that she speaks a number of different versions of Spanish that she learned from different people, in different situations. Do you speak different versions of your native language? If so, how did you learn these versions? Does the language or dialect you use depend on the situation and the people you're talking to? To investigate the ways we communicate in different environments, write a critical analysis of your linguistic experience. Identify at least one setting—at home, with your family, at work, or out with friends, for example—in which you use a different or "nonstandard" way of speaking. Include in your writing answers to the following questions.

   - What is the context for your use of this version of the language? Who are you talking to? What are your main communication goals?

   - How does this version of the language vary from a more standard version of it? In other words, what makes your version of the language different? Why is it the best choice, given the context? Support your claim by quoting and analyzing specific words and phrases.

   - To what extent is this version of the language tied to your identity? Your community? Your culture?

Firoozeh Dumas, **The "F Word"**

Firoozeh Dumas moved from Abadan, Iran, to Whittier, California, with her family when she was seven years old. In her autobiography, *Funny in Farsi: A Memoir of Growing Up Iranian in America* (2002), Dumas writes about negotiating the transition from one culture to another and about respecting traditional values while becoming part of a new and modern society. The following essay, excerpted from *Funny in Farsi,* is about Dumas's challenge of taking on a new identity while preserving her original sense of self. It is a familiar story, with a twist. Many people have childhood memories of being teased about their names. However, a person whose name is not familiar—meaning "not American"—goes through additional struggles as others use, don't use, or adapt his or her name.

> ### ▶ Mapping Your Reading
>
> As you read, pay attention to how Dumas uses humor to connect with her readers while she makes an argument about the value of diversity. Would you change your name to accommodate others? Or have you changed your name? Why is having an unusual name in America, as Dumas writes, "a pain in the spice cabinet"?

My cousin's name, Farbod, means "Greatness." When he moved to America, all the kids called him "Farthead." My brother Farshid ("He Who Enlightens") became "Fartshit." The name of my friend Neggar means "Beloved," although it can be more accurately translated as "She Whose Name Almost Incites Riots." Her brother Arash ("Giver") initially couldn't understand why every time he'd say his name, people would laugh and ask him if it itched.

All of us immigrants knew that moving to America would be fraught with challenges, but none of us thought that our names would be such an obstacle. How could our parents have ever imagined that someday we would end up in a country where monosyllabic names reign supreme, a land where "William" is shortened to "Bill," where "Susan" becomes "Sue," and "Richard" somehow evolves into "Dick"? America is a great country, but nobody without a mask and a cape has a z in his name. And have Americans ever realized the great scope of the guttural sounds they're missing? Okay, so it has to do with linguistic roots, but I

For another reading on language, see Anzaldúa, page 53.—EDS.

do believe this would be a richer country if all Americans could do a little tongue aerobics and learn to pronounce "kh," a sound more commonly associated in this culture with phlegm, or "gh," the sound usually made by actors in the final moments of a choking scene. It's like adding a few new spices to the kitchen pantry. Move over, cinnamon and nutmeg, make way for cardamom and sumac.

Exotic analogies aside, having a foreign name in this land of Joes and Marys is a pain in the spice cabinet. When I was twelve, I decided to simplify my life by adding an American middle name. This decision serves as proof that sometimes simplifying one's life in the short run only complicates it in the long run.

My name, Firoozeh, chosen by my mother, means "Turquoise" in Farsi. In America, it means "Unpronounceable" or "I'm Not Going to Talk to You Because I Cannot Possibly Learn Your Name and I Just Don't Want to Have to Ask You Again and Again Because You'll Think I'm Dumb or You Might Get Upset or Something." My father, incidentally, had wanted to name me Sara. I do wish he had won that argument.

To strengthen my decision to add an American name, I had just finished fifth grade in Whittier, where all the kids incessantly called me "Ferocious." That summer, my family moved to Newport Beach, where I looked forward to starting a new life. I wanted to be a kid with a name that didn't draw so much attention, a name that didn't come with a built-in inquisition as to when and why I had moved to America and how was it that I spoke English without an accent and was I planning on going back and what did I think of America?

My last name didn't help any. I can't mention my maiden name, because:

"Dad, I'm writing a memoir."

"Great! Just don't mention our name."

Suffice it to say that, with eight letters, including a *z*, and four syllables, my last name is as difficult and foreign as my first. My first and last name together generally served the same purpose as a high brick wall. There was one exception to this rule. In Berkeley, and only in Berkeley, my name drew people like flies to baklava. These were usually people named Amaryllis or Chrysanthemum, types who vacationed in Costa Rica and to whom lentils described a type of burger. These folks were probably not the pride of Poughkeepsie, but they were refreshingly nonjudgmental.

When I announced to my family that I wanted to add an American name, they reacted with their usual laughter. Never one to let mockery or good judgment stand in my way, I proceeded to ask for suggestions. My father suggested "Fifi." Had I had a special affinity for French poodles or been considering a career in prostitution, I would've gone with that one. My mom suggested "Farah," a name easier than "Firoozeh" yet still Iranian. Her reasoning made sense, except that Farrah Fawcett was at the height of her popularity and I didn't want to be associated with somebody whose poster hung in every postpubescent boy's bedroom. We couldn't think of any American names beginning with *F*, so we moved on to *J*, the first letter of our last name. I don't know why we limited ourselves to names beginning with my initials, but it made sense at that moment, perhaps by the logic employed moments before bungee jumping. I finally chose the name "Julie" mainly for its simplicity. My brothers, Farid and Farshid, thought that adding an American name was totally stupid. They later became Fred and Sean.

That same afternoon, our doorbell rang. It was our new next-door neighbor, a friendly girl my age named Julie. She asked me my name and after a moment of hesitation, I introduced myself as Julie. "What a coincidence!" she said. I didn't mention that I had been Julie for only half an hour.

Thus I started sixth grade with my new, easy name and life became infinitely simpler. People actually remembered my name, which was an entirely refreshing new sensation. All was well until the Iranian Revolution, when I found myself with a new set of problems. Because I spoke English without an accent and was known as Julie, people assumed I was American. This meant that I was often privy to their real feelings about those "damn I-raynians." It was like having those X-ray glasses that let you see people undressed, except that what I was seeing was far uglier than people's underwear. It dawned on me that these people would have probably never invited me to their house had they known me as Firoozeh. I felt like a fake.

When I went to college, I eventually went back to using my real name. All was well until I graduated and started looking for a job. Even though I had graduated with honors from UC–Berkeley, I couldn't get a single interview. I was guilty of being a humanities major, but I began to suspect that there was more to my problems. After three months of rejections, I added "Julie" to my résumé. Call it coincidence, but the job offers started coming in. Perhaps it's the same kind of coincidence that keeps African Americans from getting cabs in New York.

Once I got married, my name became Julie Dumas. I went from having an identifiably "ethnic" name to having ancestors who wore clogs. My family and non-American friends continued calling me Firoozeh, while my coworkers and American friends called me Julie. My life became one big knot, especially when friends who knew me as Julie met friends who knew me as Firoozeh. **I felt like those characters in soap operas who have an evil twin. The two can never be in the same room,** since they're played by the same person, a struggling actress who wears a wig to play one of the twins and dreams of moving on to bigger and better roles. I couldn't blame my mess on a screenwriter; it was my own doing.

I decided to untangle the knot once and for all by going back to my real name. By then, I was a stay-at-home mom, so I really didn't care whether people remembered my name or gave me job interviews. Besides, most of the people I dealt with were in diapers and were in no position to judge. I was also living in Silicon Valley, an area filled with people named Rajeev, Avishai, and Insook.

Every once in a while, though, somebody comes up with a new permutation and I am once again reminded that I am an immigrant with a foreign name. I recently went to have blood drawn for a physical exam. The waiting room for blood work at our local medical clinic is in the basement of the building, and no matter how early one arrives for an appointment, forty coughing, wheezing people have gotten there first. Apart from reading *Golf Digest* and *Popular Mechanics,* there isn't much to do except guess the number of contagious diseases represented in the windowless room, Every ten minutes, a name is called and everyone looks to see which cough matches that name. As I waited patiently, the receptionist called out, "Fritzy, Fritzy!" Everyone looked around, but no one stood up. Usually, if I'm waiting to be called by someone who doesn't know me, I will respond to just about any name starting with an *F.* Having been called Froozy, Frizzy, Fiorucci, and Frooz and just plain "Uhhhh . . . ," I am highly accommodating. I did not, however, respond to "Fritzy" because there is, as far as I know, no *t* in my name. The receptionist tried again, "Fritzy, Fritzy DumbAss." As I stood up to this most linguistically original version of my name, I could feel all eyes upon me. The room was momentarily silent as all of these sick people sat united in a moment of gratitude for their own names.

Despite a few exceptions, I have found that Americans are now far more willing to learn new names, just as they're far more willing to try new ethnic foods. Of course, some people just don't like to learn. One mom at my children's school adamantly refused to learn my "impossible" name and instead settled on calling me "F Word." She was recently transferred to New York where, from what I've heard, she might meet an immigrant or two and, who knows, she just might have to make some room in her spice cabinet.

▶ **Analyzing the Text**

1. What do you think the spice cabinet symbolizes in this essay?

2. What are some examples from the reading of how people responded to Dumas's Iranian name, Firoozeh? How does Dumas experience this? What actions does she take to address her experience, and why?

3. Dumas points out that only immigrants have names that include the letter *z.* Reread the essay and identify all of the attributes that the writer labels "immigrant" or "ethnic." Use the board to create a list. Through her language choice and humor, what does Dumas convey about being labeled an immigrant in America?

4. What objects, practices, and names does Dumas identify as "American"? What additional examples could you add to her list? What connects these examples to American values?

5. What overall message does Dumas convey about American culture? What, if anything, do you think she would like to change about it?

6. **Connecting to Another Reading.** In "How to Tame a Wild Tongue," Gloria Anzaldúa suggests that our language, our way of speaking, forms our sense of identity. How do you connect Anzaldúa's argument about language with Dumas's experiences as an immigrant, learning American ways? In what ways did changing her name affect Dumas's sense of identity? How did it affect the way people treated her?

Writing about Cultural Practices

7. Dumas asks readers to consider the question, "What makes someone or something American?" For this assignment, you will investigate the connections between eating habits and food choices and American culture—particularly American values and attitudes. For instance, what does American consumption of "instant" or microwavable foods say about American culture? What values are represented by a typical American breakfast? (While Americans might grab cereal bars or sit down to have eggs and bacon, many Chinese begin their day with congee, a kind of watery rice porridge.) Or a typical American late-night snack? (In countries in Africa, people snack on fresh fruit or raw sugarcane, while Americans might have ice cream, chips, or cookies.)

   Your task is to focus on a food that you identify as typically American and to write a descriptive analysis of it, connecting it to some cultural value that you think is shaped by Americans who eat it. To begin, go to a local grocery store or your school dining hall and identify foods that you consider to be very "American." Choose one or two related foods to be the focus of your essay. As you draft your analysis, consider the following questions.

   - How is the food typically prepared? When and where is it usually eaten? What is the nutritional value of the food?

   - What is the symbolic value of the food? How is the food represented in advertising images? How do advertisers connect it to particular cultural values? How does its presence in other unique contexts (like hot dogs at ballparks or pizzas in dorms) reinforce its symbolic value as an American food?

   - What about the food makes it American, in your opinion? What does it suggest about American culture and about what it means to be an American?

Russell Thornton, **What the Census Doesn't Count**

A noted writer of Native American history, Russell Thornton, a Cherokee Indian, grew up in eastern Oklahoma and has published *American Indian Holocaust and Survival: A Population History Since 1492* (1987) and *The Cherokees: A Population History* (1992). He teaches anthropology at the University of California, Los Angeles, and has also taught at the University of California, Berkeley; Dartmouth College; the University of Minnesota; and the University of Pennsylvania. This essay, which originally appeared in the *New York Times* in 2001, explores the addition of ever-widening labels of ethnic identity to the 2000 U.S. census.

▶ **Mapping Your Reading**

As Thornton points out in the following essay, the most recent national census (2000) allowed Americans their first opportunity to officially choose their racial identities. But what is racial identity? Is it something we choose, or, as Thornton asks, "Is it chosen for us?" According to this essay, what is it that the census "doesn't count"? As you read, mark the passages that address this question. Also, is it important for us to know how many of us are one race or another? Or how many of us are of mixed race? Can the census really tell us who we are?

The 2000 census was the first in which Americans could choose to identify themselves as having more than one race, and some 6.8 million people, about 2.4 percent of the population, did so. What does this identification mean for these Americans? Do others accept it? Is race really something we can choose, or is it chosen for us?

Race, we now know, is a social notion, not a biological reality. Physical appearances used to construct races—particularly skin color—are all but meaningless as indicators of important biological differences. Nevertheless, the races society has created are real to many people and have important psychological and social implications for individuals. According to the 2000 census, three of every ten Americans are members of one of four defined minority groups—African Americans, Asian Americans, Native Americans, and Latinos. Some seven of every ten Americans consider themselves white.

The 2000 census remains silent on whether the people around a given person consider him or her to be white, Asian American, or something else altogether. And that relative suspension of social judgment is the 2000 census's greatest innovation; it recognizes who you think you are as an important piece of information.

Since the census began, the government has attempted to enumerate citizens in terms of the important categories of the period. The first census, in 1790, was primarily concerned with counting landholding white males. Subsequent censuses became more inclusive. In 1890, for example, all Native Americans were first counted as part of the United States population; eighty years later the census included a question about Latinos.

All censuses through 1990 classified each American as being of only one of the designated races—except for the "mulatto" category common through the nineteenth century, which mainly concerned people who appeared to census enumerators to be somewhere between black and white. The mulatto category was the ancestor of today's mixture option, with the difference that today it is up to the individual rather than the census enumerator to name and describe the mixture.

> Race, we now know, is a social notion, not a biological reality.

The mulatto concept lived on somewhat quietly from 1900 to 1960 in the practice of having census workers split the differences themselves, so to speak, in problematic cases of mixture, or classify people in the category "all other races." In particularly difficult cases, the enumerators were to ask members of a person's community about what race that person was thought to be. This practice shows that in those years the important question was what society thought you were—not your own thoughts on who you were.

The 2000 census finally acknowledged the private reality of racially mixed citizens, capping the trend toward self-reporting begun with the 1960 census. But racial mixture in our country, of course, dates back centuries, despite the many state laws prohibiting marriages between whites and nonwhites. Among Native Americans, the story has long been—and it is not a very amusing story—that the first Indian-white child in North America was born nine months after the first white man arrived. Similarly, the mulatto census category accounted for significant percentages of the population in some states. It was not merely a demographic footnote.

The Native American case is in many ways an extreme one. In the 2000 census, 2.6 million Americans reported they were Native American. Some 1.5 million others reported that they were Native American and another race, typically white. This ratio—37 percent of a group reporting themselves as racially mixed—far exceeds percentages for other groups. For example, only about 5 percent of African Americans reported mixed ancestry.

A high percentage of racially mixed Native Americans is not surprising for those familiar with Native American history. The Native American population of what is now the United States declined from more than 5 million around 1492 to as few as 250,000 by 1900. It then began to increase, in part because of intermarriage, especially with whites; indeed, given the small numbers, it could hardly have increased without intermarriage. This situation created identity struggles for children of these marriages as they sought to define who they were and have others accept it. Children of Native American and African American intermarriages, for example, typically could not get others to accept their "Indianness" and almost always were defined as African American.

In such cases, we can see a variety of choices being made. Individuals may choose one identity for themselves, but others in society may make another choice for them. The black-Indian child may think of himself as Indian, but if no one around him does, then he has run up against the limit of his own power to choose a racial identity. And this constriction of choice extends backward in our history as it is verified by the terms we use: the racial categories themselves, black, white, and so on, were not necessarily "chosen" in the past, any more than we are completely free to choose them today.

We might imagine race as something that shifts unstably between individual freedom of choice (as in the new census) and a group's complete lack of freedom to choose. The reality of American life and our past exists between these twin poles, and the choices involved in it can perhaps never be entirely free.

A man who looks African American is typically going to be treated as an African American. That the man may also be Native American, Asian American, and/or white, and may have designated himself accordingly in the 2000 census, may be of no importance to anyone other than himself.

Americans are now relatively free to decide who they are, in racial terms, when filling out a census. But that is one of the few times when they are free to do so. Race is a social, not private, reality. And the census should not be misused to make racial policies, which have much more to do with how we act toward each other than what we think about ourselves.

▶ Analyzing the Text

1. Thornton writes, "Race, we now know, is a social notion, not a biological reality." How does he support this argument? Do you agree with him? Why or why not?

2. What does Thornton mean by the statement that "race is a social, not private, reality"? What potential conflicts are there between how we identify ourselves and how our communities or the larger society identify us? Which does Thornton think is more important? What do you think?

3. How important is Thornton's perspective as a Native American to his central argument? Does his critique apply equally to groups such as Latino, African, or Asian Americans? What about to white Americans?

4. Is it important that we identify ourselves—and that we be identified—by racial categories in the U.S. census? Why or why not?

5. **Connecting to Another Reading.** What are the differences and similarities between how Russell Thornton and Gloria Anzaldúa view the shaping of identity in terms of personal choice versus cultural factors?

6. How do students on your campus identify themselves demographically? More specifically, how do they plan to identify themselves in the 2010 census? Since conducting a full-scale census of your campus would be unmanageable for this assignment, you will develop a survey and administer it to one of your other college classes. To begin, go to the census website and download the form used for the 2000 census (see the On the Web link below for information on how to do this). Working in groups, draft a brief questionnaire that might include questions such as the following.

   - How would you identify yourself according to the racial categories of the 2000 government census? (You will need to show your respondents the racial identity portion of the U.S. census form.)

   - Do you feel it is important to identify yourself by race? Why or why not? Is the way you identify yourself different from how others see you? If so, is this important? Why or why not?

   - What do you think of the government's new "mixed race" category? Is it an important identifier? Why or why not? Are there categories missing from the census that you would like to see included? If so, what are they, and why do you think they are important?

   - As part of a particular demographic, do you feel you are adequately represented at your school? Do the administration and faculty adequately meet the needs of your demographic?

Once you have drafted your questions, use them to survey students in one of your other classes, and write an analysis of your findings. Your analysis should do the following:

   - Summarize the information you've gathered in a table or graph

   - Include a section on what findings surprised you most and why

   - Include any student critiques—of the government's racial categories or the degree to which they feel represented on campus, for example—and propose concrete actions that respond to these concerns

Michelle Lee, The Fashion Victim's Ten Commandments

Michelle Lee is a frequent contributor to women's and men's fashion magazines, including *Marie Claire, Elle, Self, Cosmopolitan, YM, Men's Health,* and *Maxim.* She has also held editorial positions at *Glamour, CosmoGIRL!,* and *Mademoiselle.* This selection is an excerpt from the first chapter of *Fashion Victim: Our Love-Hate Relationship with Dressing, Shopping, and the Cost of Style* (2002).

▶ **Mapping Your Reading**

As you read, use the margins to mark places in the text where Lee describes the role of fashion, clothes, or style in defining a person's sense of identity. Is how we dress an extension of how we see ourselves? Or is it an expression of how we want others to see us? Why do brand names carry so much cultural clout? What does Lee argue is the "sorry state we find ourselves in today"?

We Fashion Victims hold certain truths to be self-evident. Without so much as a raised eyebrow, we allow a set of ridiculous, yet compelling, rules to govern our wardrobes, our purchases, our desires, even our own sense of self-worth. It's these unquestioned tenets that have helped bring us to the sorry state we find ourselves in today.

1. Thou Shalt Pay More to Appear Poor

It takes a great deal of time and money to look as though you put no effort into dressing. Since a garment today rarely remains a popular item in our wardrobes beyond a few months, we require it to be worn out before we buy it. Fabrics are prewashed and grayed out to appear less new. Designers sew on decorative patches, slash gaping holes into the knees of jeans, and fray the hems. Dresses and shirts are prewrinkled. Jeans are stonewashed, sandblasted, acid-washed, and lightened, they're iron-creased and bleached to "whisker" at the upper-thigh as if they were passed down to you by your mother, who inherited them from her father, who had worn them in the wheat fields a century ago. Designers add "character" to clothes by messing

> It takes a great deal of time and money to look as though you put no effort into dressing.

them up, like Helmut Lang's famous $270 paint-spattered jeans. Jeans, blasted and stained dust-brown, by CK, Levi's, and Dolce & Gabbana, cost up to $200. In fact, Calvin Klein's "dirty" jeans sold for $20 more than a pair of his basic, unblemished ones. In 2001, Commes des Garçons produced a peasant dress, priced at a very unpeasantlike $495, described by discount shopping website Bluefly.com as "given a chic tattered look."

Fashion may be bent on newness, but we apparently can't stand it when something looks *too* new (who can bear the blinding whiteness of new sneakers?). The industry has taken to calling the shabby, imperfect look "distressed"—a word that carries a connotation of pain and suffering. This fashion agony doesn't come cheap, from Jean-Paul Gaultier's distressed leather pants for $1,560 and two-piece distressed leather jacket and bustier for $2,740 to Versace's distressed ball gowns and midpriced shoe maker Aldo's distressed leather pumps for $70.

2. Thou Shalt Covet Useless Utility

To the Fashion Victim, there's nothing wrong with clothes that serve no purpose other than looking cool. But if a garment can create the illusion that it's functional as well, it's all the better. A part of us knows that fashion is frivolous, so we attempt to justify our participation in it by making our clothes seem useful. We're grasping at straws to rationalize making some of our unnecessary purchases. Shirts come with hoods whose sole purpose is to hang behind one's neck. The polar fleece vest was pitched as functional in a climbing-the-Alps sort of way, but if you really wanted something to keep you warm, wouldn't you give it sleeves? Cargo pants, with their multitude of pockets, seemed infinitely useful . . . imagine all the odds and ends you could carry. Countless designers, including Calvin Klein, Gucci, and Versace, interpreted the military style for the runway, and mall retailers followed suit with their versions, like Abercrombie's Paratroops and American Eagle's Cargo Trek Pant. Ralph Lauren even produced an army-green cargo bikini with pockets at the hip (for toting beach grenades?). The fashion world's idealized image of the utilitarian future appears to involve lots of zippers, buckles, Velcro, pull closures, straps, and strings—no matter if they actually serve a purpose or not.

3. Thou Shalt Own Minutely Differing Variations of the Same Thing

Fashion Victims own duplicates of items that are just different enough to not be *exactly* the same. The average American owns seven pairs of blue jeans. Certainly, each pair could be cut and colored differently, but are those seven pairs really that different? Rosa, a twenty-six-year-old office manager in Chicago, owns more than fifteen pairs of navy-blue jeans that she's amassed over the last two years, picking up one or two pairs a month. "Some are regular-waisted, some are boot-cut, others are tapered, one has red stitching on the sides and on the pockets, some are button-fly, some are a bit darker," she explains. "Even though they all look the same, they each have their special style." All that variety means she doesn't wear each pair very often. "I have a few clothes that I have in my closet that I've only worn once or twice," she says. "But it's hard to part with them because I always feel like, 'Maybe I'll wear it *one* more time.'" Fashion Victims all share in this mind-set, and as a result, we could have two walk-in closets stuffed to the gills and still never feel like we have enough. So we continue to buy.

4. Thou Shalt Believe Submissively in the Fashion Label's Reach

Today when you buy a designer's clothes, you're also buying a lifestyle. Ralph Lauren (a.k.a. Ralph Lifschitz from the Bronx) knew this when he created Polo, a brand meant to evoke the image of the affluent, holiday-in-Hyannisport set. As a result, our favorite clothing brands can sell us practically anything else—hand cream, lipstick, perfume, nail polish, dishes, pillows, candles, duvets, music. You can not only wear Ralph Lauren, Calvin Klein, Banana Republic, Eddie Bauer, Donna Karan, Liz Claiborne, Nautica, and Versace, but you can dress your bedroom in them, too. Love how Club Monaco clothes look? Buy the retailer's line of cosmetics. Hooked on Victoria's Secret bras? Well, they must have good skin-care products if they make good bras, right? Like Armani suits? Buy their line of gourmet chocolates. Just as automakers like Jaguar, Vespa, and Harley-Davidson have their own branded clothing lines, retailers and designers have left their mark on the automotive world with special-edition cars like the Eddie Bauer Ford Explorer and Expedition, the Coach-edition Lexus, the Subaru Outback LL Bean edition, the Joseph Abboud Special Edition Buick Regal, and the Louis Vuitton edition of Chrysler's PT Cruiser.

5. Thou Shalt Require Validation of Thine Own Stylishness

The art of dress is quite frequently built on the opinions of others. We may like to think that how we dress is an extension of how we see ourselves, but more commonly, it's an expression of how we want *others* to see us. "We dress to communicate our social identities to others," says Kim Johnson, PhD, a professor at the University of Minnesota who teaches courses on the social psychology of clothing. "Dress informs others of how willing you are to participate in fashion and at what levels you're playing." In our appearance-centered society, one of the most common ways we butter up strangers and acquaintances is to compliment them on their clothes. We shower people with praise for their sense of style and expect to receive praise in return, like the sometimes sincere "You look great," which never fails to elicit the awkward yet gushing "You do *too*."

"We dress to communicate our social identities to others."

6. Thou Shalt Dress Vicariously Through Thy Children and Pets

It's not enough for Fashion Victims to dress themselves in designer clothes; they often feel it necessary to share their impeccable taste with others. Someone once told me, "You give what you want to receive." People choose items for others that reflect their own taste, rather than the recipient's. We Fashion Victims live by this. We dress our kids (and others' children when we buy gifts) in mini-me lines like Moschino kids, GapKids, babyGap, Old Navy Kids, Diesel Kids, Ralph Lauren kids, Prada kids, and Guess? Kids. Small sizes don't mean small prices. A baby leather jacket costs $200 at Polo. A jean jacket from Diesel Kids costs $109—more than a grown-up size at many stores. Then there's the $125 tulle dress for girls by Christian Dior, the $175 sweater by Missoni Kids, the pink knit pant set by Baby Dior, $93 trousers by Young Versace, and $68 bootleg jeans by Diesel. Before Dolce & Gabbana's kiddy line, D&G Junior, ran into some trouble in 2000 when its licensee Nilva went belly up, it carried several categories of clothing like "Denim Rock Star," "Lord Rapper," and "Logomania." There were gold denim jackets, tiny shearling coats, and a red leather racing-team jacket for $599. With most kids' clothes, there's not even the possibility of an outfit becoming a long-lasting part of a wardrobe because they outgrow things so quickly, so laying out exorbitant amounts of cash is truly like throwing money into a bottomless pit.

7. Thou Shalt Feign Athleticism

Most of our lives are wholly un-rugged, so we attempt to reinsert that missing ruggedness through our wardrobes. Labels like the North Face and Patagonia, which create functional garb for the mountaineering über-athlete, have become fashionable brands to traipse around town in. Timberland boots are as ideal for digging through CDs at the Virgin Megastore as they are for hiking through backwoods Montana. Columbia Sportswear recently produced a parka that de-tects when the wearer's skin temperature has dropped and releases stored body heat, which will no doubt become a must-have item for those climbing the Himalayas—or picking up an iced latte at Starbucks (*brrrr*).

Those of us who aren't triathletes or marathoners still enjoy examining the sole of a sneaker and seeing very scientific-looking springs, air pockets, gel, and pumps. Employees at the Nike Sport Research Laboratory hold PhD's or master's degrees in human biomechanics and bioengineering. In March 2002, Adidas in-troduced ClimaCool sneakers, designed to keep feet cool with a "360-degree ven-tilation system." Athletic shoe makers spend millions of dollars on research to develop supersneakers that add more bounce, absorb shock, improve traction, and cushion arches. And when the Fashion Victim buys these supersneakers, he is delighted over his purchase and can't wait to wear them when he meets his buddies for a drink, no doubt at the local sports bar.

8. Thou Shalt Be a Walking Billboard

In a way, wearing a logo is like wearing gang colors. Just as the Bloods and Crips brandish red and blue bandannas, the Fashion Victim wears the designer logo as a proud badge of membership. It's an act that's tribal at its core. "It's like schoolchildren all nagging for the coolest trainers [sneakers, for you non-Anglophiles]," says Vella. "If you're seen to be wearing the right thing, you're in."

A brand name can add immediate "worth" to two identical products. "Branding is unfortunately the cornerstone of many fashion labels today—not the design, the innovation, the cut, or any other skill honed by the designer. And what the brand stands for is everything," says Debi Hall, fashion-branding strategist for JY&A Consulting in London. "As the Japanese say, name is the first thing—without a name, a garment in today's highly capitalistic, value-added culture is worth very little. Take the vintage phenomenon: Even if a secondhand YSL dress is without a label, because it once had a name, it is still worth something. If, however, it is simply a secondhand dress with a name nobody has heard of, then it will go for pennies."

Still, not every Fashion Victim is so taken with the visible logo. Some fashion-conscious folk have been known to consider a visible label such a dealbreaker that they'll take the time to remove it. A few years back, hipsters in London started a trend by tearing the *N* off their New Balance sneakers. And according to *New York* magazine, the late Carolyn Bessette Kennedy once had employees cut the labels out of skiwear she had bought. Emily **In a way, wearing a logo is like wearing gang colors.** Cinader Woods, cofounder and chairman of J. Crew, says that unlike her friend Michael Jeffries—CEO of Abercrombie & Fitch, a company notorious for slapping its name conspicuously on everything—she's always been adamant about no logos. "There are so many brands that you might love an item or the color but the logo keeps you from buying it," she says. On the other hand, when you're around people who are familiar with various brands—as is typical for the Fashion Victim—it's possible to be a walking billboard without ever displaying the brand name on your body. I once wore a sleeveless J. Crew top to the office, and two co-workers that day remarked in passing, "I like that—J. Crew?" The brand's familiar look and prevalence in their mail-order catalogs had made the clothes recognizable enough that they didn't need an obvious swoosh, polo player, or little green alligator sewn across the chest. I had been a moving J. Crew billboard all day without the presence of any visible logos.

9. Thou Shalt Care about Paris Hilton's Gaultier Micro-mini

The socialite's role in the fashion game is to look stunning at events in couture gowns, and casually upper class when attending a summer soiree in the Hamptons. A gossipworthy socialite should be trailed by at least one rumor of out-of-control partying, like making out with someone other than her date or accidentally letting her Galliano gown slip down and flashing her fellow partygoers. Her job is to *be* the answer to the question: "Who actually wears those clothes?" These are the women who can afford the Fendi furs and Gucci pantsuits, but like celebrities, they are also the frequent recipients of loans and freebies from designers—residing below the A-List celebrity, but above B-List TV actresses and pop stars in the fashion hierarchy. In magazines, they seem somehow superhuman. Mostly whippet-thin (perfect for fitting into the sample size), the pretty and privileged attend trunk shows, where they're wined, dined, and shown exquisite new designs. Their job description also includes sitting front row at catwalk shows. Of course, these women are expected to do something in return: They are obliged to wear (and showcase) the designer's clothes.

The fashion system is built on want. Looking at socialites' clothes in *Vogue* is like drooling over the estates in *Architectural Digest* or flipping through the *DuPont Registry* to catch a glimpse of the Bentleys and Aston Martins you'll never be able to afford. We live vicariously through the socialite—who has deep enough pockets to buy designer threads of a caliber most of us will never even see in person. Perplexing as our interest may be, the Fashion Victim eats up every morsel, but not without a tinge of jealousy, of course. "I *love* looking at those rich bitches," says Rita, a 49-year-old website editor in Stamford, Connecticut. "But what kills me is that a lot of them don't really have great taste—they just have great resources. If they had to put together a wardrobe like the rest of us mere mortals—from the Gap, Banana Republic, etc.—I doubt they'd be so fabulous. But you do get good fashion ideas from looking and it's nice to daydream."

10. Thou Shalt Want Without Seeing

Curiously, selling clothes today does not always require actually *showing* the clothes. "Sex sells, sells, and keeps selling," says Marc Berger, fashion director of *GQ*. "A sexy woman in an ad will always grab the attention of a man. It's a great marketing ploy." The no-show advertising technique is frequently justified with "We're selling an image." Ads are another example of fashion's hypnotic power over us. All a company needs to do is get our attention—whether or not we love the clothes is insignificant. In recent years, Abercrombie & Fitch's controversial magalog, the *A&F Quarterly,* has raised eyebrows with its photos of tanned all-American dudes and dudettes, often with zero body fat and zero clothing—a buff naked guy holding a film reel in front of his privates, a couple wearing nothing but body paint, a group of disrobed guys flashing their smiles (and nearly everything else) by the pool. The image: cool, horny coeds. In 1999, a Sisley campaign shot by Terry Richardson simply showed the faces of two female models in a half-sexy, half-goofy liplock. Two years later, an ad for the retailer featured a self-portrait of the moustached Richardson wearing a snake around his neck and nothing else. The image: sexy, slightly dirty. Then there was an Ungaro print ad a few years back showing a werewolf licking a woman's bare body, which was widely condemned for being overly graphic. The image? Anyone's guess. Perhaps the most controversial campaign of late comes from French Connection. To announce the opening of its largest store ever, the retailer took out a full-page ad in a London paper that read, "The World's Biggest FCUK," flaunting the company's easily misread acronym (think of the poor dyslexics!).

▶ Analyzing the Text

1. Most of us hear the term "fashion victim" and think of someone who dresses very badly, but what does Lee mean by this term?

2. By creating her own version of the ten commandments, Lee makes an indirect statement about the role of fashion (of paying attention to the clothes we wear) in our lives. What statement does she make? Does this indirect strategy work? How would her message be different if she had spelled out her argument more directly, or without humor?

3. According to Lee, how does fashion help shape or define identity? How does a person's style of dress affect the conclusions you draw about him or her?

4. How effective is the way Lee constructs her argument? Working in pairs or small groups, choose a paragraph to reexamine. Then, create a list or map of the task each sentence of the paragraph accomplishes. Where in the paragraph does Lee state her main claims or points? What techniques does she use to support her claims?

5. **Interrogating Assumptions.** How does Lee's essay challenge the third assumption in this chapter's introduction that "identity is shaped by personal choices" (see p. 11)? To what extent is "how we dress . . . an expression of how we want *others* to see us," as Lee suggests in her fifth commandment? How would Lee respond to the second assumption in the introduction that "identity is shaped by culture" (see p. 9)? How do you respond?

▶ Writing about Cultural Practices

6. In the introduction to her book, Lee writes, "Our clothes are visible symbols of who we really are and who we want to be" (xiii). To reinforce her point, Lee describes the work of an artist named Lisa Greenstein who paints still-life portraits using only people's shoes. The shoes, Greenstein says, are "visual representations of [people's] personalities" (xiii). For the sake of investigation, play along with this argument and construct a written description, or portrait, of someone solely by focusing on a pair of shoes he or she wears. As you draft, consider the following questions.

   - How would you describe this pair of shoes? Pay attention to their materials and construction, and describe the styling of their brand name.
   - When and where does this person wear them? Are they for special occasions? Are they worn only with certain clothes or outfits? What conclusions do you draw from these details?
   - What do these shoes say about who this person is? What do they say about the social groups to which the person belongs?

7. Take an opposite view on the role of fashion and create a ten commandments of your own to describe a belief system for the anti-fashion point of view. For instance, an anti-fashion point of view might command people to wear the same clothes every day. When you've completed your list and described each of your

alternative commandments, compare your version to Lee's. Write a critical analysis describing the differences and similarities you find between yours and Lee's. As you write, consider these questions.

- Reviewing your commandments, how do you define "anti-fashion"? How does Lee define "fashion"?

- What is Lee's argument about how fashion affects people's sense of identity? How do your commandments compare and contrast to Lee's argument? In other words, how might having an anti-fashion attitude affect one's sense of identity?

- Given the extent to which we are surrounded by media and advertising images, is it possible to live by the principles of anti-fashion that you defined? Why or why not?

Shannon Wheeler, **I Hated Journey**

Shannon Wheeler is the creator of the *Too Much Coffee Man* cartoon strip, first published in 1993, and the creator of a bimonthly web zine of the same name. The comic strip, which has been collected in books from *Too Much Coffee Man: Guide for the Perplexed* (1998) to *How to Be Happy* (2005), is a (jittery) satire of modern life and popular culture, especially superheroes. The cartoon's main character is an everyday man who is incapable of doing anything productive. In the foreword to *Too Much Coffee Man's Parade of Tirade* (2000), Henry Rollins describes the impact of Wheeler's creation: "Too Much Coffee Man is the embodiment of our stressed urban intellectual overload smashing into a wall. He sits, grinding his teeth in the eye of the storm, deeply entrenched in the battlefield of our collective fears and neurosis."

▶ **Mapping Your Reading**

The following cartoon is a commentary about how identity and relationship to others can be shaped by our dislikes as well as our likes. What details convey the cartoonist's social commentary? Is what we choose to reject an important indicator of who we are? Do you share musical or other tastes with your social group? What do these preferences say about who you are and about how you relate to others?

TOO MUCH COFFEE MAN
BY SHANNON WHEELER

MY BEST FRIEND AND I **HATED** JOURNEY MORE THAN **ANYTHING**. AS A **JOKE**, WE WENT TO SEE THEM.

WE HAD A **BLAST** MAKING FUN OF THE **GUYS** AND CHECKING OUT THE **GIRLS**.

MULLET, 10 O'CLOCK!

HA HA HA

MID-SHOW, WHEN **JOURNEY** PLAYED THEIR **BIG HIT NUMBER ONE SONG**, WE DECIDED TO **TAKE OFF**.

THIS SUCKS!

LET'S GET OUT OF HERE!

IT FELT **GREAT** TO WALK PAST HORDES OF **FANS** THAT COULDN'T BELIEVE THAT WE WERE **LEAVING**.

NOW, WHENEVER I HEAR **JOURNEY**, THE MUSIC BRINGS BACK **GOOD MEMORIES** OF **FRIENDSHIP** AND **SUBVERSION**.

HA HA HA HA HA HA HA HA HA

I **LIKE** IT BECAUSE I USED TO **HATE** IT.

IT'S NOT FAIR! I DON'T WANT TO LIKE A CRAPPY POP BAND!

WHEN THE LIGHTS...GO DOWN IN THE CITY...

Analyzing the Text

1. What point is the cartoonist making about his memories of hating the band Journey?

2. How does the cartoon suggest that individual dislikes shape identity? Can they be more powerful than likes? What do individual and shared tastes have to do with identity and social relationships?

3. The cartoon's main character recounts a fond memory of bucking a popular fad or trend (in this case, a popular band). Do you find this attitude appealing? Why or why not? Is this a particularly American attitude?

4. One underlying message of this cartoon is that our likes and dislikes say something about who we are and directly affect our social relationships. In the cartoon, the main character's friendship is grounded in making fun of people who like something he hates. Based on this cartoon, what observations can you make about what keeps friends together?

Writing about Cultural Practices

5. Write an essay in which you respond to Wheeler's observations about the impact of dislikes and fads on identity by using your own experiences. Remember a fad that became overwhelmingly popular when you were between the ages of 8 and 13. Was it Harry Potter? Skateboarding? *The X-Files*? Britney Spears? Hello Kitty? Describe your involvement with this fad *or* your intense dislike of it. Explain how it became part of your identity at that time. As you draft your descriptive analysis, respond to the following questions.

   - When did you first notice the popularity of this particular fad? How did this fad affect the way people acted? Dressed? Entertained themselves?

   - How would you describe your involvement with this fad? Were you an avid fan or were you a critic, like Wheeler?

   - How did your love or hate of this fad influence your friendships at the time? How did it affect how you spent your time? Looking back, how did your love or hate of it shape your sense of identity at that time?

   - In your opinion, how do fads impact people's sense of identity? Do they impact all age groups on some level? Why or why not?

© Neal Preston/CORBIS

© Henry Diltz/CORBIS

© Neal Preston/CORBIS

© Bettmann/CORBIS

Mixing Words and Images

CREATING AN IDENTI-KIT

Originally, identi-kits were used by the police to develop a picture of a suspect. They were a set of transparencies of typical facial characteristics that could be superimposed on one another to build a picture of a person. Today, the word "identi-kit" more commonly is used to describe the process of creating an identity (like the process of turning a regular person into a pop singer on *American Idol*) by copying the cultural markers commonly understood as identifying such a person. During their ZooTV concert tour in the early 1990s, the rock group U2 wanted to poke fun at their own rock star status. To do this, lead singer Bono performed as an over-the-top rock star character called The Fly. In interviews he explained, "I was Robo-Bono, a kind of identi-kit rock star" (*Rolling Stone*, 9 July 2000). To create his identi-kit, he borrowed elements from past iconic rock stars, specifically Roy Orbison's glasses, Jim Morrison's leather look, and Elvis Presley's swaggering style.

Creating Your Identi-kit

Like Bono's, your identi-kit will be a kind of robo-image or hyperconscious image of yourself. To begin, identify one stereotypical image of yourself that you can convey in this assignment. What labels might others use to describe you? For example, are you an athlete? A night owl? A hip-hop fan? A girly girl? A computer geek? An indie rocker? A film buff? A vegan poet? Choose a label to use for your identi-kit picture. Next, consider which qualities or aspects about yourself help others to label you in this way. For instance, think about what symbols might convey particular messages about this side of your identity. These symbols may show your intellectual, comic, or artistic side. They may come from details about your appearance (specific brands or styles of clothes, shoes, jewelry, hairstyle, and so on) or the things you carry with you every day.

To make your identi-kit, you will create a picture of yourself that takes up an 8 × 11 inch piece of paper. Begin by cutting out a picture of your face from a photo. Next, search magazines, catalogs, newspapers, and websites for images that you can paste together to complete your picture of yourself. It's almost like creating a paper-doll version of yourself that you are "dressing up" to show how one side of your identity is constructed.

Writing about Your Identi-kit

Once you have constructed your identi-kit, draft a descriptive analysis essay that considers the following questions.

- Why did you choose these particular symbols or details to construct your identi-kit? How do the items included in your identi-kit represent particular cultural values or messages? How do they help others to identify or label you?

- How do these cultural markers, taken together, form an image of your identity for other people?

- To what extent is identity something that we perform or "put on" and "take off"?

1. How to Belong: A Critical Analysis of Cool

In her essay "High School's Secret Life," Emily White describes how people often work very hard to belong. Her point of view is as an outsider, as she analyzes what it means to belong or to fake belonging. For this assignment, you will take the outsider's point of view to write a critical analysis of "how to belong." (If you already define yourself as an outsider, see the alternative writing suggestion at the end of this assignment.) To begin, choose a social scene in your present life or from your recent past. In your essay, you will combine two equally important elements: (1) to provide readers with the kind of concrete and descriptive details that White uses to create her study of "how to belong," and (2) to explain or analyze what you think the impact of these social markers have on people's sense of identity. How important is belonging to a person's sense of self?

Consider the following questions as you draft.

- In the social scene you describe, what are the unspoken traditions of belonging or looking like you belong? What kinds of belonging are there?

ON THE WEB
For help with these assignments, go to Chapter 1, **bedfordstmartins.com/remix**

- In the social scene you describe, what traits, behaviors, or material objects mark people as belonging?
- White remarks that there are striking similarities among all the popular students at Calhoun High. In fact, she notes remarkable similarities in dress, behavior, and attitudes within each of the different tribes she describes. Do similarities and conformity help define the particular crowd or social group that is the subject of your analysis?

Assignment Alternative: How *Not* to Belong, or a Critical Analysis of Uncool

There are probably as many people making an effort *not* to belong as there are people trying to belong. Take the other side and create an analysis of "how not to belong." Are you an outsider? Is "not belonging" another way of belonging, or is it something else?

2. Looking the Part: Deconstructing Personal Fashion

In "The Fashion Victim's Ten Commandments," Michelle Lee contends that fashion is so integrated with personal identity that we can no longer think of clothes simply as layers that protect us from the elements or as "just what I like to wear." In her book's introduction, Lee writes, "Dress is used to some extent to distinguish groups—rich/poor, liberal/conservative, hip/unhip" (xvi). As a result, our particular "look" influences not only how we think of ourselves but also the way others see us. For this assignment, write a critical narrative essay that accomplishes the following tasks.

To begin, define and describe either your current look or a look you used to wear, for instance, at a job where you were required to look a particular way. In describing your look, include all relevant details such as your shoes, clothes, hair style, jewelry, and so on.

In the second half of the essay, form a judgment about how others might (or did) position you within social or cultural markers of identity based on your appearance. In other words, to what extent do (or did) people form expectations about who you are (or who you were) based on your appearance? To explain your judgment, consider the following questions.

- How do (or did) people treat you, based on your appearance?
- How or in what ways does (or did) your look conform to a particular social group? What judgments do (or did) people make about this group?

3. Interrogating Assumptions: What Makes Us Who We Are?

At the beginning of this chapter, you were introduced to three commonly held assumptions that challenged you to reflect on some of the cultural attitudes behind how we think about identity.

Identity is what we're born with.

Identity is shaped by culture.

Identity is shaped by personal choices.

For this assignment, you will develop a critical analysis of how two to three of the readings interrogate one of these assumptions about identity. In your essay, you will present the main arguments of the readings you've selected and show how they support or refute the assumption you've chosen.

As you draft, consider the following questions.

- What claim(s) does each writer make? Identify the main argument of each essay. What aspect of identity seems to be at stake in each essay?
- Which of the above assumptions does each writer focus on? According to each writer, what makes us who we are? What details in the essays lead to this observation? (Be sure to quote from the essays you discuss.)
- What does the use of supporting evidence reveal about the writer's argument about how people negotiate or develop their senses of identity? What does it reveal about the writer's assumptions about who his or her audience is? How well (or how poorly) does the writer use evidence to support his or her argument? Ultimately, are you persuaded to agree with the writer? Why or why not?

 +  =

*or, are these
your people?*

2 Community

Examining the Everyday
Community and Shoes

Every year on the third Monday in April, more than twenty thousand people from around the world come to Boston to run in the country's oldest marathon. This photo shows a billboard posted above a subway station close to the 2004 marathon's finish line. Many of the runners and the thousands of spectators streamed wearily past it on their way home that day. What makes this billboard—sponsored by Nike—such clever marketing is that the statement reflects our changing ideas about the nature of community.

The term "community" once referred primarily to our association with a town, city, or neighborhood. But what the image of the Nike billboard demonstrates is that the things that hold people together—the things that define a community—can be more broadly defined. "Running," the ad says, "is a community." The ad does not say

ON THE WEB
For additional resources for this
assignment, go to Chapter 2,
bedfordstmartins.com/remix

"Wearing Nike running shoes is a community," although that is what it also suggests. What do the following statements have in common?

Music-downloading is a community.

Listening to talk radio is a community.

Instant-messaging is a community.

Shopping on eBay is a community.

Loving the Chicago Cubs is a community.

Reading the *Times* is a community.

Voting for candidate *X* is a community.

Wearing a yellow ribbon is a community.

In all these statements, what defines community is a verb. One shared interest is expressed as an action. People belong to many different communities based on their interests, needs, and values, and, as these shift, so do the communities they identify with.

And yet, Nike's idea of community is a romanticized one. After all, only one runner crosses the finish line first and gets to claim the glory of being named the winner. Running is an individual sport in which runners have to work to find and build a sense of community.

For this initial assignment, you will look into the ways one of your daily activities connects you to a community of people. You'll also examine when and how the

differences among individuals test a group's ability to stick together.

Write a brief profile of a group and use this group to investigate what makes a community a community. To begin, identify a daily activity that you share with other people—for example, studying, taking the bus, or working out. Second, go to where people doing this activity are found. (Note: This space could be a nonphysical, online space.) Observe people and take notes as you study their actions. You may also want to take photos. How do people who share this activity interact with one another? Taking your cue from the photo on page 84, begin your profile with the sentence "_____ is a community." Your profile should answer the following questions.

- What makes this group a community? What holds the group together?

- What interests, needs, and values do these people share?

- What tensions or differences work against the cohesion of this community?

Finally, add an additional paragraph that answers these questions.

- How do you fit in with this group? What makes this community one that you want to be a part of?

The initial assignment of this chapter is meant to broaden your view of the concept of community; in part, it points out that who and what constitute a community are not as clear-cut as they seem. In this chapter, you will investigate how communities function in modern American life.

One of the first challenges to investigating the role of communities today is that a set of idealized assumptions about what defines a community tends to dominate our thinking. These idealistic notions offer a simplified view of community that makes it more difficult for us to investigate community as a concept. Consider the example of *Mister Rogers' Neighborhood,* one of the longest running and most acclaimed children's television shows on PBS. In Mr. Rogers's neighborhood, everything is peaceful, neighbors know one another, everyone gets along, and no one goes hungry, gets laid off, or suffers from any of the typical social problems of our time. *Mister Rogers' Neighborhood* provides examples of idealized assumptions about community that can get in the way of an investigation of how communities really work.

The readings in this chapter present many examples of and perspectives on communities and their roles in modern life. They will challenge you to reflect on some of the most common assumptions people make about what defines communities and how they work. Each assumption emphasizes one function of community life over others, yet as you'll see, they sometimes overlap. Here is a brief overview of these assumptions.

introduction

Assumption 1

Communities provide us with a sense of stability.

Communities maintain stability by establishing traditions and standards of behavior for those who belong to them. Traditions and standards of behavior make it easier for community members to know which practices are acceptable and which are not. "Traditions," as you will see in the following chapter, are the customs and beliefs shared by a community. Traditions are shared practices such as religious celebrations or national holidays, but they also exist in smaller contexts such as the pregame rituals of athletes or a family's custom of eating at the same restaurant every Saturday night. "Standards of behavior" include all of the mundane everyday habits that a group of people accepts as normal. For example, how people dress is often a matter of what is standard within their own community. Greetings—whether a handshake, a "Whazzup?," or a kiss—are further examples of standards of behavior within a community.

Fred Rogers (1928–2003), *creator of the PBS children's show* Mister Rogers' Neighborhood, *described his program as a "television visit" between him and his young viewers. The stories shared in his make-believe neighborhood "illustrate how people can work together and support each other. While the puppet characters have identifiable personalities, they, like all of us, have the capacity for growing." PBS explains the appeal of the show: "While some adults wonder what makes this program so fascinating, the children know: Mister Rogers brings them a one-to-one affirmation of their self-worth and offers them a place where they feel accepted and understood."*

We're Glad To Be Your Neighbors

The assumption that communities offer stability requires traditions and standards of behavior that allow community members to identify each other. In ancient times, this was a matter of survival. Societies were bound together by their uniformity and traditions. These communities changed little, and their individual members were closely related by family ties and experience.

Today, the family is perhaps the most common example of a community that falls under this first assumption. Most of us assume that the family will provide protection and shelter for our physical, mental, and emotional needs. Families may also provide us with a sense of history and teach us many of the values, traditions, and standards of behavior that help guide our actions and decisions.

On the one hand, shared traditions and history can have a positive impact on the individual. Consider the example of a family that shares an interest in local sports. This can be a very supportive and positive environment for the children of the family to grow up in because, when a family participates together in activities like sports, it often grows closer. The children may gain a feeling of purpose, stability, and even a sense of identity as a result of the shared activity. Members of the community may identify the children as the brothers of the star softball pitcher or the daughters of the coach; and, as the family socializes with other families involved in local sports, the children learn the importance of belonging to a community.

On the other hand, sometimes a community's efforts to maintain stability and uniformity come at a cost to the individual. What happens to the child of a sports-focused family if he or she doesn't share the same interest in or talent for sports? How does that child deal with the difficulty of not fitting into the expectations or traditions of his or her family? This may seem like a minor example. After all, one hopes that a family is held together by more than one shared interest and that its members see each individual as a whole person. Yet, examples of this conflict between a community's needs to maintain stability and an individual's needs for personal choice and autonomy are not altogether uncommon. In his essay, "The Amish Charter" (p. 99), John Hostetler describes in detail how the Amish community puts its needs for stability and uniformity above those of its individual members.

Consider also that some communities do not provide their members with stability. In fact, the rising popularity of online communities raises real questions about the importance of stability as a defining characteristic of communities. The ease with which people join and leave online communities leads Andrew Leonard, in "You Are Who You Know" (p. 150), to observe that "the not-so-secret secret of social networking is that *flimsy is good*!"

What questions can you ask to uncover the benefits and limitations of the assumption that communities provide stability?

- What traditions or standards of behavior do the members of a given community share?
- How do these traditions or standards of behavior help give community members a sense of purpose, identity, and stability?
- How does the community respond if a member breaks with tradition or doesn't comply with the accepted standards of behavior?

Assumption 2

Communities serve our needs.

Another popular assumption about communities is that they will support us and give us what we need to lead productive and happy lives. When we need help, the assumption is that our community will come together to offer it. If an apartment building catches fire, the fire department will come to the rescue. If there's a flood, state and national officials will arrive to help the victims rebuild their lives. These examples represent community support in its broadest sense because they describe public services, which offer identical help to individuals with identical needs because it is in the public's interest to do so.

But when people say communities will serve their needs, they aren't speaking only about public services. They are usually referring to the ways they assume communities will support their personal goals. Consider someone who wishes to apply to college. He or she expects to receive the support of family, friends, teachers, and a range of community institutions, perhaps including an educational counseling center, a test preparation center, and a bank or student loan foundation. Or how about someone who decides to lose 25 pounds after her doctor tells her she is overweight? This dieter assumes her friends will provide support, perhaps by offering encouragement, adjusting their group routines by eating at healthier restaurants, or exercising together.

When communities serve our needs, as in the previous examples, both the individual and the group benefit: a college-educated or

"So, does anyone else feel that their needs aren't being met?"

healthier person helps the community. However, built into the assumption that communities serve our needs are these beliefs: (1) Communities have only our best interests at heart. (2) Individuals in a community always know (and are free to determine) what their best interests are. In this view, the role of the community is to support the individual's vision. But what if the dieter mentioned above does not really need to lose 25 pounds, but, as Mim Udovitch writes in "A Secret Society of the Starving" (p. 109), wants to get into "the double digits" in terms of her weight? Perhaps her friends do not see her weight loss goal as potentially harmful and, instead, encourage her to purge after eating and to take diuretics. With the encouragement of images on TV and in magazines and the approval of her mother, who always seems to be on a diet, the dieter loses weight quickly. Before people really notice the danger to her health, she reaches her goal of losing 25 pounds, and the true nature of her eating disorder is not discovered until she has to be hospitalized for heart palpitations. It could be argued in this case that the community did its job—after all, it supported the young woman's goal. Here, then, is the danger of assuming that communities always act in our best interests—sometimes communities actually support behavior or attitudes that can harm us.

What questions can you ask to uncover the benefits and limitations of the assumption that communities serve our needs and are good for us?

- What roles do individuals play within a particular community?
- How does this community demonstrate its support for the individuals who are its members? How is this "support" defined?
- What underlying values—whether positive, negative, or some combination—are revealed through this support?

Assumption 3

Communities accept us for who we are.

Another popular assumption about communities is that they provide caring environments for their members—places where individuals are treated positively for expressing their personal views, talents, or interests. Although as commonly accepted as the first assumption, this view does contradict it on some level. Whereas the first assumption tends to focus on the needs or concerns of the community over the individual, this third assumption turns that view around. In this view, a community becomes stronger by accepting people as individuals.

Such a perspective is tied to long-held attitudes within American culture. For example, Americans have high regard for the rugged individual, leader, free spirit, or visionary speaking his or her mind. Americans tend to put great faith in the premise that a strong community is one that respects members' personal views and encourages them to explore their own interests.

For this reason, we may seek out communities of people who share our interests and who will accept us without trying to change us. Where we once were limited by our geography, today people use websites and chat rooms to seek out communities who understand and accept them. It seems there is a place on the Internet for almost any group of like-minded people. For example, women struggling with infertility may use the Internet to seek out others who share and understand their situation. Likewise, there are many different sites dedicated to helping people make friends or find their romantic match. Indeed, a defining characteristic of such communities is that they do not judge us or seek to change us in any fundamental way. Their sole purpose is to service the individual.

This, then, is the main limitation of this assumption about communities: It treats communities as a service that individuals "shop" for. Accordingly, when individuals' needs change they simply move on to other communities. Two things are lost if we accept this perspective without question. First, by moving from one community of interest to another, we can lose the possibility of developing more sustained relationships with others over time. Second, our relationships with others can become more superficial or two-dimensional. Ultimately, how well do the people we meet online really know us when they see us only in light of a particular shared interest? By limiting ourselves to communities whose chief purpose is to reinforce our personal interests, ideas, or problems, we can become accustomed to connecting only with like-minded people who see just one part of who we are. Such limiting could cheat us out of developing relationships that spark in us new ways of thinking and behaving.

What questions can you ask to uncover the benefits and limitations of the assumption that communities accept us for who we are?

- What holds the individuals within this community together? Is there a set of shared interests? Activities? Beliefs?
- How does the community respond to change?
- What causes individuals to stop participating in or engaging with this community?

Questioning These Assumptions

What makes these three assumptions about communities powerful is that there is *some* truth to them. At some point in our lives, each of us will experience the positive benefits of belonging to a community that respects and cares about us. However, the cultural assumptions outlined here can prevent us from truly investigating how communities function—whether positively or negatively.

Throughout this chapter, you will be asked to move beyond these idealized views about communities. In the readings and assignments, you will be asked, "How do communities function? What do they enable? What do they constrain? What roles do communities serve in our lives?"

IN THE MIX

Rosario Morales and Aurora Levins Morales, **Ending Poem**

A poet and community historian, Aurora Levins Morales was born in Puerto Rico in 1954 to a Puerto Rican mother and a Jewish father. Her mother, Rosario Morales, is the co-author of this poem. As a family they moved to the United States in 1967, lived in Chicago and New Hampshire, and now reside in California. Levins Morales's short stories and poems have appeared in many books and collections. Her most recent books are *Medicine Stories: History, Culture, and the Politics of Integrity* (1998), *Remedios: Stories of Earth and Iron from the History of Puertorriqueñas* (1998), and *Telling to Live: Latina Feminist Testimonios* (2001). Levins Morales's poetry frequently focuses on how her family and community histories affect or shape her sense of identity and community. As its title suggests, "Ending Poem" is the final poem in a collection called *Getting Home Alive* (1986), which contains poems by both mother and daughter. A unique element of this poem is the generational dialogue and "cross-fertilization," as Levins Morales describes it, between her mother's voice and her own. The result is a poem, written mostly in the first-person "I," in which this mother and daughter explore family ties as perhaps the most significant community affecting our lives.

▶ **Mapping Your Reading**

Throughout this poem, Rosario Morales and Aurora Levins Morales are writing about who they are and about their ancestors' contributions to their lives. As you read, mark lines in the poem that describe ancestors' experiences or ancestral places with a colored pencil or highlighter and mark lines that describe the writers' own lives in a different color. You may notice this isn't a straightforward task. What does the overlap of individual and communal experiences suggest about the writers' relationships to their ancestors?

I am what I am.
A child of the Americas.
A light-skinned mestiza of the Caribbean.
A child of many diaspora, born into this continent at a crossroads.
I am Puerto Rican. I am U.S. American.

I am New York Manhattan and the Bronx
A mountain-born, country-bred, homegrown jibara child,
up from the shtetl, a California Puerto Rican Jew
A product of the New York ghettos I have never known.
I am an immigrant
And the daughter and granddaughter of immigrants.
We didn't know our forbears' names with a certainty.
They aren't written anywhere.
First names only or mija, negra, ne, honey, sugar, dear

I come from the dirt where the cane was grown.
My people didn't go to dinner parties. They weren't invited.
I am caribeña, island grown.
Spanish is my flesh, ripples from my tongue, lodges in my hips,
the language of garlic and mangoes.
Boricua. As Boricuas come from the isle of Manhattan.
I am of latinoamerica, rooted in the history of my continent.
I speak from that body. Just brown and pink and full of drums inside.

I am not African.
Africa waters the roots of my tree, but I cannot return.

I am not Taína.
I am a late leaf of that ancient tree,
and my roots reach into the soil of two Americas.
Taíno is in me, but there is no way back.

I am not European, though I have dreamt of those cities.
Each plate is different.
wood, clay, papier maché, metals, basketry, a leaf, a coconut shell.
Europe lives in me but I have no home there.

The table has a cloth woven by one, dyed by another,
embroidered by another still.
I am a child of many mothers.
They have kept it all going
All the civilizations erected on their backs.
All the dinner parties given with their labor.

We are new.
They gave us life, kept us going,
brought us to where we are.
Born at a crossroads.
Come, lay that dishcloth down. Eat, dear, eat.

History made us.
We will not eat ourselves up inside anymore.

And we are whole.

▶ **Analyzing the Text**

1. A mother and daughter wrote this poem, and in part, it is about how their relationships to the people they've descended from have helped to make them who they are. Which details in this poem help them get their message across?

2. Throughout the poem, the writers play with time and voice. They write in the present tense even when describing people and places from the past, and they use the first person "I" even though there are two authors and even when they aren't speaking about their own direct experiences. What effect do these choices have on the message of the poem? Why do the authors end the piece using the plural pronoun "we"?

3. What is the tone of this poem? Is it dark? Somber? Hopeful? Reserved? What adjective(s) would you use to describe it? What details in the poem give you clues about its mood or tone?

4. Pay attention to the writers' use of metaphors to make comparisons. For instance, images of trees and of being rooted appear in several places. How do these images affect the poem's message about family as a special kind of community? What other metaphors or images do the writers use? What do these images convey about how familial communities affect or shape personal identity?

5. The purpose of this chapter is to explore the role of communities in our lives, and to ask, How do communities function? What do they enable? What do they constrain? Working from this poem, how would you say family heritage provides us with a sense of community? How do families and family histories constrain us? What do they offer us?

▶ **Writing about Cultural Practices**

6. Near the end of the poem is this line: "History made us." In what ways has your history shaped you? For this assignment, write a poem or an autobiographical essay based on "Ending Poem." To do this, you will need to consider your own background, interests, and experiences as well as those of someone in your family—preferably your mother or father, or a grandparent, an aunt, or an uncle. Here are some instructions to help you accomplish this task.

   • Whether you are drafting a poem or an essay, begin by collecting biographical information about yourself and one of your parents or older relatives. Interview your relative and be sure to take notes. If drafting a poem, begin with the line "I am what I am." Continue writing lines that alternate between your voice and the voice of your relative, but just as in "Ending Poem," use the first person "I" in this section. In your voice, provide details about your background. In your relative's voice, provide details about his or her background.

The details you choose to write about may include place of origin, socioeconomic background, religious or other family traditions, values, and languages spoken or heard as a child. If you are drafting an essay, you will use conventional essay format and tone, but you will still want to begin your essay by providing these biographical details.

- In the middle section of your poem or essay, describe traits and talents you and your ancestors share. If drafting a poem, you may wish to continue using "I" in this section, or you could switch to "we." As you write (in either genre), go back as many generations as you wish—hundreds of years or one or two generations. Specify the continents, countries, cities, or states your ancestors were from. Describe aspects of your ancestor's lives that you feel are part of you. Taking a cue from "Ending Poem," try to mention symbols that represent this family history.

- In the final section of the poem or essay begin with a phrase like "I am new" or "I move on." To conclude, describe how you are entering new territory or how you are different from your ancestors.

7. Families are not the only communities that can trace their heritage. Most colleges and universities have a heritage and a history that affects how they function. Working individually or in small groups, research the history of your school and write an essay that answers these kinds of questions.

- How was your school founded? What was its original mission?

- What need from the surrounding community did this school originally help to meet?

- What were the early groups of students who attended your school like? Describe their backgrounds and their areas of study.

- How has your school grown or changed over time? What is the school's current profile?

- Most schools consider themselves to have a particular focus and personality. What is your school's current focus? What is its current reputation?

Finally, your essay needs to address these questions.

- In what ways would you say your school's history—its heritage—has impacted the kind of institution it has become?

- How has this history been a positive force? And in what ways has its history caused your school to leave some people, or some areas of study, behind?

John A. Hostetler, **The Amish Charter**

Recognized as the leading scholar of Amish and Hutterite societies, John A. Hostetler wrote extensively about these communities before his death in 2001. His books reflect both his personal experience—Hostetler was raised in an Amish family—and his background as a sociologist—he earned a doctorate from Penn State University in 1953. The following reading comes from the third chapter of *Amish Society* (1994), a book that is considered a classic work on the subject.

Amish communities are found primarily in Pennsylvania, Ohio, Indiana, Iowa, and Ontario, Canada. They attract millions of tourists each year; however, most visitors, misled by stereotypes and commercial attractions, do not understand the Amish or how they really live and work together. The Amish migrated to the United States, starting in the early 18th century, to escape religious persecution in Europe. They are a very conservative Christian faith group. Their lives are characterized by their belief in remaining separate from the rest of the world, their rejection of involvement with the military or warfare, and their preference for rural living. As this reading explains, Amish daily life is regulated by the *Ordnung,* which is an oral tradition of rules agreed on by specific church communities. Each community maintains its own *Ordnung.*

 Mapping Your Reading

The Amish represent an example of a closed community, one that is starkly different from mainstream American life. Even so, such closed communities can reveal much about how all communities govern themselves—deciding who belongs and who doesn't and why. As you'll notice from the reading, choosing to care about the many details of daily life is one way that the Amish maintain their identity as a community. As you read, mark those passages where Hostetler details the standards for behavior within an Amish community. Why does the community set these standards? How do they benefit or hinder the community? The individual?

We turn now to the moral principles of the contemporary Amish community. By moral we mean that which is considered right and wrong, and the principles for which life is worth living. The fundamentals of right and wrong are made relevant in the life of the society. Behavior in the Amish community is oriented to absolute values, involving a conscious belief in religious and ethical ends, entirely for their own sake, and quite independent of any external rewards. This orientation to *Wert-rational*,[1] or absolute values, requires of the individual certain unconditional demands. Regardless of any possible cost to themselves, the members are required to put into practice what is required by duty, honor, personal loyalty, and religious calling. The fundamental values and common ends of the group, recognized by the people and accepted by them, have been designated as the charter.[2] A charter need not be reduced to writing to be effective in the little community; it may be thought of as the common purpose of the community, corresponding to a desire or a set of motives embodied in tradition. Although Amish life is oriented to absolute values, there is an almost automatic reaction to habitual stimuli that guides behavior in a course which has been repeatedly followed. Behavior is traditionally oriented by belief and the habit of long experience.

The Amish view of reality is conditioned by a dualistic world view. They believe, as have many other ascetic brotherhoods, that light and truth coexist with the powers of darkness and falsehood. Purity and goodness are in conflict with impurity and evil. The rejection of the world is based upon this dualistic conception of reality and is manifest in specific life situations.[3] While the Amish share this fundamental doctrine of the two worlds with other believers, it becomes a reality to the Amish, while to many Christian people it is greatly modified.

Separation from the World

To the Amish there is a divine spiritual reality, the Kingdom of God, and a Satanic Kingdom that dominates the present world. It is the duty of a Christian to keep himself "unspotted from the world" and separate from the desires, intent, and goals of the worldly person. Amish preaching and teaching draws upon passages from the Bible which emphasize the necessity of separation from the world. Two passages, perhaps the most often quoted, epitomize for the Amishman the message of the Bible. The first is: "Be not conformed to this world, but be ye transformed by the renewing of your mind that ye may prove what is that good and acceptable and perfect will of God."[4] This to the Amishman means among other things that one should not dress and behave like the world. The second is: "Be ye not unequally yoked together with unbelievers; for what fellowship hath righteousness with unrighteousness? and what communion hath light with darkness?"[5] This doctrine forbids the Amishman from marrying a non-Amish person or from being in business partnership with an outsider. It

---

[1]Max Weber, *The Theory of Social and Economic Organization*, trans. by A. M. Henderson and Talcott Parsons (The Free Press, 1947), 165.

[2]Bronislaw Malinowski, *A Scientific Theory of Culture* (University of North Carolina Press, 1944), 48, 162.

[3]Max Weber, "On Religious Rejection of the World," *Essays in Sociology* (Oxford University Press, 1958), 323–59.

[4]Romans 12:1.

[5]II Corinthians 6:14.

is applied generally to all social contacts that would involve intimate connections with persons outside the ceremonial community. This emphasis upon literalness and separateness is compatible with the Amish view of themselves as a "chosen people" or "peculiar people."[6]

The principle of separation conditions and controls the Amishman's contact with the outside world; it colors his entire view of reality and being. Bible teaching is conditioned by the totality of the traditional way of life. Compatible with the doctrine of separation is the doctrine of non-resistance. By the precepts of Christ, the Amish are forbidden to take part in violence and war. In time of war they are conscientious objectors, basing their stand on biblical texts, such as "My kingdom is not of this world: If my kingdom were of this world, then would my servants fight."[7] The Amish have no rationale for self-defense or for defending their possessions. Like many early Anabaptists they are "defenseless Christians." Problems of hostility are met without retaliation. The Amish farmer, in difficulty with the hostile world around him, is admonished by his bishop to follow the example of Isaac: After the warring Philistines had stopped up all the wells of his father Abraham, Isaac moved to new lands and dug new wells.[8] This advice is taken literally, so that in the face of hostility, the Amish move to new locations without defending their rights.

> **The Amish view themselves as a "chosen people."**

The Amish are "otherworldly" minded, in contrast to the many Christian churches that are concerned with making the world a better place in which to live. The Amish show little interest in improving the world or their environment. They profess to be "strangers and pilgrims" in the present world. The Amish interpretation of salvation also differs in emphasis from much of modern fundamentalism. Belief in predestination is taboo as is also the idea of assurance of salvation. A knowledge of salvation is complete only after the individual hears the great words at the last judgment, "Come, ye blessed of my Father, inherit the kingdom prepared for you from the foundation of the world."[9] Furthermore, the commands of obedience and self-denial are given more emphasis than is the teaching on "grace through faith alone." To assert that "I know I am saved" would be obnoxious because it smacks of pride and boasting. Pride of knowledge or personal display is held to be one of the greatest of all sins. Among the highly traditional Amish, Christ becomes a *Wegweiser*, one who shows the way, and not just one who is to be worshipped for his own sake in the way that revivalists teach.

---

[6]This concept was present in the Old Testament in the case of the Jews (Exodus 19:5, Deuteronomy 14:2) and the Amish tend to apply the concept to themselves using New Testament passages. I Peter 2:9 and Titus 2:14. Max Weber observed that the notion of the "chosen people" comes naturally with ethnic solidarity and is a means of status differentiation ("Ethnic Groups," in *Theories of Society*, Talcott Parsons, ed. [The Free Press of Glencoe, 1961], Vol. 1, 305).

[7]John 18:36.

[8]Genesis 26:15–18.

[9]Matthew 25:34.

Greetings! From The Amish Country

A souvenir postcard from southeastern Pennsylvania.

Amish preaching and moral instruction emphasize self-denial and obedience to the teaching of the Word of God, which is equated with the rules of the church. All ministers constantly warn their members to beware of worldliness. The choice put before the congregation is to obey or die. To disobey the church is to die. To obey the church and strive for "full fellowship," that is, complete harmony with the order of the church, is to have *lebendige Hoffnung*, a living hope of salvation. An Amish person simply puts faith in God, obeys the order of the church, and patiently hopes for the best.

Separation from the world is a basic tenet of the Amish charter.

Separation from the world is a basic tenet of the Amish charter; yet the Amish are not highly ethnocentric in their relationships with the outside world. They accept as a matter of course other people as they are, without attempting to convert them to the Amish way of life. But for those who are born into the Amish society, the sanctions for belonging are deeply rooted in the belief in separatism.

The people of the little community have an "inside view" as well as a contrasting "outside view" of things.[10] The doctrine of separation shapes the "outside view," and in discussing further aspects of the Amish charter we turn now to the "inside view."

---

[10]Robert Redfield, *The Little Community*, 80.

The Rules for Living

Once the individual has been baptized, he is committed to keep the *Ordnung* or the rules of the church. The rules for living tend to form a body of sentiments that are essentially a list of taboos within the environment of the small Amish community.

The following *Ordnung*[11] of a contemporary group, published in English, appears to be representative of the Old Order Amish, except for those portions indicated by brackets. That it appears in print at all is evidence of change from the traditional practice of keeping it oral. This *Ordnung* allows a few practices not typically sanctioned by the Old Order: the giving of tithes, distribution of tracts, belief in assurance of salvation, and limited missionary activity.

Ordnung of a Christian Church

Since it is the duty of the church, especially in this day and age, to decide what is fitting and proper and also what is not fitting and proper for a Christian to do, (in points that are not clearly stated in the Bible), we have considered it needful to publish this booklet listing some rules and ordinances of a Christian Church.

We hereby confess to be of one faith with the 18 articles of Faith adopted at Dortrecht, 1632, also with nearly all if not all articles in booklet entitled "Article und Ordnung der Christlichen Gemeinde."

No ornamental bright, showy form-fitting, immodest or silk-like clothing of any kind. Colors such as bright red, orange, yellow, and pink not allowed. Amish form of clothing to be followed as a general rule. Costly Sunday clothing to be discouraged. Dresses not shorter than half-way between knees and floor, nor over eight inches from floor. Longer advisable. Clothing in every way modest, serviceable, and as simple as scripturally possible. Only outside pockets allowed are one on work eber-hem or vomas and pockets on large overcoats. Dress shoes, if any, to be plain and black only. No high heels and pomp slippers, dress socks, if any, to be black except white for foot hygiene for both sexes. A plain, unshowy suspender without buckles.

> **Colors such as bright red, orange, yellow, and pink not allowed. Clothing in every way modest . . .**

Hat to be black with no less than 3-inch rim and not extremely high in crown. No stylish impression in any hat. No pressed trousers. No sweaters.

Prayer covering to be simple, and made to fit head. Should cover all the hair as nearly as possible and is to be worn wherever possible. [Pleating of caps to be discouraged.] No silk ribbons. Young children to dress according to the Word as well as parents. No pink or fancy baby blankets or caps.

Women to wear shawls, bonnets, and capes in public. Aprons to be worn at all times. No adorning of hair among either sex such as parting of hair among men and curling or waving among women.

A full beard should be worn among men and boys after baptism if possible. No shingled hair. Length at least halfway below tops of ears.

---

[11]From a tract, "Ordnung of a Christian Church," with a byline "Amish Church of Pike County, Ohio, 1950." This group has since moved to Elgin County, Ontario.

No decorations of any kind in buildings inside or out. No fancy yard fences. Linoleum, oilcloth, shelf and wall paper to be plain and unshowy. Over-stuffed furniture or any luxury items forbidden. No doilies or napkins. No large mirrors, (fancy glassware), statues, or wall pictures for decorations.

[No embroidery work of any kind.] Curtains either dark green rollers or black cloth. No boughten dolls.

No bottle gas or high line electrical appliances.

Stoves should be black if bought new.

Weddings should be simple and without decorations. [Names not attached to gifts.]

No ornaments on buggies or harness.

Tractors to be used only for such things that can hardly be done with horses. Only either stationary engines or tractors with steel tires allowed. No airfilled rubber tires.

Farming and related occupations to be encouraged. Working in cities or factories not permissible. Boys and girls working out away from home for worldly people forbidden except in emergencies.

Worldly amusements as radios, card playing [party games], movies, fairs, etc., forbidden. [Reading, singing, tract distribution, Bible games, relief work, giving of tithes, etc., are encouraged.]

Musical instruments or different voices singing not permissible. No dirty, silly talking or sex teasing of children.

Usury forbidden in most instances. No government benefit payments or partnership in harmful associations. No insurance. No photographs.

No buying or selling of anything on Sunday. It should be kept according to the principles of the Sabbath. [Worship of some kind every Sunday.]

[Women should spend time doing good or reading God's Word instead of taking care of canaries, goldfish, or house flowers.]

Church confession is to be made if practical where transgression was made. If not, a written request of forgiveness should be made to said church. All manifest sins to be openly confessed before church before being allowed to commune. I Tim. 5, 20. A period of time required before taking new members into full fellowship.

Because of great falling away from sound doctrine, we do not care to fellowship, that is hold communion, with any churches that allow or uphold any unfruitful works of darkness such as worldliness, fashionable attire, [bed-courtship, habitual smoking or drinking, old wives fables, nonassurance of salvation, anti-missionary zeal] or anything contrary to sound doctrine.

The rules of the Amish church cover the whole range of human experience. In a society where the goal is directed toward keeping the world out, there are many taboos, and customs become symbolic. There are variations in what is allowed from one community to another in the United States and Canada. Custom is regional and therefore not strictly uniform. The most universal of all Amish norms across the United States and Canada are the following: no electricity, telephones, central-heating systems, automobiles, or tractors with pneumatic tires; required are beards but not moustaches for all married men, long hair (which must be parted in the center, if allowed at all), hooks-and-eyes on dresscoats, and the use of horses for farming and travel. No formal education beyond the elementary grades is a rule of life.

The *Ordnung* is an essential part of the Amish charter. It is the way in which the moral postulates of society are expressed and carried out in life.[12] The charter is constantly subjected to forces of change, a source of conflict to be discussed later.

The Punishment of the Disobedient

A moral principle in the little Amish community is the practice of *Bann und Meidung*. These words rendered in English mean excommunication and shunning. *Meidung* was the crucial question in the controversy that gave rise to the Amish as a sect movement in their secession from the Swiss Brethren. This doctrine[13] was intrinsic in the Anabaptist movement from its very beginning and appeared in the earliest confession of faith.[14] The Anabaptist concept of the church was that it should be a pure church of believers only; persons who fall into sin must be first excommunicated, then shunned. Menno Simons taught that the ban applies to "all—great and small, rich and poor, without any respect of persons, who once passed under the Word but have now fallen back, those living or teaching offensively in the house of the Lord—until they repent."[15]

The method of dealing with a backslider is that given by Christ in Matthew 18: 15–17, and "If he neglect to hear the church, let him be unto thee as a heathen man and a publican." In other words, a person who has broken his vow and will not mend his ways must be expelled just as the human body casts off an ulcer or infectious growth.[16] Through the years the *Meidung* has been applied in different ways. The doctrine among the Mennonites of Holland and Switzerland was of a mild character, in which the offender was excluded from communion. But a stricter conception of the ban was advanced by Jakob Ammann. The strict interpretation requires shunning of all (1) members who leave the Amish church to join another and (2) members who marry outside the brotherhood. *Meidung* requires that members receive no favors from the excommunicated person, that they do not buy from or sell to an excommunicated person, that no member shall eat at the same table with an excommunicated

> No formal education beyond the elementary grades is a rule of life.

---

[12]Charles P. Loomis, *Social Systems* (Van Nostrand, 1960).

[13]See "Ban," *Mennonite Encyclopedia*, Vol. I.

[14]Not only the Schleitheim Confession of 1525 but also the Dortrecht Confession of 1632 set forth the doctrine. See J. C. Wenger, *The Doctrines of the Mennonites* (Herald Press, 1950), 69, 75.

[15]*The Complete Writings of Menno Simons* (Herald Press, 1956), 94, 961 ff. The ban is given extended treatment by Frank C. Peters, "The Ban in the Writings of Menno Simons," *M.Q.R.* (January, 1955).

[16]Other references in the Scriptures supporting the practice of shunning are: I Corinthians 5:11; Romans 16:17; II Thessalonians 3:14; Titus 3:10.

person, and if the case involves husband or wife, they are to suspend their usual marital relations.[17]

The Amish make no effort to evangelize or proselyte the outsider, nor are they concerned with the redemption of the outside society to the extent that they wish to draw members from the outer society into the brotherhood. It is their primary concern to keep their own baptized members from slipping into the outer world, or into other religious groups. With greater mobility and ease of travel and communication, isolation is breaking down, and Amish solidarity is threatened by more and more of their members wanting to become like outsiders. The Amish leaders meet this threat with the ban. Members who wish to have automobiles, radios, or the usual comforts of modern living, face the threat of being excommunicated and shunned. Thus the ban is used as an instrument of discipline, not only for the drunkard or the adulterer, but for the person who transgresses the order of the church. It is a powerful instrument for keeping the church intact and for preventing members from involvement in the wider society.

One of the purposes of excommunication is to restore the erring member by showing him his lost condition so that he will turn to repentance. The excommunication service itself is a painful and sober procedure. John Umble's description is fitting: "The excommunication of members was an awful and solemn procedure. The members to be expelled had been notified in advance and were present. An air of tenseness filled the house. Sad-faced women wept quietly; stern men sat with faces drawn. The bishop arose; with trembling voice and with tears on his cheek he announced that the guilty parties had confessed their sin, that they were cast off from the fellowship of the church and committed to the devil and all his angels (*dem Teufel und allen seinen Engeln übergeben*). He cautioned all the members to exercise 'shunning rigorously.' "[18]

Persons who fall into sin must be first excommunicated, then shunned.

Once an individual is in a state of *Bann* (or *Bond* as the Amish call it), members are to receive no favors from him. In a very real sense he is "an outcast, rejected of God and man. His only hope is not to die before he should [be] reinstated, lest he should be an outcast also in the world to come."[19]

Among the Amish communities today there are numerous divisions as a result of differing opinions on shunning. The moderate interpretation of the ban, taken by most of the midwestern groups, holds that moral transgressors should be excommunicated and shunned, but if the offender is restored to another Christian church of the non-resistant faith, then shunning should no longer be applied. But this, according to the adherents of the strict ban, is a departure from Jakob Ammann. In speaking of a former Amish member who joined the

---

[17]This literal and extreme position is still articulated by contemporary privately published writings of the Amish. *Eine Betrachtung und Erklarung über Bann und Meidung . . .* 1948.

[18]John Umble, "The Amish Mennonites of Union County, Pennsylvania," *M.Q.R.* (April, 1933), 92.

[19]*Ibid.*

Mennonites a bishop told the writer: "The only way for us to lift the ban is for him to make peace with the Old Order church, going back to one of them and living his promise he made in his baptismal vow on his knees before God and the church. It does not need to be here but in any of the churches that are in peace with us." According to this view, an excommunicated person must be shunned for life unless he restores his previous relationship with the group. The ban becomes an effective means of dispensing with the offender. By shunning him in all social relations, he is given a status that minimizes the threat to other members of the community. This perpetuation of the controversy undoubtedly aids the Old Order group to remain distinct and socially isolated.

Analyzing the Text

1. **Interrogating Assumptions.** What is the purpose of the *Ordnung* for an Amish community? According to Hostetler, why do the Amish care so much about small details such as the color of a stove, the length of a dress, or the width of a hat brim? To what extent does the *Ordnung* help provide stability for the community? How does the *Ordnung* impact the individual?

2. Hostetler writes, "In a society where the goal is directed toward keeping the world out, there are many taboos, and customs become symbolic." What does it mean that customs become symbolic? What is the importance of this for maintaining a sense of community identity? What are some examples from the reading? Do you think customs have symbolic meaning only in closed communities or also in open communities?

3. Have you ever been a part of a community with a dress code and other rules about appearance? Many people have gone to schools or held jobs that required a uniform or specific styles of dress. How did these standards of appearance affect you and others within the community? How or in what ways did those codes or uniforms become embedded with symbolic meaning? Did anyone break the code? If so, what repercussions followed?

4. According to Hostetler, what function does shunning or banning certain members serve for the community? Although the consequences are much less severe, more open communities practice their own versions of shunning. Can you think of any? What is the function of shunning in more open communities?

5. **Connecting to Other Readings.** Hostetler writes, of the Amish community, that "without unity there can be no communion." The Amish community, as he describes it, does not tolerate the dissent of the individual. What other selections in this chapter convey a sense that the needs of the individual are secondary to the needs of the group?

Writing about Cultural Practices

6. Outside of closed communities, such as the Amish, few communities maintain such stringent rules for their members. However, all communities develop their own conventions for behavior, and many organizations use a code of conduct.

Locate a copy of your school's code of conduct and write an essay in which you analyze its purpose. As you develop your analysis, consider some of the following questions.

- What is the purpose of this code of conduct? What is its role or significance?
- Who is it written for?
- What standards of behavior does your school's code of conduct outline as acceptable? Unacceptable?
- In what ways does your school's code of conduct reflect the values and practices of the community for which it was written? In what ways doesn't it reflect these values and practices?
- How or in what ways does this document differ in its content or significance from the Amish charter that Hostetler describes?

7. Choose a relatively tight-knit community that you are a committed member of and write an *Ordnung* for it. Consider using a club, a team, an organization, or even a household community that you've belonged to for some time. To begin, decide which details of daily life matter most to your community, and identify any unwritten codes that may already exist for the group. After you've drafted an *Ordnung,* write an analysis that answers the following questions.

- Why did you choose to include the types of rules that you did for this community?
- What do these rules or standards of behavior say about your community? Its purpose? Its values or principles?
- In what ways would having a written *Ordnung* change the functioning of this community? How would it affect individuals within the community? Consider both positive and negative impacts.

Mim Udovitch, **A Secret Society of the Starving**

Mim Udovitch writes about popular culture and the arts for publications including *Rolling Stone*, the *New York Times*, the *Village Voice*, and *Esquire*. This essay,
originally, printed in the *New York Times Magazine* in 2002, explores the Internet
community of pro-anas, girls and women who are pro-anorexia and who believe
anorexia nervosa is a lifestyle choice, not an illness. They use chat rooms, message boards, and other Internet sites to create a community that supports their
disorders. For this essay, Udovitch researched these websites and interviewed
several women who identify themselves as pro-anas.

While pro-ana community members don't view their destructive habits as
an illness, eating disorders (EDs) are serious mental illnesses. EDs such as
anorexia, bulimia, and compulsive eating are on the rise. Currently, about one in
ten Americans suffers from some kind of eating disorder. Among teenagers the
number is one in four or one in five, depending on which medical source you
consult. EDs lead to serious medical conditions such as bleeding gums and
tooth loss; diarrhea; weakness; low blood pressure, chest pain, and difficulty
breathing; liver and kidney damage; ulcers in the esophagus, stomach, and bow-
els; weakening of bones leading to osteoporosis; infertility; damage or loss of
muscle tissue; and an irregular heartbeat. They can be deadly. Untreated EDs
have a death rate between 10 and 20 percent, according to Linda Paulk
Buchanan, director of the Atlanta Center for Eating Disorders.

At a time when many people claim that what is good about the Internet is
its ability to link people who are dispersed geographically but who share common values and interests, Udovitch reminds us that not all kinds of community
spirit are good. (See Assumption 2 in the chapter introduction, p. 90.)

> ▶ **Mapping Your Reading**
>
> This essay challenges one of the most taken-for-
> granted assumptions about communities—that a
> caring and supportive community works in the
> best interests of its members. As you read, under-
> line quotes or statements in which Udovitch's in-
> terviewees describe how the pro-ana community
> supports them. What contradictions can you find
> in this support in terms of its effect on the indi-
> vidual?

Claire is 18. She is a pretty teenager, with long strawberry-blond hair, and she
is almost abnormally self-possessed for a girl from a small town who has
suddenly been descended upon by a big-city reporter who is there to talk to her,

in secret, about her secret life. She is sitting on the track that runs around the field of her high school's football stadium, wearing running shorts and a T-shirt and shivering a little because even though we are in Florida—in the kind of town where, according to Claire, during "season" when you see yet another car with New York plates, you just feel like running it down—there's an evening chill.

Claire's is also the kind of town where how the local high school does in sports matters. Claire herself plays two sports. Practice and team fund-raisers are a regular part of her life, along with the typical small-town-Florida teenage occupations—going to "some hick party," hanging out with friends in the parking lot of the Taco Bell, bowling, going to the beach.

Another regular part of her life, also a common teenage occupation, is anorexia—refusal to eat enough to maintain a minimally healthy weight. So she is possibly shivering because she hasn't consumed enough calories for her body to keep itself warm. Claire first got into eating disorders when she was 14 or 15 and a bulimic friend introduced her to them. But she was already kind of on the lookout for something: "I was gonna do it on my own, basically. Just because, like, exercise can only take you so far, you know? And I don't know, I just started to wonder if there was another way. Because they made it seem like, 'You do drugs, you die; be anorexic and you're gonna die in a year.' I knew that they kind of overplayed it and tried to frighten you away. So I always thought it can't be *that* bad for you."

Bulimia—binge eating followed by purging through vomiting or laxatives— didn't suit her, however, so after a little while she moved on to anorexia. But she is not, by her own lights, anorexic. And her name isn't Claire. She is, in her terms, "an ana" or "pro-ana" (shortened from pro-anorexia), and Claire is a variation of Clairegirl, the name she uses on the Web sites that are the fulcrum of the pro-ana community, which also includes people who are pro-mia (for bulimia) or simply pro-E.D., for eating disorder.

About one in 200 American women suffers from anorexia; two or three in 100 suffer from bulimia. Arguably, these disorders have the highest fatality rates of any mental illness, through suicide as well as the obvious health problems. But because they are not threatening to the passer-by, as psychotic disorders are, or likely to render people unemployable or criminal, as alcoholism and addiction are, and perhaps also because they are disorders that primarily afflict girls and women, they are not a proportionately imperative social priority.

These disorders have the highest fatality rates of any mental illness.

And now there's pro-ana, in many ways an almost too lucid clarification of what it really feels like to be eating disordered. "Pain of mind is worse than pain of body" reads the legend on one Web site's live-journal page, above a picture of the Web mistress's arm, so heavily scored with what look like razor cuts that there is more open wound than flesh. "I'm already disturbed," reads the home page of another. "Please don't come in." The wish to conform to a certain external ideal for the external ideal's sake is certainly a component of anorexia and bulimia. But as they are experienced by the people who suffer from them, it is just that: a component, a stepping-off point into the abyss.

As the girls (and in smaller numbers, boys) who frequent the pro-E.D. sites know, being an ana is a state of mind—part addiction, part obsession, and part seesawing sense of self-worth, not necessarily correlating to what you actually weigh. "Body image is a major deal, but it's about not being good enough," says Jill M. Pollack, the executive director of the Center for the Study of Anorexia and Bulimia, "and they're trying to fix everything from the outside." Clairegirl, like many of the girls who include their stats—height, weight, and goal weight—when posting on such sites, would not receive a diagnosis of anorexia, because she is not 15 percent under normal weight for her height and age.

But she does have self-devised rules and restrictions regarding eating, which, if she does not meet them, make her feel that she has erred—"I kind of believe it is a virtue, almost," she says of pro-ana. "Like if you do wrong and you eat, then you sin." If she does not meet her goals, it makes her dislike herself, makes her feel anxiety and a sense of danger. If she does meet them, she feels "clean." She has a goal weight, lower than the weight she is now. She plays sports for two hours a day after school and tries to exercise at least another hour after she gets home. She also has a touch of obsessive-compulsive disorder regarding non-food-related things—cleaning, laundry, the numeral three. ("Both anorexia and bulimia are highly O.C.D.," says Pollack. "*Highly.*")

And she does spend between one and three hours a day online, in the world of pro-ana. Asked what she likes best about the sites, Claire says: "Just really, like at the end of the day, it would be really nice if you could share with the whole world how you felt, you know? Because truthfully, you just don't feel comfortable, you can't tell the truth. Then, like, if I don't eat lunch or something, people will get on my case about it, and I can't just come out and tell them I don't eat, or something like that. But at the end of the day, I can go online and talk to them there, and they know exactly what I'm going through and how I feel. And I don't have to worry about them judging me for how I feel."

Pro-ana, the basic premise of which is that an eating disorder is not a disorder but a lifestyle choice, is very much an ideology of the early twenty-first century, one that could not exist absent the anonymity and accessibility of the Internet, without which the only place large numbers of anorexics and bulimics would find themselves together would be at inpatient treatment. "Primarily, the sites reinforce the secretiveness and the 'specialness' of the disorder," Davis says. "When young women get into the grips of this disease, their thoughts become very distorted, and part of it is they believe they're unique and special. The sites are a way for them to connect with

"The Web sites reinforce the secretiveness and the 'specialness' of the disorder."

other girls and to basically talk about how special they are. And they become very isolated. Women with eating disorders really thrive in a lot of ways on being very disconnected. At the same time, of course, they have a yearning to be connected."

Perfectionism, attention to detail, and a sense of superiority combine to make the pro-ana sites the most meticulous and clinically fluent self-representations of a mental disorder you could hope to find, almost checklists of diagnostic criteria expressed in poignantly human terms. Starving yourself, just on the basis of its sheer difficulty, is a high-dedication ailment—to choose to be an ana, if choice it is, is to choose a way of life, a hobby, and a credo. And on the Web, which is both very public and completely faceless, the aspects of the disorder that are about attention-getting and secret-keeping are a resolved paradox. "I kind of want people to understand," Clairegirl says, "but I also like having this little hidden thing that only I know about, like—this little secret that's all yours."

Pro-ana has its roots in various newsgroups and lists deep inside various Internet service providers. Now there are numerous well-known-to-those-who-know sites, plus who knows how many dozens more that are just the lone teenager's Web page, with names that put them beyond the scope of search engines. And based on the two-week sign-up of 973 members to a recent message-board adjunct to one of the older and more established sites, the pro-ana community probably numbers in the thousands, with girls using names like Wannabeboney, Neverthinenuf, DiETpEpSi UhHuh! and Afraidtolookinthemirror posting things like: "I can't take it anymore! I'm fasting! I'm going out, getting all diet soda, sugar-free gum, sugar-free candy and having myself a 14-day fast. Then we'll see who is the skinny girl in the family!"

That ana and mia are childlike nicknames, names that might be the names of friends (one Web site that is now defunct was even called, with girlish fondness, "My Friend Ana"), is indicative. The pro-ana community is largely made up of girls or young women, most of whom are between the ages of 13 and 25. And it is a close community, close in the manner of close friendships of girls and young women. The members of a few sites send each other bracelets, like friendship bracelets, as symbols of solidarity and support. And like any ideology subscribed to by many individuals, pro-ana is not a monolithic system of belief.

"Thou shall not eat without feeling guilty."

At its most militant, the ideology is something along the lines of, as the opening page of one site puts it: "Volitional, proactive anorexia is not a disease or a disorder. . . . There are no VICTIMS here. It is a lifestyle that begins and ends with a particular faculty human beings seem in drastically short supply of today: the will. . . . Contrary to popular misconception, anorexics possess the most iron-cored, indomitable wills of all. Our way is not that of the weak. . . . If we ever *completely* tapped that potential in our midst . . . we could change the world. Completely. Maybe we could even rule it."

Mostly, though, the philosophical underpinnings of pro-ana thought are not quite so Nietzschean. The "Thin Commandments" on one site, which appear under a picture of Bugs Bunny smiling his toothy open-mouthed smile, leaning against a mailbox and holding a carrot with one bite taken out of it, include: "If thou aren't thin, thou aren't attractive"; "Being this is more important than being healthy"; "Thou shall not eat without feeling guilty"; "Thou shall not eat fattening food without punishing thyself afterward"; and "Being thin and not eating are signs of true willpower and success."

The "Ana Creed" from the same site begins: "I believe in Control, the only force mighty enough to bring order into the chaos that is my world. I believe that I am the most vile, worthless, and useless person ever to have existed on this planet."

In fact, to those truly "in the disorder"—a phrase one anonymous ana used to describe it, just as an anonymous alcoholic might describe being in A.A. as being "in the rooms"—pro-ana is something of a misnomer. It suggests the promotion of something, rather than its defense, for reasons either sad or militant. That it is generally understood otherwise and even exploited ("Anorexia: Not just for suicidal teenage white girls anymore" read the home page of Anorexic Nation, now a disabled site, the real purpose of which was to push diet drugs) is a source of both resentment and secret satisfaction to the true pro-ana community. Its adherents might be vile and worthless, but they are the elite.

The usual elements of most sites are pretty much the same, although the presentation is variable enough to suggest Web mistresses ranging from young women with a fair amount of programming know-how and editorial judgment to angry little girls who want to assert their right to protect an unhealthy behavior in the face of parental opposition and who happen to know a little HTML. But there are usually "tips" and "techniques"—on the face of it, the scariest aspect of pro-ana, but in reality, pretty much the same things that both dieters and anorexics have been figuring out on their own for decades. There are "thinspirational" quotes—"You can never be too rich or too thin"; "Hunger hurts but starving works"; "Nothing tastes as good as thin feels"; "The thinner, the winner!" There are "thinspirational" photo galleries, usually pretty much the same group of very thin models, actresses, and singers—Jodie Kidd, Kate Moss, Calista Flockhart, Fiona Apple. And at pro-ana's saddest extreme, balancing the militance on the scales of the double-digit goal weight, there are warnings of such severity that they might as well be the beginning of the third canto of Dante's "Inferno": "I am the way into the city of woe. I am the way to a forsaken people. I am the way into eternal sorrow." The pro-ana version of which, from one site, is:

> PLEASE NOTE: Anorexia is NOT a diet. Bulimia is NOT a weight-loss plan. These are dangerous, potentially life-threatening DISORDERS that you cannot choose, catch, or learn. If you do not already have an eating disorder, that's wonderful! If you're looking for a new diet, if you want to drop a few pounds to be slimmer or more popular or whatever, if you're generally content with yourself and just want to look a bit better in a bikini, GO AWAY. Find a Weight Watchers meeting. Better yet, eat moderate portions of healthy food and go for a walk.
> However.
> If you are half as emotionally scarred as I am, if you look in the mirror and truly loathe what you see, if your relationships with food and your body are already beyond "normal" parameters no matter what you weigh, then come inside. If you're already too far into this to quit, come in and have a look around. I won't tell you to give up what I need to keep hold of myself.

Most of the pro-ana sites also explicitly discourage people under 18 from entering, partly for moral and partly for self-interested reasons. Under pressure from the National Eating Disorders Association, a number of servers shut down the pro-ana sites they were hosting last fall. But obviously, pretty much anyone who wanted to find her way to these sites and into them could do so, irrespective of age. And could find there, as Clairegirl did, a kind of perverse support group, a place where a group of for the most part very unhappy and in some part very angry girls and women come together to support each other in sickness rather than in health.

Then there's Chaos—also her Web name—who like her friend Futurebird (ditto) runs an established and well-respected pro-E.D. site. Chaos, whom I met in Manhattan although that's not where she lives, is a very smart, very winning, very attractive 23-year-old who has been either bulimic or anorexic since she was 10. Recently she's been bingeing and purging somewhere between 4 and 10 times a week. But when not bingeing, she also practices "restricting"—she doesn't eat in front of people, or in public, or food that isn't sealed, or food that she hasn't prepared herself, or food that isn't one of her "safe" foods, which since they are a certain kind of candy and a certain kind of sugar-free gum, is practically all food. ("You're catching on quickly," she says, laughing, when this is remarked on.) Also recently, she has been having trouble making herself throw up. "I think my body's just not wanting to do it right now," she says. "You have the tooth-brush trick, and usually I can just hit my stomach in the right spot, or my fin-gernails will gag me in the right spot. It just depends on what I've eaten. And if that doesn't work, laxis always do."

Chaos, like Clairegirl, is obsessive-compulsive about a certain number (which it would freak her out to see printed), and when she takes laxatives she either has to take that number of them, which is no longer enough to work, or that number plus 10, or that number plus 20, and so forth. The most she has ever taken is that number plus 60, and the total number she takes depends on the total number of calories she has consumed.

While it hardly needs to be pointed out that starving yourself is not good for you, bulimia is in its own inexorable if less direct way also a deadly disorder. Because of the severity of Chaos's bulimia, its long-standing nature, and the other things she does—taking ephedra or Xenadrine, two forms of, as she says, "legal speed," available at any health food or vitamin store; exercising in excess; fasting—she stands a very real chance of dying any time.

As it is, she has been to the emergency room more than half a dozen times with "heart things." It would freak her out to see the details of her heart things in print. But the kinds of heart things a severe bulimic might experience range from palpitations to cardiac arrest. And although Chaos hasn't had her kidney function tested in the recent past, it probably isn't great. Her spleen might also be near the point of rupturing.

She stands a very real chance of dying any time.

Chaos is by no means a young woman with nothing going for her. But despite her many positive attributes, Chaos pun-ishes herself physically on a regular basis, not only through bu-limia but also through cutting—hers is the live-journal page with the picture of the sliced-up arm. To be beheld is, to Chaos, so painful that after meeting me in person, she was still vomiting and crying with fear over the possible conse-quences of cooperating with this story a week later. "Some days," she says of her bulimia, "it's all I have."

While in some moods Chaos says she would do anything to be free of her eat-ing disorders, in others she has more excuses not to be than the mere lack of health insurance: She has a job, she is in school, she doesn't deserve help. And what she has, on all days, is her Web site, a place where people who have only their eating disorders can congregate, along with the people who *aspire* to having eating disorders—who for unknowable reasons of neurochemistry and personal experience identify with the self-lacerating worlds of anorexia and bulimia.

> "I can't go to a doctor. I can't tell anyone. But I can go to this site."

Futurebird, whom I also met in Manhattan, says that she has noticed a trend, repeating itself in new member after new member, of people who don't think they're anorexic *enough* to get treatment. And it's true, very much a function of the Internet—its accessibility, its anonymity—that the pro-ana sites seem to have amplified an almost-diagnostic category: the subclinical eating disorder, for the girl who's anorexic on the inside, the girl who hates herself so much that she forms a virtual attachment to a highly traumatized body of women, in a place where through posts and the adoption of certain behaviors, she can make her internal state external.

Futurebird and Chaos are sitting in a little plaza just to the south of Washington Square Park, with the sun behind them. Futurebird is a small African-American woman. As she notes, and as she has experienced when being taken to the hospital, it is a big help being African-American if you don't want people to think you have anorexia, which is generally and inaccurately considered to be solely an affliction of the white middle class. Futurebird has had an eating disorder since she was in junior high school and is now, at 22, looking for a way to become what you might call a maintenance anorexic—eating a little bit more healthily, restricting to foods like fruits and whole-grain cereal and compensating for the extra calories with excessive exercising.

Like Chaos, she is opposed, in principle, to eating disorders in general and says that she hates anorexia with a blind and burning hatred. Although she also says she thinks she's fat, which she so emphatically is not that in the interest of not sounding illogical and irrational, she almost immediately amends this to: she's not as thin as she'd like to be.

Both she and Chaos would vigorously dispute the assertion that the sites can *give* anyone an eating disorder. You certainly can't give anyone without the vulnerability to it an eating disorder. But many adolescent girls teeter on the edge of vulnerability. And the sites certainly might give those girls the suggestion to . . . hey, what the hell, give it a try.

"What I'd like people to understand," Futurebird says, "is that it is very difficult for people who have an eating disorder to ask for help. What a lot of people are able to do is to say, well, I can't go to a recovery site and ask for help. I can't go to a doctor or a friend and ask for help. I can't tell anyone. But I can go to this site because it's going to quote-unquote make me worse. And instead what I hope they find is people who share their experience and that they're able to just simply talk. And I've actually tested this. I've posted the same thing that I've posted on my site on some recovery sites, and I've read the reactions, and in a lot of ways it's more helpful."

In what ways?

"The main difference is that if you post—if someone's feeling really bad, like, I'm so fat, et cetera, on a recovery site, they'll say, that's not recovery talk. You have to speak recovery-speak."

"Fat is not a feeling," Chaos says, in tones that indicate she is echoing a recovery truism.

"And they'll use this language of recovery," Futurebird continues. "Which does work at some point in the negative thinking patterns that you have. But one tiny thing that I wish they would do is validate that the feeling does exist. To say, yes, I understand that you might feel that way. And you get not as much of that. A lot of times people just need to know that they aren't reacting in a completely crazy way."

The problem is that by and large, the people posting on these sites are reacting in a completely crazy way. There are many, many more discussions answering questions like, "What do you guys do about starvation headaches?" than there are questions like, "I am feeling really down; can you help me?" And in no case, in answering the former question, does anyone say, "Um . . . stop starving yourself." A site like Futurebird's, or like the message board of Chaos's, are designed with the best intentions. But as everybody knows, that is what the way into the city of woe, the way to a forsaken people, and the way into eternal sorrow are paved with.

▶ **Analyzing the Text**

1. Construct a profile of the pro-ana community. What practices, habits, or routines define it? Based on this reading, what would you say are the principles or values of this community?

2. Pay particular attention to the ways in which the pro-anas in this essay describe themselves. What distinctions do the pro-anas make between themselves and "outsiders" to their community?

3. The situation that gave rise to Udovitch's article is the rise in popularity of online message boards and chat rooms. In the case of pro-anas, Udovitch argues that the Internet has been a pivotal source of support: "Pro-ana, the basic premise of which is that an eating disorder is not a disorder but a lifestyle choice, is very much an ideology of the early twenty-first century, one that could not exist absent the anonymity and accessibility of the Internet, without which the only place large numbers of anorexics and bulimics would find themselves together would be at inpatient treatment." Do you agree with this statement? Why or why not? Based on your experiences and the descriptions in this essay, how does the nature of the Internet affect what types of communities flourish there and what types do not?

4. How, after reading Udovitch's essay, do you think groups engaging in high-risk behavior function as a community? What do they offer individuals? In what ways do they constrain them? Keep in mind that compulsive eating or dieting is only one kind of high-risk behavior. Other kinds include regularly skipping classes, drug use, smoking, excessive drinking, and unprotected sex.

5. **Connecting to Another Reading.** In "The Amish Charter," John Hostetler explains that the Amish believe that "it is the duty of a Christian to keep himself 'unspotted from the world' and separate from the desires, intent, and goals of the worldly person" (p. 100). In other places in the essay, Hostetler describes the importance the Amish place on acting as pilgrims in the present world. How does this sense of alienation that the Amish cultivate—this feeling of specialness—relate to the goals of the pro-ana community? What are the consequences of striving for a sense of alienation from the world for each of these communities?

▶ **Writing about Cultural Practices**

6. Peer pressure—the drive for social acceptance—affects community life by influencing people to override personal habits or inhibitions to follow a perceived group norm. This essay illustrates how finding social acceptance is a powerful—but not necessarily positive—dynamic that can hold a community together. For this assignment, describe the impact of peer pressure on college campuses. To do this, identify one example of peer pressure that you have witnessed on your campus. Consider some of these examples of peer pressure (some are negative, some are positive):

   • Drinking to celebrate school events or holidays
   • Cheating
   • Joining fraternities, sororities, or other clubs
   • Being part of a sports team or club
   • Participating in student government
   • Forming study groups

   After you choose the focus of your essay, develop a descriptive analysis of the ways in which this example of peer pressure influences community life on your campus. Consider the following questions.

   • How does the group benefit or hinder human connection?
   • Does the group provide stability?
   • How does the group serve the needs of its members?
   • Does the group value individuality, or does it insist on conformity?
   • Whose interest is most served by the group's rules?

Sampling the Old and the New

Olympic Communities in Greece: The Ancients vs. The Moderns

The ancient Olympic Games were athletic, religious, and cultural celebrations that brought athletes together from each Greek city-state. Held every four years from about 776 B.C. to A.D. 393, the games took place in the sacred valley of Olympia and included rituals honoring Zeus, the father of the Greek gods. As the games unfolded, representatives of the city-states discussed political issues, set military truces, and formed alliances. Although the games brought communities together, only men participated—in accordance with Greek law, women were not granted the rights of citizenship and thus were not allowed to compete.

The modern Olympics, revived in the late nineteenth century by the French aristocrat Pierre de Coubertin, had inauspicious beginnings in terms of diversity: "An Olympiad with females would be impractical, uninteresting, unaesthetic, and improper," said de Coubertin at the 1900 Olympics in Paris. The Olympics have since become more inclusive of women and international athletes, especially in the past 20 years. At the 1984 summer games in Los Angeles, only 23 percent of the athletes were women. However, those games introduced the first women's marathon and witnessed the first African and Muslim woman to win a gold medal. The 2004 Summer Olympics, held in Athens, Greece, hosted the largest number of athletes ever and the most women athletes to date (over 40 percent of the total competitors).

Shown above is the 2004 Greek women's 4 x 400 relay team, which appeared in the Olympic finals that year. Women competed in 135 events at the Athens games, including the shot put, which was held at Olympia, the site of the ancient games.

1. What do these images suggest about cultural attitudes toward athletic competition? What messages do they convey about how the Olympics have changed?

2. Can you think of an example from the modern Olympics in which gender politics or ethnic or racial tensions played out? Conduct some research to learn more about one or two such events in Olympic history. What do these events tell you about the attitudes and assumptions people once had about the athletes representing their country? What assumptions do people make today?

3. Beamed around the planet via satellite, can it be said that the modern Olympics create a sense of community? Of national pride? If so, what is the nature of this community? If not, why do you think they don't? How have advancements in communication technologies strengthened or weakened the goal of the Olympics to promote understanding and peace among participant nations?

Richard Rodriguez, "Blaxicans" and Other Reinvented Americans

Peabody Award-winning writer and commentator Richard Rodriguez has been publishing work for over twenty years. His often controversial essays on race and identity have been featured on *NewsHour with Jim Lehrer* and the Pacific News Service, for which he is an editor. Rodriguez is also a contributing editor for *Harper's Magazine, U.S. News & World Report*, and the Sunday Opinion section of the *Los Angeles Times*. He is the author of several books including *Hunger of Memory* (1982) and *Brown: The Last Discovery of America* (2002). This essay originally appeared in the *Chronicle of Higher Education* in 2003. In it, Rodriguez argues that classic racial and ethnic categories—like black, white, and Hispanic—are not meaningful and do not help us understand what makes people American.

> ### Mapping Your Reading
>
> "We are no longer a black-white nation," writes Rodriguez. In this essay, he argues that the United States is reinventing its sense of national identity by not relying on racial categories. As you read, use the margins to note how Rodriguez supports his argument about ethnicity and cultural identity. What makes someone American? How do immigrant groups shape a community? What is the significance of assimilation?

There is something unsettling about immigrants because . . . well, because they chatter incomprehensibly, and they get in everyone's way. Immigrants seem to be bent on undoing America. Just when Americans think we know who we are—we are Protestants, culled from Western Europe, are we not?—then new immigrants appear from Southern Europe or from Eastern Europe. We—we who are already here—we don't know exactly what the latest comers will mean to our community. How will they fit in with us? Thus we—we who were here first—we begin to question our own identity.

After a generation or two, the grandchildren or the great-grandchildren of immigrants to the United States and the grandchildren of those who tried to keep immigrants out of the United States will romanticize the immigrant, will begin to see the immigrant as the figure who teaches us most about what it means to be an American. The immigrant, in mythic terms, travels from the outermost rind of America to the very center of American mythology. None of this, of course, can we admit to the Vietnamese immigrant who served us our breakfast at the hotel this morning. In another forty years, we will be prepared to say to the Vietnamese immigrant that he, with his breakfast tray, with his intuition for travel, with his memory of tragedy, with his recognition of peerless freedoms, he fulfills the meaning of America.

We who are already here don't know exactly what the latest comers will mean to our community.

In 1997, Gallup conducted a survey on race relations in America, but the poll was concerned only with white and black Americans. No question was put to the aforementioned Vietnamese man. There was certainly no question for the Chinese grocer, none for the Guatemalan barber, none for the tribe of Mexican Indians who reroofed your neighbor's house.

The American conversation about race has always been a black-and-white conversation, but the conversation has become as bloodless as badminton.

I have listened to the black-and-white conversation for most of my life. I was supposed to attach myself to one side or the other, without asking the obvious questions: What is this perpetual dialectic between Europe and Africa? Why does it admit so little reference to anyone else?

I am speaking to you in American English that was taught me by Irish nuns—immigrant women. I wear an Indian face; I answer to a Spanish surname as well as this California first name, Richard. You might wonder about the complexity of historical factors, the collision of centuries, that creates Richard Rodriguez. My brownness is the illustration of that collision, or the bland memorial of it. I stand before you as an Impure-American, an Ambiguous-American.

In the nineteenth century, Texans used to say that the reason Mexicans were so easily defeated in battle was because we were so dilute, being neither pure Indian nor pure Spaniard. Yet, at the same time, Mexicans used to say that Mexico, the country of my ancestry, joined two worlds, two competing armies. José Vasconcelos, the Mexican educator and philosopher, famously described Mexicans as *la raza cósmica,* the cosmic race. In Mexico what one finds as early as the eighteenth century is a predominant population of mixed-race people. Also, once the slave had been freed in Mexico, the incidence of marriage between Indian and African people there was greater than in any other country in the Americas and has not been equaled since.

Race mixture has not been a point of pride in America. Americans speak more easily about "diversity" than we do about the fact that I might marry your daughter; you might become we; we might become us. America has so readily adopted the Canadian notion of multiculturalism because it preserves our preference for thinking ourselves separate—our elbows need not touch, thank you. I would prefer that table. I can remain Mexican, whatever that means, in the United States of America.

I can remain Mexican, whatever that means, in the United States of America.

I would propose that instead of adopting the Canadian model of multiculturalism, America might begin to imagine the Mexican alternative—that of a *mestizaje* society.

Because of colonial Mexico, I am mestizo. But I was reinvented by President Richard Nixon. In the early 1970s, Nixon instructed the Office of Management and Budget to identify the major racial and ethnic groups in the United States. OMB came up with five major ethnic or racial groups. The groups are white, black, Asian/Pacific Islander, American Indian/Eskimo, and Hispanic.

It's what I learned to do when I was in college: to call myself a Hispanic. At my university we even had separate cafeteria tables and "theme houses," where the children of Nixon could gather—of a feather. Native Americans united. African Americans. Casa Hispanic.

The interesting thing about Hispanics is that you will never meet us in Latin America. You may meet Chileans and Peruvians and Mexicans. You will not meet Hispanics. If you inquire in Lima or Bogotá about Hispanics, you will be referred to Dallas. For "Hispanic" is a gringo contrivance, a definition of the world according to European patterns of colonization. Such a definition suggests I have more in common with Argentine-Italians than with American Indians; that there is an ineffable union between the white Cuban and the mulatto Puerto Rican because of Spain. Nixon's conclusion has become the basis for the way we now organize and understand American society.

The Census Bureau foretold that by the year 2003, Hispanics would outnumber blacks to become the largest minority in the United States. And, indeed, the year 2003 has arrived and the proclamation of Hispanic ascendancy has been published far and wide. While I admit a competition has existed—does exist—in America between Hispanic and black people, I insist that the comparison of Hispanics with blacks will lead, ultimately, to complete nonsense. For there is no such thing as a Hispanic race. In Latin America, one sees every race of the world. One sees white Hispanics, one sees black Hispanics, one sees brown Hispanics who are Indians, many of whom do not speak Spanish because they resist Spain. One sees Asian-Hispanics. To compare blacks and Hispanics, therefore, is to construct a fallacious equation.

Some Hispanics have accepted the fiction. Some Hispanics have too easily accustomed themselves to impersonating a third race, a great new third race in America. But Hispanic is an ethnic term. It is a term denoting culture. So when the Census Bureau says by the year 2060 one-third of all Americans will identify themselves as Hispanic, the Census Bureau is not speculating in pigment or quantifying according to actual historical narratives, but rather is predicting how by the year 2060 one-third of all Americans will identify themselves culturally. For a country that traditionally has taken its understandings of community from blood and color, the new circumstance of so large a group of Americans identifying themselves by virtue of language or fashion or cuisine or literature is an extraordinary change, and a revolutionary one.

By the year 2060 one-third of all Americans will identify themselves as Hispanic.

People ask me all the time if I envision another Quebec forming in the United States because of the large immigrant movement from the south. Do I see a Quebec forming in the Southwest, for example? No, I don't see that at all.

But I do notice the Latin American immigrant population is as much as 10 years younger than the U.S. national population. I notice the Latin American immigrant population is more fertile than the U.S. national population. I see the movement of the immigrants from south to north as a movement of youth—like approaching spring!—into a country that is growing middle-aged. I notice immigrants are the archetypal Americans at a time when we—U.S. citizens—have become post-Americans, most concerned with subsidized medications.

I was at a small Apostolic Assembly in East Palo Alto a few years ago—a mainly Spanish-speaking congregation in an area along the freeway, near the heart of the Silicon Valley. This area used to be black East Palo Alto, but it is quickly becoming an Asian and Hispanic Palo Alto neighborhood. There was a moment in the service when newcomers to the congregation were introduced. Newcomers brought letters of introduction from sister evangelical churches in Latin America. The minister read out the various letters and pronounced the names and places of origin to the community. The congregation applauded. And I thought to myself: It's over. The border is over. These people were not being asked whether they had green cards. They were not being asked whether they arrived here legally or illegally. They were being welcomed within a new community for reasons of culture. There is now a north-south line that is theological, a line that cannot be circumvented by the U.S. Border Patrol.

I was on a British Broadcasting Corporation interview show, and a woman introduced me as being "in favor" of assimilation. I am not in favor of assimilation any more than I am in favor of the Pacific Ocean or clement weather. If I had a bumper sticker on the subject, it might read something like ASSIMILATION HAPPENS. One doesn't get up in the morning, as an immigrant child in America, and think to oneself, "How much of an American shall I become today?" One doesn't walk down the street and decide to be 40 percent Mexican and 60 percent American. Culture is fluid. Culture is smoke. You breathe it. You eat it. You can't help hearing it—Elvis Presley goes in your ear, and you cannot get Elvis Presley out of your mind.

I am in favor of assimilation. I am not in favor of assimilation. I recognize assimilation. A few years ago, I was in Merced, California—a town of about 75,000 people in the Central Valley where the two largest immigrant groups at that time (California is so fluid, I believe this is no longer the case) were Laotian Hmong and Mexicans. Laotians have never in the history of the world, as far as I know, lived next to Mexicans. But there they were in Merced, and living next to Mexicans. They don't like each other. I was talking to the Laotian kids about why they don't like the Mexican kids. They were telling me that the Mexicans do this and the Mexicans don't do that, when I suddenly realized that they were speaking English with a Spanish accent.

On his interview show, Bill Moyers once asked me how I thought of myself. As an American? Or Hispanic? I answered that I am Chinese, and that is because I live in a Chinese city and because I want to be Chinese. Well, why not? Some Chinese-American people in the Richmond and Sunset districts of San Francisco sometimes paint their houses (so many qualifiers!) in colors I would once have described as garish: lime greens, rose reds, pumpkin. But I have lived in a Chinese city for so long that my eye has taken on that palette, has come to prefer lime greens and rose reds and all the inventions of this Chinese Mediterranean. I see photographs in magazines or documentary footage of China, especially rural China, and I see what I recognize as home. Isn't that odd?

I do think distinctions exist. I'm not talking about an America tomorrow in which we're going to find that black and white are no longer the distinguishing marks of separateness. But many young people I meet tell me they feel like Victorians when they identify themselves as black or white. They don't think of themselves in those terms. And they're already moving into a world in which tattoo or ornament or movement or commune or sexuality or drug or rave or electronic bombast are the organizing principles of their identity. The notion that they are white or black simply doesn't occur.

And increasingly, of course, one meets children who really don't know how to say what they are. They simply are too many things. I met a young girl in San Diego at a convention of mixed-race children, among whom the common habit is to define one parent over the other—black over white, for example. But this girl said that her mother was Mexican and her father was African. The girl said "Blaxican." By reinventing language, she is reinventing America.

America does not have a vocabulary like the vocabulary the Spanish empire evolved to describe the multiplicity of racial possibilities in the New World. The conversation, the interior monologue of America cannot rely on the old vocabulary—black, white. We are no longer a black-white nation.

So, what myth do we tell ourselves? The person who got closest to it was Karl Marx. Marx predicted that the discovery of gold in California would be a more central event to the Americas than the discovery of the Americas by Columbus— which was only the meeting of two tribes, essentially, the European and the Indian. But when gold was discovered in California in the 1840s, the entire world met. For the first time in human history, all of the known world gathered. The Malaysian stood in the gold fields alongside the African, alongside the Chinese, alongside the Australian, alongside the Yankee.

That was an event without parallel in world history and the beginning of modern California—why California today provides the mythological structure for understanding how we might talk about the American experience: not as biracial, but as the re-creation of the known world in the New World.

Sometimes truly revolutionary things happen without regard. I mean, we may wake up one morning and there is no black race. There is no white race either. There are mythologies, and—as I am in the business, insofar as I am in any business at all, of demythologizing such identities as black and white— I come to you as a man of many cultures. I come to you as Chinese. Unless you understand that I am Chinese, then you have not understood anything I have said.

Analyzing the Text

1. According to Rodriguez, "assimilation happens." What does he mean by this? What does he mean when he ends this essay by saying, "Unless you understand that I am Chinese, then you have not understood anything I have said"?

2. Rodriguez points out that the ethnic label "Hispanic" was invented by the U.S. federal government in the 1970s. He argues that this term represents a revolutionary change in how Americans define themselves. Why is this? What evidence does he use to support his argument? How do you respond?

3. "Culture is fluid," writes Rodriguez. "Culture is smoke. You breathe it. You eat it." How does this relate to his argument about assimilation? According to Rodriguez, does this mean that racial and ethnic distinctions do not matter at all in America? Why or why not?

4. **Interrogating Assumptions.** Would Rodriguez agree with the assumption that communities provide stability (see p. 87)? To answer, draw on passages in the essay in which he discusses cultural identity.

5. **Connecting to Another Reading.** Maya Angelou in "Reclaiming Our Home Place" (p. 135) writes about assimilation and American cultural identity. How might she respond to Rodriguez's argument?

6. **Connecting to Another Reading.** In "How to Tame a Wild Tongue" (p. 53), Gloria Anzaldúa writes that people who grew up speaking Chicano Spanish have "internaliz[ed] how our language has been used against us by the dominant culture." For Anzaldúa, language is identity, and assimilation represents a painful process of erasing the Tex-Mex border culture in which she grew up. In your opinion, how would she respond to Rodriguez's argument about assimilation? How do their perspectives on language and identity differ? Do Anzaldúa and Rodriguez share any common ground?

Writing about Cultural Practices

7. "There is something unsettling about immigrants," writes Rodriguez in the opening paragraph of this essay. Elsewhere, he describes immigrants as "the archetypal Americans," and throughout, he peppers his stories with examples of immigrant experiences in America. Understanding the immigrant histories of a community can provide insight into what defines Americans culturally. Work in groups to trace some of the immigrant histories of the town or communities surrounding your campus. Use the local historical society, area libraries, and the archives of your local newspaper. Focus your research on the immigrant groups that originally moved to this community, on the largest local immigrant group historically, or on the most recent groups to have arrived. Then prepare a group presentation for the class. As you conduct your research and plan your presentation, consider the following questions.

   - What places did the immigrant groups come from?
   - Why did they come to America? Why did they come to this specific community?
   - What traditions and customs did these groups bring with them?

- Were they welcome here?
- What did they do when they arrived? Where did they live? What sort of work did they do when they first arrived?
- To what extent did the immigrant groups assimilate? Explain how you reach this conclusion.
- Overall, how did the immigrant groups impact the community?

Finally, address these questions:

- What does "the immigrant" symbolize for Rodriguez? How does he use the immigrant experience to make his argument about assimilation? How do you respond?

Kathleen Norris, **Can You Tell the Truth in a Small Town?**

Kathleen Norris is the critically acclaimed author of *The Cloister Walk* (1996), *Amazing Grace* (1998), and *The Virgin of Bennington* (2001). The following reading comes from her first book, *Dakota: A Spiritual Geography* (1993), a collection of essays about Norris's move from New York City to her grandparents' homestead in Lemmon, South Dakota, population 1,614. It captures both the impact of the farm crisis of the 1980s on South Dakota communities and the richness of life she found there nonetheless—in small Protestant churches, Benedictine monasteries, and other local communities.

 Mapping Your Reading

In this essay, Norris explores the nature and role of community life within small towns. As you read, mark sections where Norris notes the qualities or characteristics of these communities. How does the author answer the question at the start of her essay—that is, how *does* one tell the truth in a small town? What are the benefits or repercussions of doing so? How does Norris feel about living in a small community?

How do we tell the truth in a small town? Is it possible to write it? Certainly, great literature might come out of the lives of ordinary people on the farms and ranches and little towns of the Plains, but are the people who farm, the people working in those towns, writing it? The truth, the whole truth, tends to be complex, its contentments and joys wrestled out of doubt, pain, change. How to tell the truth in a small town, where, if a discouraging word is heard, it is not for public consumption?

Like many who have written about Dakota, I'm invigorated by the harsh beauty of the land and feel a need to tell the stories that come from its soil. Writing is a solitary act, and ideally, the Dakotas might seem to provide a writer with ample solitude and quiet. But the frantic social activity in small towns conspires to silence a person. There are far fewer people than jobs to fill. Someone must be found to lead the church choir or youth group, to bowl with the league, to coach a softball team or little league, to run a Chamber of Commerce or club

---

For another reading on place, see Angelou, page 135.—Eds.

committee. Many jobs are vital: the volunteer fire department and ambulance service, the domestic violence hotline, the food pantry. But all too often a kind of Tom Sawyerism takes over, and makes of adult life a perpetual club. Imagine spending the rest of your life at summer camp.

Women writers especially are in danger of being overwhelmed. As a rural North Dakota woman said to me at a writing workshop, "The world will continue to give more and more responsibility to any woman who will accept it." She had told friends she was at a meeting because she thought taking a writing workshop sounded frivolous. In Lemmon, it's possible for a woman to belong to one or more church groups, home extension club, Legion and hospital auxiliary, one or two women's clubs, bridge club, sewing club, country club, and several service club auxiliaries such as Jaycettes, each with their crafts projects, creeds, codes, and books of minutes, all of which read "a delicious lunch was served."

As one North Dakota writer says, "Here and there a woman has to step on a few toes and put her writing above other things." But in drawing back from the social whirl she sets herself apart from those around her, and in a small town this is hard to do. Someone who wants to write either has to break away or settle for writing only what is acceptable at a mother-daughter church banquet or a Girl Scout program.

> People write local histories "the way they wished it had been instead of the way it was."

Many writers depicting rural and small-town America, writers as diverse as Willa Cather, Sinclair Lewis, and Louise Erdrich, have found it necessary to write about that world from a distance. The distance may be mostly geographical, but it can also be the distance a profession provides: teaching in a college, for instance. In either case, the writer is insulated from the day-to-day realities of small-town or rural life. But a writer who is thoroughly immersed in Dakota's rural milieu, where nearly everyone is related, faces a particularly difficult form of self-censorship. "I'd like to write about my relatives," one North Dakota ranch woman told me, "but I'm no good at disguising things."

One popular form of writing on the Plains is the local history. These books reveal a great deal about the people who write them but do not often tell the true story of the region. In North Dakota, most homesteaders failed to remain on their land after proving up a claim, and the 1920s and 1930s brought farm bankruptcies and political upheaval, but you would never know it to read local histories, centered on those who made it. They present tales of perseverance made heroic in the context of the steady march of progress from homesteading days to the present. As one old-timer told me, "people have been writing it the way they wished it had been instead of the way it was."

The local history mentality that takes care not to offend the descendants of pioneer families who had grit enough to remain must, as anthropologist Seena Kohl says in an essay in *Plains-woman*, present the past "as a harmonious whole" that, despite its hardships, was preferable to the present. When this view of life comes off the page to dictate present reality, the consequences can be serious indeed. A fourth generation Dakotan, a high school student, wrote recently in a school theme that his family had always been here, and would always remain. "Always" in this context is less than 75 years, and with a fragile economy and a

Graduates (the only two) in a small North Dakota town.

falling population, chances are this young man will have to seek his livelihood elsewhere. Having been raised for a world that does not exist, he may, sitting in an apartment in Minneapolis, Denver, or Spokane, come to see the Dakota prairie as a lost Eden. Maybe by the fifth generation the family will produce a writer who can excavate the story.

A more immediate consequence of the local history mentality is the tendency to "make nice." If we can make the past harmonious, why not the present? Why risk discussion that might cause unpleasantness? I was once at a pastor search committee meeting when a woman said, "We don't want anyone too old." A pastor from a neighboring town who was guiding us through the bureaucratic thickets, a woman who had been ordained the week of her sixty-fifth birthday, said, amicably but firmly, "I know most churches feel that way, but maybe you should think about that." Another woman jumped in and said, "Oh, we didn't mean anything. It was all in fun."

The bluntness of the first woman was at least useful: Had she been more urbane, she would have disguised her prejudice. But the lie put forth by the other woman was intended to silence us. Thanks to the minister's persistence, we did manage a brief look at the question of what age we wanted our next pastor to be, but it was painful. Among other things, it forced us to look at the fact that our congregation is aging, and people wanted to drop the subject as quickly as possible.

And what of truth? We don't tend to see the truth as something that could set us free because it means embracing pain, acknowledging our differences and conflicts, taking our real situation into account. Instead, in the isolated, insular small-town and rural environment, truth itself can become an outside authority, like the economic and political forces we profess independence from, or the state and federal laws we so casually break when they don't fit our needs. I am indebted to the Reverend G. Keith Gunderson for this insight. He was vilified not long ago by many in his town for protesting the custom of allowing high school graduates to drink in the bars, no matter what their age. The moral issue for him was not drinking but respect for law. The reaction was mixed, but many felt that one of their own—he was raised just thirty miles away—had betrayed them. He should have known that this is simply how we do things here.

A woman in another town baffled Medicaid fraud investigators when they discovered that she had been fudging figures for a local clinic, but with no personal gain in mind. It was just that the government had plenty of money and she knew how much we needed it. A typical small-town person in many ways, she saw herself as effectively dissociated from the law of the land. Anger over the incident was directed primarily at the professionals, doctors, and clergy who cooperated in the government's investigation. Her friends and family never grasped that it was precisely their cooperation that kept the woman from going to jail.

It is a truism that outsiders, often professionals with no family ties, are never fully accepted into a rural or small-town community. Such communities are impenetrable for many reasons, not the least of which is the fact that the most important stories are never spoken of; the local history mentality has worn down their rough edges, or placed them safely out of sight, out of mind.

To learn the truth about the web of close-knit families that make up an isolated small town on the Plains, one must look back some years, to the men and women of the homesteading and early merchant generation. By now they've mostly been mythologized into the stern, hard-working papa and the overworked-mother-who-never-complained, all their passions and complexities smoothed over. But many of these people, the women especially, had an intense love/hate relationship with the Plains that lives on in their children. Some mourned the loss of European culture or ethnic roots; others the social status they'd enjoyed in cities back East. Only the toughest survived here.

These women's ambivalence—or rage—toward the Plains found expression in their relationships with their children; often they doted on the children who moved away while treating shabbily those who remained. The grandchildren growing up here developed, in self-defense, a world view in which everything from the outside world is suspect, while everything local, especially that which derives from the immediate family, is good. These are families that have an exceptionally difficult time dealing with conflict and change.

We don't tend to see the truth as something that could set us free.

Change means failure; it is a contaminant brought in by outside elements. Such families have brought the local history mentality to life, and in sufficient numbers they dictate the nature of their small towns. They are as precarious as they are deliberately, even obsessively, harmonious.

It is impossible to exaggerate how much the unconscious, the hidden story, dictates behavior in such families. If you know the story going back fifty years or so, their behavior makes sense. If you don't, and if you're an outsider, especially a teacher or pastor, someone whose profession connects with people's deepest (and most deeply embedded) needs, then God help you. You may wake one morning to find that all of the unresolved conflicts of lo these many generations have just been laid at your door.

And what if such a family produced a writer? How would it be possible to write the story, dig it out from the depths in which it is entombed? If truth has become an outside authority to be resisted in order to keep the family myths intact, then the writer seeking truth would have to become an outsider, too. This, in fact, is what often happens. One writer I know, a second generation North Dakotan who farms with her husband, was stunned to find, when she began a column in the weekly paper, that she suddenly felt insecure on her home turf. She was surprised that so many of her friends reacted with a sullen silence, as if her column did not exist. "Something drives me to do this. I'm possessed to do this," she told me. "Maybe nothing drives them. Maybe it's a sin to be possessed in North Dakota."

Robert Kroetsch, a writer from the Canadian Plains, suggests that prairie writers can learn to see in "the particulars of place," old photographs, diaries, and the like, archaeological deposits of great value. But in my area more than one family has abandoned such evidence of their past; they've walked away from farmhouses and moved to town, leaving behind not only the oak furniture but old china and handmade quilts, even family photographs. The truth was so painful it literally had to be abandoned.

> A good story tells lie after lie, and the happy ending is the happiest lie of all.

I wonder if the complex and often fragmented narrative style Kroetsch believes the prairie writer must adopt in "[trusting] to a version of archaeology" isn't squarely at odds with the local history mentality, which prefers a linear narrative, the progress model. I know from my experience working in a small-town library that writers like Larry Woiwode and Louise Erdrich are read warily by rural people on the Plains, if they are read at all. "Well, it's different," one woman said of *Love Medicine,* somewhat startled that the novel wasn't set in New York, Paris, or Hollywood, like a "real" best seller. "I didn't want anything like *this*," another woman said, returning *Beyond the Bedroom Wall;* "I just wanted a good story."

A good story is one that isn't demanding, that proceeds from A to B, and above all doesn't remind us of the bad times, the cardboard patches we used to wear in our shoes, the failed farms, the way people you love just up and die. It tells us instead that hard work and perseverance can overcome all obstacles; it tells lie after lie, and the happy ending is the happiest lie of all.

This is the reason why books like Woiwode's, or Richard Critchfield's *Those Days,* or Lois Phillips Hudson's novel of the farm crisis of the 1920s, *The Bones of Plenty,* as relevant today as it ever was, tend to be buried by Plains people, cast down into the silence. Who wants to read Hudson's depiction of a farm wife's anguish over being torn from her roots, her home, her beloved piano: "If I go over and touch it now . . . just touch the middle C above the golden lock again, I would be turned into a pillar of salt; I would never have to walk out of here and get in the front seat of the car beside my husband, where the world says I belong."

Those times were hard enough to live through; there's no desire to read about them among people who raised their children to believe those hard times could never come again. Now that they're back, they and their children are doubly impoverished by having lost a native literature as well as the land homesteaded by their grandparents.

I write on the Plains, in a small town. I am indelibly an outsider, because I write and because I spent my formative years away. I am also an insider by virtue of family connections. I have a unique role here and try to respect its complexity. I have no family in the area now, but my roots go deep. When with considerable misgivings I joined my grandmother's Presbyterian church more than ten years after she died, an old woman startled me by saying, "It's good to have a Totten in the church again." People like her have helped recall me to my inheritance.

Not long ago I visited with a gentlemanly old cowboy in a tavern. He was in town, "buying provender," as he put it, and he sought me out as a member of what he termed "one of the old families," to tell me about a sidesaddle he owns that his great-grandfather made as a wedding present nearly 150 years ago. We mused a while on the subject of our ancestors, who traveled from many places— England, Scotland, Connecticut, Virginia, Iowa, Kansas—to settle on the Plains.

"I worry about us, if we aren't producing artists here who can tell our story."

Suddenly he said: "Who are we, and where do we come from? That's the real question, isn't it?" Before I could reply, he smiled slyly and said, "And here we are, telling each other lies." "Stories," I said, laughing. "Call them stories." "Stories?" he nearly shouted back. "That's who we are!" Slapping the bar, he repeated, *"Who we are!"*

Just a small moment, the philosophical enthusiasm of a tipsy but still courtly cowboy, but I think it reveals something about the sensitivity of Plains people to their past and present identities. I am entrusted with many stories here, and I have my own to tell. What I often wonder is why the others are not telling theirs. The material is certainly here: The economic upheavals of the last ten years alone might have inspired a novel as deeply Dakotan as *The Bones of Plenty*. Instead there is silence. We have comparatively few writers in the Dakotas, most of them teaching in our colleges or universities, which, as one of them, Jay Meek, has said, makes them "not *of* the [rural] communities, however much they might be *from* them." A few people in small towns write genre fiction—cowboy poetry, historical westerns, and the like—and some wonderful indigenous writing surfaces in memoirs and devotional literature, like a ranch woman's chronicle of the current farm crisis told through the Psalms, but mostly there is silence.

This is no doubt fine with many; artists are suspect in American society, as they bring uncomfortable truths to the surface. But the silence here disturbs some who seek after truth; I've heard both clergy and board members of the North Dakota Arts Council wonder aloud what it means to have so few writers in the region. One minister told me he saw it as a kind of censorship, having a different cause than the censorship inflicted by totalitarianism or a military dictatorship, but with the same result. "I worry about us," he said, "if we aren't producing artists here who can tell our story. A people with no art has lost its soul."

Perhaps it will be another generation before the story of these days can be told. The children and grandchildren of farm people forced off their land today may well be the ones to write about it. Perhaps, given the distance that the passage of time can provide, they will give us back the truth about ourselves. Whether or not we will listen, out here on the Plains, I cannot say.

▶ **Analyzing the Text**

1. One of the themes in this essay is the tension people in small towns on the Plains feel between being part of their community and having some space for themselves. A second theme questions the tendency of small-town Plains people to "make nice" or to smooth over unpleasantness. As a class or in groups, discuss these two themes and how you see Norris working them out in this essay.

2. The title of the book from which this essay is excerpted is *Dakota: A Spiritual Geography*, and indeed, throughout this reading Norris suggests that the physical characteristics of the land shape the spirits of the communities she describes. Following Norris's lead, describe how you think geography shapes a community and what it values. As you answer this, think about your own community.

3. Norris writes, "And what of truth? We don't tend to see the truth as something that could set us free" (p. 130). As a class or in groups discuss the meaning of Norris's point in this paragraph. Then, locate several other places in the text where Norris talks about truth or telling the truth versus telling lies. What point is she making about the role of truth within a community?

4. Norris describes how a need to smooth things over in small towns influences how local family and community histories are written. Why is this smoothing over or silencing necessary for these communities and families? Why or under what conditions do unspoken agreements to block the unappealing from memory or view become more necessary for the life of a community than a commitment to being truthful or historically accurate? When can such decisions hurt a community? When can they hurt an individual?

5. Norris was a writer before she moved to this small town, and she not only taught writing there but also was inspired by her experiences in South Dakota to write this essay and several books. In this essay, what does she seem to conclude about the role of writers and other artists within a community? Do you agree with her? Why or why not?

6. **Interrogating Assumptions.** What assumptions are inherent in the attitudes of the townspeople that Norris describes, particularly their tendency to mythologize the past?

7. **Connecting to Another Reading.** Both this essay and "The Amish Charter" (p. 99) describe how communities handle conflict. The Amish have rules for shunning or banning community members whose behavior conflicts with their standards. Norris describes how small-town people ignore or "smooth over"

conflicts. What do these two approaches to handling conflict say about these communities? What assumptions about how a community ought to function are revealed by these practices?

Writing about Cultural Practices

8. Locate and study the history of the community in which you currently live or, if your instructor agrees, of the community in which you grew up. Working individually or in groups and using a local history museum, historical society, or library, research the history of your community. Next conduct individual interviews with long-standing community members. (If you live in a large city or town, you may wish to focus this project on a particular neighborhood or area.) The purpose of this assignment is to look at histories as stories that are constructed out of a particular community's needs. As you gather your findings (which you may present as either an essay or a class presentation), consider the following questions.

    • What are the most meaningful or moving aspects of the stories you've gathered? What is it about them that makes them meaningful or moving? If you gathered stories through individual interviews, explain why you think the people you interviewed chose to tell you those stories.

    • Can you back up the stories with historical facts? Do any of the stories stray from the truth? If so, how much? How do you account for this?

    • How does your experience of gathering local stories compare to Norris's?

Maya Angelou, **Reclaiming Our Home Place**

Maya Angelou, hailed as one of the great voices of contemporary American literature, grew up in St. Louis, Missouri, and rural Arkansas. She is an accomplished poet, author, historian, civil rights activist, playwright, actress, producer, and director. Among her twelve best-selling books is *I Know Why the Caged Bird Sings* (1969), which was nominated for a National Book Award. In 1993, Angelou was invited by Bill Clinton to become the second poet in history to speak at a presidential inauguration, an occasion for which she wrote and presented "On the Pulse of Morning." In the following essay, adapted by Henry Louis Gates, Jr., from an interview he conducted with the writer, Angelou describes her pleasure that many African Americans are moving to the South: "Our people have been in exile in the North for three-quarters of a century. In exile, and in many cases, not realizing it but terribly uncomfortable. . . . Wherever home is, the closer one gets to it, the more one relaxes. . . . I think this is true for all people."

 Mapping Your Reading

In this essay Angelou suggests that, for African Americans, the choice to return to the South is a move to reclaim "the gifts that our ancestors gave." As you read, underline passages where Angelou makes a particularly strong case for the South as home. Use the margins to make notes connecting these passages. What assumptions about community does she rely on to make her argument?

With liberation comes choices. One of America's worst race riots occurred in Atlanta, in 1906, yet today it is home to many African Americans who choose to live there happily.

To understand the phenomenon, one could say if there is that much evil in the history, there is bound to be that much good.

The Civil War was fought all over the South, and alas it is still being fought in some people's hearts. But the fight for Atlanta was particularly fierce and particularly ongoing. I do not know the impact *Gone with the Wind* had on the resistance to change, but I suspect that many people whose ancestors were white

---

For another reading on place, see Norris, page 127.—Eds.

sharecroppers fell in love with the romance in the novel and imagined that if we returned to slavery days, they could be served mint juleps by grinning butlers and hotcakes by loving nannies. The people, black and white, who fought to liberate Atlanta from her prison of ignorance were equal to the task. The organization the Southern Christian Leadership Conference, Martin Luther King, Maynard Jackson, Septima Clark, Andrew Young, Joe Lowery, C. T. Vivian, and others white and black won victory for Atlanta and for all people.

Martin Luther King told a story that after the Montgomery bus boycott ended and the companies capitulated, a black woman got onto the bus and walked all the way back and sat in the backseat. A young man who had been so adamant about voter registration, so adamant, and about the boycotting, went back and he said, "Ma'am, excuse me, we have walked eighteen miles so that you don't have to sit here." And she said, "Son, I walked with you, but now that I can sit anywhere, I'm sitting in the back. It's much more comfortable. I can relax, put my bags down, and stretch my legs out." Then she smiled.

With choices comes a different kind of criticism. There is surprise that in some affluent neighborhoods in Atlanta, black people have chosen to live with other affluent black people. But if your neighbor likes the same kind of music you like, and pretty much the same food and maybe goes to the same church, it's easier to go over and ask, excuse me, do you have some pinto beans, or have you got some Mahalia Jackson records, some Tabasco sauce? Most folks live in the same neighborhood with others like them and have very fine homes there where they choose to live. That should be unremarkable.

I can't imagine having a city place that wouldn't be Atlanta. After I moved from California, the first place I bought outside North Carolina was in Atlanta. I'm a country soul—not way rustic, but small town. I love my town, but 140,000 other people do so as well. But I need the city too; from time to time I need its vitality. There are city souls and country souls. I think a country soul could have been born in Times Square, but when he sees the country he says, this is where I'm supposed to live. And a city soul could have been born in the mountains of West Virginia, but when she sees the city she says, hm-mm, this is me. Wherever home is, the closer one gets to it, the more one relaxes. That's even if you're walking. If you've been on a trek, a few blocks or a few miles, you can almost spot your house. You start to breathe differently. I think this is true for all people.

Our people are coming home.

The federal census for the year 2000 tells us that far more African Americans are now choosing to migrate south than the other way around. This reverse migration has its roots, I believe, in the first move north. Not the very first, because obviously slaves were escaping slavery going north. The move in the late nineteenth and twentieth centuries to the place Robert Hayden called the "mythic northern city" was caused by people who hoped they could find a better place. People thought if they could get away north, get away from the cotton, the worn-out South, get away from all the hatred, from the mean sharecropping days, they would find milk and honey in the streets of Chicago and New York and even St.

Louis, and certainly Los Angeles. However, if the North did promise that, it never lived up to its promise, although many black people remained there.

So when the people sent their children back to the South, to the grandmothers, to the grandfathers, to Sister and Bubba, they sent them to be looked after, I believe, because of the northern disappointment. It was thanks to the Civil Rights Movement and the leveling of the playing field that we had the possibility of Maynard Jackson and Andrew Young as mayors of the great southern city. Then the congressmen and -women began coming from the South to Washington, D.C., to plan a better world. I believe that those events freed people from the painful memories of southern treatment. They began to look south again and see it as they want it to be.

Something basic and earth-shattering happened with the Civil Rights Movement. The fabric of old belief was shattered. The belief that in the South you're black get back, if you're white you're all right. That was structurally shaken, so that black people in Detroit and Philadelphia and Tucson began to look back at the South. They began to remember not only the South's beauty, but that our people's bodies and sweat and tears and blood have enriched this soil, and thought, wait a minute, maybe I belong there too.

I am saying our people have been in exile in the North for three-quarters of a century. In exile, and in many cases, not realizing it but terribly uncomfortable. There's a wonderful cartoon by the great Ollie Harrington, who drew the character Bootsie for the *Chicago Defender*. In the 1950s, in a particularly relevant drawing, he showed Bootsie and his friend standing atop a mountain in Maine. They are outfitted in ski gear with the ski poles and this heavy, heavy, heavy clothing. Bootsie turns to his friend and asks, "Do you think Martin Luther King really wanted us to do this? Is this part of our liberation?"

Our people are coming home. The South is rich with memories of kindness and courage and cowardice and brutality. It is beautiful physically, and spiritually rich.

I live in the South because it's the best place to live. It's beautiful beyond the weight and even the ecstasy of my memories. If you come as far south as North Carolina, you see the lush, almost tropical growth and the fireflies and hear the birds in the morning and the cicadas in the evening.

Come south, walk along honeysuckled paths, and listen carefully to the sounds of good southern music that will play so easily on your ears. You will be happy that you had the nerve and perspicacity to travel on a southern train.

We can reclaim our home place.

We can stand for the good. That's why we risk our lives.

From a past rooted in pain, we rise, the hope and the dream of the slave.

I see the work, the art and the music, and the lyrics of the poets, and the sculpture and the paintings, and I see that the culture is healthy. I do not believe that drugs and criminalities and venialities have total power over our youth. There is a core of health in our culture. Still we rise, out of the huts of history's shame, we rise. From a past rooted in pain, we rise. Bringing the gifts that our ancestors gave, we are the hope and the dream of the slave.

▶ Analyzing the Text

1. According to Angelou, how has what the South represents for African Americans changed in the last one hundred years? What does she suggest it represents now?

2. **Interrogating Assumptions.** This essay presents an argument for why moving to the South will allow African Americans to reclaim a truer sense of home. What underlying assumptions about what makes a community a home does Angelou use to make her argument? To answer this, consider the differences between how she describes what the North and the South offer.

3. Angelou describes Atlanta as "the great southern city." What does Atlanta represent for Angelou? Buildings, sidewalks, shops, and apartment buildings definitely help give a city its character, but as this reading illustrates, the people in a city also make it their own. In what ways do you see Angelou describing this city as a socially constructed community, that is, created by those who live in it?

4. The original title of this essay was "Choices." To what extent is "home" a choice we make instead of something that is predetermined by where we are born? And how do our histories influence the choices we make?

5. **Connecting to Another Reading.** Both this essay and Kathleen Norris's essay (p. 127) explore how place shapes a community and what it values. Although Angelou discusses the city of Atlanta, she also, like Norris, describes what it means to live in the country. Compare or contrast Angelou's description of country life with Norris's descriptions.

▶ Writing about Cultural Practices

6. Identify a Hollywood film that is set in an American city and write a descriptive analysis of how Hollywood portrays "the city," its neighborhoods, and communities. Keep in mind that, even if a movie uses a real urban neighborhood to stage its action, the set designers and movie producers carefully construct how these "real" places will appear in a scene. As you work on your analysis, consider some of the following questions.

   - Whether the film is set in the past, present, or future, how does the filmmaker use the city to set a specific tone for the movie? What details in the movie help you come to this interpretation?

   - Pay attention to the actors and extras being used in the background. As the "residents" of this city, how do these people help the filmmaker communicate a specific message about the nature of city life?

   - Is the city represented by one kind of setting or neighborhood throughout the entire movie (the entire movie is set in high-rise buildings and wealthy neighborhoods, for example), or does the action take characters into different parts of a city? If the action moves around, what visual cues does the filmmaker use to indicate the differences between these parts of the city? How is the portrayal of the city affected by these choices?

   - In your opinion, how do Hollywood's images of "the city" influence popular assumptions about life in urban America?

David Brooks, **Our Sprawling, Supersize Utopia**

David Brooks is a newspaper columnist, a political analyst on TV and radio, an editor, and a social critic. He writes for the *New York Times,* the *Weekly Standard, Newsweek,* and *Atlantic Monthly,* among others. In the following reading, taken from his latest book, *On Paradise Drive: How We Live Now (and Always Have) in the Future Tense* (2004), Brooks reflects on the meaning of suburban sprawl. He argues that critics who see these ever-expanding suburbs as signs of America's shallowness get it wrong. Instead, he argues that they represent "the latest iteration of the American dream" or a sign of an unflappable faith in the future.

 Mapping Your Reading

In the course of this essay, Brooks names and counters two of the most common criticisms of suburbs. The first criticism is that suburbs are strongholds of conformity, and the second is that they represent shallowness or lack of imagination. As you read, make notes in the margins where Brooks sets up and then responds to these criticisms. What does Brooks see as the benefits of living in suburbia? How does Brooks connect suburban communities with the American dream?

We're living in the age of the great dispersal. Americans continue to move from the Northeast and Midwest to the South and West. But the truly historic migration is from the inner suburbs to the outer suburbs, to the suburbs of suburbia. From New Hampshire down to Georgia, across Texas to Arizona and up through California, you now have the booming exurban sprawls that have broken free of the gravitational pull of the cities and now float in a new space far beyond them. For example, the population of metropolitan Pittsburgh has declined by 8 percent since 1980, but as people spread out, the amount of developed land in the Pittsburgh area increased by nearly 43 percent. The population of Atlanta increased by 22,000 during the 1990s, but the expanding suburbs grew by 2.1 million.

The geography of work has been turned upside down. Jobs used to be concentrated in downtowns. But the suburbs now account for more rental office space than the cities in most of the major metro areas of the country except Chicago and New York. In the Bay Area in California, suburban Santa Clara County alone has five times as many of the region's larger public companies as

San Francisco. Ninety percent of the office space built in America by the end of the 1990s was built in suburbia, much of it in far-flung office parks stretched along the Interstates.

These new spaces are huge and hugely attractive to millions of people. Mesa, Arizona, a suburb of Phoenix, now has a larger population than Minneapolis, St. Louis, or Cincinnati. It's as if Zeus came down and started plopping vast developments in the middle of farmland and the desert overnight. Boom! A master planned community. Boom! A big-box mall. Boom! A rec center and 4,000 soccer fields. The food courts come and the people follow. How many times in American history have 300,000-person communities materialized practically out of nothing?

In these new, exploding suburbs, the geography, the very landscape of life, is new and unparalleled. In the first place, there are no centers, no recognizable borders to shape a sense of geographic identity. Throughout human history, most people have lived around some definable place—a tribal ring, an oasis, a river junction, a port, a town square. But in exurbia, each individual has his or her own polycentric nodes—the school, the church, and the office park. Life is different in ways big and small. When the New Jersey Devils won the Stanley Cup, they had their victory parade in a parking lot; no downtown street is central to the team's fans. Robert Lang, a demographer at Virginia Tech, compares these new sprawling exurbs to the dark matter in the universe: stuff that is very hard to define but somehow accounts for more mass than all the planets, stars, and moons put together.

The food courts come and the people follow.

We are having a hard time understanding the cultural implications of this new landscape because when it comes to suburbia, our imaginations are motionless. Many of us still live with the suburban stereotypes laid down by the first wave of suburban critics—that the suburbs are dull, white-bread kind of places where Ozzie and Harriet families go to raise their kids. But there are no people so conformist as those who fault the supposed conformity of the suburbs. They regurgitate the same critiques decade after decade, regardless of the suburban reality flowering around them.

The reality is that modern suburbia is merely the latest iteration of the American dream. Far from being dull, artificial, and spiritually vacuous, today's suburbs are the products of the same religious longings and the same deep tensions that produced the American identity from the start. The complex faith of Jonathan Edwards, the propelling ambition of Benjamin Franklin, the dark, meritocratic fatalism of Lincoln—all these inheritances have shaped the outer suburbs.

At the same time the suburbs were sprawling, they were getting more complicated and more interesting, and they were going quietly berserk. When you move through suburbia—from the old inner-ring suburbs out through the most distant exurbs—you see the most unexpected things: lesbian dentists, Iranian McMansions, Korean megachurches, outlaw-biker subdevelopments, Orthodox shtetls with Hasidic families walking past strip malls on their way to shul. When you actually live in suburbia, you see that radically different cultural zones are emerging, usually within a few miles of one another and in places that are as architecturally interesting as a piece of aluminum siding. That's because in the age of the great dispersal, it becomes much easier to search out and congregate with people who are basically like yourself. People are less tied down to a factory, a mine, or a harbor. They have more choice over which sort of neighborhood to live in. Society becomes more segmented, and everything that was once hierarchical turns granular.

When you move through suburbia, you see the most unexpected things: lesbian dentists, Iranian McMansions, outlaw biker sub-developments.

You don't have to travel very far in America to see radically different sorts of people, most of whom know very little about the communities and subcultures just down the highway. For example, if you are driving across the northern band of the country—especially in Vermont, Massachusetts, Wisconsin, or Oregon—you are likely to stumble across a crunchy suburb. These are places with meat-free food co-ops, pottery galleries, sandal shops (because people with progressive politics have a strange penchant for toe exhibitionism). Not many people in these places know much about the for-profit sector of the economy, but they do build wonderful all-wood playgrounds for their kids, who tend to have names like Milo and Mandela. You know you're in a crunchy suburb because you see the anti-lawns, which declare just how fervently crunchy suburbanites reject the soul-destroying standards of conventional success. Anti-lawns look like regular lawns with eating disorders. Some are bare patches of dirt, others are scraggly spreads of ragged, weedlike vegetation, the horticultural version of a grunge rocker's face.

Then a few miles away, you might find yourself in an entirely different cultural zone, in an upscale suburban town center packed with restaurants—one of those communities that perform the neat trick of being clearly suburban while still making it nearly impossible to park. The people here tend to be lawyers, doctors, and professors, and they drive around in Volvos, Audis, and Saabs because it is socially acceptable to buy a luxury car as long as it comes from a country hostile to U.S. foreign policy.

Here you can find your Trader Joe's grocery stores, where all the cashiers look as if they are on loan from Amnesty International and all the snack food is especially designed for kids who come home from school screaming, "Mom, I want a snack that will prevent colorectal cancer!" Here you've got newly renovated Arts and Crafts seven-bedroom homes whose owners have developed views on beveled granite; no dinner party in this clique has gone all the way to dessert without a conversational phase on the merits and demerits of Corian countertops. Bathroom tile is their cocaine: Instead of white powder, they blow their life savings on handcrafted Italian wall covering from Waterworks.

You travel a few miles from these upscale enclaves, and suddenly you're in yet another cultural milieu. You're in one of the suburban light-industry zones, and you start noting small Asian groceries offering live tilapia fish and premade bibimbap dishes. You see Indian video rental outlets with movies straight from Bollywood. You notice a Japanese bookstore, newspaper boxes offering the *Korea Central Daily News*, and hair salons offering DynaSky phone cards to Peru.

One out of every nine people in America was born in a foreign country. Immigrants used to settle in cities and then migrate out, but now many head

Suburban sprawl in Baltimore.

straight for suburbia, so today you see little Taiwanese girls in the figure skating clinics, Ukrainian boys learning to pitch, and hints of cholo culture spreading across Nevada. People here develop their own customs and patterns that grow up largely unnoticed by the general culture. You go to a scraggly playing field on a Saturday morning, and there is a crowd of Nigerians playing soccer. You show up the next day and it is all Mexicans kicking a ball around. No lifestyle magazine is geared to the people who live in these immigrant-heavy wholesale warehouse zones.

You drive farther out, and suddenly you're lost in the shapeless, mostly middle-class expanse of exurbia. (The inner-ring suburbs tend to have tremendous income inequality.) Those who live out here are very likely living in the cultural shadow of golf. It's not so much the game of golf that influences manners and morals; it's the Zenlike golf ideal. The perfect human being, defined by golf, is competitive and success-oriented, yet calm and neat while casually dressed. Everything he owns looks as if it is made of titanium, from his driver to his BlackBerry to his wife's Wonderbra. He has achieved mastery over the great dragons: hurry, anxiety, and disorder.

His DVD collection is organized, as is his walk-in closet. His car is clean and vacuumed. His frequently dialed numbers are programmed into his phone, and his rate plan is well tailored to his needs. His casual slacks are well pressed, and he is so calm and together that next to him, Dick Cheney looks bipolar. The new suburbs appeal to him because everything is fresh and neat. The philosopher George Santayana once suggested that Americans don't solve problems; we just leave them behind. The exurbanite has left behind that exorbitant mortgage, that long commute, all those weird people who watch "My Daughter Is a Slut" on daytime TV talk shows. He has come to be surrounded by regular, friendly people who do not scoff at his daughter's competitive cheerleading obsession and whose wardrobes are as Lands' End–dependent as his is.

Exurban places have one ideal that soars above all others: ample parking. You can drive diagonally across acres of empty parking spaces on your way from Bed, Bath & Beyond to Linens 'n Things. These parking lots are so big that you could recreate the Battle of Gettysburg in the middle and nobody would notice at the stores on either end. Off on one side, partly obscured by the curvature of the earth, you will see a sneaker warehouse big enough to qualify for membership in the United Nations, and then at the other end there will be a Home Depot. Still, shoppers measure their suburban manliness by how close they can park to the Best Buy. So if a normal healthy American sees a family about to pull out of one of those treasured close-in spots just next to the maternity ones, he will put on his blinker and wait for the departing family to load up its minivan and apparently read a few chapters of *Ulysses* before it finally pulls out and lets him slide in.

> **Exurban places have one ideal: ample parking.**

You look out across this landscape, with its sprawling diversity of suburban types, and sometimes you can't help considering the possibility that we Americans may not be the most profound people on earth. You look out across the suburban landscape that is the essence of modern America, and you see the culture of Slurp & Gulps, McDonald's, Disney, breast enlargements, and *The Bachelor*. You see a country that gave us Prozac and Viagra, paper party hats, pinball machines, commercial jingles, expensive orthodontia, and Monster Truck rallies. You see a trashy consumer culture that has perfected parade floats, corporate-sponsorship deals, low-slung jeans, and frosted Cocoa Puffs; a culture that finds its quintessential means of self-expression through bumper stickers ("Rehab Is for Quitters").

Indeed, over the past half century, there has been an endless flow of novels, movies, anti-sprawl tracts, essays, and pop songs all lamenting the shallow conformity of suburban life. If you scan these documents all at once, or even if, like the average person, you absorb them over the course of a lifetime, you find their depictions congeal into the same sorry scene. Suburban America as a comfortable but somewhat vacuous realm of unreality: consumerist, wasteful, complacent, materialistic, and self-absorbed.

Disneyfied Americans, in this view, have become too concerned with small and vulgar pleasures, pointless one-upmanship. Their lives are distracted by a buzz of trivial images, by relentless hurry instead of contemplation, information rather than wisdom, and a profusion of unsatisfying lifestyle choices. Modern suburban Americans, it is argued, rarely sink to the level of depravity—they are too tepid for that—but they don't achieve the highest virtues or the most demanding excellences.

These criticisms don't get suburbia right. They don't get America right. The criticisms tend to come enshrouded in predictions of decline or cultural catastrophe. Yet somehow imperial decline never comes, and the social catastrophe never materializes. American standards of living surpassed those in Europe

GEORGE CARLIN
. . . on Where
He Lives

"I grew up in New York City and lived there until I was thirty. At that time, I decided I'd had enough of life in a dynamic, sophisticated city, so I moved to Los Angeles.

If you really want to understand California, forget the grief clinics and yogaholics. Disregard spirit guides, centering groups, dream workshops, pyramid energy, and primal therapy. Ignore centering, fasting, Rolfing, grounding, channeling, rebirthing, nurturing, self-parenting, and colon cleansing. And don't even think about polarity work, inversion swings, and psychocalisthenics. You also need pay no attention to nude volleyball, spinach therapy, white wine hot tubs, jogging on hot coals, and the people who sing Christmas carols to zoo animals. Forget all that. The only thing you have to know about California is this: They have traffic school for chocoholics. Okay?"

–From *Brain Droppings*, 1997

around 1740. For more than 260 years, in other words, Americans have been rich, money-mad, vulgar, materialistic, and complacent people. And yet somehow America became and continues to be the most powerful nation on earth and the most productive. Religion flourishes. Universities flourish. Crime rates drop, teen pregnancy declines, teen-suicide rates fall, along with divorce rates. Despite all the problems that plague this country, social healing takes place. If we're so great, can we really be that shallow?

Nor do the standard critiques of suburbia really solve the mystery of motivation—the inability of many Americans to sit still, even when they sincerely want to simplify their lives. Americans are the hardest-working people on earth. The average American works 350 hours a year—nearly 10 weeks—more than the average Western European. Americans switch jobs more frequently than people from other nations. The average job tenure in the U.S. is 6.8 years, compared with more than a decade in France, Germany, and Japan. What propels Americans to live so feverishly, even against their own self-interest? What energy source accounts for all this?

Finally, the critiques don't explain the dispersion. They don't explain why so many millions of Americans throw themselves into the unknown every year. In 2002, about 14.2 percent of Americans relocated. Compare that with the 4 percent of Dutch and Germans and the 8 percent of Britons who move in a typical year. According to one survey, only slightly more than a quarter of American teenagers expect to live in their hometowns as adults.

What sort of longing causes people to pick up and head out for the horizon? Why do people uproot their families from California, New York, Ohio, and elsewhere and move into new developments in Arizona or Nevada or North Carolina, imagining their kids at high schools that haven't even been built yet, picturing themselves with new friends they haven't yet met, fantasizing about touch-football games on lawns that haven't been seeded? Millions of people every year leap out into the void, heading out to communities that don't exist, to office parks that are not yet finished, to places where everything is new. This mysterious longing is the root of the great dispersal.

To grasp that longing, you have to take seriously the central cliche of American life: the American dream. Albert Einstein once said that imagination is more important than knowledge, and when you actually look at modern mainstream America, you see what a huge role fantasy plays even in the seemingly dullest areas of life. The suburbs themselves are conservative utopias, where people go because they imagine orderly and perfect lives can be led there. This is the nation of Hollywood, Las Vegas, professional wrestling, Elvis impersonators, *Penthouse* letters, computer gamers, grown men in LeBron James basketball jerseys, faith healers, and the whole range of ampersand magazines (*Town & Country, Food & Wine*) that display perfect parties, perfect homes, perfect vacations, and perfect lives.

Millions leap out into the void, to communities that don't exist, to places where everything is new.

This is the land of Rainforest Cafe theme restaurants, Ralph Lauren WASP-fantasy fashions, Civil War re-enactors, gated communities with names like Sherwood Forest, and vehicles with names like Yukon, Durango, Expedition, and Mustang, as if their accountant-owners were going to chase down some cattle rustlers on the way to the Piggly Wiggly. This is the land in which people dream of the most Walter Mitty-esque personal transformations as a result of the low-carb diet, cosmetic surgery, or their move to the Sun Belt.

Americans—seemingly bland, ordinary Americans—often have a remarkably tenuous grip on reality. Under the seeming superficiality of suburban American life, there is an imaginative fire that animates Americans and propels us to work so hard, move so much, and leap so wantonly.

Ralph Waldo Emerson once wrote that those who "complain of the flatness of American life have no perception of its destiny. They are not Americans." They don't see that "here is man in the garden of Eden; here, the Genesis and the Exodus." And here, he concluded fervently, will come the final Revelation. Emerson was expressing the eschatological longing that is the essence of the American identity: the assumption that some culminating happiness is possible here, that history can be brought to a close here.

The historian Sacvan Bercovitch has observed that the United States is the example par excellence of a nation formed by collective fantasy. Despite all the claims that American culture is materialist and pragmatic, what is striking about this country is how material things are shot through with enchantment.

The United States is a nation formed by a collective fantasy.

America, after all, was born in a frenzy of imagination. For the first European settlers and for all the subsequent immigrants, the new continent begs to be fantasized about. The early settlers were aware of and almost oppressed by the obvious potential of the land. They saw the possibility of plenty everywhere, yet at the start they lived in harsh conditions. Their lives took on a slingshot shape—they had to pull back in order to someday shoot forward. Through the temporary hardships they dwelt imaginatively in the grandeur that would inevitably mark their future.

This future-minded mentality deepened decade after decade, century after century. Each time the early settlers pushed West, they found what was to them virgin land, and they perceived it as paradise. Fantasy about the future lured them. Guides who led and sometimes exploited the nineteenth-century pioneers were shocked by how little the trekkers often knew about the surroundings they had thrown themselves into, or what would be involved in their new lives. As so often happens in American history, as happens every day in the newly sprawling areas, people leapt before they really looked.

Americans found themselves drawn to places where the possibilities seemed boundless and where there was no history. Francis Parkman, the great nineteenth-century historian, wrote of his youthful self, "His thoughts were always in the forest, whose features possessed his waking and sleeping dreams, filling him with vague cravings impossible to satisfy."

Our minds are still with Parkman's in the forest. Our imagination still tricks us into undertaking grand projects—starting a business, writing a book, raising a family, moving to a new place—by enchanting us with visions of future joys. When these tasks turn out to be more difficult than we dreamed, the necessary exertions bring out new skills and abilities and make us better than we planned on being.

And so we see the distinctive American mentality, which explains the westward crossing as much as the suburban sprawl and the frenzied dot-com-style enthusiasms. It is the Paradise Spell: the tendency to see the present from the vantage point of the future. It starts with imagination—the ability to fantasize about what some imminent happiness will look like. Then the future-minded person leaps rashly toward that gauzy image. He or she is subtly more attached to the glorious future than to the temporary and unsatisfactory present. Time isn't pushed from the remembered past to the felt present to the mysterious future. It is pulled by the golden future from the unsatisfactory present and away from the dim past.

There's a James Fenimore Cooper novel called *The Pioneers,* in which a developer takes his cousin on a tour of the city he is building. He describes the broad streets, the rows of houses. But all she sees is a barren forest. He's astonished she can't see it, so real is it in his mind already.

Mentality matters, and sometimes mentality is all that matters. The cognitive strands established early in American history and through its period of explosive growth—the sense that some ultimate fulfillment will be realized here, that final happiness can be created here, that the United States has a unique mission to redeem the world—are still woven into the fabric of everyday life. The old impulses, fevers, and fantasies still play themselves out amid the BlackBerries, the Hummers, the closet organizers, and the travel-team softball leagues.

Suburban America is a bourgeois place, but unlike some other bourgeois places, it is also a transcendent place infused with everyday utopianism. That's why you meet so many boring-looking people who see themselves on some technological frontier, dreaming of this innovation or that management technique that will elevate the world—and half the time their enthusiasms, crazes, and fads seem ludicrous to others and even to them, in retrospect.

We members of this suburban empire still find ourselves veering off into world crises, roaring into battle with visions of progressive virtue on our side and retrograde evil on the other, waging moralistic crusades others do not understand, pushing our movie, TV, and rock-star fantasies onto an ambivalent and sometimes horrified globe.

This doesn't mean all Americans, or even all suburban Americans, think alike, simply that there is a prevailing current to national life that you feel when you come here from other places with other currents. Some nations are bound, in all their diversity, by a common creation myth, a tale of how they came into being. Americans are bound, in all our diversity, by a fruition myth.

The Paradise Spell makes us heedless of the past but consumed by hope.

Born in abundance, inspired by opportunity, nurtured in imagination, spiritualized by a sense of God's blessing and call, and realized in ordinary life day by day, this Paradise Spell is the controlling ideology of national life. Just out of reach, just beyond the next ridge, just in the farther-out suburb or with the next entrepreneurial scheme, just with the next diet plan or credit card purchase, the next true love or political hero, the next summer home or all-terrain vehicle, the next meditation technique or motivational seminar; just with the right schools, the right moral revival, the right beer, and the right set of buddies; just with the next technology or after the next shopping spree—there is this spot you can get to where all tensions will melt, all time pressures will be relieved, and happiness can be realized.

This Paradise Spell is at the root of our tendency to work so hard, consume so feverishly, to move so much. It inspires our illimitable faith in education, our frequent born-again experiences. It explains why, alone among developed nations, we have shaped our welfare system to encourage opportunity at the expense of support and security; and why, more than people in comparable nations, we wreck our families and move on. It is the call that makes us heedless of the past, disrespectful toward traditions, short on contemplation, wasteful in our use of the things around us, impious toward restraints, but consumed by hope, driven ineluctably to improve, fervently optimistic, relentlessly aspiring, spiritually alert, and, in this period of human history, the irresistible and discombobulating locomotive of the world.

▶ Analyzing the Text

1. According to Brooks, what is the Paradise Spell? What is it that he believes sprawling exurbs represent? Focusing on the last few paragraphs of the reading, pull out several quotes that represent Brooks's explanation of this concept.

2. Before you read this essay, you were asked to trace how Brooks outlines the two most common criticisms of suburbs and to use the margins to make notes next to his responses to these criticisms. Use these notes to create a list of his main claims.

3. Early in his essay, Brooks describes the diversity that is found in suburbs: "At the same time the suburbs were sprawling, they were getting more complicated and more interesting, and they were going quietly berserk." As a class or in groups, work out what you think Brooks is saying in this paragraph about suburban communities (p. 140). Pay particular attention to the final sentence where he suggests that society is "more segmented" and that "everything that was once hierarchical turns granular."

4. Working from your understanding of the reading, how would Brooks argue these new suburbs, or exurbs, function as a community? What do they offer

individuals? In what ways do they constrain them? Do you agree with Brooks's argument? Why or why not?

5. **Interrogating Assumptions.**   One of the themes in Brooks's analysis of suburbia and exurbia is the tendency of Americans to move frequently and to be car-obsessed. What assumptions about how communities should work or function are revealed by these two tendencies? How does this theme tie into Brooks's overall argument?

6. **Connecting to Another Reading.**   David Brooks's essay and Maya Angelou's essay (p. 135) both explore what it is people search for in a community and what causes people to move. What connections do you see between Angelou's arguments about reclaiming a sense of home in the South and Brooks's larger argument about what people search for when they move?

▶ **Writing about Cultural Practices**

7. Is America a restless culture? One of the claims that Brooks repeats is that part of the modern American mentality is to keep moving. For Americans, moving—be it to a new neighborhood or to a new state—represents new beginnings and bigger or better possibilities. For this assignment, respond to Brooks's argument by using your own experiences moving or being new somewhere. Perhaps you moved from a house to an apartment or to a new town, or you started a new school or began a new job. As you draft your critical narrative, consider the following questions.

   • What did this move represent to you or your family? What were the reasons for this move? What expectations or hopes did you have for this move? Did the move meet them?

   • Looking back, to what extent did your experience relate to what Brooks describes as the Paradise Spell, which is "the tendency to see the present from the vantage point of the future"?

   • If you moved to the suburbs or exurbs, did your experience parallel what Brooks describes? If so, how? If not, how did it differ?

8. Brooks writes, "Despite all the claims that American culture is materialist and pragmatic, what is striking about this country is how material things are shot through with enchantment." What Brooks points out here is that people have a tendency to see material, or everyday, objects as representing our dreams or hopes for the future. Objects such as a new car may have very useful purposes, but they also have deeper symbolic value because they represent the dreams of the owner. For this assignment, find an object that you believe represents this idea of enchantment or hopefulness and write an analysis of it. Your object could be something personal, like a graduation gift, or an object of importance to your family. Or it could be a public object that you feel represents a community's enchantment, such as a baseball diamond, a statue, or a public works object such as a dam, tunnel, or bridge. As you write, consider the following questions.

   • What outward purpose does this object have?

   • What do you think is its symbolic purpose, and why?

   • What would life be without this object?

Andrew Leonard, **You Are Who You Know**
Jennifer Bishop Fulwiler, **An Ode to Friendster**

Andrew Leonard is the senior technology correspondent at Salon.com, author of *Bots: The Origin of a New Species* (1997), as well as a contributing writer for *Wired* magazine. He describes himself as a techno cultural hack whose writing focuses on the impact of technology on our everyday lives. Jennifer Bishop Fulwiler is a humorist and cultural critic who writes for a popular online newsletter called Buttafly.com. Included with these readings are images from Friendster.com. Friendster is one of the largest social networking sites on the Internet.

Both of these readings introduce you to arguments about the role of the Internet in helping individuals form and maintain a sense of community. As Leonard says, "Like e-mail, like using a search engine, social networking is a part of the Internet way of life." Both Leonard and Fulwiler agree that the Internet has changed how communities function—but have these changes all been for the better?

▶ **Mapping Your Reading**

As you read, pay attention to how both writers present their arguments about the Internet as a community-building space. Underline passages where you think the writers make strong statements about the nature or quality of people's relationships online. How has the Internet built or undermined a sense of community? Are online communities genuine communities? Do you agree or disagree with Leonard's and Fulwiler's critiques of online communities?

Marc Canter is a social networking addict. On the day I had lunch with him in a Chinese restaurant in downtown San Francisco, he boasted a whopping 558 "friends" on the Web service Orkut. For most people, that might be enough. But Canter wanted more. Not only more friends, but more *friends of friends.*

His situation was dire. In a prankish campaign for the dubious honor of most friendly man in cyberspace, he had recently lost ground to another highly connected Orkut superstar, the Japanese new-media maven Joi Ito.

"SO—that means you all need to go out and make new friends!" read an e-mail sent by Canter to his network that morning. "Try it—it's easy, just click!"

Social networking Web services are online gathering places that encourage their members to build explicit, hyperlinked networks of their friends and acquaintances. Since I am one of Marc Canter's Orkut "friends," I am connected to all of his other friends, and to all the friends of all those friends. Looking for a job or a date, or merely curious, I can point-and-click my way through the pictures, profile information, and communities of the other members of my network.

There's no question that Marc Canter is a friendly guy, both online and off. Sitting in front of me, stealing bites of Hunan pork in between one sizzling proclamation after another about the future of the digital lifestyle, Canter is the epitome of gregariousness. And Orkut isn't his only playground. On Friendster, the most popular social networking venue, he has 124 friends. On Tribe.net, a kind of Friendster spinoff, he has 444. At press time, he was up to 749 on Orkut.

But to me, Canter's numbers did not compute. How can a person have 500 friends? I struggle to keep close to half a dozen, much less half a thousand. When so many people are your friends, can those "friendships" be worth much?

When so many people are your friends, can those "friendships" be worth much?

Canter acknowledges that his Orkut network isn't what anyone would call a closely knit pack of bosom buddies. The word "friend" is a bad term for describing someone you link to online. Reducing friendship to a click on a yes/no button is, Canter notes, "a complete joke."

The accumulation of those connections on Orkut, for Canter, was part game, part marketing exercise, and part simply a test of what in early March 2004 was the newest, hottest offering in the swirling nexus of hype and hope that is online social networking. Not since the glory days of the dot-com boom has a buzzword so thoroughly captured the attention of the media, the geeky early adopters, the venture capitalists, and the mainstream. Social networking has arrived on your PC, and is coming to your phone, your favorite computer game, your chat program, and anywhere else you might consider tapping into the Net. Depending on how you define the term, there are already at least 250 social networking sites or companies, and the mergers-and-acquisition crowd is eyeing them all hungrily. (In the most recent such move, Monster.com bought Tickle, a site that includes social networking and boasts millions of users. Friendster brought in NBC Entertainment veteran Scott Sassa to run the company.)

The promises made by social networking proponents are sky-high: They'll get you jobs, get you laid, get you a party invite or a mountain-biking partner for next Tuesday. Social networking will empower communities, combat existential alienation, and, best of all, could even be the key to ending spam. Social networking software—with its idea that human relations can be hacked, that community can be programmed—is a geek wet dream.

On the flip side, the critique is equally charged. Social networking sites are a hotbed for data-miners and marketing strategists, controlled laboratories in which the question of what human beings like to do and with whom can be studied with greater accuracy and detail than ever before. That geek wet dream turns into a nightmare; the social network is a state-of-the-art Panopticon. (Not that most people appear to care. Promise someone a date, or a chance at a job, and they'll happily expose their most intimate secrets.)

Panopticon or panacea, social networking is hardly new. Most people started networking socially online, one way or another, the first time they logged on. It's the fundamental fact of network existence: You connect. But what once was done by early-adopter pioneers typing from the command line over puny modems in primitive chat rooms and bulletin board systems is now standard practice for the broadband-hooked up, digital camera-equipped, blog-and-instant-messaging obsessed masses.

The venture capitalists and start-up CEOs call this "the return of the consumer Internet," but the truth is that nothing ever went away. Our attention may have lapsed—I know mine did. After the dot-com crash, 9/11, corporate scandal, and war, what people are doing online just doesn't seem as world-changingly important as it once did, last century. But that doesn't mean that we stopped doing things online—on the contrary, more people are doing more things online than ever before, and social networking is an essential part of it. Like e-mail, like using a search engine, social networking is a part of the Internet way of life. And it's barely getting started.

One evening this spring, I attended an event at Trader Vic's in Palo Alto, sponsored by the Commonwealth Club of California. The topic was social networking, a subject that members of the club were predisposed to be interested in, since, although it bills itself as a "public affairs group," the Commonwealth Club is really an old-school social network.

The panelists that night included Jas Dhillon, CEO of ZeroDegrees.com, recently purchased by Barry Diller's Interactive Corp.; Stanford sociologist Mark Granovetter, whose 1973 paper "The Strength of Weak Ties" is a foundational document in the young discipline of networking science; Ben Smith, CEO of Spoke.com which provides social networking services to corporations; and Valerie Syme, executive vice president of Tribe.net, a company that aims to employ social networking as a tool for the delivery of local online classified ads.

A posting on Tribe.net had led me here. I found out about the event after joining a "tribe" called "social software intellectuals"—originally created by Marc Canter. A tribe, on Tribe.net, is what would be called a "group" or a "conference"

FOUND

from sanfrancisco.craigslist.com

COMMUNITIES ON CRAIGSLIST, SAN FRANCISCO

Anxiety Group (Pleasant Hill)

Artists' Support Group

Bay Area Brit Group

Bible Study in Japanese (South Beach)

Chronic Fatigue Support Group (Menlo Park)

Circle of Pagans (Bay Area)

Civil & Open Minded Thinkers' Free Form Group (Concord)

East Bay Scrapbook Group (Martinez)

Enjoy A Dream Group (Oakland)

Foreign and Indie Film Buffs Group

Gay Travel Group (East Bay)

German Conversation Group (Palo Alto)

Girl's Night Out Club (Ingleside)

GLBT Movie Buddies Club

Graphic Design Network (Mill Valley)

Healthy Living Group for Women (Oakland)

Intermediate Spanish Speaking Group (Berkeley)

Jujitsu/Martial Arts Group (Sunset/Parkside)

Kissing Club (Ingleside)

Massage Group

MBA Applicant Network

Meditation Group! This Week—Love your Body! (Richmond)

Men's Right's Activist Group (Sonoma)

Mid-life Women's Circle (Berkeley)

Mother's Support Group (Mill Valley)

Mountain Bike Group (Palo Alto)

Non-Native Singles Unite!

Online Poker Club (Northern California)

Pleasanton Newcomers Club

Relationship and Intimacy Skills Group (Financial District)

Repetitive Strain Group (Petaluma)

Restaurant Workers Group

San Francisco Stitch-n-Bitch

Santa Clara Men's Group

Science Fiction Writers Group (Berkeley)

Spiritual/Conscious Relationships Book Discussion Group (Cotati)

Stay at Home Dads (Sunnyvale)

Support Group for Lesbians Trying to Get Pregnant (Berkeley)

Tennis eGroup

Toastmasters

Transforming Body/Mind/Relationship Group (El Cerrito)

Twenty Somethings Blog Group (San Francisco)

Wealth Building Group!!

What The Bleep Group (aka "Bleepers' Anonymous") (San Rafael)

Wine Tasting Groups (San Francisco/Bay Area)

Women's Psychotherapy Group (San Mateo)

You are a GODDESS Group (Mission District)

or a "forum" on other community sites. Tribe.net is part of the second generation of social software networking sites (along with LinkedIn, Orkut, MySpace, and others) founded by people who witnessed the explosive growth of Friendster in 2003 and wanted a piece of the action. (The founders of both Tribe.net and LinkedIn were early investors in Friendster.)

If you join a tribe, notice of relevant events to that group will be posted on your Tribe.net home page. It's a simple, intuitively useful idea. Who wouldn't like to be able to check their home page and be spontaneously informed of local events of interest, as recommended by your friends, or even as advertised to the specific communities you've chosen to join? Your network becomes your filter on the world, and the more carefully you cultivate and nurture that network, the better the filter becomes.

At Trader Vic's, the audience had come for some clarity, but arrived armed with skepticism. For some Silicon Valley veterans, their carefully and painstakingly accumulated personal networks were their stock in trade, their competitive edge; why should they lay them out for all to see on the Web? For others, burned one too many times before by venture capital-spawned fool's gold rushes, social networking sounded like the latest sucker's pitch. To still others, the whole idea of linking up with friends—complete with a picture showing you to your best advantage and a profile calculated to make you look cool—seemed distastefully high-schoolish. On Orkut and elsewhere, random strangers were asking others to be friends on the flimsiest of bases. *I read your blog, can I be your friend? Like you, I'm a Yeah Yeah Yeahs fan, can I be your friend?*

But the not-so-secret secret of social networking is that *flimsy is good!* Flimsy is where the action is. Seek out flimsy, and you shall be rewarded. As Mark Granovetter explained, for what must have been the thousandth time this year, the counterintuitive key to social networking is that its value doesn't inhere in linking up to your *best* friends and soul mates. You are far more likely, argued Granovetter, to find leads on a good job or a prospective date from the networks of people you *don't* know very well.

> **The not-so-secret secret of social networking is that *flimsy is good!***

You are already probably familiar with the friends of your best friend, or spouse, or close office colleague. There's no fresh territory to plunder there. It's those people with whom you have "weak ties"—the vague acquaintances, that guy or gal you once kind of knew, a little bit—who offer a path into possibility that you didn't know was there. The essence of social software networks is that they are a clever way to organize access to the networks of people *you aren't actually friends with.*

People, especially in the business world, especially salespeople, have been trying to figure out how to do this forever. But it's a tough problem, because once you start dealing with a network that consists of the friends of the friends of your friends, you are confronting big numbers and big complexity. I have 50 "friends" on Orkut—my resulting network has 410,000 members, and is growing by 20,000 every week!

The human mind is not built to deal with networks that large. But computers make it easy. As sociologist Duncan Watts argues in *Six Degrees: The Science of a Connected Age,* serious research into network theory wasn't really feasible until the development of fast, powerful computers. Doing the math involved was simply too arduous.

In the past, the supernetworkers, the salespeople with the fat Rolodexes and the eidetic memory of names and faces, were exceptional cases. But today, creating an online Rolodex has never been easier. Point and click a few times, and boom, not only do you have a little network of your own, but you can suddenly browse through the hundreds of thousands of people you are linked to. Keeping all those hordes of almost-but-not-quite-complete strangers organized is a snap.

But if you can keep track of all those strangers, they can also keep track of you.

"There is something fascinating about collections of people," says Bernardo Huberman, the director of the Information Dynamics Lab at Hewlett Packard Laboratories. Huberman boasts a résumé that stretches back to the famous Xerox PARC and includes groundbreaking work in a multitude of disciplines. Of late, one of the things he and his team of researchers have been studying is what you can learn about people from their interactions on a computer network.

> **"There is something fascinating about collections of people."**

In 2003, Huberman, Joshua R. Tyler, and Dennis M. Wilkinson published a paper titled "E-mail as Spectroscopy: Automated Discovery of Community Structure within Organizations." In it, they reported on their analysis of a year's worth of e-mail sent back and forth between the 500 or so employees of HP Labs. They paid no attention to content; they concerned themselves only with the "to:" and "from:" sections of the e-mail header. But from that data set they were able to create an intriguing map of relationships—clusters of HP workers who e-mailed among themselves at particularly high rates.

Many of these clusters mapped directly to explicit HP Labs work groups or departments, as one might expect. But others jumped across groups and transcended departments, revealing communities that did not exist on any official corporate map.

"Discovering that you and a great bunch of other people that are not obviously in the same organization seem to be exchanging a lot of messages and have some things in common might be very interesting," says Huberman. In the paper recounting their research, the authors note that one potential application could be to identify terrorist networks.

"The Internet is a fantastic opportunity to learn about the behavior of very very large groups of users," says Huberman. "There is, wafting around all of us, a cloud of information—we have cellphones, we have PDAs, we have the e-mail that we read. . . . There is information that is implicit there . . . and we have been very interested in seeing whether we could do something with it."

A growing number of companies are already applying similar research to their social networking services. If a corporation signs up with Spoke.com, Spoke will analyze corporate e-mail traffic to see who is connecting to whom and map the networks that result. So rather than have you assemble your own network, as one might do on LinkedIn or Ryze, Spoke *derives* your actual network from an automated analysis of your behavior.

"The real value to businesses in the current groundswell of social networking services is in the potential utilization of the conceptual underpinnings of these services to help uncover and connect to, as appropriate, the human nodes in their organizations," says Judith Meskill, a technology consultant who maintains the Social Software Weblog.

Increasingly, pundits like to tell us, we live in a "network society." Our most important relationships and communities are no longer primarily determined by family and geography. Particularly in the developed world, our atomized, alienated, transient lifestyles have resulted in our seeking community from those who share the same interests, or workplace, or some other kind of tribal loyalty.

Our most important communities are no longer determined by family and geography.

"Networks," writes Duncan Watts, "are the signature of social identity—the pattern of relations between individuals is a mapping of the underlying preferences and characteristics of the individuals themselves."

"One of the main questions I start asking myself is about constructions of identity," says Danah Boyd, a graduate student at the University of California at Berkeley who is a ubiquitous pundit on the topic of social software. "How do people make sense of their identity? And over and over again it kept coming back to the fact that people make sense of their identity by the people around them."

In other words, to quote one of the panelists at the Commonwealth Club: "You are who your network is." You are who you know.

If all this is true, then online social networks are God's gift to sociology. As late as the mid-1990s, notes Watts, sociologists who wanted to research social networks—how people related to each other, who became friends with whom, how information traveled through a social network—found their job very difficult. Information had to be gathered by hand, by passing out surveys, and the data was always suspect, because people might not answer truthfully, or even if they attempted to be truthful, might not be accurate. "A much better approach is to record what it is that people actually do, who they interact with, and how they interact," writes Watts.

And that is exactly what an online social network enables. When we sign up on a social networking site, we are diving into the petri dish, and gladdening the heart of every scientist with a key to the lab. If the network can figure out what groups you are part of simply by the patterns of e-mail sent back and forth, imagine what it can learn when it knows every last bit of data you have input into a five-page profile, which might include everything from your favorite breed of dog, your sexual orientation and marital status, to your turn-ons, bedroom accessories, and tastes in music, movies, and books?

But that's only the tip of the data iceberg. What if, in addition to that, it knows everything you've ever searched for on the world's most popular search engine, it has access to your blog, and it has been scanning the content of your e-mails so as to better target ads to you? Researchers with access to that network—to that online neighborhood where modern men and women spend ever greater amounts of their disposable time—will know more about you than you do about yourself.

I don't normally recommend that people immediately leave my site and go to another one, especially not in the first sentence of an article, but this is an exception: Stop what you're doing and go to Friendster.com right now. It's the best website, nay, the best service ever to be created in the history of mankind. Why? Because it's a 24-hours-a-day, 7-days-a-week freak show in which your friends and your friends' friends are the stars.

For those of you who are not yet on Friendster (both of you), it's a website that maps out your personal network, i.e., everyone who you know through five degrees of separation or less. You create a profile of yourself, then create links to your friends' profiles, who have links to their friends' profiles, and so on and so on. You can just casually peruse through your network linearly, e.g., I go to my friend Nora's profile and click on her friend Richard and click on his friend Kelly who says in her bio that she's a die-hard Slayer fan. So now I know that there is someone in my personal network who still listens to Slayer. I would have never guessed.

But that's boring.

The real beauty of Friendster is the Gallery feature. It's where you have full access to everyone in your network. In my case I have more than 150,000 people in my network within one to five degrees of separation of the friends I've listed. To narrow it down you can search the fields in people's profiles like where they live, what their interests and hobbies are, what their occupation is, etc.

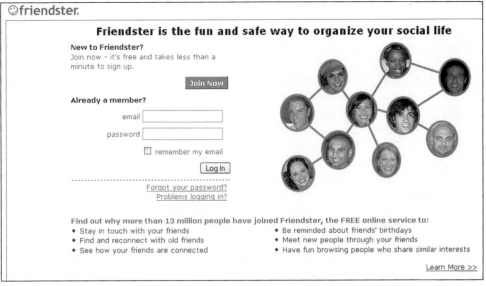

When I first discovered this feature I was excited to see what kind of interesting people my friends and their friends know. I restricted the Gallery search to people living in the Austin area, then clicked on the first profile that appeared, a guy named Milton. According to the occupation listed on his profile, Milton is a Straight-up Playa'. His interests include "talkin shit to you and your friends" and "keepin it gangsta." And evidently Milton is not alone in my network. A quick search revealed that next time I am in the mood to keep it gangsta, I can join Milton and 186 other friends of friends who have listed this under their interests.

Friendster.com is a 24-hours-a-day, 7-days-a-week freak show.

There is also a feature where you can suggest that two people meet each other if you think they'd make a good match. So I could suggest that Xster, who likes "smoking all types of ill shit," meet Josh, who lists his occupation as Rolling Fatty Bluntz. Perhaps I could even meet these people myself! After all, I am only two degrees of separation from both of them. Though I don't need anyone to roll fatty bluntz or smoke ill shit with, they both also list "sleeping" and "eating" under their interests. Though it would never have occurred to me to list bodily functions as interests, at least it's a start.

Maybe I shouldn't have been, but I was quite surprised to find my network full of people like Milton, Xster, and Josh. After a while it appeared that the collective interests of the people in my network could basically be boiled down to "creepin on hoez," "Mr. T," and the "Food Channel." With a mix of bewilderment and morbid curiosity I continued to search through my network, seeing if there was *something* so outlandish that nobody I know listed as an interest. I was unsuccessful. In the half day I wasted on this pursuit, here were some of the favorite interests I learned my friends' friends have. These are direct quotes:

What Are People in My Personal Network Interested In?

"knife fights"

"boozin it up, collecting pez"

"trying to talk like I'm one sick ass gangsta by saying, 'holla like a playa!' and typing LiKe diS 2 gEt cHO aTtenShuN"

"creepin on fools"

"being a god dam gangsta and bubblebaths and long walks on the beach"

"getting pissed about stuff, poetry, porn"

"jewish geography"

"heroin"

"big pimpin"

"bare knuckle boxing"

"i like to go online......also i like to kick it and shit......i go clubbin......and more"

"making giant cardboard heads"

Testimonials

Lisa
24, single, from New York, NY says:
Friendster is great-it should be called employmentster or apartmentster or even lovester! This site and the people I have met have here have benefited me so much! I cannot believe I found a new job on this site, but I did! I have even adopted cats, met a few men, and gone to some exciting private parties! I owe you guys a huge debt of gratitude.

David
19, single, from Redwood City, CA says:
Friendster helps me keep in touch with friends back home now that I am away at college. It is more robust than email, less expensive than the telephone and does not require stamps. At the same time, I use Friendster to tap into the university's social hotbed and connect with new people. It's not terrible either to have that girl I saw on Friendster magically appear in lecture!

Nina
28, single, from Los Angeles, CA says:
Friendster has allowed me a forum through which to express myself and tell people who I really am without the added pressure of online dating. Friendster is great, b/c it doesn't take itself too seriously and neither do I. I've also had the opportunity to spread the word about the service, by using it as a way to market and promote my one-woman show......and it worked!

Amy
27, in a relationship, from Washington, DC says:
As for Friendster, I love it! I use it to keep in touch with people I haven't seen in 10 years and with whom I might have not reconnected. I have looked up job applicants on Friendster as a way to check them out, I look up people I meet at and receptions and meetings get a little background on them, and I have even successfully facilitated some dating via Friendster.....Stop being lame already and join!

Eli
37, single, from San Francisco, CA says:
I found out that I know someone who knows someone who knows someone who is friends with Jerri from Survivor! Friendster makes me feel good because my friends write all these great testimonials about me. The bulletin board has helped keep me in the loop on parties, live music, etc. I found out my friends are friends with some attractive single women as well...

Amy
32, married, from New York, NY says:
Friendster is great for people living in New York. When looking for a restaurant, movie, or new music recommendation, I go to Friendster and ask my network of friends for advice. When I discover something new and cool to do in the city, I share it with my friends on Friendster. I also love setting up my single Friendsters with each other via Friendster!

Lesly
27, single, from Riverside, CA says:
My friend got me to join Friendster, and so far I am really having fun with it. I have already invited five people to join up with me. I invited them because I am so far from them since I moved away, so this is a fun way to keep in touch. I like Friendster because I can connect with people all over. I have already found another person who likes to scuba dive.

Christian
32, single, from San Francisco, CA says:
We all know that meeting people out in the wild is a risky proposition. With Friendster, you meet people through people that you already know and trust. So it's like having an infinite social network.

Used by permission of www.friendster.com

Testimonials at Friendster.com.

But more important than the prose of my acquaintances' bios were their pictures. One of the things that you will quickly realize is that a picture really is worth a thousand words, and this is never more true than on Friendster. Many of the users need not even waste their efforts typing their bios. Their photos speak the loose string of misspelled words and expletives for them. One could guess that PoisonSexy, who chose a photo in which she's wearing a leather bustier that emphasizes the indecipherable tattoo on her chest, lists only "PARTAYing, chillin, porn" under interests. And it's not necessary to read the Relationship Status line to know that the 30-something-year-old man dressed as a robot is "single." The picture of the fat girl kissing her somewhat attractive friend sends the message loud and clear, "I may be obese, but at least I'm bisexual, and that's hot, right?" And the countless women who post photos of themselves in bikinis that are smaller than an eye patch don't even need to write the words, "I will do pretty much anything if you'll just pay attention to me."

About every five minutes you're on this site you'll find yourself thinking, "Who the hell is friends with these freaks?" And that, in a nutshell, is the beauty of Friendster. Because the answer is always, "MY friends."

▶ Analyzing the Text

1. Leonard summarizes both the promises and the criticisms of online social networks that people commonly cite when they talk about what's good or bad about the Internet. Go back and review them. Then, working in a group, create your own list of both the positive and negative claims you have heard people make when describing how the Internet affects social interactions. Why do you think there seems to be so little middle ground when people talk about the Internet's role in our lives?

2. One of the larger points Leonard makes about any social network is that it "becomes your filter on the world, and the more carefully you cultivate and nurture that network, the better the filter becomes." What does he mean? Do all types of communities that we belong to filter the world for us? Is this ability to filter the world a characteristic that is special or unique to our online social networks?

3. In contrast to the serious tone of Leonard's essay, Fulwiler uses humor to criticize online social networks. In essence, her essay asks, "What is the difference between a freak show and the 'friendship' that exists on sites like Friendster?" How does she use humor to make her argument?

4. **Interrogating Assumptions.** Both Leonard and Fulwiler agree that people's online relationships in these social networks are flimsy. While Leonard praises this as an important positive aspect of online social networking, one that can broaden people's lives, Fulwiler cites the flimsiness of these relationships as her main criticism. What assumptions about how online communities should work or function are revealed by these critiques of flimsiness?

5. What do the images from Friendster suggest about how community life is defined on the Internet? Do these images seem to support Leonard's view or Fulwiler's view about online social networks? What makes you say so?

6. **Connecting to Another Reading.** Consider these readings in the context of Mim Udovitch's essay (p. 109). In what ways are the pro-ana communities that Udovitch describes similar to or different from the social networking communities that Leonard and Fulwiler describe?

▶ **Writing about Cultural Practices**

7. Working individually or in groups, create a social networking site—an alternative to Friendster—that follows an organizational model of your own design. As you create your own guidelines and parameters for your site, consider how you want people to use your site to meet and connect with others. Ask yourself the following questions.

   • What personal information will people share about themselves?

   • What will draw people to the site?

   • How will it be organized?

   After you create a detailed outline of how your site will work, write an essay in which you accomplish these two tasks: (1) explain the decisions you made as you designed your site, and (2) articulate what assumptions about how people form communities guided your decisions.

Bill Donahue and Peter Granser,
The Land of the Setting Sun

Bill Donahue regularly writes for *Mother Jones,* the magazine in which the following photo essay originally appeared. Peter Granser is an Austrian photographer whose portraits from his project documenting Sun City, Arizona, have won several photography awards. In their photos and text, Donahue and Granser present what they found when they visited Sun City, the oldest and largest retirement community in the country. Founded in 1960, Sun City is an age-restricted community; one member of the household must be 55 or older, and no one under the age of 18 is permitted residence. Sun City residents can spend their time at one of eleven golf courses or at several other recreation centers, which provide swimming, tennis, bowling, fishing, and other activities.

▶ **Mapping Your Reading**

As you study these photos, make notes in the margins about the symbols of retirement life in this community. How do these images challenge or confirm your assumptions about retirement communities? What images particularly stand out for you? How do the images and text work together to offer a commentary on Sun City?

Somewhere near the end of my recent stay in Sun City, Arizona, I saw a cockroach—a ghastly little brown thing flat on its back, all alone, and desperately writhing on the immaculate linoleum of Waldo Smith's garage. The 82-year-old homeowner was standing beside me, watching the spectacle. "I spray for insects," he said, "and that fellow there"—Smith pointed his rubber-tipped cane at the bug—"he got ahold of some of that stuff. It won't be long now he'll be dead."

Smith and I went inside, got some cold water, listened to the ice cubes *chonk* out of the door of the fridge. Then we came back out to the garage and a faint grin glimmered on Waldo Smith's wrinkly face. Sure enough, nature had been vanquished. And in Sun City, population 38,000, such vanquishment is holy.

As these pictures by Austrian photographer Peter Granser will attest, America's oldest adults-only community is the antithesis of a wild place. There are no weeds in the sidewalk cracks or on the manicured expanses of its seven 18-hole golf courses. The trunks of the diminutive sour orange trees are literally painted (white, against the blistering sun) and if you stroll through the cul-de-sacs at eight in the evening, all you will hear is the liquid whir of hundreds of air

Peter Granser; original photos in color

conditioners. Everyone is inside, gathering strength to do battle against the most chronic and brutal of natural forces, human decay.

In the cool, dewy dawn, they will be out there again—on ancient Schwinn bicycles, bearing quivering little Chihuahuas in their handlebar baskets, or otherwise toiling. There is an 87-year-old here who gets around pretty good on his roller skates, and when I visited a rehearsal of the Tip Top Dancers, assembled Rockette-style [on p. 164], the whole troupe swerved toward me, tap dancing and smiling so warmly that I was filled with the unnerving sense that 16 tanned septuagenarians were hitting on me at once.

Such sparkle has always been Sun City's trademark. When developer Del Webb built 27,000 houses here in 1960, back when leaving the workforce often meant hanging up the briefcase and waiting to die, he envisioned "An Active New Way of Life," as the ad jingle put it. Ever since, his successors have continued to preach the gospel of vigor, to great economic effect. The Del Webb Corp. now has 15 communities throughout the country, and as many as 10 percent of all Americans over 70 currently live in age-segregated communities.

Of course, it doesn't take a genius to recognize that places that bar youngsters (under 55, in Sun City's case) are essentially waiting rooms for the Fairway Beyond. Del Webb has his critics. In a recent book, *Prime Time,* author Marc Freedman argues that retirees shouldn't take themselves "out of circulation" but should instead remain in mixed-age communities to share their wisdom through volunteering. Others are more virulent. When I showed these photos to a friend, he dismissed Sun City as "nasty neat," as the kind of closed community

Peter Granser; original photos in color

Life in Sun City, Arizona, is not all mah-jongg and pinochle. From the synchronized swimming club, which takes the plunge four times a week, to the Tip Top Dancers—a hit at local parties—to the lawn bowlers who rise at dawn to beat the heat, Sun City attracts active seniors—and more than its share of inactive wildlife (see the flamingoes on p. 162).

Peter Granser; original photos in color

that might appeal to his Reagan-loving grandfather—a man who once cussed him out for getting cut from the football team.

My friend didn't get it. What Peter Granser has done here is celebrate, with the fresh eye of a foreigner, a distinctly American hope. The people in these photographs are believers. They are from the Midwest, many of them, and they put in their 40 years at the insurance company (hardware store, tire factory) and they got the gold watch and then moved out to the outskirts of Phoenix, determined to enjoy the leisure years they so thoroughly earned. Consider the man with the bag and the perma-press slacks [on p. 163]. Maybe he's a widower, or maybe he had to get chemo for that thing with his prostate, but he still bowls every Thursday, damn it.

Or consider Waldo Smith, the roach killer, who, when I met him at 6:30 one morning, was dressed in a fluorescent orange vest and cap and slowly making his way toward his Chevrolet pickup. Smith is a former president of the Sun City

Sunland Pet Rest, the local pet cemetery, is adjacent to the human cemetery, helping preserve the bond between Sun City residents and their animal companions.

Peter Granser; original photos in color

Prides, a volunteer group whose 300 members all wear orange vests and caps as they pluck litter from the median strips on the roadways.

"We have the privilege of doing the work to make Sun City one of the world's cleanest cities," Smith told me, "and I believe that cleanliness, honesty, and integrity all go together." We drove around for several miles, killing much of the morning in pursuit of a particular yard that was, in Smith's view, "a total catastrophe." He wanted to have a word with the homeowner, but we kept getting lost, which made him sadly chagrined. But eventually we ran into another Pride member, Stanley Jones, who was wearing a fluorescent orange pith helmet and clutching a huge orange plastic bag. In the bottom of the bag there were a few featherlike husks. Sun City was now six or eight desiccated palm fronds cleaner—a fact that brought joy to Waldo Smith's heart.

Analyzing the Text

1. After studying the images and text that make up this essay, what overall impressions do you have of life in Sun City? What impressions do you have of the attitudes and values of the retirees who live there? Provide details from the photos and text to explain your impressions.

2. In what ways are these images similar to standard images of communities anywhere?

3. **Interrogating Assumptions.** In what ways do these images present a nonstandard picture of community life? How does Sun City challenge popular assumptions about what makes a community a community?

4. No one is born into this community. Everyone who lives in Sun City is from somewhere else. How is this a mark of strength for this community? In what ways does this constrain what is possible within this community?

5. **Connecting to Another Reading.** Are there any similarities between Sun City and the Amish communities described in John Hostetler's essay (p. 99)? Sun City is a planned community, and the Amish are a closed community. Compare or contrast the function of these communities.

Writing about Cultural Practices

6. How different are online gaming communities from planned communities like Sun City? SimCity is one example of a computer simulation game in which players oversee the growth and development of systems ranging from cities to galaxies to alternate life forms. Develop a critical analysis of the structures and assumptions that hold these two kinds of communities together. As you write, consider the following questions.

   - What do you see as the working assumptions of these communities?
   - How do the simulated online communities like those in SimCity compare to planned communities like Sun City?
   - What shared ideas and desires hold these communities together?

These images are part of a photo essay assembled by students at Chicago's Westside Alternative High School, with the assistance of their teacher, Will Okun. These photos are from the Seventy-fifth Annual Bud Billiken Parade, an event that celebrates youth and education in the African American community.

Mixing Words and Images

PICTURING COMMUNITIES

For this assignment, you will create a photo essay (with text) about a community that you are a part of. A photo essay is a group of photographs arranged to explore a theme, tell a story, or make an argument. While images are the dominant component of most photo essays, in this assignment, you will create an essay in which the use of photos and text is balanced—an essay in which the text supports, explains, and gives detail or background about the images.

The photos on the facing page are part of an essay created by the students of Westside High, who publish a monthly photo essay about their community at the New Expression website. Although this photo essay contains no text, it does convey an argument about the community in which these students live. Working as a class, study these images and review the Sun City photo essay (p. 161). Pay attention to how the photographers' decisions about what to focus on and how to position people and objects reveal an overall argument about what this community values.

After studying these two photo essays, choose a specific community that you're a part of. Put together an essay of four to six photographs with text that make an argument about your community—what it values and what holds it together.

Taking Photos for Your Photo Essay

1. Include at least four to six photographs that you have taken yourself.

2. You may also include images from other photographers, but be sure to give credit to images that are not yours.

3. Your photos should work with, not against, the text of your essay. Ask yourself how each image furthers the argument you're trying to make.

4. Expect the photographic process to be recursive. Once you've decided on the point you want to make, you will start taking photos that support or demonstrate that argument. However, once you start shooting, you may begin to rethink your argument; be prepared to revise your original idea if you discover a new angle you want to pursue.

Writing the Text

1. Remember that your text is an integral part of your argument about the community you are focusing on.

2. Your text may:

   - narrate the action of the photos or give a voice to the people (or animals or objects?) being pictured.

   - describe what your images symbolize about the community they represent.

   - explain how your photos demonstrate what your community values.

ON THE WEB
For help with these assignments, go to Chapter 2,
bedfordstmartins.com/remix

Connecting to Culture ## Suggestions for Writing

1. Network Connections: Mapping Your Social Identity

The nature and impact of social networks in our lives is a topic that several readings in this chapter explore. In "You Are Who You Know," Andrew Leonard suggests that we increasingly "live in a network society," and these social networks—usually a combination of online and face-to-face communities—are what he calls "the signature of social identity."

But what is "social identity"? Social identity refers to how our relationships with others help define our own sense of identity. As Leonard puts it, the networks of people with whom we associate form a "pattern of relations between individuals." By studying this pattern, Leonard argues, we can map "the underlying preferences and characteristics of the individuals themselves."

For this assignment, create a partial map of your social network and write an essay in which you analyze or test this theory of identity. The central question of this assignment, then, is, "To what extent do the social networks we belong to shape our social identity?" To answer this question, use your map of your social network and draw on this chapter's readings.

As you create your map and write your analysis, consider the following questions.

- What connects you with the people in your network? Is it shared interests, experiences, places, or something else?
- What similarities or patterns do you notice among individuals in your net-

work? How do you account for these patterns? Are they explained, as Leonard argues, by underlying preferences and characteristics of individuals? Or by something else?

- What is the distribution of online versus face-to-face communities in your life? What do you conclude about this distribution?
- Is mapping your social connections a useful way for you to think about your social identity? Why or why not?

2. Reality Check: Evaluating Virtual Communities

The purpose of this assignment is to develop a persuasive argument in response to this question: "Are virtual communities *real* communities?" To answer this question, you will need to develop a definition of what defines a community that you can use to help support your argument about whether virtual communities are, in fact, real communities. Use the readings from this chapter to help you construct your definition of the qualities, assumptions, or characteristics of a community.

Second, you will need to investigate some examples of virtual communities such as blogs or chatrooms. For this assignment, consider investigating one such community from one of these categories:

- Virtual communities related to arts and entertainment
- Virtual communities related to college students

- Virtual communities related to a social issue (for example, gender, health, politics, protest, or cybercrime)
- Virtual communities related to your field of study or your career goals

In your essay, develop your argument using points of analysis from the readings in this chapter as well as your experience and observations of this virtual community. As you write, consider the following questions.

- In your view, and especially after reading this chapter, what defines a community? How does this definition apply to groups that interact online? Explain, drawing on examples from an online community that you've visited.
- If virtual communities are communities, how do they function? How are they like and not like face-to-face communities?
- Do virtual communities have more potential for destructiveness, supportiveness, or other qualities than face-to-face communities? Explain. Overall, what do you think of virtual communities? Do they meet their potential to serve and connect individuals? Why or why not?

3. Interrogating Assumptions: How Do Communities Function?

The introduction of this chapter explains three commonly held assumptions about how communities function.

Communities provide us with a sense of stability.

Communities serve our needs.

Communities accept us for who we are.

By exploring one or more of these assumptions, each of the readings in this chapter asks you to consider what makes a community a community. For this assignment, you will develop a critical analysis of how the readings interrogate one of these assumptions about communities. To do this, you will need to present the arguments of two or three of the readings and show how they support their claims about how communities function. As you write, consider the following questions.

- What claims about community does each writer make?
- Which assumption(s) does each writer focus on? According to each writer, what characterizes a community? How does a community function?
- What assumptions are built into the essay(s) you are analyzing?
- What does the use of supporting evidence reveal about the writer's argument about the function of communities?
- Ultimately, do you agree with the writer about what defines a community and how a community functions? Why or why not?

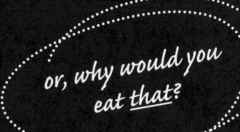

or, why would you eat that?

3 Tradition

Examining the Everyday
Tradition and Candied Apples

Each year small towns and neighbor-hoods in cities across the country organize fairs and food festivals, turning their main streets into parade routes, crowning new queens, holding cooking competitions, and offering up all manner of never-seen-anywhere-else foods. There's the Pickle Festival in Rosendale, New York; fish boils in Door County, Wisconsin; a Rock'n Ribs festival in Springfield, Missouri; a chili festival in Hatch, New Mexico; and a garlic festival in Gilroy, California, to name a few.

Each of these festivals offers a taste of regional culture, community, and tradition. Festival-goers gain more at such shindigs than a few extra pounds. Ethnic festivals celebrate heritage and promote intercultural understanding. County and state fairs and other harvest festivals remind farmers and city dwellers of their relationship

ON THE WEB
For additional resources for this
assignment, go to Chapter 3,
bedfordstmartins.com/remix

to each other and to the land. And neighborhood events like a spaghetti supper at a local firehouse or a tamale sale sponsored by a youth group bring people together to share more than dinner. When it comes to local festivals, the foods served and the act of making and sharing them are embedded in American culture and traditions.

For this initial assignment, you will examine how food traditions promote a sense of cultural identity. To begin, identify a local festival or fair. (If your area has no such festival, then identify a type of food that is special in your area.) Write a brief profile of the traditions surrounding a food from this festival and the history of why it is associated with this special event. As you write, consider the following questions.

- What are the local customs surrounding how this food is prepared, eaten, or celebrated?

- What would those attending this event for the first time learn about local or regional practices or traditions? What would they learn about the local or regional culture—its value or beliefs?

In a final paragraph, respond to these questions:

- When it comes to food, what makes a dish "traditional"? What is the difference between calling a food "traditional" and simply describing people's eating preferences?

The initial assignment helps reveal the extent to which traditions are woven into everyday life. But what exactly are traditions? The most widely accepted definition of "traditions" is that they are the means through which beliefs, customs, stories, laws, religious practices, and other cultural phenomena are handed down from one generation to the next. But this definition is only a starting place for understanding how traditions function.

In this chapter, you will investigate how traditions impact contemporary American culture. The questions that will drive this investigation include these: What makes a tradition a tradition? What are the roles of traditions in a culture? To what extent are these roles positive, and to what extent can traditions hurt or limit us?

Traditions play a role in our relationships with others. Among our family and friends, we share traditions that have special meaning just for us. One family might have a tradition of throwing backyard barbeques for friends and family to mark special occasions like birthdays. Others might share traditions among their friends, like getting together once a week to play video games or watch a TV show or sports event. Traditions are also important ways in which people honor their spiritual beliefs or cultural heritage. For example, for some eight million Muslims in North America, Ramadan is a "month of blessing" marked by prayer, fasting, and charity. Other traditions that honor cultural or ethnic heritage include Chinese New Year, Juneteenth, and Cinco de Mayo. There are also national traditions that help define Americans, such as raising the flag and singing the national anthem, and holidays like the Fourth of July and Thanksgiving that commemorate events in American history.

Identifying these traditions raises an important question: Why do some practices or routines become traditions while others don't? Consider the example of Mother's Day. The tradition of setting aside a day to honor mothers existed in ancient Greek, Roman, and Celtic cultures and was usually connected with spring planting. In America, Mother's Day celebrations began in the mid-1800s and were connected to peace movements. Horrified by the carnage of the Civil War and the Franco-Prussian War, women, who did not yet have the right to vote and had a limited ability to voice their opinions on matters of public policy, used the idea of honoring mothers to create a holiday that promoted peace. They issued Mother's Day Peace Proclamations and held events celebrating mother- and womanhood in cities across the country. In 1914, the U.S. Congress passed a joint resolution, and President Woodrow Wilson signed it, officially establishing Mother's Day. However, this holiday emphasized women's role in the family, not as activists in the public arena, as had been the case in the 1800s. Soon thereafter, florists and greeting card companies introduced the now widely accepted tradition of sending mothers flowers and cards on Mother's Day.

We may think of traditions as fixed and unchanging, yet the story of Mother's Day illustrates the complex ways in which the purposes and meanings of traditions are formed and reformed over time. The readings in this chapter will challenge you to reflect on the cultural assumptions built into how we define traditions and how they operate within American culture. Following is a brief overview of some popular assumptions about traditions. While each of these assumptions emphasizes one aspect of traditions over others, these assumptions sometimes overlap.

Assumption 1

Traditions are long-standing and static practices.

For many people, the term "tradition" has a somewhat old-fashioned connotation. From this perspective, traditions are practices that have been handed down to us by past generations. By far the most common use of the word "tradition," or "traditional," is to indicate references to the past. Add "traditional" to any number of popular culture references and you'll immediately call to mind the long-standing practices of the past:

traditional + songs

traditional + stories

traditional + dance

traditional + clothing

Each of these phrases calls to mind practices or styles that are generations old. Civil War reenactors dress and talk in the style of the original soldiers. Folk musicians play tunes that haven't changed since they were originally made popular. Although these are very specific examples, it is a widely accepted view that the label "traditional" implies long-standing practices that have remained static or unchanged as time has passed.

According to this view, traditional behavior involves repetitive behavior enacted in a particular context. To celebrate a holiday, people may retell the same stories year after year or dance the same dances that they learned as children. Consider the family traditions surrounding holidays like Thanksgiving. Garrison Keillor's essay (p. 225) describes the Thanksgiving traditions of his extended family. The same dinner was served every year, and every year the men in the family packed into the living room to watch TV while the women worked in the kitchen, preparing the meal. As they are for many families, the rituals of Keillor's Thanksgiving were unchanging. Weddings and funerals also offer examples of long-standing traditions. The memorial or religious services, music, and food chosen for these events are fundamentally defined by traditional practices. The benefit of these rituals is that they help people feel connected to something larger than themselves.

As valuable as it may be to keep traditions that honor the past, the reality is that many traditions are more recent inventions. Indeed, commercialism has done much to invent "tradition." In their book, *The Invention of Tradition* (1983), Eric Hobsbawm and Terence Ranger provide many examples of how industrialists from the nineteenth century invented new traditions in order to create a market for their goods. One example is the Scottish kilt. Most people think the kilt—a knee-length wraparound garment worn by men—is a traditional style of dress in Scotland, passed down from ancient times. In fact, it was invented in the early 1800s by an Englishman who adapted a form of Scottish peasant clothing that held no special significance into a garment that could be mass-produced in his woolen mills. It was marketed as "traditional" and soon came to be seen as an iconic image of Scottish history. Similarly, nearly all of the traditions surrounding Christmas as it is celebrated by English-speaking cultures today—the tree, the carols, Santa Claus, the greeting cards—are creations of nineteenth-century Britain.

As these examples show, many traditions are new or have changed over time. Several of the readings in this chapter explore this idea. In her essay, "A Fitting Memorial" (p. 248), Jenn Shreve considers how traditions surrounding memorials for honoring the dead in our culture are changing. Specifically, she investigates the popularity of making and wearing T-shirt memorials to honor loved ones.

When we view traditions as long-standing and static practices, we lose sight of the fact that many of them began as counter-traditions, invented to oppose practices that were seen as unfair or were believed to marginalize a particular social group. Recall the story of how Mother's Day was originally celebrated in America. It was a day for women to speak out on political matters, but when the holiday was claimed by mainstream society, it was depoliticized and commercialized, becoming instead a day to show appreciation toward mothers by sending them flowers or cards. In "It Takes a Tribe" (p. 207), David Berreby explores the origins and meanings of traditions found on college campuses, many of which began as counter-traditions.

What kinds of questions can you ask to uncover the benefits and limitations of this assumption that traditions are long-standing, static practices?

- Within traditions, what purposes do rituals serve?
- How do traditions evolve over time?
- What happens when a counter-tradition becomes popularized by the mainstream? How does it change?

Assumption 2

Traditions preserve an authentic version of the past.

According to this view, because traditions represent accurate snapshots of the past, they act to keep people connected to the past. This assumption, which builds on the first, rests on the idea that by practicing family and community traditions, people stay in touch with their true heritage.

Many organizations exist solely to preserve and celebrate the traditions of a particular culture or region. The goal of the Kentucky Center for Traditional Music at Morehead State University, for example, is to preserve traditional music by collecting and displaying historical artifacts such as original instruments, sponsoring public programs, and supporting folk musicians and instrument makers. The Cuban American Mercian Heritage Foundation in Key West, Florida, similarly wishes to preserve Key West's Cuban history. The goal of this foundation is to help younger generations take pride in their cultural roots and to explain to the public how Cuban people and traditions have influenced the area's culture and economy. From this perspective, keeping traditions alive is a positive way for people to stay connected to their heritage and to teach young people about where they come from.

However, viewing a tradition as a direct, authentic connection to the past is problematic because "past" cultures were no more monolithic or fixed than culture is today. Further, the foods, music, clothing, and values that have, over time, come to represent a past culture can give us only a partial, highly filtered view into that culture. Consider the American celebration of St. Patrick's Day. For centuries, March 17 has been celebrated as a solemn religious day among the Catholic population in Ireland. In modern-day Ireland, families traditionally spend the day attending church and gathering for family dinners; until 1995, Irish law dictated that pubs be closed in honor of the holiday. Holding parades with bagpipes and marching bands and dyeing beer green are customs that originated in America. Today, in fact, American traditions surrounding St. Patrick's Day have been adopted by Ireland's tourism industry in an effort to promote the country and its products around the world.

St. Patrick's Day in America illustrates that, in an attempt to honor the heritage of a particular culture, people are less likely to preserve the past in an authentic way than they are to construct a new hybrid version of it. Often traditions reveal more about the people who maintain them than they reveal about any "truth" about a past culture. What we miss by narrowly defining a tradition as something that connects us to the past is that a tradition can offer insight into our present. This view fails to recognize the wider significance of tradition. In an essay titled "Tradition and the Individual Talent," the poet T. S. Eliot warns against viewing tradition only as a means of preserving the past. He writes "[I]f the only form of tradition, of handing down, consist[s] . . . [of] following the ways of the immediate generation before us in a blind or timid adherence to its successes, 'tradition' should positively be discouraged."

© Ramin Talaie/CORBIS

Eliot argues that understanding and valuing the past should lead us to a better understanding of contemporary culture and its values and customs.

What kinds of questions can you ask to uncover the benefits and limitations of this assumption that traditions preserve an authentic past?

- In what ways is a particular tradition linked to the past?
- How and to what extent do traditions reflect a truth about the past? How and to what extent do they reflect practices and attitudes of the present?
- What wishes or desires are expressed by modern interpretations of past traditions and cultures?

Assumption 3

Traditions promote unity.

According to this commonly held assumption, traditions give individuals a sense of identification with and pride in their community. For example, singing the national anthem before sporting events or wearing yellow ribbons to support men and women in the military are two ways Americans show their unity. Indeed, examples all around us show traditions that are meant to promote a sense of unity and national identity among people.

College campuses use traditions to build and maintain a sense of unity, for instance, through school colors, mascots, landmarks, school songs, cheers or chants, and annual events like homecoming, alumni weekend, and the Spring fling. In their research on the history of cheerleading in schools, Natalie Guice Adams and Pamela J. Bettis, the authors of "Cheerleader! An American Icon" (p. 233), point out that early policymakers and educators believed that school activities such as sports, cheerleading, and student government "would encourage social unity among different ethnic groups" and teach the virtues of cooperation and teamwork. Many campus traditions were created with this goal in mind.

Additionally, although these types of traditions exist in some form on most campuses, most schools also have their own individual—even quirky—traditions. During home football games at Texas Tech University, students fling tortillas onto the field when the opposing team kicks off. At 9 P.M. the night before finals week at Northwestern University in Chicago, students hang out the windows of campus housing and scream. At Wells College, a women's college in upstate New York, first-year students serenade the campus with carols on an evening before winter vacation. The fact that these traditions were invented by the students themselves reinforces the notion that people seek out experiences that bind them together and promote a sense of identification with a group or place.

However, the assumption that traditions promote unity can set up an us-versus-them mindset among people. Establishing school colors and creating specific traditions around joining a campus group can lead to a clannish mentality that causes people to view anyone who doesn't belong in a derogatory

The tradition of displaying a yellow ribbon for an absent loved one may have its roots in the American Civil War. According to the late Gerald E. Parsons, folklorist for the Library of Congress, "The thing that makes the yellow ribbon a genuinely traditional symbol is . . . its capacity to take on new meanings, to fit new needs and, in a word, to evolve. And it is evolving still."

Ribbons courtesy of Jason Reblando; Designs on Demand; United for Peace and Justice

light. Sociologists studying this response have found that traditions sometimes lead people to develop biases against those who do not share their traditions, viewing them as inferior or morally suspect outsiders. To understand the function of traditions in contemporary American culture, we must examine such us-versus-them backlash.

This third assumption also overlooks the ways some traditions can silence or disenfranchise people who do not share a particular viewpoint or belief. This issue is particularly troubling when the traditions are viewed as American or patriotic. Consider the earlier example of singing the national anthem. At many sports events, the national anthem is followed by a Christian prayer. Some view this practice as a way of bringing people together; however, public prayers, particularly prayers that represent only one major religion, can disenfranchise those who don't share the beliefs represented. Such traditions assume that all people feel the same way and share the same religious beliefs. The same can be said about the tradition of wearing or displaying yellow ribbons, which are commonly understood as patriotic symbols. To some, this tradition is not just a sign of support for an individual serving in the military, but also a symbol of support for the government's military policies. Should those who don't support the display of yellow ribbons be considered outside of the mainstream and therefore less American or patriotic? The interpretation of the significance of the yellow ribbon illustrates how complex and potentially volatile the role of some national traditions are in contemporary American culture.

What kinds of questions can you ask to uncover the benefits and limitations of this assumption that traditions promote unity?

- To what extent does a particular tradition promote a sense of unity among people? What values or beliefs are being promoted by this tradition?

- How are traditions used to create an us-versus-them mentality? What are the consequences of such a mentality?

- In what ways can or do traditions actually promote disunity or marginalize people?

- What messages do national traditions convey? What if you don't agree with these messages? What are the consequences?

Questioning These Assumptions

Whether you agree or disagree with them, recognizing these assumptions will help you examine how traditions impact modern American life. Throughout this chapter, you will investigate your own attitudes and assumptions about traditions, particularly their impact on people's sense of identity. Some questions you will encounter include the following: How do traditions influence our behavior and beliefs? How do traditions represent or misrepresent the past? How do traditions evolve to reflect who we are now?

IN THE MIX

Ana Castillo, **Bowing Out**

Chicago native Ana Castillo participated in the Mexican American civil rights movement of the 1970s while teaching English and creative writing in California community colleges. She attended Northeastern Illinois University, and later received a PhD in American studies from the University of Bremen, Germany, in 1991. A leading voice of Latino writers, Castillo has published poetry, essays, and novels, including the award-winning *The Mixquiahuala Letters* (1986) and *So Far from God* (1993). Her essay "Bowing Out" appeared in 1999 on Salon.com. Ruminating on her son's maturation, Castillo explores "the first tear at the seam" in the family unit.

▶ **Mapping Your Reading**

In the following essay, Castillo describes a family tradition invented and practiced by her teenage son. As you read, pay attention to how Castillo moves back and forth from being part of the scene to observing or commenting on it. Underline those passages in which you feel the writer functions as an observer. How do traditions get their start? In what ways are family traditions different from other kinds of traditions? What is the importance of this family tradition for Castillo and her son? What does it mean, in this case, to "bow out"?

Whenever my son wants to come into my bedroom he knocks, of course. It's something he learned to do at five. But in the last couple of years, before he enters he gives me an Eastern-style bow and says something in Japanese, I think, which I don't understand. I don't even know where he learned it. Maybe from TV. You think all your child is picking up from television is how to become a cold-blooded killer. Then he comes up with an elegant ritual of respect toward his mother.

I am thinking about this because my only child is now 15 and he is beginning to separate. On the brink of adolescence I heard the first tear at the seam, but he was still a clumsy duckling returning every day to the fold of his mother's wing. Now he is nearly six feet tall and will start shaving soon.

For another reading on family, see Pillsbury, page 188.—EDS.

He gives me an Eastern-style bow and says something in Japanese, I think.

He's kind of got a girlfriend.

He comes into my room, his single mom's room, usually accompanied by his little dog, Rick. The dog is less certain that it is welcome in this forbidden domain than his master and hesitates when Marcel is invited in. I am usually not in the middle of anything that can't be interrupted, though my laptop may be propped on a pillow or frayed tarot cards out for a little nightly musing. I might be reading or writing in my journal or doing all at once and watching TV. I am always "decent," which is how a woman who sleeps alone usually dresses for bed.

Before you know it, my almost grown-up boy is sneaking under my comforter and trying to get the dog to hop in too. (Which it does not do, being that the dog is no fool and understands the hierarchy of command in our household: *Do not jump on the mama-san's bed upon pain of death!*)

We have our little chats then, my almost grown-up son and I, about his grades at school, homework, what money he needs (and for what), or about where each of us is in our lives at the moment.

"Are you in a relationship?" I ask him.

I use that word because I've overheard him use it on the telephone with his best friend. I'm trying to imagine what "relationship" could mean to a pair of 15-year-olds. Although I must admit I'm not sure what the word means for your average pair of 40-year-olds either.

"I don't know," he says. I guess he's trying to understand what it means to him too.

"You're too young," I say, predictably, as the strictest mother he knows. "You're like a green corn. You're not ready to give anything. Too green."

"And you're too old for a relationship," he says, also predictably, as a teenager who has to get the last word in no matter what.

Well, I'm not in any "relationship" so it's a moot point at the moment, but I must admit he's got a point. I'm pretty content and getting used to my ways as a bona fide bachelor. I'd say "bachelorette," but it would bring to mind *The Dating Game* show and dating is something I don't do anymore. I can't even remember when I ever did, which makes me think that maybe my wise 15-year-old is right, perhaps I have gotten too old for a relationship. If he's too green possibly you can also become so ripe you need to stand all on your own, no compromises, no 50-50 sharing, no attempts at merging your identity with anyone else's, no simple giving of yourself fully to be appreciated fully at all times. But what I say to my son is this: "Go to bed. I pay the bills around here. I can do what I want."

"I'm the man of the house," he says. I can't believe my ears. Then he adds, "I'm the man of the house because I'm the only man *in* the house."

"I'm the woman of the house," I say.

"And Rick is the dog of the house." He smiles and puts his head on my shoulder. Suddenly he is not 15 and ready to fly at any moment but a peaceful, trusting child who, like his mother (and yes, I'd even say like the dog and every other living thing on the planet), is just trying to figure out how he fits and keep everything balanced and in harmony.

"Good night," I say to my son with a kiss on his forehead, now covered with an outbreak of teen acne.

He gets up, the dog behind him, goes to the door, turns around, bows, and says his Japanese phrase. I wish I knew what it is that he says. But I've never asked him. It's one of those things about him now that is independent of me but somehow related to me. I'm not expected to ever understand; just to respect and trust and let him grow and be.

 Analyzing the Text

1. What is the meaning of the tradition that Castillo's son has invented? Does the tradition have a different significance for Castillo than it has for her son?

2. What is the dynamic between mother, son, and dog in this essay? What does Castillo's description of this dynamic suggest about the way they function as a family?

3. **Interrogating Assumptions.**   This essay challenges the assumption that traditions are long-standing practices handed down to us from past generations (see p. 176). The tradition invented by Castillo's son is based on cultural practices of an ethnic group to which they share no connection. If a family tradition is not about honoring its past, what other role can it serve?

4. Castillo's essay reminds us that some traditions revolve around everyday matters. To what extent do bedtime traditions, such as the one described here, mark an important event? To what extent do they heighten everyday experiences?

Writing about Cultural Practices

5. As this essay illustrates, family traditions can arise in unexpected ways and around something as ordinary as bedtime. These traditions often surprise us with the depth of meaning that family members can attach to them. For this assignment, develop a critical narrative of a tradition that is unique to your family. To get started, consider traditions, such as the tradition Castillo describes, that are associated with everyday family life rather than with a major holiday or special occasion. As you draft, consider the following questions.

   • At what point did your family recognize that this practice was more than a routine? In other words, how did this tradition become a tradition within your family?

   • In what ways does this tradition reveal some deeper meaning—stated or unstated—within your family?

   • Why do some family practices or routines become traditions while others do not?

Richard Pillsbury, **Thoroughly Modern Dining**

Richard Pillsbury has written extensively on American food culture. His books include *From Boarding House to Bistro: The American Restaurant Then and Now* (1990) and *No Foreign Food: The American Diet in Time and Place* (1998), both of which examine the evolution of American cuisine throughout history. In his essay "Thoroughly Modern Dining" (2002), Pillsbury examines how "dining out to celebrate special occasions is not just a new American custom; it is becoming the norm throughout the developed world." Suggesting that there has been a shift from families dining at home to dining at restaurants, Pillsbury connects the change in American dining to a larger departure from American traditions.

▶ **Mapping Your Reading**

Gathering as a family in a relative's home, writes Pillsbury, "is the stuff of our individual pasts that gives us a sense of belonging and being a part of something larger than ourselves." As you read, pay attention to how Pillsbury describes the value and importance of the at-home dinner-table experience. What argument does Pillsbury make about home cooking versus the restaurant dining experience? What assumptions does the writer make about the value of family dining at home?

The restaurant was packed. The maître d' scurried up, nodded while making a sign of ten minutes, and flowed off with a waiting group toward the already packed tables in the back of the restaurant. Sunday night was obviously a big night here. A group of eight came through the door laughing and talking; they greeted the newly returned maître d' by name, made a joke with one of the passing waiters, and then had a hurried conversation with a hostess that included a lot of head shaking and hand waving. The room was organized mayhem. Thirty-five or so white covered tables were jammed into a space big enough for twenty-five. On the other hand, the dessert case looked luscious, and the pasta flowing from the kitchen stirred fond memories of great meals in the past. Clearly the food would be worth the wait, however long it took.

It was not a good experience. We were first seated at a corner table for four and then ignored for a time. A senior waiter finally approached to ask in broken

_____

For another reading on family, see Castillo, page 185.—EDS.

English if we could move to another table toward the center of the restaurant. We agreed, and our table was transformed into a table for eight before we were even settled at the new table. Ignored again, I finally calmed my fuming wife by having us moved from the center of the melee to another table along the side of the room, though we clearly were not going to be served anytime soon at that location either.

Menus eventually arrived with yet another waiter, who obsequiously apologized for our wait and then managed to look as if he were trying to hide his disappointment at our order of a half carafe of house white. The wine appeared in short order; he didn't. Finally he returned, and we ordered too much food. It was a celebration dinner for us as well—the crowning dinner for a great vacation.

There were plenty of people to watch as we waited. And waited. The table behind us was filled by a family group of twelve with ages ranging from grandpa to the youngest grandson who must have had his first communion that day. Five courses and a cake with a candle came as we still waited for the remainder of our meal. A teenage daughter brought mom to a birthday dinner on our other side. Their pizza came, their coffee came, and their requisite cake with candle came as we waited. A young couple in love replaced them, and finally the waiter took pity and our second plates arrived.

> Mom, grandma, auntie, or spouse got out the pots and prepared the honoree's favorite foods.

We were strangers, tourists in "a place where everybody knows your name." It was to be expected that the regulars would get the greater attention. It was also a local holiday with many large families sitting around long tables celebrating their children's first communions and baptisms. They were loud. They were having a good time. These were special dinners, not at home, but at the Capri Restaurant in town. The food was good. The wine was good. The company was good. They were here to have a good time. They came. They all went. Our coffee finally arrived.

Brooklyn, Baltimore, or Sarasota? No, this was a dinner in Busto Arsizio, a blue-collar suburb of Milan, Italy. Dining out to celebrate special occasions is not just a new American custom; it is becoming the norm throughout the developed world. The issues that have accompanied these changes seem to have diffused around the world as well.

Special foods and special occasions seemingly have been synonymous from the beginning of time. The ranking cook in the household—mom, grandma, auntie, or spouse—got out the pots and prepared the honoree's favorite foods. The household gathered around the groaning board, and the family created a special time to remember the occasion for all the year and maybe a lifetime.

One learned one's place in the family and in the fabric of their community during those occasions. The foods served were always special. My mother prepared my favorite cake on my birthday and artfully left out some of the ingredients on her only written record so that she would be the only one who could ever create this special thing for her son. My wife's mother, possibly less purposefully deceptive, recorded her favorite pasta recipe as: First, cover the table with a mound of flour. . . .

Replacing the Family Dinner

This is the stuff of our individual pasts that gives us a sense of belonging and being a part of something larger than ourselves. Sharing those times at home in the United States, indeed apparently everywhere, is increasingly being replaced with a trip to the nearest nice restaurant. The good part is that mom does not have to spend the day or days preparing the food and can enjoy the event with the same relaxed ease as others. The downside is that mom no longer plays the role of the dispenser of personalized love and attention. The food served is not created by love, but by some commissary fifty miles down the road. You say that you cannot taste that, and your mom was not that great a cook. Perhaps, but it was not the taste that you remember; it was the love and effort that went into it which created an event that became an indelible image in your mind—indelible, not because the food itself was special, but indelible because of the people who were present and the contextual setting.

The replacement of the family dinner table by the restaurant has been amazingly swift. The restaurant concept, the establishment of a commercial store for selling food to be consumed upon the premises as its primary source of revenues, began in eighteenth-century France. It was not until the Industrial Revolution and the parallel rise of cities that the restaurant began to become an important form of retailing. Few women ate in commercial eating establishments before the twentieth century; indeed, women were barred from many kinds of restaurants through the late nineteenth century. The restaurant was a man's world because most early ones were created to serve meals to men who were unable to return home to lunches and other meals. Women were deemed too delicate for these male emporiums, and if one did appear, someone might wonder about her upbringing, though eventually women did begin to be allowed to enter restaurants first as escorted guests and eventually unescorted.

> The replacement of the family dinner table by the restaurant has been amazingly swift.

Restaurants rarely hosted family dining through the first half of the twentieth century. "A woman who is unable to prepare a meal for her family must be a poor housekeeper indeed" seemed to be the prevailing opinion of the day. World War II, the invasion of the workplace by women in large numbers, and the move to the rose-covered cottage in suburbia changed all of those concepts. Individuals and families increasingly found themselves too far away from home at mealtime to return there to eat. New forms of restaurants appeared that catered to family dining, especially the quick, economical hamburger and its associated fast food emporium. It is not surprising at all that McDonald's corporation, with its $15 billion in annual sales, is the largest purveyor of food in the world.

The transition, of course, was more difficult to live through than to describe. Generation gaps always exist, but in this gender and generation collision the impact was about basic relationships, and those involved were slow to adjust. In my family, for example, if my father and my uncles found themselves in town shopping at lunchtime, they would return home for lunch. If their wives were not at home when they arrived, they would sit there until someone returned to fix them a sandwich and a cup of coffee. I do not know whether they did not know how to spread peanut butter on a piece of bread or believed that the gender division of labor precluded them from fixing a sandwich. It was women's work, and men did not do it. It was all right to fix breakfast, but it was not all right to fix anything for lunch or dinner. My generation negotiated these issues and may have done some work in the kitchen. It certainly did not pretend it did not know how the can opener works. In sharp contrast to my father's generation, my children often wait to start a shopping expedition so that they can have lunch at the mall or some favorite restaurant conveniently passed on the way to the shopping center.

Today, more than half of every food dollar is spent in a restaurant.

Increasing numbers of families eat only a meal or two a week together at the dinner table. Differing school times, work times, soccer practice, choir practice, meetings, and a host of competing activities have played havoc with the structure of family dining. Today more than half of every food dollar is spent in a restaurant. While that does not represent half of the meals, as restaurant meals cost more than home-prepared ones, it also does not include home-replacement meals purchased at the grocery store on the way home from the day's activities. Home cooking, that is, actually preparing a meal—not simply opening a box or thawing a tray—has become a luxury, rather than a necessity.

Effects of This Change

This is not to suggest that there is anything wrong with this trend because many homemakers are not great cooks; nor do they care to be. The question really revolves around the issue of the impact of these actions upon family life. For most Americans growing up in the mid-twentieth century, the one time every day that was crucial for almost every kid was to be home at 6 P.M. (or whenever the evening meal was served) and to be prepared to sit down with the entire family to eat dinner. Today's young families may perceive this as a *Leave It to Beaver*, sophomoric concept, but those dinners set an indelible stamp upon family life. Whether dinners were casual and filled with banter or were more serious, family members interconnected each day in such a way that is virtually impossible to purchase. It was an opportunity for parents to try to discover what their children had been up to, to discuss plans and ideas and problems, and most importantly a chance to build bridges that would set the tone of future relationships. How many parents today will later wonder why their relationship with their children is not like that of theirs with their parents?

This does not mean that everyone at those tables saw and heard the same things in the same ways. My older brother continually tells me that we grew up with different parents in the same house. His memories of those times vary widely from mine. It is not important whose memory might be more accurate, or whether either is accurate for that matter. The point is that every single day we did share time together that built a bond between us which lasted a lifetime of living on opposite sides of the nation and leading quite different lives. Will grabbing a hamburger at McDonald's create the same depth of relationships? It is difficult to imagine that it would.

The rise in violence, mind-altering drugs, suicide, mental disorders, and similar "dropping-out" behavior patterns suggests that there is something very wrong with the United States today. Increasing numbers of people are feeling a general ennui about their lives. They have more difficulties in connecting with others. Loneliness is no longer the sole province of the elderly.

It would be too simplistic to suggest that having one's communion dinner at the local restaurant is the underlying cause of that change. Yet, one must wonder what effect it does have on the long-term memory of that event. No one would suggest that it is the sole cause of the ills that inhabit our lives today, but it does reflect a basic change in family life and our image of our relationships. Will Antonio carry the same sense of family belonging after having his important milestone memorialized at the Capri, as he would carry if he had gathered around the home dinner table with his entire family in a room of mementos of similar passages by those who have gathered on that special day? Will my grandson Trae have the same sense of unconditional love that would come from having his own birthday cake that no one else in the world could have while he is celebrating his sixth birthday at the local pizza parlor playing video games?

How many parents will wonder why their relationship with their children is not like theirs with their parents?

Restaurants certainly are not the villains, nor is such a thing suggested. There is something truly special about celebrating one's first love in front of the fireplace at a quiet inn by the seashore. It gives you a sense of peace to have a place that you know you can go to for breakfast each morning, a place where a little repartee with the waitress and chatter with others doing the same thing are a part of your toast and eggs as you get your mind organized on the business of the day away from the pressures and problems of life at home. No, restaurants are not evil. The changes that we see in our lifestyles while using them as celebration vehicles, however, tell us much about the nature of the changing family and maybe even suggests a warning about what may await us later in life.

A few years ago my brother was visiting his children, who now live in another city, for Thanksgiving. He commented later that they had Thanksgiving dinner at a Mexican restaurant because that was the only place everyone could agree upon that was open. My mind was boggled. We had grown up in an environment where Thanksgiving dinner was the single most important occasion of the entire year. There was a command appearance at Grammy and Papa's, and uncles literally came from across the entire country to be there. The meal consisted of two turkeys, thirty-five to forty relatives, and a day of stories and reaffirmation of pasts and community. It was also a day when each generation spent time together building emotional bridges. The cousins ran wild in the park. The women gathered in the kitchen and brought dinner together and shared their lives. The men washed the dishes and continued their earlier conversations about trout fishing and pheasant hunting, and about camping for months in the

Sierra Nevada during their boyhood summers. These were activities and conversations that helped one find a sense of place in ten generations of American experience. Somehow a lunch of enchiladas and beans, even with extra sauce, just does not seem to be likely to achieve these same goals.

Analyzing the Text

1. Careful to admit that food isn't necessarily better at home, Pillsbury writes, "Many homemakers are not great cooks; nor do they care to be." If it isn't the taste of home cooking that's at stake, what is it that he fears is being lost by replacing the at-home experience with a restaurant experience?

2. How does the author's opening story about eating at a busy family restaurant in Italy set the tone for the claim that the dining-out experience is less meaningful than at-home celebrations?

3. According to Pillsbury, how has the role of restaurants in people's lives changed over time?

4. To what extent is Pillsbury's argument nostalgic? Is he longing for a past that may or may not reflect people's experiences? Where in this essay do you feel he expresses this nostalgia?

5. **Interrogating Assumptions.**   Which, if any, of the assumptions in this chapter's introduction would Pillsbury reject? Support your opinion with quotes from his essay.

Writing about Cultural Practices

6. Ever since the 1970s, when many more women entered the workforce, the number of "family-style" restaurants and restaurants that advertise a home-like dining experience have grown dramatically. For example, the Olive Garden, a chain of Italian American restaurants, uses the motto "When you're here, you're family," and Bennigan's Grill & Tavern advertises itself as offering traditional Irish American food in a "family atmosphere." The goal of these restaurants is to recreate or simulate an idealized version of the home-dining experience. For this assignment, choose one such family-style restaurant—either a local or a chain restaurant—and write a critical analysis of how this restaurant employs family traditions or themes to attract families. Study the restaurant's advertising and, if possible, visit the restaurant to observe its atmosphere as well as the interactions between customers and employees. Consider the following questions as you draft.

   • How does the restaurant attempt to reproduce or simulate the home-dining experience?

   • What family traditions or themes does the restaurant rely on to create its marketing image?

   • In your experience, what does the restaurant's recreation of home dining leave out? How does it redefine the family's dining experience?

Charles Bowden, **Last Meals and the People Who Eat Them**

Celia A. Shapiro, **Last Suppers**

Charles Bowden is a contributing editor of *Esquire* and has written for a variety of other publications, such as *Harper's* and the *New York Times Book Review*. He is the author of numerous works of nonfiction, including *Juarez: The Laboratory of Our Future* (1998) and *Blood Orchid: An Unnatural History of America* (2002). Bowden, asserting that "the last meal is part of the ritual," examines the relationship between a prisoner's last meal and a government's decision to sentence death. This essay originally appeared alongside Celia A. Shapiro's photography in *Aperture* (2003). Shapiro's *Last Suppers* project began in 1999. Since then, she has recreated numerous final meals of executed prisoners and has displayed them in Kingston's Fine Arts Center at the University of Rhode Island. This selection appeared in the January/February 2004 edition of *Mother Jones*.

▶ **Mapping Your Reading**

The following essay and the accompanying photos ask you to consider what the tradition of offering last meals to condemned prisoners reveals about food's connection to American culture. As Bowden's essay points out, food plays a symbolic role in honoring those condemned to die. Why does food play a role in nearly all major life events—both positive and negative? What can you learn from Shapiro's startling photo essay about the tradition of last meals?

When they first clambered off the truck they looked dazed. Steam flared from their nostrils in the chill of the Minnesota morning. They were range stock from somewhere in the West bought to be fattened with the extra corn off his small farm. The cattle stared out dazed and we had to shoo them toward the trough where the golden kernels of corn mystified their primitive palettes. But they soon swung into the work and ballooned up toward the day of sale and slaughter. I remember once playing around the pen and getting them riled and running and my uncle came running over with dark anger on his normally friendly face. The cattle were not to be disturbed but were honored and pampered guests. Some I even took to brushing down and they got hand-tame in their captivity. My uncle said we were "finishing" them, and come one dawn when a particular fine Angus was taken to the barn, I grasped what he meant. We had the fresh liver cooked for breakfast, steaks all around for supper that day.

Of course cattle are not men, most people insist on this point, but there is some dim ancient echo in my head from that morning of slaughter, the somber nature of the men as they went down to the barn, and the feeling that rises up from our custom of giving the condemned a last grand feed. Supposedly, it comes from Christ's last supper, or from a Jewish rite, or from some similar custom of the Greeks, or maybe from somewhere else. But in the thirty-eight American states where we slaughter people in an orderly fashion with due public notice—after keeping them healthy, letting them get in shape with weights, stuffing their minds with endless books—the last meal is part of the ritual. Sometimes the condemned must pick off the prison cafeteria menu, but more often, they are allowed their heart's delight—that final savoring of steaks, lobsters, sweet desserts—which they will never live long enough to digest.

> There is some dim ancient echo in my head from that morning of slaughter.

Unlike our ancestors, we don't allow them any booze. It seems important these days to die with a clear head. And in the interest of health, we generally deny them cigarettes, cigars, or a hit off the pipe. And of course, they are allowed only dead flesh, no deep tasting of lovers is ever tolerated. We also permit them last words. We seem fascinated by what largely uneducated men—and they are almost all men—might say on the lip of the grave. But the meal's the thing, and in almost every jurisdiction the choice of the doomed is published for some reason no one seems eager to explain. The only other menus I generally see in the press are those from certain galas of presidents or movie stars.

When I was a kid, folks would speculate about things such as what they would want on a desert island if shipwrecked, or what the one book might be if they could, God forbid, have only one. But I don't recall anyone thinking about what their ideal last meal would be. Now there are at least two documentary movies on the subject of dining in by the condemned, plus various sites on the Internet that record the choices of those hung, injected, gassed, or now and then electrocuted.

The choices are not cordon bleu, perhaps because we generally fail to send many Harvard boys or great gourmands to the death house. When the state of Ohio murdered Richard Fox on February 12, 2003, he had a cheeseburger with lettuce, pickle, onion, tomato, ketchup, mustard, and mayonnaise with a side of fries and a Pepsi. John Elliot, just before the state of Texas murdered him on February 4, 2003, settled for a cup of tea and a chocolate chip cookie. The bill of fare runs toward burgers, pop, steaks, fried chicken, liver and onions: plain food for elemental appetites. Look over a hundred or so of them, and the impression rises that the government murders junk-food devotees.

Of course, quite a few prisoners do not eat much if anything of their last meals, though the wardens are not often forthcoming on this question. Once in a while, we have the odd case of one of the condemned refusing the offer of a feast as a protest of the execution. Some have at times asked for God's grace, peace, and love—but these items are not listed on the cafeteria menus, nor easily supplied by ordering in. Ricky Ray Rector, a brain-damaged Arkansas inmate murdered during the governorship of Bill Clinton, famously set aside half of his pecan pie to enjoy after his execution. Ruben Montoya in 1993 asked the state of Texas for barbecued chicken and frijoles and bubblegum. He was denied the bubblegum due to prison regulations. Sometimes the requests are short and sweet. Margie Velma Barfield, who had poisoned her lover's beer with arsenic, simply wanted a bag of Cheez Doodles, a Coke, and a Kit-Kat bar.

I've only witnessed one execution, and in that case, as I sat with the family of the condemned and various prison guards and officials, we were supplied with a large buffet of salads, cold cuts, pop, and the like. The condemned man had been slowly wandering through the legal system, a prime case of someone too crazy to execute. The legal system concluded finally that he was sane enough to murder. When he was offered his last words, strapped to the gurney a few feet from me, he merely said he wanted to get the whole thing over with so that he could have lunch.

The last meal is part of the ritual—that final savoring of steaks, lobsters, sweet desserts.

There is a dream-walk quality to an execution. No one can be murdered before their appointed hour, and so the whole thing has that frantic and yet slow quality of a big wedding. The prison officials have checklists of protocols they patiently work through. The entire affair is quite orderly and organized. In the one such murder I witnessed, the whole shebang kept more than a hundred guards busy. In that case no one said the word *execution* out loud, but simply referred to *The Event*.

There is one thing about that killing that reminds me of my boyhood slaughter of that Angus steer. They *know*. The hog, the lamb, the chicken, the steer, always know what you have in mind and this fact can be plainly seen in their eyes. A prison on execution day has that same feeling that floated through the air on that long ago butchering day of a Minnesota summer. The entire installation of men and cells and ugly buildings has both a tension and a pall over it. Conversations are muffled and the air is choked with silence.

I don't think anyone who reads the menus of the condemned is likely to get hungry. Nor do I think anyone gazing on such final feeds is likely to get angry about capital punishment. Or feel good about it, for that matter. I think the inescapable sensation is sadness, sadness for the little trays with the little treats. Perhaps, in some cases, also a sadness for the person about to be murdered, though many such diners have sorry and savage deeds charged to their souls. But mainly a sadness for this petty and small thing we do through the instrument of our governments, this calm, cold, premeditated murder that sums up not only the terrible failings of the condemned, but of ourselves. There seem to be no comforting answers in this murder-by-government business and the bleak-looking meals we spring for make this fact naked to the eye.

John William Rook, age 27, executed by North Carolina, 9/19/86

Stacey Lamont Lawton, age 31, executed by Texas, 11/14/00

Jeffery Allen Barney, age 28, executed by Texas, 4/16/86

Photos courtesy of Celia A. Shapiro/Redux Pictures

Velma Margie Barfield, age 52, executed by North Carolina, 11/2/84

Karla Faye Tucker, age 38, executed by Texas, 2/3/98

Timothy McVeigh, age 33, executed by U.S. government in Indiana, 6/11/01

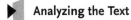

Analyzing the Text

1. What connection does Bowden make between his boyhood memory of "finishing" cattle before sending them to slaughter and prisoners' last meals?

2. Throughout his essay, Bowden describes last meals as solemn, sad, and depressing. Yet he also points out that prisoners' last meals often receive the kind of attention by the press and public typically reserved for "certain galas of presidents and movie stars." How does Bowden resolve these two cultural responses? How do you explain them?

3. Bowden observes that while people may ponder what book or CD they would want if they were stranded on a desert island, they don't generally discuss "what their ideal last meal[s] would be." Why, according to Bowden, don't people contemplate last meals in the same way?

4. **Connecting to Another Readings.** Taken together, how do Richard Pillsbury's essay (p. 188) and Bowden's essay construct a view of how food and dining traditions have evolved over time?

5. The photo essay that accompanies Bowden's essay recreates the last meals of several death-row prisoners. What impression do these meals convey about the prisoners who ordered them? What can't we know about them?

Writing about Cultural Practices

6. Develop a photo essay (with text) that offers a critical analysis of the traditions surrounding dining on college campuses. Dining on college campuses can be a very institutional experience, especially in the cafeteria setting. Or, it can be highly quirky, as students create their own concoctions using microwaves and hot plates. To begin, think about particular meals or dining environments that offer telling details about campus dining traditions and take four to six photographs that will allow you to best present your analysis. Expect the photography process to be recursive—that is, when you start taking photos, you may begin rethinking your analysis. Be prepared to revise your ideas as you work on this project. Once you have chosen the photos you want to include, draft detailed captions to accompany each one. Because your photo essay will be a balance of visual images and written text, consider the following questions as you draft the captions of this essay.

   • What college dining traditions are revealed by your photos?

   • What details about your photos bring these traditions to light?

   • What cultural values or beliefs about dining are revealed by these traditions?

Jon Stewart, **Commencement Address**

Jon Stewart has appeared in films and television and has coauthored the national best-seller, *The Daily Show with Jon Stewart Presents America (The Book): A Citizen's Guide to Democracy Inaction* (2004). Stewart joined the national stand-up comedy circuit before his breakthrough with his eponymously named talk show on MTV (1993–1995). His film credits include *The Faculty* (1998), *Half Baked* (1998), *Big Daddy* (1999), and *Death to Smoochy* (2002). Stewart currently anchors, writes, and produces the Emmy award-winning *The Daily Show with Jon Stewart* for Comedy Central.

> ▶ **Mapping Your Reading**
>
> Stewart, a 1984 graduate of the College of William and Mary in Williamsburg, Virginia, delivered the following commencement address at the school to the class of 2004. How does Stewart break from the traditional form and tone of a college graduation speech? What are his purposes for doing so? What messages does he want to convey to graduates? What rhetorical strategies does he use to do so? At what points is he ironic? In what passages, if any, is he serious or sincere? Is his talk ultimately memorable and effective? Why or why not?

Thank you, Mr. President, I had forgotten how crushingly dull these ceremonies are. Thank you.

My best to the choir. I have to say, that song never grows old for me. Whenever I hear that song, it reminds me of nothing.

I am honored to be here. I do have a confession to make before we get going that I should explain very quickly. When I am not on television, this is actually how I dress. I apologize, but there's something very freeing about it. I congratulate the students for being able to walk even a half a mile in this nonbreathable fabric in the Williamsburg heat. I am sure the environment that now exists under your robes are the same conditions in which primordial life began on this earth.

I know there were some parents that were concerned about my speech here tonight, and I want to assure you that you will not hear any language that is not common at, say, a dock workers' union meeting, or Tourrette's convention, or profanity seminar. Rest assured.

Stephen Salpukas

I am honored to be here and to receive this honorary doctorate. When I think back to the people that have been in this position before me, from Benjamin Franklin to Queen Noor of Jordan, I can't help but wonder what has happened to this place.

Seriously, it saddens me. As a person, I am honored to get it; as an alumnus, I have to say I believe we can do better. And I believe we should. But it has always been a dream of mine to receive a doctorate and to know that today, without putting in any effort, I will. It's incredibly gratifying. Thank you. That's very nice of you, I appreciate it.

I'm sure my fellow doctoral graduates— who have spent so long toiling in academia, sinking into debt, sacrificing God knows how many years for what, in truth, is a piece of parchment that in truth has been so devalued by our instant gratification culture as to have been rendered meaningless—will join in congratulating me. Thank you.

But today isn't about how my presence here devalues this fine institution. It is about you, the graduates. I'm honored to be here to congratulate you today. Today is the day you enter into the real world, and I should give you a few pointers on what it is. It's actually not that different from the environment here. The biggest difference is you will now be paying for things, and the real world is not surrounded by a three-foot brick wall. And the real world is not a restoration. If you see people in the real world making bricks out of straw and water, those people are not colonial reenactors—they are poor. Help them. And in the real world, there is not as much candle lighting. I don't really know what it is about this campus and candle lighting, but I wish it would stop. We only have so much wax, people.

Let's talk about the real world for a moment. We had been discussing it earlier, and I . . . I wanted to bring this up to you earlier about the real world, and this is I guess as good a time as any. I don't really know how to put this, so I'll be blunt. We broke it.

Let's talk about the real world for a moment. We broke it. Please don't be mad.

Please don't be mad. I know we were supposed to bequeath to the next generation a world better than the one we were handed. So, sorry.

I don't know if you've been following the news lately, but it just kinda got away from us. Somewhere between the gold rush of easy Internet profits and an arrogant sense of endless empire, we heard kind of a pinging noise, and, uh, then the damn thing just died on us. So I apologize.

But here's the good news. You fix this thing, you're the next greatest generation, people. You do this—and I believe you can—you win this war on terror, and Tom Brokaw's kissing your ass from here to Tikrit, let me tell ya. And even if you don't, you're not gonna have much trouble surpassing my generation. If you end up getting your picture taken next to a naked-guy pile of enemy prisoners and don't give the thumbs up, you've outdone us.

We declared war on terror. We declared war on terror—it's not even a noun, so, good luck. After we defeat it, I'm sure we'll take on that bastard ennui.

But obviously that's the world. What about your lives? What piece of wisdom can I impart to you about my journey that will somehow ease your transition from college back to your parents' basement?

I know some of you are nostalgic today and filled with excitement and perhaps uncertainty at what the future holds. I know six of you are trying to figure out how to make a bong out of your caps. I believe you are members of Psi U. Hey, that did work, thank you for the reference.

So I thought I'd talk a little bit about my experience here at William and Mary. It was very long ago, and if you had been to William and Mary while I was here and found out that I would be the commencement speaker 20 years later, you would be somewhat surprised, and probably somewhat angry. I came to William and Mary because as a Jewish person I wanted to explore the rich tapestry of Judaica that is southern Virginia. Imagine my surprise when I realized "The Tribe" was not what I thought it meant.

In 1980 I was 17 years old. When I moved to Williamsburg, my hall was in the basement of Yates, which combined the cheerfulness of a bomb shelter with the prison-like comfort of the group shower. As a freshman I was quite a catch. Less than five feet tall, yet my head was the same size it is now. Didn't even really look like a head, it looked more like a container for a head. I looked like a *Peanuts* character. *Peanuts* characters had terrible acne. But what I lacked in looks I made up for with a repugnant personality.

In 1981 I lost my virginity, only to gain it back again on appeal in 1983. You could say that my one saving grace was academics where I excelled, but I did not.

And yet now I live in the rarified air of celebrity, of mega stardom. My life is a series of Hollywood orgies and Kabala center brunches with the cast of *Friends*. At least that's what my handlers tell me. I'm actually too valuable to live my own life and spend most of my days in a vegetable crisper to remain fake-news-anchor-fresh.

My life is a series of Hollywood orgies and Kabala center brunches with the cast of *Friends*.

So I know that the decisions that I made after college worked out. But at the time I didn't know that they would. See, college is not necessarily predictive of your future success. And it's the kind of thing where the path that I chose obviously wouldn't work for you. For one, you're not very funny.

So how do you know what is the right path to choose to get the result that you desire? The honest answer is this: You won't. And accepting that greatly eases the anxiety of your life experience.

I was not exceptional here and am not now. I was mediocre here. And I'm not saying aim low. Not everybody can wander around in an alcoholic haze and then at 40 just, you know, decide to be president. You've got to really work hard to try to. I was actually referring to my father.

When I left William and Mary I was shell-shocked. Because when you're in college it's very clear what you have to do to succeed. And I imagine here everybody

You know what, we're gonna be OK. knows exactly the number of credits they needed to graduate, where they had to buckle down, which introductory psychology class would pad out the schedule. You knew what you had to do to get to this college and to graduate from it. But the unfortunate, yet truly exciting thing about your life is that there is no core curriculum. The entire place is an elective. The paths are infinite and the results uncertain. And it can be maddening to those who go here, especially here, because your strength has always been achievement. So if there's any real advice I can give you, it's this.

College is something you complete. Life is something you experience. So don't worry about your grade, or the results, or success. Success is defined in myriad ways, and you will find it, and people will no longer be grading you, but it will come from your own internal sense of decency, which I imagine, after going through the program here, is quite strong . . . although I'm sure downloading illegal files . . . but, nah, that's a different story.

Love what you do. Get good at it. Competence is a rare commodity in this day and age. And let the chips fall where they may.

And the last thing I want to address is the idea that somehow this new generation is not as prepared for the sacrifice and the tenacity that will be needed in the difficult times ahead. I have not found this generation to be cynical or apathetic or selfish. They are as strong and as decent as any people that I have met. And I will say this, on my way down here I stopped at Bethesda Naval, and when you talk to the young kids who are there that have just been back from Iraq and Afghanistan, you don't have the worry about the future that you hear from so many who are not a part of this generation but judging it from above.

And the other thing that I will say is, when I spoke earlier about the world being broke, I was somewhat being facetious, because every generation has its challenge. And things change rapidly, and life gets better in an instant.

I was in New York on 9-11 when the towers came down. I lived 14 blocks from the twin towers. And when they came down, I thought that the world had ended. And I remember walking around in a daze for weeks. And Mayor Giuliani had said to the city, "You've got to get back to normal. We've got to show that things can change and get back to what they were."

And one day I was coming out of my building, and on my stoop was a man who was crouched over, and he appeared to be in deep thought. And as I got closer to him I realized, he was playing with himself. And that's when I thought, "You know what, we're gonna be OK."

Thank you. Congratulations. I honor you. Good night.

▶ **Analyzing the Text**

1. What are the classic or traditional themes of commencement addresses? How does Stewart use these classic themes in his speech?

2. What are the most effective comedic moments in Stewart's speech? What makes them so effective?

3. Are there serious moments in this speech? Where do they appear? What messages does Stewart treat seriously?

4. In what way does being a comedian allow Stewart to speak on traditional commencement themes in unexpected ways? Is the address meaningful? Why or why not? What wishes or desires does Stewart express by offering a modern interpretation of a past tradition?

 Writing about Cultural Practices

5. Write a rhetorical analysis of a past commencement speech given on your campus. Search your school's website or library archives to find a copy of a past commencement speech. As you draft your analysis, consider the following questions.

   - What is the purpose or role of commencement addresses in graduation traditions?

   - Who is the speaker, and why was he or she invited to give the commencement address?

   - What classic themes are at the center of the speech? What details from the speech support these classic themes?

   - To what extent does the speech pay attention to issues or concerns that were current at the time?

   - Within the speech, what rhetorical strategies does the speaker use particularly effectively? For what purpose? How do you think the address was received by the graduates?

David Berreby, **It Takes a Tribe**
Laura Randall, **Things You Only Do in College**

David Berreby is a freelance writer who has written for numerous publications, including the *New York Times Magazine*, *New Republic*, *Slate*, and *Smithsonian Magazine*. Reporting on scientific trends and ideas, Berreby has explored topics ranging from alligator jaws to human societal hierarchies. Laura Randall is a freelance writer who has written for the *New York Times* and the *Los Angeles Times*, among other publications. Both "It Takes a Tribe" and "Things You Only Do in College" originally appeared in the *New York Times Magazine* in August 2004.

▶ **Mapping Your Reading**

These essays explore the ways in which campus traditions are invented and used to promote a sense of unity among students. However, as Berreby suggests, many of these traditions also promote an "us-versus-them" mindset. As you read, underline key passages where Berreby explains the problems he sees with campus traditions. Do you agree with Berreby—that students "don't just attend a college; they join its tribes"? And have campus rituals, as Randall argues, become more reckless? What traditions hold these groups together and keep outsiders out? What are the consequences—positive and negative—of campus traditions?

When the budding pundit Walter Lippmann coined the term "stereotype" back in 1922, he offered several examples from the America of his time: "Agitator." "Intellectual." "South European." "From the Back Bay." You know, he told the reader, when a glimpse and a word or two create a full mental picture of a whole group of people. As in "plutocrat." Or "foreigner." Or "Harvard man."

Harvard man? We know, thanks to Lippmann, that stereotypes are part of serious problems like racism, prejudice, and injustice. What is Lippmann's alma mater doing on such a list? (He even added: "How different from the statement, 'He is a Yale man.'")

Spend time on a campus in coming weeks, though, and you'll see what he meant.

At colleges across the country, from Ivy League to less exclusive state schools, students who are mispronouncing the library's name this month will soon feel truly and deeply a part of their college. They'll be singing their school songs and cherishing the traditions (just as soon as they learn what they are). They'll talk the way "we" do. (Going to Texas A&M? Then greet people with a cheerful "howdy.") They'll learn contempt for that rival university—Oklahoma to their Texas, Sacramento State to their U.C. Davis, Annapolis to their West Point.

> They'll be singing their school songs and cherishing the traditions (just as soon as they learn what they are).

They may come to believe, too, that an essential trait separates them from the rest of humanity—the same sort of feeling most Americans have about races, ethnic groups, and religions. As the writer Christopher Buckley said recently in his college's alumni magazine: "When I run into a Yale man I somehow feel that I am with a kindred spirit. A part of that kindred-ness comes from his gentility and his not being all jumped up about it. It's a certain sweetness of character."

All this sentiment comes on fast (a study last year at Ivy League campuses found freshmen even more gung-ho than older students). Yet college loyalty, encouraged by alumni relations offices, can last a lifetime—as enduring as the Princeton tiger tattooed on the buttock of former Secretary of State George P. Shultz, or the Yale sweater sported by evil Mr. Burns on "The Simpsons," a number of whose writers went to Harvard.

New identities are forged within the university as well, in elite groups like Skull and Bones at Yale or the Corps of Cadets at Texas A&M or Michigamua at the University of Michigan; in sororities and fraternities; even in particular majors and particular labs. Students don't just attend a college; they join its tribes.

"What endlessly impresses me is people losing sight of how arbitrary it is," says Robert M. Sapolsky, a Stanford biologist who specializes in the links between social life and stress. "Students understand how readily they could have wound up at another school or wound up in another lab." Yet every year, he adds, "they fall for it." For most, what Professor Sapolsky calls that "nutty but palpable" onset of college tribalism is just a part of campus life. For social scientists, it's an object of research, offering clues to a fundamental and puzzling aspect of human nature: People need to belong, to feel a part of "us." Yet a sense of "us" brings with it a sense of "them."

Human beings will give a lot, including their lives, for a group they feel part of—for "us," as in "our nation" or "our religion." They will also harm those labeled "them," including taking their lives. Far as genocide and persecution seem from fraternity hazings and Cal versus Stanford, college tribes may shed light on the way the mind works with those other sorts of groups, the ones that shape and misshape the world, like nation, race, creed, caste, or culture.

After all, a college campus is full of people inventing a sense of "us" and a sense of "them." As one junior at the University of California, Los Angeles, told her school paper before a game against the University of Southern California: "School spirit is important because it gives us a sense of belonging and being a part of something bigger. Besides," she said, "U.S.C. sucks in every way."

> A college campus is full of people inventing a sense of "us" and a sense of "them."

In an e-mail interview, Professor Sapolsky writes that "Stanford students (and faculty) do tons of this, at every possible hierarchical level." For instance, he says, they see Stanford versus Harvard, and Stanford versus the University of California at Berkeley. "Then, within Stanford, all the science wonks doing tribal stuff to differentiate themselves from the fuzzies—the humanities/social science types. Then within the sciences, the life science people versus the chemistry/physics/math geeks." Within the life sciences, he adds, the two tribes are "bio majors and majors in what is called 'human biology'—former deprecated as being robotic pre-meds, incapable of thinking, just spitting out of factoids; latter as fuzzies masquerading as scientists."

Recent research on students suggests these changes in perception aren't trivial. A few years ago, a team of social psychologists asked students at the University of California at Santa Barbara to rank various collections of people in terms of how well they "qualify as a group." In their answers, "students at a university" ranked above "citizens of a nation." "Members of a campus committee" and "members of a university social club" ranked higher than "members of a union" or "members of a political party," romantic couples, or office colleagues working together on a project. For that matter, "students at a university" and "members of a campus committee" ranked well above blacks and Jews in the students' estimation of what qualifies as a group.

Much of this thinking, researchers have found, is subconscious. We may think we care about our college ties for good and sensible reasons—wonderful classes! dorm-room heart-to-hearts! job connections!—when the deeper causes are influences we didn't notice.

Some 20 years ago, researchers asked students at Rutgers to describe themselves using only words from a set of cards prepared in advance. Some cards contained words associated with Rutgers, like "scarlet," the school color, and "knight," the name of its athletic teams. Others, like "orange," were associated with archrival Princeton. Some students took the test in a room decorated with a Rutgers pennant; others took it under a Princeton flag. A third group saw only a New York Yankees banner.

Students who saw a Princeton or Rutgers emblem were more likely to use Rutgers-related words to describe themselves. They also mentioned that they were students at Rutgers earlier than those who saw only the neutral flag. They didn't consciously decide to stand up for Rutgers. Outside their conscious minds, though, that identity was in place, ready to be released by symbols of the tribe.

More recently, three social psychologists at Harvard looked at another example of subconscious tribal beliefs. Mahzarin R. Banaji, who led the study, argues that people in similar, equivalent groups will place those groups into a hierarchy, from best to worst, even when there is no rational basis for ranking them. The psychologists tested Yale sophomores, juniors, and seniors, who live and eat together in "residential colleges." Students know that these colleges are effectively all alike and that people are assigned to them at random. Still, the team found, Yalies did indeed rank them from best to worst. (In the interests of peace and comity, the colleges were kept anonymous.) Moreover, students assigned to the less prestigious units were less enthusiastic about their homes than those from the ones with a better reputation.

What this suggests, Professor Banaji says, is that taking one's place in a tribe, and accepting the tribe's place in a larger society, are mental acts that happen regardless of the group's purpose or meaning. Once people see that they've been divided into groups, they'll act accordingly, even if they know that the divisions are as meaningless as, oh, the University of Arizona versus Arizona State. "We know that human beings identify with social groups, sometimes sufficiently to kill or die on their behalf," she says. "What is not as well known is that such identity between self and group can form rapidly, often following a psychological route that is relatively subconscious. That is, like automata, we identify with the groups in which we are accidentally placed."

> "Like automata, we identify with the groups in which we are accidentally placed."

Not all researchers agree that people care about so-called nonsense groups with the same passion they give to religion, politics, or morals. Another theory holds that the subconscious mind can distinguish which groups matter and how much. One example comes from a much-cited experiment, performed, naturally, on college students.

In 1959, the social psychologists Elliot Aronson and Judson Mills asked undergraduate women to join a discussion group after a short initiation. For one set of participants the initiation required reciting a few mild sexual words. The other group had to say a list of much saltier words about sex, which embarrassed them no end (remember, this was 1959). The discussion group was dull as dishwater, but the women who suffered to join rated it as much more valuable than those who had a mild initiation (and higher than a control group that didn't have to do anything).

A subconscious clue for perceiving a tribe as real and valuable, then, may be expending sweat, tears, and embarrassment to get in. The political activist Tom

Hayden recently recalled just such a rite at the University of Michigan, in an article on the left-wing Web site alternet.org. He was complaining about the lock that Skull and Bones has on November's election (President Bush and the Democratic nominee, Senator John Kerry, are members).

"As a junior, I was tapped for the Druids," Mr. Hayden wrote about his own campus clan, "which involved a two-day ritual that included being stripped to my underpants, pelted with eggs, smeared with red dye, and tied to a campus tree. These humiliations signified my rebirth from lowly student journalist to Big Man on Campus."

"The two-day ritual included being stripped to my underpants, pelted with eggs, smeared with red dye, and tied to a campus tree."

As for Professor Aronson, had he not wanted tight control over the experiment, he writes in his widely used textbook, *The Social Animal,* he and Professor Mills could simply have studied an initiation outside the lab—at a campus fraternity or sorority.

That kind of lumping together—studying one group to explain another—drives scholars in other fields to distraction. To them, a pep rally is different from a political rally.

Historians, trained to see big generalizations as meaningless, are often aghast at the way psychologists' theories about groups ignore the difference between, say, today's two-gendered, multiethnic, and meritocratic Harvard College and the one that gave Lippmann his degree in 1909. And anthropologists for generations have disdained psychology for ignoring cultural differences.

But one fact is clear, and college groups exemplify it well: While many creatures live in groups, humanity's are unlike anything else found in nature. Peter Richerson, a biologist at Sacramento State's rival, the University of California at Davis, likes to point out that his students, sitting quietly together on the first day of class, are an amazing exception to the general rules of animal behavior. Put chimpanzees or monkeys that don't know one another in a room, and they would be in hysterics. People team up with strangers easily.

Professor Richerson and his longtime collaborator, Robert Boyd, an anthropologist at U.S.C.'s hated enemy, U.C.L.A., argue that we will sign up for membership in tribelike groups for the same reason birds sing: It feels right because we evolved to do it. "We want to live in tribes," Professor Richerson says. Humans are "looking to be told what group they belong to, and then once they do that, they want to know, 'What are the rules?'"

The tricky part, says Professor Sapolsky of Stanford, Cal-Berkeley's bitter rival, is that humans alone among animals can think about what a tribe is and who belongs. "Humans actually think about who is an 'us' and who is a 'them' rather than just knowing it," he says. "The second it becomes a cognitive process, it is immensely subject to manipulation."

And, of course, studying the phenomenon won't make you immune. "I'm true blue," says Professor Banaji, who taught at Yale from 1986 until 2002, when she joined the Harvard faculty. "I was physically unable to sit through a women's basketball game between Harvard and Yale on the Harvard side."

I t used to be that goldfish swallowing and stuffing students in telephone booths were all the rage on campus. Today's traditions are more likely to involve nudity, fire, and intoxicants and be closely monitored by publicity-wary administrators. Some rituals have been abolished because of safety concerns or underage drinking. Recent casualties include spring couch burning at the University of Vermont and Princeton's Nude Winter Olympics. In one of the higher-profile incidents, the death of 12 people by collapsing logs in 1999 brought to an end the tradition of Texas A&M's bonfire on the eve of the annual football game against the University of Texas (the bonfire has since been revived off campus). But other traditions are going strong, sanctioned or not. Like their zanier predecessors, they are a long-remembered part of the college experience—if occasionally rowdy, childish, illegal, or all three.

> **Today's traditions are more likely to involve nudity, fire, and intoxicants.**

Setting Things on Fire

Each spring, students at the Massachusetts Institute of Technology haul a steer into a dorm courtyard, put it on a spit, and light a fire under it with a flaming roll of toilet paper lowered from the roof. Campus police considered moving the Steer Roast to a more controlled site a few years ago, but residents fought to keep it at their dorm, Senior House (they won). The three-day event, first staged in 1963, includes mud wrestling, live music, and other forms of entertainment that are not necessarily approved by school authorities.

"There are certain aspects that the administration doesn't like, such as the strippers in the basement and stuff like that," admits Gene Shuman, a Steer Roast organizer and resident of Senior House. Also not helping its case is the location: adjacent to the president's residence. Presidents and spouses have usually slept elsewhere during the roast. This year, however, the outgoing president, Charles M. Vest, showed up Sunday morning to make pancakes for the remaining partygoers, bringing back a tradition that had stopped more than a decade ago (no one seems to know why).

Coincidently, bonfires at Warren Wilson College in Asheville, North Carolina, also have a bovine component. Bonfire parties known as bubbas have been held for decades at each semester's end in cow pastures around campus. Amid concerns about alcohol abuse and sexual assault, officials are heightening security.

Drinking and Smoking

Campus festivities that center on alcohol or drugs are provoking a tug of war between students and administrators. At 4:20 P.M. every April 20 (a day when pot smokers light up nationwide, for reasons that remain murky), several hundred students at the University of Vermont would gather on the quad to bang drums and puff on pipes. In 2002, the university decided to create a diversion and took over the space for an all-day Spring Fest with bands and marijuana-free entertainment like rock climbing. In the spring of 2004, students tried to revive the pot-smoking event. About 600 people and 20 police officers showed up. The police videotaped the crowd, casting a chill on "420," as the tradition is known.

Meanwhile, at Princeton this spring, university officials, religious groups and Paul Newman himself urged students not to participate in a day of drinking known as Newman's Day. The day derives its name from a quote—"24 beers in a case, 24 hours in a day. Coincidence? I think not"—attributed to Mr. Newman during a campus visit. (Princeton has no record of the actor saying it. "We believe it's based in myth," says a spokeswoman, Patricia Allen.) The goal is to consume 24 beers in 24 hours. This year alcohol consumption was less flagrant, students report, though that could be because the event fell on a Saturday and two days after classes had ended.

Indeed, some rituals just refuse to vanish from the calendar despite best efforts: For decades, students at Wesleyan in Middletown, Connecticut, have honored the pot-smoking *Doonesbury* character Zonker Harris each spring with a day of live music, face painting, and plenty of open marijuana use.

Jumping into Water

Dunking traditions can be benign enough.

Costumed engineering students at Simon Fraser University in British Columbia throw one another in the reflection pond during February's Polar Plunge. For more than a century at Wellesley, seniors have tossed the winner of the annual spring hoop roll into chilly Lake Waban. (The winner used to be declared the first to marry; today, she is the most likely to succeed.)

At the same time, the ritual has its dark side. Ithaca College's tradition started 10 years ago as a way for seniors to celebrate their new freedom by taking a dip in a landmark campus fountain. But it soon attracted students from all grade levels and was accompanied by heavy drinking, according to David Maley, a university spokesman. "Its very popularity helped kill it off," he says. Officials cracked down in 1999 after dozens of students were treated for alcohol-related problems. Administrators switched the date from the last day of classes to senior week, so most undergraduates have gone home for the summer.

Streaking

Princeton and the University of Michigan have banned nude sprints (Michigan students who partake in the Naked Mile midnight race must now wear underwear or face charges of indecent exposure).

But the ritual remains popular at many universities. On the first rainy day of the year, students at the University of California at Santa Cruz streak en masse through campus in their birthday suits. At Yale, seniors run naked through two campus libraries at the end of each semester and toss candy at students cramming for finals.

Champions of the tradition reason that it is an innocuous way to relieve stress. "A streaking tradition is the perfect excuse to get even the most timid students to chuck inhibitions and bare it all in the name of pride," says Colleen Bayus, a

University of Pittsburgh student, in a recent column for her school paper supporting the ritual. "Let's face it, you can't exactly get away with such indecent exposure without a big, fat citation accompanying it after your college years have vanished."

▶ Analyzing the Text

1. According to Berreby, how do college traditions help promote a tribal mentality? What are the consequences of this? How does Randall's essay support Berreby's argument?

2. **Interrogating Assumptions.** Both Berreby's and Randall's essays point out that many college traditions are invented and arbitrary and have no particular rationale behind their origins. This reality challenges the assumption that traditions are long-standing practices that connect us to past generations (see p. 176). Why, according to Berreby, doesn't the arbitrariness of these traditions affect their importance as rituals?

3. To help explain the us-versus-them tribal dynamic that he observes in college life, Berreby cites a number of studies conducted by social psychologists. According to the author, what do these studies reveal about people's tribal or clannish tendencies?

4. Berreby cites a study in which students ranked "students at a university" well above ethnic groups such as African Americans or Jews as qualifying as a group. What is it about the rituals and traditions of college campuses that cause students to rank membership at a university so highly?

5. Berreby explores the negative side of campus traditions—the use of hazing, for example, or the ways in which traditions divide people and set up social hierarchies. What are some examples from either Berreby's or Randall's essays that show this negative side of college traditions?

6. Consider Berreby's statement "[As] far as genocide and persecution seem from fraternity hazings and Cal versus Stanford, college tribes may shed light on the way the mind works with those other sorts of groups, the ones that shape and misshape the world, like nation, race, creed, caste, or culture." How do you respond to this claim?

▶ Writing about Cultural Practices

7. What are the traditions or rituals on your college campus? Attend a campus event and write a critical analysis of it. Base your analysis on or respond to Berreby's theories about traditions and tribalism on college campuses. As you draft your study, consider the following questions.

   - What rituals and customs are associated with this campus event?
   - Who are the participants, and what are their goals for participating?
   - In what ways are these rituals meant to promote unity among students?
   - What values or beliefs are these traditions promoting?
   - In your experience, are these traditions used to create an us-versus-them mentality? If so, how? What are the consequences of such a mentality?

Ayana D. Byrd and Lori L. Tharps,
The Rituals of Black Hair Culture

Ayana D. Byrd has worked as a research chief at *Vibe* magazine and contributed to many publications, including *Rolling Stone* and *InStyle*. Lori L. Tharps is a reporter for *Entertainment Weekly*. In 2001, Byrd and Tharps published *Hair Story: Untangling the Roots of Black Hair in America*, which explores the social history of black hair from its African roots to present-day America. In the following essay, excerpted from *Hair Story*, the authors describe the balancing act many African Americans feel between adapting to and countering white mainstream beauty traditions.

▶ **Mapping Your Reading**

As you read, consider the various attitudes toward black hair described by Byrd and Tharps. What impact, according to the authors, do these attitudes have on individuals? How do traditions and rituals around caring for black hair function in terms of black culture? What about in terms of mainstream white culture? To what extent do the traditions and rituals described in this essay represent a counter-tradition?

Black Hair Culture 101

America was built on the myth of the melting pot, but despite the efforts of the powers that be, the ingredients never fully blended. At best there is a patchwork quilt of various ethnic groups struggling to live peacefully with one another while something called "mainstream culture"—it looks like a Norman Rockwell painting, sounds like a George Gershwin musical, and tastes like Chef Boyardee—is offered up as the national example. The pervasiveness of what bell hooks terms this "dull dish that is mainstream White culture" has succeeded in keeping many people unaware of the diversity surrounding them, including the unique culture of Black hair.

Culture is a sticky subject and can be interpreted in many ways. Anthropologists define culture as the strategies by which humans adapt to their natural environment. The many aspects of human adaptation—including language, technology, traditions, values, and social organization—are all identifiable components of the culture of Black hair in America. And although academics and laypeople alike might doubt the assertion that a culture specific to Black hair exists, the truth is self-evident.

In the United States, where the aesthetic norms are overwhelmingly based on a White European standard, Black people with any variation of kinky tresses are immediately cast as "others" in mainstream beauty culture. Since the first Black slaves set foot on the beaches of Jamestown, Virginia, their hair-raising strategies to adapt and fit in have been passed on from generation to generation. This was the beginning of Black hair culture in America. And what of those Black Americans born without the follicular stamp of Negro heritage? By virtue of their African ancestry in this one-drop-rule nation, even these kink-free, straight-haired Black citizens have a confirmed place in the social order of Black hair culture.

> "Mainstream culture" looks like a Norman Rockwell painting, sounds like a George Gershwin musical, and tastes like Chef Boyardee.

Hot Combs and Hair Grease: The Language and Technology of Hair

From day one, Black children are indoctrinated into the intricate culture of hair. Vocabulary words like *grease, kitchen* (the hair at the nape of the neck, not the room in the house), and *touch-up* are ones a Black child hears at a very early age and needs to learn in order to fully participate in the Black hair lifestyle. Phrases like *nappy-headed, tender-headed,* and *turn back* aren't so much taught as they are absorbed into the growing lexicon of a young Black mind. Before a Black child is even born, relatives speculate over the texture of hair that will cover the baby's head, and the loaded adjectives "good" and "bad" are already in the air.

Keeping in mind that culture is passed on from one generation to the next, the prevalence of the "good" hair/"bad" hair dichotomy present in modern Black hair culture is not surprising. Black men and women from all parts of the country recall hearing the labels everywhere from the playground at school to the sermons at church.

"I remember growing up with a girl named Wanda who had long, wavy hair," says a Long Island native Patricia Watson. "People always referred to her as 'Wanda with the good hair.'" Saundra Adams, who grew up in the San Francisco Bay Area, comments, "I have a best friend who is still insistent that I have 'good' hair and she has 'bad' hair. As a matter of fact, the only argument that we've had in our eleven-year friendship was over the insistence of this concept." Euphemisms for good hair also have to be learned, like "Indian hair," "curly hair," or "nice hair." Likewise, there are other monikers for "bad" hair like "peasy" (as in, the hair is so tightly curled it looks like peas) and "nappy." Cynthia Racks remembers, "I was about seven when I overheard someone say that I had 'coarse' hair and I thought that meant 'Wow! I like her hair.' I found out not long afterwards that coarse wasn't a compliment." Kathryn Benson, a young woman who grew up in the eighties in Florida, says she was taught that bad hair was "that really kinky, curly, 'woolish' type of natural hair." Thankfully, there have been efforts to strike these archaic classifications from Black hair vernacular or at the very least redefine them. "I was going to a local hairdresser," says Maya Cole of an experience in North Carolina. "She corrected me when I

> Black people with kinky tresses are immediately cast as "others."

talked about my hair as being 'bad' hair. She told me that if you have hair covering your head, and it holds a style well, that is 'good' hair."

Learning the language of Black hair culture goes hand in hand with understanding the technology. As the tools created to manipulate Black hair advance, the language continues to expand. The original tool of Black hair culture has to be the ancient hand-carved African comb, better known in America as the Afro pick. This wide-toothed invention has served as the prototype for modern utensils—from blow-dryer attachments to regular combs—used by Black people all over the world. Other equipment can be grouped according to function in the following categories: straighteners, styling tools, moisturizers, pomades (also known as grease), and accessories. Familiarity with the tools and fluidity in the language of Black hair culture do not automatically qualify a person as a member of the club, however. Certain rituals and rites of passage must also be experienced.

Rituals and Rites of Passage

The care of Black hair requires patience, time, and a healthy dose of creativity. In its natural state, kinky hair tends to be extremely dry, very fragile, and generally requires less washing than finer textured hair. Little Black girls usually get their hair washed anywhere from once a week to once a month, and then it must be arranged into some sort of style or it will be nearly impossible to manage until the next washing. Regardless of the desired look—from Afro puffs to intricate cornrows to Shirley Temple Curls—the hair has to be combed out, a small section at a time, and blow-drying is often necessary. For many Blacks, memories of early hair-care rituals are unforgettable, for reasons both bad and good. Feminist author and social critic bell hooks describes pleasurable hair-straightening days from her childhood in her memoir *bone black*. "We are six girls who live in a house together. . . . We sit in the kitchen and wait our turn for the hot comb, wait to sit in the chair by the stove, smelling grease, feeling the heat warm our scalp like a sticky hot summer sun." Regardless of age, both old and young reach back to hair rituals as seductive memories. "As a child my mother washed my hair every Saturday afternoon for church on Sunday," remembers Monisha Franklin, who grew up in Ann Arbor, Michigan. "Since it took so long, she used to give me dates to eat while she talked to me and washed my hair in the kitchen sink. I used to sit on the counter and lean back over the sink while she washed and told me stories and I ate those dates. To this day, I eat dates and feel cared for."

For many Black children, the time spent under the knowing hands of a mother, grandmother, or older sibling as they grease the scalp, then comb, braid, or twist the hair yields some of the most cherished moments of each day. "I remember when my cousin—who is extremely talented and creative—would braid my hair when I was a kid and she would come up with so many unique styles and patterns," says Shanna Little, reminiscing about her most positive hair experiences. "I would always get compliments. I felt like a peacock." Says Marcia

Gillespie, editor-in-chief of *Ms.* magazine, "I think part of the stories that bind us together as Black [people] are our hair stories. I just look forward to the time when the hair stories won't be as traumatic."

Unfortunately, for many Black people childhood hair memories are tinged with bitterness and pain, a bad omen for a positive future relationship with one's own tresses. "I remember my mother picking out my hair with an Afro pick every day," recalls Anthony Riggins. "My god, it hurt. I hated it because she was so forceful." A similar comment comes from Lynn Bracey: "When I was a child I hated to get my hair done. My mother would pull and swat me if I moved too much. She always seemed to burn me with that straightening comb."

The first date with "that straightening comb"—for some it stands as a rite of passage, for others it was the beginning of a painful relationship. "For each of us getting our hair pressed is an important ritual," bell hooks writes. "It is not a sign of our longing to be White. It is not a sign of our quest to be beautiful. We are girls. It is a sign of our desire to be women." In order to straighten the hair with a hot comb, the hair has to be clean, dry, and tangle-free. Some sort of pressing oil or grease is applied to condition the hair as well as to make it smooth and shiny. On contact with the comb, the grease will often make a sizzling sound, not unlike bacon frying in a cast-iron skillet. No matter how steady the person doing the hot-combing is, there is always the danger of hitting a trouble spot like an ear, a forehead, or the back of the neck with the red-hot piece of metal. Jamie White grew up in the eighties, and some of her worst memories revolve around the hot comb. "I would have to sit for thirty minutes to an hour being scared," she says. "It's not that my mom burned me often, but those few times she burned my ear really made an impression on me. I would flinch whenever I heard the sizzle of the grease."

"Part of the stories that bind us together as Black people are our hair stories."

When hair-care manufacturers introduced kinder, gentler relaxers especially formulated for young people in the early 1980s, many parents and children were overjoyed at the prospect of retiring the hot comb. Make no mistake, permed hair still requires a lot of time and maintenance efforts (washing, blow-drying, conditioning), but infinitely less than unpermed hair. "Both my daughters (age 11 and 18) have relaxers and it's partly because of our lifestyle," explains Mary Lewis, a bank manager. "It's really more about the convenience of being able to wash it as much as you want."

Some parents are not eager to see their young daughters become a "slave to the chemicals," for reasons varying from hair health to lingering sixties "Black is beautiful" nostalgia. "I had to beg my mother to let me get my first perm when I was twelve," says writer Lauren Epps, 26. "All my friends had gotten perms, my cousin had a perm, and I wanted one too. But my mother, who used to wear a big Afro in the sixties and seventies, had no intentions of letting me permanently straighten my hair."

Some people may wonder why parents would inflict the torture of the hot comb or a chemical relaxer on their young children, and the usual reply would fall somewhere between convenience and acceptability. It is never an easy answer, but adapting to America's visual norms often makes it easier for Black hair to move through White culture without causing a disturbance. The first time Black hair intersects with White people is a telling experience most people will never forget. "When I was in first grade I went to an after-school program with my hair in Afro puffs," says Kim Watson, who grew up in the seventies as one of only a handful of Blacks in a small town in Ohio. "The kids from another school called me 'Mickey Mouse,' and this quickly degenerated into 'nigger.' I wanted desperately to get rid of signs of my blackness, so I asked to get my hair relaxed." While not every experience is as traumatic as Watson's, the feeling of "otherness" as it relates to hair is one most Black people in America can identify with and recognize.

> **The first time Black hair intersects with White people is a telling experience most people will never forget.**

Black children, especially those who live in integrated neighborhoods and have friends of other ethnicities, realize early in life that their hair makes them different. Images they see on television and in their friends' homes prove that Black hair isn't like White hair. White people do not typically use hot combs to make their hair straight; they don't put oils and grease in their hair to make it shine; they usually wash it more often than once a week; and it does not take as long to get it into a satisfactory style. Something as innocuous as a slumber party—when all the other girls can just jump in the shower and the Black girl has to ask for a shower cap—can be an uncomfortable and awkward experience.

School is often the first place Black children learn survival skills when it comes to their hair. They are forced to defend it, explain it, and often make excuses for it as White students and teachers remain unaware of their inner turmoil. "Being the only Black child in class in my elementary school, White kids were always awed at the texture of my hair," remembers Anthony Riggins. "There were definite insecurities I had because these wretched kids would want to touch it to see what it felt like. I don't know how many times I would just glare at them, with eyes that said, 'I'm not a dog.'"

Another elementary school incident sure to test the mettle of young Black minds is when the inevitable lice epidemic breaks out. A typical reaction involves equal parts trepidation and pride. When all the students have to line up and get their hair picked over by the school nurse, many Black children feel confident that they'll be in the clear, based on the widely believed myth that Black people cannot get lice. Countless Black mothers assure their children that the little white creatures can't navigate their kinky, curly tresses or that hair grease makes Black hair inhospitable to lice. On the other hand, the trauma of having a White nurse or school volunteer poking around in their hair with a Q-Tip can be downright unnerving to a Black child because the nurse is often unaccustomed to the feel of their hair. Heaven forbid she comment aloud about the distinctive texture or the generous amount of hair grease being used for a high-gloss shine. Then the nurse continues to mess up the student's hairstyle, which cannot simply be patted back in place, so the child has to go through the rest of the day looking unkempt. Though embarrassing and sometimes painful, these trials are the ways young Black children mature in the life cycle of Black hair culture. Not much unlike the physical initiation rituals young men must go through in the New Guinea Highlands, surviving in mainstream culture with Black hair is like that insightful old refrain: What doesn't kill you makes you stronger.

The attitudes within the Black community regarding hair, some would argue, are far more damaging to a child's self-esteem and beauty image than the ignorance of mainstream White culture. For every story of a Black child like Kim Watson, who was taunted by White children about her Afro puffs, there is another story of a Black child tormented by her own family members or other Black friends. "I was a young girl with coarse hair," says Ashley Canady. "My brother and his friends would often tease me about it. Once the neighbor's cousin came to visit and she called me 'nippie nippie nap neck,' and that name kind of stuck. The teasing bothered me so bad I once took a scissors and cut out all the naps all the way up to the crown of my head." Marie Jackson started wearing her hair in a short Afro in 1968 to the chagrin of her Brooklyn neighborhood. "It was the time when everyone in my community looked at my nappy hair and was shocked," says Jackson. "Also, my church felt I needed to get a hot comb and fix my hair." For Shani Atkinson, it was her parent's commentary about her hair that wounded her the most: "My father told me that my [dred]locks looked like a pile of shit upon my head."

"My church felt I needed to get a hot comb and fix my hair."

Black children who have naturally long and wavy hair are also targeted for teasing by their Black peers. "When I was a child, some of the [Black] kids on my block harassed me because of my hair, accusing me of thinking that I was better than them because I had 'good' hair and it was long," recalls Sheila Jenkins, a 30-year-old graduate student in psychology. "I remember feeling hurt and rejected for something I had no control over." Veronica Williams says that for a few years during her adolescence in 1960s Philadelphia, she was afraid to go to school because she was told she had "good" hair. Blacks are "still quibbling around skin color and hair texture," family therapist Joy DeGruy Leary says, because the psychological injuries from slavery regarding hair have not been healed. "They didn't give us the group therapy," she says, only half-joking. Not surprisingly, the affliction shows.

All Grown Up

Adulthood in the cycle of life with Black hair feels very similar to childhood for many men and women. There are satisfying memories of a new style or a time-honored ritual, yet there are countless interactions with a White world that doesn't understand Black hair culture. Sheila Nelson, an editor at a popular fashion magazine who straightens her hair with a hot comb, says she felt as if she was at summer camp all over again when her company retreat was themed around water activities. "According to the schedule," says Nelson, "we were supposed to go swimming and then meet for dinner like 15 minutes later. I can't swim and then expect my hair to be presentable in 15 minutes. If I didn't go in the water, people would think I wasn't a team player, but if I did, I knew there would be questions about why my hair didn't look the same as before." Constance Jones echoes Nelson's dilemma. A Chicago-based consultant, Jones travels a lot with her company. Once she had to share a hotel room with a White coworker, and Jones says she automatically felt herself on the defensive as well as a little self-conscious. "Here I am 32 years old and I'm afraid this White woman is going to think less of me because I have to put rollers in my hair at night and I use oil sheen in the morning. It's ridiculous but that's how I felt." Even though many Black people spend their childhood and college years explaining their hair-care and maintenance routines to White people, it doesn't mean the whole world was taking notes. As long as hair care remains a segregated experience in this country (salon visits, retail shopping, advertisements), Black hair culture will remain foreign.

As long as hair care remains a segregated experience, Black hair culture will remain foreign.

"Unless you live with someone who is Black, as a White person you will probably remain quite ignorant of the ways in which Black hair is different from White," says Gail Jacobs, a Jewish woman who has lived with two different Black women over a period of eight years. Flipping through a mainstream magazine or watching TV or a movie, one is hard-pressed to find significant information about Black hair care, as though it were inconsequential or the same as White hair care. Jacobs says she clearly recalls witnessing Marcia Brady on the *Brady Bunch* "brushing her hair a hundred times before she went to sleep." But, Jacobs quickly counters, "I don't ever remember seeing Denise on the *Cosby Show* doing her hair in the Huxtable bathroom." As a result of this secret-society status of Black hair care in popular culture, most non-Black Americans are unable to make an educated guess about the form or function of basic Black hair tools, style techniques, or maintenance rituals. Compounding this problem is the average person's lack of knowledge regarding Black America's tangled hair history. Even with the best intentions, the constant questioning and uninformed commentary by White people can lead to frustration, hostility, and hurt. Some Blacks carry the burden like a heavy chip on their shoulder; others just wonder when they can stop worrying about how White America will interpret what's on top of their heads.

"When you answer the same damn question, even though it comes from five different people, you get a little tired," offers Marcia Gillespie. The most annoying queries Blacks are bombarded with range from "Why do you use grease in your hair?" to "How do you get your hair to stay like that?" One Black woman, in utter frustration over the steady stream of questions she received from her White coworkers regarding her hairstyle, started carrying around three-by-five-inch index cards with prepared answers to the most common questions she received. Undoubtedly some inquiries are indeed meant to be rude, racist, and offensive, which is why many Blacks are suspicious of so-called innocent questions. "One White guy in high school asked me why Black men have pubic hair on top of their head," recalls an angry Michele Meyerson, an Illinois native and PhD candidate. "My White adviser [recently] asked me what I had been spending my time on besides my hair after I had twisted it," Meyerson adds. When you consider the fact that Black women in America already have to deal with racism and sexism, the added drama of Black hair in a White world can be interpreted as a cruel twist of fate.

There is no denying that Black hair can feel like a burden rather than a blessing. Many women harbor repressed frustrations at the time, energy, and effort Black hair requires to get it into a style society deems acceptable. "Maybe we have this envy over how easy it is for the White woman to maintain her hair," says Bernice Calvin, founder of Black Hair Expo. "Even with natural styles, we have to work at it." Everything from a day at the beach to a trip overseas requires detailed planning and serious preparation. The concept of a wash-and-go style when it comes to Black hair is like pie in the sky. As Bernice Calvin intimates, Black hair is work.

It would be erroneous to assume that all Black people dislike their hair or even have problems working with it. From celebrity stylists to adolescent boys on the road to self-discovery, Black people often use their hair as a medium for celebrating creative energy. "I love my hair," says Penn State student Lois Baxter. "I wake up every day and wonder how I was able to grow [dred]locks on my head. I love to touch my hair and I love to take care of it." The texture of Black hair, in its natural form or chemically altered, is also conducive to a plethora of styling options. "Kinky hair . . . relaxes and straightens easily, and can hold curly styles with great success," writes New York-based celebrity stylist Kevin Mancuso in his book, *The Mane Thing*. "Kinky hair is also self-supportive," Mancuso writes. "What this means is that in its naturally dry state, it can be fashioned into shapes . . . and hold the style with relative ease and not need spraying." Curls, finger waves, braids, twists—the list of styling variations is endless. Black people can change their hairstyle to match their mood and satisfy their every whim. "I like to find new, unique things to do with my hair," says Habiba Anan, a Washington, D.C., native. "Before it was through the use of a combination of colors. Now it's more in terms of styles. I feel like I'm often defending my hair because it's not straight and slick, [but] I just laugh because I couldn't be happier with it."

American Beauty

While natural hair was not universally desired at the end of millennium, many Black Americans were still searching for a way to "improve" their hair naturally. In a clear case of history repeating itself, a product was introduced to the market in 1999 that promised a *natural,* chemical-free way to get "hair that moves." Using the same marketing scheme as Rio, the disaster product of the early nineties, this new miracle cure was called Copa. Via a late-night infomercial featuring product endorser and entertainer Debbie Allen and her dredlocked hairstylist Snacky, the 96 percent natural Copa "curl release system" promised to "give you freedom. Freedom from the effects of humidity, freedom to work out or swim."

Perhaps still recalling the photos of Rio victims' patchy bald heads and sandwich bags full of hair, Black women have not embraced Copa in great numbers. But the very existence of the product underlines the rut that Black America stays in regarding hair. "Freedom" is still equated with having straight hair. Neither

Ten Memorable Moments in Black Hair History

Circa 1845: The hot comb is invented in France.

1910: The first year hair-care entrepreneur Madam C. J. Walker makes the *Guinness Book of World Records* as the first Black self-made female millionaire.

1948: Mexican chemist Jose Calva discovers that the same process that turns sheep's wool into mink-like fur can turn kinky hair straight.

1969: The year Angela Davis's image—massive Afro on display—is disseminated to the masses by the FBI. Warning: Afroed and dangerous.

1981: The proud lady symbol, reminding consumers to buy Black, is introduced by the American Health and Beauty Aids Institute.

January 27, 1984: Michael Jackson's hair catches fire during the shooting of a Pepsi commercial.

July 1989: Quaker Oats removes Aunt Jemima's signature red headrag and updates her look with a no-lye relaxer.

November 1998: The first Madam C. J. Walker commemorative stamp is issued by the U.S. Postal Service.

Later in November 1998: A White teacher in Brooklyn is threatened with bodily harm for reading the book *Nappy Hair* to her third-grade students. She eventually leaves the school, fearing for her safety. The book goes on to sell a hundred thousand copies.

January 26, 1999: Tennis star Venus Williams receives a point penalty and subsequently loses at the Australian Open semifinals when some of her trademark beads fly off her braids and onto the court.

– From *Hair Story*

the product's infomercial nor the other hair straightening systems on the market mention that women and men with braids, dredlocks, and various natural styles have the freedom to swim, sweat, and walk in the rain without destroying their styles. The reason for the omission is that these manufacturers understand that the majority of Blacks would not see freedom in wearing natural hair. They would instead feel further alienated, ostracized, and unattractive.

Black men's and women's psyches still value unkinky hair much more than the type that grows out of most Black heads. Popular culture continues to be filled with Black women with long, or at least soft, moving hair. Music videos overflow with light-skinned, long-haired women or, continuing a trend that started in the early nineties, feature women who are of mixed heritage, Asian or Latina. Beauty advertising historically preys on the insecurities of those in its intended market, and the Black hair game is no exception. Since the days of the first Black newspapers, advertisements have told Black people that their hair is unacceptable and downright ugly. In 1998 a billboard campaign was introduced for Bone Strait Relaxer system. The ad showed a woman with long, straight hair, her head slightly arched back. The caption read, "My Hair. Your Man. His Fingers. Your Drama." It became a source of outrage for many (of all races) who felt that the campaign lacked cutural sensitivity and portrayed Black women as sexually licentious homewreckers. African-Americans expressed their disapproval of the campaign that so insidiously linked having long, straight, touchable hair with having not only a man but someone else's man. In a culture where women were continually made to feel that they were attractive primarily if they fit into a certain beauty mold, this ad hit a raw nerve with those Black women who always worried that no man would find their hair "touchable" and beautiful.

Ironically, the campaign was created and executed by Spike/BBDO, the ad company co-owned by filmmaker Spike Lee—the same man who once forced Black Americans to face their color and hair issues in his film *School Daze*. A spokesperson for the agency said that the ad was meant as "fun" and to show the "playful gamesmanship that exists between Black women." But surely the company knew that Black women find few things funny about hair, and even less when it comes to their men.

Children, who pick up their cultural cues from family and schoolmates, still favor long, straight hair. As bell hooks notes, "Every day of our lives in this society a Black child somewhere is slaughtering their hair with dangerous products." In recent years, little Black girls have been wearing their hair in braid extensions that often fall past the middle of their backs. Parents typically claim that the style shaves tremendous time off the morning routine. But many social critics and commentators see danger in adding long, unkinky hair to the heads of little girls who must develop an ethnic identity and self-esteem in a society that looks down on short, nappy tresses. It is seen as a way of telling these children from a very early age that what they naturally possess must somehow be amended in order to be pretty and acceptable.

> America's beauty ideal has not altered drastically since the late 1800s.

America's, including Black America's, beauty ideal has not altered drastically since the late 1800s. Large breasts, small waists, and masses of flowing hair are still the look desired by men and sought after by many women. The adoption of certain Black looks and trends by Whites does not indicate a more inclusive definition of beauty but merely offers Whites a broader range of ways to look "exotic" or "different." Black people looking to fit into the mainstream visually still overwhelmingly have to contend with the same standards as in the past.

▶ ## Analyzing the Text

1. According to Byrd and Tharps, "In the United States, where the aesthetic norms are overwhelmingly based on a White European standard, Black people with any variation of kinky tresses are immediately cast as 'others' in mainstream beauty culture." What physical characteristics are described in this essay as the mainstream beauty norm? How does this norm compare to African American beauty norms?

2. The authors write, "The first time Black hair intersects with White people is a telling experience most people will never forget." What stories does this essay share about the attitudes African Americans face about hair?

3. According to the authors, how can attitudes about hair within the African American community be more damaging to children's developing sense of identity than "the ignorance of mainstream White culture"?

4. Byrd and Tharps cite feminist scholar bell hooks, who has written about her childhood experiences having her hair straightened as a passage from childhood to womanhood: "For each of us getting our hair pressed is an important ritual. It is not a sign of our longing to be White. It is not a sign of our quest to be beautiful. We are girls. It is a sign of our desire to be women." How do the stories in this essay demonstrate that African American hair rituals can provide rites of passage?

5. **Interrogating Assumptions.** To what extent does this essay challenge mainstream traditions, arguing that they are damaging and marginalize those who do not fit into a narrowly defined (white-centered) standard of beauty? How would the authors of this essay respond to the assumption that traditions promote unity (see p. 181)?

6. **Connecting to Another Readings.** In his essay, "It Takes a Tribe" (p. 207), David Berreby describes people's need to belong. In your opinion, in what ways is the argument Berreby presents related to the arguments presented by Byrd and Tharps?

▶ ## Writing about Cultural Practices

7. Write a position paper responding to Byrd and Tharps's argument that beauty standards are narrowly defined by mainstream white culture. On page 223, they argue that the adoption of certain African American looks and trends by mainstream white culture "does not indicate a more inclusive definition of beauty but merely offers Whites a broader range of ways to look 'exotic' or 'different.' Black people looking to fit into the mainstream visually still overwhelmingly have to contend with the same standards as in the past." As you draft your paper, consider the following questions.

   • What are mainstream beauty standards in American culture? Are these standards evolving? If so, how? What physical characteristics are most highly prized?

   • What evidence from popular culture can you provide to support your description of the beauty norm in mainstream culture?

   • How are people who do not fit into these standards represented in popular culture? In what ways are they defined as an "Other," as Byrd and Tharps contend is sometimes the case for African Americans? What evidence can you provide to support your view?

Garrison Keillor, **A Wobegon Holiday Dinner**

Garrison Keillor, one of America's leading humorists, is the creator of *A Prairie Home Companion*, a radio variety show for Minnesota Public Radio. Now internationally syndicated, the show reaches millions of listeners worldwide. Keillor is also the author of more than 10 books, including *Lake Wobegon Boy* (1997) and *Me: By Jimmy (Big Boy) Valenta* (1999). His essay "A Wobegon Holiday Dinner" appeared in *The Best of the Best American Humor* (2002), but it was originally performed as one of his weekly radio show monologues. Keillor centers these monologues on a remembered experience of his past, which he usually sets in the fictional town of Lake Wobegon, an amalgam of the small towns in central Minnesota where Keillor grew up. This essay recalls memories of a Thanksgiving Day in 1965 when his entire extended family got together for dinner. Keillor's essay uses humor to tell an alternative story about families and holidays—one that does not present an idealized picture of family togetherness.

▶ **Mapping Your Reading**

Keillor's honest yet humorous portrait of his family and its Thanksgiving traditions illustrates that, in reality, family traditions aren't always all they're cracked up to be. Far from being Norman Rockwell perfect, Keillor suggests that family gatherings rarely live up to the expectations that precede the big day. How does Keillor compare his family's traditions to how he imagines other people must celebrate the day? Place checks in the margins next to passages that you find especially telling. Do you know any families like the Keillors?

My cousin Duke called me one day last week when I was in the middle of something, but I swiveled my chair back and put my feet up on the windowsill and we talked for half an hour, which was good. My relatives never call me anymore since I moved to New York because they imagine I'm busy, and when they do call, they say, "Did I catch you at a bad time? Are you busy? You're busy, aren't you? I'm sorry. I didn't mean to bother you. I can call you back later. Sorry. Bye."

This was a more normal conversation. She said it was snowing in Minnesota and was still deer-hunting season, so she was staying indoors and away from windows. She had arrived in Lake Wobegon on Halloween from Seattle where

"Since we're new here, would you mind if we cleared the forest between our encampments so we can observe how you live in harmony with nature?"

she lives, taking a month's leave to see her mother, my aunt Lois, who is ailing, though you wouldn't know this from talking to my aunt, who is no complainer. "How are you, Mary Ann?" I asked. It's hard to think of her as Mary Ann, having known her as Duke since she was tiny, but she left her Dukedom to become a Mary Ann in Seattle, I guess, and we must honor that.

She was in a good mood. She was sitting in the kitchen of her childhood home, and the sight of snow made her cheerful, but her family was always cheerful. Aunt Lois inherited it from my grandma, who spent her last years baking good bread and whistling and thinking highly of her grandchildren. Duke said, "You know something? This month, it will be 25 years since the last time I vomited."

I asked her how she planned to celebrate the anniversary, and she said she wasn't sure. I said, "I sure remember the event." So did she, vividly. Mary Ann is a slight woman, like Lois, and elegant, even in jeans and a sweatshirt, and she would rather lie very still for days on a couch than throw up. She never rides the Ferris wheel, is leery of airplanes, and doesn't drink more than one glass of wine per dinner. Other people in our family, if they feel a little queasy, think nothing of heading for the bathroom and taking matters into their own hands, but Mary Ann would rather lie very still in a dark room with a cold compress on her forehead.

The last time Duke threw up was Thanksgiving Day, 1965. It was the last year our whole family, aunts and uncles and cousins, were together at Al and Flo's house in Lake Wobegon. The next year we rented the Sons of Knute temple, and after that we broke apart into separate single-family Thanksgivings. There were simply too many of us, about 60, for that three-bedroom bungalow. There were card-tables upstairs, in the basement, and in the living room. The men wedged themselves along the blue sofa and on the floor and watched football on Al's snowy TV set. Upstairs, little kids played with Lincoln logs and plastic cowboys, quietly, after Uncle Jack threatened to lock them in the garage. Sun poured in the front window, the radiators steamed, and steam drifted out from the kitchen, which was packed with aunts.

My aunts stood shoulder to shoulder and whacked at things and chopped and slapped dinner together.

I stood by the kitchen door, next to the praying-hands plaque, talking to Aunt Marie, who wasn't allowed in the kitchen because she dropped things. My fiancée stood beside me; it was her first encounter with the family, who were trying not to look at her, and she was trying to catch my eye. She was bored to tears and needed a cigarette. "Let's go for a walk," she whispered. But it wasn't easy to escape. Poor Marie was clinging to us for dear life. She kept asking me about school, about our wedding, about anything at all—we were her life raft. She couldn't sit on the sofa, go upstairs, or enter the kitchen.

My aunts were powerful women caught up in a crusade to create vast quantities of food and stuff us with it and stuff the rest into Tupperware dishes and stuff them into the refrigerator. Marie, who married into the family, was a weak reed. She was unsure of recipes and worried about measuring accurately. My aunts stood shoulder to shoulder and whacked at things and whipped and chopped and slapped dinner together. "I have to get out of here right now," my fiancée whispered. I felt the same way, but how do you get out of your own family? "Your writing!" Marie cried. "Tell me about your writing!"

We extracted ourselves from her and put on our coats, and the moment we got out the door, I felt buoyant. We walked down the street and, free of the family, I could speak up, I could say what I thought, be vulgar, have great opinions, be original, and when I turned the corner, we could smoke a cigarette. Pall Malls. "Did you really grow up here?" my fiancée asked. I could see her point. A guy like me coming from such a dismal little town, little frame houses with dumb lawn ornaments and the people inside cooking the exact same dinners and saying the same things: Yes, I grew up here, but of course, even as a child, I had looked to distant horizons. And I regretted that my family was not more colorful. I wished we were Italians. Italians had ethnic customs. We didn't. We just had turkey for Thanksgiving. Italians had big flagons of red wine. We had pitchers of ice water. We were Sanctified Brethren.

In 1986, for my new Danish wife and stepchildren, who wanted an authentic American Thanksgiving, I fixed the traditional barbecued spareribs and the customary Thanksgiving linguini with garlic sauce on the side, and we enjoyed the old-fashioned Thanksgiving Scotch and soda. But at Thanksgiving

"I have to get out of here right now," my fiancée whispered.

1965, there was no alcohol. Not a drop. My fiancée's family in Minneapolis, who were fall Methodists, were knocking down some Manhattans, I knew, and keeping them nice and fresh, and I wished we were there, instead of among the Brethren.

"It's nothing," he said. He bled all down the front of his new white shirt.

Thanksgiving is better when you're with somebody else's family and can enjoy their little fights. Her mother and father sparred constantly, over silly things like money, whereas my parents fought with me and fought for blood, over ultimate truths and matters of faith. That day, walking back to Al and Flo's, I knew that Vietnam was bound to come up at dinner.

I could imagine my Uncle Jack saying, "Ya, well, I don't know about these protesters and this draft-card burning, but if it was up to me, I'd throw them out of college and put them to work if they don't want to go in the Army." And then I would say something about our tragic mistakes in Southeast Asia, and a few minutes later, my beloved uncle would lean forward and hiss at me and my dear aunts would purse their lips and glare and my mother would run weeping to the bathroom.

But when we got back, something else had happened, something unpleasant, everybody was very thin-lipped about it. "It's nothing," my mother said. "Don't bring it up." "What is it?" I said. "It doesn't concern you," she said. It concerned Uncle Jack and Aunt Dee. I gathered that he had gotten up from the football game and come to the kitchen for a drink of water and she said something and he said something back, something mean, just teasing, and she threw something at him, playfully, which happened to be a paring knife, and it made a deep scratch down his cheek.

Jack returned to the couch and resumed watching TV, bleeding profusely, shrugging off first aid. Aunt Lois ran for a washcloth, Uncle Al dabbed at him with a hanky. "It's nothing," he said. He bled all down the front of his new white shirt. Aunt Dee went down to the basement and cried and came back mad. The basement had reminded her of things in the past, of her historic struggle with Jack. "He's always saying things like that," she said. "He hasn't changed since he was nine years old." Jack would not look at her or anybody else. "I'm not mad," he said. "If the rest of you want to make a federal case out of it, go ahead. I'm just fine."

Either he never got over Jesus' death, the way the rest of us had, or else it was just a bad habit he couldn't stop.

The food was portioned out to all the cardboard tables and everyone sat down in a thoughtful mood. In the kitchen, Dee and Aunt Mary were still muttering at each other: "Well, he started it." "Yes, but you could have had the decency to apologize for throwing a knife at him." "I see no point in discussing it," said Dee. "You've always taken his side and you always will." Aunt Mary lowered the boom. "You never cared a bit for this family. You didn't go visit Mother before she died and nobody was a bit surprised. You've always gone your own way. And now you're ruining this Thanksgiving." Dee fled back to the basement. We could hear her long musical sobs. Mary sat down with us in the dining room, breathing hard. Vietnam seemed like a small distant event compared to this, and if I had mentioned the war, it might've come as a great relief.

Then Uncle Al dinged his glass. "We're going to return thanks now," he said, and called up the hot air vent to diners upstairs, "Time for grace now!" He must have been awfully upset, too upset to pray, because he said, "Carl, would you return thanks," and Uncle Carl stood up and cleared his throat.

Uncle Carl was the last person you'd ask to pray, ever. For one thing, he prayed longer than anybody else in the Sanctified Brethren, where prayers tended to cover a lot of theological ground and touch on all the main points of faith. Carl was endless. Scripture said, "Pray without ceasing," and he almost succeeded. He could pray until food got moldy. And, what was worse, when Carl came to the part of the prayer where he thanked God for sending His only begotten Son Jesus Christ to die on the cross as propitiation for our sins, he always wept.

Carl had wept in prayer for many years. Either he never got over Jesus' death, the way the rest of us had, or else it was just a bad habit he couldn't stop. He always stood and cried, helpless, his shoulders shaking. He was a sweet man with tidy gray hair, oiled, with comb tracks in it, a dapper dresser who favored bow ties—a good uncle, and it was painful to sit and listen to him cry.

He stood, and we stirred in our seats uneasily. I peeked at my fiancée, and saw she had already put a big dab of squash on her plate. She was not accustomed to table grace. I couldn't imagine she'd be ready for Uncle Carl.

Carl spoke in a clear voice toward the heating vent so the people upstairs could hear, thanking God for the food, for each other, for this day, and then for sending His only begotten son Jesus to die on Calvary's cross, and he started to sob, such a wrenching sound, his awful weeping, especially because he tried to keep talking about Jesus, and the words would hardly come out. He stopped and blew his nose and we all, one by one, started to get weepy. My fiancée wept, I cried, we all cried. I don't think we wept for Jesus so much as from exhaustion. Families can wear you out sometimes. Down in the basement, somebody was bawling. And right there, as Carl wiped his nose and everyone around the dining room table sniffled, my cousin Duke leaned forward and tossed her cookies.

Everyone had their eyes closed, and believe me, it's more vivid when you only hear it. Radio is a powerful medium. She vomited twice and gagged twice, two longs

DAVID SEDARIS
. . . on Being a
Macy's Christmas Elf

"My costume is green. I wear green velvet knickers, a yellow turtleneck, a forest-green velvet smock, and a perky stocking cap decorated with spangles. This is my work uniform. My elf name is Crumpet.

Young children tend to be frightened of Santa. A Photo Elf understands that, once a child starts crying, it's over. Tonight I saw a woman slap and shake her sobbing daughter, yelling, 'Goddamnit it, Rachel, get on that man's lap and smile or I'll give you something to cry about.'

I often take photographs of crying children. Even more grotesque is taking a picture of a crying child with a false grimace. It's not a smile so much as the forced shape of a smile. Oddly, it pleases the parents. 'Good girl, Rachel. Now, let's get the hell out of here. Your mother has a headache that won't quit until you're twenty-one.' "

–From *Holidays on Ice,* 1994

229

FOUND

from dyngusdaybuffalo.com

DYNGUS DAY: PREPARE TO POLKA

Polish stamp commemorating "Dyngus Day"

The Easter season in Poland ends on Monday when the traditional "Smigus-Dyngus" is observed. It is a humorous custom, during which young people break the solemnity of Easter with a burst of frivolity, visiting house to house, singing songs, and playing pranks. The tradition further evolved in more modern times when farm boys in Poland wanted to attract notice from the girls of their choice. It became customary to throw water (or cologne, if you were a more gallant lad) and to hit the girls on their legs with twigs or pussy willows. The ladies would reciprocate by throwing dishes and crockery. Over the decades, Dyngus Day has become a wonderful holiday to celebrate Polish American culture, heritage, and traditions.

Many Polish customs date back to pre-Christian practices of our Slavic ancestors, and some say that Dyngus Day is a pagan tradition. The custom of pouring water is an ancient spring rite of cleansing, purification, and fertility, as is the practice of switching with pussy willow branches. Since A.D. 966, Dyngus Day has also been associated with the baptism of Prince Mieszko I, who along with his court were baptized on Easter Monday.

Buffalo, New York, is officially the Dyngus Capital of America with the largest concentration of festival locations and live polka music. No, you do not need to be Polish to enjoy Dyngus Day. Many parties begin at noon on the Monday after Easter with a large buffet of traditional Easter foods (Kielbasa, ham, fresh breads, eggs). It is common to hear polka music on Dyngus, with the mandatory dancing of at least one polka.

Speak Like a Native: Here are a few words and sayings in Polish that you can use while celebrating Dyngus Day.

How are you?	Jak sie masz?	Can I kiss you?	Moge Cie pocalowac?
Good day.	Dzien dobry.	I want you.	Pragne Cie.
Thank you.	Dziekuja.	I love you.	Kocham Cie.
Please.	Prosze.	Let's get married.	Ozenmy sie.
Cheers!	Nazdrowie or Sto lat!	Let's pray.	Modlmy sie.
Let's dance.	Zatanczymy?	I'm broke.	Nie mam pieniedzy.
You're beautiful.	Jestes tak piekna.	I have a headache.	Boli mnie glowa.
I like you.	Lubie Cie.		

and two shorts, and staggered for the bathroom. There was some sympathetic gagging among the other children, and some men got up suddenly, even before Carl's amen, and went outdoors and leaned against the house. My aunts leaped into action and cleared the table and whipped off the tablecloth and mopped up the floor and dinner was put back in the oven while our heads settled and our appetites returned. This took about half an hour. Some people took walks, others simply stood looking out windows. Dishes were washed, the room aired out, the table reset, and eventually we came back. I felt good: Someone had vomited at the table before a meal and it was not me.

Life is good. Even when it is lousy, it is still good.

There was some question of whether to repray or not, whether the previous blessing was still in effect, and Uncle Al said a brief grace, thanking God for His mercy. We ate. Tentatively at first, but we hit our stride and finished up strong, with pumpkin pie. Duke was so mortified she began her long career of not vomiting. Twenty-five years of relative calm. Uncle Jack died a few years later, and Aunt Dee followed in 1982: May they rest in peace. Happy Thanksgiving. Life is good. Even when it is lousy, it is still good, and thank God for it.

Analyzing the Text

1. Keillor clearly chose a particularly memorable Thanksgiving to share in this essay. What does the vomit episode contribute to the larger story about how his family celebrated Thanksgiving?

2. What is Keillor's perception of the rituals and traditions surrounding his family's Thanksgiving? How do his family's traditions control the meaning of the holiday for Keillor? How do they compare to the way he imagines other people celebrate the holiday? What details in the essay best illustrate this?

3. Keillor writes, "Thanksgiving is better when you're with somebody else's family and can enjoy their little fights." How does the author contrast the differences between the tensions or fights in his family with those of his fiancée's family? How does his use of humor allow him to make this comparison?

4. In the last lines of the essay, Keillor writes, "Life is good. Even when it is lousy, it is still good." What does he mean by this? In what sense is this final statement the lesson of the essay?

5. **Connecting to Another Reading.** In "Thoroughly Modern Dining" (p. 188), Richard Pillsbury worries about the loss of family traditions caused by people not gathering in homes to mark special occasions. To what degree is Keillor's essay a response to Pillsbury's claims about the nature of family gatherings? Do you think Keillor would agree with Pillsbury? Why or why not?

Writing about Cultural Practices

6. "A Wobegon Holiday Dinner" presents a more complex view of families and holidays than is often presented in the popular media. Our popular culture is full of idealized images of family traditions formed to celebrate major holidays.

"Freedom from Want," reprinted above, is Norman Rockwell's famous image of
an American family's Thanksgiving celebration. Rockwell was an illustrator and
artist best known for his contributions to the *Saturday Evening Post,* for which he
produced 332 covers, beginning in 1916. Many of Rockwell's images epitomize
what people frequently believe family holidays should be. For this assignment,
write a critical analysis of advertising images that focus on families and holidays. To begin, search both online and print sources to locate three to four advertisements that contain images of families celebrating a holiday together. As
you draft your essay, consider the following questions.

- How does each of the ads portray families celebrating a holiday?
- Do the advertisements share themes similar to Rockwell's painting?
- In what ways do the ads idealize or romanticize family traditions? What de-
  tails in the images lead you to your conclusions?
- How complex is the characterization of the family holiday in the ads?
- What and who do the images leave out of the picture? Why?

Natalie Guice Adams and Pamela J. Bettis, Cheerleader! An American Icon

Natalie Guice Adams, an associate professor of education at the University of Alabama, and Pamela J. Bettis, an assistant professor of education at Washington State University, authored *Cheerleader! An American Icon* in 2003. In this book, from which the following essay is excerpted, Adams and Bettis explore the changing nature of cheerleading in an effort to articulate how this tradition has come to symbolize American spirit. However, as the authors make clear, they see cheerleading as representative of both the best and worst parts of that spirit: "Granted, cheerleading may be as American as apple pie for some. But for many others, it's definitely a store-bought frozen apple pie with too much sugar and not enough apples."

▶ **Mapping Your Reading**

Cheerleaders have long been associated with American traditions that are meant to promote unity and encourage feelings of pride and loyalty. As you read this essay, pay attention to how the authors describe both the optimism and the narcissism associated with images of cheerleaders. Place checks in the margins next to passages that best convey what cheerleaders represent in American culture. What role do cheerleaders play in a school or community? How does this role connect with patriotism? With American idealism? What makes cheerleading a particularly American tradition?

Hey! Hey! What do you say?
We're proud to live in the USA![1]

For many Americans, cheerleading is as American as apple pie. Maybe it's because cheerleading began in this country and has not caught on in other countries as much as other American cultural and corporate institutions, such as McDonalds and jazz. Perhaps, it's because female cheerleaders are often described as the "all-American, girl next door" and are still considered, by many, to represent the ideal American girl. Or maybe it's because cheerleading is so closely associated with the American spectacle of football, the sport beloved by

---

For another reading on American symbols, see Staples, page 243.—Eds.

so many Americans of every race, ethnicity, age, and social class. Maybe it's because "cheerleading" is used with such regularity in our American vernacular, often in contexts having nothing to do with sports, that it's part of our cultural lexicon as reflected in a recent newspaper headline, "Workers blame corporate cheerleading for huge retirement losses with BC-Enron—Investigation."[2] Cheerleading represents, for many, the American virtues they embrace: loyalty and devotion to a cause; perseverance even in the face of insurmountable obstacles; and a confidence and optimism that sometimes defy explanation.

> Cheerleading represents a confidence and optimism that sometimes defy explanation.

Granted, cheerleading may be as American as apple pie for some. But for many others, it's definitely a store-bought frozen apple pie with too much sugar and not enough apples. Take, for example, Marty Beckerman, the teenage author of *Death to All Cheerleaders* and former editor of his Alaska high school newspaper, who agrees that cheerleading does indeed represent something about our American character: its worst traits. "Cheerleading is nothing more than a perfect example, an incontestable paradigm, of what is horribly wrong with our generation. . . . Our generation, as a whole, has so much capacity, but we toss it all away on vacuous brand name loyalties and the superficial corporate blueprint for our lives that is unceasingly shoved down out throats."[3] Many would agree with Beckerman's assessment of cheerleaders as shallow in character, disingenuous, egocentric, and materialistic, and would point out that these character flaws are often the same criticisms aimed at Americans as a whole.

Whether we think cheerleaders represent the best of American culture or the worst of American culture, the fact is cheerleading is a uniquely American cultural institution that reveals much about the diverse and contradictory values of the American people. Cheerleading's origins are found in this country. Further, cheerleading has persevered through massive cultural changes since its beginnings in the late 1800s, and its popularity continues into the twenty-first century. So what can this activity tell us about some of our strengths and weaknesses as a people? What can it tell us about the American identity? More important, since cheerleading in this country is mainly a youthful activity, what can it tell us about how we socialize our young people?

Living in a Cheerocracy: American Optimism on Display

When local cheerleaders hold their fingers up and yell "We're number 1!" they bear a remarkable resemblance to the countless displays of patriotism that were seen in the immediate aftermath of the 9-11 attacks, as Americans from all walks of life proudly proclaimed, "We're still number 1!" Americans are an optimistic people, and cheerleaders represent this optimism because they are expected, above all else, to be perky and cheerful. In fact, if there is anything ubiquitous about any cheerleader, anywhere, it is their ever-present smile. That smile has been labeled in a variety of ways—as the toothpaste smiles and velcroed-on smiles. But smiling is part of the standard cheerleading uniform. Also part of the standard cheerleading look is pom pons, which also help with the cheery appearance. As Kline Boyd, vice president of Varsity Spirit Corporation, the world's most successful producer of cheerleading paraphernalia, says, "people just like pom pons. It makes people smile and makes them happy."[4] The spirit stick, the most coveted award at hundreds of cheerleading camps throughout this country, is also associated with cheerfulness and only given to those squads who most demonstrate cheerful optimism and energy. And consider the colors of the original National Cheerleading Association (NCA) spirit stick—red, white, and blue.

Repeatedly in our interviews with cheerleaders throughout this country, they referred to themselves as ambassadors for their schools. While football players may growl and shout obscenities to the opposing players, cheerleaders, as ambassadors of the school, are expected to be model citizens who are even cheerful to the opposing cheerleaders and fans. In fact, a common practice at many junior high and high school football games is that the home cheerleaders visit the other side of the stadium to greet the opposing team's cheerleaders and fans. Typically they perform a "Hello Cheer" on the opponent's side, and then their opponent's cheerleaders come back with them to be introduced to the home crowd. Shelia Angalet, spirit coordinator of Metuchen (NJ) High School, explains the importance of this ambassador role in maintaining a civil competitive environment, even when the atmosphere around the cheerleaders is less than cordial:

> **Cheerleaders, as ambassadors of the school, are expected to be model citizens.**

> It [the football game] has been a big rivalry—and sometimes a nasty one. I had warned my cheerleaders to be on their best behavior—that if anything was going to be sparked—it would be from the opposition, not us. After the game began, and things were rolling, the home team's cheerleaders came over to do their cheer. Our crowd was not overly cordial, but they were not rude either. As the other cheerleaders got closer, I encouraged my girls to welcome them and they started applauding! It caught on a little bit in the stands. The girls did their cheer nicely and there was applause for them—not rousing—but applause nonetheless. Shortly after that, we went to their side to do our Hello cheer. As we got close to the stands, the boos and cat calls started. I told my girls walk proud. Their cheerleaders were sitting waiting and applauding and cheering us! Their crowd may have been rude, but their cheerleaders were awesome and welcoming! While we lost the game, I feel the cheerleaders gained a bit of new respect and some cheer friends within our local community.[5]

Even when the chips are down—when all obstacles are stacked against us—when we're losing 66–3, the cheerleaders are expected to continue to yell "F-I-G-H-T, Fight, Eagles Fight!" Kline Boyd believes this cheerleading "can-do" mentality is at the heart of American idealism. "Cheerleaders go out there and say dad gum it, we support our team, we're going to cheer for them to win and believe they can win even if they don't have a chance."[6] In her reflection of what it was like to cheer during a miserable losing season at a small rural school, Ginger Hopkins admits that it was difficult to yell when the basketball team trailed by 58 points and their players were six inches shorter than the opposing team. However, her squad shifted to some innovative cheers such as, "Mayonnaise, mustard, relish—catch up!" and "Gimme a G, an R, an O, a W. What's that spell? . . . GROW!" And Ginger has a typical cheerleading spin on that season: "In fact, we'll probably remember that unchampionship season after other seasons are long forgotten. During it, we tried our hardest and kept our dignity, pride, and our sense of humor. The team may have lost, but we cheerleaders went undefeated!"[7]

> "The team may have lost, but we cheerleaders went undefeated!"

Such a portrayal of cheerleaders may sound corny to many people, but these sentiments are shared by many in the cheerleading world. Indeed, cheerleading has almost become a synonym for eternal optimism and is used regularly in our American vernacular to convey the ability to look on the bright side even in the midst of travails. After the economic summit called by President Bush in the summer of 2002, the *Tuscaloosa News* in Tuscaloosa, Alabama, introduced its editorial for the day with the headline, "President leads cheers at summit." The article goes on to say:

> President George W. Bush's heralded economic summit in Waco, Texas, Tuesday resembled nothing if not a pep rally meant to reassure a shaken stock market and public. And Bush, true to his roots as a prep school cheerleader, was out front leading the cheers. At times it almost seemed that he wanted to break into a rousing, "Give me an A! Give me a M! Give me an E . . ." "Even though times are kind of tough right now, we're America," Bush said. "I'm incredibly optimistic about the future of this country because I understand the strength of this country. . . . We've got a lot going for us."[8]

In the aftermath of the September 11 tragedy, the American character attributes that have been highlighted by the press and in conversations across the nation include our strength to pull together during a crisis, our faith in the future, and our optimism. In many ways, the activity of cheerleading embodies all of these qualities. We think that is why diverse groups of Americans with diverse causes and ways of presenting themselves have adopted cheerleading as the vehicle for their message. So, even radicals from the left, whose politics, one might think, would preclude their use of cheerleading, still become cheerleaders, albeit "radical cheerleaders."[9] Although their protests are bereft of short skirts and football chants, they shoulder the burdens of environmental degradation, globalization, the threat of war, patriarchy, and homophobia through clever cheers and chants such as the following:

> I don't know but I've been told
> SUV's have got to go
> They smell bad, take too much space
> They pollute all over the place
> That beast's just a passenger car
> No more two-tiered emission laws
> They think driving in a mall parking lot
> Is going off-roading, but it's not
> Sustainable transit's what we want to see
> So join me on a bike, yuppie!

As one of the groups explains on their website, "Radical Cheerleading is protest and performance! It is activism with pom-poms and combat boots! It is non-violent direct action in the form of street theatre."[10] Cheerleading, somehow, seems just as appropriate for those wearing combat boots and shaking milk jugs filled with pebbles as for those in kicky skirts who shake pom pons. Whether it's optimism for the end of global pollution or optimism for a winning football season, both groups of cheerleaders embody enthusiasm for whatever their passion. As Torrance, the captain of the Torro High School cheerleading squad in the popular cheerleading movie *Bring It On,* says, "we don't live in a democracy but a cheerocracy."[11]

Cheerleading: As American as Consumerism, Shallowness, and the Worst of American Culture

> Two, four, six, eight
> Go for a look you'll appreciate
> Body in shape and looking great
> Hurry, don't procrastinate![12]

If most people considered cheerleading only in light of the preceding discussion, there would be few, if any, criticisms of this activity and its participants. But all of us know that this is certainly not the case. In fact, cheerleaders are continually maligned in this culture, in very vicious as well as humorous ways, and are often used to highlight the worst of American culture, particularly conformity, mindlessness, and confused priorities. As Marty Beckerman notes, cheerleading is "an activity that attracts a lot of people with a lot of capacity, a lot of really energetic people who are throwing that energy away on this meaningless, pom-pom, jumping-around activity that doesn't really stand for anything. Clearly, that energy could be devoted to something more meaningful."[13] For Marty as well as countless other Americans, cheerleading represents a shallowness in intelligence and character as parodied by the Spartan Cheerleaders on *Saturday Night Live* and the innumerable "dumb cheerleader" jokes such as: "What did the Trojan cheerleader say when she learned she was pregnant? Is it mine?"[14]

> Cheerleaders are often used to highlight conformity, mindlessness, and confused priorities.

Marty's book title, *Death to All Cheerleaders,* is certainly not so far removed from reality when we consider the case of the Texas cheerleader murder plot. In 1991, a Channelview, Texas, housewife named Wanda Holloway was arrested for solicitation of murder. When the reason behind the murder solicitation was revealed, the case made national and international headlines and confirmed countless people's beliefs that the activity of cheerleading is filled with narcissistic and shallow people whose mothers are even worse. Wanda had attempted to find someone to kill her former close friend, Verna Heath, because in the past Verna's daughter had beaten out Wanda's daughter for a slot on the cheerleading squad. Wanda believed that if Verna died, her 13-year-old daughter Amber would be so distraught that she would be unable to try out for cheerleader, which would then ensure that Wanda's daughter, Shana, was selected.[15] This sensational story led to a book, two made-for-television movies, innumerable talk show discussions, and countless gossip magazine stories. Further, the story was publicized around the world; for many outside the United States, the Texas cheerleading murder plot confirmed what they had seen in the popular TV show *Dallas:* that Americans were superficial people who will do anything to win. In 1996, Wanda, Texas housewife, school and church volunteer received a 10-year sentence; 6 months of the sentence would be served in jail while the remaining time would be spent on probation. Verna's family received $150,000 compensation from Wanda's insurance company.[16]

Although most parents of cheerleaders are not plotting to murder anyone standing in their daughter's way, the California Newport Harbor High School controversy provides further ammunition for critics who blame overzealous parents for the misguided priorities taught to our young people. In 1995, the parents of a student not selected as a Newport Harbor High cheerleader filed a lawsuit against the school district, claiming the selection process had been unfair. The school district settled out of court for $50,000. As a result, a new selection process was implemented: three paid external, expert judges, votes tallied by a certified public accountant, and a representative of the League of Women Voters standing by to make sure nothing went amiss. Despite all of the precautions to ensure a fair selection process, when the squad was selected at the November 2001 tryouts, the coach, who was not a faculty member and was paid by the boosters, complained to the principal that the judges were inconsistent and showed partiality. The principal decided to reverse the judges' decisions and allow all 48 girls to be on the squad. This action incited several of the parents whose daughters had been selected; one filed a formal complaint with the school district. An investigative team was convened and determined that the selection process had been fair. Thus, the principal had to reverse his earlier decision— only the 30 originally selected would be able to cheer, but, as a compromise, tryouts would be held again and four additional cheerleaders selected.[17] The subsequent letters to the *Los Angeles Times* reflected a general disbelief that cheerleading can garner more serious attention than an economic recession, failing achievement scores, and even the war on terrorism. David Perez of Irvine wrote tongue-in-cheek: "Forget the Taliban, Al Qaeda, and Osama bin Ladin's whereabouts. No, what is of most urgency is getting to the bottom of 'pompomgate' at Newport Harbor High School."[18] Similarly, Julie Hudash, who graduated from USC on a full athletic scholarship, wrote:

> I have a few suggestions on the cheerleading "crisis" in Newport Beach. First, the administrators should skip cheerleading this year and invest their money in a way that actually benefits students. Open the High School of Second Chances for pushy and overly involved parents. Here moms and dads can pay to relive, or recreate, their own high school fantasies. Moms can be cheerleaders and homecoming queens. Competitive dads can try to be the superjock they think their kids should be. While their parents are busy, their kids can finally concentrate on what is really important: growing into responsible and mature adults.[19]

But it is not just cheerleading parents whose shallowness is highlighted in the above commentaries. Cheerleaders themselves are often associated with shallowness and narcissism. Supposedly, they are so egocentric that they even lose track of the game for which they are cheering, as the following critical cheer reflects:

Totally, for sure, I just got a manicure.
The sun, up there, is bleaching out my hair.
My makeup is smearing; I just lost an earring.
33–44, I don't know the stinking score.
Go, go, fight, fight!
Gee, I hope I look alright.

This same complaint has been made about professional cheerleaders. Scott Ostler, writing in 1994, considers the role of professional cheerleaders who are so caught up in being the center of attention that they actually detract from the game:

When it's a good game, the cheerleaders get in the way. At the Forum years ago, the Lakers went on a hellacious 14–0 run, and the other team's coach frantically called timeout. The crowd, worked into a frenzy by Magic and Showtime, went nuts. For about four seconds. Then the disco music started and the Laker Girls ran onto the court, an acre of womanhood in two square yards of Spandex.

The forum fell silent, except for the pounding disco beat and from the stands, the occasional growl or whimper. The fans not only stopped cheering, they almost stopped breathing. There's an irony for you: cheering stopped cold by cheerleaders.[20]

"Give a cheer for good looks. Plan your beauty routines as carefully as you plan your routines on the fields and look your best from kick-off until the clock runs out!"[21] This advice from an article in *Teen* magazine is what leads many critics of cheerleading to hold such disdain for the activity. They argue that cheerleading, despite claims made to the contrary, has less to do with athleticism and more to do with projecting a particular "look." That look can be seen at any regional or national cheerleading competition where spiral curl ponytails and red lipstick are part of standard uniform wear. As a recent article for coaches in *American Cheerleader Junior* reflects, achieving the right cheerleading look requires not only such essentials as uniforms, bodysuits, bloomers, and healthy snacks but also hair ribbons, bows, makeup, glitter sprays and curlers "for those crazy competition curls."[22] And if you can't get those "crazy competition curls" just right, you can now purchase them from Cheer Curls, a company that specializes in creating customized synthetic wiglets. Made to match each girl's natural hair color and texture, these synthetic curls ensure that the entire squad has the exact same curly ponytail. According to its makers, "THEY WILL NOT FALL OFF no matter how active you are. Tumble, stunt, fly . . . Your curls will stay firmly attached until you are ready to remove them."[23]

> **Synthetic curls ensure that the entire squad has the exact same ponytail.**

Besides narcissism and shallowness, cheerleading is also denigrated because of the enormous cost to participate. Many families make substantial (and some would say, foolish and selfish) financial sacrifices for their daughters to participate in a $1,000-a-year activity that many consider superfluous and more akin to wet T-shirt contests and karaoke. Why not spend money, critics ask, on violin, art, or equestrian lessons—activities that can be continued throughout one's life and represent a higher form of cultural activity? It is certainly disconcerting to many that whereas school orchestras are almost non-existent today in many small towns, 85 girls may show up to try out for 12 slots on a cheerleading squad. These misguided financial priorities are what many would say is the most American facet of cheerleading and perhaps most representative of American culture at large.

Cheerleading: Something So American

After watching *Bring it On* and the ESPN National Cheerleading Championships, a cheerleading online participant, Celso, from Brazil, thought cheerleading looked really cool. However, he notes that in Brazil, "we don't have such a thing. I don't know why. I believe that there you cheer the audience, here for a long time we have our own shouts and everything. It's also something so American that it wouldn't look good as it looks there."[24]

We agree with Celso that cheerleading is "something so American." Yet what is "so American" about it can be read in both positive and negative ways. On the one hand, cheerleading is seen, by many, as a positive representation of the patriotic American, the good citizen, who exudes optimism even in the face of adversity. On the other hand, cheerleading, for many, represents the worst of American culture with its shallow, consumer-oriented, misguided emphasis on crass entertainment over intellectual, cultural pursuits. However, as we all know, the American identity is not monolithic, nor is it fixed. It changes and adopts new ways of being American while still clinging to some of the older American markers. American institutions that can tell us something about ourselves, like jazz, baseball, and cheerleading, are also not static but being created anew with each generation. These shifts, these reconfigurations are very American.

Endnotes

1. Marcie Frazee, "Patriotic Cheers," 3 September 2002, <cheerleader@imagicomm.com> (5 September 2002).
2. Leigh Stope, "Workers Blame Corporate Cheerleading for Huge Retirement Losses with BC-Enron Investigation," *AP Worldstream*, 8 February 2002, <wysiwyg://211/http://web1.epnet.com/cit . . . 04187+sm+KS+so+b+ss+SO+6C48&fn=41&m=43> (23 August 2002).
3. John Strausbaugh, "The Anti-Cheerleader," *The New York Press* 30, 4–10 October 2000, <www.nypress.com/13/40/news&columns/publishing.cfm> (20 January 2003).
4. Kline Boyd, executive vice president/general manager, Varsity Spirit Fashions, interview with author, tape recording, Memphis, Tennessee, 25 June 2002.
5. Shelia Angalet, "Spread Good Cheer," 30 August 2002 <cheerleader@imagicomm.com> (5 September 2002).

6. Boyd, interview.

7. Ginger Hopkins, "That Unchampionship Season," *Seventeen* 38 (January 1979): 115.

8. "President Leads Cheers at Summit," *The Tuscaloosa News* (14 August 2002), 6A.

9. We discuss Radical Cheerleaders in more detail in chapter 2.

10. Radical Cheerleaders, "About Us," <www.geocities.com/radicalcheerleaders/index.html> (12 September 2002).

11. *Bring it On*, Universal Studios, Los Angeles, 2000.

12. "Let's Hear it For Pep Squad Beauty," *Teen* 27 (September 1983): 94.

13. Strausbaugh, "The Anti-Cheerleader."

14. "Jokes About $C Cheerleaders," <http://www.bol.ucla.edu/~ddacumos/cheer.html1> (22 August 2002).

15. For more details on this sensational story, see Anne McDonald Mayer, *Mother Love, Deadly Love* (Secaucus, NJ: Birchlane Press Book, 1992).

16. Gabrielle Cosgriff, "Verna Heath Puts a Murder Plot Behind Her," *People Weekly*, 15–22 March 1999, <http://proquest.umi.com/pqdweb?TS=931895&Fmt=3&Sid=1&Idx=33&Deku=1&ROT=309&Dtp=1> (13 July 1999).

17. Sandy Banks, "Inspiring Tears as Well as Cheer," *Los Angeles Times*, 15 January 2002, <wysiwyg://bodyframe.13/http://ehostvgw2 . . . =34booleanTerm=cheerleading&fuzzyTerm=> (22 May 2002).

18. "Pompomgate Is Not Worth Cheering About," *Los Angeles Times*, 13 January 2002, <wysiwyg://bodyframe.13/http://ehostvgw2 . . . =35booleanTerm=cheerleading&fuzzyTerm=> (22 May 2002).

19. Ibid.

20. Scott Ostler, "Dump the Cheerleaders," *Sport* 85 (August 1994): 20.

21. "Let's Hear it for Pep Squad Beauty," 95.

22. "Leader of the Pack," *American Cheerleader Junior* 3 (Winter 2003): 54.

23. Cheer Curls, 29 October 2002, <www.expage.com/cheercurlz> (16 September 2002).

24. Celso, "New Guy From Brazil!—This is the Tird [sic] Time I Try to Send it," 31 August 2002, <cheerleader@imagicomm.com> (16 September 2002).

▶ **Analyzing the Text**

1. According to Adams and Bettis, to what extent does cheerleading embody a can-do, enthusiastic spirit that is considered a typically American trait?

2. How does cheerleading embody narcissism and shallowness, also considered typically American traits? What examples from the reading do you find most telling regarding these traits?

3. Find the paragraph on page 236 that begins, "In the aftermath of the September 11 tragedy, . . ." What is the main message of this paragraph? What are Adams and Bettis saying about why diverse groups have adopted cheerleading to communicate messages to the public?

4. The authors write, "American institutions that can tell us something about ourselves, like jazz, baseball, and cheerleading, are also not static but being created anew with each generation. These shifts, these reconfigurations, are very American." Based on this reading, how is cheerleading being recreated as a new American tradition? What does your own experience tell you about how cheerleading fits into contemporary American traditions? What does this suggest about today's mainstream culture?

5. **Interrogating Assumptions.** According to this essay, how do the traditions and techniques of cheerleading promote unity within a community? Is there potential for cheerleading traditions to create an us-versus-them mentality? Why or why not?

▶ **Writing about Cultural Practices**

6. The impact of cheerleading—its techniques and traditions—has spread beyond sporting arenas. As Adams and Bettis observe, "Diverse groups of Americans with diverse causes and ways of presenting themselves have adopted cheerleading as the vehicle for their message." For this assignment, you will test the authors' claims about cheerleading by creating a cheer campaign for a campus or community organization and writing a critical analysis about the experience. To begin, work in groups to identify four or five campus or community organizations and, choosing one, create a cheer campaign for it that accomplishes one of the following goals.

   • Raises public awareness about a need on campus or in the community.

   • Raises funds for a nonprofit group or charity.

   • Promotes an organization or event by educating people about it.

   For your cheer campaign, create a document—flyer, poster, mailer, information sheet, etc.—that could be distributed to your intended audience. To help with this task, collect sample fundraising or promotional flyers found on campus and analyze how they use cheerleading techniques. After you've designed your document, draft a critical analysis that considers the following questions.

   • What goal or message are you conveying in your document? How did you use cheerleading techniques to accomplish this goal or communicate this message?

   • What were the benefits of using cheerleading techniques to educate people about a problem or need in the community? What were the limitations or drawbacks?

   • What goal or message is conveyed in the sample documents you located? Who is their intended audience? What cheerleading techniques do you notice being used? How effective are these documents in conveying their message or meeting their goals? What details in the documents lead you to your evaluation?

   • Considering your experience designing a cheer campaign as well as your analysis of the sample documents, how has cheerleading's impact on American culture spread beyond sporting arenas?

Brent Staples, **The Star-Spangled Hard Hat**

An editorial writer for the *New York Times* since 1983, Brent Staples holds a PhD in psychology from the University of Chicago. His articles and essays have appeared in the *Nation*, the *New York Review of Books*, and other magazines. Staples holds the Anisfield Wolff Book Award for his memoir, *Parallel Time: Growing Up in Black and White* (2000). "The Star-Spangled Hard Hat," originally published in the *New York Times* in 2001, is about patriotism and the meaning of the flag during the period following the attack on the World Trade Center on September 11, 2001. Like many communities around the country that fall, Staples's neighborhood displayed a variety of American flags.

> ▶ **Mapping Your Reading**
>
> As you read, notice how Staples compares attitudes about patriotism and the flag from the 1960s era of protest over the Vietnam War with today's post-September 11 attitudes. What traditions surround displays of the American flag? How are these traditions changing? How do these changes represent Americans' changing notions of patriotism?

The trade center disaster came to my neighborhood as a dark thunderhead of smoke that boiled over the river into Brooklyn, showering the streets with burning papers from the desks of the dead. Charred documents were still falling when the first American flag went up along our street. Within 48 hours this tree-lined block of nineteenth-century brownstones was flying more flags than it ever has. The flags have already created a new subset of petty crime. Like bicycles, they get stolen, leaving their owners to rustle up new ones in the midst of a flag shortage.

My wife is a flag purist. Tattered, ill-kept banners offend her. She tolerates the plastic, paper, and synthetic flags that have blossomed since September, but does not view them as "real." A "real" flag for my wife is made of heavy-gauge cotton, sewn together piece by piece so that the seams are visible between the stripes and the flag furls gracefully. No seams, no authenticity.

> The flags that speak to me most come in non-traditional, Pop Art designs.

I was a teenager during the Vietnam War, when the meaning of the flag was hotly disputed, and never became a flag purist. The flags that speak to me most

---

For another reading on American symbols, see Adams and Bettis, page 233.—EDS.

come in nontraditional, Pop Art designs. They were regarded as desecration when they first appeared in the 1960s but are now viewed simply as flags of another color. In my neighborhood I've seen a flag used as a garland, snaked through the railings of window grates and fire escapes, and a flag improvised from red, white, and blue bandannas. There is a spectacular flag painted across the full width of a house with glossy paint like the moist icing on a cake, with chrome yellow stripes instead of white ones. The composition speaks of patriotism with a postmodern twist.

Since September 11 conservative critics have been saying that the 60s generation has finally come round to a patriotism that it despised in the Vietnam era. But this generation did not reject patriotism. It rejected the notion that there was only one way to be patriotic. The protest era broadened the definition of patriotism and created a new, less formal identity for the American flag.

The psychedelic-flag hard hat that was worn by Dick Cheney when he visited the trade center site shows how design liberties with the flag have been embraced by groups that would have reviled them in the past. Hats like the vice president wore would have been unwelcome—and might even have gotten you roughed up—on construction sites during the late 60s. Then, the term "hard hat" referred to the working-class white ethnics who were soon to bolt the Democratic Party for Ronald Reagan. The clashes between hard hats and antiwar demonstrators were particularly nasty in New York, especially during the building of the World Trade Center. The hard hats worn when I was a shipyard worker in high school were buckets, in basic colors. The flag decals that appeared on them later in the decade were in response to criticism of the country's policy in Vietnam. A longhair who was smart went the other way when he saw a group of flagheads bunched together.

The protest era broadened the definition of patriotism.

I never burned a flag, never saw one burned. But as a teenager growing up around the shipyards on the Delaware River, I was threatened with tire irons by angry dockworkers who were incensed by flag clothing, most notably the flag that an eccentric friend made into a sash and wore to a Jimi Hendrix concert.

The art critic Jed Perl of the *New Republic* has described this as partly a fashion issue, arguing that young people wished to see the flag "as camp, as Kitsch, or retro chic." But the thing went deeper than that. When the rock diva Grace Slick was photographed nude, wrapped in a flag, during the Vietnam War she personified a generation's desire to seize ownership of a symbol from which we were profoundly estranged.

As a black teenager with a huge cloud of hair, I would have avoided a flag-draped street like the one I live on now, wanting no trouble with the kind of people who flew the colors from their homes. But cruising the same streets today, I note the funky, psychedelic banners among the "real" ones and understand that what we have now is a spacious, postmodern patriotism.

▶ Analyzing the Text

1. According to Staples, what is the relationship between the flag and patriotism? How does the acceptance of different versions of the flag demonstrate a change in how we define patriotism?

2. Why is the hard hat an important symbol for Staples? How does it represent changing attitudes about patriotism and about the flag?

3. **Interrogating Assumptions.** How would Staples likely respond to the third assumption discussed on page 181? According to Staples, how can the very symbols that are meant to promote unity create an us-versus-them backlash?

4. In Staples's view, how do changing attitudes about the flag represent "a spacious, postmodern patriotism"?

▶ Writing about Cultural Practices

5. Both Staples's "The Star-Spangled Hard Hat" and Natalie Guice Adams and Pamela J. Bettis's "Cheerleader! An American Icon" (p. 233) investigate the impact of powerful symbols of patriotism on everyday life. Both essays demonstrate the fact that people seek out experiences or symbols that bind them together to promote a sense of identification with a group or place. For this assignment, identify a common object or practice that symbolizes American patriotism. You might choose yellow ribbons, parades, or the use of red, white, and blue color-combinations on a range of everyday objects. After choosing one object or practice, write a critical analysis in which you answer the following questions.

   - How does this object or practice represent a tradition connected to patriotism?

   - To what extent does this particular tradition promote a sense of unity among people? What values or beliefs does this tradition promote?

   - How might this tradition create an us-versus-them mindset among people? What are the consequences of such a mindset? In what ways can or do traditions actually promote disunity or marginalize people?

   - What message does this tradition convey about the meaning of patriotism?

American Monuments: The Vietnam Veterans Memorial vs. The Tribute in Light

Many public memorials use traditional designs to commemorate national events and in particular to praise military victories. The Vietnam Veterans Memorial, however, broke from tradition. Designed by 21-year-old Yale undergraduate Maya Lin and completed in 1982, the "Wall of Names" (above) does not declare winners. Instead, the memorial, made of polished black granite and cut into the landscape of the Mall in Washington, D.C., simply inscribes the names of the dead. Lin writes of the Wall, "These names, seemingly infinite in number, convey the sense of overwhelming numbers . . . this memorial is meant not as a monument to

the individual, but rather as a memorial to the men and women who died during this war, as a whole."

If the Wall changed how memorials could be designed, the Tribute in Light (at right) represents a different sort of transformation. This temporary memorial, displayed in 2002, used 88 searchlights to create two vertical columns of light on the site of the September 11, 2001, attack on the World Trade Center. It was conceived by two artists, Paul Myoda and Julian LaVerdiere, who wanted the memorial to "offer consolation or a sense of security or hope." It was originally proposed as the "Phantom

Towers": "Those towers are like ghost limbs; we can feel them even though they're not there anymore," said LaVerdiere.

1. What do these images suggest about the traditions surrounding public memorials? What do they convey about how cultural attitudes toward memorials have changed?

2. How would you compare either of these memorials to public memorials on your campus or in your community? Conduct some research about a local memorial to learn what it memorializes as well as how it was conceived and designed. What is the meaning or significance of this memorial to the community? What traditions or values is it meant to represent?

3. To what extent is permanence no longer a requirement of modern memorials? Both the Tribute in Light and the essay "A Fitting Memorial" by Jenn Shreve (see p. 248) illustrate that temporary memorials are increasingly popular. Can you think of other examples of temporary memorials? What cultural attitudes might this trend convey?

Jenn Shreve, **A Fitting Memorial: The Commemorative T-Shirt**

Jenn Shreve's articles on technology, media, and popular culture have appeared in *Wired, Slate, Salon,* and *Mother Jones.* In her essay "A Fitting Memorial," which originally appeared in *Slate* in 2003, she examines the growing number of memorial T-shirts that have arisen in the post-September 11 world to commemorate national and personal grief.

> ▶ Mapping Your Reading
>
> While previous readings in this chapter investigate the role of long-standing traditions, this essay explores a new tradition in American culture—the wearing of memorial T-shirts to commemorate someone who has died tragically. As you read, underline passages where Shreve tries to explain what this recent trend means. How did this counter-tradition get its start? What is it about memorial T-shirts that people find appealing?

T-shirts have been used to commemorate everything from rock concerts to company picnics. Usually, their seams fall apart or their print fades right around the time you no longer want to admit you're old enough to have seen Talking Heads live or that you once thought wearing a picture of the Eiffel Tower was in any way sophisticated. And so, the shirt gets thrown in the trash or donated to the Salvation Army to make room in your overstuffed dresser.

But many people have a new kind of T-shirt in their drawer that they might be more reluctant to throw away: the memorial tee, worn by relatives or friends of someone whose life has come to a premature and violent end. The memorial T-shirt commemorates tragic deaths—suicides, murders, car accidents, terrorism. In other words, you aren't likely to make a memorial T-shirt for your 97-year-old grandpa who passed away in his sleep, but you might have one printed for your young niece who was killed by a drunk driver.

The strange thing about the trend is that tees are the ultimate casual attire, made for spinning class, the mall, yard work, Disneyland—they're not exactly considered appropriate funeral attire. At best, a T-shirt will hold up for a few years, whereas we usually think of memorials as being enduring. So, how did this trend begin? West Coast gangsters are believed to have started the memorial-tee trend in the early '90s as a way to remember slain gang members, most notable among them being rapper and movie actor Tupac Shakur. In the '90s, the practice of wearing the tees grew popular among urban minorities, especially teenagers. It is now so common that a friend of mine who works for the public school district in Oakland, California, where there were 117 murders last year, told me that students often say, "Don't make me put your face on a T-shirt." The Mountain View Funeral Home in Tacoma, Washington, notes that wearing a memorial T-shirt to a funeral, as teenagers often do, is an acceptable alternative to traditional expressions of grief and sympathy.

September 11 was the "tipping point" that pushed memorial T-shirts into mainstream visual vernacular. In New York and Washington, D.C., people began wearing T-shirts memorializing slain friends, family members, police officers, and firefighters. In many ways, these standard memorial tees resembled the posters that were placed around New York City when friends and families were still searching for their loved ones. In the aftermath of 9/11, many people bought T-shirts featuring the popular "crying eagle," the New York Fire Department logo, or the American flag, turning a once-ironic act into a demonstration of solidarity and mourning. (In 1968, when Abby Hoffman transformed an American flag into a shirt, he was arrested and tried for desecration. Today the Stars and Stripes are slapped onto everything from men's boxer shorts to women's string bikinis.) During the war in Iraq, the flag tee-as-memorial was adopted by the families of slain soldiers. When Army Spc. Larry K. Brown was killed in Iraq last April, his family (including his mother and father) wore T-shirts depicting Old Glory to the funeral.

West Coast gangsters are believed to have started the trend as a way to remember slain gang members.

The typical memorial T-shirt displays a homespun pixilated photograph of the deceased, the kind you might have put on a mug or a magnet when they were alive. Accompanying the image is often a message such as "You'll be missed," or simply the date of death. Friends of victims of the Chicago nightclub stampede, earlier this year, wore shirts bearing photographs with the words "In Loving Memory" and "The Good Die Young." Nowadays, most custom T-shirt shops can cheaply print memorial tees. At $10 to $15 per shirt, or around $3.50 if ordered in bulk, they're less expensive than a bouquet of lilies or many teddy bears, which may explain some of their appeal to teens. Fancier renditions of the memorial tee may use an illustration in addition to a photograph, such as those created for Brian Deneke, a punk who was murdered, or instead of a photograph, as was the case with tees for Brian E. Sweeney, a New York firefighter who died on September 11.

In some cases, the T-shirt has a utilitarian secondary purpose. Web sites, like those for Sweeney and Deneke, sell the shirts in order to raise money for

The back of this T-shirt honoring Brian Deneke, a teen murdered in Amarillo, Texas, reads, "We're at war and you're not paying attention!! December 12, 1997."

memorial funds. The funeral tee can communicate a political message, as is the case with services that customize SIDS shirts with the name and date of birth and death of your infant or those sold on the Matthew Shepard Foundation Web site. In other cases, memorial tees are explicitly intended to create a sense of solidarity among wearers, such as the "We are Columbine" tees that Columbine High School students wore when they returned to classes or those worn following the sudden death of pop singer Aaliyah, uniting strangers in grief in much the same way fans bond during a sporting event.

Still, the memorial tee raises an obvious question: What good is a memorial if it's not lasting? For those of us who were raised believing that proper funeral attire consists of somber Sunday dress and that a proper memorial should outlast the life it represents, the notion of remembering somebody with a plain old T-shirt can seem downright disrespectful. But in many ways, the memorial tee is a modern iteration of the lost practice of wearing mourning clothes for days or years after a loved one has died. Long after

What good is a memorial if it's not lasting?

the funeral suits and dresses have been returned to the closet, a T-shirt continues to show the world that grief and loss continue. Obviously a memorial T-shirt isn't meant to replace the stone monument on a plot of green grass, the engraved urn, or scenic bench. It simply adds a new dimension to the traditional memorial. Like grief and life itself, it isn't meant to last forever.

▶ Analyzing the Text

1. Memorials serve specific and sometimes controversial purposes. According to Shreve, who originated this counter-tradition of wearing memorial T-shirts?

2. **Interrogating Assumptions.** Traditionally, monuments and memorials act as a repository for memory of a person or event. According to this essay, how do T-shirt memorials serve this purpose? In what ways do they counter more conventional or traditional memorials? To what extent do they challenge the assumption that traditions are long-standing and static practices?

3. In what ways does wearing these T-shirts give people a sense of unity?

4. In the final paragraph of this essay, Shreve asks, "What good is a memorial if it's not lasting?" Reread this paragraph. What does the author suggest the T-shirt memorials say about contemporary practices and attitudes regarding memorials?

5. What has happened as memorial T-shirts have become popularized by the mainstream? When did this begin to happen? How, in Shreve's view, has their growing popularity changed the meaning or intent of these T-shirts?

▶ Writing about Cultural Practices

6. "A Fitting Memorial" investigates the development of a counter-tradition surrounding the practice of commemorating a person or event. Memorials are intended to be reminders of a person and often celebrate that person's life or work. Your task is to design a nontraditional memorial for a person or an important event from your community. Like the T-shirt memorial described in Shreve's essay, your memorial should not rely on typical practices or designs. Instead, reinvent the idea of a memorial without losing sight of commemorating a person's life. To begin, identify a person or event in your community to memorialize. Second, in order to understand the traditions you are countering in this assignment, study some existing memorials in your community. What characteristics do these traditional memorials share? Who do they commemorate? What particular values and beliefs are highlighted by these memorials? (For instance, memorials to veterans highlight service to country and other patriotic themes.)

Create a visual representation of your memorial, making as detailed a drawing as possible. Draft a critical analysis of your alternate memorial to accompany your design. Consider the following questions as you write.

- Why did you choose to memorialize this person or event? Does this person or event represent the kind of person or event that is not typically memorialized? Why or why not?
- What is the rationale behind your design decisions?
- What response are people meant to have when they visit or view your memorial?
- In what ways does your proposed memorial differ from a traditional memorial? What values or message are you able to convey with your alternate memorial that could not be conveyed as well by a traditional one?

Gamaliel Padilla, **Moshing Etiquette**

Gamaliel Padilla is a contributing writer to MundoRockero.com. Her article "Moshing Etiquette," published in *Dig*, the California State University–Long Beach monthly magazine, is a humorous essay in which a formal code of behavior is prescribed for a surprising venue—a mosh pit at a rock concert.

Etiquette is a code that defines what behavior is considered "the norm" or conventional by a particular culture or social group. It prescribes and restricts how people interact with each other in a given setting. Breaches of etiquette can lead to misunderstandings, and can even cause hurt feelings, grief, and public disgrace. As the authors of the Wikipedia.com entry on etiquette state, "One can reasonably view etiquette as the minimal politics required to avoid major conflict in polite society."

> ▶ **Mapping Your Reading**
>
> This reading offers a set of social standards for the aggressive style of dancing during a rock concert known as moshing. How has moshing become a tradition at rock music venues? How does Padilla use etiquette conventions to construct a code of conduct for moshers? What do you find surprising about this version of etiquette?

A recent study by the American Music Recreation Foundation suggested moshing is the top contributor of bruises to the upper torso region of concert goers. While the study is in fact a fallacy, I wouldn't necessarily disregard the fact that moshing can often hurt. In order to prevent you and yours from being swallowed in the pit of sweat and cheap black vinyl, I've put together, through the means of careful observation and half-assed assumptions, a few rules on proper moshing etiquette for all music fans to follow.

Every concert-goer must at all times remain alert for a mosh formation. A mosh pit is initially started by innocuous shoves from one individual to another. It progresses, growing in force and strength, ultimately leading to the participation of others in what many would deem a carnal practice, traditionally in the form of a pit.

Upon reaching the pit, participants must assess the movement of the moshing. That is, if people are pushing in a clockwise motion, participants should follow. If

Do not attempt to go against the flow of the pit. Salmon do this against the tide to lay eggs, then die. Learn from the salmon.

the flow is moving from outer to inner circle, so should you. Do not attempt to go against the flow of the pit. Salmon do this against the tide to lay eggs, then die. Learn from the salmon.

Once in the pit, you may get over-heated and eventually reek a stench so foul even Europeans would protest. In consideration for the Western Hemisphere, please deodorize your own pits before you leave the house and refrain from removing your shirts. Leave the shirt removal to the artists.

All should be aware that injuries may occur. Therefore, those attendees scared or angry the pit is forming within their space should suck it up and move away. The collective within the pit should comply with the following unwritten rules: 1) no targeted rushes towards specific individuals, 2) man-down assistance, and 3) no intentional attempts to inflict pain. Lastly, those wishing to crowd surf within the pit must also comply with weight and height restrictions. If you're 6′1″ and 310 pounds, keep your feet on the floor. Most people have grown very fond of their necks. Also, surf is a metaphorical term. There is no actual swimming in the pit, so there is no need to kick. Kicking may lead to you walking out with only tube socks, compliments of your fellow moshers.

As for the surrounding observers, you must learn to coexist with the pit. Keep your ice in your cup and find a good spot to watch the show. If a mosher happens to run into you, don't take offense.

Everyone should be allowed to enjoy themselves at a show and unfortunately, there is only so much beer to go around, so it's up to concert-goers to make it lively and entertaining in their own way. The coexistence of the rowdy mosher and the laid back observer creates an interesting dynamic. With the addition of good performers and good music, you'll have a memorable night that doesn't include three stitches above your left eye.

▶ **Analyzing the Text**

1. How does Padilla characterize appropriate moshing behavior?

2. According to Padilla, what types of behavior would be considered a breach of etiquette among moshers?

3. How does Padilla's moshing etiquette reflect an underlying ethical code of behavior that is shared by people who attend rock concerts?

4. The word "etiquette" often makes people think of a set of overly formal rules for eating soup or selecting the correct fork at the dinner table. The connotation is that etiquette enforces obsessive rules about small matters—rules that define a strict yet meaningless protocol of how people should interact. How do Padilla's etiquette rules counter this view of the term?

5. **Connecting to Another Reading.** Jenn Shreve's essay, "A Fitting Memorial" (p. 248), and Padilla's essay both describe new traditions in American popular culture. What underlying social values and beliefs are described in each of these readings? What attitudes do the two traditions described have in common? What do they reflect about this particular cultural moment?

Writing about Cultural Practices

6. As Padilla's essay points out, there are many emerging or new forums for social interaction for which we have no guide or shared sense of acceptable behavior. Follow Padilla's example and create your own etiquette to describe appropriate behavior for a social setting that has recently emerged. Before drafting your own rules of etiquette, you might study more examples of social etiquette, such as those offered by Etiquette Grrls (www.etiquettegrrls.com) or Miss Manners (syndicated in many national newspapers). As you write, consider the following questions.

   - Who is the main audience for your proposed new etiquette?

   - What is the purpose of your new etiquette? What type of behavior do you want to curtail? What type of behavior do you want to encourage? Why?

   - How would you sell the idea of your new etiquette to your intended audience? Why should they agree with you and your ideas for a guide for behavior?

Since 1991, the Canadian-based Adbusters organization has been promoting an annual Buy Nothing Day as a chance to "expose the environmental and ethical consequences of consumerism."

Mixing Words and Images

INVENTING A NEW HOLIDAY

This chapter asks you to investigate the role of traditions in contemporary America. Some of the readings—"A Wobegon Holiday Dinner," "The Rituals of Black Hair Culture," and Jon Stewart's "Commencement Address"—reflect on the purpose and power of long-standing traditions. Still others—"Bowing Out," "A Fitting Memorial," and "Moshing Etiquette"—examine how traditions get their start, often as counter-traditions.

Your task is to create a new holiday for your campus or local community, complete with its own traditions, rituals, and customs. The purpose of this assignment is for you to investigate the connections between traditions and the values or beliefs that push them into existence. To this end, the holiday you invent must originate from existing campus or community practices and values. Although your holiday doesn't have to be serious, the values that anchor it must be meaningful to your audience.

To begin, identify an event, a person, or a practice that you feel deserves to have its own holiday. What should be celebrated or honored that isn't being celebrated currently? Once you've determined what your new holiday will be, design a poster that both introduces the holiday and invites people to participate in its traditions, rituals, or customs. Then, write a descriptive analysis in which you explain why you created this poster this way, for this audience.

Designing a Poster for Your New Holiday

The size of your poster may vary, but make it large enough to include the following visual elements.

- The name and purpose of your holiday.
- A logo, icon, or other image that symbolizes this new holiday. All major holidays have an image or icon that symbolizes the meaning of the day. Your new holiday needs its own.
- A blend of visual and written elements that introduces the traditions, rituals, or customs of your new holiday and invites the community to participate in them.

Drafting Your Descriptive Analysis Essay

After you have created your poster, draft an essay to accompany it that answers the following questions.

- What traditions, rituals, or customs mark this holiday?
- Who are the main participants in this holiday? Who benefits most from it?
- What wishes or desires of the community are expressed by these traditions?
- What values or beliefs are promoted by these traditions?
- How does the tradition reflect the attitudes and needs of your campus or community?

1. Rocking the Mainstream: An Analysis of Counter-Traditions

Counter-traditions oppose or act as alternatives to the traditions of mainstream culture. At least three of the readings in this chapter—"The Rituals of Black Hair Culture," "A Fitting Memorial," and "Moshing Etiquette"—consider the role of counter-traditions. For this assignment, you will investigate a counter-tradition that you feel offers a meaningful alternative or response to mainstream American culture.

To begin, identify a counter-tradition that you are familiar with. It is not necessary that you agree with the values of the counter-tradition you choose; however, you need to be curious enough about this counter-tradition to want to learn more about it and to be able to represent it fairly. What qualifies as a counter-tradition? Any activity that makes a conscious effort to define itself as an alternative to the American mainstream constitutes a counter-tradition. There are many examples of counter-traditions in music, for instance. Also, on your college campus there may be groups and organizations that define themselves as counter to mainstream campus culture. You might look for non-university-sanctioned activities surrounding official events, or for underground magazines, websites, or clubs. Once you identify a counter-tradition, investigate how it started, who participates in it, and what aspect of mainstream culture the counter-tradition is a response to.

As you write your critical analysis, consider the following questions.

- What is the history of the counter-tradition you have identified?
- What rituals, practices, or events constitute the counter-tradition?
- How does the counter-tradition promote unity among the people participating in it? What values and beliefs does it support?
- What makes this tradition a counter-tradition? What aspects of mainstream American culture does it oppose or wish to create an alternative to?
- What is the role or importance of counter-traditions in American culture?

2. Defining America: An Analysis of Civic Rituals and Public Spectacles

In "Cheerleading: An American Icon," the authors argue that Americans "love a parade and public spectacle." From celebrations of family events to cheerleading to even the somber act of wearing memorial T-shirts, we regularly encounter and participate in many civic rituals and public spectacles that bear a particularly American stamp. Your task for this assign-

ON THE WEB
For help with these assignments, go to Chapter 3,
bedfordstmartins.com/remix

ment is to attend a public event on your campus or in your local community and analyze how its rituals or spectacle reflect or define American values and beliefs.

To begin, identify a public spectacle at which people share in specific civic rituals. A spectacle can be any public performance or display that is large or lavish, such as a pep rally, parade, fair, public concert, or holiday celebration. Attend the event as an observer and take notes. Pay attention to the rituals surrounding the event and collect any flyers or other materials distributed at the event.

As you draft your essay, consider the following questions.

- What is the purpose of the event? What occasion does it mark?

- Who participates in this event? Who comes to watch? What do the participants appear to have in common?

- What specific rituals are important to this event? What values or beliefs do they convey? What details about the event lead you to this conclusion?

- To what extent do these rituals reflect a connection to the past? How do they reflect attitudes of the present?

- Do these rituals promote unity among the participants and observers? If so, how? In what ways might this event marginalize people?

- What is it about this event and its rituals that makes them uniquely American?

3. Interrogating Assumptions: How Do Traditions Define Us?

The introduction of this chapter explains three commonly held assumptions about traditions:

> Traditions are long-standing and static practices.
>
> Traditions preserve an authentic version of the past.
>
> Traditions promote unity.

Each of the readings and visual images in this chapter questions one or more of these assumptions, asking how traditions influence our behavior and beliefs, how they represent the past and how they evolve to reflect who we are now. For this assignment, develop a critical analysis of how two or three of the readings interrogate one of these assumptions.

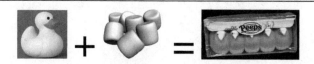

the ONION®

| VOLUME 35 ISSUE 13 | AMERICA'S FINEST NEWS SOURCE™ | 8–14 APRIL 1999 |

Romantic-Comedy Behavior Gets Real-Life Man Arrested

TORRANCE, CA—Denny Marzano, a 28-year-old Torrance man, was arrested Monday for engaging in the type of behavior found in romantic comedies.

Marzano was taken into custody after violating a restraining order filed against him by Kellie Hamilton, 25, an attractive, unmarried kindergarten teacher who is new to the L.A. area. According to Hamilton, Marzano has stalked her for the past two months, spying on her, tapping her phone, serenading her with The Carpenters' "Close To You" at her place of employment, and tricking her into boarding Caribbean-bound jets.

Hamilton made the call to police at approximately 7:30 p.m., when she discovered that the bearded cable repairman she had let into her apartment was actually Marzano in disguise.

"Thank God he's in custody, and this nightmarish ordeal is finally over," said Hamilton, a single mother struggling to raise an adorable, towheaded boy all alone in the big city. "I repeatedly told him I wasn't interested, but he just kept resorting to crazier and crazier schemes to make me fall in love with him."

Marzano, who broke his leg last week falling off a ladder leaning against Hamilton's second-story bedroom window, said he was "extremely surprised" that his plan to woo Hamilton had failed.

"She was supposed to hate me at first but gradually be won over by my incredible persistence, telling me that no one has ever gone to such wild lengths to win her love," Marzano said. "But for some reason, her irritation never turned to affection."

In addition to the stalking charges, Marzano is accused of framing Stuart Polian, a handsome Pasadena attorney and chief competitor for Hamilton's hand, for arson. Marzano denied the charge.

"While it is true that I would love to have seen my main romantic rival out of the picture, I did not burn down that animal shelter and try to pin it on Mr. Polian," Marzano said. "I believe and have always believed I can win Kellie's love without resorting to such illegalities."

Marzano had been arrested for engaging in romantic-comedy behavior on five previous occasions. The most recent arrest came in May 1998, when he pretended to be a confession-booth priest in the hopes of manipulating a Fresno, CA, woman into unwittingly revealing her love for him. ∅

Above: Police officers take Denny Marzano into custody following his latest romantic-comedy-like crime.

or, what's love got to do with it?

4 Romance

Examining the Everyday
Romance and Ladders

This piece of satire was published in the *Onion* (onion.com), a magazine that uses scathing humor to comment on current events, cultural trends, and human behavior. In this fake news story, the *Onion* writers critique popular notions of romance, especially those promoted by Hollywood romantic comedies. The basic plot of a romantic comedy is that two people meet, are clearly attracted to each other, but for various reasons do not get involved. Typically, the two separate for a period of time, during which one partner realizes they are meant for each other. After a series of elaborate attempts by that partner to gain the other's affection, along with plenty of coincidence, they meet again, pronounce their love, and go on to live happily ever after. Some popular romantic comedies include *When Harry Met Sally, Sleepless in Seattle, The Wedding Planner*, and *50 First Dates*. Reread the *Onion* article, and you will undoubtedly notice that the writers borrow character details and

© Royalty-Free/CORBIS

plot points from the romantic-comedy genre to tell a crime story.

This story offers a good starting point for this chapter because it brings to light some popular assumptions about the search for love and romance and offers an opportunity for us to reconsider cultural notions of romantic love and behavior. For example, one assumption about romantic love played on by the *Onion* is that instant attraction or "chemistry," whether felt by one or both people, equals love. Other assumptions played on are that love will overcome all obstacles, and that persistence and elaborate gestures (the ladder to the window, for example) are always welcomed and rewarded. Skim through the article again, and you will recognize these and other assumptions that people make about romance, including the assumption that love can make us crazy.

For this initial assignment, you will begin examining cultural assumptions about romance by identifying examples of "romantic love" or romantic behavior from the popular media. Concentrate on finding examples of romantic love or romantic behavior in advertisements (print or online). Choose two examples that you think are most interesting and, in one page, write a description that answers these questions.

- What makes these images romantic? How do they represent romance?

- Who is the presumed audience of the ads?

- What do the writers of the ads assume about their audience?

As you write, be sure to pay attention to details in the images and the text of the ads to help answer these questions. Finally, add a paragraph that answers this question:

- If these examples show what we think of when we think of romance, what types of behaviors or actions, or kinds of people, are often left out of the picture?

"The Truth about Love at First Sight"—*Ebony*

"Bring Out Her Wild Side"—*Men's Health*

"Find Your Best Match!"—*Glamour*

"What's Your Sexual IQ?"—*Esquire*

"Turn a Friend into a Lover"—*Details*

"Sexy Secrets for Staying in Love Forever"—*Redbook*

These headlines from popular magazines highlight the deep interest (and even fascination) with which Americans approach the topics of love, sex, and romance. The reader's attention can hardly turn elsewhere, bombarded as it is with images and messages about romance in the popular media—from songs on the radio to love stories on television to pop-up ads for online dating to advertising that uses seduction to sell everything from perfume to SUVs.

But what exactly is this thing called love? And what does love mean now? In this chapter, you will be asked to consider: "What's at stake in the way Americans define romance?"

To answer this question, you will first explore some of the most commonly accepted assumptions people share about romance. Foremost among these assumptions is the notion that of all the possible forms love takes—puppy love, platonic love, or lust— one form stands above the rest: true love. True love is a common label for describing the ultimate form of love, one that combines passion and friendship and elevates them to a kind of spiritual union between two people. In countless love stories and movies, we have been educated in romance and true love. From Helen of Troy and Paris in the ancient Greek epic, *The Iliad,* to Romeo and Juliet in Shakespeare's tragedy, to Ross and Rachel on the television show *Friends,* true love is seen as beautiful, sensual, and somehow fated to be (even if it's not fated to last).

The readings in this chapter will challenge you to reflect on the cultural assumptions built into how we define romance or true love— and how our expectations about romance shape our relationships with others. Following is a brief overview of some popular, idealized notions about romance. Each of these assumptions emphasizes one aspect of love over others, yet these assumptions can overlap at times.

Assumption 1

Love conquers all.

According to this assumption, true love will survive in the face of any differences or obstructions that could potentially keep two people apart. The idea that is central here is that nothing else matters if there is love, *true* love. On some level, this perspective suggests that love exists on a spiritual plain that rises above the mundane or the everyday. True love, in this view, is almost beyond human control. Rather, it is ruled by fate.

In movies and fairy tales, there are many examples of true love conquering all. Consider the stories of Cinderella and Snow White. Here are classic tales that illustrate that true love is fated and that nothing—not poverty in Cinderella's case nor death in Snow White's—can stop true love from its course. Although most people don't believe that their lives should follow the plots of fairy tales, the messages and morals of the stories told to us as children may continue to have an impact on us as adults. Their popularity has endured even in modern times, and updated versions of the Cinderella story are retold every few years (some recent examples: *Pretty Woman, The Princess Bride, The Princess Diaries,* and *The Prince and Me*).

In the realm of the real world, the popular media values stories that offer examples of how true love overcomes all obstacles. The story of the late Christopher Reeve is one such example. A tragic horseback riding accident left the movie star paralyzed from the neck down, and yet, both he and his wife explained in interviews that the accident brought them closer together as they combined forces to campaign for a cure for spinal injuries.

On the one hand, the assumption that love overcomes all obstacles can lead people to develop a positive perspective toward romance and love—namely, that love can tackle problems. When jobs or family background or circumstances get in the way of a romantic relationship, some couples find a way to stay connected, even when distance, illness, differences in backgrounds, or other pressures bear down on them. The Christopher Reeve story is one well-known example of the positive benefit of this assumption. In fact, many people in love have experienced what it means to endure a hardship or to fight the disapproval of others in order to stay together. They believe that such obstacles become insignificant in the face of true love.

On the other hand, believing that true love conquers all can lead people to conclude wrongly that all differences between two people can or should be overlooked. For example, when two people don't share common ground on the issues, beliefs, or values that matter most to them, it is foolish to overlook such differences. Too often people chalk up serious differences as insignificant because they believe love will prevail in the end. This can lead people to ignore anything about their partner that does not mesh with their values, lifestyle, or belief system.

A second downside to buying into this assumption is that it can lead people to give problems a misguided place of importance in their relationships. Believing that love conquers all can lead people to think that love isn't love unless it's difficult—in other words, some people equate the presence of obstacles or a struggle of some kind with true love. Without the presence of an obstacle, such relationships may grow unfocused and fizzle out.

What questions can you ask to uncover the benefits and limitations of the assumption that love conquers all obstacles?

- How do classic themes about love from fairy tales and other popular stories influence how people develop their own expectations about romance?
- What role do conflicts play for the people in the love stories we encounter on television, at the movies, or in novels? How do conflicts come to define these fictional relationships?

Assumption 2

"Chemistry" = love.

Without a spark, can there be true love? According to this assumption, the answer is no. Chemistry is another term people use to describe the connection between physical attraction and love. Good chemistry can equal love. At the very least, it leads people to want to see each other again. But a lack of chemistry leads people to say, politely, "I just couldn't see myself with him" or "I'm just not that into her." And so the possibility for a relationship is not explored beyond that initial point.

The importance of physical attraction in finding love is reinforced to us in marketing pitches. Spend a little time paging through your favorite magazines and ignore everything but the advertising copy. You are likely to find that most ads assume that readers or viewers, with the help of various consumer products, seek to spark attraction that may lead to love.

Is the spark of attraction based in biology? Benedict Carey raises this question in "The Brain in Love" (p. 341). Scientists have learned that the effect on the brain of the rush of instant attraction is similar to the feeling of a drug-induced high. Such a state warps our brains, sends us reeling, and leaves us feeling like we are walking on air. Biologically speaking, what could be the benefit from such a departure from reality? One theory is that this euphoria may allow people to overlook or even adore the flaws or "quirks" of their significant other long enough to establish a relationship instead of giving up or losing interest. Does this state of euphoria contribute to the notion that love must be "sparked"? That true love requires instant attraction?

What happens, then, if chemistry and passion fade? Does love fade as well? We are inundated with novels and films that depict the passionate beginnings of relationships—but can you think of examples about couples in long-term relationships? They are rare indeed. Arguably, we are educated about the relationship of attraction to love by stories and advertising images—and we've learned to expect sparks and passion when we meet our true love.

What questions can you ask to uncover the benefits and limitations of the assumption that true love must be sparked by physical attraction?

- What significance does physical attraction have in how we define romantic love?
- What do you notice in media representations about what typically defines couples who have chemistry? Who lack chemistry?

Assumption 3

My true love will be my soul mate.

Another popular assumption is that true love partners understand us in ways that no one else can. This belief centers on the idealized notion that love is deeper than outward appearances. It is also centered on the idea that for everyone in the world there is one person with whom they are truly connected—one person with whom they share a true gift of understanding. In some ways, this third assumption about love contradicts the previous assumption

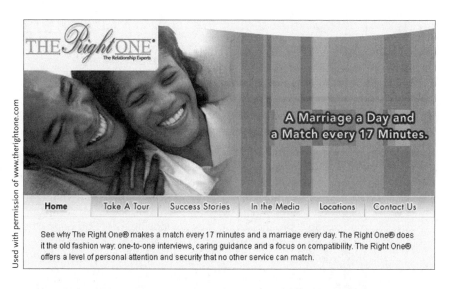

THE *Right* ONE®
The Relationship Experts

A Marriage a Day and a Match every 17 Minutes.

| Home | Take A Tour | Success Stories | In the Media | Locations | Contact Us |

See why The Right One® makes a match every 17 minutes and a marriage every day. The Right One® does it the old fashion way: one-to-one interviews, caring guidance and a focus on compatibility. The Right One® offers a level of personal attention and security that no other service can match.

GAY-SINGLES.US

HAVE YOU EVER FOUND THE ONE?

LOOKING FOR LOVE AND ROMANCE?   GAY-SINGLES.US

"She's on her fifth soul mate."

about the importance of chemistry. While that viewpoint idealizes the importance of instant reactions and physical attraction, this viewpoint suggests that a person's "true love" sees past surface impressions of us and loves us for who we "really" are.

Most Internet dating sites provide a space within the profile template for members to describe who they are seeking. And what do many people say about who they are looking for? "Someone who will love me just the way I am." "The real thing." "The right one." "My true love." "The love of my life." "My soul mate." Behind each of these statements is the assumption that real love is about finding that one true partner we are each "destined" to be with.

However, such an assumption causes people to develop unrealistic expectations of romantic love and even affects relationships with friends and family. Consider, for example, the young woman in college who falls in love and suddenly her roommates and friends barely see her; her parents can never reach her. People in love can also lose a sense of their own individuality and of having interests separate from those of their significant others. Why, they may wonder, would they and their soul mate ever want to be apart? Or pursue separate interests?

What questions can you ask to uncover the benefits and limitations of the assumption that a true love is a soul mate who sees us as we really are?

- What do depictions of soul mates in music or in movies suggest to us about the nature of true love?
- Does having a soul mate imply that people in love do or don't have to work at their relationships?
- To what extent does being in love lead people to become less individual, less free to express their own interests? To what extent does being in love lead people to become more free, more truly who they imagine themselves to be?

Assumption 4

True love is forever.

This final assumption folds all of the previous assumptions about love together into one package—the struggles, the passion, and the search for a soul mate. Each of the previous three assumptions finds some home in this fourth guiding principle of romance and romantic love, which suggests that true love lasts forever.

Consider the DeBeers diamond company slogan: "A diamond is forever." DeBeers's commercials portray dedicated husbands going to great lengths to show their wives that their love has grown stronger over time. In one commercial, a husband rents out an entire movie theater so he can show the couple's wedding video. As the tears stream down his surprised wife's face, he presents her with a three-diamond anniversary ring. The commercial ends with the announcement, "The three-stone anniversary ring. For your past, your present, and your future." Over the years, DeBeers has used many different versions of this commercial to sell diamonds by selling the idea that true love and marriage—divorce rates not withstanding—last forever. Despite the fact that close to 50 percent of all marriages end in divorce, our culture places a great emphasis on that institution and on the idea of true, lasting, monogamous relationships. Indeed, the assumption that true love should last forever demonstrates the importance people place on needing stability in their love relationships.

Yet, one negative impact of this view is that this places the single person—who may be single by choice—at odds with mainstream attitudes. Consider the ways single people are portrayed in the media. For example, the entertainment media hunts single celebrities in order to catch them with their secret loves. And numerous novels and films make it clear that being single, especially for women, is a temporary, undesirable state, and that only a relationship and marriage can bring true happiness.

Additionally, the assumption that true love is forever fails to recognize the fallibility of romantic relationships. Sometimes they just don't work out.

What questions can you ask to uncover the benefits and limitations of this assumption about romantic love?

- What role does this idealized notion of true love play in messages from popular media about what true love should be?
- Based on your experience, what differences do you notice between these examples from the media of true love and the real-life experiences of couples you know who have been together over many years?
- In what ways is being single presented as a problem in the popular media? In what ways is being single glorified?

Questioning These Assumptions

These assumptions offer a starting point for examining how romance is defined in modern America. Through the readings and assignments in this chapter you will investigate how these assumptions function and manifest themselves in everyday life. Some questions you will encounter include, "To what extent do idealized notions of romance reflect American cultural values?" and "What is the meaning of romance in modern America?" On the following page are a few more questions to get you thinking about some of the issues raised in this chapter.

IN THE MIX

David Sedaris, **The End of the Affair**

David Sedaris's scathing and hilarious accounts of his life have been published in a series of memoirs including *Naked* (1997), *Me Talk Pretty One Day* (2000), and *Dress Your Family in Corduroy and Denim* (2004). He is also a regular commentator on National Public Radio. In his personal essays, Sedaris offers poignantly funny and unflinching stories about his dysfunctional family, his youth and coming to terms with his sexuality, his bizarre series of jobs, and his move to France with his partner, Hugh.

This essay was published in *Dress Your Family in Corduroy and Denim*. In it, Sedaris describes going to the movies with Hugh to see the romantic drama *The End of the Affair*. The film leads Sedaris to reflect on the disconnect many people feel between their real-life relationships and those they see on the movie screen.

> ### ▶ Mapping Your Reading
>
> Throughout this essay, Sedaris compares himself and his relationship to the ones we see on the movie screen. As you read, pay attention to the way Sedaris's self-deprecating descriptions of himself help him draw distinctions between his long-term relationship and the fiery passion of the lovers in the movie. In this essay, how is "real love" different from the love portrayed in movies?

On a summer evening in Paris, Hugh and I went to see *The End of the Affair*, a Neil Jordan adaptation of the Graham Greene novel. I had trouble keeping my eyes open because I was tired and not completely engaged. Hugh had trouble keeping his eyes open because they were essentially swollen shut: He sobbed from beginning to end, and by the time we left the theater, he was completely dehydrated. I asked if he always cried during comedies, and he accused me of being grossly insensitive, a charge I'm trying to plea-bargain down to simply obnoxious.

They rarely make movies about long-term couples, and for good reason: Our lives are boring.

Looking back, I should have known better than to accompany Hugh to a love story. Such movies are always a danger, as unlike battling aliens or going undercover to track a serial killer, falling in love is something most adults have actually experienced at some point in their lives. The theme is universal and encourages the viewer to make a number of unhealthy comparisons, ultimately raising the question "Why can't *our* lives be like that?" It's a box best left unopened, and its avoidance explains the continued popularity of vampire epics and martial-arts extravaganzas.

The End of the Affair made me look like an absolute toad. The movie's voracious couple was played by Ralph Fiennes and Julianne Moore, who did everything but eat each other. Their love was doomed and clandestine, and even when the bombs were falling, they looked radiant. The picture was fairly highbrow, so I was surprised when the director employed a device most often seen in TV movies of the week: Everything's going along just fine and then one of the characters either coughs or sneezes, meaning that within 20 minutes he or she will be dead. It might have been different had Julianne Moore suddenly started bleeding from the eyes, but coughing, in and of itself, is fairly pedestrian. When she did it, Hugh cried. When I did it, he punched me in the shoulder and told me to move. "I can't wait until she dies," I whispered. I don't know if it was their good looks or their passion, but something about Julianne Moore and Ralph Fiennes put me on the defensive.

I'm not as unfeeling as Hugh accuses me of being, but things change once you've been together for more than 10 years. They rarely make movies about long-term couples, and for good reason: Our lives are boring. The courtship had its moments, but now we've become the predictable Part II no one in his right mind would ever pay to see. ("Look, they're opening their electric bill!") Hugh and I have been together for so long that in order to arouse extraordinary passion, we need to engage in physical combat. Once, he hit me on the back of the head with a broken wineglass, and I fell to the floor pretending to be unconscious. That was romantic, or would have been had he rushed to my side rather than stepping over my body to fetch the dustpan.

Call me unimaginative, but I still can't think of anyone else I'd rather be with. On our worst days, I figure things will work themselves out. Otherwise, I really don't give our problems much thought. Neither of us would ever publicly display affection; we're just not that type. We can't profess love without talking through hand puppets, and we'd never consciously sit down to discuss our relationship. These, to me, are good things. They were fine with Hugh as well, until he saw that damned movie and was reminded that he has other options.

The picture ended at about 10, and afterward we went for coffee at a little place across the street from the Luxembourg Gardens. I was ready to wipe the movie out of my mind, but Hugh was still under its spell. He looked as though his life had not only passed him by but paused along the way to spit in his face. Our coffee arrived, and as he blew his nose into a napkin, I encouraged him to look on the bright side. "Listen," I said, "we maybe don't live in wartime London, but in terms of the occasional bomb scare, Paris is a pretty close second. We both love bacon and country music, what more could you possibly want?"

What more could he want? It was an incredibly stupid question and when he failed to answer, I was reminded of just how lucky I truly am. Movie characters might chase each other through the fog or race down the stairs of burning buildings, but that's for beginners. Real love amounts to withholding the truth, even when you're offered the perfect opportunity to hurt someone's feelings. I wanted to say something to this effect, but my hand puppets were back home in their drawer. Instead, I pulled my chair a few inches closer, and we sat silently at our little table on the square, looking for all the world like two people in love.

▶ Analyzing the Text

1. According to Sedaris, how do the lovers in the movie *The End of the Affair* symbolize romantic love? "I don't know if it was their good looks or their passion, but something about Julianne Moore and Ralph Fiennes put me on the defensive," he writes. Why does Sedaris feel challenged by them?

2. Throughout the essay, Sedaris jokes about how these love stories usually end tragically, with a sudden death or tragic separation. Why does the tragic ending seem to be a required element of the classic romantic love story?

3. "They rarely make movies about long-term couples," Sedaris writes, "and for good reason: Our lives are boring." How does he go on to describe what love is like for couples who have been together a long time?

4. One important detail that Sedaris does not grapple with directly is who these classic love stories, particularly Hollywood love stories, usually fail to include. What kind of people generally make up classic love stories and what kind of people do not?

5. **Interrogating Assumptions.** What, in Sedaris's view, are some of the problems with the love stories typically portrayed in movies? How do the problems he identifies connect with the assumptions outlined in this chapter's introduction (pp. 263–70)?

▶ Writing about Cultural Practices

6. As a class, expand on Sedaris's description of romance in the movies by choosing a romantic film to view and analyze. Before watching, outline the main characteristics of the classic romantic love story. After viewing the movie, write an analysis of how the love story portrayed in the film supports or departs from the tradition of classic romantic love stories. As you write, consider the following questions.

   - To what extent does the story rely on a familiar formula? Were you surprised by anything regarding the characters or plot? If so, explain.

   - What assumptions does the film's story rely on? Support your answer with evidence from the film.

   - How would you improve the film's script?

Jennifer Egan, **Love in the Time of No Time**

Jennifer Egan is a writer whose work has appeared in the *New York Times Magazine*, *Slate*, *Harpers*, and *GQ*. Her novels include *Look at Me* (2001), *The Invisible Circus* (1994), and a collection of short stories titled *Emerald City* (1996). In the following essay, which originally appeared in the *New York Times Magazine* in 2003, Egan investigates how the quest for love has changed as modern American life has become increasingly fast paced and technologically advanced. She argues that traditional community-based contexts for dating or finding romance are being replaced by the Internet, and that online dating is changing the way we look for romance or companionship.

> ▶ **Mapping Your Reading**
>
> What interests Egan about online dating sites is *not* the question of whether or not online dating is "good" or "bad." Instead, she says, "Better questions might be, How do [dating websites] work and how is the way they work changing the nature of courtship?" How has online dating changed the way people look for love or companionship? How has it affected how people identify and portray themselves? As you read, use the margins to note passages where Egan addresses these questions.

The city is full of people we can't reach. We pass them on sidewalks, sit across from them in the subway and in restaurants; we glimpse their lighted windows from our own lighted windows late at night. That's in New York. In most of America, people float alongside one another on freeways as they drive between the city and the places where they live. To lock eyes with a stranger is to feel the gulf between proximity and familiarity and to wish—at least sometimes, briefly, most of us—that we could jump the hedges of our own narrow lives and find those people again when they drift out of sight.

In a sense, the explosion of online personals speaks to the fervency of that wish. In the first half of 2003, Americans spent $214.3 million on personals and dating sites—almost triple what they spent in all of 2001. Online dating is the most lucrative form of legal paid online content. According to comScore Networks, which monitors consumer behavior on the Internet, 40 million Americans visited at least one online dating site in August—27 percent of all Internet users for that month. The sites they visited range from behemoths like

Yahoo! Personals and Match.com, which boasts 12 million users worldwide, to smaller niche sites catering to ethnic and religious groups and to devotees of such things as pets, horoscopes, and fitness. In between are midsize companies like Spring Street Networks, which pools the personals ads for some 200 publications nationwide, including Salon.com, the *Onion,* and *Boston Magazine,* and sites like Emode and eHarmony, which specialize in personality tests and algorithms for matching people. One entrant, Friendster, conceived of as a site for dating and meeting new people through mutual friends, has become a raging fad among the younger set and now claims more than three million members.

The societal reasons for this fury of activity are so profound that it's almost surprising that online dating didn't take off sooner: Americans are marrying later and so are less likely to meet their spouses in high school or college. They spend much of their lives at work, but the rise in sexual harassment suits has made workplace relationships tricky at best.

Online personals are a natural outcropping of our historical and technological landscape.

Among a more secular and mobile population, social institutions like churches and clubs have faded in importance. That often leaves little more than the "bar scene" as a source of potential mates. (Many single people I spoke to saw this as their only option, aside from online dating.)

Improved technology—namely, the proliferation of broadband and the abrupt ubiquity of digital cameras—partly explains online dating's surge in popularity. More critical still is the fact that the first generation of kids to come of age on the Internet are now young adults, still mostly single, and for them, using the Web to find what they need is as natural as using a lung to suck in air. They get jobs and apartments and plane tickets online—why not dates?

Still, a fair number of people continue to feel a stigma about dating online, ranging from the waning belief that it's a dangerous refuge for the desperate and unsavory to the milder but still unappealing notion that it's a public bazaar for the sort of people who thrive on selling themselves. The shopping metaphor is apt; online dating involves browsing and choosing among a seemingly infinite array of possible mates. But those who see a transactional approach to coupling as something new and unseemly would do well to pick up a novel by Jane Austen, where characters are introduced alongside their incomes. There is nothing new about the idea of marriage as a business transaction. Serendipitous love is what's new, love borne of chance, love like what engulfed my grandparents after my grandfather, then a resident physician at a Chicago hospital emergency room, happened to remove my grandmother's appendix. Serendipitous love as a romantic ideal is a paean to cities and their dislocations, the unlikely collisions that result from thousands of strangers with discrete histories overlapping briefly in time and space. And online dating is not the opposite of this approach to love, but its radical extension; if cities erase people's histories and cram them together in space, online dating sites erase both cities and space, gathering people instead under the virtual rubric of a brand.

The defining fact of online dating is that it begins outside any context—historical, temporal, physical. To compensate, dating sites offer the old-fashioned comfort of facts: income, life goals, tastes in music, attitudes toward having children—the sorts of things you might wonder about a stranger you locked eyes with. To ask whether this lack of real-world context is "good" or "bad" is to oversimplify; online personals are a natural outcropping of our historical and technological landscape—one more proof of the fact that time and space are ceding their primacy as organizers of our experience. Better questions might be, How do they work and how is the way they work changing the nature of courtship?

First Impressions

Online dating profiles may begin as jokes or time wasters at work or good deeds on behalf of single, lonely friends whose digital picture you happen to have in your hard drive. But for the serious online dater, the personal profile—the page allotted to each client on dating Web sites—quickly assumes a pivotal importance. Whether visible or hidden (meaning people can see it only if you contact them first), profiles are as intrinsic to online dating as cards are to poker. The profile does the legwork of materializing before potential love interests and braving with a smile their contemplation, dismissal, exegesis, mockery, or the whiplash of being zapped among friends as an e-mail attachment whose subject heading reads, "Check this one out." The profile never sleeps. It keeps vigil day and night, dutifully holding your place in the queue of romantic prospects drummed up by the thousands of searches all over the world whose criteria you happen to meet. What this means is that tens of millions of Americans, a great many of whom have never gone near a virtual-reality game, find themselves employing "avatars," or digital embodiments of themselves, to make a first impression in their absence.

The profile never sleeps.

Dating profiles are works in progress, continually edited and tweaked, fortified with newer, more flattering pictures. If they were physical documents, they would have the velvety, dogeared texture of beloved children's books or nineteenth-century family Bibles. Often they're made collaboratively, with friends, or at least vetted by someone of the same sex as their target audience. Many online daters have more than one profile, sometimes on the same dating site. (Before Spring Street Networks limited the number of profiles a single person could post, lone individuals were known to have a few dozen.)

Greg, a 23-year-old secretary and aspiring rock singer who lives in Brooklyn, has two profiles on Nerve.com. Recently, his profile answered the question "Why you should get to know me" with a short paragraph ending: "Because I have condoms in my back pocket but don't hit on anyone. I'm quiet, complacent, pretty, and utterly diabolical." Greg acknowledged in an e-mail message to me that his approach was "pretty risky": "The ad will attract fewer women, most definitely, but the ones who respond will be very likely candidates for a good date. . . . If I was bored and looking to go on a lot of dates, I'd have a different picture and a funnier, more verbose ad." His earlier profile was indeed more expansive and earnest—the headline reads, "Make sure she gets home safe." And as any online dater will tell you, the picture is the most crucial profile component. (Among the several cottage industries that have sprung up around online dating is that of personal profile photography.) "I'm no photographer," Greg writes (my weeks of conversation with Greg have occurred entirely by e-mail; we have never spoken or met), "but I've spent a lot of time trying to take sexy pictures of myself for these ads, and the good ones have produced lots of responses." Greg estimates that he has gone out with between 30 and 50 women he met online since he first posted a profile nearly three years ago. His second meeting, through amihot.com—one of several dating sites where members can rate one another's pictures—led to a relationship that lasted a year and a half.

Greg is 6-foot-4 and, judging by his pictures, possessed of a tousled rock 'n' roller handsomeness. Like a lot of online daters I corresponded with, he doesn't have Internet access at home; his online activity occurs almost exclusively at work (he minimizes the screen when his boss walks by) or at Internet cafes on weekends. "It is impossible to draw the line between my online social life and my real-world social life," Greg says. "Without online personals, there is no telling where I would be living, who I'd be hanging out with, what clothes I'd be wearing, or how busy my nightlife and sex life would be (believe me, they are busy)."

> "It is impossible to draw the line between my online social life and my real-world social life."

Notice that Greg refers to his profile as an "ad." This is common parlance and helps to explain why a lot of people—especially those older and less Web-inclined than Greg—are squirmy about posting one. Lorraine, a 39-year-old mortgage officer in Cherry Hill, N.J., and the divorced mother of three teenagers, had no photo posted on her original profile with Match.com, and her descriptions of herself were vague. A tepid response spurred her on. She uploaded a photo and wrote a lengthy profile, whose "about me" section includes: "My ideal man is someone who respects a truly good woman and knows how to make her feel special, important, and loved. . . . A man who would give of himself before he gives to himself. (Ouch! I bet that hurt)."

Lorraine was honest, she says, in her choice of picture and report of her physical dimensions, but this isn't always the case; most online daters have at least one cranky tale of meeting a date who was shorter or fatter or balder or generally less comely than advertised. Small lies may even be advisable; by dropping a year or two off her age, a 40-year-old woman will appear in many more men's searches, and the same is true for a man shorter than 5-foot-11 who inflates his height even slightly. But for all the fibbing and fudging that go on, outright lying about who you are is generally regarded as uncool and self-defeating. Think about it: If all goes well, the person will ultimately agree to meet you, at which point they'll discover you're not a race-car driver from Monaco who speaks five languages and owns an island in the Caribbean. Evan Marc Katz, a screenwriter and veteran online dater, has started a business called E-Cyrano.com that will actually write someone's personal profile in his or her own voice after a lengthy interview. Katz, 31, favors another popular metaphor for online dating: job hunting. "It is really a résumé," he says of the profile. "You're taking the available facts, and you're cleaning them up."

But for all the metaphorical aptness of shopping and job hunting to describe online personals generally, they neglect the most basic truth of the profile itself: regardless of its tone—hipster irony in Greg's case, gushy sincerity in Lorraine's—making and posting a profile is an act of faith. Like throwing coins into a well, there is an earnestness about doing it at all. Which is why even people with a cynical view of personals tend to speak about their own profiles with disconcerting pride. Yasmeen, a 26-year-old recent law-school graduate, went on only one date in three years in Columbus, Ohio, where she says her ethnicity (she is half Indian, half Filipino) made her "invisible." She posted a profile through *Jane Magazine,* but chose not to meet any of her respondents for a year and a half. Still, she said: "When I'm lonely, it helps to know there is someone out there who is looking for me. . . . And while my ad may not be 'the real me,' at least there is potential for me to be that best version of myself. Even for just a small part of a day."

Flirting

Here is part of the expansive introductory e-mail message Greg wrote to Sam, a 23-year-old graphic designer, in response to her profile:

> "Subject: Hi.
>
> "It's weird. I'm in the middle of noting to myself how you misused 'perceptively' (shoulda been perceptibly) when I get to a word I've never seen before: 'ideationally.' Everyone always tells me I shouldn't be so harsh when grading the grammar, spelling, etc. in people's ads and responses, but I can't help it. . . . If you like to go out to dirty rock shows and drink at bars from time to time, or if you think you'd like to let my roommate cook for you while we all act like retards, you and I could get along. Please respond."

Sam did, in an e-mail that began: "And here I was congratulating myself on my 170 I.Q. Dammit. . . . I am all about dirty rock shows and bars." Referring to Greg's remark in his profile that he carries condoms in his back pocket, Sam concluded: "P.S. You know, you have to use the condoms, or discard and replace. . . . Just F.Y.I., so you can start hitting on bar skanks before it's too late."

There is no shortage of ways to flirt online. The most obvious are codified right into the dating sites as nonverbal signals people can click at each other: "winks," "smiles," "breaking the ice," depending on the site. While women are generally more comfortable approaching men online than in bars, men still tend to make the first moves, and since women with attractive pictures (Sam is 5-foot-11 with long blond hair) are usually besieged with responses—she's had several hundred since posting her first ad last spring—it behooves a man to think hard about his opening salvo. Greg's style has evolved over time: "It used to be: 'I like your ad. Check out mine. Hope to hear from you.' . . . But I've found that long-winded and entertaining messages get responses more than half the time, while boring, mass-mailed messages can't beat a 1-to-5 response/message ratio."

FOUND

from 1-true-love.com

PERSONAL-AD SHORTHAND

Don't know what all the abbreviations in personal ads mean? Here's a list. Remember, you can say a lot with abbreviations in your ad. Instead of saying "Non Smoking Non Drinking Single White Male In Search of Non Smoking Non Drinking Single White Female" you could just put this in: NSNDSWMISONSNDSWF. You could use the above as part of your ad title. Just say, "Fun Loving NSNDSWMISONSNDSWF25-30YO" as your ad title.

A = Asian

B = Black

BI = Bisexual

C = Christian

D = Divorced

DDF = Drug/Disease Free

FTA = Fun Travel Adventure

G = Gay

GSOH = Good Sense of Humor

H = Hispanic

HWP = Height Weight Proportional

ISO = In Search Of

J = Jewish

LD = Light Drinker

LDS = Latter Day Saint

LS = Light Smoker

LTR = Long Term Relationship

MM = Marriage Minded

NA = Native American

NBM = Never Been Married

ND = Non Drinker

NS = Non Smoker

P = Professional

S = Single

SD = Social Drinker

SI = Similar Interests

SOH = Sense of Humor

W = White

W/ = With

Wi = Widowed

W/O = With Out

YO = Years Old

Online daters are constantly innovating ways to shanghai the technology into flirtatious use: A 34-year-old opera singer and actor created a new profile of himself, "Brooklynboy," that was entirely a response to a particular woman's profile, "Brooklyngirl," that had smitten him. But if flirting in the real world consists of no-strings banter between two people who feel a mutual attraction, online flirtation is its inverse—it happens in the presence of everything but physical attraction. Two people who have read each other's profiles may know each other's hobbies, income, turn-ons, religious affiliations, political views, and whether or not they want children, but they have no idea whether the frisson these avatars of themselves manage to whip up in the void will translate into life. When Brooklynboy met Brooklyngirl after a week of strenuous flirtation, there was so little mutual attraction that they never made it to a second date. Online flirting happens, then, in the conditional voice, and there's a general sense that it shouldn't go on for too long.

The exact progression from first contact to in-the-flesh-meeting varies among daters and age groups. For younger people, who grew up with instant-messaging programs, e-mail will often lead to an instant-message exchange (or several), followed by a meeting; those over 30 tend to prefer the phone. David Ezell, 39, who is gay and runs a rare-book business online, refuses to exchange more than two or three e-mail messages before moving to the telephone. "There's a lot of men who are on the fence about their sexuality. . . . this is their sexual outlet: writing personals ads," he says. "They're never going to meet anybody, and they don't want to. . . . That's the first step in intimacy, swapping phone numbers." Ezell had a serious long-term relationship with a physician he met online, and when that relationship failed a year and a half ago, he returned to the personals.

Making a timely segue from virtual to real-world flirtation is hardest when two people are talking across a physical distance. Angel, a 42-year-old divorced father who lives in Boston, made contact with Carmen, a 39-year-old divorced woman who had just moved from Puerto Rico to Connecticut, on LatinSingles.com, where his profile is posted in Spanish. Angel was skittish about relationships; after separating from his wife of 18 years, he spent several months homeless, sleeping in city shelters and in his car because his job at a printing company didn't pay enough for him to afford an apartment of his own. He and Carmen communicated by e-mail and then moved to the phone. "I did not go by the looks of her, because she had no photo posted on her profile," Angel said. "I was basically just going with what the heart said." After a month of e-mail messages and phone calls, they made a plan for Carmen to drive to Boston so they could meet.

"We met at South Bay shopping center in the parking lot, right in front of Toys 'R' Us," Angel said. When he first saw her, he recalled, "I said: 'Wow. Damn, I'm good.' Because she is a very attractive lady. I was definitely speechless. We were both shy, but slowly we started to loosen up and get to the same type of conversation we were having over the phone. We got a bite to eat, and then we went to get a drink, and she stayed over that night." They slept in separate rooms, and Carmen went back to Connecticut the next day. She now visits every weekend and plans to move to Boston in December.

Chemistry

Angel and Carmen had it; Brooklynboy and Brooklyngirl didn't. "Chemistry" is a word you hear a lot among online daters: sine qua non of the enterprise and the object of a fair bit of fetishization. Here, for example, is an excerpt from a dating log kept by Regan, a 37-year-old technical writer in Atlanta, since she posted an ad a year and a half ago on Salon.com. "M: Sang in the car; zero chemistry; started writing me poems and stories. A: Too young, too tiny, had roommate problems and bored me. C: Zero chemistry; I was sure he was gay. K: Great chemistry, but too straight for me. Lives in my building, of all things. R: Had had a recent bankruptcy and actually skipped out on his bar tab, appalling me. M.P: Came from California to meet me. A waste of a few days—there was zero attraction."

The early stages of an online acquaintance happen on spec, with the mutual understanding that chemistry will be required in order for things to proceed. This puts a fair amount of pressure on that first meeting—both parties tend to arrive with chemistry sensors keyed to a quivering state of alertness. When chemistry is absent, on both sides or (more painfully) just one, a cut-your-losses mentality prevails. "Sorry but it just wasn't there for me" e-mail messages are the polite response to a chemically inert date; just as often, the disappointed party will simply fade away, a conventional rudeness that is especially jarring to newcomers.

Being on the receiving end of these rejections can be bruising, because the rejection comes not from a total stranger but from a person you've e-mailed and talked to and possibly become fond of. In September, Lorraine, the New Jersey divorcée, had tea on a Sunday afternoon with an attorney she had spoken with at some length on the phone. She said that on first seeing him, "My initial reaction was: shorter than I like, he's not great looking but he's O.K. looking. I would have given him a chance and gone out again." But the attorney sent her an e-mail message that began, "I think you're a wonderful woman, but. . . ." A week later, Lorraine was still trying to figure it out. "You think, what is wrong with me?" she said. "I'm 90 percent sure it's physical, that I'm just not the perfect body. I try. I wear a small size, but I'm probably not what he's looking for." Or was the problem that, as a way of making conversation, she had mentioned a conflict she was having with a neighbor—did the lawyer think she was grubbing for free legal advice? Or could it have been her personality? "On a first date I laugh, I smile, but I don't crack jokes," she reflected. "So I was thinking, Maybe he wanted someone who was fun immediately." Lorraine's failed marriage began with love-at-first-sight, so she is wary of instant chemistry. "A lot of times that spark is just lust anyway," she said. She's looking for something that will evolve and endure, but fears that in the chemistry-fixated world of online dating, that sort of bond would never have time to flourish.

> **"There was zero attraction."**

And there are those who say that the culture of online dating is itself inimical to the chemistry its practitioners crave. Someone actively dating online may have as many as five or six dates in a week ("serial dating" is the term for this), which can make for some fuzzy-headed folks beholding one another across tables. Just organizing that much dating activity is a challenge; at one point, David Ezell had his dates and prospective dates arranged on an Excel spreadsheet. Leslie Hill, 34, who works in human resources in Silicon Valley, estimates that she went on 100 online dates before meeting her second husband on Match.com. She kept track of the multitude in a dating binder, printing out the profiles of every man who contacted her and filing them under different headings: "Under Consideration," "Chatting Online," "Chatting and Going to Meet," "Met and Would Like to See Again" and, for men she didn't want to see again, "NMF," or "Not Moving Forward," a category borrowed from human resources. During phone conversations with prospective dates, Hill would scribble notes about their lives: "I would write it down: 'has two sisters and a brother,' 'worked there and there,' and if I went out, I would go through my binder and refresh myself: 'O.K., this is Bob. He went to Chico.' I hoped that when I got to meet the person, I was real and genuine."

For Greg, who isn't looking for a serious relationship, the chemistry issue is less acute. In late July, he had a first date with a woman he met online. "I just don't spend much time trying to figure out where the date will go," he said that afternoon, when I asked about his expectations. "I think she'll be attractive. I think she'll be just a bit heavier than she looks in her pictures, since she did not list her weight anywhere. I think we will get along very quickly. It would be out of line to assume that we're going to have sex, but I think it's a definite possibility. . . . She's told me that my e-mails make her laugh, which might be good or bad, as it is difficult for me to be funny in person before the conversation has gained momentum, and I've actually had dates comment that I'm much quieter than they expected. . . . The key is fun. Intense mutual attraction is optional. Playful lust will do."

"A lot of times that spark is just lust anyway."

Sex

The next day, Greg sent me this account of his date: "Well, she was a little on the heavy side, as I expected, but wearing it well. She was well dressed and drank quickly at first. I wouldn't say there was an immediate comfort level; she seemed maybe just a little nervous at first." They hit a couple of bars on Manhattan's Lower East Side, played pool and ate grilled-cheese sandwiches. The evening ended like this: "We took the cab to my place and made out during the entire ride, except when I needed to direct the driver. My place is a wreck. My bed is in the living room. It's a good thing that my roommate was already asleep, because I have absolutely no privacy when he decides to walk through the apartment. . . . We got naked, I left the light on, we had some really good sex for around 40 minutes and passed out by about 1:30." He concluded: "I'd say she'd see me again. It will probably happen at some point."

I remarked to Greg that by virtually any standard, it sounded like a successful date and asked for his evaluation. "This was a run-of-the-mill date, or maybe a notch better than that," he said. "I liked her, but not enough to merit fireworks. Given the seemingly endless selection, I get to be a little less forgiving."

Until the late 1960's, marriage was the best guarantor of regular sex. Thereafter, it was being in a steady relationship. But online dating may be on its way to eliminating that particular incentive for commitment. Sites like men4men4sex.com and adultfriendfinder.com or the "Casual Encounters" area of Craig's List exist purely to coordinate sex dates among interested parties with complementary tastes, often on very short notice. But even at the more mainstream sites, one-night stands are commonplace and easy to arrange. L., a 31-year-old information-technology specialist, had several one-night stands during the three years he lived in New York. (He moved to Paris last August.) He let me log into one of his accounts and scour the old e-mail exchanges, a typical one of which (to "sexyangelina") reads: "Let me know if you're interested. . . . I think we could have fun." The woman's response: "Where yah goin'?" He: "Moving to Paris." She: "Whoa! Why is that? You're such a cutie! Good luck to you, though." This time, "sexyangelina" included a private e-mail address, so the communication could bypass the dating site. "It starts with a few e-mails," L. said, "and goes to I.M. More pictures are exchanged, then it goes to a phone call, and that's when the deal is usually closed. Typically, it doesn't take very long if both people are interested in the same thing. . . . On two occasions the women have come to my place, had sex with me, and we haven't had one paragraph of conversation."

> "Given the seemingly endless selection, I get to be a little less forgiving."

The ability to prospect anonymously for lovers who have no overlap with your actual life is something of a Valhalla for married people inclined toward extramarital sex, and by all accounts, the dating sites are teeming with them. Many are disguised as singles, while some operate quite openly, usually—though not always—without a picture. (Friendster and Spring Street Networks allow "open marriage" and "discreet," respectively, in their choices of "relationship status.")

Greg may not be looking for a serious relationship, but he's not after no-strings sex, either. An ideal date for Greg is a woman he can see casually, sleep with for as long as possible, and stay friends with when the sex ends. The lack of context around women he meets online doesn't trouble him. "We had enough in common, I guess," he said of the woman he slept with on the first date the previous night. "I tend to focus more on the fun at hand—I'm not preoccupied with matching up with a person's life goals or hobbies or anything." By the end of that week, he had gone on four dates with women he'd met online (one indirectly; she was the friend of another online date) and had slept with three of them—a busy week, Greg said, though not extraordinary. He practices safe sex. "It's more or less understood with everyone that condoms are mandatory," he explained. "I even have a brand. There is also a brand I hate. Also, it's extremely rare for the girl not to have condoms. The one time I forgot mine because of a last-minute pants change, my date had a whole box in her purse."

Those disillusioned with online dating will tell you that its promise of a no-muss relationship attracts people with intimacy and commitment problems. This is probably true. A 50-year-old American magazine editor who lives in Paris says that he has used online personals over the past 10 years to orchestrate "adventures"—rendezvous in foreign locales with women from various European countries. "There are periods when a frenzy comes upon you," he said. "You really feel yourself in the grip of something that's kind of like a 'high.' The problem comes when you try to make that happen again and the feeling gets progressively more tepid and less exciting each time around. And before you know it, you're looking for somebody new." This man calls his present relationship, of one year, "a record for me." Yet he recently posted profiles on two French dating sites. "This is kind of made for people like me, who prefer fantasy to reality," he said of online dating. For this man, though, the promise of a no-strings attachment has often proved illusory. "Whatever people say, they tend to get involved," he told me. "People tend to lose their hearts."

> "Whatever people say, they tend to lose their hearts."

Rejection

Relationships begun online have a tendency to end there too. This generally happens one of two ways: by e-mail or by no e-mail—i.e., someone disappears. Regan, the Atlanta technical writer whose dating log I excerpted above, fell in love last spring with a man she met online: a journalist living in Atlanta. "We e-mailed and talked on the phone for about a year before we met," she told me. "We set up a meeting two times. He stood me up both times." The reason was guilt: He had a live-in girlfriend. In April, Regan happened to pass this man on the street, and they recognized each other from the many digital photos they'd exchanged. "We circled each other, in slow motion, in disbelief," she remembered. "Everything in me relaxed, calmed, stilled. . . . It was IT. The thunderbolt. And he was going through exactly the same thing." They began a relationship that flourished despite the fact that the journalist kept postponing the promised breakup with his girlfriend. On Regan's birthday, he sent a gift and a love letter from Europe and left her three messages. "His heart is completely open, visible at all times, this one," she said.

Then silence. Days and then weeks began to pass. Because there was no overlap in their work or social or daily lives, Regan had no idea whether the man was still in Europe or had returned to Atlanta, and they had no friends in common to ask. "I feel like I'll never smile again, let alone laugh," she told me. "Everything weighs eight million pounds. . . . I guess anyone can do anything to you at any time."

The journalist resurfaced several weeks later with an unsatisfying explanation and hopes of resuming the relationship. Regan agreed to see him and continues to, but repairing the gouge left by his sudden absence has been difficult.

People in fledgling relationships begun online can vanish from one another's lives with the same breathtaking efficiency as a line of text deleted from a word processing document, leaving no hole, no gap in one another's daily lives to mark the fact that they were ever there. For some, an awareness of this exit strategy permeates the enterprise, allowing them to skimp on the niceties they would more or less have to extend toward a person they were likely to meet again. Newcomers to online dating either acclimate themselves to these occasional early evaporations or abandon the practice altogether. "I'm totally irritated at how disrespectful it is to just disappear," a 27-year-old TV producer fumed after the man she had been dating for three weeks failed to call and then stopped answering her e-mail messages. "I really don't have the energy or the self-esteem to continue to meet guys whose backgrounds I don't know." She was one of several people who renounced online dating in the course of my interviewing them for this article, although the paucity of alternatives soon drove her back and she has since become seriously involved with a man she met on Friendster.

Because online relationships begin in a state of mutual absence, "disappearance" may be the wrong word for a sudden lack of contact between two people who meet this way; more, these are failures to reappear from the digital murk that came first. And because the avatars who reside in that digital realm often hang about long after their makers have ceased to communicate, it is possible for people to keep distant, prolonged track of one another. Lynn Ross, a clothing merchandiser in her 40's, was involved for three months with a married man who deceived her into believing he was single. The relationship ended nine months ago, but she still checks his profile, noting recently that he continues to update it every week. And Marie, the designer, takes comfort from the fact that a man she loved and was rejected by is often logged into the dating site where they met. "Sometimes when I see him online late at night," she said, "I think: Good. Another night he's home alone."

Getting Serious

Online dates that lead to love—and they are legion—are a little like Tolstoy's happy families: for all their quirky particularity, they end up sounding strangely alike. There's Kellie Smith, 33, from outside Boston, an occupational therapist who whimsically clicked "Love on AOL" during her lunch break and found herself on Match.com, where she dashed off e-mail messages to several men who interested her. Michael DuGally, 35, a partner in a Massachusetts furniture manufacturing company, was her first online date; they met for lunch and never really parted. Last summer, the couple asked Match.com for a logo banner so they could be photographed with it on their wedding day.

They aren't the only ones making such requests, according to Trish McDermott, vice president for romance at Match.com; the company has forked over baseball caps and matchbooks to give away at weddings, along with well wishes and toasts to be read aloud. One couple designed their wedding cake in the shape of a computer, with the top section decorated to look like the

Match.com welcome page. Michael and Kellie, whom I met for a drink in Manhattan just after their honeymoon in Greece, call themselves lucky, as if a fluke of chance had brought them together. There was no intersection at all between their worlds, yet the connection they feel, they say, is "spooky." Neither wants children. Both practice Bikram yoga. They don't like making plans, but are very neat. They love to shop. They even drink the same cocktail: Grey Goose orange vodka on the rocks, with two wedges of lime.

Relationships begun online have a tendency to end there too.

There are scads of stories like this from every walk of life, so that even the most jaundiced view of online personals must contend with the fact that people manage to find one another this way—again and again and again. So far in 2003, McDermott says, more than 140,000 Match.com members said they were leaving the site "because they found the person they were seeking there."

As of December, Angel and Carmen, the couple who met on LatinSingles.com, plan to be living together in Boston. But removing their profiles from the dating site—the watermark of commitment in a relationship begun online—is something neither wants to do. A community of sorts has sprung up among the single people posting on the message boards, Angel says. "My girlfriend and I, we did create a lot of friendships on this board. We have created a ganglike type of thing." There are even plans for "gang" members, many of whom have never met, to convene in New York this winter. So rather than remove their profiles, Angel and Carmen hope to bend the genre and create a joint profile of some sort—as Angel puts it, "something that will reflect both of us."

The circularity here is intriguing: an absence of real-world community fuels a schematic, inorganic online ritual that spawns a network of online friendships that ultimately pushes back out into the real world. No context becomes, in effect, a context all its own—an avatar, if you will, of the city itself. This is how the Internet was supposed to work, and it suggests that the deep impulse behind the success of online dating could reach well beyond dating itself. Friendster lets people search for one another using book titles, band names, and TV shows, among other things, as keywords, and its "interested in meeting people for" category offers not only "friends" and "dating" but also "activity partners" and "just here to help." Greg used Nerve.com to research nightlife before a weekend trip to San Francisco; he arrived with two prearranged dates and a list of 19 bars he was interested in checking out. The chairman of Spring Street Networks, Rufus Griscom, sees the company as not even being in the business of online dating so much as "purchasing access to like-minded people." The long-term vision, here, looks like something out of a Borges story: a virtual clearinghouse where potential lovers, friends, business associates, audience members, and devotees of all forms of culture—invisible to one another in the shadowy cracks of cities around the world—are registered, profiled, and findable. An alternate dimension where the randomness and confusion of urban life are at last sorted out.

1. Has dating in the traditional sense disappeared altogether? How have dating practices transformed into something completely new? From Egan's perspective, what does it mean to date someone today?

2. According to Egan, how is online dating like the following:
   - Job-hunting?
   - Shopping or marketing oneself?
   - Playing a game?

   Find examples from the reading that explain how the principles behind these activities affect the expectations people bring to online dating.

3. According to Egan, how does the online profile, which she refers to as an avatar, impact modern dating? An avatar is a version of ourselves that we project into digital spaces like the Internet. An avatar represents a person in cyberspace. How has the use of avatars benefited the dating process? How have avatars created limitations or hurt the dating process?

4. Throughout the essay, Egan suggests that the online world, which includes virtual profiles, emailing, and instant messaging, frequently clashes with the "real world" when people use online dating services. According to this essay, how have online practices or attitudes begun to change "real-world" dating?

5. **Connecting to Another Reading.**   David Sedaris's "The End of the Affair" (p. 272) begins this chapter because it provides a starting point for defining the classic themes of romantic love in American culture. Egan's essay takes the next step by asking, "How has courtship—or finding romance—changed today?" Having read her essay, how would you answer this question? How would you compare people's expectations about romance today to the classic views about romance that you identified for the Sedaris essay?

▶ **Writing about Cultural Practices**

6. Every online profile presents an argument for why readers should be interested in meeting its author. Choose one online dating or social networking site and analyze how the site structures the profiles appearing within it. One chief question is: How do the websites dictate how people can represent themselves? Begin by exploring several different sites, paying particular attention to the questions the site asks its members to respond to when creating a profile and the advice the site gives for writing a successful profile. As you draft your essay, consider these questions.
   - What kinds of facts, features, or qualities about a person are emphasized by the structure of the profiles? What about a person is deemed most important or attractive?
   - How much emphasis is placed on photographs?
   - What facts, features, or qualities about a person *cannot* be conveyed in a profile because of the structure imposed?
   - How does the site determine whether a profile is acceptable?

7. Egan's essay illustrates how important and sometimes complicated emails or instant messages can become between people looking for romance. Work with a partner or in a group to create a guide that explains the unspoken rules of using email versus instant messaging versus phone calls for communicating with a potential love interest.

- To begin, create a list of eight to ten reasons people use these methods to initiate communication. (For example, to introduce themselves? To flirt? To ask someone out? To turn someone down? To talk to someone the day after a date?)

- In one section of your guide, explain which medium—email, IM-ing, or phone calling—is most appropriate for communicating each of these eight to ten messages effectively. Provide examples to illustrate your advice.

- Next, include a second section in which you identify five common social blunders people make when using one of these methods to communicate. Be sure that you explain both the benefits and the drawbacks for using email versus IM-ing versus phone calls.

Inviting Love: A Vintage Valentine vs. An Online Profile

St Valentine's Greeting

Cupid has long,
with smiling art,
Invited me to
yield my heart.

"I wake filled with thoughts of you. Your portrait and the intoxicating evening which we spent yesterday have left my senses in turmoil. Sweet, incomparable Josephine, what a strange effect you have on my heart!" These words were written by Napoleon Bonaparte (1769–1821) in a love letter to his then-fiancée Josephine in December 1795. In those more socially rigid—and less technologically advanced—times, letters were a vital means for two people to romance—or court—each other. Written expressions of love like the Valentine's Day card pictured above became popular in America in the nineteenth century.

Today's approaches to courtship—such as email, instant-messaging, and online dating profiles, like the one at right—haven't so much removed the old rules as transposed them into a digital environment. Although trying hard to suggest otherwise, the book *Online Dating for Dummies* (2003) demonstrates a fundamental similarity between love letters and online dating: "A dating site . . . [is] a means to get into the prospect's character and personality by virtue of an ongoing exchange that takes place before you meet! . . . When you finally do meet your prospect in person, you aren't strangers. The date is with someone who is a suitable match

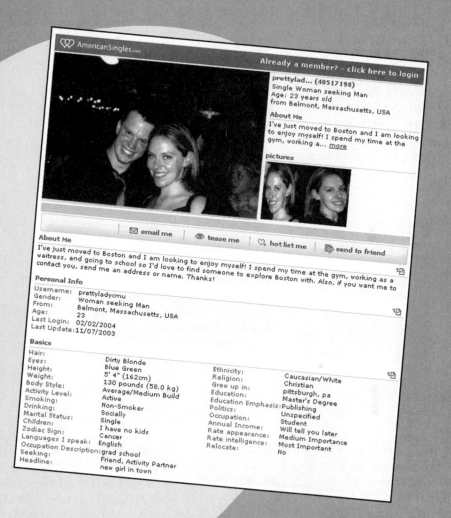

with respect to age, values, and future goals."
Jane Austen would've been right at home.

1. What do these images suggest about the rituals surrounding courtship? What do they convey about how cultural attitudes toward courtship and romance have changed?

2. Do you agree or disagree that today's digital methods of dating rely on many conventional attitudes toward courtship and finding love? To answer this, conduct some research using the Internet, or your library, to locate archives of valentines or love letters written before 1950, as well as a sampling of

online profiles from dating websites. What similarities and differences do you notice between these forms of correspondence?

3. One difference between nineteenth- and twenty-first-century courtship is that instead of a kindly aunt or clergy member performing the introductions, the dating website now acts as the intermediary between two people. Having examined two or more online dating sites, what assumptions about courtship do these sites' formats for profiles (including the use of pictures) create or reinforce?

Sasha Cagen, **People Like Us: The Quirkyalones**

Sasha Cagen's essays have appeared in the *Village Voice* and *Utne,* and she is the founding editor of *To-Do List* magazine. In this essay, which is excerpted from her book *Quirkyalone: A Manifesto for Uncompromising Romantics* (2004), Cagen introduces a new term—the quirkyalone—to describe the single person who'd rather be alone on a Saturday night than out on an uninteresting date. Quirkyalones, she suggests, are people who are attracted to the freedom that comes with being single. They are also, Cagen writes, "romantics of the highest order."

> ▶ **Mapping Your Reading**
>
> So far in this chapter, you have considered how popular assumptions about romance influence or guide how people date or seek the attention of others. This essay, in contrast, is about being single. As you read, mark passages where Cagen redefines what it means to be single. What is a quirkyalone? What are the drawbacks and benefits of being a quirkyalone?

I am, perhaps, what you might call deeply single. Almost never ever in a relationship. Until recently, I wondered whether there might be something weird about me. But then lonely romantics began to grace the covers of *TV Guide* and *Mademoiselle.* From *Ally McBeal* to *Sex in the City,* a spotlight came to shine on the forever single. If these shows had touched such a nerve in our culture, I began to think, perhaps I was not so alone after all.

The morning after New Year's Eve (another kissless one, of course), a certain jumble of syllables came to me. When I told my friends about my idea, their faces lit up with instant recognition: the quirkyalone.

If Jung was right, that people are different in fundamental ways that drive them from within, then the quirkyalone is simply to be added to the pantheon of personality types assembled over the twentieth century. Only now, when the idea of marrying at age 20 has become thoroughly passé, are we quirkyalones emerging in greater numbers.

We are the puzzle pieces who seldom fit with other puzzle pieces. Romantics, idealists, eccentrics, we inhabit singledom as our natural resting state. In a world where proms and marriage define the social order, we are, by force of our personalities and inner strength, rebels.

For the quirkyalone, there is no patience for dating just for the sake of not being alone. We want a miracle. Out of millions, we have to find the one who will understand.

Better to be untethered and open to possibility: living for the exhilaration of meeting someone new, of not knowing what the night will bring. We quirkyalones seek momentous meetings.

By the same token, being alone is understood as a wellspring of feeling and experience. There is a bittersweet fondness for silence. All those nights alone— they bring insight.

Sometimes, though, we wonder whether we have painted ourselves into a corner. Standards that started out high only become higher once you realize the contours of this existence. When we do find a match, we verge on obsessive—or we resist.

> **All those nights alone— they bring insight.**

And so, a community of like-minded souls is essential.

Since fellow quirkyalones are not abundant (we are probably less than 5 percent of the population), I recommend reading the patron saint of solitude: German poet Rainer Maria Rilke. Even 100 years after its publication, *Letters to a Young Poet* still feels like it was written for us: "You should not let yourself be confused in your solitude by the fact that there is something in you that wants to break out of it," Rilke writes. "People have (with the help of conventions) oriented all their solutions toward the easy and toward the easiest side of easy, but it is clear that we must hold to that which is difficult."

Rilke is right. Being quirkyalone can be difficult. Everyone else is part of a couple! Still, there are advantages. No one can take our lives away by breaking up with us. Instead of sacrificing our social constellation for the one all-consuming individual, we seek empathy from friends. We have significant others.

And so, when my friend asks me whether being quirkyalone is a life sentence, I say, yes, at the core, one is always quirkyalone. But when one quirkyalone finds another, oooh la la. The earth quakes.

Analyzing the Text

1. According to Cagen, how do quirkyalones view romance and dating? How do they view being single?

2. To what extent is Cagen's label for one type of single person the same as another common label: "the hopeless romantic"? How are these two labels different?

3. How does Cagen use the quote from the German writer Rainer Maria Rilke to help construct her manifesto on being single? How does her reference to Rilke—who believed that embracing suffering and cultivating solitude made someone a better writer—help shape her own manifesto?

4. To what extent is Cagen's manifesto a response to cultural pressures that label being single a problem?

5. **Interrogating Assumptions.**   Which of the assumptions outlined in this chapter's introduction (see pp. 263–70) would Cagen and other quirkyalones most identify with? What details in the essay lead you to your conclusion?

Writing about Cultural Practices

6. Attend a social event on your campus by yourself—no date, no buddy, no meeting with friends once you are there. Afterwards, write an essay that reflects on the experience. As you write, consider the following questions.

   - What did you notice, throughout the event, about how you behaved? Where you stood or sat? Who you talked to, and who talked to you?
   - What are some of the unspoken rules of going single to a social event? How are single people expected to behave?
   - What did you notice about how others treated you? What did you notice about how other single people were treated?
   - To what extent is being single acceptable in social contexts? What details about your experience lead you to this analysis?
   - To what extent is being single in social contexts socially unacceptable? What details about your experience lead you to this analysis?

Ellen Fein and Sherrie Schneider,
Don't Talk to a Man First

Samantha Daniels, **20 Simple Tips for
the Perfect Date**

Dave Singleton, *From* **The MANdates:
25 Real Rules for Successful Gay Dating**

Unlike the 1950s, gender roles are not so narrowly defined today. The sexual rev-olution of the 1960s and '70s encouraged less rigid views about dating, being sexually active, and getting married. Modern America, then, has essentially dropped most of the codes that once made clear how men and women should conduct themselves when it comes to romance. Into this vacuum of guidelines has rushed a plethora of dating tips, advice columns, and how-to guides for people looking for love.

The following readings represent three examples of contemporary dating advice. "Don't Talk to a Man First" is Rule #2 of the 35 rules outlined in the best-selling dating guide for women titled *The Rules: Time-Tested Secrets for Capturing the Heart of Mr. Right* (1995), by Ellen Fein and Sherrie Schneider. The second reading is a how-to essay by Samantha Daniels, a columnist for *Men's Health* and founder of Samantha's Table, a New York– and Los Angeles–based dating service. The third selection offers dating advice for gay men. This essay is the introduction from the book *The MANdates: 25 Real Rules for Successful Gay Dating* by Dave Singleton, published in 2004.

> ▶ Mapping Your Reading
>
> These readings—each written for a different audi-ence—offer a set of cultural documents that give a sense of how we discuss, and apply rules to, ro-mance. What assumptions do the authors of these pieces make about their readers? What assump-tions do they make about romantic love? What do these rules say about American culture today?

Never? Not even "Let's have coffee" or "Do you come here often?" Right, not even these seemingly harmless openers. Otherwise, how will you know if he spotted you first, was smitten by you and had to have you, or is just being polite?

We know what you're thinking. We know how extreme such a rule must sound, not to mention snobbish, silly, and painful; but taken in the context of *The Rules,* it makes perfect sense. After all, the premise of *The Rules* is that we never make anything happen, that we trust in the natural order of things— namely, that man pursues woman.

By talking to a man first, we interfere with whatever was supposed to happen or not happen, perhaps causing a conversation or a date to occur that was never meant to be and inevitably getting hurt in the process. Eventually, he'll talk to the girl he really wants and drop you.

Yet, we manage to rationalize this behavior by telling ourselves, "He's shy" or "I'm just being friendly." Are men really shy? We might as well tackle this question right now. Perhaps a therapist would say so, but we believe that most men are not shy, just not *really, really* interested if they don't approach you. It's hard to accept that, we know. It's also hard waiting for the right one—the one who talks to you first, calls, and basically does most of the work in the beginning of the relationship because he must have you.

> **We trust in the natural order of things—namely, that man pursues woman.**

It's easy to rationalize women's aggressive behavior in this day and age. Unlike years ago when women met men at dances and "coming out" parties and simply waited for one to pick them out of the crowd and start a conversation, today many women are accountants, doctors, lawyers, dentists, and in management positions. They work with men, for men, and men work for them. Men are their patients and their clients. How can a woman not talk to a man first?

The Rules answer is to treat men you are interested in like any other client or patient or coworker, as hard as that may be. Let's face it, when a woman meets a man she really likes, a lightbulb goes on in her head and she sometimes, without realizing it, relaxes, laughs, and spends more time with him than is necessary. She may suggest lunch to discuss something that could be discussed over the phone because she is hoping to ignite some romance. This is a common ploy. Some of the smartest women try to make things happen under the guise of business. They think they are too educated or talented to be passive, play games, or do *The Rules.* They feel their diplomas and paychecks entitle them to do more in life than wait for the phone to ring. These women, we assure you, always end up heartbroken when their forwardness is rebuffed. But why shouldn't it be? Men know what they want. No one has to ask *them* to lunch.

So, the short of it is that if you meet men professionally, you still have to do *The Rules.* You must wait until he brings up lunch or anything else beyond business. As we explain in *Rule #17,* the man must take the lead. Even if you are making the same amount of money as a man you are interested in, he must bring up lunch. If you refuse to accept that men and women are different romantically, even though they may be equal professionally, you will behave like men—talk to them first, ask for their phone number, invite them to discuss the case over dinner at your place—and drive them away. Such forwardness is very risky; sometimes we have seen it work, most of the time it doesn't and it *always* puts the woman through hell emotionally. By not accepting the concept that the man must pursue the woman, women put themselves in jeopardy of being rejected or ignored, if not at the moment, then at some point in the future. We hope you never have to endure the following torture:

Our dentist friend Pam initiated a friendship with Robert when they met in dental school several years ago by asking him out to lunch. *She spoke to him first.* Although they later became lovers and even lived together, he never seemed really "in love" with her and her insecurity about the relationship never went away. Why would it? *She spoke to him first.* He recently broke up with her over something trivial. The truth is he never loved her. Had Pam followed *The Rules*, she would never have spoken to Robert or initiated anything in the first place. Had she followed *The Rules*, she might have met someone else who truly wanted her. She would not have wasted time. *Rules* girls don't waste time.

Here's another example of a smart woman who broke *The Rules:* Claudia, a confident Wall Street broker, spotted her future husband on the dance floor of a popular disco and planted herself next to him for a good five minutes. When he failed to make the first move, she told herself that he was probably shy or had two left feet and asked him to dance. The relationship has been filled with problems. She often complains that he's as "shy" in the bedroom as he was that night on the dance floor.

A word about dances. It's become quite popular these days for women to ask men to dance. Lest there is any doubt in your mind, this behavior is totally against *The Rules*. If a man doesn't bother to walk across the room to seek you out and ask you to dance, then he's obviously not interested and asking him to dance won't change his feelings or rather his lack of feelings for you. He'll probably be flattered that you asked and dance with you just to be polite and he might even want to have sex with you that night, but he won't be crazy about you. Either he didn't notice you or you made it too easy. He never got the chance to pursue you and this fact will always permeate the relationship even if he does ask you out.

We know what you're thinking: What am I supposed to do all night if no one asks me to dance? Unfortunately, the answer is to go to the bathroom five times if you have to, reapply your lipstick, powder your nose, order more water from the bar, think happy thoughts, walk around the room in circles until someone notices you, make phone calls from the lobby to your married friends for encouragement—in short, anything but ask a man to dance. Dances are not necessarily fun for us. They may be fun for other women who just want to go out and have a good time. But you're looking for love and marriage so you can't always do what you feel like. You have to do *The Rules*. That means that even when you're bored or lonely, you don't ask men to dance. Don't even stand next to someone you like, hoping he'll ask you, as many women do. You have to *wait* for someone

> You're looking for love and marriage. You can't always do what you feel like. You have to do *The Rules*.

to notice you. You might have to go home without having met anyone you liked or even danced one dance. But tell yourself that at least you got to practice *The Rules* and there's always another dance. You walk out with a sense of accomplishment that at least you didn't break *The Rules*!

If this sounds boring, remember the alternative is worse. Our good friend Sally got so resentful of having to dance with all the "losers" at a particular party that she finally decided to defy *The Rules* she knew only too well and asked the best-looking man in the room to dance. Not only was he flattered, but they danced for hours and he asked her out for the next three nights. "Maybe there are exceptions to *The Rules*," she thought triumphantly. She found out otherwise, of course. It seems Mr. Right was in town for just a few days on business and had a girlfriend on the West Coast. No wonder he hadn't asked anyone to dance that night. He probably just went to the party to have fun, not to find his future wife. The moral of the story: Don't figure out why someone hasn't asked you to dance—there's always a good reason.

Men aren't interested in women who are witty in a negative way.

Unfortunately, more women than men go to dances to meet "The One." Their eagerness and anxiety get the best of them and they end up talking to men first or asking them to dance. So you must condition yourself not to expect anything from a dance. View it simply as an excuse to put on high heels, apply a new shade of blush, and be around a lot of people. Chances are someone of the opposite sex will start to talk to *you* at some point in the evening. If and when he does, and you're not having such a great time, don't show it. For example, don't be clever or cynical and say, "I would have been better off staying home and watching *Seinfeld*." Men aren't interested in women who are witty in a negative way. If someone asks if you're having a good time, simply say yes and smile.

If you find all of this much too hard to do, then don't go to the dance. Stay home, do sit-ups, watch *Seinfeld*, and reread *The Rules*. It's better to stay home and read *The Rules* than go out and break them.

1. It's okay to suggest a drink instead of dinner for a first date. She dreads a boring four-course ordeal, too.
2. Call her by early evening on Monday to confirm a Tuesday get-together. (Weekends aren't for first dates.)
3. Leave your home and work numbers. No home number and she'll assume you have a wife or girlfriend.
4. If you want to keep the plans a surprise, at least clue her in as to what to wear. You do not want an overdressed, overstressed woman navigating the Talladega pits in high heels.
5. Yes, she'll notice if the date location you've chosen is conveniently around the block from your place.
6. Don't assume that just because you're out with a beautiful woman, she knows how pretty she looks—she wants to hear it from you.
7. Ask if she's too cold or too warm, and if changing the temperature is in your power, fix it.
8. Men judge women according to whether they can picture having sex with them; women judge men by whether they can imagine kissing them. White teeth, fresh breath, and unchapped lips make her more apt to pucker up.
9. Do not ask her, "So, what kind of music do you like?" The last 25 guys asked that. Be original.
10. She loves when you insist on ordering dessert. Sharing = extra sexy.
11. Tip well: Grab the check, mentally divide the bill by 10, double that number, and throw down the tip. Do it quickly but casually. Believe me, she'll be watching.
12. If she touches your arm, she's interested; if she touches your leg, she's interested tonight.
13. When in doubt, hold her hand.
14. Very small protective gestures go a long way and show her you're a gentleman: Offer your arm as she's stepping from a curb, direct her away from shards of broken glass. She'll notice if you wait until she's safely in her car or house before you leave. Wait the extra 90 seconds, and next time you might be going in with her.
15. She expects you to know her eye color after the first date.
16. Women need momentum—without it, they lose interest or wonder if you have. Momentum = a minimum of one date a week, plus a couple of phone calls in between.
17. She knows that when you invite her over for a homemade meal or to watch a movie, it's code for "tonight is hook-up night." Don't play this card any earlier than date three.
18. A Friday or Saturday night is required by date four. Otherwise, she'll wonder who else you're seeing.
19. Rule of Groping: If anything happens that couldn't be shown on prime-time TV, call her the next day. Otherwise, she'll feel cheap and used.
20. Don't say, "I'll call you," if you have no intention to. She'd prefer that you say nothing at all.

Of course, you don't know anything about gay dating until you're out there on the frontlines. I certainly didn't.

To borrow from the opening of *Great Expectations:* I was born. I lived. I came out. I started "dating," which I defined as an often slow, tedious process of getting acquainted with a variety of men. Once you meet someone who shares your attraction and interests, then you consider dating him on an increasingly intense level leading perhaps, one day, to a relationship.

But I didn't like dating back then. I didn't know what I was doing and there were no guidelines, so I hit plenty of bumps and potholes on the road to love. I soon chose "immediate serial monogamy" as my dating alternative since it felt less bumpy and more romantic. After all, you meet a guy you like, and after fifteen minutes of mutual sustained attraction, you become a couple. What's wrong with that? Didn't it work for Loretta Lynn in *Coal Miner's Daughter?*

I'd jump into relationships faster than a paratrooper.

Maybe, but after a few attempts, I learned it didn't work for me. I'd jump into relationships faster than a paratrooper, then emerge from monogamist seclusion a year or two later, shake off the dust, and wonder what the hell happened when it was obvious to everyone else how mismatched my partner and I were. I'd take a break, chalk it up to fate, and start the cycle over. That's the life of a gay serial monogamist. I don't recommend it. When you jump into relationships that quickly, with only a shred of postbreakup analysis in between, you often end up with lovers whose interests, personality, values, and goals don't match yours at all.

After a therapist assured me I wasn't really a lesbian, despite my penchant for Sapphic insta-relationships (lifetime commitment by the second date, moving in with U-Haul on the third) and fierce Stevie Nicks CDs, I decided to quit making the same mistakes and dive into the dating pool.

I spent many nights at coffee houses, dinners, and movies with a variety of guys I met at parties, the gym, and work. I noticed that all my gay male friends were dating constantly, too, but spending an even greater amount of time talking about it.

I logged hours listening to tales of jerks, losers, the one who got away, the hot one at the bar last night, the one who wouldn't leave the house the next day, the one who seemed so sweet before he went into a drug-induced rage, and the one who came on strong like a hurricane and left without a trace. I'd like to say that we did *not* resemble the cast of *The Broken Hearts Club,* but, unfortunately, like them, we spent our Saturday mornings at coffee shops pouring over Friday's dates, and anticipating the three-ring dating circus that would follow on Saturday and Sunday. Sunday evening, we'd retrench with drinks and more dating rehash than a greasy-spoon diner.

What did I learn from all this?

I learned that there are 8 million gay men, and four stories.

I learned that tales of dating woe poured out before my required-and-stipulated-clearly-in-my-contract morning coffee made my eyes glaze over.

I learned how to get the most out of a "screener" drinks date in 30 minutes or less. This lopped off an hour and a half off my initial two-hour time. It was all about asking the right questions.

I learned that the Alcoholics Anonymous definition of insanity is on target: "repeating the same behavior over and over and expecting a different outcome."

Most important, I realized that the stories I was hearing were strikingly similar to my own. Like characters in an all-male cast of *Groundhog Day,* we were experiencing and doing the same things again and again. My friends and I discussed other men as if there were somehow two different species, "us" and "them," which, of course, made no sense.

Here we were, reasonably attractive gay guys with more opportunities than previous generations ever had, more places to be open, and certainly more coffee- and beer-induced "date talk" than I ever imagined. Thanks to the magic of the Internet, we quickly located gay neighborhoods, bars, and restaurants anywhere in the world, as well as found the actual men via phenomenally packed chat rooms and increasingly popular on-line personals. Popular Web portals such as PlanetOut.com, Gay.com, and AOL.com (the mother of all Internet love) became virtual one-stop shops for romance.

So with all these new ways for gay guys to meet and interact, why weren't we happier about it? Were there now too many options? An oft-repeated criticism of the '90s Information Age boom was that too many options do not, in and of themselves, improve anything. You need to learn to pay attention to commonsense guidelines so you can navigate through all those choices.

Where were our rules?

During an all-guy dinner full of laughs, empathizing head nods, impatient eye rolls, and attempts at advice for tale upon tale of dating woe, I asked myself the following question: With so many gay guys experiencing the same damn dating patterns, where were our rules?

Putting the Date in Mandate

Let's do some "dating" math. There are 95 million men over the age of 18 in the United States, according to the Census Bureau. Forty-two percent, or 40 million, of them are unmarried (27 percent have *never* been married—the really suspicious ones). That means up to 4 million of them are gay and single, if you believe the Kinsey study that claimed one in ten men are gay.

Aside from a few stray loners, celibate closet cases, and inmates, many of them are dating. But it's a sad, twisted tale of men alone in the cold, wreaking havoc on each other, and lost without dating guidelines.

Can a conscience rest with news like this? Historically, no civilized society has ever been without codes or norms for dating. From Australia to Zimbabwe, every society has rules about courtship, rules that young people absorb before they wade into the swamp of dating. But across the world, eligible gay men are still "social outlaws," a ragtag gang of hormonally driven cowboys riding into romantic battle with guns, "ammo," and no clue.

Gay men are in the early years of a new millennium with a whole new century of possibility. But it'll be a new century full of Friday nights alone at bars, hunched over computers virtually propositioning chat-room habitués, or watching television repeats of *Buffy the Vampire Slayer*, unless we learn how to put the "date" in mandate.

Dating Rules: Not Just for Straight Women Anymore

All the single people I know (sadly, some of the married ones, too) want to date more successfully. Straight or gay, most singles want to rise from the muck and mire to win the dating game. But somehow, straight women are the only ones getting advice on how to do this.

In fact, women have been inundated with romantic rules lately. Don't call him. Don't seem desperate. Be "a creature unlike any other," whatever the hell that means. Fool the hell out of him if you want your shot at the goal, which, according to *The Rules*, is a *Leave It to Beaver* marriage with bread-winner husband, lovely children, fidelity forever, and a yellow brick road.

Thankfully, after *The Rules* came a vicious backlash. Independent women revolted at those outdated notions of how to nab a man, wrangle a ring out of him, and then ease the poor worm down the aisle. Then—surprise, surprise—an author of *The Rules* announced her divorce after publishing a sequel of "time-tested" marriage guidelines. As I watched late-night comics have a field day with the irony, I thought to myself, "At least straight people have rules to complain about." And if we were going to have rules, what would they be? What kind of rules would work for gay people? I wouldn't want them to mirror typical straight rules. It's clear that they are no panacea for dating woes.

> **From Australia to Zimbabwe, every society has rules about courtship.**

Dating rules, and the backlash, focused on straights, missing completely the other 10 percent of the population who endure the messy dating process. Why? Well, you can argue that openly discussed gay life is a relatively new concept. How can you examine gay dating habits and develop dating rules and goals when gay people are in a closet? About 30 years ago at the Stonewall riots, the first martyred drag queen put her oversize high heel down, kicking off the gay rights movement (with great style and bearing I am sure). Until then, we lived in a shadowy, secret society with no distinct goals. Now, we're pioneering pilgrims of another age, but please, without the buckle shoes.

What's the Dating Goal for Gay Men?

So three cheers and two shakes of a feathered tambourine for all this newfound dating freedom, but what the hell do we do with it now? Traditionally, marriage with children is the long-standing goal for straight relationships, as well as the benchmark for "girl gets boy" dating rules. But what's the dating goal for gay men? How could there be just one?

Gay marriage is certainly one possible goal for those with access to Amsterdam, Canada, and possibly one day New England, where ten thousand gays with rainbow rings will descend on Ben & Jerry's country, standing before each other, God, and a field of cows to say "We do."

But since marriage isn't a realistic option right now, maybe relationship-oriented gays can anticipate celebrating that all-important milestone—the first-year dating anniversary. If you measure gay relationships in dog years (seven for every one), you'll be hitting the 25-year mark in no time.

If long-term commitment is your goal, you can always strive to co-invest in real estate, a much harder union to dissolve than marriage. Ask anyone who's ever bought a home with a significant other and then suffered through the traumas of a breakup. That's when the promise "till death do us part" becomes a dare.

Straight dating rules have one goal: the "together forever till death do us part" marriage vow. But that isn't the only gay dating goal. Gay men are too diverse to share one common dating goal. We are not subject to the same societal pressure for us to marry. Many of us wouldn't want to if we could.

Instead, the real goal is for men to date successfully. That means finding a man who attracts you, sustains your interest, makes you as happy as you make him, and wants the same level of dating as you.

That doesn't necessarily mean celebrating your fiftieth anniversary together surrounded by your grandchildren, though a few gay couples may be able to do that. That doesn't mean all the traditional trappings of straight rules, with their white weddings and promises of love everlasting. Rules shouldn't set you up for failure or set unrealistic expectations or promise impossible things. Life doesn't work like that. But rules for gay people can be guidelines and that's better than anything we've had.

Dating is difficult for anyone, but it's harder for gay men for a few reasons:

It's a numbers game. From a sheer numbers standpoint, the population of available men is relatively smaller for gays than straights (though if you live in Chelsea, the Castro, or Dupont Circle, my gay friend Steve argues, "You can't swing a cat by the tail without hitting ten of us").

We've had few role models. Off the top of your head, think of five current or past gay dating relationships you can point to and say, "I want that!"

There's a disproportional focus on youth and beauty. This doesn't apply to all, of course, but there's a gay culture emphasis on youth and beauty that often eclipses other important elements of a dating relationship. The gay "biological clock" is linked to aging, not ovaries.

It's a straight, straight, straight world. Almost all the romantic images we grew up with are straight, so we must reinvent romance for ourselves. That can be a slow process. The baggage that gay guys initially bring to dating—such as negative gay stereotypes we grew up with, and expectations based on what we saw in our

There's a gay culture emphasis on youth and beauty that often eclipses other elements of a dating relationship.

families, society, movies, and television—gets lighter as the trip gets longer. But, despite more positive images than ever before, gays still have fewer role models on which to base our romantic interactions. Since we are pioneers, it probably takes us more time and more tries to find Mr. Right than it does the average straight. Hopefully, we figure it out before we end up gumming Jell-O during singles night at the old gay folks' home.

Matchmaking and fix-ups are a rarity. Where is your "Auntie Yenta" when you need her? In addition to a smaller gay single population, even fewer gay couples are willing to play matchmaker. And with your single gay pals, you can pretty much bet that if some hot guy comes along, they aren't likely to wrap him up as your birthday surprise fix-up. More likely, they'll nab him if they can. Men, after all, are taught to go after what we want.

Gay men have a propensity toward dysfunction. Okay, it's a broad generalization, but find me one gay man who will refute it. I am speaking more of emotional dysfunction than other kinds of dysfunction. No one would dispute that gay men in general are very functional within the community. For example, no one can gentrify a neighborhood better than we can. While there's no mistaking that gay men are functional in many ways, studies show that our community has higher instances of alcoholism, drug addiction, and self-loathing than the straight population. All of which make dating tougher, unless your dream guy is a Tennessee Williams character.

There's a wide range of dating goals. Want a challenge? In a community with such diverse dating goals, try to pinpoint the guy who wants what you want. Despite headline-catching battles for legalized gay marriage, many gay guys have zero interest in getting married. No societal pressure on gays to marry is a curse for some, but a blessing for others who relish freedom from traditional social constraints. Since a long-term relationship with a lifetime commitment isn't the only gay dating norm, you have to figure out what you want and then find an emotionally and physically compatible guy who wants the same.

So Many Men, So Many Options, So Much Confusion!

To paraphrase that Miguel Brown disco anthem, there are "so many men, so many options!" Options can confuse rather than focus. Based on observations from men interviewed for this book, dating goals range widely from superficial (looks, money, sex, casual hookups) to deep (common interests and companionship) to all points in between. More to the point, many guys either don't know what they want, say they want one thing but pursue something else, or are too paralyzed by options to decide on a goal.

Unless you've been cloistered in a monastery or are a recently "out" dating virgin (we call these newbies), you've encountered guys who have confused, tortured, or mysteriously abandoned you. Maybe you've even been the person responsible for a former date's psychiatrist bills. In either case, some of these typical gay archetypes might ring a bell:

Peter Pan–sexual. As Andrew, a 32-year-old Princeton grad from New Jersey who runs his own consulting business, said, "I met what I thought was the perfect guy for me. We were a good fit in every way from sexual to social, loved doing the same things, even finished each other's sentences. But, at the end of the day, he wanted to settle down, and I didn't—and still don't—want that. Nothing against it, but I just want a fun guy to hang out with and date, not move in with and settle down." Andrew wants lots of intimacy and will come on strong, but don't get too close. His little green flying suit is never far, far away.

The poetic "bait and switch" body Nazi. Bill, an athletic 31-year-old from Minnesota, says, "Having a boyfriend these days is all about your body fat percentage." His idea of a perfect date is sharing one of those tasteless MET-Rx nutrition bars after a romantic "his and his" caliper test. But in his personal ad, he claims he's interested in "reading, writing poetry, long walks on the beach at night, and guys who take care of themselves emotionally as well as physically." There is no truth in this advertising.

The young, restless, and clueless. Aaron, a 24-year-old bartender in Ft. Lauderdale, thinks dating is "all about money, looks, and social status. When guys see I am a bartender, they want a fling but nothing real." Aaron wants a relationship with a guy around his own age who shares common interests like music and art history, but hasn't found one who takes him seriously. Then again, most of the guys Aaron meets are older and hang out at the bar, where Aaron spends 60 percent of his free time.

Mr. Too Old to Be Looking for Love in All the Wrong Places. Kevin, a 38-year-old association executive, says, "I want a boyfriend to create a life together, not some occasional sex buddy." Though he attracts enough guys to keep his dating stream steady, the dates consistently fizzle after the first or second one. He isn't sure if he comes off too desperate or too aloof. It's dawning on him that, at his age, he might be looking for love in all the wrong places, like gay bars and clubs, but he doesn't realize that there are alternative meeting places. He's sitting home alone on Saturday nights questioning a new approach before dating anymore.

The "bi-curious" male who's as straight as a circle. Tim, a 36-year-old lobbyist from Washington, D.C., wants "a guy to fool around with once in a while, somebody who's more like my straight college roommate," so Tim ends up dumping any guy who exhibits stereotypically gay characteristics from Clinique in the medicine cabinet to a fondness for dance music. He meets lots of gay guys at the gym and through work, but he's quick to point out that dating isn't satisfying. Though he can't see himself actually dating a guy, he still craves the sex long after any "curiosity" should have been satisfied. Tim is typical of many gay men who say they are bi-curious, just experimenting, or want a guy who's "straight acting," which usually just means they dislike themselves.

From the "young, restless, and clueless" to the "too old to be looking for love in all the wrong places," you'll encounter many different types of guys. One guy wants to date so he can find a life partner, the sooner the better. Another guy wants to find his match for "no strings" hookups. Many want to break bad patterns and just eliminate psychos from their comfortable, casual dating repertoire. Understand what motivates you so that you can understand what motivates him! As you learn more about yourself, and your nature, you'll understand your dates better.

Forget the psychobabble for just a minute, and face one fact: Gay or straight, men are men. Successfully dating a man, when you *are* a man, takes special skills, insight, and understanding that this book aspires to provide.

So if you're gay, throw out whatever dating rules you've heard. Most make no sense for gay men since they were created to give women a leg up, so to speak, on straight men. Their success depends on a woman's ability to trick a man into total surrender and holy matrimony. The dating rules you've heard are all about gender differentiation. Not much help for you, are they?

What makes sense, however, is for gay men to learn through other gay men's dating experiences. Sharing our common "war" stories is one of the benefits from gay men coming out in droves since the 1970s. Maybe that's why I refer to *The Mandates* as "lessons learned from the frontlines of gay dating." Learning these funny and true rules will help you gain perspective on your dating goals, target your best type, weed out losers earlier, and avoid common pitfalls.

▶ Analyzing the Text

1. Why do you think dating rules and tips are so popular? What assumptions about romantic love do they use to persuade their readers?

2. When it comes to romance, how do each of these readings define gender roles? How are women supposed to behave? How are straight men supposed to behave? How are gay men supposed to behave? What details in each of the readings reveal the gender politics behind the assumptions of the authors?

3. One common rhetorical technique of dating guides is that they offer to let the reader in on "how the other half thinks." Identify examples for all three readings of this. Why is this such a powerful technique for dating rules?

4. One of the central assumptions that drives *The Rules* is that women want to find "the one" and "capture" him. According to its authors, how should women do this? What do these authors assume a successful love relationship is like?

5. Although *The Rules* was met with heavy criticism when it was published because of its built-in assumptions about women's roles, doesn't "20 Simple Tips for the Perfect Date" operate under the same sets of beliefs? Why, then, might some readers find *The Rules* unacceptable, but "20 Simple Tips" palatable?

6. According to Dave Singleton, why do gay men need a dating guide? How are cultural expectations for finding romance or love the same for gay and straight men? How are they different? What details in *The MANdates* lead you to your observations?

7. What is Singleton's critique of straight dating guides, particularly *The Rules*? How successfully does he avoid the pitfalls or problems associated with those dating guides in this excerpt from *The MANdates*?

8. **Interrogating Assumptions.** Consider the advice given by these selections. On what assumptions about romance—including those outlined in this chapter's introduction (pp. 263–70) and any others you can think of—are each of these how-to readings based? Are the readings based on the same assumptions? Different ones? How do you account for this?

▶ Writing about Cultural Practices

9. Develop a rhetorical analysis of a dating how-to guide. To begin, visit your library or local used bookstore to find a copy of a guide to romance that you can use for this assignment. As you develop your critique, consider the following questions.

   - When was the guide published? Who is the intended audience for the guide?
   - What assumptions does the author make about his or her intended audience? What details in the guide lead you to these observations?
   - How does the guide define potential significant others? According to the author, what qualities or values are preferred in a potential mate?
   - How does the author's formula for finding romance or love rely on idealized notions about romance or love?

Laura Kipnis, **Against Love**

Laura Kipnis is a professor of media studies at Northwestern University. She has published many essays on sexual politics and contemporary culture. This essay, originally published in the *New York Times Magazine* in 2001, is an excerpt from her book, *Against Love: A Polemic* (2003). In her book, Kipnis examines the meaning and cultural significance of adultery. She argues that the real question isn't "Why do people commit adultery?" but "Why do we believe we can only find happiness or completeness in long-term, monogamous relationships?" In this essay, Kipnis argues that our society's commonly accepted notions of romantic love snow people into remaining in coupled relationships that lack passion and squelch individuality.

▶ **Mapping Your Reading**

Whereas previous readings in this chapter have offered an opportunity for you to identify, label, and understand some commonly accepted assumptions about romance, this essay offers a critique of these assumptions. As you read, highlight or underline passages in which Kipnis describes her problem with modern love. In the author's view, what expectations are placed on today's relationships? What rules and language characterize them? And how much freedom do couples really have?

L ove is, as we know, a mysterious and controlling force. It has vast power over our thoughts and life decisions. It demands our loyalty, and we, in turn, freely comply. Saying no to love isn't simply heresy; it is tragedy—the failure to achieve what is most essentially human. So deeply internalized is our obedience to this most capricious despot that artists create passionate odes to its cruelty, and audiences seem never to tire of the most deeply unoriginal mass spectacles devoted to rehearsing the litany of its torments, fixating their very beings on the narrowest glimmer of its fleeting satisfactions.

Yet despite near total compliance, a buzz of social nervousness attends the subject. If a society's lexicon of romantic pathologies[1] reveals its particular anxi-

---

[1]**society's lexicon of romantic pathologies:** A lexicon is a vocabulary, or stock of words, shared by a group of people. In this phrase, Kipnis suggests that our commonly accepted notions of romance are unreasonable.

eties, high on our own list would be diagnoses like "inability to settle down" or "immaturity," leveled at those who stray from the norms of domestic coupledom either by refusing entry in the first place or, once installed, pursuing various escape routes: excess independence, ambivalence, "straying," divorce. For the modern lover, "maturity" isn't a depressing signal of impending decrepitude but a sterling achievement, the sine qua non[2] of a lover's qualifications to love and be loved.

> Most of us pledge ourselves to unions that will far outlast the desire that impelled them into being.

This injunction to achieve maturity—synonymous in contemporary usage with 30-year mortgages, spreading waistlines, and monogamy—obviously finds its raison d'être[3] in modern love's central anxiety, that structuring social contradiction the size of the San Andreas Fault: namely, the expectation that romance and sexual attraction can last a lifetime of coupled togetherness despite much hard evidence to the contrary.

Ever optimistic, heady with love's utopianism, most of us eventually pledge ourselves to unions that will, if successful, far outlast the desire that impelled them into being. The prevailing cultural wisdom is that even if sexual desire tends to be a short-lived phenomenon, "mature love" will kick in to save the day when desire flags. The issue that remains unaddressed is whether cutting off other possibilities of romance and sexual attraction for the more muted pleasures of mature love isn't similar to voluntarily amputating a healthy limb: a lot of anesthesia is required and the phantom pain never entirely abates. But if it behooves a society to convince its citizenry that wanting change means personal failure or wanting to start over is shameful or simply wanting more satisfaction than what you have is an illicit thing, clearly grisly acts of self-mutilation will be required.

There hasn't always been quite such optimism about love's longevity. For the Greeks, inventors of democracy and a people not amenable to being pushed around by despots, love was a disordering and thus preferably brief experience. During the reign of courtly love, love was illicit and usually fatal. Passion meant suffering: The happy ending didn't yet exist in the cultural imagination. As far as togetherness as an eternal ideal, the twelfth-century advice manual "De Amore et Amor is Remedio" ("On Love and the Remedies of Love") warned that too many opportunities to see or chat with the beloved would certainly decrease love.

The innovation of happy love didn't even enter the vocabulary of romance until the seventeenth century. Before the eighteenth century—when the family

---

[2]**sine qua non:** A prerequisite. In this phrase, the writer observes that, in order to love and be loved, a person must "be mature."

[3]**raison d'être:** The justification or reason for something's existence. Here the writer is arguing that people use their belief that "romance and sexual attraction can last a lifetime" to justify their acceptance of "adult" responsibilities.

was primarily an economic unit of production rather than a hothouse of Oedipal tensions[4]—marriages were business arrangements between families; participants had little to say on the matter. Some historians consider romantic love a learned behavior that really only took off in the late eighteenth century along with the new fashion for reading novels, though even then affection between a husband and wife was considered to be in questionable taste.

Historians disagree, of course. Some tell the story of love as an eternal and unchanging essence; others, as a progress narrative over stifling social conventions. (Sometimes both stories are told at once; consistency isn't required.) But has modern love really set us free? Fond as we are of projecting our own emotional quandaries back through history, construing vivid costume dramas featuring medieval peasants or biblical courtesans sharing their feelings with the post-Freudian savvy of lifelong analysands,[5] our amatory[6] predecessors clearly didn't share all our particular aspirations about their romantic lives.

We, by contrast, feel like failures when love dies. We believe it could be otherwise. Since the cultural expectation is that a state of coupled permanence is achievable, uncoupling is experienced as crisis and inadequacy—even though such failures are more the norm than the exception.

For the Greeks, love was a disordering and thus preferably brief experience.

As love has increasingly become the center of all emotional expression in the popular imagination, anxiety about obtaining it in sufficient quantities—and for sufficient duration—suffuses the population. Everyone knows that as the demands and expectations on couples escalated, so did divorce rates. And given the current divorce statistics (roughly 50 percent of all marriages end in divorce), all indications are that whomever you love today—your beacon of hope, the center of all your optimism—has a good chance of becoming your worst nightmare tomorrow. (Of course, that 50 percent are those who actually leave their unhappy marriages and not a particularly good indication of the happiness level or nightmare potential of those who remain.) Lawrence Stone, a historian of marriage, suggests—rather jocularly, you can't help thinking—that today's rising divorce rates are just a modern technique for achieving what was once taken care of far more efficiently by early mortality.

Love may or may not be a universal emotion, but clearly the social forms it takes are infinitely malleable. It is our culture alone that has dedicated itself to allying the turbulence of romance and the rationality of the long-term couple,

---

[4]**Oedipal tension:** According to the psychoanalytic theory of Sigmund Freud, Oedipal tension exists when a child unconsciously superimposes his or her love for the parent of the opposite sex with sexual tension. Usually this is expressed in the child's jealousy over attention given to the same sex parent.

[5]**analysands:** A term used to describe people who are undergoing counseling or regularly meeting with a therapist.

[6]**amatory:** Relating to, expressing, or typical of physical love.

convinced that both love and sex are obtainable from one person over the course of decades, that desire will manage to sustain itself for 30 or 40 or 50 years and that the supposed fate of social stability is tied to sustaining a fleeting experience beyond its given life span.

Of course, the parties involved must "work" at keeping passion alive (and we all know how much fun that is), the presumption being that even after living in close proximity to someone for a historically unprecedented length of time, you will still muster the requisite desire to achieve sexual congress on a regular basis. (Should passion fizzle out, just give up sex. Lack of desire for a mate is never an adequate rationale for "looking elsewhere.") And it is true, many couples do manage to perform enough psychic retooling to reshape the anarchy of desire to the confines of the marriage bed, plugging away at the task year after year (once a week, same time, same position) like diligent assembly-line workers, aided by the occasional fantasy or two to help get the old motor to turn over, or keep running, or complete the trip. And so we have the erotic life of a nation of workaholics: If sex seems like work, clearly you're not working hard enough at it.

But passion must not be allowed to die! The fear—or knowledge—that it does shapes us into particularly conflicted psychological beings, perpetually in search of prescriptions and professional interventions, regardless of cost or consequence. Which does have its economic upside, at least. Whole new sectors of the economy have been spawned, with massive social investment in new technologies from Viagra to couples' porn: capitalism's Lourdes for dying marriages.

Our culture alone is convinced that both love and sex are obtainable from one person over the course of decades.

There are assorted low-tech solutions to desire's dilemmas too. Take advice. In fact, take more and more advice. Between print, airwaves, and the therapy industry, if there were any way to quantify the G.N.P. in romantic counsel, it would be a staggering number. Desperate to be cured of love's temporality, a love-struck populace has molded itself into an advanced race of advice receptacles, like some new form of miracle sponge that can instantly absorb many times its own body weight in wetness.

Inexplicably, however, a rebellious breakaway faction keeps trying to leap over the wall and emancipate themselves, not from love itself—unthinkable!—but from love's domestic confinements. The escape routes are well trodden—love affairs, midlife crises—though strewn with the left-behind luggage of those who encountered unforeseen obstacles along the way (panic, guilt, self-engineered exposures) and beat self-abashed retreats to their domestic gulags, even after pledging body and soul to newfound loves in the balmy utopias of nondomesticated romances. Will all the adulterers in the audience please stand up? You know who you are. Don't be embarrassed! Adulterers aren't just "playing around." These are our home-grown closet social theorists, because adultery is not just a referendum on the sustainability of monogamy; it is a veiled philosophical discussion about the social contract itself. The question on the table is this: "How much renunciation of desire does society demand of us, versus the degree of gratification

**Steve Carroll, 60, and
Chuck Maisel, 74**

Secastocol, California
Together for 30 years

Steve (top): *"When we got together, we immediately merged our finances. Chuck owned a lovely home in Sausalito, and to my total astonishment, he made me joint tenant with him. We have always maintained one checking account, and all of our investments and everything are in both our names. That is about as formal as a gay couple can get. And I think, like a lot of couples, it has helped us get through rough spots in life. When your lives are totally intertwined, it makes more sense to resolve issues than to start cutting things apart most of the time.*

"At this point, after 30 years, Chuck and I have very few rules in our relationship. We don't have a rule, for instance, that you can never go out on the other one. We realized from time to time the opportunity would present itself, and we also realized that if we turned down every opportunity that presented itself to us, eventually we might begin to resent each other. So we said, O.K., you can go ahead and do it, but never make a date that leaves me sitting at home while you are out with someone else. And we have never done that. From time to time we have had affairs with other people, or moments of sexual release, but they were recreational."

Chuck: *"Jealousy probably breaks up more gay people than anything in the world. I guess that goes for all couples. And jealousy is caused by a lack of trust. The one who lacks trust the most and is accusing the other of cheating, he's usually the one who is cheating. Jealousy is based on guilt, an awful lot. But if you are absolutely convinced that the person you are with is totally open to you, that nothing is hidden, there won't be problems, ever. I know that Brad Pitt could not walk in this house and take Steve away from me. I am absolutely convinced of that. I have total confidence in that. In my case, it is Michael York, but I go way back. And when you know that, sex is really an unimportant aspect, in terms of the deep emotions of your relationship. There is a movie called* Relax . . . It's Just Sex—*I love that title. It is only sex: It has no deep-seated meaning. It may seem to be a part of romance— certainly it jump-starts it—but as the years go by, it becomes more of a bonus to the relationship. There are no earthquakes that can happen as a result of sex."*

it provides?" Clearly, the adulterer's answer, following a long line of venerable social critics, would be, "Too much."

But what exactly is it about the actual lived experience of modern domestic love that would make flight such a compelling option for so many? Let us briefly examine those material daily life conditions.

Fundamentally, to achieve love and qualify for entry into that realm of salvation and transcendence known as the couple (the secular equivalent of entering a state of divine grace), you must *be* a lovable person. And what precisely does being lovable entail? According to the tenets of modern love, it requires an advanced working knowledge of the intricacies of *mutuality*.

Mutuality means recognizing that your partner has needs and being prepared to meet them. This presumes, of course, that the majority of those needs can and should be met by one person. (Question this, and you question the very foundations of the institution. So don't.) These needs of ours run deep, a tangled underground morass of ancient, gnarled roots, looking to ensnarl any hapless soul who might accidentally trod upon their outer radices.[7]

Still, meeting those needs is the most effective way to become the object of another's desire, thus attaining intimacy, which is required to achieve the state known as psychological maturity. (Despite how closely it reproduces the affective conditions of our childhoods, since trading compliance for love is the earliest social lesson learned; we learn it in our cribs.)

You, in return, will have your own needs met by your partner in matters large and small. In practice, many of these matters turn out to be quite small. Frequently, it is the tensions and disagreements over the minutiae of daily living that stand between couples and their requisite intimacy. Taking out the garbage, tone of voice, a forgotten errand—these are the rocky shoals upon which intimacy so often founders.

Mutuality requires *communication*, since in order to be met, these needs must be expressed. (No one's a mind reader, which is not to say that many of us don't expect this quality in a mate. Who wants to keep having to tell someone what you need?) What you need is for your mate to understand you—your desires, your contradictions, your unique sensitivities, what irks you. (In practice, that means what about your mate irks you.) You, in turn, must learn to understand the mate's needs. This means being willing to hear what about yourself irks your mate. Hearing is not a simple physiological act performed with the ears, as you will learn. You may think you know how to *hear*, but that doesn't mean that you know how to *listen*.

With two individuals required to coexist in enclosed spaces for extended periods of time, domesticity requires substantial quantities of compromise and adaptation simply to avoid mayhem. Yet with the post-Romantic ideal of unconstrained individuality informing our most fundamental ideas of the self, this can prove a perilous process. Both parties must be willing to jettison whatever aspects of individuality might prove irritating while being simultaneously allowed to retain enough individuality to feel their autonomy is not being sacrificed, even as it is being surgically excised.

Having mastered mutuality, you may now proceed to *advanced intimacy*. Advanced intimacy involves inviting your partner "in" to your most interior self. Whatever and wherever our "inside" is, the widespread—if somewhat metaphysical—belief in its existence (and the related belief that whatever is in there is dying to get out) has assumed a quasi-medical status. Leeches once served a

---

[7]**radices:** The beginning of a root system in a plant. Taken here, *radices* refers to the roots or points where a person's emotional needs begin.

similar purpose. Now we "express our feelings" in lieu of our fluids because everyone knows that those who don't are far more prone to cancer, ulcers, or various dire ailments.

With love as our culture's patent medicine, prescribed for every ill (now even touted as a necessary precondition for that other great American obsession, longevity), we willingly subject ourselves to any number of arcane procedures in its quest. "Opening up" is required for relationship health, so lovers fashion themselves after doctors wielding long probes to penetrate the tender regions. Try to think of yourself as one big orifice: Now stop clenching and relax. If the procedure proves uncomfortable, it just shows you're not open enough. Psychotherapy may be required before sufficient dilation can be achieved: the world's most expensive lubricant.

If you love me, you'll do what I want—or need, or demand—and I'll love you in return.

Needless to say, this opening-up can leave you feeling quite vulnerable, lying there psychically spread-eagled and shivering on the examining table of your relationship. (A favored suspicion is that your partner, knowing exactly where your vulnerabilities are, deliberately kicks you there—one reason this opening-up business may not always feel as pleasant as advertised.) And as anyone who has spent much time in—or just in earshot of—a typical couple knows, the "expression of needs" is often the Trojan horse[8] of intimate warfare, since expressing needs means, by definition, that one's partner has thus far failed to meet them.

In any long-term couple, this lexicon of needs becomes codified over time into a highly evolved private language with its own rules. Let's call this couple grammar. Close observation reveals this as a language composed of one recurring unit of speech: the interdiction—highly nuanced, mutually imposed commands and strictures extending into the most minute areas of household affairs, social life, finances, speech, hygiene, allowable idiosyncrasies, and so on. From bathroom to bedroom, car to kitchen, no aspect of coupled life is not subject to scrutiny, negotiation, and codes of conduct.

A sample from an inexhaustible list, culled from interviews with numerous members of couples of various ages, races, and sexual orientations:

You can't leave the house without saying where you're going. You can't not say what time you'll return. You can't go out when the other person feels like staying at home. You can't be a slob. You can't do less than 50 percent of the work around the house, even if the other person wants to do 100 percent more cleaning than you find necessary or even reasonable. You can't leave the dishes for later, load them the way that seems best to you, drink straight from the carton, or make crumbs. You can't leave the bathroom door open—it's offensive. You can't leave the bathroom door closed—your partner needs to get in. You can't not

---

[8]**Trojan horse:** The term comes from a mythological episode of the Trojan war. A "trojan horse" is something that appears to be a gift, talent, or advantage, but that is actually a curse; trojan horse tactics are disruptive, underhanded, or ruthless.

shave your underarms or legs. You can't gain weight. You can't watch soap operas. You can't watch infomercials or the pregame show or Martha Stewart. You can't eat what you want—goodbye Marshmallow Fluff; hello tofu meatballs. You can't spend too much time on the computer. And stay out of those chat rooms. You can't take risks, unless they are agreed-upon risks, which somewhat limits the concept of "risk." You can't make major purchases alone, or spend money on things the other person considers excesses. You can't blow money just because you're in a bad mood, and you can't be in a bad mood without being required to explain it. You can't begin a sentence with "You always. . . ." You can't begin a sentence with "I never. . . ." You can't be simplistic, even when things are simple. You can't say what you really think of that outfit or color combination or cowboy hat. You can't be cynical about things the other person is sincere about. You can't drink without the other person counting your drinks. You can't have the wrong laugh. You can't bum cigarettes when you're out because it embarrasses your mate, even though you've explained the unspoken fraternity between smokers. You can't tailgate, honk, or listen to talk radio in the car. And so on. The specifics don't matter. What matters is that the operative word is "can't."

Thus is love obtained.

Certainly, domesticity offers innumerable rewards: companionship, child-rearing convenience, reassuring predictability, and many other benefits too varied to list. But if love has power over us, domesticity is its enforcement wing: the iron dust mop in the velvet glove. The historian Michel Foucault has argued that modern power made its mark on the world by inventing new types of enclosures and institutions, places like factories, schools, barracks, prisons, and asylums, where individuals could be located, supervised, processed, and subjected to inspection, order, and the clock. What current social institution is more enclosed than modern intimacy? What offers greater regulation of movement and time, or more precise surveillance of body and thought, to a greater number of individuals?

Of course, it is your choice—as if any of us could really choose not to desire love or not to feel like hopeless losers should we fail at it. We moderns are beings yearning to be filled, yearning to be overtaken by love's mysterious power. We prostrate ourselves at love's portals, like social strivers waiting at the rope line outside some exclusive club hoping

CHRIS ROCK
. . . on Marriage

"Men are always complaining: 'How come I get only one wife? I want another wife.' What man wouldn't? Every one of us has visions of harems dancing in our pointed little heads. But you know, I'd be willing to give up that fantasy if my wife could have another husband—or two.

This is how it would work: One husband would be normal—in other words, me. The other one would be one of those platonic friends who is always hanging around. I wouldn't even have to approve of him. He could be her choice. And all he would have to do is take her to the stuff I don't want to go to.

Like the Ice Capades. There is no way I want to watch somebody skate. I don't give a damn about Nancy Kerrigan or Brian Boitano. Her: 'Do it for me.' Me: 'Hell, no! I'm not sitting through ice-skating!' "

–From *Rock This!*, 1997

to gain admission and thereby confirm our essential worth. A life without love lacks an organizing narrative. A life without love seems so barren, and it might almost make you consider how empty the rest of the world is, as if love were vital plasma and everything else just tap water.

Exchanging obedience for love comes naturally—after all, we all were once children whose survival depended on the caprices of love. And there you have the template for future intimacies. If you love me, you'll do what I want—or need, or demand—and I'll love you in return. We all become household dictators, petty tyrants of the private sphere, who are, in our turn, dictated to.

And why has modern love developed in such a way as to maximize submission and minimize freedom, with so little argument about it? No doubt a citizenry schooled in renouncing desire instead of imagining there could be something more would be, in many respects, advantageous. After all, wanting more is the basis for utopian thinking, a path toward dangerous social demands, even toward imagining the possibilities for altogether different social arrangements. But if the most elegant forms of social control are those that came packaged in the guise of individual needs and satisfactions, so wedded to the individual psyche that any opposing impulse registers as the anxiety of unlovability, who needs a soldier on every corner? We are more than happy to police ourselves and those we love and call it living happily ever after. Perhaps a secular society needed another metaphysical entity to subjugate itself to after the death of God, and love was available for the job. But isn't it a little depressing to think we are somehow incapable of inventing forms of emotional life based on anything other than subjugation?

▶ Analyzing the Text

1. What is Kipnis's main argument about modern love?

2. To clarify your understanding of Kipnis's argument, work through each of the "tenets of modern love" she describes. They are mutuality, communication, and advanced intimacy. How does she use these concepts to build her critique of long-term relationships?

3. Kipnis writes, "Why has modern love developed in such a way as to maximize submission and minimize freedom, with so little argument about it?" What do you think of this question? Do you agree with Kipnis? Why or why not?

4. How does Kipnis use historical references to help support her claim that modern society's notion of "mature love" is a recent invention? Reread the early section of her essay and discuss these historical examples. How does the author contrast historical views of love to her view of modern love?

5. How does Kipnis use the example of people who cheat on their partners to help support her argument against long-term relationships? To answer this question, find the paragraph that begins, "Inexplicably, however, a rebellious breakaway faction keeps trying to leap over the wall and emancipate themselves, not from love itself—unthinkable!—but from love's domestic confinements." What is Kipnis saying in this paragraph about adultery?

Writing about Cultural Practices

6. Kipnis is not alone in suggesting that romantic love is fraught with unrealistic contradictions and foolish expectations about achieving ultimate happiness. Follow up on her argument by finding examples from popular culture that similarly critique the idea that love is all roses, candlelit dinners, and long walks. Locate examples of song lyrics that represent this view of love, and draft a critical description that explains how these songs debunk the traditional themes of romantic love. As you write, consider the following questions for each song.

- Who wrote the song? Who sings it? How would you characterize the song's primary target audience?

- Describe the song. What is its main argument about love?

- What cultural assumptions about romance does the song rely on to communicate its message about love? What references, if any, does it make to other love stories or common romantic themes?

- How does the song make this argument? Does it include examples from life or other details that make it particularly convincing and persuasive?

- How would you compare this song's approach to love or romance with other similar songs in the same musical genre? What patterns, if any, exist in how these songs define love or romance?

bell hooks, **Baba and Daddy Gus**

Cultural critic and feminist writer bell hooks was born in Kentucky in 1952 and graduated from Stanford University. She continued her education at the University of California at Santa Cruz where she received her PhD and has taught in the English departments at Yale University and Oberlin College. Hooks has written numerous essays and books and has been named one of *Utne*'s "100 Visionaries Who Could Change Your Life." In an interview with *O Magazine*, hooks said of writing and books, "Life-transforming ideas have always come to me through books." In the following essay, hooks explains her choice of a pen name as she writes about her grandparents.

While Laura Kipnis's essay, "Against Love," clearly stands against marriage and long-term monogamy, this essay offers another view of marriage and explores how and why people stay together.

▶ **Mapping Your Reading**

As you read, notice hooks's detailed descriptions of her grandparents Baba and Daddy Gus and the contrasts she points out between them. Underline those passages in which the author explains how this marriage works. How do the differences between Baba and Daddy Gus serve their relationship?

There are family members you try to forget and ones that you always remember, that you can't stop talking about. They may be dead—long gone—but their presence lingers and you have to share who they were and who they still are with the world. You want everyone to know them as you did, to love them as you did.

All my life I have remained enchanted by the presence of my mother's parents, Sarah and Gus Oldham. When I was a child they were already old. I did not see that then, though. They were Baba and Daddy Gus, together for more than 70 years at the time of his death. Their marriage fascinated me. They were strangers and lovers—two eccentrics who created their own world.

More than any other family members, together they gave me a worldview that sustained me during a difficult and painful childhood. Reflecting on the eclectic writer I have become, I see in myself a mixture of these two very different but equally powerful figures from my childhood. Baba was tall, her skin so white and her hair so jet black and straight that she could have easily "passed" denying all traces of blackness. Yet the man she married was short and dark, and sometimes his skin looked like the color of soot from burning coal. In our childhood the fireplaces burned coal. It was bright heat, luminous and fierce. If you got too close it could burn you.

Together Baba and Daddy Gus generated a hot heat. He was a man of few words, deeply committed to silence—so much so that it was like a religion to him. When he spoke you could hardly hear what he said. Baba was just the opposite. Smoking an abundance of cigarettes a day, she talked endlessly. She preached. She yelled. She fussed. Often her vitriolic rage would heap itself on Daddy Gus, who would sit calmly in his chair by the stove, as calm and still as the Buddha sits. And when he had enough of her words, he would reach for his hat and walk.

Together Baba and Daddy Gus generated a hot heat.

Neither Baba nor Daddy Gus drove cars. Rarely did they ride in them. They preferred walking. And even then their styles were different. He moved slow, as though carrying a great weight; she with her tall, lean, boyish frame moved swiftly, as though there was never time to waste. Their one agreed-upon passion was fishing. Though they did not do even that together. They lived close but they created separate worlds.

In a big two-story wood frame house with lots of rooms they constructed a world that could contain their separate and distinct personalities. As children one of the first things we noticed about our grandparents was that they did not sleep in the same room. This arrangement was contrary to everything we understood about marriage. While Mama never wanted to talk about their separate worlds, Baba would tell you in a minute that Daddy Gus was nasty, that he smelled like tobacco juice, that he did not wash enough, that there was no way she would want him in her bed. And while he would say nothing nasty about her, he would merely say why would he want to share somebody else's bed when he could have his own bed to himself, with no one to complain about anything.

I loved my granddaddy's smells. Always, they filled my nostrils with the scent of happiness. It was sheer ecstasy for me to be allowed into his inner sanctum. His room was a small Van Gogh–like space off from the living room. There was no door. Old-fashioned curtains were the only attempt at privacy. Usually the curtains were closed. His room reeked of tobacco. There were treasures everywhere in that small room. As a younger man Daddy Gus did odd jobs, and sometimes even in his old age he would do a chore for some needy lady. As he went about his work, he would pick up found objects, scraps. All these objects would lie about his room, on the dresser, on the table near his bed. Unlike all other grown-ups he never cared about children looking through his things. Anything we wanted he gave to us.

Daddy Gus collected beautiful wooden cigar boxes. They held lots of the important stuff—the treasures. He had tons of little diaries that he made notes in. He gave me my first wallet, my first teeny little book to write in, my first beautiful pen, which did not write for long, but it was still a found and shared treasure.

When I would lie on his bed or sit close to him, sometimes just standing near, I would feel all the pain and anxiety of my troubled childhood leave me. His spirit was calm. He gave me the unconditional love I longed for.

"Too calm," his grown-up children thought. That's why he had let this old woman rule him, my cousin BoBo would say. Even as children we knew that grown-ups felt sorry for Daddy Gus. At times his sons seemed to look upon him as not a "real man." His refusal to fight in wars was another sign to them of weakness. It was my grandfather who taught me to oppose war. They saw him as a man controlled by the whims of others, by this tall, strident, demanding woman he had married. I saw him as a man of profound beliefs, a man of integrity. When he heard their put-downs—for they talked on and on about his laziness—he merely muttered that he had no use for them. He was not gonna let anybody tell him what to do with his life.

They lived close but they created separate worlds.

Daddy Gus was a devout believer, a deacon at his church; he was one of the right-hand men of God. At church, everyone admired his calmness. Baba had no use for church. She liked nothing better than to tell us all the ways it was one big hypocritical place: "Why, I can find God anywhere I want to—I do not need a church." Indeed, when my grandmother died, her funeral could not take place in a church, for she had never belonged. Her refusal to attend church bothered some of her daughters, for they thought she was sinning against God, setting a bad example for the children. We were not supposed to listen when she began to damn the church and everybody in it.

Baba loved to "cuss." There was no bad word she was not willing to say. The improvisational manner in which she would string those words together was awesome. It was the goddamn sons of bitches who thought that they could fuck with her when they could just kiss her black ass. A woman of strong words and powerful metaphors, she could not read or write. She lived in the power of language. Her favorite sayings were a prelude for storytelling. It was she who told me, "Play with a puppy, he'll lick you in the mouth." When I heard this saying, I knew what was coming—a long polemic about not letting folks get too close, 'cause they will mess with you.

Baba loved to tell her stories. And I loved to hear them. She called me Glory. And in the midst of her storytelling she would pause to say, "Glory, are ya listenin'. Do you understand what I'm telling ya." Sometimes I would have to repeat the lessons I had learned. Sometimes I was not able to get it right and she would start again. When Mama felt I was learning too much craziness "over home" (that is what we called Baba's house), my visits were curtailed. As I moved into my teens I learned to keep to myself all the wisdom of the old ways I picked up over home.

Baba was an incredible quilt maker, but by the time I was old enough to really understand her work, to see its beauty, she was already having difficulty with her eyesight. She could not sew as much as in the old days, when her work was on everybody's bed. Unwilling to throw anything away, she loved to make crazy quilts, 'cause they allowed every scrap to be used. Although she would one day order patterns and make perfect quilts with colors that went together, she always collected scraps.

Long before I read Virginia Woolf's *A Room of One's Own* I learned from Baba that a woman needed her own space to work. She had a huge room for her quilting. Like every other space in the private world she created upstairs, it had her treasures, an endless array of hatboxes, feathers, and trunks filled with old clothes she had held on to. In room after room there were feather tick mattresses; when they were pulled back, the wooden slats of the bed were revealed, lined with exquisite hand-sewn quilts.

In all these trunks, in crevices and drawers were braided tobacco leaves to keep away moths and other insects. A really hot summer could make cloth sweat, and stains from tobacco juice would end up on quilts no one had ever used. When I was a young child, a quilt my grandmother had made kept me warm, was my solace and comfort. Even though Mama protested when I dragged that old raggedy quilt from Kentucky to Stanford, I knew I needed that bit of the South, of Baba's world, to sustain me.

Like Daddy Gus, she was a woman of her word. She liked to declare with pride, "I mean what I say and I say what I mean." "Glory," she would tell me, "nobody is better than their word—if you can't keep ya word you ain't worth nothin' in this world." She would stop speaking to folk over the breaking of their word, over lies. Our mama was not given to loud speech or confrontation. I learned all those things from Baba—"to stand up and speak up" and not to "give a good goddamn" what folk who "ain't got a pot to pee in" think. My parents were concerned with their image in the world. It was pure blasphemy for Baba to teach that it did not matter what other folks thought—"Ya have to be right with yaself in ya own heart—that's all that matters." Baba taught me to listen to my heart—to follow it. From her we learned as small children to remember our dreams in the night and to share them when we awakened. They would be interpreted by her. She taught us to listen to the knowledge in dreams. Mama would say this was all nonsense, but she too was known to ask the meaning of a dream.

In their own way my grandparents were rebels, deeply committed to radical individualism. I learned how to be myself from them. Mama hated this. She thought it was important to be liked, to conform. She had hated growing up in such an eccentric, otherworldly household. This world where folks made their own wine, their own butter, their own soap; where chickens were raised, and huge gardens were grown for canning everything. This was the world Mama wanted to leave behind. She wanted store-bought things.

My grandparents were rebels, deeply committed to radical individualism.

Baba lived in another time, a time when all things were produced in the individual household. Everything the family needed was made at home. She loved to tell me stories about learning to trap animals, to skin, to soak possum and coon in brine, to fry up a fresh rabbit. Though a total woman of the outdoors who could shoot and trap as good as any man, she still believed every woman should sew—she made her first quilt as a girl. In her world, women were as strong as men because they had to be. She had grown up in the country and knew that country ways were the best ways to live. Boasting about being able to do anything that a man could do and better, this woman who could not read or write was confident about her place in the universe.

My sense of aesthetics came from her. She taught me to really look at things, to see underneath the surface, to see the different shades of red in the peppers she had dried and hung in the kitchen sunlight. The beauty of the ordinary, the everyday, was her feast of light. While she had no use for the treasures in my granddaddy's world, he too taught me to look for the living spirit in things—the things that are cast away but still need to be touched and cared for. Picking up a found object he would tell me its story or tell me how he was planning to give it life again.

Connected in spirit but so far apart in the life of everydayness, Baba and Daddy Gus were rarely civil to each other. Every shared talk begun with goodwill ended in disagreement and contestation. Everyone knew Baba just loved to fuss. She liked a good war of words. And she was comfortable using words to sting and hurt, to punish. When words would not do the job, she could reach for the strap, a long piece of black leather that would leave tiny imprints on the flesh.

There was no violence in Daddy Gus. Mama shared that he had always been that way, a calm and gentle man, full of tenderness. I remember clinging to his tenderness when nothing I did was right in my mother's eyes, when I was constantly punished. Baba was not an ally. She advocated harsh punishment. She had no use for children who would not obey. She was never ever affectionate. When we entered her house, we gave her a kiss in greeting and that was it. With Daddy Gus we could cuddle, linger in his arms, give as many kisses as desired. His arms and heart were always open.

In the back of their house were fruit trees, chicken coops, and gardens, and in the front were flowers. Baba could make anything grow. And she knew all about herbs and roots. Her home remedies healed our childhood sicknesses. Of course she thought it crazy for anyone to go to a doctor when she could tell them just what they needed. All these things she had learned from her mother, Bell Blair Hooks, whose name I would choose as my pen name. Everyone agreed that I had the temperament of this great-grandmother I would not remember. She was a sharp-tongued woman. Or so they said. And it was believed I had inherited my way with words from her.

Families do that. They chart psychic genealogies that often overlook what is right before our eyes. I may have inherited my great-grandmother Bell Hooks's way with words, but I learned to use those words listening to my grandmother. I learned to be courageous by seeing her act without fear. I learned to risk because she was daring. Home and family were her world. While my grandfather journeyed downtown, visited at other folks' houses, went to church, and conducted affairs in the world, Baba rarely left home. There was nothing in the world she needed. Things out there violated her spirit.

As a child I had no sense of what it would mean to live a life, spanning so many generations, unable to read or write. To me Baba was a woman of power. That she would have been extraordinarily powerless in a world beyond 1200

Broad Street was a thought that never entered my mind. I believed that she stayed home because it was the place she liked best. Just as Daddy Gus seemed to need to walk—to roam.

After his death it was easier to see the ways that they complemented and completed each other. For suddenly, without him as a silent backdrop, Baba's spirit was diminished. Something in her was forever lonely and could not find solace. When she died, tulips, her favorite flower, surrounded her. The preacher told us that her death was not an occasion for grief, for "it is hard to live in a world where your choicest friends are gone." Daddy Gus was the companion she missed most. His presence had always been the mirror of memory. Without it there was so much that could not be shared. There was no witness.

> **Without Daddy Gus there was so much that could not be shared. There was no witness.**

Seeing their life together, I learned that it was possible for women and men to fashion households, arranged around their own needs. Power was shared. When there was an imbalance, Baba ruled the day. It seemed utterly alien to me to learn about black women and men not making families and homes together. I had not been raised in a world of absent men. One day I knew I would fashion a life using the patterns I inherited from Baba and Daddy Gus. I keep treasures in my cigar box, which still smells after all these years. The quilt that covered me as a child remains, full of ink stains and faded colors. In my trunks are braided tobacco leaves, taken from over home. They keep evil away—keep bad spirits from crossing the threshold, like the ancestors they guard and protect.

 Analyzing the Text

1. What does hooks conclude about what kept her grandparents' marriage working, despite the substantial differences between them?

2. Hooks explains, "I see in myself a mixture of these two very different but equally powerful figures from my childhood." How does hooks describe the differences between Baba and Daddy Gus? What examples does she provide about how their differences were played out?

3. **Interrogating Assumptions.** According to hooks, what are the advantages of being in a marriage where the two people are so different? What are the drawbacks? In what ways does the story of hooks's grandparents challenge popular assumptions about romance (see this chapter's introduction)?

4. **Connecting to Another Reading.** Is Baba and Daddy Gus's marriage an exception to what Laura Kipnis says happens in long-term relationships (see p. 308)?

5. **Connecting to Other Readings.** David Sedaris's "The End of the Affair" (p. 272) looks at romance from the perspective of the long-term relationship. Like hooks, Sedaris tries to answer the questions, "What keeps people together? What is true romance?" Explore the similarities and differences between the theories Sedaris and hooks develop about what love means for couples in long-term relationships. How do they form a response to Kipnis's "Against Love" (p. 308) stance?

6. One theme of hooks's essay is that opposites attract. Analyze this assumption as it is expressed in popular culture by identifying one to two examples from popular love stories (perhaps on television or in the movies, or from novels) that either support the view that opposites attract or reject it. When writing your analysis, consider the following questions.

- What attracts people to each other in your examples? What keeps them apart?

- In the examples you identify for this essay, what characteristics about the couple are considered "opposite" and lead to the attraction they feel for each other? What characteristics are merely differences and not factors influencing whether a couple stays together?

- In what ways does the statement "opposites attract" support popular assumptions about romance that this chapter investigates? (See pp. 263–70 in this chapter's introduction.)

Jon Katz, **Petophilia**

As a contributor to magazines such as *Wired, Slate,* and *Rolling Stone,* Jon Katz has written numerous articles on technology, politics, and culture. His books include the memoirs *Running to the Mountain* (1999), which is about reaching middle age, and *Dog Year* (2002), which focuses on Katz's other pet subject: dogs. "Dogs," Katz once wrote, "make me a better human." Originally published in *Slate* in 2004, "Petophilia" is an essay about the implications of human-dog love.

> ▶ **Mapping Your Reading**
>
> What is the impact of pets in our lives? How do our relationships with pets shape or reflect back on our ability to connect with other people? As you read, mark passages that you strongly agree with.

I encountered Sam, a 34-year-old investment banker, and his dog, Namath, when Sam responded to a column I wrote. He told me he loves his dog "to death," so much that it sometimes unnerves him. Sam and Namath, a German shepherd/husky mix adopted three years ago from a shelter in Brooklyn, jog together, play Frisbee, take long hikes in the Catskills. Sam was planning a Caribbean vacation last year but decided instead to rent a cabin in New Hampshire so that Namath could come along. "I have to say it was great, one of the best times I've ever had," he reported. He's considering leaving New York City so that Namath can have more space to run.

Human companionship? Sometimes Sam dates, but he's increasingly inclined to stay home with Namath, who's more fun to be with than most of his dates, he says. He's rarely more content than when he and Namath are relaxing on the sofa with a bowl of popcorn, watching ESPN. "There is nothing I wouldn't do for him, nothing he wouldn't do for me," Sam says. "We understand each other."

A few weeks ago I also heard from a married California couple in their late 20s who doubt they'll have children "because [they] are so content" with one another and their two Rottweilers. "We could not love any children more than we love our dogs, to be honest," the husband explained. "We see the dogs as the glue that helps keep our relationship strong."

And Jane, whom I've known for years, is a former computer programmer who just sold her suburban Boston home and moved to a ranch house on five acres in upstate New York with her seven golden retrievers—all rescued dogs with cancer, heart disease, or bone disease. She intends, she says, "to spend the rest of my life with these dogs. I want to take care of them and make them happy. Often in my life I've felt let down by people, but never by my dogs."

"I've felt let down by people, but never by my dogs."

I've been living with my border collies on a farm this winter and spring. There have been moments—I think of one bitter, black winter night when the dogs and I sat huddled together in front of a wood stove while the wind wailed outside—that I, too, felt that love beyond words, pure and powerful.

Dog love can be comic or disturbing, painful or uplifting, neurotic, joyful, all of the above. Since the dog cannot put any limits on it, dog love can be boundless, sometimes growing beyond our intentions.

For everyone—dog owners and non-dog owners alike—loving human beings is difficult, unpredictable, and often disappointing. Dog love is safer, perhaps more satisfying: Dogs can't betray us, undermine us, tell us they're angry or bored. Dogs can't leave.

Our voiceless companions, dogs are a blank canvas on which we can paint anything we wish. When it comes to love, that's a powerful temptation. Are dog and human love compatible? Dog love can lead human beings away from one another and from the painstaking work of coming to terms with our own species. But dogs can teach wounded people how to trust and love again. They can ease loneliness, buffer pain.

Behavioral research suggests that men and women love dogs equally, but often in different ways. Men usually love dogs because they don't talk, which makes them the perfect pals. A guy can have an intense relationship, like Samuel does with Namath, and never have to discuss it. Women are more likely to see dogs as emotionally complex creatures; it's disturbingly common to hear them say their dogs understand their moods better than their boyfriends; that their dogs know when they're upset, but their husbands don't.

There are various kinds of dog love. Some I've noticed:

Partner love: Working dogs—herders, hunters, bomb sniffers, agility and obedience performers, search and rescue dogs, therapy dogs—have a particular kind of connection with their owners and handlers, forged by years of training and working together. My border collie Rose and I have spent months together herding sheep. We anticipate each other, communicate without words. We are almost telepathic.

Dog love is safer. Dogs can't leave.

Victim love: Dog rescuers—those tens of thousands of people, overwhelmingly female, who scour animal shelters for dogs in trouble—see a lot of ugly human behavior and its consequences, too much, sometimes. The bonds between rescued dogs and those who heal and adopt them are among the strongest of human-animal attachments. This love often taps into the owner's own anger, painful history, and sense of victimization—as well as her need to nurture and heal, and to be nurtured and healed.

Surrogate love: Certain people treat their dogs like family members rather than pets—substitutes for the children or spouses they don't have or don't like. Such owners lavish all the toys, food, activities, and affection on their dog that they would customarily give children. But the dogs don't talk back, drink and smoke pot in the basement, or discover and point out our stupidity and failings. In surrogate love, unlike partner or victim love, the dog can sometimes be a one-for-one replacement for a human.

The intensity of dog love can sometimes be disturbing. People and dogs have been boon companions for thousands of years, but these contemporary kinds of dog love are new. A recent Yankelovich study for *American Demographics* found that nearly a third of respondents—and half of all single people—said that of everyone in their lives, they relied most on pets for companionship and affection. Distressingly often, owners have confessed to me that they could survive the loss of a companion or spouse, but they're not sure how they could live without their dog.

I've become a dog-love rationalist: Love them all you want, but maintain some perspective on what they are and where your love comes from.

A couple of years back, a University of Kentucky psychiatrist who studies human-animal bonds sent me a classic work, *Twins,* by the late British analyst and author Dorothy Burlingham. Burlingham wrote about the power of fantasies in very young children, especially during moments when they are lonely or frightened. A child, she wrote, may take "an imaginary animal as his intimate and beloved companion; subsequently he is never separated from his animal friend. This animal offers the child what he is searching for: faithful love and unswerving devotion. The two share everything, good and bad experiences, and complete understanding of each other; either speech is not necessary, or they have a secret language; the understanding between them goes beyond the realm of consciousness."

This yearning, then, is part of many of our lives from our earliest years. What begins as a potent, comforting fantasy later ripens. Dogs now at our sides, we escape from loneliness and solitude, find "faithful love and unswerving devotion." We feel, rightly or not, as if we share complete understanding; certainly we have a secret language. Our love goes beyond the words we have. We finally find our intimate and beloved companions.

▶ Analyzing the Text

1. What are Katz's theories about dog love? Do you agree with him? Why or why not?

2. What is the impact of dog love on human love relationships? According to Katz, what are the connections between dog love and human love? How does one kind of love inform the other?

3. **Interrogating Assumptions.** Katz describes three types of dog love that he has observed: partner love, victim love, and surrogate love. What assumptions—about what love is or should be—do each of these types of dog love reveal? What do you think of Katz's three categories? Has he left out other forms of dog love that you have either experienced or observed in others?

4. In this essay, Katz is only interested in describing dog-human love. But what about cat owners? Or horse owners? Do his theories about dog love translate to all forms of pet love? Why or why not?

5. **Connecting to Another Reading.** How does this essay about dog love support or counter Laura Kipnis's argument in "Against Love" (p. 308)? As you answer this question, consider some of the details in Katz's essay. For instance, he cites a study from *American Demographics* in which a large number of people report that "of everyone in their lives, they relied most on pets for companionship and affection."

▶ Writing about Cultural Practices

6. To what extent has your relationship with pets shaped your view of what love is or should be? Write a critical narrative in which you define pet love and support your definition with an example from your experiences as a pet owner. As you write, consider the following questions.

   • How has your connection with your pet affected your expectations of human relationships? How do you account for this impact, or lack of impact?

   • Do you identify with any of the people quoted in Katz's essay? Explain.

   • Do you see yourself fitting into any of the three categories Katz identifies? If so, identify which ones and explain why you would include yourself in it/them.

Scott Russell Sanders, **Looking at Women**

Scott Russell Sanders is a distinguished professor in the Indiana University department of English. He has written numerous award-winning books on spirituality, philosophy, and the environment, including *Secrets of the Universe: Scenes from the Journey Home* (1991), *Staying Put: Making a Home in a Restless World* (1993), and *The Force of Spirit* (2000). His writing also appears regularly in the *Georgia Review, Orion, Audubon,* and numerous anthologies. "Looking at Women" originally appeared in the *Georgia Review* in 1989.

Previous readings in this chapter explore questions and assumptions about love—whether love can last, how the search for love has changed. In this essay, Sanders takes a different interest in the question of romance. He analyzes the factors of physical attraction and explores how gender roles play out on the field of courtship by asking, "How should a man look at women?"

> ▶ **Mapping Your Reading**
>
> Throughout this essay, Sanders describes specific episodes from his own life. As you read, use the margins to make notes about what each episode is meant to convey to readers. As a boy and a young man, what messages does Sanders get about sex? How does he connect sexuality with morality, and what contradictory attitudes about sex and women does Sanders point out? What does he think is the purpose of pornography?

On that sizzling July afternoon, the girl who crossed at the stoplight in front of our car looked, as my mother would say, as though she had been poured into her pink shorts. The girl's matching pink halter bared her stomach and clung to her nubbin breasts, leaving little to the imagination, as my mother would also say. Until that moment, it had never made any difference to me how much or little a girl's clothing revealed, for my imagination had been entirely devoted to other mysteries. I was 11. The girl was about 14, the age of my buddy Norman who lounged in the back seat with me. Staring after her, Norman elbowed me in the ribs and murmured, "Check out that chassis."

His mother glared around from the driver's seat. "Hush your mouth."

"I was talking about that sweet Chevy," said Norman, pointing out a souped-up jalopy at the curb.

"I know what you were talking about," his mother snapped.

No doubt she did know, since mothers could read minds, but at first I did not have a clue. Chassis? I knew what it meant for a car, an airplane, a radio, or even a cannon to have a chassis. But could a girl have one as well? I glanced after the retreating figure, and suddenly noticed with a sympathetic twitching in my belly the way her long raven ponytail swayed in rhythm to her walk and the way her fanny jostled in those pink shorts. In July's dazzle of sun, her swinging legs and arms beamed at me a semaphore I could almost read.

As the light turned green and our car pulled away, Norman's mother cast one more scowl at her son in the rearview mirror, saying, "Just think how it makes her feel to have you two boys gawking at her."

How? I wondered.

"Makes her feel like hot stuff," said Norman, owner of a bold mouth.

"If you don't get your mind out of the gutter, you're going to wind up in the state reformatory," said his mother.

Norman gave a snort. I sank into the seat, and tried to figure out what power had sprung from that sashaying girl to zap me in the belly.

Only after much puzzling did it dawn on me that I must finally have drifted into the force-field of sex, as a space traveler who has lived all his years in free fall might rocket for the first time within gravitational reach of a star. Even as a bashful 11-year-old I knew the word *sex*, of course, and I could paste that name across my image of the tantalizing girl. But a label for a mystery no more explains a mystery than the word *gravity* explains gravity. As I grew a beard and my taste shifted from girls to women, I acquired a more cagey language for speaking of desire, I picked up disarming theories. First by hearsay and then by experiment, I learned the delicious details of making babies. I came to appreciate the urgency for propagation that litters the road with maple seeds and drives salmon up waterfalls and yokes the newest crop of boys to the newest crop of girls. Books in their killjoy wisdom taught me that all the valentines and violins, the waltzes and glances, the long fever and ache of romance, were merely embellishments on biology's instructions that we multiply our kind. And yet, the fraction of desire that actually leads to procreation is so vanishingly small as to seem irrelevant. In his lifetime a man sways to a million longings, only a few of which, or perhaps none at all, ever lead to the fathering of children. Now, 30 years away from that July afternoon, firmly married, twice a father, I am still humming from the power unleashed by the girl in pink shorts, still wondering how it made her feel to have two boys gawk at her, still puzzling over how to dwell in the force-field of desire.

How should a man look at women? It is a peculiarly and perhaps neurotically human question. Billy goats do not fret over how they should look at nanny goats. They look or don't look, as seasons and hormones dictate, and feel what they feel without benefit of theory. There is more billy goat in most men than we care to admit. None of us, however, is pure goat. To live utterly as an animal would make the business of sex far tidier but also drearier. If we tried, like

> **What power had sprung from that sashaying girl to zap me in the belly?**

Rousseau,[1] to peel off the layers of civilization and imagine our way back to some pristine man and woman who have not yet been corrupted by hand-me-down notions of sexuality, my hunch is that we would find, in our speculative state of nature, that men regarded women with appalling simplicity. In any case, unlike goats, we dwell in history. What attracts our eyes and rouses our blood is only partly instinctual. Other forces contend in us as well: the voices of books and religions, the images of art and film and advertising, the entire chorus of culture. Norman's telling me to relish the sight of females and his mother's telling me to keep my eyes to myself are only two of the many voices quarreling in my head.

If there were a rule book for sex, it would be longer than the one for baseball (that byzantine sport), more intricate and obscure than tax instructions from the Internal Revenue Service. What I present here are a few images and reflections that cling, for me, to this one item in such a compendium of rules: How should a man look at women?

Well before I was to see any women naked in the flesh, I saw a bevy of them naked in photographs, hung in a gallery around the bed of my freshman roommate at college. A *Playboy* subscriber, he would pluck the centerfold from its staples each month and tape another airbrushed lovely to the wall. The gallery was in place when I moved in, and for an instant before I realized what I was looking at, all that expanse of skin reminded me of a meat locker back in Newton Falls, Ohio. I never quite shook that first impression, even after I had inspected the pinups at my leisure on subsequent days. Every curve of buttock and breast was news to me, an innocent kid from the Puritan back roads. Today you would be hard pressed to find a college freshman as ignorant as I was of female anatomy, if only because teenagers now routinely watch movies at home that would have been shown, during my teen years, exclusively on the fly-speckled screens of honky-tonk cinemas or in the basement of the Kinsey Institute.[2] I studied those alien shapes on the wall with a curiosity that was not wholly sexual, a curiosity tinged with the wonder that astronomers must have felt when they pored over the early photographs of the far side of the moon.

The paper women seemed to gaze back at me, enticing or mocking, yet even in my adolescent dither I was troubled by the phony stare, for I knew this was no true exchange of looks. Those mascaraed eyes were not fixed on me but on a camera. What the models felt as they posed I could only guess—perhaps the boredom of any numbskull job, perhaps the weight of dollar bills, perhaps the sweltering lights of fame, perhaps a tingle of the power that launched a thousand ships.

Whatever their motives, these women had chosen to put themselves on display. For the instant of the photograph, they had become their bodies, as a

---

[1]Jean-Jacques Rousseau (1712–1778), French philosopher, composer, and political theorist. His theory of the noble savage contends that people are good by nature but become corrupted by the imposition of society's conventions.

[2]**The Kinsey Institute** for Research in Sex, Gender, and Reproduction was founded by Alfred Charles Kinsey (1894–1956) and is located at Indiana University.

prizefighter does in the moment of landing a punch, as a weightlifter does in the moment of hoisting a barbell, as a ballerina does in the whirl of a pirouette, as we all do in the crisis of making love or dying. Men, ogling such photographs, are supposed to feel that where so much surface is revealed there can be no depths. Yet I never doubted that behind the makeup and the plump curves and the two dimensions of the image there was an inwardness, a feeling self as mysterious as my own. In fact, during moments when I should have been studying French or thermodynamics, I would glance at my roommate's wall and invent mythical lives for those goddesses. The lives I made up were adolescent ones, to be sure; but so was mine. Without that saving aura of inwardness, these women in the glossy photographs would have become merely another category of objects for sale, alongside the sports cars and stereo systems and liquors advertised in the same pages. If not extinguished, however, their humanity was severely reduced. And if by simplifying themselves they had lost some human essence, then by gaping at them I had shared in the theft.

What did that gaping take from me? How did it affect my way of seeing other women, those who would never dream of lying nude on a fake tiger rug before the million-faceted eye of a camera? The bodies in the photographs were implausibly smooth and slick and inflated, like balloon caricatures that might be floated overhead in a parade. Free of sweat and scars and imperfections, sensual without being fertile, tempting yet impregnable, they were Platonic ideals of the female form, divorced from time and the fluster of living, excused from the perplexities of mind. No actual woman could rival their insipid perfection.

The swains who gathered to admire my roommate's gallery discussed the pinups in the same tones and in much the same language as the farmers back home in Ohio used for assessing cows. The relevant parts of male or female bodies are quickly named—and, the *Kamasutra* and Marquis de Sade[3] notwithstanding, the number of ways in which those parts can be stimulated or conjoined is touchingly small—so these studly conversations were more tedious than chitchat about the weather. I would lie on my bunk pondering calculus or Aeschylus and unwillingly hear the same few nouns and fewer verbs issuing from one mouth after another, and I would feel smugly superior. Here I was, improving my mind, while theirs wallowed in the notorious gutter. Eventually the swains would depart, leaving me in peace, and from the intellectual heights of my bunk I would glance across at those photographs—and yield to the gravity of lust. Idiot flesh! How stupid that a counterfeit stare and artful curves, printed in millions of copies on glossy paper, could arouse me. But there it was, not the first proof of my body's automatism and not the last.

Nothing in men is more machinelike than the flipping of sexual switches. I have never been able to read with a straight face the claims made by D. H.

---

[3]The **Kamasutra** is an ancient Indian text on human sexual behavior, written by Vatsyayana sometime between the first and sixth centuries A.D. The **Marquis de Sade** (1740–1814) was a French aristocrat and writer of often violent pornography. The word "sadism" came from his name.

Lawrence[4] and lesser pundits that the penis is a god, a lurking dragon. It more nearly resembles a railroad crossing signal, which stirs into life at intervals to announce, "Here comes a train." Or, if the penis must be likened to an animal, let it be an ill-trained circus dog, sitting up and playing dead and heeling whenever it takes a notion, oblivious of the trainer's commands. Meanwhile, heart, lungs, blood vessels, pupils, and eyelids all assert their independence like the members of a rebellious troupe. Reason stands helpless at the center of the ring, cracking its whip.

While he was president, Jimmy Carter raised a brouhaha by confessing in a *Playboy* interview, of all shady places, that he occasionally felt lust in his heart for women. What man hasn't, aside from those who feel lust in their hearts for other men? The commentators flung their stones anyway. Naughty, naughty, they chirped. Wicked Jimmy. Perhaps Mr. Carter could derive some consolation from psychologist Allen Wheelis, who blames male appetite on biology: "We have been selected for desiring. Nothing could have convinced us by argument that it would be worthwhile to chase endlessly and insatiably after women, but something has transformed us from within, a plasmid has invaded our DNA, has twisted our nature so that now this is exactly what we *want* to do." Certainly, by Darwinian logic, those males who were most avid in their pursuit of females were also the most likely to pass on their genes. Consoling it may be, yet it is finally no solution to blame biology. "I am extremely sexual in my desires: I carry them everywhere and at all times," William Carlos Williams[5] tells us on the opening page of his autobiography. "I think that from that arises the drive which empowers us all. Given that drive, a man does with it what his mind directs. In the manner in which he directs that power lies his secret." Whatever the contents of my DNA, however potent the influence of my ancestors, I still must direct that rebellious power. I still must live with the consequences of my looking and my longing.

> Whatever my DNA, I must live with the consequences of my looking and longing.

Aloof on their blankets like goddesses on clouds, the pinups did not belong to my funky world. I was invisible to them, and they were immune to my gaze. Not so the women who passed me on the street, sat near me in classes, shared a table with me in the cafeteria: It was risky to stare at them. They could gaze back, and sometimes did, with looks both puzzling and exciting. It only complicated matters for me to realize that so many of these strangers had taken precautions that men should notice them. The girl in matching pink halter and shorts who set me humming in my eleventh year might only have wanted to keep cool in the sizzle of July. But these alluring college femmes had deeper designs. Perfume, eye shadow, uplift bras (about which I learned in the Sears catalog), curled hair,

---

[4]**David Herbert Lawrence** (1885–1930), English writer who explored themes of sexuality and the primal instincts of the unconscious.

[5]**William Carlos Williams** (1883–1963), American poet and physician.

stockings, jewelry, lipstick, lace—what were these if not hooks thrown out into male waters?

I recall being mystified in particular by spike heels. They looked painful to me, and dangerous. Danger may have been the point, since the spikes would have made good weapons—they were affectionately known, after all, as stilettos. Or danger may have been the point in another sense, because a woman teetering along on such heels is tipsy, vulnerable, broadcasting her need for support. And who better than a man to prop her up, some guy who clomps around in brogans wide enough for the cornerstones of flying buttresses? (For years after college, I felt certain that spike heels had been forever banned, like bustles and foot-binding, but lately they have come back in fashion, and once more one encounters women teetering along on knife points.)

Back in those days of my awakening to women, I was also baffled by lingerie. I do not mean underwear, the proletariat of clothing, and I do not mean foundation garments, pale and sensible. I mean what the woman who lives in the house behind ours—owner of a shop called "Bare Essentials"—refers to as "intimate apparel." Those two words announce that her merchandise is both sexy and expensive. These flimsy items cost more per ounce than truffles, more than frankincense and myrrh. They are put-ons whose only purpose is in being taken off. I have a friend who used to attend the men's-only nights at Bare Essentials, during which he would invariably buy a slinky outfit or two, by way of proving his serious purpose, outfits that wound up in the attic because his wife would not be caught dead in them. Most of the customers at the shop are women, however, as the models are women, and the owner is a woman. What should one make of that? During my college days I knew about intimate apparel only by rumor, not being that intimate with anyone who would have tricked herself out in such finery, but I could see the spike heels and other female trappings everywhere I turned. Why, I wondered then and wonder still, do so many women decorate themselves like dolls? And does that mean they wish to be viewed as dolls?

On this question as on many others, Simone de Beauvoir[6] has clarified matters for me, writing in *The Second Sex*. "The 'feminine' woman in making herself prey tries to reduce man, also, to her carnal passivity; she occupies herself in catching him in her trap, in enchaining him by means of the desires she arouses in him in submissively making herself a thing." Those women who transform themselves into dolls, in other words, do so because that is the most potent identity available to them. "It must be admitted," Beauvoir concedes, "that the males find in woman more complicity than the oppressor usually finds in the oppressed. And in bad faith they take authorization from this to declare that she has *desired* the destiny they have imposed on her."

---

[6]**Simone de Beauvoir** (1908–1986), French author and philosopher whose major work is *The Second Sex* (1949), in which she observes that, throughout history, women have been considered less capable, irrational, and a deviation from the norm. Having been cast as "the Other," de Beauvoir asserts that women need to fight against this assumption about male dominance.

Complicity, oppressor, bad faith: such terms yank us into a moral realm unknown to goats. While I am saddled with enough male guilt to believe three-quarters of Beauvoir's claim, I still doubt that men are so entirely to blame for the turning of women into sexual dolls. I believe human history is more collaborative than her argument would suggest. It seems unlikely to me that one-half the species could have "imposed" a destiny on the other half, unless that other half were far more craven than the females I have known. Some women have expressed their own skepticism on this point. Thus Joan Didion: "That many women are victims of condescension and exploitation and sex-role stereotyping was scarcely news, but neither was it news that other women are not: nobody forces women to buy the package." Beauvoir herself recognized that many members of her sex refuse to buy the "feminine" package: "The emancipated woman, on the contrary, wants to be active, a taker, and refuses the passivity man means to impose on her."

Since my college years, back in the murky 1960s, emancipated women have been discouraging their unemancipated sisters from making spectacles of themselves. Don't paint your face like a clown's or drape your body like a mannequin's, they say. Don't bounce on the sidelines in skimpy outfits, screaming your fool head off, while men compete in the limelight for victories. Don't present yourself to the world as a fluff pastry, delicate and edible. Don't waddle across the stage in a bathing suit in hopes of being named Miss This or That.

A great many women still ignore the exhortations. Wherever a crown for beauty is to be handed out, many still line up to stake their claims. Recently, Miss Indiana Persimmon Festival was quoted in our newspaper about the burdens of possessing the sort of looks that snag men's eyes. "Most of the time I enjoy having guys stare at me," she said, "but every once in a while it makes me feel like a piece of meat." The news photograph showed a cheerleader's perky face, heavily made-up, with starched hair teased into a blond cumulus. She put me in mind not of meat but of a plastic figurine, something you might buy from a booth outside a shrine. Nobody should ever be seen as meat, mere juicy stuff to satisfy an appetite. Better to appear as a plastic figurine, which is not meant for eating, and which is a gesture, however crude, toward art. Joyce[7] described the aesthetic response as a contemplation of form without the impulse to action. Perhaps that is what Miss Indiana Persimmon Festival wishes to inspire in those who look at her, perhaps that is what many women who paint and primp themselves desire: to withdraw from the touch of hands and dwell in the eye alone, to achieve the status of art.

By turning herself into (or allowing herself to be turned into) a work of art, does a woman truly escape men's proprietary stare? Not often, says the British critic John Berger. Summarizing the treatment of women in Western painting, he concludes that—with a few notable exceptions, such as works by Rubens and

> **Nobody should ever be seen as meat. Better to appear as a plastic figurine.**

---

[7]**James Joyce** (1882–1941), Irish novelist.

Rembrandt—the woman on canvas is a passive object displayed for the pleasure of the male viewer, especially for the owner of the painting, who is, by extension, owner of the woman herself. Berger concludes: "Men look at women. Women watch themselves being looked at. This determines not only most relations between men and women but also the relation of women to themselves. The surveyor of woman in herself is male: the surveyed female. Thus she turns herself into an object—and most particularly an object of vision: a sight."

That sweeping claim, like the one quoted earlier from Beauvoir, also seems to me about three-quarters truth and one-quarter exaggeration. I know men who outdo the peacock for show, and I know women who are so fully possessed of themselves that they do not give a hang whether anybody notices them or not. The flamboyant gentlemen portrayed by Van Dyck are no less aware of being *seen* than are the languid ladies portrayed by Ingres.[8] With or without clothes, both gentlemen and ladies may conceive of themselves as objects of vision, targets of envy or admiration or desire. Where they differ is in their potential for action: the men are caught in the midst of a decisive gesture or on the verge of making one; the women wait like fuel for someone else to strike a match.

I am not sure the abstract nudes favored in modern art are much of an advance over the inert and voluptuous ones of the old school. Think of two famous examples: Duchamp's *Nude Descending a Staircase* (1912), where the faceless woman has blurred into a waterfall of jagged shards, or Picasso's *Les Demoiselles d'Avignon* (1907), where the five angular damsels have been hammered as flat as cookie sheets and fitted with African masks. Neither painting invites us to behold a woman, but instead to behold what Picasso or Duchamp can make of one.

The naked women in Rubens, far from being passive, are gleefully active, exuberant, their sumptuous pink bodies like rainclouds or plump nebulae. "His nudes are the first ones that ever made me feel happy about my own body," a woman friend told me in one of the Rubens galleries of the Prado Museum. I do not imagine any pinup or store-window mannequin or bathing-suited Miss Whatsit could have made her feel that way. The naked women in Rembrandt, emerging from the bath or rising from bed, are so private, so cherished in the painter's gaze, that we as viewers see them not as sexual playthings but as loved persons. A man would do well to emulate that gaze.

I have never thought of myself as a sight. How much that has to do with being male and how much with having grown up on the back roads where money was scarce and eyes were few, I cannot say. As a boy, apart from combing my hair when I was compelled to and regretting the patches on my jeans (only the poor wore patches), I took no trouble over my appearance. It never occurred to me that anybody outside my family, least of all a girl, would look at me twice. As a young man, when young women did occasionally glance my way, without any

---

[8]**Anthony Van Dyck** (1599–1641), Flemish painter who settled in England in 1632; **Jean-Auguste-Dominique Ingres** (1780–1867), French painter.

prospect of appearing handsome I tried at least to avoid appearing odd. A standard haircut and the cheapest versions of the standard clothes were camouflage enough. Now as a middle-aged man I have achieved once more that boyhood condition of invisibility, with less hair to comb and fewer patches to humble me.

Many women clearly pass through the world aspiring to invisibility. Many others just as clearly aspire to be conspicuous. Women need not make spectacles of themselves in order to draw the attention of men. Indeed, for my taste, the less paint and fewer bangles the better. I am as helpless in the presence of subtle lures as a male moth catching a whiff of pheromones. I am a sucker for hair ribbons, a scarf at the throat, toes leaking from sandals, teeth bared in a smile. By contrast, I have always been more amused than attracted by the enameled exhibitionists whom our biblical mothers would identify as brazen hussies or painted Jezebels or, in the extreme cases, as whores of Babylon.

Many women pass through the world aspiring to invisibility.

To encounter female exhibitionists in their full glory and variety, you need to go to a city. I never encountered ogling as a full-blown sport until I visited Rome, where bands of Italian men joined with gusto in appraising the charms of every passing female, and the passing females vied with one another in demonstrating their charms. In our own cities the most notorious bands of oglers tend to be construction gangs or street crews, men who spend much of their day leaning on the handles of shovels or pausing between bursts of riveting guns, their eyes tracing the curves of passersby. The first time my wife and kids and I drove into Boston we followed the signs to Chinatown, only to discover that Chinatown's miserably congested main street was undergoing repairs. That street also proved to be the city's home for X-rated cinemas and girlie shows and skin shops. LIVE SEX ACTS ON STAGE. PEEP SHOWS. PRIVATE BOOTHS. Caught in a traffic jam, we spent an hour listening to jackhammers and wolf whistles as we crept through the few blocks of pleasure palaces, my son and daughter with their noses hanging out the windows, my wife and I steaming. Lighted marquees peppered by burnt-out bulbs announced the titles of sleazy flicks; life-size posters of naked women flanked the doorways of clubs: leggy strippers in miniskirts, the originals for some of the posters, smoked on the curb between numbers.

After we had finally emerged from the zone of eros, eight-year-old Jesse inquired, "What was *that* place all about?"

"Sex for sale," my wife Ruth explained.

That might carry us some way toward a definition of pornography: making flesh into a commodity, flaunting it like any other merchandise, divorcing bodies from selves. By this reckoning, there is a pornographic dimension to much advertising, where a charge of sex is added to products ranging from cars to shaving cream. In fact, the calculated imagery of advertising may be more harmful than the blatant imagery of the pleasure palaces, that frank raunchiness which Kate Millett refers to as the "truthful explicitness of pornography." One can leave the X-rated zone of the city, but one cannot escape the sticky reach of commerce, which summons girls to the high calling of cosmetic glamor, fashion, and sexual display, while it summons boys to the panting chase.

You can recognize pornography, according to D. H. Lawrence, "by the insult it offers, invariably, to sex, and to the human spirit." He should know, Millet argues in *Sexual Politics*, for in her view Lawrence himself was a purveyor of patriarchal and often sadistic pornography. I think she is correct about the worst of Lawrence, and that she identifies a misogynist streak in his work; but she ignores his career-long struggle to achieve a more public, tolerant vision of sexuality as an exchange between equals. Besides, his novels and stories all bear within themselves their own critiques. George Steiner reminds us that "the list of writers who have had the genius to enlarge our actual compass of sexual awareness, who have given the erotic play of the mind a novel focus, an area of recognition previously unknown or fallow, is very small." Lawrence belongs on that brief list. The chief insult to the human spirit is to deny it, to claim that we are merely conglomerations of molecules, to pretend that we exist purely as bundles of appetites or as food for the appetites of others.

Men commit that insult toward women out of ignorance, but also out of dread. Allen Wheelis again: "Men gather in pornographic shows, not to stimulate desire, as they may think, but to diminish fear. It is the nature of the show to reduce the woman, discard her individuality, her soul, make her into an object, thereby enabling the man to handle her with greater safety, to use her as a toy. . . . As women move increasingly toward equality, the felt danger to men increases, leading to an increase in pornography and, since there are some men whose fears cannot even so be stilled, to an increase also in violence against women."

Make her into an object: All the hurtful ways for men to look at women are variations on this betrayal. "Thus she turns herself into an object," writes Berger. A woman's ultimate degradation is in "submissively making herself a thing," writes Beauvoir. To be turned into an object—whether by the brush of a painter or the lens of a photographer or the eye of a voyeur, whether by hunger or poverty or enslavement, by mugging or rape, bullets or bombs, by hatred, racism, car crashes, fires, or falls—is for each of us the deepest dread; and to reduce another person to an object is the primal wrong.

Caught in the vortex of desire, we have to struggle to recall the wholeness of persons, including ourselves. Beauvoir speaks of the temptation we all occasionally feel to give up the struggle for a self and lapse into the inertia of an object: "Along with the ethical urge of each individual to affirm his subjective existence, there is also the temptation to forgo liberty and become a thing." A woman in particular, given so much encouragement to lapse into thinghood, "is often very well pleased with her role as the *Other.*"

> **Caught in the vortex of desire, we have to struggle to recall the wholeness of persons, including ourselves.**

Yet one need not forgo liberty and become a thing, without a center or a self, in order to become the Other. In our mutual strangeness, men and women can be doorways one for another, openings into the creative mystery that we share by virtue of our existence in the flesh. "To be sensual," James Baldwin writes, "is to respect and rejoice in the force of life, of life itself, and to be *present* in all that one does, from the effort of loving to the breaking of bread." The effort of loving is reciprocal, not only in act but in desire, an *I* addressing a *Thou,* a meeting in that vivid presence. The distance a man stares across at a woman, or a woman at a man, is a gulf in the soul, out of which a voice cries, *Leap, leap.* One day all men may cease to look on themselves as prototypically human and on women as lesser miracles; women may cease to feel themselves the targets for desire; men and women both may come to realize that we are all mere flickerings in the universal fire; and then none of us, male or female, need give up humanity in order to become the *Other.*

Ever since I gawked at the girl in pink shorts, I have dwelt knowingly in the force-field of sex. Knowingly or not, it is where we all dwell. Like the masses of planets and stars, our bodies curve the space around us. We radiate signals constantly, radio sources that never go off the air. We cannot help being centers of attraction and repulsion for one another. That is not all we are by a long shot, nor all we are capable of feeling, and yet, even after our much-needed revolution in sexual consciousness, the power of eros will still turn our heads and hearts. In a world without beauty pageants, there will still be beauty, however its definition may have changed. As long as men have eyes, they will gaze with yearning and confusion at women.

When I return to the street with the ancient legacy of longing coiled in my DNA, and the residues from a thousand generations of patriarchs silting my brain, I encounter women whose presence strikes me like a slap of wind in the face. I must prepare a gaze that is worthy of their splendor.

▶ Analyzing the Text

1. At the beginning and end of this essay, Sanders suggests that a "force-field of sex" surrounds all our interactions with others. Working through the essay, explain how Sanders uses each example or episode from his past to discuss the impact of this force-field of sex.

2. In one early episode from his past, Sanders describes the experience of viewing pinups and centerfolds of women from magazines like *Playboy.* How, in his view, do these images "severely reduce" the humanity of the women in the photographs? How did the prevalence of these images in his college dorm affect his way of seeing women?

3. In the middle of this essay, Sanders introduces the theories of feminist scholar Simone de Beauvoir. Review those paragraphs and develop your own explanation of what her theories are regarding how men and women define each other's sexuality.

4. What role does Sanders suggest women play in allowing themselves to be objectified by men's attention? What examples does he provide? Do you think that women contribute to their own objectification by men? Why or why not?

5. In the end, what is Sanders's answer to the question, "How should a man look at women?" Where does he provide it?

6. **Interrogating Assumptions.** How might Sanders respond to the second assumption discussed in this chapter's introduction—that "chemistry" equals love (see p. 265)? Support your response by quoting from Sanders's essay. In addition, identify any assumptions about men and women that are suggested in this essay.

Writing about Cultural Practices

7. How has the rise of online dating services and other social networking sites reinforced the role of "the gaze" in whether people get together? As you work on this essay, challenge the assumption that true love is about finding a soul mate who will "see the real me" (see p. 267). Write an essay in which you develop a critical analysis of the common poses and styles of photographs that accompany people's profiles. Begin by visiting a dating site and printing out three to five profiles of men and three to five profiles of women that include photos. To analyze these photos, consider the following questions.

   - Notice details of the person's clothing, facial expression, and body language. What do these details convey about that person? How would you describe the "real me" that the person is trying to convey?

   - What does the person in the photo seem to assume about his or her audience?

   - What are the differences between how women and men portray themselves in the photos? What are the similarities? Consider women vs. other women, men vs. other men, and then women as a group vs. men as a group.

Benedict Carey, **The Brain in Love**

Benedict Carey writes about psychology and human behavior for the *New York Times'* weekly science section. He wrote "The Brain in Love" in 2002 while working as a staff writer for the *Los Angeles Times*. Like Scott Russell Sanders's "Looking at Women" (p. 329), this selection explores questions about the role of attraction in love. But while Sanders focuses on how men and women are socialized into specific gendered roles, Carey focuses on the roles of biology to determine matters of attraction. In the following essay, Carey presents several studies by scientists who argue that romantic attraction is a biologically based human drive, like hunger.

> ▶ **Mapping Your Reading**
>
> Throughout this essay, Carey cites a range of different scientific studies. As you read, use the margins to take notes about these scientists' claims. Do they agree with each other? Where don't they agree? Do you agree that biology drives attraction?

For generations scientists have studied the peacock feathers of human mating, the swish and swagger that advertise sexual interest, the courtship dance at bars, the public display. They've left the private experience—what's happening in the brain when we fall for someone—mostly to poets.

We know there's an inborn human urge to mate, after all. Love is a mystery, a promise, an arrow from Cupid's bow.

Yet recent research suggests that romantic attraction is in fact a primitive, biologically based drive, like hunger or sex, some scientists argue. While lust makes our eye wander, they say, it's the drive for romance that allows us to focus on one particular person, though we often can't explain why. The biology of romance helps account for how we think about passionate love, and explain its insanity: why we might travel cross-country for a single kiss, and plunge into blackest despair if our beloved turns away.

This view of romantic attraction rests on observations of passionate behavior across cultures, studies of animals during courtship and, most recently, findings by scientists studying the human brain. Using magnetic resonance imaging, or MRI, machines to peer into the brains of college students in the throes of early love—that crazed, can't-think-of-anything-but stage of romance—scientists have developed some of the first direct evidence that the neural mechanisms of romantic attraction are distinct from those of sexual attraction and arousal.

"What we're seeing here is the biological drive to choose a mate, to focus on one person to the exclusion of all others," said Helen Fisher, an anthropologist at Rutgers University in New Jersey, who spells out the biological basis for romantic attachment in a paper appearing this month in the journal *Neuroendocrinology Letters*. "Let's say you walk into a party and there are several attractive women or men there. Your brain is registering this attraction for each one; then you talk to the third or fourth one, and whoosh—you feel something extra."

Unique Brain Activity

Fisher's group is analyzing more than 3,000 brain scans of 18 recently smitten college students, taken while they looked at a picture of their beloved. She expects the results to build upon the findings of English researchers who recently completed a similar study of young men and women in love. When shown a picture of their romantic partner, their brain activity pattern was markedly different from when they looked at a picture of a close friend, reported neurobiologists Andreas Bartels and Semir Zeki of University College London. The pictures showed that the experience of romantic attraction activated those pockets of the brain with a high concentration of receptors for dopamine, the chemical messenger closely tied to states of euphoria, craving, and addiction.

Biologists have linked high levels of dopamine and a related agent, norepinephrine, to heightened attention and short-term memory, hyperactivity, sleeplessness, and goal-oriented behavior. When they're first captivated, Fisher argues, couples often show the signs of surging dopamine: increased energy, less need for sleep or food, focused attention, and exquisite delight in smallest details of this novel relationship.

The neural mechanisms of romantic attraction are distinct from those of sexual attraction.

Bartels and Zeki compared their MRI images to brain scans taken from people in different emotional states, including sexual arousal, feelings of happiness, and cocaine-induced euphoria. The pattern for romantic love was unique. But there was some overlap with and close proximity to other positive states. "This makes sense," said Zeki. "These were young people who were practically willing to die for their lover. You would expect that the images would reflect many strong emotions all at once."

MRI machines can't read people's minds, psychiatrists say. The pictures are not nearly sensitive enough to separate and measure each of the emotions that comprise romantic feeling, as if they were on a color-by-numbers map. Yet the images' emotional complexity itself reflects how many people think about being in love, some psychologists say.

In one recent study, University of Minnesota researcher Ellen Berscheid asked a group of young men and women to make four lists: of all their friends; of the people they loved; of everyone they thought sexually attractive; and finally, of those with whom they were "in love." As expected, the last list was the shortest, usually just one name. That same person, however, appeared on all the lists. "It's this combination of friendship, affection, and lust," Berscheid said, "that makes it so powerful."

This power is enough to warp judgment in otherwise sensible people, just as a spike in dopamine activity might. As psychologists have demonstrated in several studies, newly smitten lovers often idealize their partner, magnifying the other's virtues and explaining away their flaws: She is the funniest person I've ever met. He's moody because of his job. This behavior, sometimes called the "pink lens effect," is often sharply at odds with the perceptions of friends and family, psychologists say. New couples also exalt the relationship itself. "It's very common; they think they have a relationship that's more special, closer, than anyone else's," said Berscheid, a leading researcher on the psychology of love.

Yet some idealization may be crucial to building a longer-term relationship, said Pamela Regan, a researcher at Cal State L.A. and author of the recently released *The Mating Game*, a book about relationships. "If you don't sweep away the person's flaws to some extent, then you're just as likely to end a relationship or not even try," she said. "This at least gives you a chance. If you think of romantic attraction as a kind of drug that alters how you think, then in this case it's allowing you to take some risks you wouldn't otherwise."

> Some idealization may be crucial to building a longer-term relationship.

Passionate love's euphoria is certainly enough to push many people through the first two stages of courtship: self-disclosure, the up-all-night storytelling; and interdependence, when lovers are continually together, often contentedly doing nothing. But that pink lens effect might also help people through stage three: conflict, when tension and doubts about the couple's future prompt arguments and soul-searching.

Healthy Romanticizing

In a 1996 experiment, psychologists at the State University of New York at Buffalo followed a group of 121 dating couples. Every few months, the couples answered questionnaires designed to determine how much they idealized their partner, and how well the pair was doing. The researchers found that the couples who were closest one year later were those who idealized each other the most. The idealizing seemed to help carry these couples through the inevitable rough spots. "Intimates who idealized one another," concluded the researchers in the paper, "appeared more prescient than blind, actually creating the relationships they wished for as romances progressed."

Short-term studies of courtship mean little for the issue that most people confront: What are the ingredients of a long-term, loving relationship? Psychologists at the University of Texas in Austin have been looking at the subject for more than a decade, following 168 couples who were married in 1981. What they're finding is that idealization of a kind can keep people happily married. "Usually, this is a matter of one person putting good spin on the partner, seeing the partner as more responsive than he or she really is," said Ted Huston, the study's lead investigator. "People who do that tend to stay in relationships longer than those who can't or don't."

But the findings are mixed. Huston's research also has identified three paths through early courtship: fast and passionate, slow and rocky, and in-between.

The fast-track group, about 25 percent of the total, usually were interdependent within weeks, tended to ignore or forget their initial problems, and were committed to marriage within several months. By contrast, the slow-motion group took an average of two years to reach a commitment, spending up to six painstaking months in each stage.

Yet when it came to success at the 13-year mark, the tortoises won out. "The more boring and deliberate the courtship, the better the prospects for a long marriage, I'm afraid," he said. "People who had very intense, Hollywood-type romances at the beginning were likely to have a big drop-off later on, and this often changed their view of the other's character."

> **If passionate romance is like a drug, then it's bound to lose its kick.**

That's the rub. If passionate romance is like a drug, as the MRI images suggest, then it's bound to lose its kick. Studies of dating and engaged couples find that feelings of passionate love and infatuation tend to fade quickly in the first year, and a year or two later often are all but gone, said Regan. What's more, simply having a strong romantic drive says nothing about how wisely you'll use it—or on whom. "The drive is there simply to focus your energy on one person," said Fisher. "People make wrong choices all the time."

The emotional fallout from that kind of decision is no less awful for its being wrong, of course. But seeing romance as a biologically based, drug-like state can at least provide some balm for a broken heart. "Like a drug addict would tell you," said Regan, "the highs don't last, but neither does the withdrawal. With time the craving and pain go away and the brain returns to normal."

▶ Analyzing the Text

1. According to Carey's essay, what have scientists discovered is the effect of love on the brain? Does this news surprise you? Why or why not?

2. Although philosophers, poets, and writers have speculated on the nature of love through the ages, the topic of love only recently has begun to gain the attention of scientists. What do you think might account for this?

3. Do you think the attention of the scientific community has helped or hindered our understanding of love and romantic attraction? Draw from Carey's essay to support your view.

4. **Connecting to Another Reading.** Compare Carey's argument with the argument posed by Scott Russell Sanders (p. 329). Both writers investigate assumptions about the origins of romantic attraction. What are the intersections of these arguments? In what ways do they support each other?

▶ Writing about Cultural Practices

5. Working in groups, locate the studies that Carey cites. Each group should summarize and analyze the findings of one study and present what they've discovered to the class. As you prepare your oral presentation, consider these questions.

- How was the study conducted? What questions are driving the researchers? What, if anything, does the study conclude?
- How does the design of the study shape its outcome? Are there any important or relevant questions that are left unaddressed by this study?
- Do your interpretations of this study align with Carey's? If not, explain any discrepancies.

6. The noted psychologist R. J. Sternberg, author of *The Psychology of Love* (1989) and *Cupid's Arrow: The Course of Love through Time* (1998), has developed a theory that explains all types of love relationships. To do this, he names eight types of love relationships, which he conceptualizes in terms of three basic components of love. The first component is *intimacy*. It refers to the emotional bond, connection, or closeness two people feel for each other. The second component, *passion*, refers to the physical attraction and sexual chemistry that two people experience. The third component, *decision/commitment*, refers to the conscious decision people make when they realize they love someone or when they decide to commit to one person. (See the table below.)

   For this assignment, select two relationships you have seen portrayed in a movie or on television and develop a psychological analysis of them based on Sternberg's theory. As you draft your essay, consider the following questions.

- Which type of love does each relationship illustrate?
- How does each relationship rely on the three components of love?
- In what ways does this scientific model of love help to explain people's relationships?
- What aspects and defining qualities of people's relationship get ignored or left out of Sternberg's model?

Table 4.1 Sternberg's Typology of Love Relationships

Type of Love Relationship	Love Component		
	Intimacy	Passion	Decision/Commitment
Nonlove	Low	Low	Low
Liking	High	Low	Low
Infatuation	Low	High	Low
Empty love	Low	Low	High
Romantic love	High	High	Low
Companionship love	High	Low	High
Irrational love	Low	High	High
Consummate love	High	High	High

Caitlin Leffel, **The Look of Love: Wedding Announcements**

New York Times, **Announcement: Victoria Dunn and Terrance Jones**

New York Times, **Announcement: Daniel Gross and Steven Goldstein**

The final set of readings in this chapter examines how wedding announcements in newspapers act as a sign of our changing cultural assumptions about marriage. In Caitlin Leffel's essay, first published in *Annabelle Magazine* in 2004, she suggests that wedding announcements sections of newspapers create "a record (if a highly edited one) of who mates in our culture, evidence of the ongoing evolution of marriage."

The two wedding announcements included in this chapter were originally published in the Weddings & Celebrations section of the *New York Times.* The first example, Victoria Dunn and Terrance Jones, details how one couple was married in a ceremony that used video-teleconferencing to bring bride, groom, and their families "together." The second announcement is of the first gay commitment ceremony to appear in the paper. Since September 2002, the *Times* has regularly included gay commitment ceremonies and marriages in this section, and other major newspapers have begun to follow suit. At the time, however, there was much debate about whether the paper should print such announcements. In the week after Daniel Gross and Steven Goldstein's announcement broke this new ground, the *New York Times* editors explained that newspapers have an obligation to report "what is happening."

▶ Mapping Your Reading

In "The Look of Love," Leffel argues that the weddings section of the *New York Times,* and indeed any paper, "serves as an immutable record of contemporary love." As you read, use the margins to create a list of details from the announcements that represent what today's weddings and commitment ceremonies look like. As Leffel asks, what do weddings have to do with "actual love"? And how does the wedding announcement serve as a cultural artifact? As a document about contemporary love?

Since the moment Jacob had his Old Testament altar-side surprise—tricked into marrying the ugly sister Leah instead of his beloved Rachel—love and marriage have had a capricious relationship. Over the years, this mysterious emotional force and the institution that legitimizes it have pursued each other through cultural obstacles and the disapproving eye of countless societies. Today, while not completely uncontroversial, these two entities amicably cohabit in many a contemporary society. Marrying for love is timidly viewed as the ideal—one that fortunately, we Americans have a much better shot of attaining thanks to the absence of dowries, the loosening of social, religious and ethnic constraints, and cell phones.

Weddings, on the other hand, can be seen as having very little to do with actual love. While marriage is premised on the romantic notion of committing oneself to another (and ostensibly to raise a family), the wedding has only indirect relations with the underlying emotion. It is the art that decorates the love, and the vehicle that promotes it, but the traditional wedding is so draped with tradition and presentation that the love itself can easily be obscured behind the pomp. Still faithful to ceremony and seduced by self-celebration, the wedding flirts with the forces of love, but is ultimately unwilling to commit.

No vestige of matrimony more smacks of shameless self-promotion than the infamous newspaper wedding announcement. While ceremonies can be personalized, vows written, printed wedding announcements betray the pretense of genuine ardor just by appearing in the "society pages." Here, one can advertise the "specs" of their forthcoming union, realize a childhood dream of having their picture in the paper (and a posed one, no less), and indulge that delicious fantasy that the boy or girl who broke your heart might come across your glorious triumph over their Wheaties.

For the purposes of this piece I am going to stick with the industry standard (and the form I know best): the *New York Times*. Each week, the Gray Lady offers us a breath of levity from inside the heft of the Sunday paper. The Weddings & Celebrations section is a comforting grounding amidst more pressing issues—from the Gaza Strip to Michael Jackson's bedroom—and a seductively voyeuristic glimpse inside an exclusive segment of our society. But more than that, these notices are a record (if a highly edited one) of who mates in our culture, evidence of the ongoing evolution of marriage and they capture the increasing emergence of true love within this glorious institution.

For the rest of us, the Weddings & Celebrations section has a certain voyeuristic appeal. Readers can amuse themselves with an admirably accomplished crop of intendeds, (mostly) youngsters whose roster reads like an Ivy League admission list. But looking past the Asian violinists, WASPy blondes flashing pearly Nantucket whites, and the occasional beaming same sex couple, the section, I would argue, actually serves as an immutable record of contemporary love. The most recent revolution of this is the inclusion of same sex unions. The *Times* began printing same sex unions in August 2002 and unlike the State of New York, the *Times* gave gay couples the same treatment as their straight counterparts from the beginning. They adhere to the same submission and editing guidelines, and their unions are presented in the same format as the weddings.

The only detail that sets apart their announcements is the addition of direction-als in the text if there is a picture, so readers can identify each member of the couple. I do not mean to suggest this as an example of activism on the *Times'* part (or that they came to this on their own sense of equanimity). Rather, that with-out visible struggle, Weddings & Celebrations independently—almost organi-cally—evolved to the changing notion of love, to reflect what indeed turned out to be an increasing public acceptance of homosexual love.

But the grand foray of gay couples into Weddings & Celebrations has by no means been the only change of note to this journalistic institution. Though it has been accompanied by less fanfare, the other evidence of modern love can be seen in the details that have crept in—or have been left out. A round-up of any given Sunday will offer a bevy of lawyers, doctors, actors, journalists, MBAs, Fulbright scholars, Peace Corps volunteers, divorcées (and divorcés), senior citizens, philan-thropists, and yes, those ubiquitous violinists. While the selection of couples veers towards the particularly accomplished, there is an interesting level of diversity: Many of those MBAs are women, the Peace Corps volunteer met his fiancée while they were both sta-tioned in Uganda working with AIDS patients, and that corporate lawyer was married in an outdoor Hindu ceremony officiated by a rabbi.

> **Evidence of modern love can be seen in the details that have crept in—or have been left out.**

Further, because of their loyalty to impeccably clean and formulaic wording, the section has normalized certain "love practices" into the vernacular by the in-corporation of phrases into the section's rigid code of syntax. For example, re-placing the "who was until recently" after the bride's married name with "who will be using her name professionally" says in Weddings & Celebrations' cryptically euphemistic jargon not that the *Times* is actively trying to promote a more diverse face of marriage, but rather that readers understand, accept, and enjoy these kinds of unions as, if not the norm, than perhaps as embodying much of it.

Weddings & Celebrations should not be charged with either adhering to a nor-mative standard or setting the ideal—it is not the job of a newspaper to issue lifestyle edicts. (*Martha* and *Oprah* take care of that already, thank you very much.) Yet by incorporating elements of both the normal and the admirable, what it can (and does) do is inform readers of the prevalence of love across traditionally im-penetrable barriers, and, in doing so, serve as evidence of the state of modern love.

On a recent episode of *The Sopranos*, the quintessential post-modern family man, Tony Soprano, quipped that wedding announcements are like the women's sports pages. I disagree. To me, they seem a lot more like the obituaries. Like the obits, wedding announcements offer an edited but unbiased account of life on a human level (rather than on a political, regional, or theoretical level, like the rest of the paper). They both deliver news of record, in an unhesitatingly respectful way.

The tradition of publishing wedding announcements is arguably antiquated, undeniably rooted in elitism, of questionable social value, and yet they endure as a reflection of contemporary love. In the end, the Weddings & Celebrations sec-tion may not inform in the same way as the rest of the newspaper does, but it still upholds the same standards and performs its requisite function by showing us exactly what's fit to print.

Walking into the wedding of Victoria Dunn and Terrance Jones on July 25 was like entering a NASA control room experiencing some technical difficulties.

Ms. Dunn and Mr. Jones, both 51, were married in a videoconference wedding held in a thundercloud-gray meeting room at the Kinko's print and copy shop on East 52d Street. Besides the 7 guests in New York, 20 more gathered to watch the proceedings, carried live via television monitors at Kinko's locations in Portland, Oregon, Seattle, and Berkeley, California.

In New York, a technician with bleached-blond hair and multiple silver hoops in each ear fiddled with the controls and said, "Portland, can you hear me?" After a half-hour of adjustments, the bridegroom joked, "I think I'll dispense with the prayer for technical success."

The couple, who work out of their home-office in Haddonfield, New Jersey, feel as comfortable among copiers and fax machines as other people do among armoires and down couches. Mr. Jones, a regional sales director for Access Publishers Network, a book distribution company, is often on the road and uses copy shops as drop-in offices.

He is also a practicing Buddhist who even fishes in a Zen way—he uses a fly but no hook. "It's catch and release without the catch," said Tim Campbell, a guest in Berkeley.

Mr. Jones and Ms. Dunn, a freelance office manager who looks like the actress Melanie Griffith with cloud-white hair, have a personal story more complicated than a four-way video hookup. In 1986, between her second and third marriages and his first and second, they met at work and fell in love over a cup of coffee. They lived together for three years, celebrated their 40th birthdays together, but split up because of "midlife crisis issues," Mr. Jones said. Then, having not spoken for nearly a decade, they got together for another cup of coffee last summer and fell in love again.

After the technician corrected the video problems, their deconstructionist wedding began. In Portland, the bride's niece read lyrics from a John Denver song; the "best woman," Jane Mathewson, spoke from Seattle; the ring bearers pretended to deliver the rings from Portland, and in New York, the Rev. James Wentz, a Unitarian Universalist minister, declared the couple married.

The videoconference added a few new twists to the wedding experience. At the New York site, there were two large television screens, one that switched between the West Coast locations and another that carried the New York scene. As soon as guests walked in, they saw themselves on the monitors. At most weddings, if someone has a wrinkled skirt or messy hair, you might not notice. Here, flaws were magnified and then beamed to Portland, Berkeley, and Seattle.

Attending the wedding also felt like being inside an Andy Warhol print with many versions of the same image. At each site, the catering was the same: turquoise tablecloths, cheesecake, and sparkling wine, all shipped by the couple.

At Kinko's in New York, the couple (at top) and guests (above) check the monitors.

"This wedding is the equivalent of being a kid and seeing Dick Tracy talk to his watch," Mr. Campbell said. "It felt strange to be in Berkeley and have guests all over the country. We had our cheesecake, we had our sparkling wine, but it was just the four of us all dressed up and looking at each other."

There are plenty of advantages to a videoconference wedding, the bridegroom said.

Compared with a traditional ceremony, for example, the price was quite reasonable, and as Mr. Jones pointed out, it is a great way to avoid confrontations between feuding family members. His divorced parents happily attended—in separate locations hundreds of miles apart.

"But the real benefit," he said, "is you don't have to spend so much time with all of your relatives. You spend an hour and then you push a button."

THE NEW YORK TIMES **WEDDINGS/CELEBRATIONS** *SUNDAY, SEPTEMBER 1, 2002*

Daniel Gross,
Steven Goldstein

Courtesy of Daniel Gross and Steven Goldstein

Daniel Andrew Gross and Steven Goldstein will affirm their partnership today in a civil union ceremony at the Shore Acres Inn and Restaurant in North Hero, Vt. Assistant Judge Barney Bloom of State Superior Court in Montpelier will preside. Last evening, Rabbi David M. Steinberg led an exchange of Jewish vows at the Musée des Beaux-Arts of Montreal.

Mr. Goldstein, 40, is the founder and owner of Attention America, a public affairs consulting firm in Manhattan. He was a co-manager of Jon S. Corzine's campaign in 2000 for the Senate from New Jersey. A summa cum laude graduate of Brandeis, Mr. Goldstein holds a master's degree in public policy from Harvard and a master's in journalism and a law degree from Columbia.

He is a son of Carole and Dennis Goldstein of Bayside, Queens. His mother is a fund-raiser for the Friends of the Lukas Foundation, which she helped found to support the Lukas Community, a village for adults with developmental disabilities in Temple, N.H. His father is the founder and senior partner of the

Barrister Reporting Service, a court transcription concern in Manhattan.

Mr. Gross, 32, is a vice president of GE Capital in Stamford, Conn., working on the financing of international projects like power plants and pipelines. He graduated cum laude from Yale, from which he also received an M.B.A. and a master's degree in environmental management. He was a Fulbright scholar in 1994-95 in Thailand, studying and teaching natural resources management at the Asian Institute of Technology near Bangkok.

He is a son of Merle and Barry Gross of Chicago. His mother ran Merle Ltd., a former coat manufacturer in Chicago. His father retired as a partner in Shefsky & Froelich, a Chicago law firm.

The couple met in October 1992 in Washington, where Mr. Goldstein was working as a television news producer and Mr. Gross as a consultant. Mr. Goldstein was one of 35 respondents to a personal ad that Mr. Gross had placed in Washington City Paper. It read: "Nice Jewish boy, 5 feet 8 inches, 22, funny, well-read, dilettantish, self-deprecating, Ivy League, the kind of boy Mom fantasized about." They arranged to meet one evening at Kramerbooks & Afterwords, and had their second date the next night.

That Thanksgiving, Mr. Gross went home to visit his parents. "My mom said, 'You seem like everything's great,' " he recalled. " 'You seem like you're in love.' I said, 'I am.' They said, 'That's great.' I said, 'His name is Steven.' My mother said, 'Oy,' and was silent for a while."

Both sets of parents now support the relationship. While Mr. Gross was in Thailand, Mr. Goldstein had a $1,500 telephone bill one month. They were apart again while Mr. Gross was in graduate school. Finally, in 1998, they moved to New York together.

They postponed a commitment ceremony until leaders of Reform Judaism had voted to support rabbis who perform same-sex unions and Vermont had given legal recognition to civil unions, both events in 2000.

"Sept. 11 accelerated the process," Mr. Goldstein said. "We all began to think of our own mortality."

 ### Analyzing the Text

1. Leffel writes, "The tradition of publishing wedding announcements is arguably antiquated, undeniably rooted in elitism, of questionable social value, and yet they endure as a reflection of contemporary love." How do you respond to these seemingly contradictory statements about newspaper wedding announcements? If they are antiquated and elitist, how can they also reflect contemporary love?

2. Leffel focuses her analysis on the wedding announcements printed in the *New York Times*. She argues that, because the *Times* editors use a spare writing style and "formulaic wording" in the announcements they publish, they have "normalized certain love practices." As you study the two sample announcements, what kind of information appears to be conventional? What patterns do you notice in how the announcements present the couples or ceremonies?

3. What do these wedding announcements indicate about the nature of contemporary love? Draw from the lists you created for the Mapping your Reading assignment and use details from Leffel's own argument.

4. **Interrogating Assumptions.** Leffel explains that adding gay unions to the announcements page of the newspaper is only the most recent example of changing attitudes and assumptions about modern love. Particularly, she suggests that wedding announcements show changing attitudes about women's and men's roles in a marriage. What do the details in the sample announcements reveal about the changing nature of gender roles in a marriage? What examples does Leffel provide in her essay?

5. Consider the announcement for Victoria Dunn and Terrance Jones. Clearly, the use of video-teleconferencing has not swept the nation's wedding chapels, so this wedding cannot be viewed as a typical modern wedding. On the other hand, in a culture that is increasingly technologically advanced, how have weddings—from the planning stages to the day itself—also become more technologically advanced? What does all this technological support buy us? How has it altered our expectations of what weddings should be like?

6. **Connecting to Other Readings.** Many of the other readings in this chapter explore how dating practices have changed. Some of these readings include Jennifer Egan's "Love in the Time of No Time" (p. 275) and the excerpts from dating how-to guides. Based on the readings, how have assumptions about love gone beyond changing dating to changing wedding practices and even the concept of marriage?

▶ Writing about Cultural Practices

7. Draft a critical analysis of the wedding announcements page from a local newspaper. Begin by determining which day your local newspaper publishes wedding and celebration announcements. Collect both the most current and several back issues of this section of the paper. To help develop greater critical distance on how these announcements reveal cultural attitudes about love, marriage, and the traditional roles of men and women, you may wish to find sample wedding announcements that were printed in this paper before you were born. As you draft your analysis, consider the following questions.

   • How have the editors developed a syntax or formula for constructing these announcements?

   • What do the details in these announcements reveal about people's assumptions about love and marriage?

   • What do these details reveal about the changing nature of gender roles in a marriage?

Mixing Words and Images

CREATING AN ALTERNATIVE VALENTINE

www.despair.com

Valentine's Day is a holiday that is intended to celebrate romance, and yet, as the company selling the BitterSweets candy hearts pictured here claims, "While a tiny fraction of the population can look forward to a holiday of wine and roses, poetry and song—the vast majority of us can anticipate a day of nausea and grief." These pretty candy hearts with their dejected or dysfunctional sayings combine the light and dark sides of the Valentine's Day experience—the romance and the realism.

The purpose of this assignment is for you to create a Valentine's Day card that juxtaposes romance and realism in order to convey a visual argument. Juxtaposition—the act of placing two or more ideas, objects, choices, or options side by side so as to encourage comparison—is a common analytical technique used in art, graphic design, and advertising. As critical commentaries on valentines, the BitterSweets candies are perfect examples of juxtaposition. On the one hand, they are heart-shaped, cutesy, and sweet-tasting. On the other hand, where you'd expect to see a romantic saying like "Be Mine," you find cynical messages like "Prenup okay?" and "Peaked at 17." Used effectively, juxtaposition conveys an argument visually. It can be a powerful way to get people's attention and to get them thinking.

Creating Your Alternative Valentine

- Gather and study examples of conventional valentines (contemporary and/or antique).
- Consider which assumption(s) about romance or true love you want to get people to question.
- Collect or create visuals that further your point and integrate them with your text to present a unified visual argument.

Writing about Your Alternative Valentine

Once you have constructed your alternative valentine, draft a descriptive analysis to accompany it. First, describe the objects or details used in your valentine and explain (a) the cultural message it conveys and (b) how it creates a juxtaposition between romance and realism. Second, consider these two questions in your analysis.

- To what extent is romance something that is socially constructed? That is, to what extent are our views on romance not individually determined but something that we gradually absorb from our social surroundings?
- To what extent do popular assumptions about romance lead people to unrealistic expectations of their love relationships?

ON THE WEB
For help with these assignments, go to Chapter 4,
bedfordstmartins.com/remix

1. What Is Love Now?
A Dialogue Essay on Romance

Construct a conversation between yourself and three or four authors from this chapter that addresses this question: "What is the meaning of romantic love in modern America?"

What is a dialogue essay?

A dialogue essay does not follow the structure or organization of a conventional essay. Instead it resembles a script for a play. Speakers' names introduce their spoken parts, and all physical actions are described in parentheses. Here is an example:

> TOM: Hey Sara! How are you?
> SARA: (*walks toward him*) Terrible. Joe dumped me last night.

The challenge for this assignment is to create a focused dialogue in which you do not play the part of a narrator or an interviewer. Your part of the conversation must be as substantial as the dialogue of the authors from this chapter.

How do you organize your dialogue essay?

- Begin your essay with a paragraph that sets the scene and introduces the speakers. Where does this conversation take place? What time of day is it? Who are the speakers?
- Each speaking turn must be a minimum of 100 words—no one-word answers.

- Eighty percent of what the three authors say in their dialogue must be direct quotes from their readings, which you may edit as long as you don't change the meaning. Use the remaining 20 percent of their speaking parts to paraphrase their views or give the author a question to ask. This will help you draft a smoother conversational flow in your dialogue.
- After the dialogue ends, write a closing paragraph that explains your argument about the meaning of romantic love as conveyed in your dialogue.

2. "Are You Hot or Not?":
Investigating Attraction

Two essays in this chapter investigate the nature of attraction: "Looking at Women" by Scott Russell Sanders and "The Brain in Love" by Benedict Carey (pp. 329, 341). Both of these readings present one, if not multiple, theories to explain how attraction works and what part attraction plays in the search for love. For this assignment, draw on one or more of the theories from these essays to help you develop your own critical analysis of attraction. Chief among the questions your essay will address are these:

- How do you know if you're "hot"? What social cues do people use to signal they are attracted to someone?
- To what extent are factors of attraction influenced by social contexts?

- To what extent is "hotness" a behavior or attitude that people can learn?

Finally, consider testing your theory about attraction by studying the profiles of users of online dating sites like facethejury.com, hotornot.com, Friendster.com, Faces.com, Yahoo.com/personals, Match.com, and so on.

3. Is TV Love like Real-life Love? A Critical Analysis

Select two relationships you have seen portrayed in television shows and draft a critical analysis of them by drawing on theories about love from one of the readings in this chapter. As you write, you need to answer the questions, "How do these relationships illustrate the theories about love from one of this chapter's authors?" and "What details about these relationships lead you to your analysis?" To help focus your analysis, consider choosing two relationships from the same category of TV shows: sitcoms, dramas, soap operas, or reality-based shows. As you develop your essay, work with the following questions.

- What is the nature of the love relationships between these characters? Is it a flirtation? Are the couples newlyweds? Long married? What social cues do the actors and the producers of the show rely to "tell" viewers what kind of relationships they are?

- What assumptions about romance appear to drive these love relationships forward? Will they last? What details in the interactions between the characters lead you to your conclusions?

- In what ways do these relationships support a particular theory about romance from one of the readings in this chapter?

4. Interrogating Assumptions: What's Love Got to Do with It?

At the beginning of this chapter, you were introduced to four commonly held assumptions that challenged you to reflect on some of the cultural attitudes influencing how we think about romance. They are:

> Love conquers all.
>
> "Chemistry" = love.
>
> My true love will be my soul mate.
>
> True love is forever.

Each of the readings in this chapter questions one or more of these assumptions, asking "How do idealized notions of romance reflect American cultural values?" and "What is the meaning of romance in modern America?" For this assignment, develop a critical analysis of how two or three readings interrogate one of these assumptions.

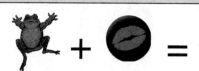

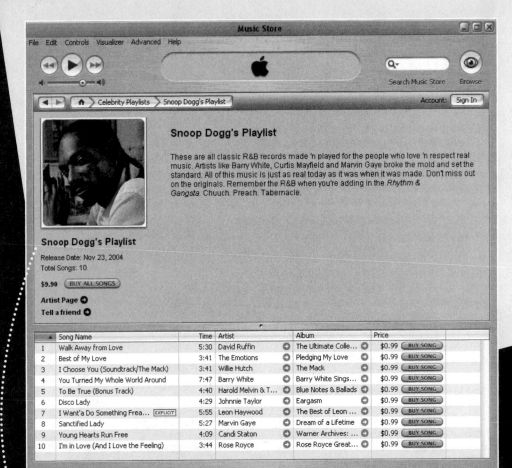

Music Store

File Edit Controls Visualizer Advanced Help

Search Music Store   Browse

Celebrity Playlists > Snoop Dogg's Playlist   Account: Sign In

Snoop Dogg's Playlist

These are all classic R&B records made 'n played for the people who love 'n respect real music. Artists like Barry White, Curtis Mayfield and Marvin Gaye broke the mold and set the standard. All of this music is just as real today as it was when it was made. Don't miss out on the originals. Remember the R&B when you're adding in the *Rhythm & Gangsta*. Chuuch. Preach. Tabernacle.

Snoop Dogg's Playlist

Release Date: Nov 23, 2004
Total Songs: 10

$9.90 BUY ALL SONGS

Artist Page ●
Tell a friend ●

	Song Name	Time	Artist		Album		Price	
1	Walk Away from Love	5:30	David Ruffin	●	The Ultimate Colle...	●	$0.99	BUY SONG
2	Best of My Love	3:41	The Emotions	●	Pledging My Love	●	$0.99	BUY SONG
3	I Choose You (Soundtrack/The Mack)	3:41	Willie Hutch	●	The Mack	●	$0.99	BUY SONG
4	You Turned My Whole World Around	7:47	Barry White	●	Barry White Sings...	●	$0.99	BUY SONG
5	To Be True (Bonus Track)	4:40	Harold Melvin & T...	●	Blue Notes & Ballads	●	$0.99	BUY SONG
6	Disco Lady	4:29	Johnnie Taylor	●	Eargasm	●	$0.99	BUY SONG
7	I Want'a Do Something Frea... EXPLICIT	5:55	Leon Haywood	●	The Best of Leon ...	●	$0.99	BUY SONG
8	Sanctified Lady	5:27	Marvin Gaye	●	Dream of a Lifetime	●	$0.99	BUY SONG
9	Young Hearts Run Free	4:09	Candi Staton	●	Warner Archives: ...	●	$0.99	BUY SONG
10	I'm in Love (And I Love the Feeling)	3:44	Rose Royce	●	Rose Royce Great...	●	$0.99	BUY SONG

10 songs

or, why are we so bored?

5 Entertainment

Examining the Everyday
Entertainment and Playlists

The image on the facing page presents hip hop artist Snoop Dogg's playlist as it appears on the iTunes Music Store website. Celebrity and music playlists form a natural combination in contemporary American culture. What music inspires Snoop Dogg? What keeps Jennifer Garner moving during her workouts? What songs does President Bush dial up on his MP3 player? Celebrities and public officials are seemingly endless sources of interest.

What's more, their personal music choices offer us a peek into their lives and into who they are.

As a form of entertainment, music is a matter of personal taste and of cultural influence, an idea central to celebrity playlists. People love a certain kind of music for how it makes them feel, or how it connects them to others, or how it reminds them of special memories or life experiences. Music does more than

ON THE WEB
For additional resources for this
assignment, go to Chapter 5,
bedfordstmartins.com/remix

give us enjoyment; it reveals parts of our identity. But our tastes in music and this aspect of our identities are deeply influenced by the cultures around us. Our musical tastes are influenced not only by our social relationships—the preferences of our friends and families—but also by the values and tastes of the larger culture, for example, radio playlists and the artists and music promoted on MTV. We don't experience music (or any form of entertainment) in a vacuum. Our musical tastes also reflect the larger cultural contexts within which we live.

To begin examining cultural assumptions about entertainment, create a list of 8 to 10 songs and artists that you could use to make a mix that can serve to introduce you to your classmates. Then write a brief description of your mix that answers the following questions.

- Why are these songs important to you? How or where did you first encounter them? (Through a friend? The radio, television, the Internet, or magazines?)

- What does your mix say about who you are? How much do your musical choices reflect your sense of yourself?

- What would people learn about you by listening to your mix? What wouldn't they be able to learn about you?

Add a final paragraph that answers this question:

- What does your mix indicate about your connection to something larger?

The initial assignment of this chapter asks you to consider the connection between personal tastes in entertainment and larger cultural forces. But what about the purposes of entertainment? As several of the readings in this chapter illustrate, entertainment is not solely about pleasure. This chapter will ask you to investigate the purposes and impact of entertainment on American culture. One question that will drive your investigation is, What does mainstream entertainment say about everyday life in America?

Living in one of the wealthiest and most technologically advanced countries in the world means Americans are constantly bombarded with new ways to spend money on entertainment. Across the country, people spend millions of dollars every weekend going to the movies. And, according to the NPD Group, a market information company, total U.S. retail sales of video game hardware, software, and accessories in the year 2002 generated $10.3 billion in record-breaking sales.[1] But what do we find entertaining? And why?

Before you encounter the readings in this chapter, it will be valuable first to survey some common assumptions about entertainment.

Assumption 1

Entertainment is just for fun.

Why do we listen to music or play video games or go to the movies? "To have fun" is the usual answer. Entertainment, according to this view, is meant to give us enjoyment and to divert our attention away from the routines and problems of everyday

---

[1] To read NPD reports on entertainment and other industries, go to npd.com.

life. To satisfy these simple purposes, entertainment does not need to tax us by requiring deep thought or reflection. Like cotton candy, some entertainment is meant to be sugary and fluffy. It is not meant to make a grand or lasting impact on us.

According to this assumption, entertainment, to be entertaining, must offer the promise of fun. Whether people are in search of fantasy and action, the scary fun of horror movies and thrill rides, the wholesome fun of campfire sing-alongs, or the nightclub fun of crowds and music, people just want to have a good time. But why is having fun so important? The ancient Greeks left us with one answer: They believed that entertainment offers emotional release. Like a pressure valve, people need entertainment to help them vent pent-up energy and emotion and refresh the spirit. The Greeks called this emotional release *catharsis.*

But while entertainment might not burden us with obligations, it does bombard us with many powerful messages about who we are or want to be and about "the American way of life." Consider the example of the Miss America beauty pageant as a popular form of entertainment. The first pageant was devised in 1921 by a group of hotel owners in Atlantic City, New Jersey, as a

The first Miss America: "Miss Margaret Gorman— Miss America—awaits the arrival of 'Neptune' on the yacht club dock, on the opening day of the National Beauty Pageant." [original caption, 1921] Bettmann/CORBIS

promotional event to persuade summer tourists to stay in town past Labor Day. The fall festival or "pageant" included a "National Beauty Tournament" on the beach to select "the most beautiful bathing beauty in America." Margaret Gorman, who represented Washington, DC, won. The sixteen-year-old school-girl (pictured on p. 362) bore an uncanny resemblance to the reigning film star of the time, Mary Pickford. Begun as a pro-motional gimmick, even the first Miss America pageant reveals important cultural values about standards of beauty, about the roles of women in society, and about celebrity worship. Beauty pageants, as forms of entertainment, are layered with judg-ments about what defines beauty. They encourage a standard based on physical appearance rather than intellect against which girls or women are meant to measure themselves. Though they are billed as fun events, beauty pageants clearly have deeper influences on American life.

The role of comedy and comics provides perhaps the best ex-ample of how entertainment conveys more than pure fun. Jon Stewart, Jay Leno, and David Letterman—all hosts of late-night TV shows—and comics like Chris Rock and Wanda Sykes demon-strate the role of comedy as a form of both cultural and political critique. For instance, Jon Stewart's *The Daily Show* develops news stories about the strange obsessions of everyday people. In one such segment, *Daily Show* correspondent Stephen Colbert interviewed a man who built a UFO welcome center in his front yard. On *The Tonight Show,* Jay Leno has a regular segment in which he quizzes people on the street about current events or American history. By doing so, he pokes fun at people who can tell you who was recently kicked off of *Survivor* but who can't name the vice president of the United States. However, in most instances, comedy and comedians take aim at the rich and pow-erful. In one essay in this chapter, Alain de Botton (see p. 390) suggests that humor acts as an important form of cultural criti-cism: "[A]s humorists and their targets have long recognized, jokes are an enormously effective means of anchoring a criti-cism. At base, they are another way of complaining: about arro-gance, cruelty, or pomposity, about departures from virtue or good sense." As de Botton illustrates, there is more to comedy than getting a laugh.

Arguably, entertainment conveys cultural values and criticism and defines human experience—but is entertainment always in-teresting? The assumption that entertainment is "just for fun" fails to acknowledge that much entertainment actually bores people. We have become a culture of "been there, done that." Media critic Kenneth Gergen describes this response in his book, *The Saturated Self: Dilemmas of Identity in Contemporary Life* (1991). In his view, the popular media provides a map of human experiences and emotions. Experiences from the everyday— falling in love, starting a new job, winning a game—to the momentous—births, deaths, affairs, divorces—have all been taught to us by movies, TV shows, advertising, music, and so on. In one form of entertainment or another, we have witnessed the complete range of human emotion and experience. This, Gergen suggests, is the cause of our boredom. "Having seen it all before," he writes, "one approaches a state of ennui." In this state of ennui, or boredom, most entertainment cannot live up to the hype surrounding it. What this suggests is that by reflecting on how we use entertainment, we gain insights into the purpose of entertainment in American life.

What kinds of questions can you ask to uncover the benefits and limitations of the assumption that entertainment is just for fun?

- What makes a form of entertainment "fun"? And why or under what conditions does entertainment stop being entertaining?
- What is under the surface of "fun"? That is, what cultural values or messages does a given form of entertainment convey?
- In what ways do different forms of entertainment act as cultural criticism? What groups or entities are being critiqued?

Assumption 2

Entertainment is merely a reflection of culture.

Unlike the first assumption, this view openly acknowledges that there is more to entertainment than "having fun." According to this assumption, the role or purpose of entertainment is to reflect ourselves back to us. In this way, entertainment acts as a kind of mirror, and the goal of entertainers like singers or video game designers or movie producers is to create songs, games, and movies that will succeed because they mirror popular values, attitudes, and desires.

Consider the history of rock and roll music. Most versions of this history could be summed up like this: "We just gave the kids what they wanted." In the 1930s and '40s, most types of blues, boogie woogie, and rhythm and blues (R & B) music was relegated to what the music industry euphemistically referred to as "race music" radio outlets that targeted mainly African American audiences. Then, in 1951, Alan Freed, a disc jockey in Cleveland, Ohio, began to play this music for his predominantly white audience; it is Freed who is credited with coining the phrase "rock and roll" to describe the music he brought to the airwaves. His radio show became so popular that, in September 1954, Freed was hired by WINS radio in New York City. The following January he held a landmark dance there, promoting African American performers as rock and roll artists. Within a month, the music industry was advertising "rock and roll" records to mainstream America.

The early history of rock and roll music demonstrates how the entertainment industry does reflect the interests and attitudes of a culture. Much as it still does today, rock music in its early days reflected its youthful audience and that audience's interest in having fun and questioning authority. Also much like today, that audience didn't want its musical choices to be hindered by racial divisions. So, it might be said that the music industry simply followed or reflected what people were demanding.

However, even the history of rock and roll reveals cracks in the assumption that entertainment acts as a mirror, reflecting popular interests and desires. Rock music, after all, did more than mirror back "what the kids wanted." In the 1960s, rock music helped transform race relations in America. In the 1970s it helped sparked the sexual revolution, transforming gender relations, and throughout its history it has been a platform for social and political critique—consider punk rock, rap, and hip hop. In fact, many times entertainment has even sparked change.

Of course, not everyone is comfortable with change. Some culture critics argue that the entertainment media is to blame for what they see as a breakdown in moral or cultural values in modern society. Few contemporary artists have attracted more criticism than shock-rocker Marilyn Manson; however, in his music and in interviews, he defends artistic endeavors that challenge people's assumptions and the status quo. Manson has some experience debating the purpose of entertainment in a society. He is the controversial musician whose music was widely blamed, along with the movie *The Matrix* and violent video games, as sources of inspiration for the two teenagers who

© Getty Images/Vince Bucci

I don't like the media, but the media likes me.
—MARILYN MANSON, MAY 28, 1999,
ROLLING STONE *MAGAZINE*

gunned down students and teachers at Columbine High School in Littleton, Colorado, in 1999. One month after the tragedy, *Rolling Stone* magazine published Manson's response to his critics. In "Columbine: Whose Fault Is It?" Manson writes that "responsible journalists have reported with less publicity that Harris and Klebold were not Marilyn Manson fans—that they even disliked my music. Even if they were fans, that gives them no excuse, nor does it mean that music is to blame." He concludes the essay:

> I think that the National Rifle Association is far too powerful to take on, so most people choose *Doom, The Basketball Diaries*, or yours truly. This kind of controversy does not help me sell records or tickets, and I wouldn't want it to. I'm a controversial artist, one who

dares to have an opinion and bothers to create music and videos that challenge people's ideas in a world that is watered-down and hollow. In my work I examine the America we live in, and I've always tried to show people that the devil we blame our atrocities on is really just each one of us.

What Manson and even the early history of rock and roll music represent is the ways in which entertainers and entertainment, rather than reflecting culture, can spark a change in, or at least an examination of, cultural values and attitudes.

What kinds of questions can you ask to uncover the benefits and limitations of the assumption that entertainment merely reflects cultural values?

- What messages do particular forms of entertainment convey about modern American life? Who is conveying the messages? Are the ideas behind the messages mainstream? Or do they somehow counter mainstream ideas?
- In what ways do particular forms of entertainment reflect cultural values and attitudes or assumptions about race, class, or gender?
- In what ways do these forms of entertainment challenge or question cultural attitudes about race, class, or gender?

Assumption 3

Entertainment is a personal choice.

In this view, entertainment is understood ultimately to be a matter of personal taste. Unlike work, school, or family obligations, entertainment is a personal preference—something people choose. Indeed, in these media-saturated times, options for selecting the entertainment that most satisfies personal tastes, as offered on television and the Internet, for example, are virtually unlimited.

As this chapter's initial assignment points out, entertainment *is* largely a matter of individual taste. People feel a personal stake in the books, music, games, movies, sports, or hobbies that entertain them. From high school students forming garage bands and making their own CDs to gamers forming gaming communities to retirees joining quilting groups and attending quilting retreats,

On a building ledge in Los Angeles, cutouts of Lisa and Bart Simpson commemorate the 350th episode of The Simpsons.

© Getty Images/Stephen Shugerman

what starts as an interest can become a passion. In this way, entertainment can give people a sense of purpose and fulfillment.

The flip side of this idea, however, is that, if entertainment is simply a personal choice, then people are free to opt out of or not participate in any type of entertainment that does not appeal to them. What happens if someone does not like reality TV, for example? According to this viewpoint, nothing—people are free to avoid it and in doing so will not be affected either way.

However, what this assumption fails to take into account are the ways in which popular forms of mass entertainment have a substantial impact on the American popular imagination or consciousness, which far exceeds an individual's ability to opt in *or* out of it. As any fourth-grader who's *not* allowed to watch *South Park* or *The Simpsons* can explain, he or she is still very much affected by these extremely popular shows. Everything from the shows' jokes to the attitudes they convey about authority figures to the merchandising of their products permeates the social life of school-aged children. The same can be said about all forms of mass entertainment. Consider the impact music videos and MTV have had on the music industry. Not only have they changed how songwriters write and producers produce, but, with their editing style of quick "cuts" and constant movement, they have also revolutionized modern storytelling more generally. Thus, people who've never watched any music videos still experience their influence in other forms of mass media. Similarly, the trend of reality TV shows has in its own way also influenced the American popular imagination. People who have never watched *Survivor* can talk about "alliances" and use the phrase "the tribe has spoken" with the ease of someone who's an avid fan of the show. When it comes to popular forms of mass entertainment, people cannot choose to simply "turn it off."

What kinds of questions can you ask to uncover the benefits and limitations of this assumption about entertainment as a personal choice?

- Which forms of entertainment most saturate our culture right now? Why do you think this is the case?
- What messages do these forms of entertainment convey?
- How have these particular forms of entertainment become a part of the American popular imagination or consciousness?
- What causes artists and celebrities to respond to criticism of their work with the response, "If you don't like it, you don't have to watch/listen to it"?
- Are we truly free of the impact of entertainment, even if we don't choose to engage in it?

Questioning These Assumptions

As these assumptions illustrate, because mass entertainment has a wide-reaching influence on the American popular imagination, we need to reflect on how it impacts everyday life. Throughout this chapter, you will investigate how these and other assumptions about the role of entertainment shape modern American life. Chief among the questions you will encounter are the following: What makes entertainment entertaining? How does entertainment reflect American cultural values? and To what extent does the entertainment industry help construct these values?

IN THE MIX

Adam Sternbergh, Britney Spears: The Pop Tart in Winter

Adam Sternbergh has written for the *New York Times Magazine* and is co-creator of the pop culture reference website Fametracker.com. In the following essay, originally published in *Slate* in 2004, Sternbergh argues that Britney Spears represents a prime example of how female sexuality is packaged and sold by the pop music industry. Spears, who first gained fame in 1993 as a cast member of the Disney Channel's *New Mickey Mouse Club*, became a pop music superstar while still a teenager. Although her increasingly sexualized image has drawn criticism, her albums have sold millions of copies, and her life has become regular fodder for entertainment media outlets. In part to respond to her critics and explain why she needed a break from her career, Spears published a letter to her fans on her website on October 15, 2004. Both Sternbergh's essay and the caption on page 373 quote from her letter. To read the letter in its entirety, go to Britneyspears.com.

> ▶ **Mapping Your Reading**
>
> Sternbergh begins his essay with a description of Spears's music video for the song "My Prerogative." Pay attention to how he uses this description as a starting point for his argument about the star's refusal to see herself as a sex symbol. "Spears just *is* a series of contradictions," he writes, suggesting that she has no discernible identity. Why is Spears such an icon in popular American culture? What does she represent?

A few months ago, Lynne Spears wrote in an online column that her daughter Britney's new video—for the single "My Prerogative"—possessed "an element of old Hollywood glamour and mystery." Her statement may puzzle some viewers; namely, those with eyes. In the video, Britney drives her car into a swimming pool; emerges from the water, dripping and squirming; writhes on a bed in her undies; and poses in lingerie and garters, stroking herself while a man puffing a cigar ogles her. That final scene, in particular, is a uniquely Spearsian take on adult-child arousal: all smoke and leerers.

Sadly, the singer herself seems unaroused. "My Prerogative" arrives along with a disarmingly candid message on Spears' Web site. In this self-described "Letter of Truth," the pop star declares her need for a break. "My prerogative right now is to just chill & let all of the other overexposed blondes on the cover of *Us Weekly* be your entertainment. GOOD LUCK GIRLS!!" She continues, "I understand now what they mean when they talk about child stars. . . . It's amazing what advisors will push you to do, even if it means taking a naive, young, blonde girl & putting her on the cover of every magazine."

> **Spears has elevated inauthenticity to a Warholian level.**

Spears has already taken a lot of flack for her vigorously punctuated *cri de coeur*. But the fact is, she's absolutely right. She *is* tragically overexposed. Perhaps it's time for the pop tart to go home and eat some Pop-Tarts (which she has publicly longed for), and ponder what happened to her—or her publicists'—masterful navigation of the fine line between self-exposure and self-destruction. Having made an art of inviting viewers to wonder just how knowingly she has participated in her own hyper-sexualization, Spears can't find anyone willing to cut her the break accorded to most young naifs in the world of showbiz.

From the start, Spears' career was built on her ability to be authentically inauthentic. When the 17-year-old Spears first showed up on MTV in 1999—a pigtailed, kilt-wearing kitten who purred, "Hit me, baby, one more time"—it seemed unlikely she'd wind up as the most scrutinized pop star of her era. Critics never regarded her as much more than a singer of middling talent. And she's hardly a beauty for the ages—she's pretty in the way the best-looking girl at your high school was (ask her first husband, Jason Alexander).

But, unlike, say, Ashlee Simpson, whose *Saturday Night Live* meltdown was a mere gaffe, Spears has elevated inauthenticity to a Warholian level. She's never had to take responsibility for her sexy persona because she refuses to acknowledge she has a persona, sexy or otherwise. Consider the evidence: "[T]he record label wanted me to do certain kinds of songs, and I was like, 'Look, if you want me to be some kind of sex thing, that's not me.'" This is Spears, quoted in an *Esquire*, alongside photos of her naked, save for white panties and strings of pearls that magically conceal (with the apparent aid of an airbrush) her nipples and little else. "I'm not gonna come out on this record and show my crotch or anything. That's not me. I would never do anything like that." This from an issue of *Rolling Stone*, in which Spears appeared topless on the cover, humping a wall. "I don't want to be part of someone's Lolita thing. It kind of freaks me out." This in response to questions about her first *Rolling Stone* photo shoot, in 1999, in which the 17-year-old Britney stood in a bedroom in short-shorts and a push-up bra, surrounded by baby dolls.

Spears didn't invent sexual doublespeak—every teen star does the dance of posing in her underwear while talking up her chastity. But she speaks it more fluently than most. Her jujitsu-like ability to deflect all criticism by turning it back on the accuser—if you ask her about her Lolita-esque antics, you're the one who's a perv—has allowed her to exploit contradictions that have felled lesser stars.

"I've actually learned to say 'NO!,'" announces Britney Spears in a letter to her fans published on her website on October 15, 2004. *"With this newly found freedom, it's like people don't know how to act around me. Should we talk to her like we did when she was 16 or like the Icon everyone says she is?"* Spears opens the letter saying she wants to speak directly to her fans, giving access to those *"who have stuck by me and who continue to support me."* As Spears tells it, she has long been overexposed by her advisors, but now wants to live the simple life *"watch[ing]* Saved with Mandy Moore *and reruns of* Sex and the City*" and planning a family with her husband. To read the entire letter, go to Britneyspears.com.

Spears learned her lessons from her acknowledged master, Madonna. Madonna stirred controversy by attaching herself to (some might say exploiting) marginalized subcultures: voguing drag queens, S & M fetishists, etc. Madonna was interested—however glancingly—in contradictions: in, say, dressing as a man and grabbing her crotch. But there was never any doubt that she was calling the shots, working the levers of her own career. Spears, on the other hand, has managed to adopt a "What? Me? Duplicitous?" pose. Spears just *is* a series of contradictions. As such, she can only peel her own layers away.

Which makes her "letter of truth" and her video cry for freedom all the more interesting. The girl who always claimed she'd never been packaged now says she wants to break free of her packaging. Perhaps Spears senses that the perma-bubble of cognitive dissonance surrounding her has finally been punctured—that there are only so many times you can invite viewers to wonder just how knowing you are before they decide, in fact, that you should know better. (It's never a good sign when a look-alike of you is killed in a movie promo, to great cheers, as Britney is in the trailer for the upcoming *Seed of Chucky.*) The problem, now, is that just when she wants to point to her own innocence—her manipulation at the hands of her PR staff—the public is likely to conclude that even her declaration of desperation smacks of a stay-on-message memo. She's referred to her online missive as "The Letter of Truth: I Hope You Can Handle It," which echoes oddly the opening words of the "Prerogative" video: "They can never take away your truth. The question is: Can you handle mine?" It seems Britney can break free from everything except her own talking points. But then, that's always been her greatest trick: She strips and strips and strips, yet never reveals a thing.

Analyzing the Text

1. How does Sternbergh support his argument that, although Britney Spears did not invent "sexual doublespeak," she has raised it to new levels? He goes on to suggest that Spears has "elevated inauthenticity to a Warholian level." How do you respond to his assessment?

2. **Interrogating Assumptions.** According to Sternbergh, what makes Spears's deflection of criticism over her highly sexualized image so successful is that she turns the criticism back on the accuser: "If you ask her about her Lolita-esque antics, you're the one who's a perv." How does this tactic rely on a commonly accepted assumption that views entertainment as a personal choice (see p. 367)?

3. Sternbergh characterizes Spears's letter to her fans as "disarmingly candid." Do you agree with him? How does the pop singer come off in quotes from her "Letter of Truth"? (See the caption on p. 373 and the second paragraph of this essay.) What do her language choices reveal about how she sees herself or wants others to see her?

4. To what extent does Spears's explanation of being naive and at the mercy of her advisors further reinforce the very image she seems to want to dismantle in her letter?

Writing about Cultural Practices

5. As Sternbergh and Spears would probably agree, we live in a culture obsessed with youth and saturated with teen stars. But what exactly makes someone a pop star? Gather three to five images of teenaged or young celebrities and use them to write a critical analysis of what it means to be a pop star in our culture. If possible, find published interviews with the stars you choose in which they discuss their feelings about their fame (for example, to what extent they feel exploited or in charge of their own careers) and their images as stars (to what extent they control their images). As you draft, consider the following questions.

   - What messages do these images (and the interviews) convey about what it means to be a pop star in our culture?

   - How do the young artists explain their stardom or any contradictions about their image in interviews?

   - What cultural attitudes or assumptions (about celebrity? about beauty? about talent?) do the images you collected rely on to appeal to their audience?

   - How and why do you think the mass media constructs images that are at once hypersexual yet innocent?

Katie Roiphe, **Profiles Encouraged**

Katie Roiphe's writings on feminism and pop culture have appeared in *Harper's*, *Esquire*, and the *New York Times*. She has published three books, *The Morning After: Fear, Sex, and Feminism on Campus* (1994), *Last Night in Paradise: Sex and Morals at the Century's End* (1997), and *Still She Haunts Me* (2002). In the following essay, which first appeared in *Brill's Content* (December 2000/January 2001), Roiphe asks, "If all celebrity profiles sound exactly the same, why does the reading public keep asking for more?"

> ▶ **Mapping Your Reading**
>
> Roiphe makes her argument perfectly clear in her opening paragraph: "*All movie-star profiles are the same.*" As you read, underline passages in which Roiphe names specific techniques used to write celebrity profiles. Why are Americans so fascinated with celebrities? Why are entertainment magazines so packed with these profiles? How do celebrity profiles connect with cultural assumptions about entertainment?

In May, a freelance writer named Tom Kummer was caught fabricating movie-star profiles for one of Germany's most respected newspapers, *Süddeutsche Zeitung*. He wrote graceful articles about stars he had never met. He had been doing it for years. *The Times* of London reported that his interviews were so good that *Marie Claire* interviewed him about "the secrets of his success," which he ironically said was demanding at least 45 minutes with his subjects. What eventually betrayed him was his inability to be banal, his desire to put ideas into people's mouths that they would never actually utter. In other words, his fatal mistake was to make the celebrity profile interesting. *The Times* of London also reported that he had Sharon Stone saying she is trying "to irritate men from wholly different classes of society," and Courtney Love saying she felt: "Empty, depressed, rather dumb." The fact that he was able to carry on for so long tells us less about Kummer than it does about the genre itself. The style of celebrity profiles has become so rigid, so absolutely predictable, that the substance, the poor ephemeral star herself, is wholly superfluous. That was the piece of information Tom Kummer passed along, the valuable contribution he made to the journalistic community, the point he dramatized as no one had before: *All movie-star profiles are the same.*

Our celebrity culture has become so greedy and wild that it overwhelms and consumes the writer's individual voice. It feels, sometimes, like the writer gives up, thinks of the rent bill, and types on a kind of automatic pilot, giving the magazine or the reader or the movie publicists what they want—and nothing more. Our appetite for the same photograph of a movie star in a spaghetti-strap dress is insatiable, and so, it seems, is our appetite for the same article. But why do we continue to read it over and over, why are we interested in it when we could generate it from thin air as easily as Tom Kummer? It may be because the celebrity profile is not about information, it is not about journalism, it is not about words; it is a ritual.

No matter who the celebrity is, the pieces follow the same narrative arc. There is the moment when the movie star reveals himself to be just like us. (In *Vanity Fair*, "Pitt, then, turns out to be that most surprising of celebrities—a modest man" and "Paltrow jumps up to clear the table and has to be told almost sternly not to do the dishes.") There is the moment when the movie star is not mortal after all. (In *Entertainment Weekly*, Julia Roberts has "a long, unbound mass of chocolate-brown curls—just the kind of Julia Roberts waterfall tangle of tresses that makes America think of bumper crops and Wall Street rallies and $100 million at the box office.") There is the fact that the movie star was funny-looking and gawky as a child ("'I had braces, and I was skinny,'" says Gwyneth Paltrow in *People*. Winona Ryder told *Life* she was taken "'for an effeminate boy'"). There is the J. D. Salinger book the movie star is reading (*Entertainment Weekly* reports that Julia Roberts "has a book of J. D. Salinger stories . . . on the coffee table," and Winona Ryder tells *In Style*, "'I have every edition, every paperback, every translation of *The Catcher in the Rye*'"). And then there is the moment when the author of the piece wryly acknowledges the artificiality of the situation. ("I have firm instructions from your people to make you comfortable," a *Harper's Bazaar* writer says to Brad Pitt, "so perhaps you should choose where you'd like to sit.") There is the disbelief on the part of both the celebrity and the author about how rich and famous and successful the movie star has become. In the end, it's not hard to see why Tom Cruise might not be essential to a Tom Cruise profile. With the pieces themselves as strictly styled as a geisha's makeup, the face behind them ceases to matter.

Tom Cruise might not be essential to a Tom Cruise profile.

Start with the way the movie star looks. How should the aspiring plagiarist describe her? What should she be wearing? In *Esquire*, Winona Ryder was "in jeans, cowboy boots, and a clingy Agnes B.–type jersey," in *Life* she was "in jeans and a long-sleeved undershirt," and in *In Style* she was "makeup-free, hair swept up in a headband." In *Harper's Bazaar*, Gwyneth Paltrow "is wearing jeans, a blue cotton-fleece sweatshirt. . . . Her hair is held back by a wide black headband," and in *Vanity Fair*, she wears "her long blond hair pulled back in a simple ponytail and no trace of makeup." Julia Roberts wears "Levi's, a snug blue top. . . . Her hair is pulled back" in *Vanity Fair* and "Levi's, a white shirt, boots, and no makeup" in *In Style*. In *Vanity Fair*, Renée Zellweger wears "jeans, a T-shirt, sneakers, and no makeup." A stripped-down wardrobe is offered as proof of the stars' unpretentiousness, their surprising accessibility.

If glossy magazines are to be believed, movie stars also have a limited number of character traits, one of which is vulnerability. Somebody in nearly every profile comments on that surprising aspect of the fabulous person's psyche, and if somebody else doesn't, the writer will. The mother of Jack Nicholson's child, for instance, is quoted in *Cosmopolitan* as saying, "'He's very strong yet very vulnerable.'" Julia Roberts is described in *Vanity Fair* as being "boldly vulnerable," and in *Cosmopolitan*, "her vulnerability brought Marilyn Monroe to mind," whereas in *Good Housekeeping*, "that same vulnerability that made her a star almost destroyed her." In *Rolling Stone*, she "show[s] some vulnerability." In *Vanity Fair*, Meg Ryan has a "compelling vulnerability," and Rupert Everett says of Madonna "'she has a lot of vulnerability'"; in the *New Yorker*, Regis Philbin is described by a fan as "'totally vulnerable.'" And why not? Vulnerability is the natural counterpoint to the sublime perfection that the profiler has gone out of his way to chronicle. It is a vague way of satisfying the need for the movie star to be "human" without detracting from her glamour with undue specificity.

And then there is the physical illustration of vulnerability: the mere presence of a magazine writer makes actresses turn every shade of red. In *Vanity Fair*, Renée Zellweger is "pink," and Meg Ryan's "face flushes." In *Harper's Bazaar*, Gwyneth Paltrow's "cheeks flush," in a *Vanity Fair* article, she "concedes with a blush," and in a *Vogue* article, "Paltrow turns crimson." *Esquire* reports a story in which Winona Ryder "turns scarlet." In *Newsweek*, the mention of her boyfriend's name causes Julia Roberts to blush and in *In Style* "reduced her to almost girlish blushes." Even Madonna blushes in *Vanity Fair*.

Not only do they blush; they glow. *Redbook* gushes, "It's really true: when you see Julia Roberts in person, she just . . . glows." *Vanity Fair* refers to her as "a lovely young woman glowing amid the flashbulbs," and *People* says, "[F]ans can't get enough of her glowing face." In *Newsweek*, the writer doesn't think Gwyneth Paltrow needs to lighten her hair because "[s]he's glowing already," and *Vogue* rhapsodizes about her "big, glowing smile." Other hackneyed phrases pop up regularly: in *Good Housekeeping* Julia Roberts is "like the proverbial deer caught in headlights," and in *Vanity Fair*, Meg Ryan "looked like a deer in headlights." There is no need in movie-star profiles to dispense with clichés because clichés—red carpet, flashbulbs, incandescence—are what stardom consists of: the role of the movie-star profile is to reinforce and sell that stardom, not to examine or undermine it. Which is also why almost all movie-star profiles from *People* to the *New Yorker* are peppered with superlatives—they add to the breathiness of the piece, the tone of worshipful trashy love and sheer commerce. *Cosmopolitan* calls Julia Roberts "the most desirable and successful actress in the world." *Redbook* calls her "the biggest female star on the planet." And *People* declares that "Roberts is, quite simply, the most appealing actress of her time." In *Vogue*, Gwyneth Paltrow is "The Luckiest Girl Alive," and in *Time* she is "the most beguiling actress of her young generation." In the *New Yorker* Tom Hanks is "the most disarming and successful of American movie stars." In *People*, Brad Pitt is "Hollywood's hottest hunk," and Tom Cruise is "The Sexiest Man Alive."

It is rare that one reads about a moderately successful actress, or the second sexiest man in Hollywood.

Every actress over the age of 20 is also depicted as girlish, childlike, or adolescent. Take the description of Julia Roberts in *Vanity Fair* ("[b]y turns childlike and sophisticated"), or Renée Zellweger (who has "little-girl moxie") in *Vanity Fair*, or Meg Ryan ("whose adult allure is redolent of adolescence") in *Vanity Fair*, or Sharon Stone (whose "childlike sexual greediness was perhaps the most eerily enticing quality about her *[Basic] Instinct* work") also in *Vanity Fair*. In *In Style*, the 28-year-old Winona Ryder is like a "defiant teen," and in *Life* she "sits like a kid." Fiftysomething Goldie Hawn, *In Style* informs us, looks as "youthful as a teenager," and a look of "childlike glee overtakes" Julia Roberts. *Cosmopolitan* compares Madonna to a "restless child," while *Vanity Fair* describes "the little girl . . . behind the woman." Male actors are invariably described as boyish. "Part of Hanks's appeal," the *New Yorker* explained, "is his boyishness." *GQ* talks about how Tom Cruise "projects a sexuality that is boyish." Even 61-year-old Warren Beatty appears "tousled and boyish" in the *New York Times Magazine*.

It often seems that the writers of magazine profiles have spent one too many Saturday nights watching *Breakfast at Tiffany's* on late-night cable, because nearly every movie star is compared to Audrey Hepburn or Holly Golightly, as Charlize Theron is in *Vanity Fair* and Julia Ormond is in the *New York Times Magazine*. In *Newsweek*, Gwyneth Paltrow's neck "brings Audrey Hepburn to mind," and other qualities of hers provoke the same comparison in *Vogue* and *In Style*. Julia Roberts is compared to Audrey Hepburn in both *In Style* and *Vanity Fair* (in 1993 and again in 1999), and *Redbook* reports that " 'she is the only actress now who can lay claim to Audrey Hepburn's mantle.' "

It is increasingly common for a magazine profile to include a pious denunciation or mockery of the tabloids, where, the highbrow writer points out, every little thing the celebrity does is being followed, every detail of what she eats and whom she dates is being observed—what an outrage to human dignity and privacy! And yet one wonders how the *Vanity Fair* or *Vogue* or *Entertainment Weekly* article is so wildly different. Indeed, it is often the same gossip, the same mundane details wrapped up and delivered in a different tone. But highbrow writers, and even not-so-highbrow writers, continue to be outraged by the tabloids, as if a slightly more literary turn of phrase changes the fundamental moral tenor and cultural worthiness of the venture. The anti-tabloid moment serves a definite function: It justifies the profile as more than just gossip. One writer in *Vanity Fair* makes fun of an item from the *New York Post* about Julia Roberts eating brunch with Benjamin Bratt at Caffe Lure on Sullivan Street, and then proceeds to report in all seriousness that she shops for soy milk at Korean delis. The qualitative difference between these two observations is unclear. It may be a certain amount of self-contempt projected onto the "tabloids" for their invasive curiosity, or it may be that the highbrow writer really believes that his pursuit is more legitimate simply because it is juxtaposed with such psychological insights as "she's no shrinking violet," and printed on higher-quality paper.

Clichés are what stardom consists of.

There are certain stylistic guidelines that immediately present themselves to the aspiring plagiarist. One of the transparent rhetorical tricks employed by movie-star profilers across the country is a hip, *Bright Lights, Big City* second-person voice. A *Newsweek* profile of Julia Roberts states, "On the way to her house, [Julia] Roberts drags you into a lingerie shop and tries to persuade you to buy a nightgown for your wife." And in *Entertainment Weekly*, "As you walk in the door, Roberts tells you she's in her panic state." In *Rolling Stone*, "[y]ou opt to look out the trailer door and take in the view of the mountains. After a bit, Pitt joins you in contemplation." And again in *Rolling Stone*, "[w]hat really throws you is what happens when Cruise puts the pedal to the metal." This is a cheap way of drawing the reader into the encounter: offering the illusion that it is you who is admiring the view with the luminous cluster of glamour that is Brad Pitt. So much of the movie-star profile is premised on the perception of the reader's desperate desire to "meet" the movie star that it is no surprise that the fantasy should be so literally reflected in the style. The writer does not feel called upon to make the scene so vivid that we feel as if we are there; instead, he lazily types out three words: *You are there.*

One of the most important moments in the movie-star profile is the moment of intimacy. That is, the moment when the writer proves that he has really contacted his celestial subject and has forged a genuine connection, distinguishing himself from the sycophantish hordes and servers-up of celebrity fluff. In the *New York Times Magazine,* the profiler writes, "Minutes after the plane lands, Ormond and I are slumped in the backseat of a limousine. We're tired. We're angry. We are about to have our first fight." Or it can be something smaller, along the lines of this Julia Roberts profile in *Newsweek:* "Later she takes your arm. And crosses Union Square." Or this one in *Vogue,* "One last hug. Paltrow, after two hours of this fashion madness, smells very eau de fresh." Or it can be a flirtatious voice-mail message, like the one Regis Philbin leaves a *New Yorker* writer: "(The next day, I received a message on my voice mail: 'Spend a whole day with you. Sing my guts out onstage for you. Do everything I can for you, and not even a goodbye.')" The writer reports the flirtation, the few seconds of intimacy, the subtext of which is that he or she has really made an impression on the star, has penetrated the defenses. In the *New York Times Magazine,* the writer says that Warren Beatty "studied the artifacts of my life as if they were long-lost Mayan ruins." Julia Roberts says to a *Vanity Fair* writer, "'You've got a pretty good pair of lips there yourself.'" These flirtations are never offered as evidence of the star's manipulative powers but rather suggest the ability of this particularly charming and attractive writer to get beyond the routine and glitter and impress the real person.

In a *Vanity Fair* profile of Renée Zellweger, "the look on her face is one that a grown woman gets that lets a man know that the night is now over." Often, the sexual overtone, the very datiness of the interview, is played up by the writer. It is fawning fandom taken to its logical extreme. There is a flirtation between the interviewer and the interviewee, a play of power, an adoration mingled with hostility that resembles nothing more than a 15-year-old's courtship. Here is *Vanity*

Fair's Kevin Sessums, the consummate highbrow profile writer and intellectual provocateur, with Julia Roberts: "'[Y]ou're famous because you're a good actress. You're *infamous* for the actors that you've f—ked,' I challenged, trying to shock a response from her. Roberts flashed her eyes at me the way she can flash them on-screen when someone has gotten her attention. Seduction lay in her un-shockable stare; she cocked her head and waited." One can hear what he is say-ing to the reader: I have gotten Julia Roberts's attention! Seduction lay in her stare! But comments like this are often laced with a sadism—a certain resent-ment, perhaps, of having to sit there with an important person and record every minor dietary habit you are lucky enough to observe—that makes its way into the prose. Take the moment Sessums says to Meg Ryan, "'Cocaine may harden one's heart, but it makes one, well, less hard in other places,' I venture. 'If you were intimate with him—and I assume you were—how could you not know he was snorting coke?'"

Because fawning laced with irony somehow seems cooler and more palat-able, the paradox of writers like Kevin Sessums—who has written more than 30 celebrity profiles for *Vanity Fair* alone—emerges. The tone is knowing and flir-tatious and world-weary. But what is strange is how the world-weariness meshes with naïve fascination. It is, in a way, a perfect reflection of the culture—a faux intellectual distance masquerading as the real thing, irony that is really adoration in a new form. The complexities of the tone make celebrity worship less de-meaning, giving it a kind of chic allure it would not otherwise have. These com-plexities allow the intelligent, critical reader to interest herself in the exact beige of the movie-star's furniture, to read about the blush and glow without shame. There is often a stunned incredulity, tinged with sexual attraction, that seems to render the writer comparatively speechless, so that the profile is dotted with banal statements of wonder that seem out of place in otherwise competent writ-ing, as when a *Vanity Fair* reporter quotes Madonna as saying, "'I wanted to be *somebody*,'" and then adds, "And boy is she." That "boy is she" would not have made it into a piece about Alan Greenspan or Madeleine Albright or Al Gore; its wide-eyed wonderment would not have a place in any form of journalism other than that of the celebrity profile. It's as if the presence of Madonna had dazzled and almost drugged the writer (and the reader) into a haze of inarticulateness, a baby patter of awe.

But why are we willing to put up with it, to wade through the stock phrases, to pick up the same article on the newsstand again and again? Because, in the end, we are not interested in Winona Ryder; we are interested in fame: its pure, bright, disembodied effervescence. And what these articles do is strip down the particu-lars to give us the excitement itself. They provide us with the affect of excitement, the sound and feel of it. It is a primitive thing, this form of admiration, one that paints in fuzzy lines and speaks in hackneyed terms. True mystery doesn't interest us; the statement "she had an aura of mystery" does. The clichés are what we crave and continue to expect. What makes glamour like lights on a marquee, is the rep-etition of the familiar sounds of adoration, the same babble of fawning irony, the same vulnerable perfect creature we don't really want to read about.

Analyzing the Text

1. According to Roiphe, what is the narrative arc that dictates both the content and the tone of movie-star profiles? Create a list of each of her points. How does she use examples to support her claims?

2. Do you agree with Roiphe that "the role of the movie-star profile is to reinforce and sell . . . stardom, not to examine or undermine it"? To what extent is the point of the celebrity profile really about the worship of fame and not actually about the movie star profiled? How does Roiphe support this claim with her analysis of celebrity profiles?

3. **Interrogating Assumptions.** This chapter's introduction describes three common assumptions about entertainment (see pp. 361–69). How does Roiphe's essay challenge the first assumption described there, that "entertainment is just for fun"? Now, consider the second assumption, that "entertainment is merely a reflection of culture." To what extent do entertainment magazines, television channels, and Internet websites reflect our desire to worship celebrities? How do they cultivate or create celebrity worship?

4. **Connecting to Other Readings.** What connections, if any, do you see between Roiphe's argument about celebrity profiles and Adam Sternbergh's critique of Britney Spears? In "Britney Spears: The Pop Tart in Winter" (p. 371), Sternbergh suggests that Spears is not so much an actual person as she is a hyperstylized pop star. Does Spears's own "Letter of Truth" (quoted in Sternbergh's essay and published in full on Britneyspears.com) follow any of Roiphe's dictates about how profiles must be written?

Writing about Cultural Practices

5. Test Roiphe's formula for writing a celebrity profile by writing one yourself. Before beginning, review the formula and techniques Roiphe describes and choose a popular celebrity. You will write your profile as if you are really in a hotel room or restaurant interviewing this famous person. After drafting your invented profile, write a critical analysis essay that considers these questions.

   - What is the goal or purpose of the celebrity profile?
   - Why are celebrity profiles so pervasive in the media?
   - Why are they written in such similar ways?
   - What is the relationship between the portrayal of celebrity and the consumption of entertainment?

Pete Rojas, **Bootleg Culture**

Pete Rojas is a technology journalist who has written for *Wired News, Slate*, the *Guardian, Village Voice*, and the *New York Times*. He is also editor-in-chief of Engadget.com, an online consumer technology magazine. The conventional definition of the term "bootleg" means to make an illegal copy of someone else's work. However, as Rojas explores in this essay, originally published in *Salon* in 2002, the ease with which people can burn, rip, or mix other people's music, images, or movies is driving people to rethink concepts like bootlegging and authorship. Rojas concludes, "Eventually recombining and remixing is likely to become so prevalent that it will be all but impossible to even identify the original source of [music] samples, making questions about authorship and origins largely irrelevant, or at least unanswerable."

> ▶ **Mapping Your Reading**
>
> In the following essay, Rojas explores the ways in which music bootlegging challenges assumptions about authorship and creativity. As you read, underline passages in which the writer makes major points about authorship. How are cultural attitudes about authorship changing? How do copyright laws protect authors? How do they limit the creativity of this new form of expression? Is it becoming impossible, as Rojas writes, "not to quote, reference, or sample the world around us" when we create something new?

When the Belgian DJ duo 2ManyDJs were creating their own album of "bootlegs"—hybrid tracks that mix together other people's songs to create new songs that are at once familiar yet often startlingly different—they decided to get permission to use every one of the hundreds of tracks they mashed together. The result: almost a solid year of calling, e-mailing, and faxing dozens and dozens of record labels all over the world. (Creating the album itself only took about a week.) In the end, about a third of their requests were turned down, which isn't surprising. Many artists and their labels have become reluctant to allow any sampling of their work unless they are sure the new work will sell enough copies to generate large royalty checks.

What is surprising are the names of some of the artists who turned them down: the Beastie Boys, Beck, Missy Elliott, Chemical Brothers, and M/A/R/R/S—

artists whose own careers are based on sampling and who in some cases have been sued in the past for their own unauthorized sampling. For whatever reason these artists decided not to license their material, the net effect is that more entrenched, "legitimate" sampling artists are preventing lesser known, struggling sampling artists from doing what the legitimate artists probably wish they could have done years ago: sample without hindrance to create new works.

Typically consisting of a vocal track from one song digitally superimposed on the instrumental track of another, bootlegs (or "mash-ups," as they are also called) are being traded over the Internet, and they're proving to be a big hit on dance floors across the U.K. and Europe. In just the past couple of years, hundreds if not thousands of these homebrewed mixes have been created, with music fans going wild over such odd pairings as Soulwax's bootleg of Destiny's Child's "Bootylicious" mixed with Nirvana's "Smells Like Teen Spirit," Freelance Hellraiser's mix of Christina Aguilera singing over the Strokes, and Kurtis Rush's pairing of Missy Elliott rapping over George Michael's "Faith." Bootlegs inject an element of playfulness into a pop music scene that can be distressingly sterile.

While there have been odd pairings, match-ups, and remixes for decades now, and club DJs have been doing something similar during live sets, the recent explosion in the number of tracks being created and disseminated is a direct result of the dramatic increase in the power of the average home computer and the widespread use on these computers of new software programs like Acid and ProTools. Home remixing is technically incredibly easy to do, in effect turning the vast world of pop culture into source material for an endless amount of slicing and dicing by desktop producers.

So easy, in fact, that bootlegs constitute the first genre of music that truly fulfills the "anyone can do it" promises originally made by punk and, to lesser extent, electronic music. Even punk rockers had to be able write the most rudimentary of songs. With bootlegs, even that low bar for traditional musicianship and composition is obliterated. Siva Vaidhyanthan, an assistant professor of culture and communication at New York University and the author of *Copyrights and Copywrongs*, believes that what we're seeing is the result of a democratization of creativity and the demystification of the process of authorship and creativity.

> What we're seeing is the result of a democratization of creativity.

"It's about demolishing the myth that there has to be a special class of creators, and flattening out the creative curve so we can all contribute to our creative environment," says Vaidhyanthan.

The debate over what bootlegs are and what they mean is taking place within the wider context of a culture where turntables now routinely outsell guitars, teenagers aspire to be Timbaland and the Automator, No. 1 singles rework or sample other records, and DJs have become pop stars in their own right, even surpassing in fame the very artists whose records they spin. Pop culture in general seems more and more remixed—samples and references are permeating more and more of mainstream music, film, and television, and remix culture appears to resonate strongly with consumers. We're at the point where it almost seems unnatural not to quote, reference, or sample the world around us. To the teens buying the latest all-remixes J.Lo album, dancing at a club to an unauthorized two-step white-label remix of the new Nelly single, or even hacking together their own bootleg, recombination—whether legal or not—doesn't feel wrong in the slightest. The difference now is that they have the tools to sample, reference, and remix, allowing them to finally "talk back" to pop culture in the way that seems most appropriate to them.

The recording industry instinctively fears such unauthorized use of copyrighted materials. But instead of sending out cease-and-desist orders, it should be embracing bootlegs. In a world of constantly recycled sounds and images, bootleg culture is no aberration—it's part of the natural evolution of all things digital.

Bootleg culture is part of the natural evolution of all things digital.

Bootlegs don't contain any specific audible element of originality in the track, in the sense that one can identify any specific original vocal or musical composition created by the remixer. The only original element of a bootleg is the selection and arrangement of the tracks to be blended into a new work. Scottish bootlegger Grant Robson, who goes by the name Grant McSleazy, responsible for such tracks as Missy Elliott versus the Strokes, readily admits this: "There is a creative aspect, because not all songs work well together, but all the lyric writing and music composition has been done for you. You may rearrange the segments of an instrumental/a capella, but that's just production work."

Even so, isn't production work what constitutes most of what goes into crafting most hip-hop, electronic music, and pop these days? Because of this, bootlegs highlight the increasing difficulty in distinguishing between musicians, DJs and producers. Is there really all that much difference, on a technical level, between McSleazy, DJ Shadow, Moby, and P. Diddy? Putting aside any qualitative judgments, on one level or another they are all just appropriators of sound. They are all combining elements of other people's works in order to create new ones, in effect challenging the old model of authorship that presupposes that the building blocks of creativity should spill forth directly from the mind of the artist.

Already we've seen that our notion of what makes a song "creative" has widened in the case of hip-hop. Early on, hip-hop—constructed largely with snippets of other songs—faced similar charges that it lacked a creative element. Eventually, because a great deal of arrangement is involved (usually a large number of samples are blended together to create just a single hip-hop track), and because the rapping itself contributes an original element, pop culture at large has found it easier to acknowledge some aspect of originality and creativity within hip-hop. Bootlegs challenge this notion even further, but it is almost inevitable that as they grow in popularity, something similar will happen, and our definition of creativity will expand to accommodate them.

Existing copyright laws mean that, for the most part, this movement will remain underground. Consequently bootlegs may be the first new genre of music that is almost entirely contraband, and most bootlegs now can only be found on a few Web sites or on file-sharing networks like KaZaA and Gnutella. The bootleggers behind these audio mismatches know they will never get permission from the artists they sample and haven't even bothered to try to get it. Though 2ManyDJs tried to go legit and get permission for as many songs as possible, they still were unable to get clearance for a significant number of samples they used on their album—and even the permissions and clearances they do have are so restricted that it will be impossible to release the album in the United States. Despite the tremendous amount of energy poured into these desktop productions, the fact remains that because the original works cut and pasted together are used without the original artists' permission, bootlegs have stayed, well, bootlegs.

While everyone (particularly the companies touting the technologies that make all this possible) predicted a flood of original movies and music spewing forth from the desktops of bedroom auteurs, no one anticipated that large numbers of people would be more interested in using their computers to combine, mash together, or remix other people's work. Sharing one's unauthorized creations via the Net is even easier. It's a dramatic change from just a few years ago, when a bootlegger's sole option would have been to have vinyl or CDs manufactured and then distributed, something that would risk arousing the attention, and legal action, of the record labels of the remixed artists.

This phenomenon hasn't been limited to music: Remixing has begun to infect film as well. Last year copies of a home-edited version of *Star Wars Episode 1: The Phantom Menace* began circulating on the Internet to widespread acclaim from fans who declared *Star Wars Episode 1.1: The Phantom Edit* the superior of the two versions. It's probably only a matter of time until someone creates a fan edit of *Attack of the Clones*. Inspired by the *Phantom* edit, DJ Hupp, a freelance film editor in Sacramento, California, has created his own "Kubrick edit" of Spielberg's *A.I.*, and it is unlikely that his will be the last fan edit we see of a major motion picture.

Such fan edits are also, technically, illegal, but from the perspective of the turntablists, remixers, and home editors at the forefront of the explosion of bootleg culture, copyright laws don't look like anything other than the means by which one group of artists limits the work of another.

Illegality can actually be a large part of the allure of bootlegs. Much underground cultural expression takes place at the margins of the law—rave culture, for example, has its origins in illegal warehouse parties. Using other people's music without permission used to be the point of mash-ups. Back in the '80s and early '90s, when culture-jamming sound collagists like Negativland and the Evolution Control Committee released their first works, mash-ups had a decidedly subversive edge to them. Mash-ups were typically created as statements about pop culture and the media juggernaut that surrounds us, not as fodder for the dance floor. Pasting together elements swiped from the top 40 and placing them together in a new form was supposed to snap us out of what these sonic outlaws saw as our media-induced trance and make a point about copyright in the process.

Traces of that element remain in the bootlegs being made today. One Australian bootlegger, a 26-year-old who goes by the name Dsico, and for legal reasons prefers that his identity be withheld, sees bootlegs as akin to the kitschiness and pastiche of pop art. "The reinterpretation and recontextualization of cultural icons like Britney Spears or the Strokes is fun and good for a laugh. But if I can grab an a cappella track of Mandy Moore and mix it with something like 'Roxanne' by the Police, while that juxtaposition may be trite, it still works as a commentary on pop music today."

And at a time when it has become increasingly difficult for pop music to be shocking (witness the mainstream acceptability, however grudging, of Eminem), it may be that the only way to write a transgressive pop song is to flat-out steal it from someone else. In other words, the only way left to shock is not through controversial content, but by subverting the very form and structure of the song itself.

Even though making music out of other people's songs without permission may appear to pose a threat to the business model of the recording industry, killing off this nascent genre may not ultimately be in the industry's best interests. Radio stations in Britain that have played bootlegs have found themselves on the receiving end of cease-and-desist orders. Hip-hop got its start using preexisting music in innovative and not always legal ways. It is arguable that had the music industry clamped down on sampling earlier than it did (it wasn't until a 1991 suit against rapper Biz Markie that sampling without permission was established as illegal), the industry's top-selling genre would never have gotten off the ground commercially. Now legendary hip-hop albums, such as Public Enemy's It Takes a Nation of Millions to Hold Us Back, and the Beastie Boys' Paul's Boutique, would be impossible to release today.

Just as with every other subcultural movement that has threatened the status quo, the music industry's best response may be to let the genre flourish online and on the margins. So far no one is really making any money from bootlegs—if anything, bootlegs stimulate demand for the original songs. Rather than threaten bootleggers with legal action, a sounder strategy would be to co-opt the scene by skimming the best ones off the top and re-releasing them as "official" bootlegs. This has already produced one No. 1 hit, with Richard X's mash-up of new waver Gary Numan and soul singer Adina Howard. The track follows in the footsteps of DNA's bootleg dance remix of Suzanne Vega's "Tom's Diner," which Vega ended up authorizing and re-releasing to much chart success in 1990.

As computers and software programs get more and more powerful with each passing year, as file-sharing networks make it simple for anyone to share their work with the world, and as it is next to impossible to outlaw digital editing software (which has plenty of legitimate uses), bootlegs and remixes will likely be a part of the cultural landscape for years to come. Bootlegging may even evolve into something of a hobby for tens of thousands of desktop producers who will spend their free time splicing together the latest top 40 hits for kicks, like model-airplane builders. The record industry could even respond by selling its own do-it-yourself bootleg kits, complete with editing software and authorized samples. In a sense bootlegs are music fans' response to the current disposability of pop culture. Effortlessly easy to create, with an infinite number of combinations possible, bootlegs are even more perfectly disposable than the pop songs they combine—by the time the novelty and the cleverness have worn off there will always be new hit singles to mash together.

Eventually recombining and remixing is likely to become so prevalent that it will be all but impossible to even identify the original source of samples, making questions about authorship and origins largely irrelevant, or at least unanswerable. We're already seeing the beginnings of that, like the hip-hop song that samples an older hip-hop song that samples a '70s funk song. Some artists, most notably David Bowie, are already proclaiming the death of authorship altogether. Technology has not only expanded who can create; in blurring the distinction between consumers and producers, these new digital tools are also challenging the very ideas of creativity and authorship. They are forcing us to recognize modes of cultural production that often make it impossible to answer such once simple questions as, Who wrote this song? The cultural landscape that emerges will be a plural space of creation in which it may even become pointless to designate who created exactly what, since everyone will be stealing from and remixing everyone else. The results might be confusing, but it'll probably be a lot more fun and worth listening to than a world where only those with the financial resources to pay licensing fees (e.g., P. Diddy) get to make songs with sampling.

 Analyzing the Text

1. Rojas writes, "Pop culture seems more and more remixed." Do you agree with his claim? Why or why not? What examples from pop culture can you provide to support this observation? Which of his pop culture examples do you find particularly compelling?

2. According to Rojas, how is it that bootlegs highlight the increasing difficulty in distinguishing between musicians, DJs, and producers?

3. Rojas observes, "Home remixing is technically incredibly easy to do, in effect turning the vast world of pop culture into source material for an endless amount of slicing and dicing by desktop producers." What are the implications of the ease with which so many can now mix their own music? How has technology changed how we think about authorship? About bootlegging?

4. To understand what Rojas suggests about how ideas of authority and creativity are changing, work through the meaning of the paragraph that begins, "So easy, in fact, that bootlegs constitute the first genre of music that truly fulfills the 'anyone can do it' promises." What does Vaidhyanthan mean by the "democratization of creativity"? What examples does Rojas provide to support this view?

5. According to Rojas, what aspects of bootleg culture should remain underground or at the fringes of mainstream pop culture? Is this really possible, given as Rojas himself admits, that bootlegging has become too widespread? And what argument does he make about how the music industry should respond to bootlegging?

6. **Connecting to Another Reading.** In her essay, "Profiles Encouraged" (p. 376), Katie Roiphe outlines the formula she claims all journalists—whom she refers to as plagiarists—use to write celebrity profiles. What connections do you see between Rojas's argument about the blurring of concepts like authorship and creativity and Roiphe's argument?

Writing about Cultural Practices

7. Create a multimedia project in which you create your own collage, drawing from musical, visual, and/or textual sources in popular culture. Your collage will be your own statement about the meaning of authorship in contemporary American culture. Your project can take the form of an audio recording, website, PowerPoint presentation, or paper document. Then, in a brief critical analysis, provide a statement of purpose—why you developed your collage in this way—and explain the choices of the materials you've remixed. As you write your analysis, consider the following questions.

   • What does your collage say about the meaning of authorship?

   • Why did you choose the individual sources that you drew on to create your collage?

   • Ultimately, what do you think about the impact of bootlegging in American culture?

Alain de Botton, **Comedy**

Alain de Botton writes books that tackle questions of everyday life, including *The Consolations of Philosophy* (2000) and *The Art of Travel* (2002), as well as three books about relationships: *On Love* (1993), *The Romantic Movement* (1996), and *Kiss & Tell (1997)*. In February 2003, de Botton was made a Chevalier de l'Ordre des Arts et Lettres, one of France's highest artistic honors. This reading is an excerpt from *Status Anxiety* (2004). In it, de Botton argues that comedy and comics provide an outlet for cultural and political critique.

> ▶ **Mapping Your Reading**
>
> De Botton begins his essay with a story about a humorist imprisoned in 1831 by a French king, Louis-Philippe, for drawing cartoons that depicted the king's head as a pear. "Louis-Philippe," writes de Botton, "would likely not have responded so vehemently if humor were just a game." As you read this essay, pay attention to how de Botton uses both historical and contemporary examples of humor to demonstrate why it has always been more than a game. How is comedy used to poke fun at and undermine the powerful? To address everyday concerns or anxiety about social status?

The summer of 1831 found King Louis-Philippe of France in a confident mood. The political and economic chaos of the July Revolution, which had brought him to power the year before, was gradually giving way to prosperity and order. He had in place a competent team of officials led by his prime minister, Casimir Périer, and on tours around the northern and eastern parts of his realm had been given a hero's welcome by the provincial middle classes. He lived in splendor in the Palais-Royal in Paris; attended weekly banquets in his honor; loved eating (especially foie gras and game) and had a vast personal fortune and a loving wife and children.

But there was one cloud on Louis-Philippe's otherwise sunny horizon: In late 1830, an unknown 28-year-old artist by the name of Charles Philipon had launched a satirical magazine, *La Caricature,* in which he now graphically transformed the head of the king (whom he also accused of corruption and incompetence on a grand scale) into a pear. Unflattering as Philipon's cartoons were, depicting Louis-Philippe with swollen cheeks and a bulbous forehead, they carried

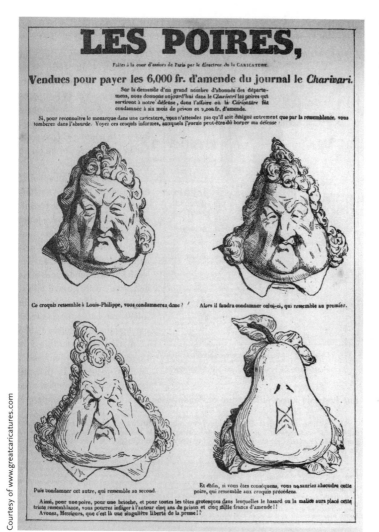

The cartoon for which the early nineteenth-century artist Charles Philipon was sentenced to two years in prison.

an additional, implied disparagement: the French word *poire*, meaning not only "pear" but "fathead" or "mug," neatly conveyed a less-than-respectful sentiment regarding the monarch's administrative abilities.

Enraged by the dig, Louis-Philippe instructed his agents to stop production of the magazine and to buy up all unsold copies from Parisian kiosks. When these measures failed to deter Philipon, prosecutors in November 1831 charged him with having "caused offense to the person of the king," and summoned him to appear in court. Speaking before a packed chamber, the caricaturist sardonically thanked the government for arresting such a dangerous man as himself, but then he suggested that the prosecutors had been negligent in their pursuit of the king's detractors. They should make it their priority, he insisted, to go after

This 1771 engraving from the Oxford Magazine *pokes fun at an extreme hairstyle that became popular among the fashionable classes in England in the late eighteenth century.*

Courtesy of www.greatcaricatures.com

anything in the shape of a pear; indeed, even pears themselves should be locked up. There were thousands of them on trees all over France, and every one a criminal fit for incarceration. The court was not amused. Philipon was sentenced to six months in prison, and when he dared to repeat the pear joke in a new magazine, *Le Charivari*, the following year, he was sent straight back to jail. In all, he spent two years behind bars for drawing the monarch as a piece of fruit.

Louis-Philippe would likely not have responded so vehemently if humor were just a game. In fact, as humorists and their targets have long recognized, jokes are an enormously effective means of anchoring a criticism. At base, they are another way of complaining: about arrogance, cruelty, or pomposity, about departures from virtue or good sense.

The most subversive comedy of all may be that which communicates a lesson while seeming only to entertain. Talented comics never deliver sermons outlining abuses of power; instead, they provoke their audiences to acknowledge in a chuckle the aptness of their complaints against authority.

Furthermore (the imprisonment of Philipon notwithstanding), the apparent innocence of jokes enables comics to convey with impunity messages that might be dangerous or impossible to state directly. Historically, for example, court jesters could poke fun at royals over serious matters that could never even be alluded to by other courtiers. (When King James I of England, who presided over a notoriously corrupt clergy, had trouble fattening up one of his horses, Archibald Armstrong, the court fool, is said to have advised him that all he had to do was make the creature a bishop, and it would rapidly gain the necessary pounds.) Noting the same impulse in his *Jokes and Their Relationship to the Unconscious* (1905), Freud wrote, "A joke will allow us to exploit something ridiculous in our enemy which we could not, on account of obstacles in the way, bring forward openly or consciously." Through jokes, Freud suggested, critical messages "can gain a reception with the hearer which they would never have found in a non-joking form . . . [which is why] jokes are especially favored in order to make criticism possible against persons in exalted positions."

That said, not every exalted person is ripe for the comic plucking. We rarely laugh, after all, at a doctor who is performing an important surgical operation. Yet we may smile at a surgeon who, *after* a hard day in the operating room, returns home and tries to intimidate his wife and daughters by talking to them in pompous medical jargon. We laugh at what is outsized and disproportionate. We laugh at kings whose self-image has outgrown their worth, whose goodness has not kept up with their power; we laugh at high-status individuals who have forgotten their humanity and begun abusing their privileges. We laugh at, and through our laughter criticize, evidence of injustice and excess.

At the hands of the best comics, laughter hence acquires a moral purpose, jokes become attempts to cajole others into reforming their character and habits. Jokes are a way of sketching a political ideal, of creating a more equitable and saner world. Wherever there is inequity or delusion, space opens up for humor-clad criticisms. As

LAURA BUSH
. . . on Being Married to the President

"George always says he's delighted to come to these press dinners. Baloney. He's usually in bed by now. I'm not kidding. I said to him the other day, 'George, if you really want to end tyranny in the world, you're going to have to stay up later.'

Here's our typical evening: Nine o'clock, Mr. Excitement here is sound asleep, and I'm watching *Desperate Housewives*—with Lynne Cheney. Ladies and gentlemen, I am a desperate housewife. I mean, if those women on that show think they're desperate, they oughta be with George.

George and I are complete opposites—I'm quiet, he's talkative, I'm introverted, he's extroverted, I can pronounce 'nuclear' . . .

The amazing thing, however, is that George and I were just meant to be. I was the librarian who spent 12 hours a day in the library, yet somehow I met George."

– From her speech at the 2005 White House Correspondents' Association dinner

"No, I have to stay here and work. I'm unloading copper."

Samuel Johnson saw it, satire is only another method, and a particularly effectual one, of "censuring wickedness or folly." In the words of John Dryden, "The true end of satire is the amendment of vices."

History reveals no shortage of jokes intended to amend the vices of high-status groups and shake the mighty out of their pretensions or dishonesty.

In the late twentieth-century United States, there was more than enough "wickedness and folly" among Manhattan's elite to keep the cartoonists of the *New Yorker* occupied. In business, many chief executives had a new interest in seeming friendly to their employees—*seeming* being, unfortunately, the operative word here. Instead of changing many of their more brutal practices, they contented themselves with camouflaging them with bland technocratic language, which they hoped might lend some respectability to an exploitation not so very different from that perpetrated by the satanic mills of old. The cartoonists, though, were not fooled. At heart, business remained committed to a starkly utilitarian view of employees, wherein any genuine, rather than ritualistic, talk of those employees' fulfillment, or of their employers' responsibilities to them, was tantamount to heresy.

The most subversive comedy may be that which communicates a lesson while seeming only to entertain.

So great were the demands of business that many high-ranking executives, particularly lawyers, permitted the clinically efficient mind-set of their jobs to permeate all areas of their lives, usually at the expense of any spontaneity or sympathy.

Meanwhile, a military class was enjoying unparalleled prestige based on its power to destroy the globe. Cartoonists encouraged their audiences to smile critically at the deathly serious demeanor of the generals.

Beyond being a useful weapon with which to attack the high-status of others, humor may also help us to make sense of, and perhaps even mitigate, our own status anxieties.

A great deal of what we find funny has to do with situations or feelings that, were we to experience them in our own, ordinary lives, would likely cause us either embarrassment or shame. The greatest comics shine a spotlight on vulnerabilities that the rest of us are all too eager to leave in the shadow; they pull us out of our lonely relationship with our most awkward sides. The more private the flaw and the more intense the worry about it, the greater the possibility of laughter—laughter being, in the end, a tribute to the skill with which the unmentionable has been skewered.

Unsurprisingly, therefore, much humor comprises an attempt to name, and thereby contain, anxiety over status. Comedy reassures us that there are others in

Created by South Park masterminds Matt Stone (left) and Trey Parker, the 2004 film Team America: World Police *offers a contemporary critique of international governments and military power. The movie features a band of international terrorism-fighting marionettes who, with the help of a Broadway star, try to apprehend a power hungry "axis of evil" dictator.*

Getty Images/Kevin Winter

"Of course they're clever. They have to be clever.
They haven't got any money."

the world no less envious or socially fragile than ourselves; that other fellow spirits wake up in the early hours feeling every bit as tormented by their financial performance as we do by our own; and that beneath the sober appearance society demands of us, most of us are daily going a little bit out of our minds, which in itself should give us cause to hold out a hand to our comparably tortured neighbors.

Rather than *mocking* us for being so concerned with status, the kindest comics *tease* us: they criticize us while simultaneously implying that our basic selves are essentially acceptable. If they are both acute and tactful enough, we may acknowledge with an openhearted laugh bitter truths about ourselves from which we might have recoiled in anger or hurt had they been leveled at us in an ordinary—which is to say, accusatory—way.

Comics, no less than other artists, hence fit rewardingly into Matthew Arnold's° definition of art as a discipline offering criticism of life. Their work strives to correct both the injustices of power and the excesses of our envy of those positioned above us in the social hierarchy. Like tragedians, they are motivated by some of the most regrettable aspects of the human condition.

The underlying, unconscious aim of comics may be to bring about, through the adroit use of humor, a world in which there will be a few less things for us to laugh about.

Matthew Arnold (1822–1888), English poet, critic, and educator.

Analyzing the Text

1. At the end of his essay, de Botton favorably compares comics to other artists. What does he see as the role or purpose of art—particularly comedy—in a society?

2. De Botton observes that "the apparent innocence of jokes enables comics to convey with impunity messages that might be dangerous or impossible to state directly." What examples does he give to support this claim? What examples can you think of from your own experience or from the popular media to support this view?

3. What does de Botton mean when he writes, "Beyond being a useful weapon with which to attack the high-status of others, humor may also help us to make sense of, and perhaps even mitigate, our own status anxieties"? How do you respond to this statement?

4. How do the visuals that accompany this reading support de Botton's argument that comedy acts as a vital form of cultural and political critique in a society? How do these images extend his argument?

5. **Interrogating Assumptions.** How would de Botton respond to the first assumption discussed in the chapter's introduction—that "entertainment is just for fun" (see p. 361). Would he agree with the second assumption, that entertainment is a "reflection of culture" (see p. 364)? Why or why not?

6. **Connecting to Another Reading.** Consider Jon Stewart's "Commencement Address" (p. 201) in light of de Botton's observation that comics can "convey with impunity messages that might be dangerous." What points does Stewart make using humor that might be too "dangerous" to address using a different rhetorical technique?

Writing about Cultural Practices

7. Who says cultural and political critique can't be funny? Write a critical analysis of a late-night comedy television show. Your class may work together to watch and analyze a particular show such as Jon Stewart's *The Daily Show,* Jay Leno's *The Tonight Show,* or David Letterman's *Late Night* in order to discuss the impact and purpose of its humor. The following questions should drive your analysis.

   - To what extent does humor in this venue act as a tool (or weapon) for cultural critique for Americans?

   - What issues, entities, and/or individuals are most frequently lampooned? How do you account for this?

   - What makes this type of humor successful? Unsuccessful? Support your answer by drawing in specific examples from the show you studied.

John Margolies, **Amazing! Incredible! The Roadside Attraction**

John Margolies is a photographer, author, and lecturer on American popular culture and architecture. His most recent books include *Hitting the Road: The Art of the American Road Map* (1996), *Fun Along the Road: American Tourist Attractions* (1998), and *See the USA: The Art of the American Travel Brochure* (2000). His photographs and articles have been published in *Smithsonian, Esquire, Architectural Record,* and the *New York Times Magazine.* Margolies, a recipient of a Guggenheim fellowship, curates exhibitions and gallery shows and gives lectures and seminars on college campuses. The following essay, excerpted from the first chapter of *Fun Along the Road,* blends cultural history with examples of popular architecture to describe and analyze an array of roadside attractions designed to tempt travelers to pull over and spend their time and money.

> ▶ **Mapping Your Reading**
>
> As you read, pay attention to how effectively Margolies paints a picture of a roadside America. Use the margins to take notes about what the images reveal to you about American culture and what Americans find (or found) entertaining. How and why did the first roadside attractions come to be? Is the roadside attraction on the decline? If so, what, if anything, do you think has replaced the roadside attraction as a form of American entertainment? What do roadside attractions—past and present—say about life in America?

When Americans first took to the road behind the wheels of their cars in the beginning of the twentieth century, a new set of facilities had to be invented to serve these happy wanderers. Shrewd entrepreneurs realized that the automotive nomads passing in front of their properties were a source of potential income, and very early on American ingenuity and the free enterprise system took hold at curbside. The most essential services for tourists were gas, food, and lodging: garages and blacksmith shops became gas stations; eating and drinking establishments, from the sublime to the mundane,

On the way to Wall Drug, South Dakota.

popped up to satiate nearly every taste; and tents and campgrounds evolved into motels.

But in this explosion of commerce beside the road, there was a fourth type of establishment that had nothing whatsoever to do with fulfilling basic needs. The tourist attraction, in an almost infinite variety of manifestations, was conceived as a way to divert and amuse travelers along the way. The beginnings of the phenomenon are shrouded in the mists of the past, and just where and when these businesses began to appear is at best a matter of conjecture.

As one drove along almost any road in the early years, some form of roadside amusement would inevitably appear. It might be there one year and gone the next, only to be replaced by another attraction just a few miles away. Because of the ad hoc and nonsequential nature of roadside attractions, a straightforward and chronological explanation of their development is an impossible task. To present a panorama of this phenomenon, I will highlight examples of a wide variety of road-side attractions, each with its own chronological development and special history. An overview of the entire genre, therefore, can be gleaned by considering the to-tality of these histories of some of the most significant, bizarre, and typical examples.

The automotive nomads were a source of potential income.

One theory about how tourist attractions began is that people involved in serving up essentials added "amusement" facilities as a means of attracting attention and income, and to distin-guish themselves from their competitors. In the 1920s a menagerie was added to Young's Rainbow Garden Tourist Cottage Camp in Council Grove, Kansas; two bear cubs were staked out and caged in front of a gas station in Belleville, Kansas; and at another auto camp near Macon, Georgia, there was a small zoo that featured a large black bear trained to guzzle bottles of soda pop provided by spectators.

Because roadside attractions were hardly a necessity, the people who built them had to scream all the louder to attract customers. Intriguing and some-times mysterious messages appeared on billboards throughout the United States to forewarn and seduce automotive explorers. Based upon the business histories of some major American attractions—places like Rock City, South of the Border, and Wall Drug—the key to their success has been the sheer number of billboards set out for the tourist to see and ponder.

The architectural expression of early roadside attractions ranged from the extravagant and outrageous to the deliberately bland. Programmatic buildings shaped as sculptural renditions of what was being offered—like a huge alligator or an orange—or enormous statues and entrance signs, made some roadside amusement facilities very hard to miss. Other attractions used the opposite ap-proach. After miles and miles of billboards, they presented only a tall and other-wise featureless blockade by the side of the road. The curious tourists would have to stop, go inside, and pay an admission charge to see just what they'd been tempted by for miles and miles.

These "unnecessary" places also fulfilled needs as temporary way stations to stretch and relax, and they also provided very necessary rest rooms. Nearly al-ways the bathrooms were made accessible even to those tourists not paying ad-mission. But in order to get to them, the tourist would have to venture deep into the gift shops (which were also the final features on the tour of paying cus-tomers) through a maze of aisles chock-full of souvenirs, candy, and other as-sorted doodads.

Garnet Carter, an early roadside entrepreneur, came to own one of the great scenic overlooks in the United States when he and a partner purchased property on Lookout Mountain in Georgia near Chattanooga, Tennessee, in 1924. Mr. Carter and his wife, Frieda, a designer interested in horticulture, developed the ten acres atop the mountain, which became known as Rock City Gardens when it was opened to the public in 1932. At Rock City were paths meandering through gardens of specimen plants, and culminating in a scenic overlook called Lover's Leap from which one could marvel at an awesome view of seven states. To get to

Lover's Leap, visitors can still walk across a solid rock bridge, or they can walk on the wild side and try the "swing along" suspension bridge across the abyss. Like other depression-era operations, business was not good at first. But then Garnet Carter came up with the slogan "See Rock City" and an idea: to proclaim this message on painted barns. The number of Rock City barns proliferated, and so did the tourists. At one time Rock City maintained over 900 barns in the eastern United States. Now, fewer than 100 remain.

Down the road from Rock City is Ruby Falls, with two caves, one with a remarkable underground waterfall that Leo Lambert, the owner, named in honor of his wife, Ruby. In 1928 Lambert had an elevator shaft drilled through rock to shuttle tourists to the wondrous world below. The leftover limestone quarried from the shaft was used to construct a three-story-high observation tower above the cave, providing a panoramic view down upon the city of Chattanooga—the view in the opposite direction from Lover's Leap.

In other instances, ordinary businesses mutated into operations that overwhelmed their original functions. C.M. "Dad" Lee, a shrewd operator, became known as the "King of the Desert" when he operated a Shell gas station along the Victory Highway in Oreana, Nevada. "Dad," as he was always called, claimed to be a relative of Robert E. Lee, and he sported a goatee and tall brimmed hat. But there was much more than gas at Dad Lee's gas station. He assembled a group of rescued old buildings along the road in the 1920s and called them Lee Center, and he stocked them with a collection of Nevada relics and curios. And in his obituary in a local paper in 1934, we learn that Dad Lee was a bootlegger as well: "It was also a matter of considerable satisfaction to many thirsty travelers to discover, upon visiting 'Dad,' that gas and water were not all that was sold in the curio shop."

James Earl "Doc" Webb was another early businessman who transformed a once humble business into what was literally almost a "three-ring circus." Webb opened his original drugstore in St. Petersburg, Florida, in 1925 with a 3-foot counter in a 17-by-25-foot space. He went on to develop a retailing empire called Webb's City, the "World's Most Unusual Drug Store," with seven buildings covering ten blocks of downtown St. Petersburg. Doc Webb could be found in and about his stores wearing one of his 150 custom-made suits with matching silk ties, and he would shout special prices into a microphone. In addition, he offered such other thrills as circus acts in the parking lot, in which Webb sometimes put in a guest appearance, shows featuring a chorus line of Webb's famous Florida poster girls, or a man milking a rattlesnake.

It's hard to imagine that the same type of thing could have happened to more than one drugstore. But it began to happen again in 1931 when Ted Hustead bought a 24-by-60-foot building containing a patent medicine store and soda fountain on the Main Street of Wall, South Dakota, for $3,000. This coincided with the depths of the Depression, and not surprisingly, business was not good at the beginning. But in 1936, Ted's wife, Dorothy, inspired by some Burma Shave signs she had seen,

John Margolies Archive

One of the ubiquitous highway signs for South of the Border, an attraction in Dillon, South Carolina.

thought that it would be a good idea to put up a series of signs on nearby Route 16A to attract tourists to the store: "Get a soda/Get root beer/Turn next corner/Just as near/To Highway 16 And 14/Free Ice Water/Wall Drug." The signs helped business, and as they proliferated nearly endlessly, so did the number of customers. Wall Drug, in this town of 800 people, became a huge complex of stores—60,000 square feet, with the main building 149 by 249 feet—drawing 10,000 visitors or more a day during the summer season to see life-size, carved wooden statues of historical personages, groups of animated figures such as the Cowboy Orchestra, photographic exhibitions, a western clothing store, a pharmacy museum, a rock shop, oodles of souvenirs, of course, a travelers chapel, and even prescriptions for medicine in this the only drugstore within a 6,000-square-mile area. Now over 60 years old, Wall Drug is an American institution run by Ted's son Bill, and two of his grandsons. And even Ted himself still comes into work three days a week.

South of the Border in Dillon, South Carolina, a Mexican-theme attraction operated by Alan Schafer beside the interstate just south of the North Carolina border, is nearly as hectic as Wall Drug. It began in the 1950s as an 18-by-36-foot beer stand, and then a 10-seat grill was added. In 1964, a 20-unit motel was built, and the whole works assumed its present identity as South of the Border. As part of the motel experience, Mexican (and later non-Mexican) boys all named "pedro" (with a generic small "p") showed surprised guests to their rooms by leading them there on bicycles. But perhaps better known than the attraction itself are its humorous and outrageous billboards. By now, there are over 250 billboard messages, full of puns and jokes, stretching along the eastern United States from Philadelphia to Daytona Beach, tempting people to stop and shop at a conglomeration of buildings spread across some 350 acres.

Many of the earliest attractions were begun in the friendly climates in the southernmost locations in the United States, particularly in the tourist-frenzied states of Florida and California where endless summer prevails. Alligator farms and ostrich farms were popular draws in the first decade of the twentieth century. In addition to allowing amazed tourists to ride on a saddle perched upon the backs of ostriches, or to see other brave souls wrestling alligators, these very same operations were also in the business of making and selling shoes, handbags, and feather boas. The Arkansas Alligator Farm and Petting Zoo in Hot Springs, Arkansas, founded in 1902, celebrates its early history by proclaiming that "in all probability your Great Grandparents visited the farm. It is truly one of the oldest show places in Hot Springs."

Other zoos and animal attractions sprang up nearly everywhere. Perhaps the most fascinating of them all was the I.Q. Zoo in Hot Springs, Arkansas. It was founded by two expert animal psychologists, Keller and Marian Breland, who based their work with animals upon B. F. Skinner's concept of "operant conditioning" (Mrs. Breland was Skinner's second graduate student at the University of Minnesota). They discovered that the best way to train most animals was to give them an immediate reward of food for a specific task that would be repeated over and over. Instead of remaining in their ivory tower, the Brelands decided in 1947 to open a commercial business, Animal Behavior Enterprises, based upon their expertise. The Brelands opted for a warmer climate and moved to a 260-acre farm outside Hot Springs in 1950, and Marian Breland (now Bailey) reports that "Finally, in 1955, somewhat in desperation, we opened the I.Q. Zoo in downtown Hot Springs to satisfy local curiosity and attract tourists seeking entertainment."

A visit to the I.Q. Zoo must have been a real treat. There, in a variety of entertaining and clever displays, some of which were coin-operated, could be found: Bert Backquack and his Barnyard Band; Chickey Mantle, the baseball-playing chicken; Romeo Rabbit, the kissing bunny; Priscilla Pig, who put large coins in a piggy bank; and many more animals performing astonishing feats. In addition, the Brelands designed shows for large corporations such as General Mills, and also provided training methods and show design to other animal

"Clara" at the I.Q. Zoo in Hot Springs, Arkansas.

John Margolies Archive

attractions throughout the country, including Marineland of Florida with its great performing dolphins, Parrot Jungle in Miami, and Knott's Berry Farm in Buena Park, California. Keller Breland died in 1965, and his widow remarried and continued to operate the I.Q. Zoo until 1990.

An animal attraction of an entirely different sort can still be found in San Antonio, Texas. It is now called the Lone Star Buckhorn Museum, and since 1956 it has been installed adjacent to the Lone Star Brewery. This location is entirely appropriate because this institution began as the Buckhorn Saloon in 1881, the very same place immortalized by Larry McMurtry in *Lonesome Dove*. A man named Albert Friedrich, whose father made furniture from animal horns, began his own collection of animal horns as he opened the saloon. As the years went by and as the saloon prospered, he collected hundreds upon hundreds of sets of mounted horns and heads. During Prohibition the business became known as Albert's Curio Store and then the Buckhorn Curio Store and Café. As a souvenir shop, it sold a curious batch of products, including such items as armadillo baskets, abalone pearl manicure sets, postcards, horn chairs, and rattlesnake hatbands.

The collection is certainly extraordinary—horns and mounted animal heads from all over the world, with Texas and other North American species having the greatest representation. Perhaps the most outstanding examples are the Brady Buck, a seventy-eight-point deer head, and "the largest mass of horns in the world" from an African oxen with a twenty-one-inch diameter where the horns attach to the skull. Another mind-boggling part of the collection is a grouping of over 32,000 rattlesnake rattles, some of which were arranged by Mrs. Friedrich into "pictures" of such subjects as a life-size antlered deer and another depicting two Indian heads.

In Florida as in Texas, attractions continued to pop up nearly everywhere in the 1940s and 1950s, and not all of them were that entertaining or inspired. At least a few of them even put human beings on display. Some of these places, perhaps unintentionally, reinforced the ethnic and racial stereotyping prevalent in the 1940s and 1950s. Black people and especially Seminole Indians were exploited and used as the lure for many "exotic" attractions. An old brochure, probably from the 1940s, for Musa Isle, a small place in the heart of Miami, which boasted that it was the "home of the Seminole Indians," goes on to tell the tourists that: ". . . here you will see the 'Silent Seminoles' living and working in their own primitive way, making curios and novelties in their own crude and interesting way."

Black Americans made out little better at Wakulla Springs, near Tallahassee.

As Margolies points out, the Lewis Plantation and Turpentine Still in Brooksville, Florida, was "more than a step behind the times" in its portrayal of slavery in the Old South.

At Wakulla, a glass-bottom boat place, we are told about a black bass that jumped over a pole, Henry the Pole Vaulting Fish. "Seeing's Believing," claims the brochure, which then goes on to explain that "a great understanding grew between the Negro guides and Henry. Today Henry will not perform for anyone else."

But at the Lewis Plantation and Turpentine Still in Brooksville, Florida, Pearce Lewis latched on to a really bad idea and then went on to promote it to the tourist trade. This attraction showed, as described briefly in one brochure, "Plantation days just as they existed in pre-civil [sic] War and antebellum days. Turpentine is distilled, Negroes dance and sing in their natural environment." A

As Margolies notes in Fun Along the Road, *Paul Domke spent four decades constructing approximately thirty statues at his Dinosaur Gardens in Ossineke, Michigan. The largest statue, begun in the 1940s and completed in the 1980s, is an 85-foot-long, walk-in brontosaurus.*

John Margolies/Esto

more detailed brochure for the attraction itself elaborates that "in addition to an actual, hale, and hearty ex-slave, some 200 happy descendants of former slaves" can be seen. "Pickaninnies are at play in the sand, . . . a carefree darky plaintively strums a guitar with a melody to his lady love," and "typical mammies are washing clothes in primitive black iron boilers. . . ."

Some places reinforced the ethnic and racial stereotyping prevalent in the 1940s and 1950s.

There was another genre of tourist attractions that were purposely designed to be incredible—the so-called Mystery Spots and Spook Hills. In these places, we are told that the laws of gravity are defied. People stand atilt at a pronounced angle, as numerous postcards show. Water runs up. Cars back up hills with their motors turned off. All very mysterious, and all very explainable. In the specially built mystery houses, the optical illusion of gravity gone berserk is achieved by slightly tilted floors within a closed environment with pictures hung at the same angle as the floors and similar trompe l'oeil feats of deception. Spook Hills are harder to explain in a few words, but they work on the same principle as the Mystery Spots within carefully chosen outdoor locations.

Finally, another carefully crafted form of tourist attraction, examples of so-called folk art constructed by dedicated and idiosyncratic artists, were often opened to visitors for an admission charge. Simon Rodia's Watts Towers in Los Angeles are the best-known example of this phenomenon. But there were many more, including Edward Leedskalnin's cosmic and ethereal Coral Castle in Homestead, Florida, and Father Dobberstein's Grotto of Redemption in West Bend, Iowa.

With the approach of the millennium, the standardization and sterilization wrought by the Interstate Highway System, and the growing sophistication of parents and children alike, one might surmise that these artifacts of the good old days of tourism might have become an endangered species. But this is not the case. Yes, some of the smaller and funkier examples have fallen by the wayside as the people who built them beside now bypassed highways have come and gone. But other attractions have thrived by making themselves bigger and "better." Some, which began as places where fairy tales came to life, have become huge amusement parks. Storytown U.S.A. in Lake George, New York, while retaining much of its early charm, has now become The Great Escape Fun Park with the addition of an enormous roller coaster and other elaborate and sophisticated thrill rides. And in Santa Claus, Indiana, the old Santa Claus Land attraction has now become known as the very "cool" Holiday World and Splashin' Safari.

It is interesting to note that small theme parks like Storytown and Santa Claus Land were precursors to the new super theme park amusement industry, which began in Southern California on July 17, 1955, when Walt Disney opened Disneyland, where the thematic ideas of storybooks and Main Streets were combined with other spectacular rides and experiences based upon new technologies that were just then evolving.

Although the names, faces, and attractions themselves have changed, the basic idea and function of these tourist meccas remain the same. The people who have operated roadside amusements

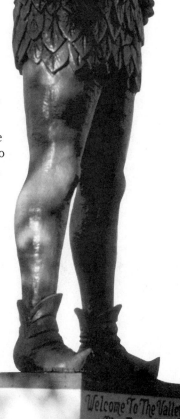

Jolly Green Giant, Blue Earth, Minnesota.

John Margolies/Esto

throughout the years are in the business of providing fun and entertainment. Roadside attractions are a popular American tradition of nearly unfathomable proportions; they have the same kind of appeal as sideshows at the circus. Often these facilities are targeted not only to the children riding in the backseats but also to the children living within the adults in the front seat as well. And so, life along the road, full of surprises and adventures, continues as American families keep on taking vacations in their cars, exploring the wonders, both scenic and man-made, in the far corners of the United States.

The very lifeblood of a roadside attraction is its means of proclaiming itself beside the road. In the old days, before the interstates, this process was much eas-

Paul Bunyan is one of the great folk legends of America. The exact origins of this giant woodsman and his famous blue ox, Babe, are unknown. But their cultural popularity is proven by an endless array of tall tales and folderol that embellish this legend. Since he is an oversized figure of our collective imaginations, tall Paul has become a perfect roadside commercial symbol. Huge apparitions of Paul Bunyan have been used to promote numerous businesses throughout the United States through the years. And since Paul is the epitome of fun and nonsense, he has become the silly symbol of choice for tourist attractions of many sorts. Shown here are the classic Paul Bunyan and Babe in Bemidji, Minnesota. These statues have been attracting tourists since the 1930s.

ier than it is today: set up your business and then strategically place a number of billboards in the line of traffic, increasing the number and the intensity of the messages as the irresistible whatever comes closer. Sometimes these messages were conveyed by artfully rendered, hand-painted images which, in and of themselves, were notable examples of commercial folk art. Artful or not, these signs had to gain the attention of the passersby, especially the children riding along, anxious only to alleviate the boredom of a long trip and to see something that was "neat" and "cool."

Not only did businesses use oversized icons to achieve their objectives, but small towns throughout the United States have used this trick to help to create an immediately recognizable identity for themselves: an enormous peach-shaped water tower by an interstate in South Carolina exuberantly celebrates this important local crop; the world's largest buffalo, a gargantuan statue, can be found on the outskirts of Jamestown, North Dakota, to delight the passing parade; and a large Superman statue helps to define where else but Metropolis, Illinois.

▶ **Analyzing the Text**

1. **Interrogating Assumptions.** What is entertaining about roadside attractions? What assumptions about entertainment do they reveal?

2. What categories of roadside attractions does Margolies describe? What do each of these different types of attractions reveal about what people find (or found) amusing or entertaining?

3. What do these attractions suggest about attitudes toward race in past decades of American life? How is "nature" presented in these attractions?

4. According to Margolies, how have roadside attractions, which were invented before the era of massive interstate highways and before McDonald's could be found in every town, kept up with modern times? How have they changed over time? What does the modern roadside attraction do to attract tourists and travelers today?

▶ **Writing about Cultural Practices**

5. Visit a roadside attraction in your area and write a descriptive analysis of it. The question your analysis should answer is, "What does this attraction reveal about the purpose or impact of 'amusements' in American life?" The particular roadside attraction you visit could be a kitschy roadside statue or a locally or regionally well-known landmark. You may want to work in groups to analyze the same setting and visit the attraction together. While you are there, take notes about the nature of the attraction and the behavior of tourists, tour guides, and others at the site. Also, collect any flyers or pamphlets describing the attraction. (Note: an alternative to this assignment is to use the Internet to take a virtual tour of an attraction.) As you draft your analysis, consider the following questions.

- Using the categories Margolies devised for describing different types of attractions, what type of roadside attraction is this?
- What is the context or setting for this attraction? What relationship does this attraction have to the place where it exists?
- Who established this attraction? Who runs it now?
- What are the people who visit this attraction like? What, if anything, do they appear to have in common with each other?
- What do the major elements of this attraction represent? What or who are they honoring, promoting, or celebrating?
- What cultural attitudes are reflected by the attraction? Is there anything potentially objectionable about it—that is, would anyone be offended by it? What leads you to this conclusion?

David Nasaw, The Pernicious "Moving Picture" Abomination

David Nasaw is a professor of history and American studies at the Graduate
Center of the City University of New York, where he chairs the doctoral history program. He has served as a historical consultant for several television documentaries, and his writing has appeared in the *New Yorker, The Nation,* and Condé
Nast's *Traveler.* The following reading, from Nasaw's book, *Going Out: The Rise
and Fall of Public Amusements* (1993), offers an opportunity to reflect on the cultural values and assumptions of a past time period. Nasaw gives an account of
the rise of the nickelodeon, or "nickel theater," in American cities around 1900, an
institution that was targeted by the anti-vice crusaders of the time as a threat to
public morals and health. What attitudes held by the early twentieth-century censors are shared by censors (or would-be censors) of today's entertainment?

 Mapping Your Reading

As you read, notice how carefully researched
Nasaw's account of the attempts by anti-vice crusaders to control movies and movie houses is.
Place checkmarks next to incidents that you find
particularly telling regarding the crusaders' assumptions about the purposes—and especially
the audiences—of the moving picture. What did
the crusaders' assume about immigrants and
people of the working class? How do these concerns connect with those who seek to control or
censor the media today?

For the critics of [nineteenth-century] commercialized popular culture who
had for [years] complained about—and organized against—the evils of sa-
loons, bawdy houses, honky-tonks, variety theaters, cheap vaudeville, prize
fights, dime novels, and story papers, the nickel show presented an unparalleled
danger to civic morality. Never before had so many innocent children and working people been placed in such immediate danger by unscrupulous (often immigrant) purveyors of commercial filth.[1]

---

[1]The definitive work on the critics of commercial culture remains Paul Boyer, *Urban Masses and
Moral Order in America, 1820–1920* (Cambridge, Mass., 1978). See, in particular, 120, 162–66. The
phrase used as the essay title is taken from the New York Society for the Prevention of Cruelty to
Children, *Thirty-fourth Annual Report* (New York, 1909), 23–24.

Although the theater had once, wrote John Collier of the People's Institute and the National Board of Censorship, served as a "moral agent of religion" and "a patriotic agent of the state," it had in twentieth-century America become an entirely "commercialized institution . . . ministered to at this day almost wholly by irresponsible, money-making agencies. . . . Commercialized recreation means dissipation. . . . It means the theater dominated by financial speculation and the moving picture reduced to the general level of yellow journalism."[2]

What made the discourse on the moving pictures cataclysmic in tone was the changed nature of the audience. Vaudeville and live theater had deadened the taste, moral sensibilities, and intellectual capacities of relatively prosperous, English-speaking audiences; moving pictures "demoralized" working people, immigrants, and children who lacked the intellectual, educational, and cultural resources to resist or counterbalance their effects. Edward Chandler of Boston likened moving pictures to a "disease" that was poisoning "beyond recovery . . . the very life blood of the city." The Ohio Humane Society, which viewed 250 films in early 1910, found 40 percent of them "unfit for children's eyes." Working-class and immigrant children whose family backgrounds and lack of educational and financial capital condemned them to unskilled, probably manual labor, were identified as being particularly susceptible to the temptations exhibited in such pictures. They would learn from viewing them not only that crime paid but also that it paid handsomely and required much less toil than labor in factory, mine, or mill.[3]

> Working-class and immigrant children were identified as being susceptible to such pictures. They would learn that crime paid.

While dedicated to protecting children from the moral dangers of the moving-picture show, the antivice crusaders were not above also using them as a Trojan Horse to invade the theaters and censor the moving pictures seen by adult working people. In 1907, Chicago passed a censorship ordinance requiring police permits for films shown in nickel and dime theaters. Jake Block, a Chicago theater owner, and his colleagues challenged the law in the Illinois Supreme Court, arguing that legislation requiring only nickel theater owners to secure prior approval of their shows was discriminatory and unconstitutional. The Court denied their contentions: "The ordinance applies to five and ten cent theaters . . . which, on account of the low price of admission, are frequented and patronized by a large number of children, as well as by those of limited means who do not attend

---

[2] John Collier, "Leisure-Time, the Last Problem of Conservation," National Recreation Association of America, *Publication 99* (1912), 8, 11.

[3] For an excellent discussion of the censorship issue in general and the historical relationship between film and theatrical censorships, see Daniel Czitrom, "The Politics of Performance: From Theater Licensing to Movie Censorship in Turn-of-the-Century New York," *American Quarterly* 44 (December 1992), 525–53; Edward H. Chandler, "How Much Children Attend the Theater, the Quality of the Entertainment They Chose and Its Effect on Them," *Proceedings of the Children's Conference for Research and Welfare* (1909), 56–57; the Ohio Humane Society study is cited in Charles Matthew Feldman, "The National Board of Censorship (Review) of Motion Pictures 1909–1922" (Ph.D. diss., University of Michigan, 1975), 43.

LADIES AND CHILDREN
ARE CORDIALLY INVITED
TO THIS THEATRE
NO OFFENSIVE PICTURES
ARE EVER SHOWN HERE

Slides like this were intended to set a proper tone in the theater.

the productions of plays and dramas given in the regular theaters. The audiences include those classes whose age, education, and situation in life specially entitle them to protection against the evil influence of obscene and immoral representations. The welfare of society demands that every effort of municipal authorities to afford such protection shall be sustained." The cheap theaters, in other words, had to be regulated and the moving pictures censored because they were patronized by children and childlike adults who required the special protection of the law.[4]

The fact that a good number of nickelodeon owners were, like Jake Block, Jewish or Catholic, and of working-class and immigrant backgrounds, made it easier for civic-minded reformers and public officials to castigate them for their foul deeds, interfere with their rights as businessmen, and threaten their

---

[4]Kathleen D. McCarthy, "Nickel Vice and Virtue: Movie Censorship in Chicago, 1907–1915," *Journal of Popular Film* V (1976), 45; *Block v. City of Chicago*, Supreme Court of Illinois, February 19, 1909, cited in 87 N.E. 1011.

[The matinee (c. 1900)] Ten-cent gallery seats meant boys like the one pictured here could see a vaudeville or picture show.

property. In May 1908, the *Moving Picture World* reported that a special bill was going to be introduced at the 1909 session of the New York State Assembly mandating that moving-picture theater licenses be issued only to citizens. "It is . . . aimed . . . at the horde of foreigners who operate the moving picture shows in New York and the other large cities in the State." The bill, if introduced, was never passed, but the threat remained.[5]

The ethnicity of the exhibitors, although seldom attacked this blatantly, remained an underlying subtext in the critique of the new medium. At a public hearing on the nickelodeons held by Mayor McClellan in December of 1908, former Assemblyman Cyrus W. Gale, now an exhibitor and because of his ethnic background and political standing, able to speak more freely in public, addressed the mayor directly on the question of discrimination. Why, he wanted to know, were

---

[5] *Moving Picture World* 2 (May 30, 1908), 473.

the "clergymen" objecting only to the moving-picture shows, when there were many other theaters and concert halls that also stayed open on Sundays?° "Would you be so unjust as to close one portion of amusement in this city and not close the rest? I say the poor have just as much right as the rich. If you are going to close the moving picture shows which are good and conducted right and have a tendency to raise and not to corrupt the morals, I am going to ask you isn't it just as fair . . . that you close the Metropolitan Opera House on Sunday or the theaters that show picture shows and the Y.M.C.A. which does the same thing."[6]

While the antivice crusaders railed against the immoral content of the films and demanded that the picture shows be closed down on Sundays, more moderate progressive reformers and politicians worried more about the unsafe conditions inside the theaters. They feared, and rightly, that overcrowded theaters with blocked exits would one day result in a tragedy comparable to the 1903 Iroquois Theater fire in Chicago that had taken 600 lives in fifteen minutes. When in December of 1908, in response to the antivice crusaders' complaints about immoral films, Mayor George B. McClellan, Jr., and Chief Oliver of the Bureau of Licenses personally inspected dozens of theaters,

> "I say the poor have just as much right as the rich."

they found the most deplorable conditions. "The exit facilities of almost all of the places . . . examined are inadequate to safeguard human life. Passageways are unlighted, exit doors are locked or blocked, and are not large enough for the large number of people who, in an emergency, would be compelled to use them." Had a fire broken out or even a spark appeared, hundreds would have been burned alive or trampled to death trying to escape.[7]

On December 24, 1908, Mayor McClellan issued executive orders revoking the licenses of the city's nickel theaters until they had been inspected and their owners had stipulated "in writing" that they would not open on Sundays. Although the theater owners eventually won an injunction against the mayor's action, the city had served notice on the nickel show proprietors that they would be held accountable for adhering to minimum fire-safety regulations. In the months that followed, many of the worst fire traps were closed down and new legislation was written enforcing minimal fire-safety standards and prohibiting nickel shows from opening in tenement buildings.[8]

Legitimate theaters, concert halls, and even vaudeville halls flouted the blue laws by presenting educational programs or "sacred concerts" on Sundays. [Nasaw's note.]

[6] *New-York Daily Tribune*, December 24, 1908, 4; partial typescript of public hearing, 150, Mayors' Papers, George B. McClellan, Box MGB 51, MA-NYC.

[7] On theater fires, see "Looking Backward: The Iroquois Theatre Fire of 1903," *Chicago History* 17 (1978–1979), 238; Czitrom, "Politics of Performance," 537; letters from Frances V. C. Oliver, Jr., Chief, Bureau of Licenses, to Mayor McClellan, December 14, 15, 18, 1908, and partial transcript of public hearing on closing the theaters, dated December 23, 1908, in Mayors' Papers, George McClellan, Box MGB 51, Departmental Correspondence Received, Mayor's Office, Bureau of Licenses, MA-NYC.

[8] *New-York Daily Tribune*, December 25, 1908, 1; *New York Times*, December 25, 1908, 1.

On January 12, 1909, with the theaters reopened but the debate on immoral films, unsafe theaters, and Sunday closings still current, the People's Institute, a progressive reform group that had earlier investigated the nickel shows and found the theaters dirty but the pictures "rarely, almost never, indecent," tried to inject a note of moderation into the controversy. In a letter to the editor of the *New York Times*, the Institute affirmed the right of the government to exercise its "police powers" to safeguard the public from overt physical or moral endangerment but emphasized that the nickel theaters fulfilled a singular and important purpose. "There is no other form of amusement at prices sufficiently low which meets the amusement needs of the workingmen's or immigrant's entire family. The possibility of cheap, wholesome, dramatic amusement for the people is involved in the moving picture problem. Let us remember this in our efforts at reform."[9]

Such a sympathetic voice must have immediately appealed to the nickelodeon owners who had won the battle to stay open but could not be sure about the larger war. To protect themselves from the antivice crusaders, the owners, joined by the movie producers, signed an agreement with the People's Institute in March 1909 to establish a National Board of Censorship.[10]

The agreement did not satisfy those who wanted to protect the morals of the young by keeping them out of the movie theaters. In 1909, the City's Board of Aldermen and the New York State Legislature passed legislation banning children unaccompanied by parent or guardian from the picture shows. *The Nickelodeon*, commenting on the legislation, remarked caustically that with a censorship board already organized to keep the movies "clean," laws barring unaccompanied children had lost their utility. "Perhaps it has never occurred to the municipal lawmakers who seek to legislate the children out of one of their greatest enjoyments, how absurdly anomalous their position is. Why have we gone to the trouble and expense of censoring pictures for the sake of those who will not be permitted to see them?"[11]

What was as galling to the antivice crusaders as the proliferation of nickel theaters was their owners' blithe disregard of the blue laws that mandated theaters be closed on Sundays. Because the storefront shows were not licensed as "theaters," they did not fall under these laws. In Chicago, Jane Addams and her associates kept their experimental Hull House nickel show open on Sundays,

[9]*New York Times*, January 12, 1909, 5; John Collier, "Cheap Amusement Shows in Manhattan: Preliminary Report of Investigation," January 31, 1908, in Subjects Papers, Records of the National Board of Review of Motion Pictures, Rare Books and Manuscripts Division, The New York Public Library (hereafter abbreviated as NBR-NYPL); John Collier, "Special Report on Cheap Amusements," in *People's Institute Eleventh Annual Report* (New York, 1908), 21–23; Czitrom, "Politics of Performance," 537–39.

[10]Robert Fisher, "Film Censorship and Progressive Reform: The National Board of Censorship of Motion Pictures, 1909–1922," *Journal of Popular Film* IV (1975), 142–56; Nancy J. Rosenbloom, "Between Reform and Regulation: The Struggle over Film Censorship in Progressive America, 1909–1922," *Film History* I (1987), 309–11.

[11]Daniel Czitrom, "The Redemption of Leisure," *Studies in Visual Communication* 10 (Fall 1984), 3–4; "Admitting Children," *Nickelodeon* II (November 1909), 135–36.

without protest of any sort. In New York City, Adoph Zukor and Marcus Loew rented legitimate playhouses from the Shuberts for special Sunday film shows.[12]

The New York City antivice forces fought back with a citywide petition drive in 1911 demanding that all nickel theaters be closed on Sunday and all pictures be censored by a board administered by a city agency (the Board of Education was suggested). The Board of Aldermen, overwhelmed by petitions from civic and religious groups, voted almost unanimously for the censorship and Sunday-closing ordinance. Mayor Gaynor, a former judge, staunch First Amendment supporter, and astute politician who knew that there were more movie fans than censorship advocates, vetoed the ordinance. While never directly taking issue with the clergymen's claims that they were acting "in behalf of the children," he exposed the censorship measure for what it was, "class" legislation aimed at the working people and immigrants who owned, operated, and patronized the nickel theaters. "These moving picture shows are attended by the great bulk of the people, many of whom cannot afford to pay the prices charged by the theaters. They are a solace and an education to them. Why are we singling out these people as subjects necessary to be protected by a censorship? Are they any more in need of protection by censorship than the rest of the community?"[13]

While the antivice crusaders failed to close the movie theaters on Sunday or establish mandatory government censorship, moderate progressive reformers fared better in their attempts to pass legislation establishing fire-safety and health standards. They were supported in this effort by the trade journals, whose editors were convinced that dirty, dangerous theaters threatened the future of the picture industry. As the *Moving Picture World* warned in early 1911, "The justified criticism of the health authorities may prove disastrous one of these days. Should a malignant epidemic strike New York City, and these conditions prevail, the result might be a wholesale closing down of these germ factories."[14]

The massing of individuals in the store shows was unlike that in any other public space, greater than in the most congested sweatshops, flophouses, and multifamily tenement flats. Worse yet, in the storefront theaters there were no lobbies, vestibules, entryways, or staircases to ease congestion; no windows, skylights, or doorways to provide light or air. In March of 1911, Commissioner of Accounts Raymond Fosdick, at Mayor Gaynor's request, sent investigators into fifty picture shows chosen at random in Brooklyn, the Bronx, and Manhattan.

---

[12]Eileen Bowser, *The Transformation of Cinema: 1907–1915* (New York, 1990), 48–49; *Moving Picture World* I (June 1, 1907), 198; Brooks McNamara, *The Shuberts of Broadway: A History Drawn from the Collections of the Shubert Archive* (New York, 1990), 75; Robert Grau, *The Theatre of Science* (New York, 1914), 33–34.

[13]For copies of these petitions and handbills, see Box 20, folder 6, Subject Correspondence: Children and Motion Pictures, NBR-NYPL; and Mayors' Papers, James G. Gaynor, Box GWJ 89, folder 3, "Protests," MA-NYC. Gaynor's correspondence on censorship is found in Box GWJ 80, Subject Files, Censorship, MA-NYC. The full text of his veto message was reprinted in *Moving Picture World* 15 (January 11, 1913), 134–36.

[14]*Moving Picture World* 8 (March 11, 1911), 539.

Over two-thirds of the theaters visited were found to be dangerously overcrowded, "in some instances, indeed, with the aisles completely blocked by standing spectators, so that it was impossible for our inspectors to force their way into the hall." On Fulton Street, in Brooklyn, all the seats were "filled and standing in the rear were 61 persons completely blocking the aisles. As a matter of fact, including the persons standing, there were 373 people in attendance at the time of inspection and a panic or fire could not but have resulted disastrously."[15]

Even had fire not broken out, antivice crusaders and progressives alike feared that congestion of this sort would endanger the health and morals of assembled audience members. In his marvelous essay on nineteenth-century utopian fiction, Neil Harris has described the "consciousness of crowding which invaded the late nineteenth-century mind." Urban reformers, housing experts, public health authorities, child savers, journalists, and novelists were worried about the effects of overcrowding in urban dwellings, on the streets, and in public spaces. "Continual contiguity led to aggression, loss of control, and social decline. 'Contact breeds contagion and decay,' wrote Captain Nathan Davis in *Beulah*. Dense 'populations which are in constant contact breed moral contagion and deadly corruption.'"[16]

Nowhere were there more congested spaces with staler air than in nickel theaters.

As the Chicago Vice Commission reported in 1911, the young and innocent were likely to be "influenced for evil by the *conditions surrounding* [the nickel shows]. . . . Many liberties are taken with young girls within the theater during the performance when the place is in total or semi-darkness. Boys and men slyly embrace the girls near them and offer certain indignities." The New York Society for the Prevention of Cruelty to Children, in its annual reports, press releases, and lobbying efforts before governmental bodies, presented case after case of such depravities. "This new form of entertainment," it claimed in its 1909 *Annual Report*, "has gone far to blast maidenhood. . . . Depraved adults with candies and pennies beguile children with the inevitable result. The Society has prosecuted many for leading girls astray through these picture shows, but GOD alone knows how many are leading dissolute lives begun at the 'moving pictures.'"[17]

The moral dangers of overcrowding, though severe, paled in comparison to the health hazards. Even in the darkness, audience members could protect themselves from mashers, perverts, and their own temptations. Not even the strongest resolve, however, could save them from the dangers that floated unseen through the air. Decades of urban epidemics and the pronouncements of

---

[15]Raymond B. Fosdick, Commissioner of Accounts, "Report on *Moving Picture Shows* in the City of New York," March 22, 1911, 10–13, in Mayors' Papers, William J. Gaynor, Box GWJ 22, Departmental Correspondence, Accounts Commissioner, 1911, MA-NYC.

[16]Neil Harris, *Cultural Excursions: Marketing Appetites and Cultural Tastes in Modern America* (Chicago, 1990), 165.

[17]Chicago Vice Commission, *The Social Evil in Chicago* (Chicago, 1911), 247–51; New York Society for the Prevention of Cruelty to Children, 23–24.

[1900] *This slide, flashed on the screen during intermission was intended, as Nasaw writes, to be "a subtle reminder" that the balconies provided privacy for young couples.*

public health reformers and journalists had, by the turn of the century, begun to convince the public (or at least that portion of it that went to public school, had contact with the settlement houses, or read the daily newspapers or general interest magazines) that, as Harris puts it, "dangerous microbes—insidious, omnipotent, invisible enemies of humanity, able to attack anyone and anywhere" flourished in overcrowded, unventilated spaces. And nowhere in the city were there more congested spaces with staler air than in the nickel theaters. As the *Independent* reported in early 1910, the city's "moving picture places [had] become foci for the dissemination of tubercle bacilli."[18]

Robert Bartholomew, inspecting the movie houses in Cleveland in 1913, was appalled by the "condition of the air." In some of the larger theaters, attendants

---

[18]Harris, *Cultural Excursions*, 169; *Independent* 67 (March 17, 1910), 590. See also Arthur Meier Schlesinger, *The Rise of the City, 1878–1898* (New York, 1933), 244–46.

using "large atomizers squirted a solution around the room to allay the odor of the foul air." In others, fans were supposed to provide fresh air but did little more than circulate the foul air already accumulated. Bartholomew concluded, in what was otherwise an extremely favorable report, that "probably 35,000 people are daily subjected to the dangers of contracting disease from the foul air laden with death-dealing germs. In ten theaters the air was found to be so foul that the investigators could not stay more than a few moments and even this short stay resulted in sneezing, coughing and the contraction of serious colds. One theater was visited at the opening of an evening performance after having been closed one and one-half hours succeeding the afternoon performance. The air was then so bad that three patrons left within a few moments complaining of faintness and headache."[19]

In many cities, progressive reform groups called for government intervention to protect the health and safety of moving-picture audiences. Legislation passed in New York State in 1911 required that all new "public entertainments or exhibitions by cinematograph or any other apparatus for projecting moving pictures," no matter how large or small, enclose their projectors in "fireproof booths." An additional state law, also from 1911, established a special licensing procedure for the operators of these projectors. In Chicago, a special ordinance forbid moving-picture theaters, no matter how safely constructed, from being built above the first floor of non-fireproof buildings.[20]

The effect of these laws on the exhibitors cannot be underestimated. The fire-safety laws passed by the Pennsylvania state legislature were so stringent, *Film Index* reported in July 1909, that a large number of the smaller theaters in the state, unable to meet them, were closing down. In Chicago, the Juvenile Protective Association reported in 1911 that, as a result of better laws and cooperation between the reformers and the police, "there has been a great improvement in the physical conditions of the theatres. The exits are now much better and the ventilation has been much improved."[21]

Unfortunately for the reform community, it was easier to pass laws than to get them enforced. The reformers were particularly stymied when it came to enforcing the laws barring underage, unaccompanied children from the nickel shows. As a confidential investigator for the Kehillah, a Jewish reform agency, reported of the Lower East Side movie houses in 1913, "Minors go in here with anyone who act as their guardian and once they get inside they take care of themselves."[22]

---

[19]Robert O. Bartholomew, "Report of Censorship of Motion Pictures and of Investigation of Motion Picture Theatres of Cleveland, 1913," filed with Council of City of Cleveland, April 7, 1913, 12–13.

[20]*Birdseye's Consolidated Laws of New York, 1909*, vol. 3, 2906–9, 2996–97; *Motography* IX (February 15, 1913), 120.

[21]See, for example, on the effect of the new regulations in Pennsylvania, *Film Index* IV, no. 29 (July 17, 1909), 3; Juvenile Protective Association, "Five and Ten Cent Theatres" (n.p., n.d.), JPA-UIC.

[22]See, for example, letter to Mayor Gaynor from President Board of Education, May 31, 1910, in Mayors' Papers, William J. Gaynor, Subjects File Censorship: Motion Pictures, MA-NYC; *New York Times*, November 12, 1911, 8; John Collier, "'Movies' and the Law," *Survey* 27 (January 20, 1912), 1629; final quotation is from "Moving Picture Houses," November 23, 1913, 36, in Magnes Papers, Hebrew University, Jerusalem, Israel (hereafter abbreviated MP-HU).

The exhibitors paid the law no attention at all. The New York City Commissioner of Accounts reported in March of 1911 that it had become "a common practice in most of the shows to admit children under sixteen years of age unaccompanied by a guardian or parents in spite of the provisions of section 484 of the Penal Code. Indeed, one important official of the Moving Picture Exhibitors Association stated in his testimony before us that 75 per cent of the moving picture shows of this city would be driven out of business if this law were strictly enforced." The problem was, of course, not confined to New York City. A 1913 survey in Cleveland found that more than one-half of the children attending the moving-picture theaters were unaccompanied by adults. For the evening performances, the percentage exceeded two-thirds.[23]

Not only did the reformers fail to keep the children out of the nickel shows, but their attempts to improve the pictures they saw were only minimally successful. When Jane Addams and her associates—under the impression that the children would patronize any moving-picture show provided the price was right—opened their Hull House theater, the first in what was supposed to have been a "settlement-house circuit" of wholesome nickelodeons, they were surprised to find only thirty-seven children in the audience. (The experiment was soon terminated.) When questioned about the "clean" show they had seen at Hull House, the children responded that they had enjoyed watching Cinderella and travel scenes of Japan and Java, but their tastes ran in other directions. According to Jimmy Flaherty, twelve years old (his words recorded by the reformers who did all they could to make them sound cute and tough), "Things has got ter have some hustle. I don't say it's right, but people likes to see fights, 'n' fellows getting hurt, 'n' love makin', 'n' robbers, and all that stuff. I like to myself, even. This here show ain't even funny, unless those big lizards from Java was funny." Had the choice been between Cinderella and nothing, the children would have paid their nickels to see Cinderella. But, with dozens of local nickelodeons anxious to attract their nickels, the children could, for the same price, see The Pirates, The Defrauding Banker, The Adventures of an American Cowboy, An Attack on the Agent, and The Car Man's Danger, all playing within a few blocks of Hull House.[24]

The reformers struggled valiantly to convince the producers to produce and the exhibitors to exhibit "educational" and "uplifting" pictures for the children. But their powers of persuasion were never sufficient to supersede the logic of the marketplace. Because the children bought more tickets than the reformers, the pictures that they wanted to see were produced and exhibited more regularly than the educational fare.

Even the crime pictures that had earlier been banned because of their supposed evil influence on the impressionable young soon returned to the theaters, as producers and exhibitors found ways to reintroduce them without violating censorship board restrictions. By 1910, according to John Collier, 20 percent of all the movies being produced presented characters who were "tempted to

---

[23]Fosdick, "Report on Moving Picture Shows in the City of New York," 11–12. On Cleveland, see Bartholomew, "Report of Censorship," 10, 27–28.

[24]Moving Picture World I (June 27, 1907), 262–63.

commit crimes, and sometimes do commit crimes," though none of these films, Collier proudly reported, portrayed crime "for its own sake" or allowed a criminal to go unpunished. In fact, crimes committed on the moving-picture screen were "invariably dealt with by a stern justice which is far more certain and terrible with its lightnings than is human justice in real life."[25]

Despite the reformers' attempts to protect them, the children remained an important segment of the moving-picture audience. The calculus of commercial amusements dictated that the show businessmen—with their cheap prices and abbreviated shows—empty and refill their houses several times a day. The children were an essential part of their audience, because they filled the theaters during fallow periods in the late afternoons, in early evenings, and for weekend matinees. The producers and owners consequently did all that was necessary to hold on to them. To disarm their critics, they followed the advice of the National Board of Censorship and cooperated with the local state and municipal censorship boards that were organized in the early 1910s. But they continued to sidestep the laws barring underage, unaccompanied children from their theaters and ignored the reformers' pleas that they substitute educational films for trashy crime melodramas and slapstick comedies.[26]

> **Legislation "hastened the demise of the nickelodeon."**

The nickelodeon's critics in the long run, achieved both more and less than they had bargained for. While the antivice crusaders never succeeded in instituting mandatory government censorship, Sunday closing, or age restrictions, their continual attack on "the pernicious 'moving picture' abomination" provided more moderate reformers with leverage to push for industry self-censorship and regulatory legislation. And that legislation, according to the film historian Charlotte Herzog, "hastened the demise of the nickelodeon" as new building codes and fire-safety ordinances made it more costly and less efficient to operate movie theaters in tiny, airless storefront theaters.[27]

▶ **Analyzing the Text**

1. Near the beginning of the essay, Nasaw explains that what made public officials and anti-vice crusaders so certain that moving pictures represented a threat to public morality was "the changed nature of the audience." According to Nasaw, who made up the audience in nickel movie houses? What assumptions did public officials have about these people? What examples does Nasaw use to support his view?

2. According to Nasaw's research, what role did the ethnicity or working class background of the theater owners play in how public officials and anti-vice crusaders acted at the time?

---

[25]John Collier, "The Motion Picture," *Proceedings of the Children's Conference for Research and Welfare* 2 (1910), 116.

[26]Richard Koszarski, *An Evening's Entertainment* (New York, 1990), 201–3.

[27]Charlotte Herzog, "The Nickelodeon Phase (1903–c. 1917)," *Marquee* 13 (First Quarter 1981), 8.

3. **Interrogating Assumptions.**   Based on Nasaw's research, what arguments did reformers attempt to use against movies and movie theaters? What assumptions did the anti-vice crusaders have about the purposes and audiences of entertainment? What assumptions outlined in the chapter's introduction (pp. 361–69) would the anti-vice crusaders have agreed with? What details in the essay lead you to your analysis?

4. In this day and age, have you heard similar arguments made by individuals or groups seeking greater control of popular entertainment? How closely do modern-day reformers mirror the assumptions and values of the anti-vice crusaders Nasaw describes? In what ways do they differ from past reformers?

5. How successful were reformers in changing moving pictures or the theaters that showed them? On what issues did they make an impact? On what issues were they completely unsuccessful?

6. **Connecting to Another Reading.**   How would you compare the attitudes about race and class reflected in some roadside attractions described in John Margolies's essay, "Amazing! Incredible! The Roadside Attraction" (p. 398), with those described in Nasaw's essay?

 Writing about Cultural Practices

7. As this reading demonstrates, at regular intervals in American history, so-called reformers have come onto the national scene to argue that a particular form of popular entertainment is corrupting the nation's youth. For this assignment, trace the arguments of a group that has argued for greater restrictions of some form of popular entertainment in the recent past and construct a rhetorical analysis of their arguments. In the last decade, debates have arisen over the rating systems and availability of video games, song lyrics, and the violence and sexual content found on television, to name a few. To start, you'll need to do some research to identify such a group, and then locate materials including articles, interviews, or transcripts from congressional hearings. Consider the following questions as you draft your analysis of the group's main argument(s).

   • What type of entertainment does the group consider to be a threat, and to whom? How does the group define the entertainment?

   • What kind of language and rhetorical strategies does the group use to support its claims? What evidence does the group cite? How persuasive are the arguments it puts forth?

   • What type of outreach campaign, if any, does the group have? Who is the intended audience in the campaign—that is, who are they trying to reach? What do they want to persuade their audience to do or not do?

   • How do other groups or individuals who oppose these "reformers" respond to them? What assumptions form the basis of *their* arguments?

David Sterritt, **Face of an Angel**
Samuel L. Jackson, **In Character**

David Sterritt is a professor of theater and film at Long Island University, a member of the film studies faculty at Columbia University, and chair of the New York Film Critics Circle. He has been a film critic for the *Christian Science Monitor* for more than 30 years and also reviews movies for National Public Radio's *All Things Considered.* In his essay "Face of an Angel," originally published in 2003 in the *Christian Science Monitor,* Sterritt argues that recent trends in mainstream Hollywood movies demonstrate how African Americans, typically cast as thugs or maids, now have a new stock character to play: the angel.

Actor Samuel L. Jackson graduated from Morehouse College in Georgia with a bachelor of arts in drama. In the 1970s, Jackson joined the Negro Ensemble Company with Morgan Freeman and, since then, has appeared in over 80 films, including *Do the Right Thing* (1989), *Mo' Better Blues* (1990), *Pulp Fiction* (1994), and *Coach Carter* (2005). "In Character" appears in *America Behind the Color Line* (2004), edited by Henry Louis Gates, Jr. In this piece, Jackson discusses race in Hollywood and identifies new challenges facing the film industry.

▶ Mapping Your Reading

Both Sterritt and Jackson argue that Hollywood's portrayals of African Americans continue to be stereotyping, patronizing, and even racist. As you read, mark passages that you find particularly compelling or effective. What ideas do the authors have for changing attitudes of Hollywood filmmakers regarding the roles they assign to African American actors?

What do the films *Bruce Almighty* and *The Green Mile* have in common with *The Family Man*, the *Matrix* movies, and *Ghost?*

All feature black characters whose main function is to help a white hero through magical or supernatural means. These are Hollywood's "black angels," whose popularity has surged in recent years—so much so that in a recent episode of *The Simpsons*, Homer mistook a black man in a white suit for an angelic visitor, all because (according to his embarrassed wife) he'd been seeing too many movies lately.

Of course, there are many films aimed at African-Americans that star blacks in a variety of parts, from villainous to heroic. But casting blacks as angelic characters has become an increasingly common trend in mainstream movies.

For their part, many African-Americans see this heavenly designation as less than beatific. Filmmakers like Spike Lee have spoken out against such roles, calling them patronizing and unrealistic.

"Black-angel movies appeal to a genuine desire for reconciliation among whites and blacks. But they also exploit a distorted fascination with blacks that many whites have," says film historian Krin Gabbard, who explores this subject in his book *Black Magic: White Hollywood and African-American Culture* [2004]. "In vast amounts of entertainment and culture, whites have trouble regarding blacks as real people. That's depressing, but true."

The record supports Dr. Gabbard's charge. In one tradition of American filmmaking, dating to D.W. Griffith's epic *The Birth of a Nation* in 1915, black people are portrayed as villains and monsters—like the lust-crazed Gus who forces Mae Marsh's character to choose death before dishonor.

This practice lives on in many films that still cast black performers as criminals or thugs. Denzel Washington played a crooked cop in *Training Day*—and won an Oscar for it. (Halle Berry also won in 2002, causing many to hope that African-Americans had finally written themselves a bigger part in Hollywood.)

In another tradition, exemplified by *Gone with the Wind* in 1939, blacks are often lovable, but also ignorant and subservient, like the characters played by Butterfly McQueen and Hattie McDaniel. In the most common tradition of all, African-Americans are excluded altogether or allowed a few seconds of screen time to lend local color or comic relief. They may also be depicted as anonymous hordes, as in war pictures such as *Zulu* and *Black Hawk Down*.

For decades, most film historians agreed that these traditions served to reinforce the racial prejudices of their times, and that little or nothing can be said in their favor. More recently, revisionist critics have noted that at least such roles allowed black performers to hold careers in the entertainment industry and to display their talents for large audiences.

"Why should I complain about making $7,000 a week playing a maid?" asked Ms. McDaniel, referring to the character type that dominated her career. "If I didn't, I'd be making $7 a week being one."

Viewed in this context, black-angel movies can be seen as an attempt at compromise, giving on-screen blacks more dignity—without taking much of the action away from the white hero. Key examples include *The Green Mile*, where black death-row inmate John Coffey heals a white prison guard and his wife before marching obediently to his execution, and the *Matrix* series, where a black "oracle" (the late Gloria Foster) dispenses prophecy and wisdom to the white "chosen one" (Keanu Reeves). The *Matrix* films, however, can't be accused of tokenism, since they also feature African-American actors, such as Laurence Fishburne and Jada Pinkett-Smith, in prominent roles.

And overall, African-American stars, from Queen Latifah to Will Smith, are commanding higher salaries and headlining more movies than in the past. (Certainly, no one is going to claim that Bill Pullman and Randy Quaid were the main heroes of *Independence Day*.)

But the list of heavenly visitations could stretch all the way down the Walk of Fame. In 1998's *What Dreams May Come*, Cuba Gooding Jr. plays an angel who leads Robin Williams, who is in heaven, on a quest to rescue his wife from hell. That same year Andre Braugher provided comfort to fallen angel Nicolas Cage in *City of Angels*. A seminal film was *Ghost*, where a psychic played by Whoopi Goldberg helps a murder victim (Patrick Swayze) communicate with his widow, Demi Moore. Ms. Goldberg won an Oscar for her role.

"Hollywood has to tread a very fine line," Gabbard says. "It can't keep putting blacks into subservient positions . . . because that would turn off the huge black audience. So in these [black-angel] movies, at some moments [a black character] gets to have total control over the white people. That way blacks don't feel demeaned, and whites don't feel . . . threatened, because the blacks aren't really from their world, they're from heaven."

> **"[Hollywood] can't keep putting blacks into subservient positions."**

"And heaven appears to be administered by white people," he adds, "because the black people [in these films] only give their help to whites. John Coffey only helps one character who isn't a white person in *The Green Mile*, and that's a mouse!"

The racial dimensions of films like *The Green Mile* have deep roots in U.S. culture, says Linda Williams, author of *Playing the Race Card: Melodramas of Black and White from Uncle Tom to O.J. Simpson*.

"They come from the tradition of melodrama," Dr. Williams explains, "where to suffer is to acquire virtue. The person who suffers is Christlike and has the moral authority to forgive and offer absolution. The black man's initials in [*The Green Mile*] are J.C., and he seems to exist for the purpose of serving and redeeming white people. You see similar things in *Bruce Almighty*, where a black person redeems a white person, even though the white person's problems are of the most trivial kind."

Williams says the "black angel" movies can be traced back 200 years to *Uncle Tom's Cabin*. "That novel came out of a moment when a certain kind of strict Calvinism was in crisis, and the solution was a more loving kind of approach," she says. "Today . . . there is a feeling that we need some kind of spiritual redemption, and we turn to black people because they're the ones who have suffered."

A key quality of the black-angel movies is that they're not realistic stories but overt, often flamboyant fantasies. Hollywood's ideal black angel [has been] embodied by Morgan Freeman, whose many authoritative roles—the president in *Deep Impact*, a judge in *The Bonfire of the Vanities*—culminate in *Bruce Almighty*, where he plays God as a white-suited gentleman bent on making the life of a self-indulgent journalist (Jim Carrey) more fulfilling.

"There's an unspoken agreement in American culture that blacks are more spiritual, more in touch with the Divine than whites," Gabbard says. "Freeman manages to project that, along with an authenticity, a folksiness, a lack of pretension. He's a man of wisdom, but not an intellectual—a guy who feels the pain of the world. There's compassion in his face, his speech, his manner. . . . This suits our fantasies of how God would act."

Too patronizing? Gabbard points out that the film also gives Freeman's character an above-the-fray quality that other black angels share. Such figures are isolated from the black community, and also from the complicated world of politics, dissension, and difficult moral questions.

Hollywood's recent pattern of casting blacks in idealistic roles and evading "the real world," is exasperating, say many race-conscious critics and filmmakers. "These movies don't really deal with race," says Armond White, an African-American cultural critic for the *New York Press*, a weekly newspaper. "They deal with the desire of white filmmakers to patronize black people . . . by portraying them as kindly, beneficent helpmates."

"These aren't progressive ideas," he adds. "They're a fantasy sold mainly to people over 40, whose thinking is a vestige of the civil rights era. Younger people are less interested in this, because the commercial media encourage them to think racism doesn't exist anymore. 'Eminem showed anyone can be black!' But he's really Elvis redux—another white performer appropriating black styles to get fame and money." (As the rapper himself boasted in last year's hit song "Without Me.")

> "These movies don't deal with race. They deal with the desire of white filmmakers to patronize black people."

Another black observer with a critical view of black-angel movies is filmmaker Spike Lee, who expressed his outrage in a March 2001 interview with *Cineaste* magazine. He called Coffey of *The Green Mile* a reworking of the "old grateful slave," and showed even more anger at 2000's *The Legend of Bagger Vance*, with Matt Damon as a (white) golfer who's supernaturally aided by his (black) caddy, played by Mr. Smith. Observing that the story takes place in the Deep South during the 1930s, when violence against blacks was common, Lee posed a pointed question: "If this magical black caddy has all these powers, why isn't he using them to try and stop some of the brothers from being lynched and [mutilated]? . . . I don't understand this!"

I think it's significant for the growth of the [movie] business that a black actor like me is being cast in race-neutral parts when 20 years ago I wouldn't have been. It's significant for young actors who have aspirations to be things other than criminals and drug dealers and victims and whatever rap artist they have to be to get into a film. The things I've done and Morgan's done and Denzel's done, that Fish has done, that Wesley's° done, everybody's done, have allowed us to achieve a level of success as other kinds of people. We've been successful in roles as doctors, lawyers, teachers, policemen, detectives, spies, monsters—anything that we have been able to portray on-screen in a very realistic way that made audiences say, I believe that, and that brought them into the theaters to see us do it. This has allowed young black actors the opportunity to become different kinds of characters in the cinematic milieu we're a part of.

Before, I used to pick up scripts and I was criminal number two and I looked to see what page I died on. We've now demonstrated a level of expertise, in terms of the care we give to our characters and in terms of our professionalism—showing up to work on time, knowing our lines, and bringing something to the job beyond the lines and basic characterizations. Through our accomplishments and the expertise we have shown, studios know there is a talent pool out there that wants to be like us, and hopefully, these young actors will take care to do the things we did.

As the fabric of our society changes in certain ways, the fabric of the cinematic world changes in the same ways. For a very long time, the people that were in power were white men. They tended to hire other white men, and when they saw a story, the people in those stories were white men or specific kinds of white women. As we get younger producers and younger people in the studios, we have a generation, or several generations, of people who have lived in a society where they have black friends. They have Asian friends. They have Hispanic friends who do a wide variety of jobs, who went into a wide variety of vocations. When the studio heads look at a script now, they can see their friend Juan or they can see their friend Kwong or they can see their friend Rashan. So all of a sudden you see a different look in the movies, as they reflect the way this younger generation of producers and studio executives live their lives. And consequently, through the worldwide network of cinema, you meet other top-quality actors from other cultures. The world of cinema brings us all together. And we've started to cast films in a whole other way that reflects the way we live and the pattern of our society. Outside of *Spider-Man*, all the big action heroes now seem to be ethnic. The new Arnold Schwarzenegger is The Rock, and the new Bruce Willis is about to be Vin Diesel. So we're doing something right. But it's difficult to do a film that's of a serious nature and that does not have guns, sex, and explosions in it if it's ethnic.

Fish . . . Wesley refers to Laurence Fishburne and Wesley Snipes.

Samuel L. Jackson

There are many ways to answer the question whether Hollywood is racist. The direct and honest answer, I guess, is yes, only because Hollywood is anti anything that's not green. If something doesn't make money, they don't want to be bothered with it. Therefore, it's still difficult to get a movie about Hispanics made; it's difficult to get a movie about blacks made that doesn't have to do with hip-hop, drugs, and sex. You can get a black comedy made. Eddie Murphy's funny, Will Smith is funny, Martin Lawrence is funny. We have huge black comics. But getting a film like *Eve's Bayou* made is practically impossible. For five years, nobody knew what that movie was. Like, what is it? It's a family drama. Yeah, but how do we market that? Nobody wanted to be bothered with it. Or *Caveman's Valentine*. What is it? It's a mystery, a murder mystery. But it's a black murder mystery. No, there's white people in it; it just happens that a black person is the lead. So Hollywood is racist in its ideas about what can make money and what won't make money. They'll make Asian movies about people who jump across buildings and use swords and swing in trees, like *Crouching Tiger,* but we can't sell an Asian family drama. What do we do with that? Or if we're going to have Asian people in the film, they've got to be like the tong, or they're selling drugs and they got some guns and it's young gang members. It's got to be that. And Hollywood is sexist in its ideals about which women are appealing and which women aren't. It's a young woman's game. Women have got to be either real old or real young to be successful. If they're in the middle, it's like, what do we do with her? Put her in kids' movies, you know, with some kids.

> There are many ways to answer the question whether Hollywood is racist.

Hollywood can be perceived as racist and sexist, because that's what audiences have said to them they will pay their money to come see. It's difficult to break that cycle, because it's a moneymaking business and it costs money to make films. Hollywood tends to copy things that make lots of money. The first thing they want to know is how many car chases are there and what's blowing up. They're over the how-many-people-die thing, because of 9/11. Now it's like, how many people can we kill and get away with it? We can't blow up anything right now unless it's in the right context. We can blow something up over there, and the bad guy can be a guy with a turban. So there's all kinds of things that go into what people say about Hollywood being racist. There have been times I had to go in a room and convince people I'm the right person for their script and the fact that I'm black will not impact on the script in a negative way. I've had to explain that my being black won't change the dynamics of the interaction; it won't change the dynamics of the story in terms of my character's interaction with the other characters. I'll just happen to be a black guy who's in that story doing those things.

We [African Americans] need to produce our own films. We need to own our own theaters in addition to producing our own films. The more theaters we own, the sooner we can have our own distribution chain. It's a matter of us having that kind of network [as major Hollywood studios do], so when we do make small films that we want to distribute to a specific group of people or to a wider audience, we're able to do it.

I want to be able to produce films for friends of mine who haven't had the opportunity to be seen in the way I've been seen. They're good at what they do, and they deserve an opportunity to be seen by a greater public.

Analyzing the Texts

1. Why are there so few Hollywood films that tell stories of nonwhites? Or, to borrow from Jackson's piece, why can't Hollywood make an Asian family drama or show people of color dealing with everyday problems?

2. To help make his argument, Sterritt presents the perspectives of film historian Krin Gabbard and culture critic Linda Williams. How do these two critics explain why Hollywood casts African Americans as angels? Do you agree? Why or why not?

3. Although Jackson points out the positive changes in Hollywood that have allowed him and several other African American stars to play race-neutral parts, he still believes the movie industry is racist and sexist. How does he support this claim? How do you respond to it?

4. According to Jackson, how do economics play into the decisions Hollywood makes about the type of movies it produces? Who is to blame for this state of affairs—the ticket-buying public? The movie industry?

5. **Interrogating Assumptions.** Connect the assumptions that Sterritt and Jackson reveal about Hollywood's attitudes toward entertainment. What assumptions outlined in the chapter's introduction (pp. 361–69) best describe the most common assumptions in the Hollywood described by Sterritt and Jackson?

Writing about Cultural Practices

6. Develop a critical analysis about the images Hollywood constructs of people of color. Your instructor may decide to have the entire class focus on the same one or two films, which you will watch together. Consider the following questions as you develop your written analysis.

   - What kind of characters do the actors of color play in this film? What roles do their characters play in the overall plot or action of the film?

   - What is the context or setting within which these actors are encountered in this film?

   - What are the relationships between the actors of color and the white actors?

   - Do the interactions between characters of different races change in some way as the story develops? If so, how? What details in the movie support your interpretation?

   - How is humor used in the film? Is it in any way derogatory?

   - Do you consider the film to be stereotyping, patronizing, or racist? If so, support your opinion with evidence from the film. What major changes would you make to the film to remove these attitudes?

   - What is the relationship between the portrayal of people of color in this film and any assumptions or stereotypes about these groups that exist in American culture?

Ira Glass, **Howard and Me**

Ira Glass has hosted *This American Life* for National Public Radio since 1995. The success of *This American Life*, which broadcasts to over 400 radio stations and reaches over one million weekly listeners, prompted writer David Mamet to claim that "Glass seems to have reinvented radio."

After the infamous Janet Jackson/Justin Timberlake "wardrobe malfunction" during the half-time show of the 2003 Superbowl, the U.S. Congress and the Federal Communications Commission (FCC) made news with their decisions to establish tougher regulations on "indecent" material on television and radio. The following commentary by Glass, published in 2004 in the *New York Times*, makes the case that free speech—even if it is raunchy—is protected by the Constitution. The title of this essay refers to shock-jock Howard Stern whose radio show has been the target of record-breaking obscenity fines from the government. In part to free himself from FCC restrictions, Stern moved his popular radio show to the subscriber-based Sirius satellite radio network. Stern's rights have been defended by many TV and radio commentators. Referring to Stern as a "garbage man humorist," Joe Honig defended his right to free speech in the *Christian Science Monitor* (2004), saying, "Journalism, commentary, and drama are not always PG-rated endeavors."

> ### Mapping Your Reading
>
> In "Howard and Me," Glass relates his feeling of kinship to fellow radio personality Howard Stern. What is striking about this connection is that Glass hosts a thoughtfully researched and edited show on public radio while Stern represents for most people the quintessential shock-jock. As you read, pay attention to how Glass relates himself to Stern, someone who works in polar opposition to himself. How are these two radio hosts affected by tougher new FCC regulations? Why should we care about whether Stern is fined again or not? How does censorship affect everyday life in America?

L ast night I dreamed about Howard Stern again. He was disappointed in me, and ordered me out of his car. In my dreams, I never live up to Howard's standards.

I'm the host of a show on public radio, and when my listeners tell me they don't care for Stern, I always think it reveals a regrettable narrowness of vision. Mostly, they're put off by the naked girls. But Stern has invented a way of being on the air that uses the medium better than nearly anyone. He's more honest, more emotionally present, more interesting, more wide-ranging in his opinions than any host on public radio. Also, he's a fantastic interviewer. He's truly funny. And his staff on the air is cheerfully inclusive of every kind of person: black, white, dwarf, stutterer, drunk, and supposed gay. What public radio show has that kind of diversity?

Ira Glass

Getty Images/Scott Olson

Recently, in a show about testosterone, we stole the format Stern invented. On the air, our staff debated who among us probably has the most testosterone. Then we were tested. Then we opened the results on the air and tussled some more. That, in a nutshell, is the genius of Stern: You put all your regular characters into some situation; they argue; the situation takes a turn; they argue some more.

Sadly, lots of smart people shrug off the recent government crackdown on Howard Stern—and on other "indecency"—as if it were nastiness going on in some bad neighborhood of the broadcast dial, one that doesn't concern them, one that they'd never stoop to visit.

But the recent FCC rulings make me Stern's brother as I've never been before. Here are just a few of the things we've broadcast on our show that now could conceivably result in fines of up to a half million dollars for the 484 public stations that run the program: assorted curse words, people saying "damn" and "goddamn" (a recent FCC decision declared that "profane" and "blasphemous" speech would now come under scrutiny); various

Howard Stern

Getty Images/Paul Skipper

prison stories; and a very funny story by the writer David Sedaris that takes place in a bathroom and that violates all three FCC criteria for "indecency."

It's explicitly graphic in talking about "excretory organs or activities"; Sedaris repeats and dwells on the descriptions at length, and he absolutely means to pander and shock. That's what makes it funny.

In the past, the FCC would have considered context, the possible literary value or news value of apparently offensive material. And the agency still gives lip service to context in its current decisions. But when the commissioners declared in March that an expletive modifying the word "brilliant" (uttered by Bono at the Golden Globe Awards) was worthy of punishment, it made a more radical change in the rules than most people realize. Now context doesn't always matter. If a word on our show could increase a child's vocabulary, if some members of the public find something "grossly offensive," the FCC can issue fines.

> The FCC rulings make me Howard Stern's brother as I've never been before.

Because the whole process is driven by audience complaints, enforcement is arbitrary by design. Political expediency also seems to play a role. Stern has pointed out how a recent *Oprah* featured virtually the same words he uses but drew no fine. He urged his listeners to file complaints, to test whether the FCC will penalize only those it sees as vulnerable. Agency aides told *The Hollywood Reporter* that Oprah Winfrey was probably untouchable.

What's craziest about this new indecency witch hunt is that it's based on the premise that just one exposure to filthy words will damage a child. (I've yet to hear of a scientific study proving even that repeated exposure affects children.) Recently on my show, I asked one of the people who organizes write-in campaigns to the FCC, Brent Bozell, what harm it did anyone to see Janet Jackson's breast for a fleeting second, or to hear Stern use the phrase "anal sex," and he said it destroyed the "innocence of childhood." In our talk, Bozell used the phrase "anal sex" himself, presumably doing exactly as much harm to young people as Stern did on April 9, 2003.

That day, a brief conversation about the act on Stern's show drew $495,000 in fines. Bozell and I received no fines. No wonder Howard kicks me out of the car.

▶ **Analyzing the Text**

1. What does Glass admire about Stern and Stern's show? What does Stern represent for Glass, and why does Glass wish more people shared his view of Stern?

2. One of Glass's chief criticisms of the FCC's obscenity regulations is that they are enforced arbitrarily. How does Glass explain this, and why does he consider it to be a problem? What examples does he provide to support his point?

3. **Interrogating Assumptions.** In what ways do the points raised by Glass act as responses to the assumptions about entertainment that are described in the introduction to this chapter (pp. 361–69)?

Writing about Cultural Practices

4. How are FCC regulations interpreted on your campus or in your community? Investigate how federal regulation of the airwaves has affected your college radio station or public access television station. If your school does not have its own radio or television station, identify one within your community that you can use for this assignment. After investigating FCC and campus (or community) policies, write a position paper that takes a stand on FCC regulations regarding indecency versus protecting free speech. If possible, interview station managers and broadcasters from your campus or local community to ask their opinions about FCC regulations. Have they encountered any problems with FCC speech codes? As you research and write, consider the following questions.

   - How does the FCC define "indecency" for radio or television? What are the consequences for a radio or television station of being charged with indecency?

   - How have these regulations influenced your school or community's station? Provide examples from your research.

   - Can free speech be "indecent"? In other words, should indecent language be protected by the First Amendment?

   - What, if anything, would you change about the FCC's practices?

Sampling the Old and the New

TV Families: The Partridges vs. The Osbournes

On the television show *The Partridge Family*, actress Shirley Jones portrayed the single mother and bandleader of five musically gifted and remarkably wholesome children. The show costarred David Cassidy as the heart-throb Keith, Susan Dey as the fresh-faced Lori, and Danny Bonaduce as the wisecracking Danny, who, along with the band's bus driver and manager, Mr. Kincaid, represented the show's comic relief. The popularity of *The Partridge Family*, which premiered in September 1970, launched a number of hit records and a product line that included the ubiquitous Partridge-themed lunchbox.

In contrast to the Partridges are the Osbournes, a real and arguably self-promoting musical family. Starring as themselves on their notorious "reality" show, *The Osbournes*, Sharon and Ozzy, along with two of their children, Kelly and Jack, and various pooches, give us a look at the home life of the bleary-eyed, bat-biting, heavy-metal rocker Ozzy Osbourne. First airing in 2000 on MTV, the tagline of the show is "they put the funk into dysfunctional."

1. What do these very different portrayals of musical families—one from 1970 and one from 2000—suggest about changing our cultural attitudes toward family? What messages do these images suggest about popular notions of conformity and nonconformity?

2. Can you think of a contemporary TV family that is similar in some way to *The Partridge Family*? If so, compare the typical problems faced by the Partridges versus the modern

TV family. How are the families' conflicts resolved? What conclusions can you draw about the different time periods that produced these shows?

3. Can you think of a TV family from the past that is parallel to *The Osbournes*? If so, choose an episode of each show and compare the plot lines and jokes. What are the differences and similarities between how the shows convey humor? Explain, using specific quotes.

Kevin Arnovitz, **Virtual Dictionary**

Kevin Arnovitz is an editor and contributor to *Slate*. Overseeing *Slate*'s readers' forum, Arnovitz has compiled weblog responses for National Public Radio's *Day to Day*. "Virtual Dictionary" was published in *Slate* on September 14, 2004. As the subtitle of the original piece suggests, this essay offers "a guide to the language of reality TV."

Mapping Your Reading

Arnovitz's glossary explains the production language that he had to learn when he was hired as a writer for a reality television show. As you read, pay attention to how this insider's view deconstructs what appears to be "reality" in these shows. What about reality television is "real"?

In what was later determined to be a network clerical error, I was hired [one] summer as a writer and producer on a political reality series. A writer on a reality show must, as a means of professional survival, have a healthy sense of self-irony—writing for reality is sort of like being a fluffer on *The Sorrow and the Pity*.

As the only member of a 50-person crew who had never worked on a reality show, I had to learn the language of reality TV, which, like most professional worlds, has a nomenclature all its own. For the layman watching *The Amazing Race* or *Big Brother* at home each week, here's a list of terms that may help you better understand the reality behind the reality on your television.

Frankenbite (n): An edited reality show snippet, most often found in contestant testimonials, that splices together several disparate strands of an interview, or even multiple interviews, into a single clip. A frankenbite allows editors to manufacture "story" (see definition below) efficiently and dramatically by extracting the salient elements of a lengthy, nuanced interview or exchange into a seemingly blunt, revealing confession or argument. While the frankenbite's origins certainly don't reside in reality TV, this is a reality show editor's most potent tool for manipulating viewer perception of a contestant. Usage: *"Man, they amped up that catfight with that vicious frankenbite of Margo."*

For another reading on reality TV, see Pozner, page 442.—Eds.

Challenge Producer (n): A tactician brought in by a reality show to produce a game within the larger framework of the program, say a reward challenge in *Survivor* involving an intricate obstacle course or a gross-out buffet. The challenge producer's responsibilities include creating said game, testing the game, explaining the game to the contestants, and overseeing the running of the game. Many of the first challenge producers came from the game show world. Today, many are coming into the industry as segment producers from previous reality shows.

Date Producer (n): A specialist—similar, in this sense, to a **challenge producer**—who excels in the creative orchestration of rendezvous for reality dating shows. The responsibilities of a date producer often include coaxing confessions from the participants, cultivating jealousies, and ensuring that the participants becomes sufficiently wasted so that they will make all the miscues essential to a dating show—hooking up, revealing intimate details about their sexual histories, and otherwise behaving sordidly. A persistent reality-TV-world myth is that attractive people are passed over for positions as date producers because production companies fear that a contestant may fall for the date producer instead of his or her intended date.

OTF (n) ["On the Fly"]: A quick, impromptu interview of a reality show contestant intended to convey the contestant's emotions and actions in the moment, as opposed to the more reflective sit-down interview. An OTF is always shot with a handheld camera, sometimes even in motion—while walking and talking—and often in a moving vehicle. Usage: *"Brian, make sure the field crews get some OTFs of the candidates back at the hotel after the debate."* If an OTF spirals out of control and lasts really, really long, it becomes a **hybrid**—something between an OTF and a formal interview. This really pisses off the camera operator because he's holding about 15 or 20 pounds of equipment on his shoulder.

Money Shot (n): The pivotal footage from a reality show shoot that will provide a dramatic climax for an episode's key segment. Money shots often consist of a clip showing a reality show contestant breaking down and crying during his or her post-elimination OTF or, say, visibly failing in the face of adversity in a physical or mental challenge—i.e., tripping and falling on an obstacle course, or cursing out a fellow housemate in an impromptu argument. Usage: *"Gary, did you get the money shot of Sarah tearing up after she was voted off?"*

Pelco (n): A camera mounted inside a room—especially popular on "house shows"—and controlled by a joystick from a behind-the-scenes control room. The Pelco's main function is surveillance, but it records as well. And since the Pelco is impossible for contestants to hide from, it provides invaluable broadcast-quality footage for producers. As if this weren't creepy and Orwellian enough, the Pelco also has night-vision capacity, which allows producers to peek in on contestants after dark. Usage: *"If that segment isn't working as is, then see if we can work in some of the Pelco stuff to jazz it up."*

Pre-Cap (n): An interview of a reality show contestant before (often en route to) a major event—say, a press conference—that captures the anticipatory giddiness of the contestant. If the crew is able to get some film on the contestant in the course of the event, that's called a **mid-cap.** A snippet from a mid-cap might be, "It's going really well here! I'm really surprised at how well people are responding to what I have to say!" A reflective interview after the fact is called, quite sensibly, a **recap.**

Reality (n) [also *Vérité*]: Footage of reality show contestants going about their business, generally in their natural habitat—the tribal camp, the common space of "the house," the war room, etc. The purpose of "reality" is to capture spontaneous interactions, conversations, machinations, and expressions of the contestants. For this reason, producers sometimes orchestrate reality shots in various other casual settings, such as restaurants, bars, or parties where contestants are encouraged to unwind (occasionally through the use of alcohol). Usage: *"After we take care of the scripted beats, let's make sure we shoot some reality—and see if we can catch Simon dishing on the other contestants."* Note: Some more highbrow reality companies, whose principals' origins are rooted in legitimate documentary work, use the terms "*vérité*" and "reality" interchangeably.

Sequester (v): To quarantine reality show contestants in their hotel rooms/campgrounds/house without access to telephone or the Internet. A producer's decision to sequester contestants is often driven by crew schedules: crews, charged with the responsibility of chaperoning contestants virtually around the clock, require some downtime—even on a non-union reality production. But sequestering is seldom used, because most producers worry that, were contestants to roam freely, unmiked and unfilmed, substantial plot could materialize and be lost. Being sequestered also infuriates reality show contestants who will invariably bitch that sequestering violates the very spirit of "reality" TV. Because, after all, shouldn't they be able to behave as they would in, you know, reality? Usage: *"Field crews A, B, D, and F have been on the clock since 7 this morning. What are we gonna do with their contestants tonight? Sequester them, I guess."*

Story (n): What drives a reality show narrative, including but not limited to: conflict, character, gamesmanship, and "heart." "Story" is the small percentage of stuff that can be shaped into a narrative from the hundreds of hours of tape collected by field crews. The term, as used by reality show producers, often refers to an attribute or skill, much like gravitas or charisma—i.e., a producer who has the ability to anticipate what that material will be while still in the field "knows story." Senior editors and executive producers are forever on the lookout for resourceful young field producers who "really understand story"—in other words, who get which images and sound bites will make a narrative work. Usage: *"If we're talking about which field producers to hang onto, we gotta consider Omar; that dude really gets story."*

Analyzing the Text

1. Having read Arnovitz's glossary of the inner workings of reality television production, what would you say is *real* about reality television?

2. In the production of reality television, the term "reality" actually refers to specific types of footage. How does Arnovitz explain this? And in turn, how should viewers interpret what they are watching?

3. Which terms in the glossary most reveal how producers manipulate people and situations to create the storylines they want?

4. How do editing and the use of specific camera shots provide different effects that producers can use to help them tell a particular story?

5. Arnovitz uses the format of dictionary entries to provide his explanation of how reality television is produced. How effective is this, rhetorically? How would his argument change—what would be lost or gained—if he had written in a conventional essay style?

Writing about Cultural Practices

6. Develop a critical analysis of a reality TV show that answers the question, What assumptions about the role or purpose of entertainment does this show rely on to keep people watching? To begin, watch several episodes of a reality show of your choice and investigate additional information on the show's official website. As you develop your analysis, consider the following questions.

   - How does this show use techniques described in "Virtual Dictionary"?

   - What is "real" about this reality show? To what extent does it construct a particular "reality"?

   - What specific beliefs and relationships does this show encourage? What details about the show lead you to your analysis?

Jennifer L. Pozner, **The Unreal World**

Jennifer L. Pozner is executive director of Women In Media & News, a media monitoring, education, and advocacy organization. She has published articles for *Ms.*, the *Chicago Tribune*, and *Salon*. Pozner has appeared as a commentator on Comedy Central's *The Daily Show with Jon Stewart* and on Fox News Network's *The O'Reilly Factor*, and has lectured to audiences across the country about media and gender issues. In "The Unreal World," originally published in *Ms.* in 2004, Pozner argues that reality TV presents harmful messages about the intrinsic worth of women and men as people. Using detailed descriptions from reality TV shows, she concludes, "Underneath their pretty promises of 'true love' and 'fairytale' transformations, producers construct these shows to drive home the notion that no emotional, professional, or political accomplishment can possibly compare with the twin vocations of beauty and marriage."

▶ **Mapping Your Reading**

In the following essay, Pozner analyzes how women are portrayed on reality TV shows. As you read, pay attention to the basic categories or stereotypes of women she identifies, and underline passages in which Pozner names and explains these stereotypes most effectively. What specific beliefs and assumptions about women does reality television encourage? What specific beliefs and assumptions about race or class does reality television encourage?

In the recently defanged revamp of *The Stepford Wives*, impossibly thin, impeccably dressed, and intellectually vapid women exist for no other reason than to cater to their husbands' every desire, delivering fresh-baked cookies and midday nookie with equal aplomb.

The film banked over $30 million in its first week of release, but if viewers wanted to watch independent women reduced to domestic drones they could have kept their cash and turned on "reality TV." Nearly every night, on every network, dating, mating, and makeover shows routinely glorify the same stereotypes lampooned in *Stepford*.

For another reading on reality TV, see Arnovitz, page 438.—EDS.

On ABC's *The Bachelor,* a husband-hunting harem competes to marry a hunky lunkhead. "Ugly ducklings" risk their health to be surgically altered on Fox's *The Swan* and ABC's *Extreme Makeover.*

Women of color are ostracized for being "difficult" on UPN's *America's Next Top Model,* while slurs like "bitch" and "beaver" are tossed around freely on NBC's *Average Joe* and *For Love or Money.*

The more profitable so-called unscripted programming grows, the more poisonous its representations of women become. Back in 2000, when Darva Conger wed (and quickly ditched) a purportedly rich stranger on Fox's *Who Wants to Marry a Multi-Millionaire,* the stunt was roundly criticized as cheap and chauvinistic, and the network promised to stop airing such exploitative fare.

Yet by February 2003, Fox was devoting 41 percent of its "sweeps" offerings to reality shows. *Multi-Millionaire* producer Mike Darnell was promoted to executive VP of alternative programming, creating *Married by America* (women get engaged to strangers by slipping their ring fingers through a hole in a wall on a TV soundstage) and *Joe Millionaire* (a supposedly rich guy turns out to be a financial Average Joe).

> The more profitable the programming becomes, the more poisonous its representations of women.

Forty million viewers made the latter show's finale Fox's highest rated entertainment program ever. It's easy to understand what network execs see in reality shows—high ratings, low production costs, and lucrative product-placement revenues—and why they deny that the shows are meaningful in any other way.

Occasionally, though, someone unwittingly tells the truth, as Darnell did when he informed *Entertainment Weekly* that the formula for every successful reality show is an easily understandable premise steeped in some social belief that provokes an audience reaction of "Oh, my god! . . . What's wrong with you?"

Brainiac in a Bikini?

Viewers may be drawn to reality TV by a sort of cinematic schadenfreude, but they continue to tune in because these shows frame their narratives in ways that both reflect and reinforce deeply ingrained societal biases about women, men, love, beauty, class, and race. The genre teaches us that women categorically "are" certain things—for example, no matter their age, they're "hot girls," not self-aware or intelligent adults.

To prove them desirably dumb, old-time game-show host Wink Martindale conducted a condescending "smarts test" on NBC's *Meet My Folks,* scolding female contestants who incorrectly answered questions like "When was the War of 1812?" or "How many days are there in a typical year?"

Yet when women aren't embarrassingly stupid, they're condemned for being smart: Just before eliminating medical student Elyse from UPN's *America's Next Top Model,* host Tyra Banks chided, "One thing with [your] intelligence is that it can intimidate people."

No one wants to see a brainiac in a bikini in reality television. In this unreal world, women aren't just stupid—they're also catty and bitchy.

"The backstabbing begins!" a *Bachelor* promo announces. Cats hiss as a *Joe Millionaire* preview promises, "The claws come out." "Girls can be conniving, deceiving, and vicious," one harem girl says; "I know better than to trust women," another echoes.

Extended intros and "stay-tuned" teasers teach us that women are "money-grubbing, gold-digging whores," as one *Bachelor* babe was described. If reality TV portrays women as whores, then the networks are their pimps, providing men with sexy singles in hopes they'll get frisky on cue, as on Fox's tawdry *Temptation Island*.

> **"The backstabbing begins! The claws come out. Who will get sent home brokenhearted?"**

Media profit off of women's humiliation, as in *Married by America*'s climactic money shot, where cameras close in on the tear-soaked face of a jilted bride as she stares off into space, glassy-eyed and broken, whispering, "I'm a joke."

The Bachelor's cheerfully cruel teaser, "Who will get sent home brokenhearted? Find out!" is repeated ad nauseum, and in reunion specials, alumnae rejectees are forced to watch mortifying montages of their most pitiful moments ("I'm a loser!"), while the host says in mock concern: "Wow, that must be uncomfortable for you."

Weepers, Sluts, and Divas

The same themes pop up, often verbatim, in nearly every reality series, belying claims of unscripted storytelling. Producers cast for type, choosing contestants they can mold into a predetermined slate of characters.

There's the Antagonizer, who declares she's "not here to make friends"; the naive Waif, who's "searching for my Prince Charming"; the Slut who plots to "take our connection to the next level" in the "fantasy suite"; and the wretched Weeper who wonders, when she's dumped, "What's so wrong with me that someone cannot love me?"

These characters behave as crassly as they do in large part because producers of shows such as *The Bachelor* deprive them of all contact with the outside world (participants are not allowed to read newspapers, watch TV, listen to the radio, or make phone calls while filming) and ply them with alcohol, then goad them to unleash their petty grievances in filmed "confessionals."

Misleading production tricks top off the editorial sleight of hand. According to the Bravo exposé *The Reality of Reality*, when Joe Millionaire ditched the cameras to sneak off into the woods with one woman, producers threw the words "ummm," "slurp," and "gulp" on-screen, along with "chikachika-pow-wow" music and dialogue recorded on another day, all to (falsely) imply that his date performed oral sex to get her hands on his, er, cash.

Not only are the women cast on these shows supposed to be hot, dumb, and licentious, but they're also, for the most part, white. Producers manufacture a fractured reality that looks nothing like America.

Women of color are tokenized and often eliminated shortly after each series debut. Non-Western features are reprimanded, then "corrected": A black woman's lips were reduced on *Extreme Makeover*, *The Swan* "softened" an Asian woman's eyes, and *American Idol* judge Simon Cowell repeatedly asserted that African American singer Kimberly Locke didn't have the right "image" to become a pop star—until *Idol* stylists relaxed her kinky hair.

"Ever since you got rid of that weird hair, you got better. You look cute now!" Cowell crowed.

When included in any prolonged way, women of color are used to stroke classic racial stereotypes. On *Profiles from the Front Line*, a show that followed U.S. troops in Afghanistan, the only black woman featured was portrayed as the military's mammy—a cook who described herself as "a bitch in the kitchen" who enjoys keeping soldier boys "happy and fed."

More common is the hypersensitive "sista with attitude" whom everyone hates, such as *Apprentice* villain Omarosa Manigault-Stallworth and *Top Model* diva Camille McDonald.

Ethnicity isn't the only cultural indicator whitewashed on reality TV, where modern fairy tales marinate in socioeconomic anxiety. On NBC's *Meet My Folks*, parents choose their sons' dates from among a gaggle of girlie girls who sleep in the "folks" lavish homes, languish by their pools, and make out in their hot tubs.

The catch? The mini-mansions do not belong to "the folks," whom producers relocate so as to erase any trace of an ordinary, middle-class lifestyle.

But that's not surprising, since love and finance are inextricably linked in these shows. A bevy of gorgeous "girls" is invariably matched with one "rich, successful" bachelor (or a penniless poser). During their "romantic journeys," hopeful brides are decked out in expensive gowns, ferried about in horse-drawn carriages, and festooned with Harry Winston diamonds.

> Love and finance are inextricably linked in these shows.

The call of these luxury contrivances is powerful—and infantilizing. There's something ridiculous about watching grown women masquerading as would-be Cinderellas hoping to snag some suburban Prince Charming.

Where women are valued as "perfect 10s" simply for being pretty, passive, and intellectually unthreatening, reality TV tells us that all men need is wealth— their own, or an illusion borrowed from producers—to be Mr. Right. Sometimes they literally ride in on a white horse, other times in a pricey sports car.

Forget about decency, honesty, or intelligence—the primary criteria to qualify as a reality-TV Prince is a firm ass and a firmer financial portfolio. This standard not only demeans women, but thoroughly underestimates men's inherent worth as people.

Further, reality-TV "studs" are praised when they're downright degrading to their female pursuers. Joe Millionaire made his dates shovel horse shit in their fancy clothing, while one of NBC's Average Joes called the woman he was wooing a "beaver" behind her back ("It's a slang term meaning a very beautiful, hot, sexy girl," he insisted).

Most egregious was *For Love or Money*'s Rob Campos, who got drunk and made a woman bend over and remove his boots while he kicked her in the ass. Producers might have predicted such behavior if they'd done a background check: Campos was booted out of the Marines for groping a female officer while intoxicated.

Flaw Finders

Dangerous beauty myths are fundamental to the reality universe, where women are unworthy of love and happiness if they're not stereotypical hot babes. This was confirmed on *Married by America* when cameras followed a couple into their bedroom and spied the woman begging her withholding "fiancé" for sex.

Women are unworthy of love if they're not stereotypical hot babes.

"I don't understand," she whispered to him, her insecurities amplified in subtitles. "I'm successful. I have a good personality. Or, do you want me to wear sexier clothes and lose 30 pounds, too?"

Women's reality-TV worth is literally weighed and measured, as when judges on ABC's short-lived *Are You Hot?: The Search for America's Sexiest People* aimed a laser "flaw finder" at the bodies of scantily clad women to determine who scored a 9.9 for "face, body and sex appeal," and who rated only a lowly 5.3.

On *America's Next Top Model*, frighteningly underweight girls were praised for their gangly physiques, while standard-sized contestants were derided as "plus-sized" at 5 foot 8 and 130 pounds.

The Swan—which shows women going under the knife for an absurd number of potentially dangerous plastic surgery procedures—institutionalizes eating disorders by forcing women who are barely overweight to exercise excessively and go on 1,300-calorie-a-day diets.

When one contestant protests because "I think I look really damn good," her coach—series creator Nely Galan—angrily labels her self-acceptance as laziness.

More disturbingly, *The Swan* promises to transform emotionally at-risk women "from the inside out" by sending them to a therapist—who actually got her Ph.D. from an unaccredited "diploma mill."

Perhaps that's why "counseling" sessions seemed more like harassment ("Stick to the program!" "Stop complaining!"), and why this "doctor" endorsed liposuction as a way to help a former battered woman "break the cycle of violence."

New-Millennium Backlash

Frivolous as reality TV may seem, the psychological browbeating these shows engage in has political ramifications. They reinforce insecurities bred into women by decades of inaccurate media reports of "man shortages" and broken-down biological clocks.

"You always hear those horror stories: 40 and single! I don't want that!" said one booted bachelorette. The genre's scare message to self-sufficient women is that they need to make themselves as attractive and nonthreatening as possible, or else Mr. Right will be snatched up by one of 24 cuter and more compliant chicks, and they will be left alone and miserable.

Welcome to the backlash, new-millennium style.

Underneath their pretty promises of "true love" and "fairytale" transformations, producers construct these shows to drive home the notion that no emotional, professional, or political accomplishment can possibly compare with the twin vocations of beauty and marriage.

They want women to think like June Cleaver, look like Miss America, and—in a nod to modernity—have sex like Madonna. Hello, Stepford.

Apologists claim reality TV isn't sexist because no one *forces* women to appear on these shows. But the impact on the shows' participants is almost beside the point: The real concern is the millions of viewers, scores of whom are young girls, who take in these misogynistic spectacles uncritically, learning that only the most stereotypically beautiful, least independent women with the lowest-carb diets will be rewarded with love, financial security, and the ultimate prize of male validation.

Perhaps saddest of all, real love is almost wholly absent from these artificial mating dances. What little girl dreams of being whisked away by a callous, egotistical dimwit who sticks his tongue down 15 other women's throats before he reluctantly settles for her?

After all the happily-ever-after buildup, every bachelor has dumped his "chosen girl" shortly after their series wrapped production. That's the thing about fairy tales . . . *they're not real*.

In the end, these programs present a trivial and depressing depiction of the concept of love itself. The equation Fat Wallet + Skinny Chick = Love robs us all of our humanity, and erases the possibility of true emotional connection.

> # FOUND
>
> from beonrealitytv.com
>
> ## MTV REALITY SHOW AUDITIONS
>
> - Want to Work for a Hollywood Heavyweight?
> - Want Revenge on Someone Who Has Done You Wrong?
> - Need Help with a Life-Altering Decision?
> - Can You Keep a Secret?
> - How Are You Spending Your Spring Break?
> - Got No Game with the Ladies?
> - Got Amazing Game with the Ladies?
> - Ever Wish You Could Contact the Dead?
> - Do You Work a Crazy Job in Vegas?
> - Are You the Ultimate Hook-Up Artist?
> - Are You into Your Car, and We Mean Waaaay into Your Car?

Analyzing the Text

1. Pozner argues that the women on reality TV fall into one of three categories: Weepers, Sluts, and Divas. How does she support this claim? How do you respond to it?

2. According to Pozner, how are issues of race whitewashed by reality TV shows?

3. Why do so many reality TV shows take place in mansions or feature lavish lifestyles for the contestants? In Pozner's view, how do these settings add to the constructedness of the "reality" in these shows? What do they suggest about contemporary attitudes or anxieties about financial status?

4. How are men presented in these programs? What does Pozner find most troubling about how men are portrayed?

5. **Connecting to Another Reading.** In "Virtual Dictionary" (p. 438), Kevin Arnovitz explains many of the editing techniques used to construct or create the storylines of reality TV shows. Working with both the Arnovitz and Pozner readings, what conclusions can you make about what specific beliefs, actions, and relationships these shows encourage?

▶ **Writing about Cultural Practices**

6. Can reality television show positive images of social relationships? Write a persuasive description of a brand-new concept for a reality TV show that would be an alternative to those currently on the air. Your persuasive description (also known as a "treatment," in TV terms) should begin with a paragraph that conveys the basic premise of your show, why it is a good idea, and what it will do that other shows do not. Your audience for your document is a group of network television producers; your purpose in writing your document is to persuade them to pilot your show. Consider the following questions as you develop your treatment.

   - What is the context of the show?
   - What activities would the participants engage in? How would they be encouraged or expected to interact?
   - What would the goals of your alternative show be? What beliefs and assumptions about social relationships would it rely on?
   - What attitudes about gender, race, and social status would your program convey? Explain.
   - Who is your target audience? How would your show meet some need not already met by other programming?

Hemal Jhaveri, **Queer Eye: Searching for a Real Gay Man**

Hemal Jhaveri is a Web designer and writer. Her article "Searching for a Real Gay Man" was originally published in 2003 on PopPolitics.com, a site that explores the connections between popular culture and politics. Previously relegated to supporting roles or minor storylines, today's television programming includes examples of sitcoms, dramas, talk shows, and reality TV shows that feature gays and lesbians in central roles. In 2005, media conglomerate Viacom is set to launch a gay- and lesbian-themed television network called Logo. Yet many critics, like Jhaveri, argue that images of gays in the mainstream media remain rooted in unhelpful, and ultimately damaging, stereotypes.

> ▶ **Mapping Your Reading**
>
> In this essay, Jhaveri examines how television and popular media represents gay men. As you read, pay attention to the author's analysis of gay stereotypes, and underline passages where she makes her case most effectively. As Jhaveri points out, the number of gay-themed shows and characters continues to grow, but how effective are they at "changing and challenging long-held stereotypes"?

A few weeks ago, over a mostly liquid Sunday brunch of Bloody Mary's and Mimosa's, a friend of mine leaned across the table and exclaimed, "You so wish you were a gay man." The comment, while a little out of the blue, was not entirely off target.

There are plenty of straight women, who, like me, harbor some version of the same fantasy. With the current media frenzy over gay culture presenting images that are irresistible, can you blame us?

Gay male characters on television are something of a hip staple these days, but despite their ubiquitous presence, the representations of gay men have been disconcertingly one-dimensional. Few shows, if any, and certainly none on network TV, have presented well-defined, complicated gay characters that might challenge existing perceptions of gay culture and masculinity. Unfortunately, by only reinforcing perceptions

Few shows have presented well-defined, complicated gay characters.

that viewers are already comfortable with, a vast majority of these shows preserve the status quo rather then challenge it.

When it debuted, jumping into an already over-crowded genre, the "make better, not over" reality show *Queer Eye for the Straight Guy* brought the joys of being gay to a whole new audience. Carson, Thom, Kyan, Jai, and Ted, the queer eyes who seem to have kicked off the current cultural infatuation with gayness, function like ambassadors of homosexuality to the straight world. They seem to have woo-ed an entire nation (or at least a large portion of straight women) with their charm and wit, as if daring Middle America to dislike them.

The men are bitingly funny and catty and snarky in the way that your best girlfriends are, but with much better punch lines. In one episode Thom snipes about the décor of a straight guy's apartment: "You've heard of minimalism right? Well . . . this is bleak." And then there's Carson on a newly made over space: "Oh look! You put a living room where the crack den used to be." Watching the show, you can't help but giggle along.

Queer Eye treads lightly when it comes to acknowledging the stereotypes to which all five guys play. Kyan (the grooming guy) approached the topic with make-over candidate John, as he received a day at the spa. Kyan asks, "What would your friends back in Virginia say if they saw you like this?" The fully wrapped and relaxed John replies, "That probably can't be repeated on TV." Indeed, while John appears genuinely grateful to have the experience, he acknowledges the perception that it seems "kind of girly."

With *Queer Eye*, the underlying message seems to be that "if you just got to know us, you'd love us," and this strikes me as being quite possibly true. With its affable hosts, disarming charm, and bitchy, but well-meaning, wit, *Queer Eye* feels like an especially well-executed marketing campaign for homosexuality. I'll admit that I've been won over. *Queer Eye* makes for great television viewing, but it's wholly dismissive (and far too easy) to assume that's where gay culture begins and ends.

By clinging to existing stereotypes, and mainly seeing all gay people as savants of style, we marginalize and dilute the complicated lives of many. In ignoring gay men's sexuality, we project a condescending tolerance of a lifestyle, implying that homosexuality is all well and good, unless it actually involves sex.

> **Homosexuality is all well and good, unless it actually involves sex.**

Queer Eye seems to be the rule for gay men on TV: cute, white, charming, and totally asexual. But there are a few, though not very prominent, exceptions that challenge the rules.

Keith, from HBO's *Six Feet Under,* is one of the most compelling and well-developed gay characters on TV. A gay, African American ex-cop with a mean temper, he hardly fits into the mold that is currently being fashioned via *Queer Eye.* While Keith's sexuality is important in defining him, it isn't the only characteristic we view him with. We're shown the complete picture of a man, with depth, dimension, and ambiguity. In addition to being gay, Keith is also a loving father figure, a son, and an officer with his own authority issues.

In a scene from last season, Keith and his partner David attended a brunch with mostly other gay men, where they play a party game called Leading Ladies. The game embodies a stereotypical camp factor, asking party-goers to guess the names of various Hollywood starlets. David, Keith's partner, quickly dispenses with his turn, while Keith struggles. By the end, Keith is so uncomfortable and obviously out of place, that a woman mockingly asks, "Are you sure you're gay?" The brunch scene underscores tensions already building up in David and Keith's volatile relationship, but we're subtly shown that there exists an established culture that not everyone fits into. It's this depiction of a gay character existing outside of his sexuality and the stereotypes that come with it that is fascinating to watch and so rarely seen on television.

Cable networks like HBO and Showtime have embraced the same sex relationship, but one of the rare instances on network TV was found, surprisingly enough, on CBS's reality show *The Amazing Race*. While *Will and Grace* gets credit for breaking the genre wide open, and NBC now runs half-hour versions of *Queer Eye* in a prime time slot, neither of these shows present an extended look at a committed same sex relationship (although Will does try periodically). *The Amazing Race* flew in under the radar this summer and offered viewers the voyeuristic pleasure of spying on relationships under pressure.

Chip and Reichen, the gay couple that won the race around the world, were identified as "married." Whether the labeling was a calculated move to generate interest in the show or not, it caused a ripple of controversy with conservative action groups like the American Decency Association and sparked more than a few heated discussions on Internet forums about the validity of such a claim.

Despite some grumbling, viewers had the opportunity to see the internal dynamics of a committed gay relationship, and surprise surprise; it wasn't that different from what we'd expect from a heterosexual one. If anything, Reichen and Chip's relationship differed in that it was annoyingly perfect and—except for a brief incident involving Reichen's foot being run over—conflict-free. They exhibited none of the dysfunction (Mille and Chuck) and bickering (Kelly and Jon) that marked almost every other romantic couple on the race. At one point, describing his relationship with Reichen, Chip sweetly said: "Reichen and I are just clicking without even asking, which is a really nice thing. We just do things for each other and don't step on each other's toes and realize that it's all for the same goal."

Filtered through the magic of editing or not, what viewers were left with on screen was a portrait of a healthy, supportive, loving, and mutually respectful relationship. We should all be so lucky. The show presented them as fiercely competitive, aggressive in nature, and physically fit. Reichen and Chip challenged the stereotypes that all gay men are good for is fashion advice and snarky remarks.

While Reichen and Chip are married, though, we never saw them exchange a kiss. The gay-themed programming we're seeing now offers up a straight sanitized version of homosexuality, one that excludes all mention of, well, sex. Bravo, for example, kept *Boy Meets Boy* as asexual as possible. It may be the only dating show that had an explicit "no sex" rule. Participants were allowed to kiss each other, but a few episodes in and viewers had yet to see a simple smooch between any of the gay (or straight, when that turned out to be the case) participants and James. The only person James repeatedly kissed was gal pal Andra.

The social taboo that exists between same sex couples kissing or showing any kind of physical affection towards each other is so strong that it's presented a somewhat warped perspective on homosexuality. The current line of programming seems to suggest that gay men are only different from heterosexual men in that they have a better sense of style and a better sense of humor. While acts of lesbian sexuality have held a more accepted and erotic image in the sexual mythology of American culture, there still exist strong social taboos surrounding men kissing other men. Showtime's *Queer as Folk,* a series about a group of gay men, can be intimidating with its aggressive sexuality, but the explicit portrayals present an honest look at the characters' lives, one that viewers aren't always comfortable with.

By prime time standards, gay sexuality is something that audiences don't seem to be ready for. Yet, if networks continue to ignore the topic and treat sex as the dirty little secret of homosexuality, that's best not seen or heard of, it sends the message that homosexuality is indeed something best swept under the rug and not discussed honestly.

This inequality between what's presented on TV and accepted in real life is all the more apparent when the issue of legalizing gay marriages comes up. One of the reasons I so enjoyed watching Chip and Richen on *The Amazing Race* was seeing them interact as a couple and realizing that behind the label of being gay, there existed two individuals, not caricatures, which is what a lot of shows seem to present us with.

This current trend in programming may just be a passing fad, or it could lead to a more lasting, even-handed reflection of the gay community (one that may actually include a lesbian), but as of now they do little to combat people's preexisting prejudices.

Unfortunately, it looks like this static trend in programming will continue. ABC's sitcom *It's All Relative* has two gay parents at the center of its show, but it, too, is contrived and stereotypical. As expected, the gay men are shown as uptight, flamboyant, neat freaks paired with equally stereotypical Irish in-laws, presented as loud, crass, buffoonish drunks. Bring on the laughs!

The number of gay themed programs and gay characters on television continues to grow, but how effective they are at changing and challenging long-held stereotypes is debatable. The problem now isn't one of exposure, but of seeing more complicated and varying depictions of gay men and women.

▶ Analyzing the Text

1. According to Jhaveri, how does the mainstream entertainment media represent gay people and gay culture? What passages best illustrate her argument about the media's portrayal of gays?

2. Jhaveri describes the reality show *Queer Eye for the Straight Guy* as an "especially well-executed marketing campaign for homosexuality." Do you agree? Why or why not? According to Jhaveri, what assumptions or beliefs about homosexuality does *Queer Eye* market?

3. What issues or aspects about gay culture are not made visible on gay-themed television programs? How does this absence affect the overall view mainstream America has on what it means to be gay?

4. **Connecting to Another Reading.**   Kevin Arnovitz's "Virtual Dictionary" (p. 438) provides a glossary of camera work and storytelling devices used in reality television. What connections do you see between that reality TV glossary and how Jhaveri argues gay men are portrayed on reality TV?

5. **Connecting to Another Reading.**   What, if any, connections do you see between the critique Jennifer Pozner makes in "The Unreal World" (p. 442) about how women are portrayed in reality television and Jhaveri's analysis of how gay culture is portrayed?

▶ Writing about Cultural Practices

6. Originally published at poppolitics.com, the online version of Jhaveri's essay includes links to additional perspectives on the portrayal of gays and lesbians in the media, including a link to the website of the Media Awareness Network. Go to bedfordstmartins.com/remix, Chapter 5, to read a collection of brief essays published by Media Awareness, beginning with "Representations of Gays and Lesbians on Television." Then, choose one additional essay from the Media Awareness collection on how the media stereotypes one of these groups: ethnic minorities, aboriginal people, girls and women, men and masculinity, or whiteness and white privilege. Write a critical analysis in which you compare the portrayal of gays and lesbians with one of the groups listed above. As you write, consider the following questions.

   • How are characters on television defined by their ethnicity, gender, or sexuality? What tactics or common practices do popular television shows use to identify a character as gay or as belonging to the other group you have chosen?

   • What cultural assumptions and attitudes about these two groups do television producers rely on to create their characters?

   • What cultural values or messages do these stereotypes help to support? What is the impact of these stereotypes?

ON THE WEB
For more on stereotypical representations in the media, go to Chapter 5,
bedfordstmartins.com/remix

Sarah Vowell, **Pop-A-Shot**

Sarah Vowell is a best-selling author and contributing editor of National Public Radio's *This American Life*. Recognized by the *New York Times* for her "funny querulous voice and shrewd comic delivery," Vowell has published articles on popular culture and politics for *Esquire*, *GQ*, *Artforum*, *Spin*, and the *Los Angeles Times*. She has authored four books: *Radio On: A Listener's Diary* (1997), *Take the Cannoli: Stories from the New World* (2001), *The Partly Cloudy Patriot* (2003), and *Assassination Vacation* (2005). This reading is an excerpt from *The Partly Cloudy Patriot*. In it, Vowell provides a humorous look at the role of the game Pop-A-Shot in her life and the lives of her friends.

> ▶ **Mapping Your Reading**
>
> In this essay, Vowell praises what she calls our "innate American ability to celebrate the civic virtue of idiocy." Her description of playing hooky with friends to play a game called Pop-A-Shot is driven by the question, "Why do people love pointless activities so much?" As you read, place checkmarks beside passages in which Vowell offers answers to this question: Does an activity have to be "socially redeeming" to have entertainment value? What needs does Pop-A-Shot fulfill for Vowell?

A long with voting, jury duty, and paying taxes, goofing off is one of the central obligations of American citizenship. So when my friends Joel and Stephen and I play hooky from our jobs in the middle of the afternoon to play Pop-A-Shot in a room full of children, I like to think we are not procrastinators; we are patriots pursuing happiness.

Pop-A-Shot is not a video game. It involves shooting real, if miniature, basketballs for 40 seconds. It's embarrassing how giddy the three of us get when it's our turn to put money into the machine. (Often, we have to stand behind some six-year-old girl who bogarts the game and whose father keeps dropping in quarters even though the kid makes only about 4 points if she's lucky and we are forced to glare at the back of her pigtailed head, waiting just long enough to start questioning our adulthood and how by the time our parents were our age they were beholden to mortgages and PTA meetings and here we are, stuck in an episode of *Friends*.)

Finally it's my turn. A wave of balls slide toward me and I shoot, making my first basket. I'm good at this. I'm not great. The machine I usually play on has a high score of 72, and my highest score is 56. But considering that I am five foot four, that I used to get C's in gym, and that I campaigned for Dukakis, the fact that I am capable of scoring 56 points in 40 seconds is a source of no small amount of pride. Plus, even though these modern men won't admit it, it really bugs Joel and Steve to get topped by a girl.

> **Goofing off is one of the central obligations of American citizenship.**

There are two reasons I can shoot a basketball: black-eyed peas and Uncle Hoy. I was a forward on my elementary school team. This was in Oklahoma, back when girls played half-court basketball, which meant I never crossed over to the other team's side, which meant all I ever had to do was shoot, a bonus considering that I cannot run, pass, or dribble. Blessed with one solitary athletic skill, I was going to make the most of it. I shot baskets in the backyard every night after dinner. We lived out in the country, and my backboard was nailed to an oak tree that grew on top of a hill. If I missed a shot, the ball would roll downhill into the drainage ditch for the kitchen sink, a muddy rivulet flecked with corn and black-eyed peas. So if the ball bounced willy-nilly off the rim, I had to run after it, retrieve it from the gross black-eyed pea mud, then hose it off. So I learned not to miss.

My mother's brother, Hoy, was a girls' basketball coach. Once he saw I had a knack for shooting, he used to drill me on free throws, standing under the hoop at my grandmother's house, where he himself learned to play. And Hoy, who was also a math teacher—he had gone to college on a dual math-basketball scholarship—revered the geometrical arc of the swish. Hoy hated the backboard, and thought players who used it to make anything other than layups lacked elegance. And so, if I made a free throw that bounced off the backboard before gliding through the basket, he'd yell, "Doesn't count." Sometimes, trash-talking at Pop-A-Shot, I bark that at Joel and Stephen when they score their messy bank shots. "Doesn't count!" The electronic scoreboard, unfortunately, makes no distinction for grace and beauty.

I watch the NBA. I lived in Chicago during the heyday of the Bulls. And I have noticed that in, as I like to call it, the moving-around-basketball, the players spend the whole game trying to shoot. There's all that wasted running and throwing and falling down on cameramen in between baskets. But Pop-A-Shot is basketball concentrate. I've made 56 points in 40 seconds. Michael Jordan never did that. When Michael Jordan would make even 40 points in a game it was the lead in the eleven o'clock news. It takes a couple of hours to play a moving-around-basketball game. Pop-A-Shot distills this down to less than a minute. It is the crack cocaine of basketball. I can make 28 baskets at a rate of less than two seconds per.

Joel, an excellent shot, also appreciates this about Pop-A-Shot. He likes the way it feels, but he's embarrassed by how it sounds stupid when he describes it to other people. (He spent part of last year working in Canada, and I think it rubbed off on him, diminishing his innate American ability to celebrate the civic virtue of idiocy.) Joel plays in a fairly serious adult basketball league in New York. One night, he left Stephen and me in the arcade and rushed off to a—this hurt my feelings—"real" game. That night, he missed a foul shot by two feet and made the mistake of admitting to the other players that his arms were tired from throwing miniature balls at a shortened hoop all afternoon. They laughed and laughed. "In the second overtime," Joel told me, "when the opposing team fouled me with four seconds left and gave me the opportunity to shoot from the line for the game, they looked mighty smug as they took their positions along the key. Oh, Pop-A-Shot guy, I could hear them thinking to their smug selves. He'll never make a foul shot. He plays baby games. Wa-wa-wa, little Pop-A-Shot baby, would you like a zwieback biscuit? But you know what? I made those shots, and those sons of bitches had to wipe their smug grins off their smug faces and go home thinking that maybe Pop-A-Shot wasn't just a baby game after all."

> **Pop-A-Shot is basketball concentrate. It is the crack cocaine of basketball.**

I think Pop-A-Shot's a baby game. That's why I love it. Unlike the game of basketball itself, Pop-A-Shot has no standard socially redeeming value whatsoever. Pop-A-Shot is not about teamwork or getting along or working together. Pop-A-Shot is not about getting exercise or fresh air. It takes place in fluorescent-lit bowling alleys or darkened bars. It costs money. At the end of a game, one does not swig Gatorade. One sips bourbon or margaritas or munches cupcakes. Unless one is playing the Super Shot version at the ESPN Zone in Times Square, in which case, one orders the greatest appetizer ever invented on this continent—a plate of cheeseburgers.

In other words, Pop-A-Shot has no point at all. And that, for me, is the point. My life is full of points—the deadlines and bills and recycling and phone calls. I have come to appreciate, to depend on, this one dumb-ass little passion. Because every time a basketball slides off my fingertips and drops perfectly, flawlessly, into that hole, well, swish, happiness found.

▶ **Analyzing the Text**

1. Vowell describes Pop-A-Shot as a pointless activity from which she gets immense enjoyment and satisfaction. Why does she love pointless entertainment so much?

2. Vowell declares that "goofing off is one of the central obligations of American citizenship." How does she support her claim? How do you respond to this argument?

3. Vowell recounts how she learned to shoot baskets during her childhood. Why does she include this information in the essay?

4. What are the differences between Pop-A-Shot and NBA basketball? Why does Vowell call Pop-A-Shot the "crack cocaine of basketball"?

Writing about Cultural Practices

5. Is wasting our time on pointless activities our patriotic duty as Americans, as Vowell argues in this humorous essay? Develop a critical analysis of the purpose of pointless, time-wasting amusements in your life. As you develop your analysis, consider the following questions.

   - What purpose or need does this amusement fulfill? Why is it important to you?

   - What redeems it as entertainment?

   - What, if anything, makes it particularly American?

A Tyrannosaurus Rex at Dinosaur World in Eureka Springs, Arkansas.

Mixing Words and Images

DESIGNING A ROADSIDE ATTRACTION

In his essay "Amazing! Incredible! The Roadside Attraction" (p. 398), John Margolies explores a roadside America that is a fantasy world of dinosaur parks, rock gardens, storybook lands, miniature villages, and animal parks. Margolies argues that these attractions can provide important insights into what people find entertaining, and such attractions reveal messages about American cultural values and beliefs.

For this assignment, design an entirely new roadside attraction that could be built in your area. To make your attraction particularly meaningful to your local community, first identify some aspect of local history or culture (real or imagined) that is worthwhile and entertaining at the same time. Draft your design on paper or use a software program to create plans for your roadside attraction.

Designing Your Roadside Attraction

- Visit roadside attractions in your area or go to RoadsideAmerica.com to study them more closely.

- Consider your audience and location. What entertains the people you want to attract? Do they hold assumptions or ideas about themselves that you may want to address in your attraction? For example, how does your audience show pride in local history, lore, figures, or events?

- Consider your purpose. What purpose will your attraction serve for the community? What do you want to persuade visitors to think, feel, or do after experiencing it? What insights into local history or culture will your attraction offer? How will it be different from other attractions?

Writing about Your Roadside Attraction

Once you have created a design for your roadside attraction, draft a descriptive analysis essay in which you do the following.

- Describe the objects and details used in your design.

- Identify your purpose (why this attraction, this way?) and target audience.

- Explain the cultural messages you mean to convey. What does your attraction say about the meaning or purpose of entertainment in modern American life?

Connecting to Culture Suggestions for Writing

1. From Production Codes to Ratings Systems: Hollywood and Censorship

"The Pernicious 'Moving Picture' Abomination," by David Nasaw (p. 411), examines the history and impact of censorship on Hollywood. In the early years, Hollywood was largely unregulated or controlled, but by the 1920s, "production codes" were developed. These were the precursors of modern-day ratings systems and other forms of controlling the content of Hollywood movies. For this assignment, investigate the history and purposes of censorship in Hollywood. To begin, use your library to conduct research about censorship in Hollywood. Identify books or articles that describe both contemporary struggles with censorship and sources that describe the censorship struggles of the 1920s and '30s. For research about current practices, study the Motion Picture Association of America's (MPAA) website: mpaa.org/home.htm. Use the following questions to help research and write your essay.

- What are the main differences between the production code developed by the Motion Picture Producers and Distributors of America (MPPDA) and the rating system developed under the leadership of Jack Valenti after 1968 by the MPAA?
- The MPAA describes its system as a voluntary movie rating system. Is it voluntary? Is it a form of censorship?
- How does the ratings system affect the creators of American film?
- How does the ratings system affect your choice of films?

2. Why This Does(n't) Matter: Making Your Case about Reality TV

Three essays in this chapter investigate reality television as a form of mass entertainment: "Virtual Dictionary" by Kevin Arnovitz (p. 438), "The Unreal World" by Jennifer L. Pozner (p. 442), and "Queer Eye: Searching for a Real Gay Man" by Hemal Jhaveri (p. 449). These readings offer arguments about the impact of reality TV on the cultural landscape. Draft a position paper in which you make your own case about the impact and function of reality television. As you draft your position, consider the following questions.

- What is "real" about reality television?
- What specific attitudes, actions, and relationships do these shows encourage?
- How has reality TV become a part of the American popular imagination or consciousness? What evidence supports your claim?

ON THE WEB
For help with these assignments, go to Chapter 5, bedfordstmartins.com/remix

- How has reality TV changed or affected our assumptions about what's entertaining?
- How do you account for the popularity of these shows?

3. Defining Modern American Humor

In his essay "Comedy" (p. 390), Alain de Botton argues that throughout history, comedy and comics have played an important role in society. Among other things, they provide a safe avenue for criticizing the powerful:

> At the hands of the best comics, laughter hence acquires a moral purpose, jokes become attempts to cajole others into reforming their character and habits. Jokes are a way of sketching a political ideal, of creating a more equitable and saner world. (393)

For this assignment, write a critical analysis of modern American humor that answers the question, "What purpose or function does modern American humor serve in our culture?" To focus your analysis, choose two to three examples of the work of comedians or specific comedic TV shows, cartoons, or movies that will help you answer this question.

4. Interrogating Assumptions: Why Is(n't) This Entertaining?

The introduction of this chapter explains three commonly held assumptions about the purpose and impact of entertainment in everyday life. They are

> Entertainment is just for fun.
>
> Entertainment is merely a reflection of culture.
>
> Entertainment is a personal choice.

Each of the readings in this chapter questions one or more of these assumptions, asking "How does entertainment reflect American cultural values?" and "In what ways does the entertainment industry help construct these values?" For this assignment, develop a critical analysis of how two or three readings interrogate one of these assumptions.

99 44/100% pure® . . . The Soap That Floats.
—Ivory Soap, ca. 1878; 1891

Conscious choices. Healing traditions. Caring for you and the earth.
The Art and Science of Pure Flower and Plant Essences.
—Aveda

There's clean and then there's honest clean.
—Earth Friendly Products

or, what's so natural about nature?

6 Nature

Examining the Everyday
Nature and Soap

In an increasingly technological, fast-paced, and urban-centered culture, how do we stay truly connected to the natural world? Perhaps we visit a public garden or park, see animals at the zoo, or take up gardening. But what about other options, like shopping "responsibly"? Products branded as "all natural," "pure," "real," "organic," or "earth friendly" represent one of the fastest growing segments of consumer spending today. The rising popularity of these products seems to reflect something about a desire to connect to nature or to feel more "natural."

The trademarked slogans for household and beauty products on the opposite page, including the Ivory soap slogan, which is more than 100 years old, reveal some of the cultural meanings and symbolic value we place on nature. They convey a belief that natural products are pure, good for you, and healing. For

ON THE WEB
For additional resources for this
assignment, go to Chapter 6,
bedfordstmartins.com/remix

example, in the nineteenth century, the makers of Ivory soap wanted consumers to associate cleanliness, purity, and even holiness with their product. One of the makers of the soap, Harley Procter (of Procter and Gamble), was inspired by Psalm 45:8, read one Sunday at his church, to name the soap "Ivory": "All thy garments smell of myrrh and aloes and casseia, out of the ivory palaces whereby they have made thee glad." Among the other epigraphs, the phrase "There's clean and then there's honest clean" is perhaps the most direct in sending the message that natural products are both morally superior and truly better for us than other products.

The design, packaging, and marketing of natural products go beyond simply selling a particular product. They also sell or reinforce cultural assumptions about nature and what it means to call something "natural." For instance, nature is connected to a pure and less complicated state of being. Nature is presented as a source for renewal and healing.

For this initial assignment, you will begin examining cultural assumptions surrounding the terms "nature" and "natural" by identifying how marketers sell a particular "all-natural" product. Because this is a short introductory assignment, concentrate on finding advertising examples of natural products on the Internet or in print ads. To search for examples on the Internet, use a search phrase such as the following:

dish soap + natural product

hand lotion + natural product

dog food + natural product

Pay attention to the slogans, marketing materials, and philosophy statements as well as the visual images used at the websites or in the print ads to connect a particular product to cultural assumptions and attitudes about nature. Find one or two examples that you think are most interesting and write a one-page description of them that answers these questions.

- What is the central message of the ad or website? What audience does it target?

- What are the assumptions or attitudes about nature that these products and their marketing materials convey? What specific language and images does the ad or website use to promote these assumptions?

Finally, add an additional paragraph that answers these questions.

- What does it mean to call something "natural"? What is implied by this description?

- Conversely, what does it mean to call something "unnatural"?

In this chapter, you will investigate the assumptions that dominate the understanding of nature and the term "natural" in American culture. As the readings in this chapter illustrate, these terms are unexpectedly difficult to define because they mean different things to different people and within different contexts. Some of the questions that will drive your investigation are these: What is nature? What makes something natural? How is our relationship to nature shaped by cultural attitudes? To what extent are our ideas about nature constructed? How much can we shape or control nature?

At its core, the study of nature is the investigation of the complex interrelationships of people, animals, plants, objects, space, and the environment. The natural sciences—biology, botany, chemistry, astronomy, geology, and ecology—are, in fact, chiefly interested in the study of relationships. This chapter asks you to examine these interrelationships by considering the discourse surrounding nature in our popular culture. By paying attention to what people say when they discuss nature or when they label something as natural, you will uncover some taken-for-granted ideas about nature.

Following is a brief overview of some of the most common assumptions people hold about the meaning and importance of nature. Each assumption emphasizes one view of nature over others; yet, as you will see, they sometimes overlap.

Assumption 1

Nature is a spiritual and nurturing force.

For many people, the word "nature," like the word "home," calls to mind mostly positive and nurturing images. "Mother Nature" is often spoken of as a mythic force that sustains life on Earth. Natural landscapes, too, are spoken of with emotion and are tied

introduction

"I have a spiritual side, but mostly I'm an eating machine."

to the concept of home and national identity. Consider, for example, the landscapes evoked by the songs "America the Beautiful" and "God Bless America." In these songs, love of country and the idea of home are clearly connected to love of the land.

The natural world is also often described in spiritual ways. In the popular media, references to nature are frequently used to evoke images of purity, innocence, and peace. Of course, drawing connections between nature and spirituality is nothing new—most ancient belief systems valued and even worshipped the natural world. Writers, spiritual leaders, and naturalists throughout history have given moving accounts of the power of nature as a source of life and as a source for learning important life lessons. Among Native American cultures, there is a long tradition of speaking in spiritual ways about humankind's relationship to nature. Luther Standing Bear, at one time chief of the Oglala Sioux, wrote several books in which he describes the reverence his people felt for the natural world. For the Lakota people, he wrote in *Land of the Spotted Eagle*, "Kinship with all creatures of the earth, sky, and water was a real and active principle." These views have been expanded on by many naturalists and environmental activists. In the opening chapter of his book, *Our National Parks* (1901), American naturalist John Muir describes the public's embrace of national parks in terms of a religious conversion:

Thousands of tired, nerve-shaken, over-civilized people are beginning to find out that going to the mountains is going home; that wildness is a necessity; and that mountain parks and reservations are useful not only as fountains of timber and irrigating rivers, but as fountains of life. Awakening from the stupefying effects of the vice of over-industry and the deadly apathy of luxury, they are trying as best they can to mix and enrich their own little ongoings with those of Nature, and to get rid of rust and disease.

In Muir's view, nature can save people from materialism and destructive habits; it can cleanse us and help us lead better lives. There is no doubt that people draw much wisdom about life from the natural world.

Nevertheless, one pitfall of assuming that nature is spiritual or nurturing is that such a view romanticizes nature. In his essay "The American Geographies" (p. 486), Barry Lopez observes American pride in "our rolling prairies, free-flowing rivers, and 'purple mountains' majesty.'" Yet, Lopez argues, these images of a national geography are in fact creations—fictions constructed by politicians, marketing firms, and the entertainment industry—meant to give people a false vision of an unspoiled, untroubled landscape. What is lost in this view is the hard reality that humans have—for both good and ill—permanently altered the natural landscape. Prairies have been fenced and forests clear-cut. Rivers have been dammed or diverted to bring water to arid regions. Cities and industries have created new mini-climate zones. Farming practices have become increasingly high-tech and involve the use of genetically modified crops. Lakes and rivers have been invaded by nonnative plants and fish, brought in on the hulls of ships from international waters. "The real American landscape," contends Lopez, "is a face of almost incomprehensible depth and complexity."

A further consequence of the romanticization of nature is that it can lead to thinking of natural disasters like droughts, hurricanes, blizzards, tsunamis, and tornados as examples of Mother Nature's dark side. Again, such a view masks humankind's impact on the natural world and any human responsibility for the overtaxing of the environment, through industrial practices, for example, that may lead to some destructive natural events. Although humans do not cause tornadoes or tsunamis, there is no doubt that human practices, such as unregulated industry, alter the environment. The temperature of the ocean is rising, the use of fossil fuels is affecting the planet's climate zones, and the interdependence of the world's economies has had a far-reaching impact on the plant and animal world.

Love and respect for the land and for nature resonate in the American national consciousness, but this very set of emotions should encourage us to question our assumptions about nature. Romanticization of nature can prevent a real investigation of the complex and conflicted relationships humankind has with the natural world.

What questions can you ask to uncover the benefits and limitations of the assumption that nature is a spiritual and nurturing force?

- What kind of imagery do writers use when they describe nature? How does the use of spiritual language affect or shape a writer's claims about nature?
- What kind of imagery do writers use when they describe human interaction with the natural world? In other words, how are humans portrayed? What is humankind's role or responsibility to the natural world?

Assumption 2

Nature is a person's essential character.

This second assumption highlights the use of the term "nature" to describe the chief characteristics and qualities of a person or thing. Consider these examples:

> Luis is a natural athlete.
>
> Trista is a natural leader.
>
> It's in his nature to be kind.

As these simple statements illustrate, the words "nature" or "natural" can be powerful ways to describe a person. These terms are sometimes used to identify a skill or talent—like singing or swinging a baseball bat—that seems to come effortlessly to someone. For example, to many people, Tiger Woods is the epitome of a "natural" on the golf course. From the age of 2, Woods made television appearances that showcased his talent, and as a junior amateur, he won almost every tournament he entered. In 1997, at the age of 21, he set a record at the Masters with a 12-stroke victory and won three other tournaments.

In other cases, people use the terms "nature" or "natural" to sum up a person's character. Calling someone "naturally" brave, or shy, or loyal implies that a given characteristic is at the heart of who that person is. Think back to your high school days and remember the kid whom everyone knew as the class clown. He

or she just seemed to know how to make people laugh. Or, conversely, recall the kid who always seemed to get in trouble. Both of these students certainly had other personality traits, but those traits rarely exceeded the chief impression people had of them. One was viewed as a natural comic, the other as a natural instigator.

However, regarding talents, skills, or personality traits as "natural" implies that these attributes are beyond a person's ability to control or change. This assumption does not take into account that abilities and traits may be the result of hard work, practice, and the support of others. Tiger Woods, for instance, frequently takes sports analysts to task for calling him a "natural," pointing out that as he grew up, his father coached him intensely and that he spent long hours practicing shots. By labeling someone a natural, what is overlooked is the extent to which a talent is the product of conscious effort and the support of others.

Another potential problem of using the terms "nature" and "natural" to describe a person's abilities or qualities is that it gives us permission to look no further. (Q: Why is your cousin so shy? A: That's just the way she is. It's her nature.) Human behavior can be left unexamined or underexamined if it is labeled "natural." In his essay "Save Lives! Defy Nature!" (p. 524), Jason D. Hill criticizes the assumption that people should procreate. His argument is that not everyone is cut out to be a parent, and the notion that parenting is a natural instinct can be harmful to the children involved.

The assumption that certain abilities or traits are natural can lead people away from developing a better understanding of human behavior.

What questions can you ask to uncover the benefits and limitations of the assumption that nature is the essential or inherent temperament of a person?

- When and how do writers use the term "natural" to describe a person's skills or abilities? What precisely is natural about them?
- When and how do writers use the term to describe behavior more broadly? What does this leave out?
- In what ways is the idea of natural abilities or traits a fiction?

Assumption 3

Nature cannot be improved upon.

This third assumption grows out of the first two. If people view nature as spiritual and nurturing and also as the essential character of a person, then it might also be assumed that nature cannot and should not be enhanced or improved upon. But is it possible or desirable to make something "more natural" or to improve upon "nature" through science? For example, if we have the ability to improve or prolong someone's "natural" life through medicine, shouldn't we do so? Or, if we have the ability to manufacture food faster and more cheaply than it can be produced "naturally," shouldn't we do so?

A number of the readings in this chapter take up these questions. In "American Bioscience Meets the American Dream" (p. 508), Carl Elliott discusses the use of "enhancement technologies" such as facelifts, personality makeovers, and Prozac as tools for "finding our true selves." In "You—Only Better" (p. 517), Christine Rosen notes, quoting a colleague, that "one way to deny our dependence on nature is to invent technologies designed to make ourselves masters of nature." She writes, "This is what cosmetic surgery promises to do." In his essay, "Why McDonald's Fries Taste So Good" (p. 552), Eric Schlosser examines the efforts of the food industry to appeal to consumer tastes by creating "natural" flavoring through the use of chemicals to enhance processed food.

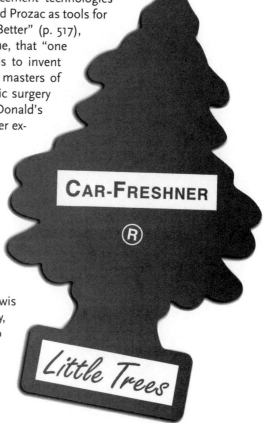

One of the problems with the assumption that nature cannot be improved upon is that it may restrict the use of science that can improve human life. However, the idea that humans can improve or control nature can lead, as Lewis Thomas argues in his famous 1973 essay, "On Cloning a Human Being" (p. 532), to the misuses of medical technologies and to a host of ethical dilemmas. It can also

The Tree design, Little Trees, and CAR-FRESHNER are registered trademarks of Julius Sämaan Ltd. and are used with permission.

lead to unrealistic desires, as Susan McCarthy notes in her essay "On Immortality" (p. 544): "We want to be 100 years old *and* dewy fresh."

What questions can you ask to uncover the benefits and limitations of the assumption that nature cannot be enhanced or improved upon?

- Can nature be "improved" by science? If so, how?
- What are the benefits of using medical science to improve or prolong our lives? What are the drawbacks?
- Are "enhancement technologies" good for us? At what point, if any, should we limit our use of them?
- How much should we attempt to alter "nature" through artificial means, especially, for example, when it comes to producing food?

Questioning These Assumptions

The readings and assignments throughout this chapter ask you to discover and examine cultural assumptions about nature. On the next page are a few questions to get you thinking about some of the issues raised in this chapter.

IN THE MIX

Susan Orlean, **Lifelike**

Susan Orlean is a literary journalist who has been a staff writer at the *New Yorker* since 1992. Her articles have also appeared in the *Atlantic Monthly*, *Outside*, *Rolling Stone*, *Vogue*, and *Esquire*. Her best-selling novel *The Orchid Thief* (2000) inspired the Spike Jonze and Charlie Kaufman film *Adaptation* (2003). Originally published in the *New Yorker*, "Lifelike" is part of a book of Orlean's collected essays titled *My Kind of Place: Travel Stories from a Woman Who's Been Everywhere* (2004). In the following essay, Orlean recounts her experience at a national convention of taxidermists in Springfield, Illinois.

▶▌ **Mapping Your Reading**

Taxidermy (a Greek word for "the arrangement of the skin") is the art of mounting or reproducing animals for display or study. As you read this essay, pay attention to Orlean's use of detail in her descriptions of the people and events surrounding the World Taxidermy Championships, and underline passages in which Orlean uses these details to make an argument about what motivates these people. What examples of stuffed animals, birds, or fish have you personally encountered? What is your reaction to these objects? How is our perception of nature shaped or influenced by the work of taxidermists?

As soon as the 2003 World Taxidermy Championships opened, the heads came rolling in the door. There were foxes and moose and freeze-dried wild turkeys; mallards and buffalo and chipmunks and wolves; weasels and buffle-heads and bobcats and jackdaws; big fish and little fish and razor-backed boar. The deer came in herds, in carloads, and on pallets: dozens and dozens of white-tail and roe; half deer and whole deer and deer with deformities, sneezing and glowering and nuzzling and yawning; does chewing apples and bucks nibbling leaves. There were millions of eyes, boxes and bowls of them; some as small as a lentil and some as big as a poached egg. There were animal mannequins, blank-faced and brooding, earless and eyeless and utterly bald: ghostly gray duikers and spectral pine martens and black-bellied tree ducks from some other world. An entire exhibit hall was filled with equipment, all the gear required to

Early twentieth-century taxidermists Thomas (left) and Ted Sparrow.

bring something dead back to life: replacement noses for grizzlies, false teeth for beavers, fish-fin cream, casting clay, upholstery nails.

The championships were held in April at the Springfield, Illinois, Crowne Plaza hotel, the sort of nicely appointed place that seems more suited to regional sales conferences and rehearsal dinners than to having wolves in the corridors and people crossing the lobby shouting, "Heads up! Buffalo coming through!" A thousand taxidermists converged on Springfield to have their best pieces judged and to attend such seminars as "Mounting Flying Waterfowl," "Whitetail Deer— From a Master!," and "Using a Fleshing Machine." In the Crowne Plaza lobby, across from the concierge desk, a grooming area had been set up. The taxidermists were bent over their animals, holding flashlights to check problem areas like tear ducts and nostrils, and wielding toothbrushes to tidy flyaway fur. People milled around, greeting fellow taxidermists they hadn't seen since the last world championships, held in Springfield two years ago, and talking shop:

"Acetone rubbed on a squirrel tail will fluff it right back up."

"My feeling is that it's quite tough to do a good tongue."

"The toes on a real competitive piece are very important. I think Bondo works nicely, and so does Super Glue."

"I knew a fellow with cattle, and I told him, 'If you ever have one stillborn, I'd really like to have it.' I thought it would make a really nice mount."

That there is a taxidermy championship at all is something of an astonishment, not only to the people in the world who have no use for a Dan-D-Noser and Soft Touch Duck Degreaser but also to taxidermists themselves. For a long time, taxidermists kept their own counsel. Taxidermy, the three-dimensional representation of animals for permanent display, has been around since the eighteenth century, but it was first brought into popular regard by the Victorians, who thrilled to all tokens of exotic travel and especially to any domesticated representations of wilderness—the glassed-in miniature rain forest on the tea table, the mounted antelope by the front door. The original taxidermists were upholsterers who tanned the hides of hunting trophies and then plumped them up with rags and cotton, so that they reassumed their original shape and size; those early poses were stiff and simple, and the expressions fairly expressionless. The practice grew popular in this country, too: by 1882, there was a Society of American Taxidermists, which held annual meetings and published scholarly reports, especially on the matter of preparing animals for museum display. As long as taxidermy served to preserve wild animals and make them available for study, it was viewed as an honorable trade, but most people were still discomfited by it. How could you not be? It was the business of dealing with dead things, coupled with the questionable enterprise of making dead things look like live things. In spite of its scientific value, it was usually regarded as almost a black art, a wholly owned subsidiary of witchcraft and voodoo. By the early part of the twentieth century, taxidermists such as Carl E. Akeley, William T. Horneday, and Leon Pray had refined techniques and begun emphasizing artistry. But the more the techniques of taxidermy improved, the more it discomfited: Instead of the lumpy moose head that was so artless that it looked fake, there were mounts of pouncing bobcats so immaculately and exactly preserved they made you flinch.

Taxidermy was regarded as almost a black art.

For the next several decades, taxidermy existed in the margins—a few practitioners here and there, often self-taught, and usually known only by word of mouth. Then, in the late 1960s, a sort of transformation began: The business started to seem cleaner and less creepy—or maybe, in that messy, morbid time, popular culture started to again appreciate the messy, morbid business of mounting animals for display. An ironic reinterpretation of cluttered, bourgeois Victoriana and its strained juxtapositions of the natural and the man-made was in full revival—what hippie outpost didn't have a stuffed owl or a moose head draped with a silk shawl?—so, once again, taxidermy found a place in the public eye. Supply houses concocted new solvents and better tanning compounds, came out with lightweight mannequins, produced modern formulations of resins and clays. Taxidermy schools opened; previously, any aspiring taxidermist could only hope to learn the trade by apprenticing or by taking one of a few correspondence courses available. In 1971, the National Taxidermy Association was formed (the old society had moldered long before). In 1974, a trade magazine called *Taxidermy Review* began sponsoring national competitions. For the first time, most taxidermists had a chance to meet one another and share advice on how to glue tongues into jaw sets or accurately measure the carcass of a squirrel.

The competitions were also the first time that taxidermists could compare their skills and see who in the business could sculpt the best moose septum or could most perfectly capture the look on a prowling coyote's face. Taxidermic skill is a function of how deft you are at skinning an animal and then stretching its hide over a mannequin and sewing it into place. Top-of-the-line taxidermists sculpt their own mannequins; otherwise they will buy a ready-made polyurethane-foam form and tailor the skin to fit. Body parts that can't be preserved (ears, eyes, noses, lips, tongues) can be either store-bought or handmade. How good the mount looks—that is, how alive it looks—is a function of how assiduously the taxidermist has studied reference material (photographs, drawings, and actual live animals) so that he or she knows the particular creature literally and figuratively inside out.

To be good at taxidermy, you have to be good at sewing, sculpting, painting, and hairdressing, and mostly you have to be a little bit of a zoology nerd. You have to love animals—love looking at them, taking photographs of them, hunting them, measuring them, casting them in plaster of Paris when they're dead so that you have a reference when you're, say, attaching ears or lips and want to get the angle and shape exactly right. Some taxidermists raise the animals they most often mount, so they can just step out in the back yard when they're trying to remember exactly how a deer looks when it's licking its nose, especially because modern taxidermy emphasizes mounts with interesting expressions, rather than the stunned-looking creations of the past. Taxidermists seem to make little distinction between loving animals that are alive and loving ones that are not. "I love deer," one of the champions in the Whitetail division said to me. "They're my babies."

Taxidermy is now estimated to be a $570-million annual business, made up of small operators around the country who mount animals for museums, for decorators, and mostly for the thirteen million or so Americans who are recreational hunters and on occasion want to preserve and display something they killed and who are willing to shell out anywhere from $200 to mount a pheasant to several thousand for a kudu or a grizzly bear. There are state and regional taxidermy competitions throughout the year and the world championships, which are held every other year; two trade magazines; a score of taxidermy schools; and three thousand visits to Taxidermy.net every day, where taxidermists can trade information and goods with as little self-consciousness as you would find on a knitting Web site:

"I am in need of several pair of frozen goat feet!"

"Hi! I have up to 300 sets of goat feet and up to 1000 set of sheep feet per month. Drop me an email at frozencritters.com . . . or give me a call and we can discuss your needs."

"I have a very nice small raccoon that is frozen whole. I forgot he was in the freezer. Without taking exact measurements I would guess he is about twelve inches or so—very cute little one. Will make a very nice mount."

"Can I rinse a boar hide good and freeze it?"

"Bob, if it's salted, don't worry about it!"

"Can someone please tell me the proper way to preserve turkey legs and spurs? Thanks!"

"Brian, I inject the feet with Preservz-It . . . Enjoy!"

The word in the grooming area was that the piece to beat was Chris Krueger's happy-looking otters swimming in a perpetual circle around a leopard frog. A posting on Taxidermy.net earlier in the week declared, "EVERYTHING about this mount KICKS BUTT!!" Kicking butt, in this era of taxidermy, requires having a mount that is not just lifelike but also artistic. It used to be enough to do what taxidermists call "fish on a stick" displays; now a serious competitor worries about things like flow and negative space and originality. One of this year's contenders, for instance, Ken Walker's giant panda, had artistry and accuracy going for it, along with the element of surprise. The thing looked 100 percent pure panda, but you can't go out and shoot a panda, and you aren't likely to get hold of a panda that has met a natural end, so everyone was dying to know how he had done it. The day the show opened, Walker was in the grooming area, gluing bamboo into place behind the animal's back paws, and a crowd had gathered around him. Walker works as a staff taxidermist for the Smithsonian. He is a breezy, shaggy-haired guy whose hands are always busy. One day, I saw him holding a piece of clay while waiting for a seminar to begin, and within 30 seconds or so, without actually paying much attention to it, he had molded the clay into a little minklike creature.

"I just took two black bears and bleached one of them— I think I used Clairol Basic."

"The panda was actually pretty easy," he was saying. "I just took two black bears and bleached one of them—I think I used Clairol Basic. Then I sewed the two skins together into a panda pattern." He took out a toothbrush and fluffed the fur on the panda's face. "At the world championship two years ago, a guy came in with an extinct Labrador duck. I was in awe. I thought, What could beat that—an extinct duck? And I came up with this idea." He said he thought that the panda would get points for creativity alone. "You can score a ninety-eight with a squirrel, but it's still a squirrel," he said. "So that means I'm going with a panda."

"What did you do for toenails, Ken?" someone asked.

"I left the black bear's toenails in," he said. "They looked pretty good."

Another passerby stopped to admire the panda. He was carrying a grooming kit, which appeared to contain Elmer's glue, brown and black paint, a small tool set, and a bottle of Suave mousse. "I killed a blond bear once," he said to Ken. "A two-hundred-pound sow. Whew, she made a beautiful mount."

"I'll bet," Ken said. He stepped back to admire the panda. "I like doing recreations of these endangered animals and extinct animals, since that's the only way anyone's going to have one. Two years ago, I did a saber-toothed cat. I got an old lioness from a zoo and bleached her."

The panda was entered in the Re-Creation (Mammal) division, one of the dozens of divisions and subdivisions and sub-subcategories, ranging from the super-specific (Whitetail Deer Long Hair, Open Mouth division) to the sweepingly colossal (Best in World), that would share in $25,000 worth of prizes. (There is even a sub-sub-subspecialty known as "fish carving," which uses no natural fish parts at all; it is resin and wood sculpted into a fish form and then painted.) Nearly all the competitors are professionals, and they publicize their awards wherever possible. For instance, instead of ordering just any Boar Eye-Setting Reference Head out of a taxidermy catalogue, you can order the Noonkester's #NRB-ERH head sculpted by Bones Johnson, which was, as the catalogue notes, the 2000 National Taxidermy Association Champion Gamehead.

The taxidermists take the competition very seriously. During the time I was in Springfield, I heard conversations analyzing such arcane subjects as exactly how much a javelina's snout wrinkles when it snarls and which molars deer use to chew acorns as opposed to which ones they use to chew leaves. This is important because the ultimate goal of a taxidermist is to make the animal look as if it had never died, as if it were still in the middle of doing ordinary animal things like plucking berries off a bush or taking a nap. When I walked around

©David Bocking

with the judges one morning, I heard discussions that were practically Talmudic, about whether the eyelids on a bison mount were overdetailed, and whether the nostrils on a springbok were too wide, and whether the placement of whiskers on an otter appeared too deliberate. "You do get compulsive," a taxidermist in the exhibit hall explained to me one afternoon. At the time, he was running a feather duster over his entry—a bobcat hanging off an icicle-covered rock—in the last moments before the judging would begin. "When you're working on a piece, you forget to eat, you forget to drink, you even forget to sleep. You get up in the middle of the night and go into the shop so you can keep working. You get completely caught up in it. You want it to be perfect. You're trying to make something come back to life."

> "When you're working on a piece, you get completely caught up in it. You want it to be perfect."

I said that his bobcat was beautiful, and that even the icicles on the piece looked completely real. "I made them myself," he said. "I used clear acrylic toilet-plunger handles. The good Lord sent the idea to me while I was in a hardware store. I just took the handles and put them in the oven at four hundred degrees." He tapped the icicles and then added, "My wife was pretty worried, but I did it on a nonstick cookie sheet."

So who wants to be a taxidermist? "I was a meat cutter for fifteen years," a taxidermist from Kentucky said to me. "That whole time, no one ever said to me, 'Boy, that was a wonderful steak you cut me.' Now I get told all the time what a great job I've done." Steve Faechner, who is the president and chairman of the Academy of Realistic Taxidermy, in Havre, Montana, started mounting animals in 1989, after years spent working on the railroad. "I had gotten hurt, and was looking for something to do," he said. "I was with a friend who did taxidermy and I thought to myself, I have got to get a life. And this was it." Larry Blomquist, who is the owner of the World Taxidermy Championships and of *Breakthrough*, the trade magazine that sponsors the competition, was a schoolteacher for three years before setting up his business. There are a number of women taxidermists (one was teaching this year's seminar on Problem Areas in Mammal Taxidermy), and there are budding junior taxidermists, who had their own competition division, for kids 14 and younger, at the show.

The night the show opened, I went to dinner with three taxidermists who had driven in from Kentucky, Michigan, and Maryland. They were all married, and all had wives who complained when they found one too many antelope carcasses in the family freezer, and all worked full time mounting animals—mostly deer, for local hunters, but occasional safari work, for people who had shot something in Africa. When I mentioned that I had no idea that a person could make a living as a taxidermist, they burst out laughing, and the guy from Kentucky pointed out that he lived in a little town and there were two other full-time taxidermists in business right down the road.

"What's the big buzz this year?" the man from Michigan asked.

"I don't know. Probably something new with eyes," the guy from Maryland answered. "That's where you see the big advances. Remember at the last championship, those Russian eyes?" These were glass animal eyes that had a reflective

FOUND

from taxidermy.net

2005 WORLD TAXIDERMY CHAMPIONSHIP WINNERS: AARDVARKS TO WILD PIGS

Ribbons Awarded for Life-Size Mammals

Aardvark, 1st place, Ray Hatfield, Cody, WY
Baby Skunk, 1st place, Terry Reed, Mantorville, MN
Badger, 1st place, Tadd Galgan, Zion, IL
Black Bear, 2nd place, Darrick Bantley, Summerhill, PA
Black Mink (freeze-dried category), 2nd place, Kurt Polus, Trempealeau, WI
Blue Fox, 2nd place, Kurt Polus, Trempealeau, WI
Bobcat, 1st place, Denny Cutright, Mill Creek, WV
Colobus Monkey, 3rd place, Dale Selby, Nicollet, MN
Cougar, 2nd place, Mike Olszanowski, Douglasville, PA
Cross Fox, 2nd place, Mark Pillion, Loxley, AL
European Stoat, 1st place, David Hollingworth, Glossop, U.K.
Fawn (freeze-dried category), 2nd place, Kurt Polus, Trempealeau, WI
Fisher Cat, 2nd place, Leonard Gums, Burlington, WI
Fox Squirrel (freeze-dried category), 1st place, Rod Connelly, Pittsburgh, PA
Grey Fox, 2nd place Randal R. Waites, Mount Morris, MI
Ground Hog, 1st place, Rick Starostki, St. Charles, MO
House Mouse, 1st place, Birger Nordahl, Uppsala, Sweden
Lynx, 1st place, Mike Olszanowski, Douglasville, PA
Mole, 1st place, Shawn Poe, Leachville, AR
Moose Calf, 1st place, Best of Category, Mark Dufresne, Gray, ME
Mountain Lion Cub, 1st place, Ron Levin, Beach Park, IL
Otter, 1st place, Ray Barbour, Bay Minette, AL
Raccoon, 1st place, Rick Starostki, St. Charles, MO
Red Duiker, 3rd place, Izell Nolan, Pretoria, South Africa
Red Fox, 1st place, Wayne Miller, Waterford, MI
Red Fox Pup, 2nd place, Terry Reed, Mantorville, MN
River Otter, 2nd place, Melissa Phillips, Fort Mill, SC
Russian Boar, 3rd place, Jackie Niccum, Milan, MO
Short Telid Visel, 1st place, Birger Nordahl, Uppsala, Sweden
Squirrel (freeze-dried category), 1st place, Roxanne Civitts, McVeytown, PA
Tiger, 3rd place, Cindy Cunningham, Kansas City, KS
Whitetail Deer, 1st place, Mike Olszanowski, Douglasville, PA
Wild Pig, 2nd place, Bob Schnettgoecke, Grafton, IL

*In November 2004 Scott Bibus, Sarina Brewer, and Robert Marbury of Minnesota
formed a group of "rogue taxidermists" to explore the artistic (and humorous)
possibilities of stuffing and mounting animal remains. (See also facing page.)*
© Minnesota Association of Rogue Taxidermists/www.roguetaxidermy.com webpage designed
by Paul Stroot and Robert Marbury

paint embedded in them, so that if you shone a light they would shine back at
you, sort of like the way real animals' eyes do. The men discussed those for a
while, then talked about the new fish eyes being introduced this year, which have
photographic transfers of actual fish eyes printed on plastic lenses. We happened
to be in a restaurant with a sports theme, and there were about a hundred televisions on around the room, broadcasting dozens of different athletic events, but
the men never glanced at them, and never stopped talking about their trade. We
had all ordered barbecued ribs. When dinner was over, all three of them were fid-
dling around with the bones before the waitress came to clear our plates.

"Look at these," the man from Kentucky said, holding up a rib. "You could
take these home and use them to make a skeleton."

In the seminars, the atmosphere was as sober and exacting as a tax-law collo-
quium. "Whiskers," one of the instructors said to the group, giving them a stern
look. "I pull them out. I label them. There are left whiskers and
there are right whiskers. If you want to get those top awards,
you're going to have to think about whiskers." Everyone took
notes. In the next room: "Folks, remember, your carcass is your
key. The best thing you can do is to keep your carcass in the
freezer. Freeze the head, cast it in plaster. It's going to really help
if your head is perfect." During the breaks, the group made jokes
about a T-shirt that had been seen at one of the regional competitions. The shirt
said "PETA" in big letters, but when you got up close you saw that PETA didn't spell
out People for the Ethical Treatment of Animals, the bane of all hunters and, by

**"Folks, remember,
your carcass is
key. Keep it in
the freezer."**

extension, all taxidermists; it spelled out People Eating Tasty Animals. Chuckles all around, then back to the solemn business of Mounting Flying Waterfowl: "People, follow what the bird is telling you. Study it, do your homework. When you've got it ready, fluff the head, shake it, and then get your eyes. There are a lot of good eyes out there on the market today. Do your legwork, and you can have a beautiful mount."

It was brisk and misty outside—the antler venders in the parking lot looked chilled and miserable—and the modest charms of Springfield, with its mall and the Oliver P. Parks Telephone Museum and Abraham Lincoln's tomb, couldn't compete with the strange and wondrous sights inside the hotel. The mere experience of waiting for the elevator—knowing that the doors would peel back to reveal maybe a man and a moose, or a bush pig, or a cougar—was much more exciting than the usual elevator wait in the usual Crowne Plaza hotel. The trade show was a sort of mad tea party of body parts and taxidermy supplies, things for pulling flesh off a carcass, for rinsing blood out of fur—a surreal carnality, but

all conveyed with the usual trade-show earnestness and hucksterism, with no irony and no acknowledgment that having buckets of bear noses for sale was anything out of the ordinary. "Come take a look at our beautiful synthetic fur! We're the hair club for lions! If you happen to shoot a lion who is out of season or bald, we can provide you with a gorgeous replacement mane!" "Too many squirrels? Are they driving you nuts? Let us mount them for you!" "Divide and Conquer animal forms—an amazing advance in small-mammal mannequins, patent pending!"

The big winner at the show turned out to be a tiny thing—a mount of two tree sparrows, submitted by a strapping German named Uwe Bauch, who had grown up in the former East Germany dreaming of competing in an American taxidermy show. The piece was precise and lovely, almost haunting, since the more you looked at it the more certain you were that the birds would just stop building their nest, spread their wings, and fly away. Early one morning, before I left Springfield, I took a last walk around the competition hall. It was quiet and uncanny, with hundreds of mounts arranged on long tables throughout the room; the deer heads clustered together, each in a slightly different pose and angle, looked like a kind of animal Roman forum caught in mid-debate. A few of the mounts were a little gory—a deer with a mail-box impaled on an antler, another festooned with barbed wire, and one with an arrow stuck in its brisket—

The "Jackalope," mythical offspring of the jackrabbit and antelope, which according to legend mate only during lightning storms. The back of this postcard notes: "Rumor has it that the Jackalope sings at night in a voice that sounds almost human."

and one display, a coyote whose torso was split open to reveal a miniature scene of the destruction of the World Trade Center, complete with little firemen and rubble piles, was surpassingly weird. Otherwise, the room was biblically tranquil, the lion at last lying down with the Corsican lamb, the family of jackdaws in everlasting, unrequited pursuit of a big green beetle, and the stillborn Bengal tiger cub magically revived, its face in an eternal snarl, alive-looking although it had never lived.

Analyzing the Text

1. What is Orlean's opinion of the taxidermists attending this convention? What details in the essay reveal her attitude toward them? Why does she portray taxidermists as she does?

2. What role does taxidermy play in modern popular culture? How do examples of taxidermy—which can be found in museums, zoos, restaurants, tourist attractions, and people's homes—contribute to popular conceptions of the natural world? What view of nature do they project?

3. Orlean points out that the obsession of taxidermists is their search for perfection—to make an animal look as if it had never died. What is the impact of their passion for recreating a perfect simulation of the natural world? How does this passion impact their perspective on nature?

4. Given their obsession for accuracy and for making their stuffed animals lifelike, how do you make sense of the taxidermists' fascination with creating weird, extinct, or fantasy animals—animals that do not exist today or never existed in the first place? To answer this question, consider both the "jackalope" pictured in the accompanying photograph and descriptions in the essay. What seem to be underlying themes about humankind's relationship to nature in these fantastic examples of taxidermy?

Writing about Cultural Practices

5. In her essay, Orlean explains that the origins of taxidermy lead back to the nineteenth century. The timing of the rise of popularity in taxidermy corresponds to the rise of the Industrial Age in Europe and North America. Use Orlean's essay as a starting point and conduct some research into this period of history to learn how people's attitudes and assumptions about the natural world changed or evolved during the Industrial Age. Write a critical analysis essay that answers these questions.

   - How does the rise of taxidermy's popularity in the nineteenth century reflect the cultural shifts brought about by the rise of the Industrial Age?

   - In what ways can the changing nature of taxidermy in our time be connected to shifts in the broader culture regarding our attitudes and assumptions about nature?

   - What cultural values are preserved through taxidermy, past and present?

6. How do we simulate the natural world? Visit a local zoo, animal exhibit, museum, or even a theme-based restaurant to locate examples of human-made representations of nature—either in displays of stuffed and mounted animals or in live exhibits of animals in recreated "natural" environments. Take notes and photos, if possible, to record how these simulations are presented to the public and collect any flyers or pamphlets that describe the purpose or intent of this exhibit. Following your visit, write a critical description of the exhibit. As you write, consider the following questions.

   - What assumptions or attitudes about the natural world (and humankind's relationship to it) are revealed in this exhibit? What details in the exhibit lead you to your conclusion? As you work through this, consider the assumptions about nature described in this chapter's introduction (pp. 465–72).

   - In your opinion, to what extent have such simulations of the natural world replaced real encounters with nature for the average person? Is this a problem? Why or why not?

Barry Lopez, **The American Geographies**

Known for his writings about the environment and natural history, Barry Lopez
has published over 10 books of nonfiction and fiction, including *Desert Notes:
Reflections in the Eye of a Raven* (1976), the National Book Award–winning *Arctic
Dreams* (1986), and *Field Notes: The Grace Note of Canyon Wren* (1994). He is a
contributing editor at *Harper's* and has published articles for the *Paris Review,
Orion,* and the *Georgia Review*. "The American Geographies" appears in *About
This Life: Journeys on the Threshold of Memory* (1998). In this essay Lopez discusses the lack of geographical awareness in America while making a case for
its relevance. He suggests that people are increasingly detached from the natural world and do not know the real American landscape. He writes that in nature specials, nature-themed calendars, and slick magazine layouts, "the essential wilderness of the American landscape is reduced to attractive scenery."

> ### Mapping Your Reading
>
> As you read, mark the passages in which Lopez
> uses his observations to support his arguments
> about the contemporary American landscape.
> What is the "real" American landscape? To what
> extent is it constructed and commodified, and to
> what purpose? What are the implications of loving
> a national geography that doesn't actually exist?
> What should the relationship between people and
> the land be?

It has become commonplace to observe that Americans know little of the geography of their country, that they are innocent of it as a landscape of rivers,
mountains, and towns. They do not know, supposedly, the location of the
Delaware Water Gap, the Olympic Mountains, or the Piedmont Plateau; and, the
indictment continues, they have little conception of the way the individual components of this landscape are imperiled, from a human perspective, by modern
farming practices or industrial pollution.

I do not know how true this is, but it is easy to believe that it is truer than
most of us would wish. A recent Gallup Organization and National Geographic
Society survey found Americans woefully ignorant of world geography. Three out
of four couldn't locate the Persian Gulf. The implication was that we knew no
more about our own homeland, and that this ignorance undermined the integrity of our political processes and the efficiency of our business enterprises.

As Americans, we profess a sincere and fierce love for the American landscape, for our rolling prairies, free-flowing rivers, and "purple mountains' majesty"; but it is hard to imagine, actually, where this particular landscape is. It is not just that a nostalgic landscape has passed away—Mark Twain's Mississippi is now dammed from Illinois to Louisiana and the prairies have all been sold and fenced. It is that it's always been a romantic's landscape. In the attenuated form in which it is presented on television today, in magazine articles and in calendar photographs, the essential wildness of the American landscape is reduced to attractive scenery. We look out on a familiar, memorized landscape that portends adventure and promises enrichment. There are no distracting people in it and few artifacts of human life. The animals are all beautiful, diligent, one might even say well behaved. Nature's unruliness, the power of rivers and skies to intimidate, and any evidence of disastrous human land management practices are all but invisible. It is, in short, a magnificent garden, a colonial vision of paradise imposed on a real place that is, at best, only selectively known.

> We profess a love for "purple mountains' majesty"; but it is hard to imagine where this particular landscape is.

The real American landscape is a face of almost incomprehensible depth and complexity. If one were to sit for a few days, for example, among the ponderosa pine forests and black lava fields of the Cascade Mountains in western Oregon, inhaling the pines' sweet balm on an evening breeze from some point on the barren rock, and then were to step off to the Olympic Peninsula in Washington, to those rain forests with sphagnum moss floors soft as fleece underfoot and Douglas firs too big around for five people to hug, and then head south to walk the ephemeral creeks and sun-blistered playas of the Mojave Desert in southern California, one would be reeling under the sensations. The contrast is not only one of plants and soils, a different array, say, of brilliantly colored beetles. The shock to the senses comes from a different shape to the silence, a difference in the very quality of light, in the weight of the air. And this relatively short journey down the West Coast would still leave the traveler with all that lay to the east to explore—the anomalous sand hills of Nebraska, the heat and frog voices of Okefenokee Swamp, the fetch of Chesapeake Bay, the hardwood copses and black bears of the Ozark Mountains.

No one of these places, of course, can be entirely fathomed, biologically or aesthetically. They are mysteries upon which we impose names. Enchantments. We tick the names off glibly but lovingly. We mean no disrespect. Our genuine desire, though we may be skeptical about the time it would take and uncertain of its practical value to us, is to actually know these places. As deeply ingrained in the American psyche as the desire to conquer and control the land is the desire to sojourn in it, to sail up and down Pamlico Sound, to paddle a canoe through Minnesota's boundary waters, to walk on the desert of the Great Salt Lake, to camp in the stony hardwood valleys of Vermont.

To do this well, to really come to an understanding of a specific American geography, requires not only time but a kind of local expertise, an intimacy with place few of us ever develop. There is no way around the former requirement: If you want to know you must take the time. It is not in books. A specific geographical understanding, however, can be sought out and borrowed. It resides with men and women more or less sworn to a place, who abide there, who have a feel for the soil and history, for the turn of leaves and night sounds. Often they are glad to take the outlander in tow.

These local geniuses of American landscape, in my experience, are people in whom geography thrives. They are the antithesis of geographical ignorance. Rarely known outside their own communities, they often seem, at the first encounter, unremarkable and anonymous. They may not be able to recall the name of a particular wildflower—or they may have given it a name known only to them. They might have forgotten the precise circumstances of a local historical event. Or they can't say for certain when the last of the Canada geese passed through in the fall, or can't differentiate between two kinds of trout in the same creek. Like all of us, they have fallen prey to the fallacies of memory and are burdened with ignorance; but they are nearly flawless in the respect they bear these places they love. Their knowledge is intimate rather than encyclopedic, human but not necessarily scholarly. It rings with the concrete details of experience.

Politics and advertising must project a national geography, often romantic and therefore frequently misleading.

America, I believe, teems with such people. The paradox here, between a faulty grasp of geographical knowledge for which Americans are indicted and the intimate, apparently contradictory familiarity of a group of largely anonymous people, is not solely a matter of confused scale. (The local landscape is easier to know than a national landscape—and many local geographers, of course, are relatively ignorant of a national geography.)

And it is not simply ironic. The paradox is dark. To be succinct: The politics and advertising that seek a national audience must project a national geography; to be broadly useful that geography must, inevitably, be generalized and it is often romantic. It is therefore frequently misleading and imprecise. The same holds true with the entertainment industry, but here the problem might be clearer. The same films, magazines, and television features that honor an imaginary American landscape also tout the worth of the anonymous men and women who interpret it. Their affinity for the land is lauded, their local allegiance admired. But the rigor of their local geographies, taken as a whole, contradicts a patriotic, national vision of unspoiled, untroubled land. These men and women are ultimately forgotten, along with the details of the landscapes they speak for, in the face of more pressing national matters. It is the chilling nature of modern society to find an ignorance of geography, local or national, as excusable as an ignorance of hand tools; and to find the commitment of people to their home places only momentarily entertaining. And finally naïve.

If one were to pass time among Basawara people in the Kalahari Desert, or with Tikuna on the upper Amazon, or with Pitjantjatjara Aborigines in Australia, the most salient impression they might leave is of an absolutely stunning knowledge

Two views of Washington's Mount Rainier—a 1940s postcard and a contemporary, industrial view.

of their local geography—geology, hydrology, biology, and weather. In short, the extensive particulars of their intercourse with it.

In forty thousand years of human history, it has only been in the last few hundred years or so that a people could afford to ignore their local geographies as completely as we do and still survive. Technological innovations from refrigerated trucks to artificial fertilizers, from sophisticated cost accounting to mass air transportation, have utterly changed concepts of season, distance, soil productivity, and the real cost of drawing sustenance from the land. It is now possible for a resident of Kansas City to bite into a fresh mango in the dead of winter; for someone in San Francisco to travel to Atlanta in a few hours with no worry of how formidable might be crossings of the Great Basin Desert or the Mississippi River; for an absentee farmer to gain a tax advantage from a farm that leaches poisons into its water table and on which crops are left to rot. The Pitjantjatjara might shake their heads in bewilderment and bemusement, not because they are primitive or ignorant people, not because they have no sense of irony or are incapable of marveling, but because they have not (many would say not yet) realized a world in which such manipulation of the land—surmounting the imperatives of distance it imposes, for example, or turning the large-scale destruction of forests and arable land into wealth—is desirable or plausible.

In the years I have traveled through America, in cars and on horseback, on foot and by raft, I have repeatedly been brought to a sudden state of awe by some gracile or savage movement of animal, some odd wrapping of a tree's foliage by the wind, an unimpeded run of dew-laden prairie stretching to a horizon flat as a coin where a pin-dot sun pales the dawn sky pink. I know these things are beyond intellection, that they are the vivid edges of a world that includes but also transcends the human world. In memory, when I dwell on these things, I know that in a truly national literature there should be odes to the Triassic reds of the Colorado Plateau, to the sharp and ghostly light of the Florida Keys, to the aeolian soils of southern Minnesota and the Palouse in Washington, though the modern mind abjures the literary potential of such subjects. (If the sand and floodwater farmers of Arizona and New Mexico were to take the black loams of Louisiana in their hands they would be flabbergasted, and that is the beginning of literature.) I know there should be eloquent evocations of the cobbled beaches of Maine, the plutonic walls of the Sierra Nevada, the orange canyons of the Kaibab Plateau. I have no doubt, in fact, that there are. They are as numerous and diverse as the eyes and fingers that ponder the country—it is that only a handful of them are known. The great majority are to be found in drawers and boxes, in the letters and private journals of millions of workaday people who have regarded their encounters with the land as an engagement bordering on the spiritual, as being fundamentally linked to their state of health.

One cannot acknowledge the extent and the history of this kind of testimony without being forced to the realization that something strange, if not dangerous, is afoot. Year by year, the number of people with firsthand experience in the land dwindles. Rural populations continue to shift to the cities. The family farm is in a state of demise, and government and industry continue to apply pressure on the native peoples of North America to sever their ties with the land. In the wake

This c. 1940 postcard reads, "Yippee! Let 'er Buck."

of this loss of personal and local knowledge, the knowledge from which a real geography is derived, the knowledge on which a country must ultimately stand, has become something hard to define but I think sinister and unsettling—the packaging and marketing of land as a form of entertainment. An incipient industry, capitalizing on the nostalgia Americans feel for the imagined virgin landscapes of their ancestors, and on a desire for adventure, now offers people a convenient though sometimes incomplete or even spurious geography as an inducement to purchase a unique experience. But the line between authentic experience and a superficial exposure to the elements of experience is blurred. And the real landscape, in all its complexity, is distorted even further in the public imagination. No longer innately mysterious and dignified, a ground from which experience grows, it becomes a curiously generic backdrop on which experience is imposed.

In theme parks the profound, subtle, and protracted experience of running a river is reduced to a loud, quick, safe equivalence, a pleasant distraction. People only able to venture into the countryside on annual vacations are, increasingly, schooled in the belief that wild land will, and should, provide thrills and exceptional scenery on a timely basis. If it does not, something is wrong, either with the land itself or possibly with the company outfitting the trip.

People in America, then, face a convoluted situation. The land itself, vast and differentiated, defies the notion of a national geography. If applied at all it must be applied lightly, and it must grow out of the concrete detail of local geographies. Yet Americans are daily presented with, and have become accustomed to talking about, a homogenized national geography, one that seems to operate independently of the land, a collection of objects rather than a continuous bolt of fabric. It appears in advertisements, as a background in movies, and in patriotic calendars. The suggestion is that there *can* be a national geography because the constituent parts are interchangeable and can be treated as commodities. In day-to-day affairs, in other words, one place serves as well as another to convey one's point. On reflection, this is an appalling condescension and a terrible imprecision, the very antithesis of knowledge. The idea that either the Green River in Utah or the Salmon River in Idaho will do, or that the valleys of Kentucky and West Virginia are virtually interchangeable, is not just misleading. For people still dependent on the soil for their sustenance, or for people whose memories tie them to those places, it betrays a numbing casualness, a utilitarian, expedient, and commercial frame of mind. It heralds a society in which it is no longer necessary for human beings to know where they live, except as those places are described and fixed by numbers. The truly difficult and life-long task of discovering where one lives is finally disdained.

The knowledge from which a real geography is derived has become something sinister.

If a society forgets or no longer cares where it lives, then anyone with the political power and the will to do so can manipulate the landscape to conform to certain social ideals or nostalgic visions. People may hardly notice that anything has happened, or assume that whatever happens—a mountain stripped of timber and eroding into its creeks—is for the common good. The more superficial a society's knowledge of the real dimensions of the land it occupies becomes, the more vulnerable the land is to exploitation, to manipulation for short-term gain. The land, virtually powerless before political and commercial entities, finds itself finally with no defenders. It finds itself bereft of intimates with indispensable, concrete knowledge. (Oddly, or perhaps not oddly, while American society continues to value local knowledge as a quaint part of its heritage, it continues to cut such people off from any real political power. This is as true for small farmers and illiterate cowboys as it is for American Indians, native Hawaiians, and Eskimos.)

The intense pressure of imagery in America, and the manipulation of images necessary to a society with specific goals, means the land will inevitably be treated like a commodity; and voices that tend to contradict the proffered image will, one way or another, be silenced or discredited by those in power. This is not new to America; the promulgation in America of a false or imposed geography has been the case from the beginning. All local geographies, as they were defined by hundreds of separate, independent native traditions, were denied in the beginning in favor of an imported and unifying vision of America's natural history. The country, the landscape itself, was eventually defined according to dictates of Progress like Manifest Destiny, and laws like the Homestead Act which reflected a poor understanding of the physical lay of the land.

When I was growing up in southern California, I formed the rudiments of a local geography—eucalyptus trees, February rains, desert cottontails. I lost much of it when my family moved to New York City, a move typical of the modern, peripatetic style of American life, responding to the exigencies of divorce and employment. As a boy I felt a hunger to know the American landscape that was extreme; when I was finally able to travel on my own, I did so. Eventually I visited most of the United States, living for brief periods of time in Arizona, Indiana, Alabama, Georgia, Wyoming, New Jersey, and Montana before settling years ago in western Oregon.

The astonishing level of my ignorance confronted me everywhere I went. I knew early on that the country could not be held together in a few phrases, that its geography was magnificent and incomprehensible, that a man or woman could devote a lifetime to its elucidation and still feel in the end that he or she had but sailed many thousands of miles over the surface of the ocean. So I came into the habit of traversing landscapes I wanted to know with local tutors and reading what had previously been written about, and in, those places. I came to value exceedingly novels and essays and works of nonfiction that connected human enterprise to real and specific places, and I grew to be mildly distrustful of work that occurred in no particular place, work so cerebral and detached as to be refutable only in an argument of ideas.

These sojourns in various corners of the country infused me, somewhat to my surprise on thinking about it, with a great sense of hope. Whatever despair I had come to feel at a waning sense of the real land and the emergence of false geographies—elements of the land being manipulated, for example, to create erroneous but useful patterns in advertising—was dispelled by the depth of a single person's local knowledge, by the serenity that seemed to come with that intelligence. Any harm that might be done by people who cared nothing for the land, to whom it was not innately worthy but only something ultimately for sale, I thought, would one day have to meet this kind of integrity, people with the same dignity and transcendence as the land they occupied. So when I traveled, when I rolled my sleeping bag out on the shores of the Beaufort Sea or in the high pastures of the Absaroka Range in Wyoming, or at the bottom of the Grand Canyon, I absorbed those particular testaments to life, the indigenous color and songbird song, the smell of sun-bleached rock, damp earth, and wild honey, with some crude appreciation of the singular magnificence of each of those places. And the reassurance I felt expanded in the knowledge that there were, and would likely always be, people speaking out whenever they felt the dignity of the earth imperiled in these places.

The promulgation of false geographies, which threaten the fundamental notion of what it means to live somewhere, is a current with a stable and perhaps growing countercurrent. People living in New York City are familiar with the stone basements, the cratonic geology, of that island and have a feeling for birds migrating through in the fall, their sequence and number. They do not find the city alien but human, its attenuated natural history merely different from that of rural Georgia or Wisconsin. I find the countermeasure, too, among Eskimos who cannot read but who might engage you for days on the subtleties of sea-ice topography. And among men and women who, though they have followed in the footsteps of their parents, have come to the conclusion that they cannot farm or fish or log in the way their ancestors did; the finite boundaries to this sort of wealth have appeared in their lifetime. Or among young men and women who have taken several decades of book-learned agronomy, zoology, silviculture and horticulture, ecology, ethnobotany, and fluvial geomorphology and turned it into a new kind of local knowledge, who have taken up residence in a place and sought, both because of and in spite of their education, to develop a deep intimacy with it. Or they have gone to work, idealistically, for the National Park Service or the fish and wildlife services or for a private institution like the Nature Conservancy. They are people to whom the land is more than politics or economics. These are people for whom the land is alive. It feeds them, directly, and that is how and why they learn its geography.

In the end, then, if you begin among the blue crabs of Chesapeake Bay and wander for several years, down through the Smoky Mountains and back to the bluegrass hills, along the drainages of the Ohio and into the hill country of Missouri, where in summer a chorus of cicadas might drown out human conversation, then up the Missouri itself, reading on the way the entries of Meriwether Lewis and William Clark and musing on the demise of the plains grizzly and the sturgeon, cross west into the drainage of the Platte and spend the evenings with Gene Weltfish's *The Lost Universe*, her book about the Pawnee who once thrived there, then drop south to Palo Duro Canyon and the irrigated farms of the Llano Estacado in Texas, turn west across the Sangre de Cristo, southernmost of the Rocky Mountain ranges, and move north and west up onto the slickrock mesas of Utah, those browns and oranges, the ocherous hues reverberating in the deep canyons, then go north, swinging west to the insular ranges that sit like battleships in the pelagic space of Nevada, camp at the steaming edge of sulphur springs in the Black Rock Desert, where alkaline pans are glazed with a ferocious light, a heat to melt iron, then cross the northern Sierra Nevada, waist-deep in summer snow in the passes, to descend to the valley of the Sacramento, and rise through groves of elephantine redwoods in the Coast Range, to arrive at Cape Mendocino, before Balboa's Pacific, cormorants and gulls, gray whales headed north for Unimak Pass in the Aleutians, the winds crashing down on you, facing the ocean over the blue ocean that gives the scene its true vastness, making this crossing, having been so often astonished at the line and the color of the land, the ingenious lives of its plants and animals, the varieties of its darknesses, the intensity of the stars overhead, you would be ashamed to discover, then, in yourself, any capacity to focus on ravages in the land that left you unsettled. You would have seen so much, breathtaking, startling, and outsize, that you might not be able for a long time to break the spell, the sense, especially finishing your journey in the West, that the land had not been as rearranged or quite as compromised as you had first imagined.

After you had slept some nights on the beach, however, with that finite line of the ocean before you and the land stretching out behind you, the wind first battering then cradling you, you would be compelled by memory, obligated by your own involvement, to speak of what left you troubled. To find the rivers dammed and shrunken, the soil washed away, the land fenced, a tracery of pipes and wires and roads laid down everywhere, blocking and channeling the movement of water and animals, cutting the eye off repeatedly and confining it—you had expected this. It troubles you no more than your despair over the ruthlessness, the insensitivity, the impetuousness of modern life. What underlies this obvious change, however, is a less noticeable pattern of disruption: acidic lakes, skies empty of birds, fouled beaches, the poisonous slags of industry, the sun burning like a molten coin in ruined air.

The land finds itself with no defenders.

It is a tenet of certain ideologies that man is responsible for all that is ugly, that everything nature creates is beautiful. Nature's darkness goes partly unreported, of course, and human brilliance is often perversely ignored. What is true is that man has a power, literally beyond his comprehension, to destroy. The lethality of some of what he manufactures, the incompetence with which he stores it or seeks to dispose of it, the cavalier way in which he employs in his daily living substances that threaten his health, the leniency of the courts in these matters (as though products as well as people enjoyed the protection of the Fifth Amendment), and the treatment of open land, rivers, and the atmosphere as if, in some medieval way, they could still be regarded as disposal sinks of infinite capacity, would make you wonder, standing face to in the wind at Cape Mendocino, if we weren't bent on an errand of madness.

The geographies of North America, the myriad small landscapes that make up the national fabric, are threatened—by ignorance of what makes them unique, by utilitarian attitudes, by failure to include them in the moral universe, and by brutal disregard. A testament of minor voices can clear away an ignorance of any place, can inform us of its special qualities; but no voice, by merely telling a story, can cause the poisonous wastes that saturate some parts of the land to decompose, to evaporate. This responsibility falls ultimately to the national community, a vague and fragile entity to be sure, but one that, in America, can be ferocious in exerting its will.

Geography, the formal way in which we grapple with this areal mystery, is finally knowledge that calls up something in the land we recognize and respond to. It gives us a sense of place and a sense of community. Both are indispensable to a state of well-being, an individual's and a country's.

One afternoon on the Siuslaw River in the Coast Range of Oregon, in January, I hooked a steelhead, a sea-run trout, that told me, through the muscles of my hands and arms and shoulders, something of the nature of the thing I was calling "the Siuslaw River." Years ago I had stood under a pecan tree in Upson County, Georgia, idly eating the nuts, when slowly it occurred to me that these nuts would taste different from pecans growing somewhere up in South Carolina. I didn't need a sharp sense of taste to know this, only to pay attention at a level no one had ever told me was necessary. One November dawn, long before the sun rose, I began a vigil at the Dumont Dunes in the Mojave Desert in California, which I kept until a few minutes after the sun broke the horizon. During that time I named to myself the colors by which the sky changed and by which the sand itself flowed like a rising tide through grays and silvers and blues into yellows, pinks, washed duns, and fallow beiges.

It is through the power of observation, the gifts of eye and ear, of tongue and nose and finger, that a place first rises up in our mind; afterward it is memory that carries the place, that allows it to grow in depth and complexity. For as long as our records go back, we have held these two things dear, landscape and memory. Each infuses us with a different kind of life. The one feeds us, figuratively and literally. The other protects us from lies and tyranny. To keep landscapes intact and the memory of them, our history in them, alive, seems as imperative a task in modern time as finding the extent to which individual expression can be accommodated before it threatens to destroy the fabric of society.

> I would want the sense of a real place—to know that I was not inhabiting an idea.

If I were to now visit another country, I would ask my local companion, before I saw any museum or library, any factory or fabled town, to walk me in the country of his or her youth, to tell me the names of things and how, traditionally, they have been fitted together in a community. I would ask for the stories, the voice of memory over the land. I would ask to taste the wild nuts and fruits, to see their fishing lures, their bouquets, their fences. I would ask about the history of storms there, the age of the trees, the winter color of the hills. Only then would I ask to see the museums. I would want first the sense of a real place, to know that I was not inhabiting an idea. I would want to know the lay of the land first, the real geography, and take some measure of the love of it in my companion before I stood before the paintings or read works of scholarship. I would want to have something real and remembered against which I might hope to measure their truth.

Analyzing the Text

1. According to Lopez, what are the important features of the "national geography"?

2. **Interrogating Assumptions.** How does Lopez's essay challenge the first assumption in this chapter's introduction that "nature is a spiritual and nurturing force" (see p. 465)? What does Lopez suggest we do about the contradiction between our professed love of the landscape and our ignorance about it?

3. What distinguishes people who, according to Lopez, are experts or "local geniuses of American landscape"? What defines their relationship to the natural world as compared to that of the average person?

4. According to Lopez, what are the important characteristics of "local geographies"? Why does he refer to local geographies in the plural?

5. Throughout this essay, Lopez warns readers of the cost of our ignorance of the American landscape. What are his chief concerns, both for people and for the natural world?

 Writing about Cultural Practices

6. Write a critical narrative about a local geography that is particularly important to you or your family. This may be a country road outside of town that leads to a relative's house, a specific vacation spot, a park, or another location within your neighborhood or city that holds special meaning to you. Once you have identified this local geography, consider the following questions as you write.

   - How would you describe this local geography to someone who has never visited it? What details about the landscape or its plant or animal life make this space important to you?

   - Why is this landscape especially important to you, aside from what you've described about its landscape or its plant or animal life?

   - To what extent might you or others take this local geography for granted? Why do you think this is so? What is the impact of taking it for granted?

   - Is the landscape likely to change (or to be changed) significantly? Why or why not?

Diane Ackerman, **We Are All a Part of Nature**

Diane Ackerman is author of over 20 works of poetry and nonfiction, including *Cultivating Delight: A Natural History of My Garden* (2001), *Origami Bridges: Poems of Psychoanalysis and Fire* (2002), and *An Alchemy of the Mind* (2004). Her essays about nature and human nature have appeared in the *New York Times, Parade,* the *New Yorker,* and *National Geographic,* among other journals. She has received many awards, including a Guggenheim Fellowship and the John Burroughs Nature Award, and has the rare distinction of having a molecule named after her: dianeackerone. She has taught at several universities, including Columbia, the University of Richmond, and Cornell. This essay originally appeared in *Parade* magazine in 2004.

> ### Mapping Your Reading
>
> Ackerman writes, "All of our being—juices, flesh, and spirit—is nature." As you read, pay attention to how she blends a reverence for nature with a natural scientist's knowledge of biology. Underline passages in which her descriptions of nature are particularly effective. How do human beings fit into the natural order of things?

A film starts running across my mind's eye, accompanied by the sound of heartbeats and birdsong. It contains my whole experience of Earth, including all the oceans I've floated on or swum under, the skies I've flown through, the lands I've walked upon, the humans and other animals I've known, lots of nature I've never witnessed firsthand but glimpsed in documentaries or read about, and the Earth seen from space.

Naturally, that film would take lifetimes to explore, because nature means the full sum of creation, from the Big Bang to the whole shebang. It includes: spring moving north at about 13 miles a day; afternoon tea and cookies; snow forts; pepper-pot stew; pink sand and confetti-colored cottages; moths with fake eyes on their hind wings; emotions both savage and blessed; tidal waves; pogo-hopping sparrows; blushing octopuses; scientists bloodhounding the truth; memory's wobbling aspic; the harvest moon rising like slow thunder; fat rainbows beneath spongy clouds; tiny tassels of worry on a summer day; the night sky's distant leak of suns; an aging father's voice so husky it could pull a sled; the courtship pantomimes of cardinals whistling in the spring with "what cheer, what cheer, what cheer!"

Sometimes we forget that nature also means us. Termites build mounds; we build cities. All of our being—juices, flesh and spirit—is nature.

Sometimes we forget that nature also means us.

Nature surrounds, permeates, effervesces in and includes us. At the end of our days, it deranges and disassembles us like old toys banished to the basement. There, once living beings, we return to our nonliving elements, but we still and forever remain a part of nature. Not everyone agrees with me. Many people harbor an us-against-them mentality in which nature is the enemy and the kingdom of animals doesn't really include us. Then we can attribute to animals all the things about ourselves that we can't stand.

True, we build more elaborate habitats than other animals who, to the best of my knowledge, don't require anything like electric cow-milk frothing machines, beeswax on a flaming string, or vaporized flower essence mixed with musk from the anal sac of civets to encourage breeding. But I could be wrong. Maybe the wren's liquid melody is equally fantastic. And I'm reluctant to hazard a guess about the necking and petting of alligators, whose cheeks are studded with exquisitely sensitive pleasure nodes. Even at our most domesticated and tame, we're like pet zebras or grizzly bears—dangerous to anger, always flirting with a tantrum just under the well-behaved surface. We're remarkable animals, erudite and loving, but, like circus lions, we will always be wild and fiercely unpredictable.

Each day, I wake startled to be alive on a planet packed with so much life. No gasp of sunlight goes unused. Life homesteads every pore and crevice, including deep dark ocean trenches. Life's rule seems to be variations on every possible theme: And so we have tree frogs with sticky feet, marsupial frogs, poisonous frogs, toe-tapping frogs, frogs that go peep and many more.

The leafy green abundance we usually think of as nature began with Earth's earliest life-forms, blue-green algae. Their gift was the cell, a microscopic circus that still is the basis of a cougar, bombardier beetle, and one's nephew. Their genius was inventing photosynthesis. Around 2.4 billion years ago, they began building solar power plants under their walls, digesting their surroundings and, in the process, excreting oxygen, a poisonous gas.

Over time, the algae sheathed the planet, and oxygen fizzed through the oceans, saturating them. Then the bubbles rose, breathing life into a slaggy sky, whose cloudbanks thinned as the blues appeared. Hydrogen ballooned away into space, while heavier oxygen stayed home. Earth became a planet rich in poisonous, flammable oxygen.

Meanwhile, evolution tinkered with creatures immune to oxygen, including some willing to pool their DNA. Complex animals evolved. And the rest is history. In every flake of skin, we still resemble those one-celled pioneers. If they didn't excrete oxygen, we wouldn't be here. So, no matter how politely one puts it, we owe our existence to the flatulence of blue-green algae.

Nature deranges and disassembles us like old toys banished to the basement.

That should humble us and remind us that we share our origins and future with the rest of life on Earth. We need a healthy environment if we hope to stay healthy.

Most days, I make time to play outside, usually in the garden or on a bike or taking a walk. I live in the country, but nature also means the manicured wilderness of a large city, where flimsy blades of grass crack through cement and fragile snowflakes halt traffic. What feats of strength! A city park lures countless animals from miles away to its bustling green oasis. Surrounded by trees and sky, it's easier to feel a powerful sense of belonging to the pervasive mystery of nature, of being molded by unseen forces older than our daily concerns. Without that, life would feel flat as a postage stamp.

But nature also means comfort, heritage, and seasoned home. Indoors, a sensuous activity I heartily recommend is what I think of as "spanieling." Find a shaft of sunlight pouring through a window on a cold day, curl up in the puddle of warmth it creates, relish the breath of sun on your skin, and nap with doglike dereliction. If you have trouble turning off your mind-theater, picture yourself as a squirrel, bear, or cocker spaniel enjoying a simple sunbath.

Steep yourself in nature. The world will wait.

▶ Analyzing the Text

1. What is Ackerman's chief message? How does she relate humankind with the natural world?

2. How does Ackerman characterize nature? What specific language does she use to describe it? Do you agree with her ideas about nature? Why or why not?

3. **Interrogating Assumptions.** There is at once a spiritual quality and a reverence of scientific study in her descriptions of the natural world. What assumptions about nature does Ackerman rely on in this essay? How are these assumptions related to the reverence she conveys for nature?

4. **Connecting to Another Reading.** How would you relate Barry Lopez's argument about the disappearing natural landscape in "The American Geographies" (p. 486) to Ackerman's essay, which attempts to reposition humankind in relationship to the larger natural world?

▶ Writing about Cultural Practices

5. Both "The American Geographies" and "We Are All Part of Nature" investigate how the natural world is presented in popular culture. Yet neither essay specifically considers what we learn about nature as children from popular literature. For this assignment, investigate the themes or assumptions about nature that are found in popular fairy tales or children's stories. Write a critical analysis of representations of the natural world found in a work of children's literature. To begin, visit your library to locate children's fairy tales or stories in which the natural world is depicted. Choose the story that you find most interesting. In your essay, consider the following questions.

   • How does this fairy tale or story depict nature or the natural world? What details in the story lead you to your observations?

   • What is the relationship between people and nature in the story?

   • What themes or assumptions about nature does this fairy tale or story present?

Wangari Maathai, **Trees for Democracy**

In the late 1970s, as a professor of veterinary anatomy at the University of Nairobi, Kenya, Wangari Maathai became a leader in two political movements: the National Council of Women, which sought to improve the lives of women, and the Green Belt Movement, which sought to repair environmental damage caused by years of deforestation. Over the past 25 years, Maathai has been politically active, fighting against the former oppressive regime in Kenya. She has addressed the United Nations' General Assembly, has published widely, and has had her methods adopted by other countries. In 2002, she was elected to the Kenyan parliament with an overwhelming majority. She was subsequently appointed as assistant minister for environment, natural resources, and wildlife. Maathai was named the 2004 Nobel Peace Prize winner "for her contribution to sustainable development, democracy, and peace." She is the first woman from Africa and the first environmentalist to win this award. The following is a transcript of her lecture at the award presentation ceremony on December 10, 2004.

 Mapping Your Reading

Before he introduced Wangari Maathai, Professor Ole Danbolt Mjøs, the chair of the Norwegian Nobel Committee, explained, "Peace on earth depends on our ability to secure our living environment." As you read Maathai's speech, pay attention to how she argues that environmental practices can address social and political problems. How can planting trees impact human life and society?

Your Majesties
Your Royal Highnesses
Honorable Members of the Norwegian Nobel Committee
Excellencies
Ladies and Gentlemen
I stand before you and the world humbled by this recognition and uplifted by the honor of being the 2004 Nobel Peace Laureate.

As the first African woman to receive this prize, I accept it on behalf of the people of Kenya and Africa, and indeed the world. I am especially mindful of women and the girl child. I hope it will encourage them to raise their voices and take more space for leadership. I know the honor also gives a deep sense of

Wangari Maathai

Getty Images/Johannes Eisele

pride to our men, both old and young. As a mother, I appreciate the inspiration this brings to the youth and urge them to use it to pursue their dreams.

Although this prize comes to me, it acknowledges the work of countless individuals and groups across the globe. They work quietly and often without recognition to protect the environment, promote democracy, defend human rights, and ensure equality between women and men. By so doing, they plant seeds of peace. I know they, too, are proud today. To all who feel represented by this prize I say use it to advance your mission and meet the high expectations the world will place on us.

This honor is also for my family, friends, partners, and supporters throughout the world. All of them helped shape the vision and sustain our work, which was often accomplished under hostile conditions. I am also grateful to the people of Kenya—who remained stubbornly hopeful that democracy could be realized and their environment managed sustainably. Because of this support, I am here today to accept this great honor.

I am immensely privileged to join my fellow African Peace laureates, Presidents Nelson Mandela and F. W. de Klerk, Archbishop Desmond Tutu, the late Chief Albert Luthuli, the late Anwar el-Sadat, and the UN Secretary General, Kofi Annan.

I know that African people everywhere are encouraged by this news. My fellow Africans, as we embrace this recognition, let us use it to intensify our commitment to our people, to reduce conflicts and poverty and thereby improve their quality of life. Let us embrace democratic governance, protect human rights, and protect our environment. I am confident that we shall rise to the occasion. I have always believed that solutions to most of our problems must come from us.

In this year's prize, the Norwegian Nobel Committee has placed the critical issue of environment and its linkage to democracy and peace before the world. For their visionary action, I am profoundly grateful. Recognizing that sustainable development, democracy, and peace are indivisible is an idea whose time has come. Our work over the past 30 years has always appreciated and engaged these linkages.

My inspiration partly comes from my childhood experiences and observations of nature in rural Kenya. It has been influenced and nurtured by the formal education I was privileged to receive in Kenya, the United States, and

Germany. As I was growing up, I witnessed forests being cleared and replaced by commercial plantations, which destroyed local biodiversity and the capacity of the forests to conserve water.

Excellencies, ladies and gentlemen, in 1977, when we started the Green Belt Movement, I was partly responding to needs identified by rural women, namely lack of firewood, clean drinking water, balanced diets, shelter, and income.

Throughout Africa, women are the primary caretakers, holding significant responsibility for tilling the land and feeding their families. As a result, they are often the first to become aware of environmental damage as resources become scarce and incapable of sustaining their families.

Women are often the first to become aware of environmental damage.

The women we worked with recounted that unlike in the past, they were unable to meet their basic needs. This was due to the degradation of their immediate environment as well as the introduction of commercial farming, which replaced the growing of household food crops. But international trade controlled the price of the exports from these small-scale farmers and a reasonable and just income could not be guaranteed. I came to understand that when the environment is destroyed, plundered, or mismanaged, we undermine our quality of life and that of future generations.

Tree planting became a natural choice to address some of the initial basic needs identified by women. Also, tree planting is simple, attainable, and guarantees quick, successful results within a reasonable amount of time. This sustains interest and commitment.

So, together, we have planted over 30 million trees that provide fuel, food, shelter, and income to support their children's education and household needs. The activity also creates employment and improves soils and watersheds. Through their involvement, women gain some degree of power over their lives, especially their social and economic position and relevance in the family. This work continues.

Initially, the work was difficult because historically our people have been persuaded to believe that because they are poor, they lack not only capital, but also knowledge and skills to address their challenges. Instead they are conditioned to believe that solutions to their problems must come from "outside." Further, women did not realize that meeting their needs depended on their environment being healthy and well managed. They were also unaware that a degraded environment leads to a scramble for scarce resources and may culminate in poverty and even conflict. They were also unaware of the injustices of international economic arrangements.

In order to assist communities to understand these linkages, we developed a citizen education program, during which people identify their problems, the causes, and possible solutions. They then make connections between their own personal actions and the problems they witness in the environment and in society. They learn that our world is confronted with a litany of woes: corruption, violence against women and children, disruption and breakdown of families, and disintegration of cultures and communities. They also identify the abuse of drugs and chemical substances, especially among young people. There are also devastating diseases that are defying cures or occurring in epidemic proportions. Of particular concern are HIV/AIDS, malaria, and diseases associated with malnutrition.

The destruction of ecosystems contributes to excruciating poverty.

On the environment front, they are exposed to many human activities that are devastating to the environment and societies. These include widespread destruction of ecosystems, especially through deforestation, climatic instability, and contamination in the soils and waters that all contribute to excruciating poverty.

In the process, the participants discover that they must be part of the solutions. They realize their hidden potential and are empowered to overcome inertia and take action. They come to recognize that they are the primary custodians and beneficiaries of the environment that sustains them.

Entire communities also come to understand that while it is necessary to hold their governments accountable, it is equally important that in their own relationships with each other, they exemplify the leadership values they wish to see in their own leaders, namely justice, integrity, and trust.

Although initially the Green Belt Movement's tree planting activities did not address issues of democracy and peace, it soon became clear that responsible governance of the environment was impossible without democratic space. Therefore, the tree became a symbol for the democratic struggle in Kenya. Citizens were mobilized to challenge widespread abuses of power, corruption, and environmental mismanagement. In Nairobi's Uhuru Park, at Freedom Corner, and in many parts of the country, trees of peace were planted to demand the release of prisoners of conscience and a peaceful transition to democracy.

Through the Green Belt Movement, thousands of ordinary citizens were mobilized and empowered to take action and effect change. They learned to overcome fear and a sense of helplessness and moved to defend democratic rights.

In time, the tree also became a symbol for peace and conflict resolution, especially during ethnic conflicts in Kenya when the Green Belt Movement used peace trees to reconcile disputing communities. During the ongoing re-writing of the Kenyan constitution, similar trees of peace were planted in many parts of the country to promote a culture of peace. Using trees as a symbol of peace is in keeping with a widespread African tradition. For example, the elders of the Kikuyu carried a staff from the *thigi* tree that, when placed between two disputing sides, caused them to stop fighting and seek reconciliation. Many communities in Africa have these traditions.

Such practices are part of an extensive cultural heritage, which contributes both to the conservation of habitats and to cultures of peace. With the destruction of these cultures and the introduction of new values, local biodiversity is no longer valued or protected and as a result, it is quickly degraded and disappears. For this reason, the Green Belt Movement explores the concept of cultural biodiversity, especially with respect to indigenous seeds and medicinal plants.

As we progressively understood the causes of environmental degradation, we saw the need for good governance. Indeed, the state of any country's environment is a reflection of the kind of governance in place, and without good governance there can be no peace. Many countries, which have poor governance systems, are also likely to have conflicts and poor laws protecting the environment.

In 2002, the courage, resilience, patience, and commitment of members of the Green Belt Movement, other civil society organizations, and the Kenyan public culminated in the peaceful transition to a democratic government and laid the foundation for a more stable society.

Excellencies, friends, ladies and gentlemen, it is 30 years since we started this work. Activities that devastate the environment and societies continue unabated. Today we are faced with a challenge that calls for a shift in our thinking, so that humanity stops threatening its life-support system. We are called to assist the Earth to heal her wounds and in the process heal our own—indeed, to embrace the whole creation in all its diversity, beauty, and wonder. This will happen if we see the need to revive our sense of belonging to a larger family of life, with which we have shared our evolutionary process.

In the course of history, there comes a time when humanity is called to shift to a new level of consciousness, to reach a higher moral ground. A time when we have to shed our fear and give hope to each other.

That time is now.

The Norwegian Nobel Committee has challenged the world to broaden the understanding of peace: There can be no peace without equitable development; and there can be no development without sustainable management of the environment in a democratic and peaceful space. This shift is an idea whose time has come.

I call on leaders, especially from Africa, to expand democratic space and build fair and just societies that allow the creativity and energy of their citizens to flourish.

Those of us who have been privileged to receive education, skills, and experiences and even power must be role models for the next generation of leadership. In this regard, I would also like to appeal for the freedom of my fellow laureate Aung San Suu Kyi so that she can continue her work for peace and democracy for the people of Burma and the world at large.

The tree became a symbol for the democratic struggle in Kenya.

Culture plays a central role in the political, economic, and social life of communities. Indeed, culture may be the missing link in the development of Africa. Culture is dynamic and evolves over time, consciously discarding retrogressive traditions, like female genital mutilation (FGM), and embracing aspects that are good and useful.

Africans, especially, should re-discover positive aspects of their culture. In accepting them, they would give themselves a sense of belonging, identity, and self-confidence.

Ladies and Gentlemen, there is also need to galvanize civil society and grassroots movements to catalyze change. I call upon governments to recognize the role of these social movements in building a critical mass of responsible citizens, who help maintain checks and balances in society. On their part, civil society should embrace not only their rights but also their responsibilities.

Further, industry and global institutions must appreciate that ensuring economic justice, equity, and ecological integrity are of greater value than profits at any cost.

The extreme global inequities and prevailing consumption patterns continue at the expense of the environment and peaceful co-existence. The choice is ours.

I would like to call on young people to commit themselves to activities that contribute toward achieving their long-term dreams. They have the energy and creativity to shape a sustainable future. To the young people I say, you are a gift to your communities and indeed the world. You are our hope and our future.

The holistic approach to development, as exemplified by the Green Belt Movement, could be embraced and replicated in more parts of Africa and beyond. It is for this reason that I have established the Wangari Maathai Foundation to ensure the continuation and expansion of these activities. Although a lot has been achieved, much remains to be done.

Excellencies, ladies and gentlemen, as I conclude I reflect on my childhood experience when I would visit a stream next to our home to fetch water for my mother. I would drink water straight from the stream. Playing among the arrowroot leaves I tried in vain to pick up the strands of frogs' eggs, believing they were beads. But every time I put my little fingers under them they would break. Later, I saw thousands of tadpoles: black, energetic and wriggling through the clear water against the background of the brown earth. This is the world I inherited from my parents.

Today, over 50 years later, the stream has dried up, women walk long distances for water, which is not always clean, and children will never know what they have lost. The challenge is to restore the home of the tadpoles and give back to our children a world of beauty and wonder.

Thank you very much.

▶ **Analyzing the Text**

1. How does Maathai's interest in improving women's lives intersect with her environmentalism? How does she connect planting trees with democracy?

2. What is Maathai's chief argument about humankind's responsibility to the natural world?

3. **Interrogating Assumptions.** Use Maathai's Nobel lecture to identify her process in forming the grassroots movement called the Green Belt Movement. How does this movement "move" people or encourage changes in their assumptions about the environment?

4. Consider the audience for Maathai's speech. What is her main objective? What does she wish to persuade her audience of? Is she successful in making her argument?

▶ Writing about Cultural Practices

5. Maathai argues that concern for the environment is also concern for the social welfare of a community. Her example of grassroots activism is powerful evidence of this. For this assignment, propose a project for developing a more sustainable use of natural resources at your school or in your area. For help, go to the website of Maathai's organization, the Green Belt Movement, which has published principles and suggestions for how others can form their own grassroots organizations. Go to this book's companion website to read a collection of brief essays published by Maathai and the Green Belt Movement. Then, working in groups, research and draft a proposal for developing a project that improves some aspect of your local environment and that also benefits the community. Consider proposing more effective or wider use of recycling, recycled products, or alternative sources of power. As you draft your proposal, consider the following questions.

- What is the purpose of your project? Why is it a good idea, and what specific problem(s) will it solve? How will it do so?
- Who will benefit from your project?
- What resources will be needed to complete your project?

ON THE WEB
To access Maathai's Green Belt Movement, go to Chapter 6, **bedfordstmartins.com/remix**

Carl Elliott, **American Bioscience Meets the American Dream**

Carl Elliott is a professor of bioethics and philosophy at the University of Minnesota. He has published articles on the ethics of enhancement technologies and the philosophy of psychiatry for the *American Prospect*, the *Hedgehog Review*, and the *Atlantic Monthly*. His books include *A Philosophical Disease: Bioethics, Culture, and Identity* (1998), *Better Than Well: American Medicine Meets the American Dream* (2003), and, most recently, *Prozac as a Way of Life* (2004). This essay offers an excerpt from *Better Than Well* in which Elliott argues, "Medical technology has become, in the popular imagination, a way of revealing and displaying an identity that has been hidden by nature, circumstance, or pathology."

> ▶ **Mapping Your Reading**
>
> This essay examines a trend in which people increasingly are turning to medicine as a tool for "working on the self." As you read, pay attention to how Elliott uses a series of case studies to illustrate a shift in people's attitudes about the connection between medicine and identity. What drives people to make changes in their appearance? To what extent is someone's personal sense of fulfillment connected to the physical? Can medicine help us feel more like our "true" or "natural" selves?

"Whoever wants to know the heart and mind of America had better learn baseball." When Jacques Barzun made this famous diagnosis of American life in 1954, Wallace Laboratories was preparing to introduce the nation to a new drug called Miltown. Marketed as a "tranquilizer," Miltown was the first prescription drug developed specifically for the anxiety of ordinary life. Within two years of its introduction, Miltown had become the most popular prescription drug in America. It would remain popular into the 1960s, when it gradually ceded its place as America's favorite to Valium, another tranquilizer. By the early 1990s, another psychopharmacology boom had begun: American consumers, mostly children, were ingesting 90 percent of the world's supply of Ritalin. Today, the pharmaceutical industry has settled comfortably into its place as the most profitable business in America, and its most profitable class of drugs is an-

---

For another reading on medicine, see Rosen, p. 517.—EDS.

tidepressants. Barzun's heart was in the right place but his mind was on the wrong subject. If you want to understand America, you must first understand Prozac.

If you want to understand America, you must first understand Prozac.

Over the past half-century, American doctors have begun to use the tools of medicine not merely to make sick people better but to make well people better than well. Bioethicists call these tools "enhancement technologies," and usually characterize them as "cosmetic" technologies or "lifestyle" drugs. But terms such as "enhancement" can be misleading, and not just because most enhancements can also be accurately described as treatments for psychological injuries or illnesses. They are misleading because the people who use the technologies often characterize them not merely as a means of enhancement but as a means of shaping identities. These are tools for working on the self.

Yet there is something puzzling about these tools. Even as we use medical technologies to transform ourselves, often in the most dramatic ways—face-lifts, personality makeovers, extreme body modifications—we describe these transformations as a way of finding our true selves. Medical technology has become, in the popular imagination, a way of revealing and displaying an identity that has been hidden by nature, circumstance, or pathology. If you want to understand America, you must first understand how a country whose citizens are known the world over for their outgoing self-confidence should emerge as a leading consumer of drugs for social anxiety; how a nation dedicated to the freedom of the individual should enforce standards for physical beauty with such rigidity that grown women race to restaurant toilets to throw up their dinners; and how a nation famed for its dedication to the pursuit of happiness should also be such a fertile market for antidepressant medication.

This vocabulary of identity is not uniquely American, of course. People in other countries talk this way as well. But a vocabulary of identity may well be *typically* American, like the technologies we use it to describe.

But as clinicians say, the cases speak for themselves. What are the users of these so-called enhancement technologies telling us?

Case One: Steroids. In his memoir *Muscle,* Samuel Fussell describes how, at the age of 26, he found himself working at a New York City publishing house. But Fussell had a problem with New York: The city terrified him. He was terrified of the crime, of the deranged strangers on the streets. It was this terror that led Fussell to bodybuilding. Fussell's moment of realization came when he read the Arnold Schwarzenegger autobiography, *Arnold: The Education of a Bodybuilder.* Soon Fussell was working out with free weights, reading bodybuilding magazines, and buying 70 eggs a week at the supermarket. He quit his publishing job and moved to southern California, where he was soon taking anabolic steroids—or, as his bodybuilder friends called it, "the juice."

The transformation in Fussell's appearance is astonishing. Photographs in his memoir show a shy-looking 22-year-old man, bony and longhaired, legs crossed and seated in a lawn chair. Several years later, they show a man so changed it is difficult to imagine it is the same person: an enormous, oiled, steroid-enhanced bodybuilder with a buzz cut, muscles bulging freakishly, eyes glazed, veins popping out all over his body, strutting and preening on a stage in southern California. But how does Fussell describe the change? As a transformation into his true self. It was his need to discover and reveal himself that drove him to steroids. "I, for one, couldn't wait three or four or five more years to become myself," Fussell writes. "I was so uncomfortable not being me that I had to have (steroids) now."

Case Two: Paxil. "I was 23, a millionaire, and had everything, yet I was never more unhappy in my life," said Ricky Williams, an NFL running back. Williams's problem was his pathological shyness, or, as his official diagnosis had it, his "social anxiety disorder." So intense was his fear of public scrutiny that Williams had become known for giving media interviews with his football helmet on. He dreaded the thought of going to the grocery store or unexpectedly meeting a fan.

When Williams began giving public interviews about his condition several years ago, it was as a paid spokesman for GlaxoSmithKline, the makers of Paxil, the first antidepressant approved by the Food and Drug Administration for social anxiety disorder. Williams explained to the press that medication had allowed his true identity to emerge. "As part of my treatment program," Williams said, "my physician prescribed the antidepressant Paxil, in combination with therapy. Soon thereafter I was able to start acting like the real Ricky Williams."

Case Three: LSD. Cary Grant was not ordinarily an easy man to interview, writes Jay Stevens in his popular history, *Storming Heaven,* but as reporters gathered around Grant for questions on the set of the 1959 movie *Operation Petticoat,* the actor was uncharacteristically forthcoming. "I have been born again," he told the astonished group. "I have been through a psychiatric experience which has completely changed me." The psychiatric experience to which Grant was referring was the result of LSD, which he claimed to have used more than 60 times. As he sat tanning himself on the deck of a pink submarine, Grant described the way that LSD had put him in touch with his inner self. "I found I was hiding behind all kinds of defenses, hypocrisies, and vanities," Grant said. LSD allowed him to get past the mask that had hidden his true nature. "I had to face things about myself which I had never admitted," Grant said. "I was an utter fake." Only with LSD was he able to overcome this fakery and become who he really was inside.

Case Four: Ritalin. By the mid-1990s Americans had become accustomed to the idea of schoolchildren on Ritalin, but we were just beginning to hear about Ritalin for adults. Newsmagazines and self-help books such as *Driven to Distraction* told us that adults, too, could suffer from Attention Deficit/Hyperactivity Disorder (ADHD). Many parents of children with ADHD began to suspect that they also had the disorder, and that their distractibility and poor concentration could be remedied with stimulant drugs. To many adults, the knowledge that their problems were due to an illness came as a relief. "I know this is not a personality flaw," said one executive who had begun taking stimulants.

"I'm rewriting the tapes of who I thought I was to who I really am."

Many people concluded that stimulants had restored to them a true self that had been hidden by pathology. One patient taking Ritalin told *Time* magazine, "I had 38 years of thinking I was a bad person. Now I'm rewriting the tapes of who I thought I was to who I really am."

Case Five: Sex-reassignment surgery. "I was three or perhaps four years old when I realized that I had been born into the wrong body, and should really be a girl." This is the opening sentence of Jan Morris's memoir, *Conundrum.* For the first 35 years of her life, Jan Morris was James Morris, a celebrated Welsh writer. The transition from James to Jan began when Morris came across a book called *Man into Woman,* which tells the story of a Danish painter who had undergone sex-reassignment surgery. Realizing that a transition from male to female was a medical possibility, Morris started taking female hormones and using the name Jan

The benefits and risks of the "tummy tuck."

in 1964. In 1972, at the age of 45, Morris traveled to Casablanca, Morocco, and underwent sex-reassignment surgery. After the operation, Morris felt clean, felt normal, and, most of all, felt like herself. "I was not to others what I was to myself," Morris writes. "All I wanted was to live as myself, to clothe myself in a more proper body, and achieve Identity at last."

Case Six: Voluntary amputation. In 2000, British newspapers announced that a surgeon in Scotland had amputated the limbs of two physically healthy people at their own requests. When asked to justify the amputations, the surgeon explained that some people "genuinely feel that their body is incomplete with their normal complement of four limbs." He and colleagues in psychiatry compared these patients to people who needed sex-reassignment surgery. One of the patients, explaining his desire for amputation, told a BBC interviewer, "I felt like at the age of 14, 'I'm in the wrong body and I should have a leg amputated.'" Another patient who had not yet undergone surgery said, "For me to have been born without my lower right leg would have been more the perfect theme of what I see my body as. It's almost a deformity. It's a wrongness, it's not a part of who I am."

As jarring as the language of authenticity and fulfillment may sound in some of these stories, it is the product of a moral ideal that is deeply rooted in modern Western culture. The philosopher Charles Taylor describes that ideal like this: "There is a certain way of being human that is *my* way. I am called upon to live my life in this way and not in imitation of anyone else's life." Taylor traces the ideal of authenticity to the eighteenth-century notion that each of us has a moral sense or conscience, a feeling for what is right and wrong. Over time, being in touch with your feelings came to be a moral ideal in itself. Authenticity eventually came to be something we must attain if we are to be true and full human beings.

As Taylor points out, it is important to acknowledge the *moral* pull of this idea. To say that people are using these technologies in pursuit of self-fulfillment is not necessarily to say that they are being selfish or narcissistic. Many people today feel *called* to pursue self-fulfillment. They have the sense that a fulfilled life is somehow a higher life, that if they do not discover a path that is true to themselves, they are missing out on what life could be. It is in pursuit of self-fulfillment that many people devote themselves single-mindedly to a career, for example, or cultivate their looks through severe diets and punishing workouts, even if it means ignoring their children, their partners, their God, their communities, or any of the other things that people at other times have thought essential to a good life. When Morris writes that all of her fellow patients in Casablanca were deliriously happy, having finally achieved fulfillment, she is articulating something of this ideal. True happiness cannot be attained without fulfillment, and fulfillment requires being true to yourself.

In medicine, the ethic of authenticity has given the pursuit of psychological well-being the same kind of moral imperative once reserved for treating illnesses. Doctors used to find it relatively easy to draw a sharp ethical line between interventions for treating illnesses and those for cosmetic purposes. But today those lines have been hopelessly blurred. Once we take seriously the idea that people can be genuinely harmed if their aspirations to self-fulfillment are blocked, interventions that used to look like cosmetic procedures start to look a lot like medical treatments.

A good example of this transformation is cosmetic surgery. At the beginning of the twentieth century, cosmetic surgery was a marginal practice, performed mainly by hucksters and quacks. By the end of the century, it had become a multibillion-dollar industry, performed by reputable surgeons. The turning point, according to Elizabeth Haiken in her superb history of cosmetic surgery, *Venus Envy*, was the notion of the "inferiority complex." The inferiority complex came out of ideas developed in the 1930s by the psychologist Alfred Adler, who argued that people could develop a sense of personal inferiority—and, as a result, psychological problems—because of the way they looked. The inferiority complex gave surgeons the ideal ethical justification for cosmetic surgery. Soon cosmetic surgery was not merely cosmetic; it was a medical treatment for the inferiority complex. As Haiken puts it, cosmetic surgery became "psychiatry with a scalpel."

Known as "the tiger woman," socialite Jocelyne Wildenstein underwent a series of operations—one of which caused her to lose her peripheral vision—to transform herself into "a replica of [her] husband's favorite jungle animal." Her advice to women who can't afford plastic surgery? "Develop a personality and learn how to bake." Beauty tips? "Nothing gives you a lift like a little collagen."

Getty Images/Astrid Stawiarz

It is easy to laugh at that phrase now because nobody talks about beauty doctors and the inferiority complex anymore. What we talk about instead is stigma. Our ethical debates today are about using medical technology to prevent people from being ashamed or humiliated. We give short boys synthetic growth hormones because short stature is stigmatized; we perform surgery on intersexed children because ambiguous genitalia is stigmatized; we prescribe Paxil because shyness is stigmatized; we give Botox injections because being old is stigmatized. This is not psychiatry with a scalpel; it is sociology with a scalpel. No longer do we simply see the possibility of treating social problems with medical technology; we see an ethical rationale for doing it. People who are stigmatized, unhappy, or unfulfilled are genuinely suffering, and their suffering can be addressed by doctors.

This is sociology with a scalpel.

Which is not to say that their suffering is not truly felt. In a famous passage in *The Souls of Black Folk,* W. E. B. DuBois wrote about the "double consciousness" of African Americans, the sense of "looking at one's self through the eyes of others." African Americans always feel their "twoness," DuBois thought, because the way they see themselves is distorted by the way they are seen by others. This distortion has not gone unnoticed by cosmetic surgeons or cosmetics manufacturers, of course. From plastic surgery for the "Jewish nose" or "Asian eyes" to skin lighteners and hair straighteners for African Americans, the market for enhancement technologies has always had an uneasy relationship with American racism.

Skeptical doctors sometimes attribute the extraordinary popularity of enhancement technologies to the FDA's 1997 relaxation of its ban on direct-to-consumer advertising of prescription drugs. According to a recent study, GlaxoSmithKline spent more money—$91 million—in direct-to-consumer advertising for its antidepressant Paxil in 2001 than Nike spent advertising its top shoes. Yet direct-to-consumer advertising remains only a fraction of the drug industry's advertising budget, most of which is aimed not at patients but at doctors. The pharmaceutical industry plies doctors with gifts, meals, trips, entertainment, drug samples, honoraria, consulting fees, even money for signing their names to ghostwritten articles. Doctors have become the instruments by which the pharmaceutical industry sells its products.

How has this happened? One example can be found in the history of the antidepressants. Before the 1960s, as the psychiatrist David Healy has pointed out, clinical depression was thought to be an extremely rare problem. The drug industry stayed away from depression because there was no money to be made there. Anxiety was where the money was. So when Merck started to produce its new antidepressant, amitriptyline, in the early 1960s, it realized that to sell antidepressants it needed to sell depression. To that end, Merck bought and distributed 50,000 copies of a book by Frank Ayd called *Recognizing the Depressed Patient,* which instructed general practitioners how to diagnose depression. The strategy worked. Prescriptions for amitriptyline

To sell antidepressants, Merck needed to sell depression.

took off, though amitriptyline was not even the first antidepressant on the market. (Imipramine, a drug of the same class, had been on the market since the mid-1950s.)

Yet it would be a mistake to think this is merely a matter of the market creating an illness. It is also a matter of a *technology* creating an illness. Wherever we can make the tools of medicine work, the condition that we are working on tends to be reconceptualized as a medical problem. It used to be the case that some people could not have children. This was not a medical problem; it was an unfortunate fact of nature. But once new reproductive technologies—such as in vitro fertilization and sperm donation—came on the scene, that fact of nature was reconceptualized as a medical problem. Now it is called "infertility" and is treated by medical specialists. This kind of reconceptualization runs throughout the history of psychiatry. When the new disorder of "neurasthenia" arose in the nineteenth century, we also got the new treatment of "rest cures" in private clinics. When the new disorder of "gender dysphoria" arose in the mid-twentieth century, we also got new surgical techniques for sex reassignment. When anxiety disorders became widespread in the 1950s and '60s, we also got "minor tranquilizers" such as Miltown and Valium. And when the concept of hyperactivity became widespread in the 1970s, we also got an upsurge in prescriptions for Ritalin.

For people who worry about the extent to which enhancement technologies are being used nowadays, it is tempting to look for something or someone—the pharmaceutical industry, psychiatrists, cosmetic surgeons, the fashion industry, or sometimes simply "the culture"—to blame. In the end, however, these technologies could not have taken off in the way they have without the traction provided by the American sense of identity. In America, technology has become a way for some people to build or reinforce their identity (and their sense of dignity) while standing in front of the social mirror. We all realize how critically important this mirror is for identity. Most of us can keenly identify with the shame that a person feels when society reflects back to him or her an image that is degrading or humiliating. But the flip side to shame is vanity. It is also possible to become obsessed with the mirror, to spend hours in front of it, preening and posing, flexing your biceps, admiring your hair. It is possible to spend so much time in front of the mirror that you lose any sense of who you are apart from the reflection that you see.

Some people call this narcissism, but if they are right, it is a kind of narcissism that is peculiarly dependent on things outside ourselves; that is to say, what other people are saying and thinking about us. This is not just a matter of your looks or personality failing to meet the standards of the culture. It is an underlying set of social structures that demand so much of the way you present yourself to others. In America, your social status is tied to your self-presentation, and if your self-presentation fails, your status will drop. If your status drops, so does your self-respect. Without self-respect, you cannot be truly fulfilled. If you are not fulfilled, you are not living a truly meaningful life.

Such is the cruel logic of our particular moral system.

Analyzing the Text

1. What does Elliott mean by "the ethic of authenticity" that he claims pervades American culture? How is this ethic driving people to seek medical solutions to achieve self-fulfillment?

2. How does Elliott use the case studies to help support his argument about how people alter themselves to reveal their true self?

3. Elliott believes that fear of social stigmas sends people to the pharmacy or to the surgeon's table. He suggests that "this is not psychiatry with a scalpel; it is sociology with a scalpel." According to this essay, how has this attitude about stigma become a rationale for body "enhancements"?

4. In the concluding paragraphs of this essay, Elliott writes, "In America, technology has become a way for some people to build or reinforce their identity (and their sense of dignity) while standing in front of the social mirror." In a cruel twist, then, he contends that one's personal sense of self-fulfillment is directly related to one's social status. Do you agree with Elliott's argument? Why or why not? What are the implications of this perspective?

Writing about Cultural Practices

5. Develop a rhetorical analysis of the selling of self-image in the popular media. Locate advertisements or promotional materials from companies and businesses that sell the kind of enhancement technologies Elliott discusses. These materials may include ads for any number of drugs, from over-the-counter muscle-building supplements to prescription drugs, or medical treatments such as Botox injections or hair restoration. To help focus your analysis, locate two to three examples of products that are marketed to alleviate one type of social stigma such as anxiety, impotence, or aging. As you develop your rhetorical analysis, consider the following questions.

   - Who is the intended audience for this product or procedure?

   - What assumptions do the ads make about their intended audience? What details in the ads lead you to these observations?

   - What type of self-image are these ads promoting or "selling"? In other words, in what ways is the intended drug or procedure presented as a path to achieving self-fulfillment?

   - What attitudes or assumptions about what defines happiness are revealed in these ads? To what extent is one's happiness connected to one's social status?

Christine Rosen, **You—Only Better**

Christine Rosen is a fellow at the Ethics and Public Policy Center in Washington, DC, and is a senior editor of the *New Atlantis*. Her publications include *Preaching Eugenics: Religious Leaders and the American Eugenics Movement* (2004), and her articles have appeared in the *Wall Street Journal, National Review,* and the *New England Journal of Medicine.* In this essay, originally published in the *New Atlantis* in 2004 under the title "The Democratization of Beauty," Rosen argues that "we have succeeded in crafting a narrative of cosmetic surgery as a modern democratic solution . . . to a most undemocratic problem."

> ▶ **Mapping Your Reading**
>
> Rosen observes that American culture has shifted from shaming those who have cosmetic surgery to celebrating them. She coins a label, *Vanitus Democratus,* to describe those people who celebrate cosmetic surgery as "evidence of our country's commitment to equality, prosperity, and individual autonomy." As you read, mark passages in which she argues the moral implications of cosmetic surgery. How does America's acceptance of cosmetic surgery relate to its democratic value system? How has the growing acceptance of cosmetic surgery affected attitudes about "natural" or "unenhanced" appearances?

Mention plastic surgery and the more judgmental among us immediately rattle off a list of traits its devotees probably share: vanity, frivolousness, narcissism, low self-esteem. We imagine shallow socialites or vain movie stars desperately trying to forestall the ravages of time. But in fact, cosmetic surgery is not an industry built on vanity alone, but also on two much more powerful emotions: denial and envy. Cosmetic surgery thrives on our collective denial of aging and on our refusal to accept physiological limits. It feeds our envy of those who embody nature's most powerful but fleeting charms—youth, strength, beauty, and fertility. Its supporters praise its ability to change lives and its critics denounce it as the expression of our society's worst impulses. It is a useful fathometer for assessing the state of our democracy and a Rorschach test for people's views about much broader social currents: the glorification of youth, the tenor of

For another reading on medicine, see Elliot, p. 508.—Eds.

popular culture, the peculiar but strenuous American anxiety about identity. It is also a wildly successful industry—one based on ingenuity and an array of constantly evolving techniques and products, overseen by an army of trained professionals eager to protect and enhance their market prestige.

In recent years, a peculiar species of thought has emerged—call it *Vanitus Democratus*—that doesn't merely tolerate, but embraces cosmetic surgery as evidence of our country's commitment to equality, prosperity, and individual autonomy. "Envy is the basis of democracy," as Bertrand Russell observed, but since beauty is a valuable commodity that is unfairly distributed (what political theorists call "the injustice of the given") it can prompt extremes of envy about its undemocratic effects. Americans loathe such unfairness, but ours is not a society that would tolerate—à la "Harrison Bergeron"—a beauty handicapper who would force-feed the svelte and inflict male pattern baldness on those with thick tresses. Our solution is to democratize beauty, to make it something that, fueled by envy and with enough money and effort, anyone can attain. This blunts its force as an instrument of inequality.

We have succeeded in crafting a narrative of cosmetic surgery as a modern democratic solution (in that it endorses the free market, personal fulfillment, and individual autonomy) to a most undemocratic problem. As cultural historian Sander Gilman has noted, "In a world in which we are judged by how we appear, the belief that we can change our appearance is liberating. We are what we seem to be and we seem to be what we are!" This narrative also feeds into the longstanding American belief in individual transformation and the reinvention of self: Unmoored from the traditional hierarchies, we are free to pursue our bliss.

> "One way to deny our dependence on nature . . . is to make ourselves masters of nature."

But cosmetic surgery is not without potential harms—both to individuals and to society as a whole. Since cosmetic surgery is, as historians David and Sheila Rothman have noted, "enhancement at its most pure," it is a troubling case study of how American culture grapples with techniques designed for therapy that can be used to fulfill our personal desires. Buried in the logic of cosmetic surgery are some disturbing truths about what our culture believes: that it is acceptable to be satisfied by the external markers of success; that the pursuit of such markers is, in and of itself, a useful and psychologically healthy goal for people; that what used to be encouraged—a lifelong process of moral education—is less useful, in the long term, than the appearance of success, health, and beauty; and that if we can overcome the limits nature places on our physical bodies, we should. "One way to deny our dependence on nature," Christopher Lasch wrote many years ago in *The Culture of Narcissism*, "is to invent technologies designed to make ourselves masters of nature." This is what cosmetic surgery promises to do.

You—Only Better

In the end, cosmetic surgery is in some sense self-defeating, since it cannot permanently stop the process of aging. And yet, many of us know formerly dewlapped matrons and love-handled forty-something rogues who are objectively much happier after their surgeries; indeed, some people experience more satisfaction from a "marriage abdominoplasty" (combination lipo and tummy tuck) than they do in their own marriages. In a free society, why should anyone stand in the way of another person's transformation from tatterdemalion to goddess? Isn't this simply the laudable and democratic pursuit of happiness?

If opponents of cosmetic surgery are too quick to dismiss those who claim great psychological benefits, boosters are far too willing to dismiss those who raise concerns. Cosmetic surgery might make individual people happier, but in the aggregate it makes life worse for everyone. By defining beauty up—50 is *literally* the new 40 if a critical mass of people are getting face-lifted and Botoxed— the pressure to conform to these elevated standards increases. So, too, does the amount of time and money we spend on what is ultimately a futile goal: cheating time.

FOUND

from wikipedia.org

PLASTIC SURGERY: A BRIEF HISTORY

Plastic surgery is a general term for operative manual and instrumental treatment which is performed for functional or aesthetic reasons. The word "plastic" derives from the Greek *plastikos* meaning to mold or to shape; its use here is not connected with modern plastics.

The history of cosmetic surgery spans back to the ancient world. The Romans were able to perform simple techniques such as repairing damaged ears. In the Middle Ages, there were techniques to restore a severed nose by attaching the arm to the face and letting a blood supply form, then removing the arm from the new nose. Nevertheless, it was not until modern times that its use became commonplace.

Reconstructive surgical techniques were developed rapidly in the period after the First World War when patients with survivable but disfiguring injuries required new approaches. The English military hospitals of the period trained surgeons from the world over in these new techniques. The main advances were with flap surgery—moving tissue from one location to another with an intact blood supply.

Even for men and women who have objectively achieved success—the award-winning novelist, the highflying CEO—the refusal to meet these beauty standards will brand you as uncompetitive, evidence to the contrary notwithstanding.

The risk is not a society of beautiful but homogeneous mannequins. "Most of my patients want to look more like themselves than they've looked in a long time," Dr. Weston told me. "They don't want to look like someone else." The danger is a growing intolerance for what we would naturally look like without constant nipping, tucking, peeling, and liposuctioning. In the process, it contributes to that "philosophy of fatigue" and "disappointment with achievements" that Paul Nystrom, an early and astute critic of modern marketing techniques, argued led to society's embrace of "more superficial things in which fashion reigns."

"Most of my patients want to look more like themselves."

In part, the discomfort some people have with cosmetic surgery is a discomfort about the particular form of denial it represents: a denial of bodily limits. The language of cosmetic surgery does everything to obscure this. Something "cosmetic" is not supposed to be a permanent alteration, as plastic

"Honey, let's lay off the Botox for a while, shall we?"

surgery is. And humans are not "plastic," but beings embodied in tissue, flesh, and bone that will, at a certain point, resist our efforts to remold it. But the freedom to do what we will with ourselves, which is the model for cosmetic surgery, presents a real challenge when we start thinking about permanent alterations to the human body. As a case study for how we might act in the genetic future, cosmetic surgery—which is individualistic, consumer-oriented, largely unregulated, and invokes the therapeutic language so popular today—is hardly a reassuring model.

In the 1990s, a French performance artist named Orlan embarked on a multi-stage cosmetic surgery art installment that involved having surgery performed that would give her the chin of the Venus de Milo, Mona Lisa's forehead, and Psyche's nose, among other things. Pictures of one of her "performances" show a partially anesthetized Orlan reclining on an operating room table, draped in a surreal, mirrored gown and speaking into a cordless microphone. Buzzing about are surgeons and nurses decked out in scrubs designed by Issey Miyake and Paco Rabanne. But Orlan has other enthusiasms. As the *New York Times* noted, she "grandly proclaims her work to be 'a fight against nature and the idea of God' and also a way to prepare the world for widespread genetic engineering." Orlan offers us a disturbing peek into our future.

In the end, the questions raised by cosmetic surgery pose a special challenge for conservatives. Conservatives advocate free markets and individual autonomy (albeit linked to personal responsibility), but profess horror at the logical excesses of this view. We cringe when commercial culture throws up a Michael Jackson or an *Extreme Makeover,* but on what grounds do we argue for their end?

Like our new reproductive technologies, cosmetic surgery collides with intimate, personal choices about the kind of lives we want to lead. And it becomes difficult to argue against the exercise of choice either legally or politically.

Perhaps this is the point at which culture becomes more important than policy, and the direct engagement with our cultural extremes a way of helping us find a more rational center. In the end, democratic culture seeks authenticity, but it doesn't always find it in the old forms where conservatives tend to feel more comfortable. And so we need to ask less threatening but no less fundamental questions—questions about the excesses of individualism and the extremes of democracy, questions about what are and what are not genuine social goods, and questions about how we measure success and failure.

We are not yet a nation of Narcissi, content to stare happily into the pool, our surgically enhanced self-esteem intact but our character irrevocably compromised. But we would do well to be more engaged in the culture that is encouraging us to move in that direction. "There are no grades of vanity, there are only grades of ability in concealing it," Mark Twain purportedly wrote. Concealing our desire for physical perfection behind a mask of democratic or therapeutic rhetoric will ultimately do us no good. We should, instead, bring cosmetic surgery out into the open, not merely to please our taste for voyeurism, but to understand how we might handle new and increasingly sophisticated techniques for empowering our vanity—techniques which stand to make that vanity much harder to conceal and to control.

▶ Analyzing the Text

1. What assumptions or attitudes about nature are behind the rising popularity of cosmetic surgery?

2. At one point, Rosen suggests that "[b]uried in the logic of cosmetic surgery are some disturbing truths about what our culture believes." What rationales do people use for seeking out cosmetic surgery? What principles have been linked to the "right" to cosmetic surgery?

3. Why do middle class men and women seem particularly obsessed with seeking out surgical solutions to physical imperfections? How does this relate to Rosen's claim that beauty has become "democratized"?

4. **Connecting to Another Reading.** In "American Bioscience Meets the American Dream" (p. 508), Carl Elliott examines how the search for self-fulfillment leads people to define personality traits—such as shyness, anxiety, or lack of concentration—as treatable illnesses. How do you relate his argument to Rosen's, which examines our culture's obsession with outward appearances?

▶ Writing about Cultural Practices

5. Both "American Bioscience Meets the American Dream" and "You—Only Better" investigate the growing practice of seeking medical "fixes" to find self-fulfillment. Yet, neither specifically considers how these practices relate to attitudes about

beauty and race. A 2004 *Newsweek* article, "Smooth Operations," reports that use of cosmetic enhancement is rising in popularity among African Americans.

What beauty ideals are reflected in the surgical enhancements chosen by different racial groups? For this assignment, investigate how the cosmetic surgery industry attempts to attract potential clients from different racial groups. To begin, find websites sponsored by cosmetic surgery clinics, and pay attention to philosophy statements, sales pitches, and visual images. As you write your critical analysis, consider the following questions.

- Which specific kinds of cosmetic procedures are most promoted at the sites? Are these the same for all racial groups, or are some types of surgeries or procedures specifically aimed at particular racial groups?
- Are there differences in the way different races are marketed to at the sites?
- What standards or definitions of beauty do these websites seem to promote?
- How, if at all, do these sites respond to criticism that cosmetic surgery promotes one standard of beauty over others?

Jason D. Hill, **Save Lives! Defy Nature!**
Four Letters Responding to "Save Lives! Defy Nature!"

Jason D. Hill is assistant professor of philosophy at DePaul University and has been a Fellow at Cornell University's Society for the Humanities. In his essay "Save Lives! Defy Nature!," first published in 2001 on Salon.com, Hill reacts to news stories about parents who murdered their young children. He contends that these tragedies should spark a national debate on the right to procreate: "We need to probe deeply this absurdly folksy idea that the deep need to have children is simply a call of nature."

Hill is the latest in a line of writers who have openly questioned society's responsibility to its children. The most famous of these is Jonathan Swift (1667–1745), who wrote "A Modest Proposal" in 1729. This essay is a biting satire, or critique, of the callous disregard of English landlords for the people of Ireland. In it, Swift proposes that the solution to alleviating starvation, poverty, and homelessness in Ireland is to eat Irish children. Much as Swift used satire to attract people's attention to serious social problems in Ireland, Hill writes with a strident tone to provoke readers' interest in his argument.

> ▶ **Mapping Your Reading**
>
> As the essay's title indicates, Hill believes that having children demands a level of moral responsibility that is lacking in today's culture. "Save Lives! Defy Nature!" spurred several responses from Salon.com readers, including the four reprinted here following the essay. Hill's abrasive tone serves to call attention to a topic he believes should be treated seriously. As you read, use the margins to make notes about the supporting evidence Hill uses to build his argument. Should reproduction be viewed as a call of nature? Is everyone equally fit to be a parent?

R ecently, a father of three was shot and killed by police after he reportedly stabbed his sons for no apparent reason, killing two and leaving one seriously wounded.

This horrible news was made worse by two earlier events: the brutal killing by Andrea Yates of her five children, and the nauseating argument made by Susan Kushner Resnick, in which she defends Yates—reportedly the victim of postpartum syndrome—under the guise of moral abstention.

Why are so many compassionate, hand-wringing sentimentalists rushing to the defense of people who should have had their reproductive organs removed years ago?

The Yates murders prompted a friend of mine, a quintessential yuppie juggling fatherhood, a profitable business, and a marriage, to send me an e-mail in which he sympathizes deeply with Yates. He claims that we are all walking a thin line between sanity and insanity and that sometimes people kill their kids out of love. Oh yeah, and you, like the rest of this culture, insist on siding with these solipsistic narcissists called modern-day parents who need a good dose of Critical Thinking 101. In an imperfect world, crucial distinctions have to be made. Most of us, even if we walk a fine line between sanity and insanity, do not kill our children. The difference in our fine line lies in the action itself, not the potentiality. What happened in Yates's case was a crucial lapse in the judgment of those in her inner circle. Few of us ever have the chance to be prognosticators on such a level; they had it and they blew it. Yates's husband, her family, and her friends should all be brought in for questioning and charged with failing to provide this woman with a lifetime of birth control pills. Her husband should be castigated for not considering a vasectomy after the second pregnancy.

I am not a supporter of governmental intrusion into the reproductive lives of human beings, but this tragedy leaves me questioning my deep liberal convictions on many levels. My fondest hope, however, is that this disaster will lead to a national debate on the so-called right to reproduce. We need to probe deeply this absurdly folksy idea that the deep need to have children is simply a call of nature.

Even if it is, so what? Nature beckons us in the direction of a great many urges, such as unbridled rage and anger, reckless sexual licentiousness, and gluttony. In the context of our life situations, we judiciously cast many of these callings into the waste bins of depravity where they belong.

Unreflective indulgence into this "need" to reproduce is a narcissistic conceit designed to give meaning to one's life at the expense of innocent children. Oprah is right! Get a dog. It will change your life and, depending on the breed, it need not be too demanding. If it is, you may turn it in to your nearest shelter with a clear conscience and a casual out: "This creature was not what I had in mind."

We have mistakenly taken the allegedly natural human desire to reproduce, which in so many ways is nothing more than old-fashioned tribalism, as a given.

It escapes the moral scrutiny of qualifying principles. We do not allow everyone who has a desire to fly a plane, to perform surgery, this automatic freedom. They must satisfy certain conditions and demonstrate competence. They must be *qualified.* Why? Because, among other things, the consequences of unchecked desires are too great for the rest of us.

> The "need" to reproduce is a narcissistic conceit.

"Who are you or I to judge what is a responsible number of children to have?" my friend fires off in his righteous e-mail, smarting, no doubt, from the guilt he feels over whether he has enough bonding time to give his three children. "If five is too many, is three OK? Is one child too many if not raised in a perfect nurturing home?" And on and on he goes, indicting Americans for needing to despise people like Yates.

"Help!" I want to say to someone out there. My conscience as an ethicist pricks me. Do I call some hot line and voice my concern that this average hard-working man may go over the brink soon? He won't go, though. Most people don't; but I will inherit their children in the classroom. As a university professor, I see it all—grown college students breaking down in my office, sobbing and sobbing. It's all about Mama and Papa and lost love and the evidence that Freud is and has always been right on target.

I am childless by choice and I will remain so, partly because at 36 I feel burned out from taking care of the kids these parents have neglected. When I ask these students why they can't talk to their parents, it's like unlocking a cistern of acidic sour grapes. What comes out is hatred. Kids in America hate their parents! There, I've said it. The ubiquitous chant ("I hate you, I hate you!") of children to their parents means just what it says. No, it's not the unreflective free association of little Billy and his sister subconsciously rehearsing one-liners for a soap opera 20 years down the road.

I think a declaration of war should be made on parents. Don't have more kids than you can afford to nurture and take care of! Who cares about your pathetic need to fulfill something deep inside of you? The problem is that once you eject that child into the world, people like me have to go about cleaning up after your messy needs. Child rearing is like a science; it is a career choice and should be treated as such. If you are not willing to devote everything, and I mean everything, do not have children.

But that's too demanding a condition to make of parents—I can hear the whining rebuttals. You know what? Life is tough and demanding. Get a grip. A right to give in to the urgings of Mother Nature cannot take moral precedence over the criteria for good stewardship of children, who cannot care for themselves. The crisis in American schools is not about crime or corporate downsizing; it's not even about underpaid teachers. It is a crisis in parenting, which the collective consciousness dares not name because it is too deeply complicit in this state of bankruptcy.

The collapse of serious devotional parenting, which coincides with the rise of families with two working parents, needs to be addressed openly and honestly, once and for all, in a serious nonpartisan manner. This part-time job of parenting

There [are] 120,000 children of poor parents annually born. The question therefore is, how this number shall be reared and provided for? which, under the present situation of affairs, is utterly impossible by all methods hitherto proposed. . . .

[I] am assured by a very knowing American of my acquaintance in London, that a young healthy child well nursed is at a year old a most delicious, nourishing, and wholesome food, whether stewed, roasted, baked, or broiled; and I make no doubt that it will equally serve in a fricassee or a ragout. I do therefore humbly offer it to public consideration that of the [1]20,000 children already computed, 20,000 may be reserved for breed . . . [and] that the remaining 100,000 may at a year old, be offered in sale to the persons of quality and fortune through the kingdom. . . .

—From "A Modest Proposal," 1729

has overtaxed our school system, and believe it or not, our universities as well, where teachers are forced to assume the role of surrogate parents and all the problems associated with it. Hillary Clinton was right. It does take a village. But let us not fool ourselves. The village in any realistic sense is the school, which assists in the socialization process begun by the parent and ensures the continued matriculation of the child into adult life.

But guess what? The village collapsed because it took on more than its fair share and lacked the crucial support of ambitious wannabes who deposited their loads without even thinking: "Gee, how can the village do all these things when I've placed all these restrictions on it, like, don't discipline my child; don't spank his rowdy butt when it needs to be; don't fail him because I'm paying for his education (private or public: I pay my taxes) and hell, I'm not paying for a failing grade; don't demand that he respect you when just last night he threw the cereal in my face; monitor all his playground activities while preparing your lesson plans, if you don't and he falls and scrapes the sheen off his fingernail I'll sue you all?"

These people disgust me. What they want is a moral blank check endorsing their perversions. An individual who is unable to gauge the huge divide between his desires and the means required to achieve them in a healthy way is called a child. An adult who fails to realize this has a cognitive handicap. But an adult who actually executes his or her desires in full knowledge of such circumstances is an unconscionable pervert.

Gays and lesbians, once heroic outlaw souls who bravely took up the responsibility of morally challenging hegemonic notions of conventional sex, family life, and relationships, are putting this alleged call of nature into high libidinal drive. They, along with all the other child-hungry breeders, are leading the nation in the multiple-birth craze. Multiple births, once viewed as an exception in nature, are now uncritically accepted as a personal preference and the price of fertility treatment. If you feel the need, buy two, technologically generate three, or four, or even seven. Hey, for your bravery and contribution to the wear and tear on your collapsible uterus we'll throw in tons of free stuff— diapers, baby food, and even a house or two.

The antidotes to this are too numerous to mention. But I have a couple of recommendations to ethically minded people who actually care a great deal about children: From now on, your response to anyone announcing a pregnancy other than their first should be a stern and formidable look. Let the full weight of this gaze fall like apocalyptic brimstone on their gooey-eyed attempts at wonder and innocence. Follow the gaze with the comment: "You have my deepest sympathies," and let the unconcealed moral accountability to which you are holding them reverberate clearly so that your remark sounds more like reproach than condolence.

The crisis in American schools is a crisis in parenting.

After the child (or children) is born, send a gift (use your imagination but keep it very respectful), which underscores your initial consternation, along with a note that simply reminds them of the following: The magic of life does not start in utero or during labor or even at conception. Nothing in nature is magical. It can't be. Nature simply is. The magic, or rather the hard dose of realism out of which mature, responsible lives are made, begins in the small, devoted, and deeply thought-out steps you take in life to ensure that your playtimes with Nature turn into something stable, healthy, and a hell of a lot more significant than 10 fingers and 10 toes.

Four Letters Responding to "Save Lives! Defy Nature!"

I have just one question about Jason Hill's Modest Proposal for the new millennium: Since no one seems able to agree, from year to year and month to month, how to define good parenting, who exactly is going to decide who gets to have children and who doesn't?

–Jeff Crook

The fact is, most parents I know are devoted to their children, to an incredible degree. I'm only guessing, but I think the ungodly pressure put upon this Texan woman to be a perfect homeschooling baby-machine (coupled with severe mental illness) might have put her over the edge. I have never wanted to kill my kids, ever. I've never even entertained the thought. Indeed, like most parents, I would throw myself in front of a train to save them from the slightest harm.

–Dorothy Nixon

Jason Hill, have you been reading my mind? How encouraging it was to read what needs to be shouted but is only mentioned in whispers. I am a Texas court-appointed guardian ad litem for children in CPS custody. In my current case, the mother is 25 and has 5 children she can't take care of. Nothing will keep her from getting pregnant again, not even the termination of her parental rights. Based on experience, I fully expect her to have more children. Those of us who work in protective services are truly like the boy sticking his finger in the dyke. If nothing changes, our society will only worsen due to the abundance of unwanted, unplanned, unsupervised poor souls.

–Denise Havard

I'm sure Hill's article will receive a tidal wave of angry response, but I found it a refreshing counterattack to the constant barrage of procreation propaganda we're treated to in the news and in advertising these days. There's nothing outlandish in suggesting that people, rich and poor, should give serious thought to how many children they can reasonably support.

–Elizabeth Bass

Analyzing the Text

1. Hill's tone is meant to get readers' attention, but it is his argument that he hopes will stick in people's minds. How does the author build the supporting evidence for his argument? How effective is his argument?

2. How does Hill characterize people who have more children than he believes they should have? What is his problem with them? How do you react to his perspective?

3. What should qualify a person to become a parent, in Hill's view? What role should nature play?

4. Which of Hill's claims do the response letters react most to—either positively or negatively? How effectively do the letter writers make their claims about Hill's argument?

Writing about Cultural Practices

5. The introduction to this essay connects Hill's argument with that of Jonathan Swift's "A Modest Proposal." Both essays respond to a specific social crisis, and both offer rather harsh assessments of society's failures toward children. Develop a comparative analysis of "Save Lives! Defy Nature!" and Swift's classic essay. Before you write, read both essays carefully, paying attention to the structure of the arguments and the tone each writer employs. As you draft your essay, consider the following questions.

   - The question that both writers address is "What is society's responsibility toward the raising of children?" But what is the central claim (or thesis) of each essay? Is this central claim stated directly or indirectly?

   - How does Swift's use of satire affect his argument? What is the impact of Hill's more direct approach?

   - How does each writer build support for his argument?

   - How does the tone of each essay affect the overall arguments being made?

ON THE WEB
To read the full text of "A Modest Proposal," go to Chapter 6,
bedfordstmartins.com/remix

Unlocking the Human Mind: Phrenology vs. The MRI

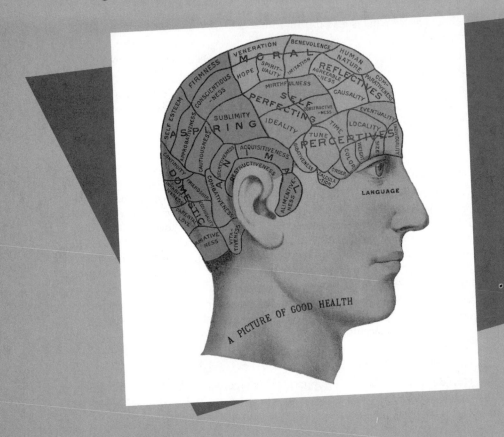

What gives us our personality? Where does the soul reside? Questions like these led German physician Franz Joseph Gall to develop his theory of phrenology in 1800. As the above diagram illustrates, Gall believed that the mind is divided into separate departments, each specialized for certain tendencies such as combativeness, secretiveness, cautiousness, benevolence, conscientiousness, wit, and individuality. Consequently, phrenologists claimed to be able to discern a person's character and personality traits—even criminality—by examining the shape and unevenness of the head. At best, phrenology is remembered as a fairground attraction; at worst, it is considered a precursor to craniometry, the anthropological study of

skull size and shape that racist groups have infamously misused.

The path from phrenology to present-day brain imaging marks humankind's desire to understand the human mind. Early attempts to literally see inside the living brain involved dangerous procedures; however, the 1970s saw the introduction of magnetic resonance imaging, or MRI scanning, which reads signals produced in the body when the head is placed in a strong magnetic field. On receiving the 2003 Nobel Prize in Physiology or Medicine for his discoveries concerning MRI, Sir Peter Mansfield described letters he and his cowinner have received from patients: "What comes through in much of the correspondence is the strong

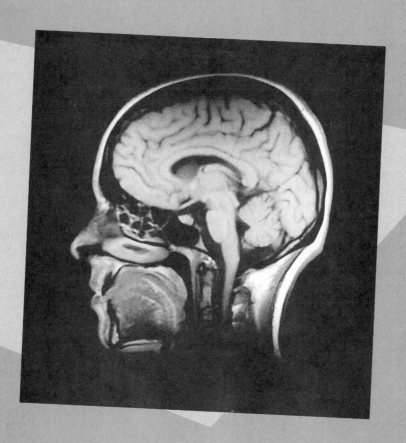

sense of relief at knowing the details of their illness and the hope inspired by the rigorous evaluation of their problem using MRI."

1. What do these images suggest about humankind's desire to understand the mind? What do they convey about cultural attitudes toward science as a key to unlocking human nature?

2. The rise of scientific medicine over the past two centuries replaced older cultural beliefs that attributed illness to demons or other spiritual forces. Conduct some research to learn the history of Chinese, Greek, Egyptian, or Indian medicine. What similarities and differences do you notice between the ways these ancient cultures sought to understand the human mind and body? Are there any cultural attitudes from these ancient societies surviving in modern medicine?

3. Though phrenologists deny it, many regard phrenology as a protoscience, barely one step above quackery. Can you think of current examples of quack treatments for mental ailments? What assumptions do proponents of quack medicine rely on to sell their wares? To learn more about quack medicine, visit Quackwatch.org on the Internet.

Lewis Thomas, **On Cloning a Human Being**

Lewis Thomas (1913–1993) attended Princeton University when he was 15, and then Harvard Medical School. His work ranged from performing medical research at Tulane University to academic administration as Dean of New York University's School of Medicine. In 1973 he led the Sloan-Kettering Institute in New York in its cancer research, and in 1982 was called "the father of modern immunology and experimental pathology" at a ceremony honoring his work. Throughout his medical career, Thomas composed volumes of short essays that connect his interests in biology with literature. Thomas wrote in *The Youngest Science* that his essays liberated him from science writing's "relentlessly flat style required for absolute unambiguity in every word." His essay collections include *The Lives of a Cell: Notes of a Biology Watcher* (1974), *The Medusa and the Snail* (1979), and *Late Night Thoughts on Listening to Mahler's Ninth Symphony* (1984). As you read the following essay on cloning, keep in mind that Thomas wrote it in the late 1970s, before the successful cloning of animals. When Thomas wrote this piece, he was addressing the question of cloning on philosophical and ethical grounds, not as a matter of scientific actuality.

> ### Mapping Your Reading
>
> Cloning represents perhaps the ultimate example of humans attempting to control nature. As you read, pay attention to how Thomas, speaking as a scientist, approaches the ethical debates over cloning. Underline those passages where he makes his argument most effectively. What is the impact of cloning living creatures on our relationship to nature?

It is now theoretically possible to recreate an identical creature from any animal or plant, from the DNA contained in the nucleus of any somatic cell. A single plant root-tip cell can be teased and seduced into conceiving a perfect copy of the whole plant; a frog's intestinal epithelial cell possesses the complete instructions needed for a new, same frog. If the technology were further advanced, you could do this with a human being, and there are now startled predictions all over the place that this will in fact be done, someday, in order to provide a version of immortality for carefully selected, especially valuable people.

The cloning of humans is on most of the lists of things to worry about from Science, along with behavior control, genetic engineering, transplanted heads, computer poetry, and the unrestrained growth of plastic flowers.

Cloning is the most dismaying of prospects, mandating as it does the elimination of sex with only a metaphoric elimination of death as compensation. It is almost no comfort to know that one's cloned, identical surrogate lives on, especially when the living will very likely involve edging one's real, now aging self off to the side, sooner or later. It is hard to imagine anything like filial affection or respect for a single, unmated nucleus; harder still to think of one's new, self-generated self as anything but an absolute, desolate orphan. Not to mention the complex interpersonal relationship involved in raising one's self from infancy, teaching the language, enforcing discipline, instilling good manners and the like. How would you feel if you became an incorrigible juvenile delinquent by proxy, at the age of 55?

The public questions are obvious. Who is to be selected, and on what qualifications? How to handle the risks of misused technology, such as self-determined cloning by the rich and powerful but socially objectionable, or the cloning by governments of dumb, docile masses for the world's work? What will be the effect on all the uncloned rest of us of human sameness? After all, we've accustomed ourselves through hundreds of millennia to the continual exhilaration of uniqueness; each of us is totally different, in a fundamental sense, from all the other four billion. Selfness is an essential fact of life. The thought of human nonselfness, precise sameness, is terrifying, when you think about it.

> The public questions are obvious. Who is to be selected, and on what qualifications?

Well, don't think about it, because it isn't a probable possibility, not even as a long shot for the distant future, in my opinion. I agree that you might clone some people who would look amazingly like their parental cell donors, but the odds are that they'd be almost as different as you or me, and certainly more different than any of today's identical twins.

The time required for the experiment is only one of the problems, but a formidable one. Suppose you wanted to clone a prominent, spectacularly successful diplomat, to look after the Middle East problems of the distant future. You'd have to catch him and persuade him, probably not very hard to do, and extirpate a cell. But then you'd have to wait for him to grow up through embryonic life and then for at least 40 years more, and you'd have to be sure all observers remained patient and unmeddlesome through his unpromising, ambiguous childhood and adolescence.

Moreover, you'd have to be sure of recreating his environment, perhaps down to the last detail. "Environment" is a word which really means people, so you'd have to do a lot more cloning than just the diplomat himself.

This is a very important part of the cloning problem, largely overlooked in our excitement about the cloned individual himself. You don't have to agree all the way with B. F. Skinner to acknowledge that the environment does make a difference,

The idea of cloning humans existed in science fiction long before it became experimentally feasible. *The Clones* (1973), produced around the time that Thomas wrote his essay, was among the first sci-fi films to capitalize on cloning.

They duplicated one man too many.

They had to find him.

And kill him.

THE CLŌNES

It may seem like science fiction...But it is based on science fact.

Used with permimssion of Lamar Card; movie poster distributed by Phoenix Fidelity, L.A.

and when you examine what we really mean by the word "environment" it comes down to other human beings. We use euphemisms and jargon for this, like "social forces," "cultural influences," even Skinner's "verbal community," but what is meant is the dense crowd of nearby people who talk to, listen to, smile or frown at, give to, withhold from, nudge, push, caress, or flail out at the individual. No matter what the genome says, these people have a lot to do with shaping a character. Indeed, if all you had was the genome, and no people around, you'd grow a sort of vertebrate plant, nothing more.

So, to start with, you will undoubtedly need to clone the parents. No question about this. This means the diplomat is out, even in theory, since you couldn't have gotten cells from both his parents at the time when he was himself just recognizable as an early social treasure. You'd have to limit the list of clones to people already certified as sufficiently valuable for the effort, with both parents still alive. The parents would need cloning and, for consistency, their parents as well. I suppose you'd also need the usual informed-consent forms, filled out and signed, not easy to get if I know parents, even harder for grandparents.

But this is only the beginning. It is the whole family that really influences the way a person turns out, not just the parents, according to current psychiatric thinking. Clone the family.

Then what? The way each member of the family develops has already been determined by the environment set around him, and this environment is more people, people outside the family, schoolmates, acquaintances, lovers, enemies, car-pool partners, even, in special circumstances, peculiar strangers across the aisle on the subway. Find them, and clone them.

But there is no end to the protocol. Each of the outer contacts has his own surrounding family, and his and their outer contacts. Clone them all.

To do the thing properly, with any hope of ending up with a genuine duplicate of a single person, you really have no choice. You must clone the world, no less.

We are not ready for an experiment of this size, nor, I should think, are we willing. For one thing, it would mean replacing today's world by an entirely identical world to follow immediately, and this means no new, natural, spontaneous, random, chancy children. No children at all, except for the manufactured doubles of those now on the scene. Plus all those identical adults, including all of today's politicians, all seen double. It is too much to contemplate.

Moreover, when the whole experiment is finally finished, 50 years or so from now, how could you get a responsible scientific reading on the outcome? Somewhere in there would be the original clonee, probably lost and overlooked, now well into middle age, but everyone around him would be precise duplicates of today's everyone. It would be today's same world, filled to overflowing with duplicates of today's people and their same, duplicated problems, probably all resentful at having had to go through our whole thing all over, sore enough at the clonee to make endless trouble for him, if they found him.

The thought of human non-selfness, precise sameness, is terrifying.

And obviously, if the whole thing were done precisely right, they would still be casting about for ways to solve the problem of universal dissatisfaction, and sooner or later they'd surely begin to look around at each other, wondering who should be cloned for his special value to society, to get us out of all this. And so it would go, in regular cycles, perhaps forever.

I once lived through a period when I wondered what Hell could be like, and I stretched my imagination to try to think of a perpetual sort of damnation. I have to confess, I never thought of anything like this.

I have an alternative suggestion, if you're looking for a way out. Set cloning aside, and don't try it. Instead, go in the other direction. Look for ways to get mutations more quickly, new variety, different songs. Fiddle around, if you must fiddle, but never with ways to keep things the same, no matter who, not even yourself. Heaven, somewhere ahead, has got to be a change.

Analyzing the Text

1. What does Thomas see as the scientific community's responsibility to the natural world? How does the issue of cloning highlight this responsibility?

2. In the middle of his essay, Thomas describes a hypothetical case of cloning that quickly becomes absurd. What is the effect of this imagined scenario on his overall argument?

3. As a biologist, Thomas writes as an expert. How would you react to this essay differently if it were written by a nonscientist? What is the effect of his argument, knowing that it was written in the late 1970s, long before the cloning of living creatures had been successfully attempted?

4. **Connecting to Another Reading.** One of Thomas's chief worries about cloning humans is that it will create a terrifying sameness among human beings and uniqueness, as a characteristic, will disappear. How might you relate this argument against cloning to Christine Rosen's argument about the effects of cosmetic surgery in "You—Only Better" (p. 517)? What connections do you find between these two essays?

Writing about Cultural Practices

5. How have the arguments about cloning changed in the decades since Thomas's essay was originally published? Working as a class, identify five or six essays about cloning by other prominent scientists or bioethicists. Working in groups, develop an oral report in which you describe one of the essays you have identified and compare it to Thomas's essay. As you plan your presentation, consider the following questions.

   - How has the debate about cloning changed since Thomas's essay was originally published?

   - What does the essay you've selected identify as the key issues to consider in debates over cloning?

Steven Pinker, **Against Nature**

Steven Pinker is the Johnstone Family Professor in psychology at Harvard University and writer of popular science books. Named one of the most influential people in 2004's *Time* magazine, Pinker has published award-winning books on language and cognitive science. For 21 years, Pinker was a professor in the Department of Brain and Cognitive Sciences at the Massachusetts Institute of Technology. He has published numerous books in his field, including *Visual Cognition* (1985), *The Language Instinct* (1994), and *The Blank Slate: The Denial of Human Nature in Modern Intellectual Life* (2002). "Against Nature" was originally published in *Discover* magazine in 1997. In this essay, Pinker explores questions surrounding human behavior and survival.

> ▶ **Mapping Your Reading**
>
> Pinker writes, "Much of human behavior is a recipe for genetic suicide, not propagation." How, then, can we explain human survival and evolution? This is the central question of "Against Nature." As you read, pay attention to how Pinker uses the first half of the essay to build up to what he suggests is the best explanation of human behavior. Underline passages that critique other theories of human behavior. Then, put checkmarks near passages in which Pinker states his own explanation. From an evolutionary perspective, how are we to make sense of human behavior that doesn't appear to promote the continuation of the human species?

There is an old song by Tom Paxton in which an adult reminisces about a wonderful childhood toy:

It went ZIP! when it moved,
And POP! when it stopped,
And WHIRRR! when it stood still.
I never knew just what it was
And I guess I never will.

The whimsy of the song comes from the childlike pleasure in a complicated object with an inscrutable function. When we grow up, we demand to know what an artifact is designed to do. Coming across a contraption in an antique store, we ask what it is, and when we are told that it is a cherry pitter, the springs, hinges, and levers all suddenly make sense in a satisfying rush of insight. This is called reverse engineering. In forward engineering, one designs a machine to do something; in reverse engineering, one figures out what a machine was designed to do.

The human body is a wonderfully complex assembly of struts, springs, pulleys, hinges, sockets, tanks, pipes, pumps, and filters, and since the seventeenth century, when William Harvey deduced that the valves in veins are there to make the blood circulate, we have understood the body by reverse engineering it. Even today we can be delighted to learn what mysterious parts are for. Why do we have wrinkled, asymmetrical ears? Because they filter sound waves coming from different directions in different ways. The sound shadow tells the brain whether the source of the sound is above or below, in front of or behind us.

We have understood the body by reverse engineering it.

The rationale for reverse engineering living things comes, of course, from Charles Darwin. He showed how "that perfection of structure and coadaptation which most justly excites our admiration" arises not from God's foresight but from natural selection operating over immense spans of time. Organisms vary, and in each generation the lucky variants that are better adapted to survival and reproduction take up a larger proportion of the population. The complicated machinery of plants and animals thus appears to have been engineered to allow them to survive and reproduce.

The human mind, which produces our behavior, is a product of the brain, another complex organ shaped by natural selection, and we should be able to reverse engineer it too. And so we have, for many parts of our psychology. Perception scientists have long realized that our sense of sight is not there to entertain us with pretty patterns but to grant us an awareness of the true forms and materials in the world. The selective advantage is obvious: Animals that know where the food, the predators, and the cliffs are can put the food in their stomachs, keep themselves out of the stomachs of others, and stay on the right side of the cliff tops. Many of our emotions are also products of natural engineering. Fear keeps us away from heights and dangerous animals; disgust deters us from eating bodily wastes and putrefying flesh.

But reverse engineering is possible only when you have an inkling of what a device was designed to accomplish. We don't understand the cherry pitter until we catch on that it was designed as a machine for removing pits from cherries rather than as a paperweight or wrist exerciser. The same is true in biological reverse engineering. Through the 1950s, many biologists worried about why organisms have body parts that seem to do them no good. Why do bees have a barbed stinger that pulls the bee's body apart when dislodged? Why do mammals have mammary glands, which skim nutrients from the mother's blood and package them as milk for the benefit of another animal?

Today we know that these are pseudo-problems, arising from the wrong idea of what the bodies of organisms are for. The ultimate goal of a body is not to benefit itself or its species or its ecosystem but to maximize the number of copies of the genes that made it in the first place. Natural selection is about replicators, entities that keep a stable identity across many generations of copying. Replicators that enhance the probability of their own replication come to predominate, regardless of whose body the replicated copies sit in. Genes for barbed stingers can predominate because copies of those genes sit in the body of the queen and are protected when the worker suicidally repels an invader. Genes for mammary glands can predominate because copies of those genes sit in the young bodies nourished by the milk.

The goal of the body is to maximize the number of copies of the genes that made it in the first place.

So when we ask questions like "Who or what is supposed to benefit from an adaptation?" and "What is a design in living things a design for?," the theory of natural selection provides the answer: the long-term stable replicators, genes. This has become a commonplace in biology, summed up in Richard Dawkins's book title *The Selfish Gene* and in Samuel Butler's famous quip that a hen is an egg's way of making another egg.

What difference does all this make to reverse engineering the mind? For many parts of the mind, not much. Vision and fear seem clearly to benefit the perceiver and fearer. But when it comes to our social lives, where our actions often do not benefit ourselves, it makes a big difference who or what we take to be the ultimate beneficiary. Mammary glands were demystified when we realized that they benefit the genes for making the mammary glands—not the copies in the mother but the copies likely to be found in the milk drinker. In the same way, kind acts toward our children can be demystified when we realize that they can benefit copies of the genes that build a brain that inclines a person toward such kind acts—not the copies in the kind actor but the copies likely to be found in the beneficiaries. We nurture our children and favor our relatives because doing so has a good chance of helping copies of the genes for nurturance and nepotism inside the children and the relatives.

In the case of altruistic behavior toward nonrelatives, a different explanation is needed, but it still hinges on an ultimate benefit to the genes for the altruistic behavior. People tend to be nice to those who are nice to them. Genes for trading favors with other favor traders can prosper for the same reason that the partners in an economic trade can prosper: both parties are better off if what they gain is worth more to them than what they give up.

The theory that human social behavior is a product of natural engineering for gene propagation came to be known in the 1970s as sociobiology and was summed up by saying that the brain is a fitness maximizer, or that people strive to spread their genes. It offered a realization of Darwin's famous prediction in *Origin of Species* that psychology would be based on a new foundation, fully integrated into our understanding of the natural world.

But there was one problem with the theory. When we look at human behavior around us, we discover that the brain-as-fitness-maximizer theory is obviously, crashingly, stunningly wrong. Much of human behavior is a recipe for genetic suicide, not propagation.

People use contraception. They adopt children who are unrelated to them. They take vows of celibacy. They watch pornography when they could be seeking a mate. They forgo food to buy heroin. In India some people sell their blood to

THE FAR SIDE® By GARY LARSON

"I know you miss the Wainwrights, Bobby, but they were weak and stupid people—and that's why we have wolves and other large predators."

buy movie tickets. In our culture people postpone childbearing to climb the corporate ladder, and eat themselves into an early grave.

What are we to make of this Darwinian madness? One response is to look for subtle ways in which behavior really might aid fitness. Perhaps celibate people have more time to raise large broods of nieces and nephews and thereby propagate more copies of their genes than they would if they had their own children. Perhaps priests and people in childless households make up for their lack of legitimate offspring by having many clandestine affairs. But these explanations feel strained, and less sympathetic observers have come to different conclusions: Human behavior has nothing to do with biology and follows arbitrary cultural norms instead.

To anyone with scientific curiosity, it would be disappointing if human behavior had to be permanently walled off from our understanding of the natural world. The founders of a new approach called evolutionary psychology—the anthropologists Donald Symons and John Tooby and the psychologist Leda Cosmides, all at the University of California at Santa Barbara—have shown that it needn't be. When you think it through, they argue, you find that the gene-centered theory of evolution does not predict that people are fitness maximizers or gene propagators.

First, natural selection is not a puppet master that pulls the strings of behavior directly. The targets of selection, the genes buried in eggs and sperm, cannot control behavior either, because obviously they are in no position to see the world or to move the muscles. Naturally selected genes can only design the generator of behavior: the package of neural information—processing and goal-pursuing mechanisms called the mind.

That is why it is wrong to say that the point of human striving is to spread our genes. With the exception of the fertility doctor who artificially inseminated patients with his own semen, the donors to the sperm bank for Nobel Prize winners, and other weirdos, no human being (or animal) really strives to spread his or her genes. The metaphor of the selfish gene must be taken seriously: People don't selfishly spread their genes; genes selfishly spread themselves. They do it by the way they build our brains. By making us enjoy life, health, sex, friends, and children, the genes buy a lottery ticket for representation in the next generation, with odds that were favorable in the environment in which we evolved (because healthy, long-lived, loving parents did tend, on average, to send more genes into the next generation). Our goals are subgoals of the ultimate goal of the genes, replicating themselves. But the two are different. Resist the temptation to think of the goals of our genes as our deepest, truest, most hidden motives. Genes are a play within a play, not the interior monologue of the players. As far as we are concerned, our goals, conscious or unconscious, are not about genes at all but about health and lovers and children and friends.

Once you separate the goals of our minds from the metaphorical goals of our genes, many problems for a naturalistic understanding of human behavior evaporate. If altruism, according to biologists, is just helping kin or exchanging favors, both of which serve the interests of one's genes, wouldn't that make altruism merely a form of hypocrisy? Not at all. Just as blueprints don't necessarily specify blue buildings, selfish genes don't necessarily specify selfish organisms. Sometimes the most selfish thing a gene can do is to build a selfless brain—for example, one that gives rise to a loving parent or a loyal friend.

People don't selfishly spread their genes; genes selfishly spread themselves.

Take another example. In a review of three books on sexuality in the *New York Times Book Review,* the linguist Derek Bickerton wrote: "When a bird practices what zoologists call 'extra-pair copulation,' can we really call this adultery? . . . The intent of the two activities is completely different. Those who engage in extra-pair copulation usually aim to make babies; adulterers usually try to avoid them."

This is a perfect example of the confusion I am trying to cure—when birds fool around, they are most definitely not trying to "make babies," since birds have not had sex education and presumably do not engage in conscious family planning. They are trying to have sex, and building a desire for sex (including extra-pair copulation) into bird brains is the genes' way of making more genes.

But if a desire for sex serves the interests of the genes, are we condemned to an endless soap opera of marital treachery? Not if you remember that human behavior is the product of a complex brain with many components, which can be thought of as distinct circuits, modules, organs, or even "little agents," in the metaphor of the MIT computer scientist Marvin Minsky. Perhaps there is a component for sexual desire that serves the long-term interests of the genes by making more children, but there are, just as surely, other components that serve the interests of the genes in other ways. Among them are a desire for a trusting spouse (who will help bring up the copies of one's genes inside one's children), and a desire not to see one's own body—genes included—come to an early end at the hands of a jealous rival.

There is a second reason that behavior should not and does not maximize fitness. Natural selection operates over thousands of generations. For 99 percent of human existence, people lived as foragers in small nomadic bands. Our brains are adapted to that long-vanished way of life, not to brand-new agricultural and industrial civilizations. They are not wired to cope with anonymous crowds, written language, modern medicine, formal social institutions, high technology, and other newcomers to the human experience.

Since the modern mind is adapted to the Stone Age, not the computer age, there is no need to strain for adaptive explanations for everything we do, such as pornography, drugs, movies, contraception, careerism, and junk food. Before there was photography, it was adaptive to receive visual images of attractive members of the opposite sex because those images arose only from light reflecting off fertile bodies. Before opiates came in syringes, they were synthesized in the brain as natural analgesics. Before there were movies, it was adaptive to witness people's emotional struggles because the only struggles you could witness were among people you had to psych out every day. Before there was effective contraception, children were difficult to postpone, and status and wealth could be converted into more children and healthier ones. Before there was a sugar bowl, saltshaker, and butter dish on every table, and when lean years were never far away, you could never get too much sweet, salty, and fatty food.

And, to come full circle, right now you and I are co-opting yet another part of our minds for an evolutionarily novel activity. Our ancestors evolved faculties of intuitive engineering and intuitive science so that they could master tools and make sense of their immediate physical surroundings. We are using them today to make sense of the universe, life, and our own minds.

Reverse engineering our minds—figuring out what they are "designed" to accomplish—could be the fulfillment of the ancient injunction to know ourselves, but only if we keep track of who is designed to accomplish what. People don't have the goal of propagating genes; people have the goal of pursuing satisfying thoughts and feelings. Our genes have the metaphorical goal of building a complex brain in which the satisfying thoughts and feelings are linked to acts that tended to propagate those genes in the ancient environment in which we evolved. With that in mind, we might make better sense of the mysterious ways in which we humans pop, zip, and whir.

Analyzing the Text

1. According to Pinker, why doesn't Darwin's theory of natural selection help us understand human behavior?

2. One theory that Pinker argues is "crashingly, stunningly wrong" is that of sociobiology, that the brain is a "fitness maximizer"—that "social behavior is a product of natural engineering for gene propagation." Do you agree with his critique of this theory? Why or why not?

3. If, as Pinker suggests, "Genes are a play within a play, not the interior monologue of the players," how can we explain human behavior? And how does Pinker's theory explain why people often behave in self-destructive ways?

Writing about Cultural Practices

4. Adaptation is an important concept in biology. A common misconception about the theory of evolution is that it explains how human beings, through a process of continual and steady progress, became the species we are today. Evolution is not progress. Instead, species evolve by simply adapting to their current surroundings. They do not necessarily become better in any absolute sense over time. A trait or strategy that is successful at one time may be unsuccessful at another. For this assignment, you will consider the implications of adaptation as it relates to social behavior.

   How do people adapt to new environments? What are the processes through which a person transitions from being "new" to being an accepted member of a group or organization? Write a critical analysis of how a person adapts to life as a college student. As you write, consider the following questions.

   - What strategies did you use to adapt to college life? How did you learn these strategies?
   - What was the role of trial and error in your attempts to adapt?
   - In what ways are you still adapting to college life?
   - In what ways might the skills or abilities necessary to adapt to college life be unhealthy?

Susan McCarthy, **On Immortality**

A leading researcher of animal behavior and emotions, Susan McCarthy holds degrees in biology and journalism. She regularly writes for Salon.com and has contributed to *Best American Science Writing*. Her books include *When Elephants Weep: The Emotional Lives of Animals* (1996), which she cowrote with Jeffrey Moussaieff Masson, and *Becoming a Tiger* (2004). Her essay "On Immortality," originally published in 2000 on Salon.com, questions the ethical and moral implications of advances in genetic research that may slow the natural process of aging. As researchers begin to identify and learn to halt the work of genes that age us, McCarthy's central question is, "Is there any theoretical limit that would keep [the goal of] increased longevity from becoming immortality?"

▶ **Mapping Your Reading**

While McCarthy's tone is sometimes playful, she carefully draws on the perspectives of scientists regarding the possibility that genetic research will one day allow humans to live forever. As you read, make notes in the margins about both the potential benefits and limitations of the research advances described in this essay. To what extent is our culture's interest in living longer ultimately really about staying young longer?

One of the pleasing prospects that's ballyhooed as a future benefit of the Human Genome Project is increasing human longevity. The trouble with longevity is that if you go waltzing far enough down the path of long life you might find that you have merged with the highway of immortality without stopping at the weigh station of wisdom. Is that a perfectly good thing?

Can longevity extension go past combating diseases and address the very process of aging itself? If not, longevity will be less attractive. If, on the other hand, we can stay forever young, we may never want to leave the party. Should all of us be allowed to hang around as long as we want? Even creeps?

Research that may bear on the practical end of these matters is proceeding with startling speed.

Dr. Francis Collins, director of the National Human Genome Research Institute at the NIH, told the Washington Post that within 30 years we'll know all the genes involved in the human aging process.

He cited an experiment in which manipulating one gene in a mouse extended the mouse life span by 30 percent. "Without manipulation, it seems that the maximum human life span is about 100 years. It is possible that could be extended if we understand the pathways of aging better," he said. He added that there are many ethical questions "that would have to be addressed before applying this on a broad scale." (I know people who already wish to sign up for the narrow scale.)

The elderly mice in question are Italian, and were engineered to be deficient in p66shc, a protein that tells a cell to self-destruct when it has sustained too much damage from free radicals (molecules produced throughout the body in the process of oxygen metabolism). This is thought to be a defense against the possibility that the damaged cells will become cancerous. But without p66shc, the mice live 30 percent longer. (Being mice, whose lives are brief, this means a few extra months of mousy joys.)

Dr. Huber Warner, director of the biology of aging program at the National Institute on Aging (NIA) is also optimistic about the Human Genome Project and the outlook for living longer. "The fruit-fly genome has just been sequenced. Now, if you look at genes known to be involved in diseases, two-thirds of those genes are found in the fruit fly, including some very important genes that are tumor-suppressor genes."

NIA is investing millions in research to find genes in animals like fruit flies or mice "which when mutated or expressed differently will alter the life span of those species," says Warner. "Now if you can identify those genes in model organisms, then the sequence of the human genome will give you the information you need to begin to extrapolate. We will figure out ways to manipulate the genes in the model organism and it'll suggest how those genes can be manipulated in humans."

Organizations like the NIA and the American Federation for Aging Research emphasize that they are not interested in increasing life span so much as increasing "health span," the years people can live with vitality, dignity, and comfort.

Another avenue age scientists are racing down is telomere research. Telomeres are tasteful strands of nonsense DNA that decorate ends of chromosomes. Each time a cell divides, a bit of the telomere is clipped off. Eventually, when the telomere is a mere buzz-cut stubble, the cell stops dividing. There's a way around telomere loss: an enzyme called telomerase, which adds on extra telomere each time it's snipped shorter, so that it stays the same length, and the cell is not signaled to stop dividing. *Scientific American* has said telomerase "may well be the elixir of youth."

Some human tissues that divide indefinitely, such as reproductive cells producing sperm and eggs, contain telomerase. So do cells in embryos, but the telomerase gene is inactivated in most cells after birth.

Reactivating telomerase could replenish lost cells. Warner mentions the possibility of restoring epithelial cells in the retinas to restore lost eyesight. Telomerase genes have been successfully reactivated in retinal epithelial cells grown in tissue culture, in work done at the University of Texas Southwestern Medical Center and the Geron Corporation. Geron has filed for patents on hTRT, the telomerase reverse transcriptase protein. Warner notes, "The problem with turning telomerase back on is that's one of the things that happens in cancer." Cancer cells are all about telomerase and unrestricted cell division.

Steven Austad is a zoologist who studies aging. In his lucid, engaging book *Why We Age,* he describes his study of opossums on a Georgia barrier island— Methuselah opossums who had smaller families, often bred two years in a row instead of one, and aged more slowly, living a whopping three years instead of two.

Austad notes that when we discover and examine genes in the human genome that can increase longevity, they may prove to come with trade-offs. "Of all these genes in these small animals [that extend longevity], none of them are ever found in nature. And they all have downsides. People have not been eager to investigate the nature of their downsides."

Cancer obviously could be a downside, as could altered fertility.

Austad says he's been snorted at by other scientists when he argues that we should study the cells of long-lived animals like whales and elephants instead of short-lived ones like mice and fruit flies if we want to understand how we might live longer. "Elephants contain about 40 times the numbers of cells we do, and whales as many as 600 times as many cells. Yet elephants and whales live, to a reasonable approximation, just as long as we do. Therefore, their cells must be 40 to 600 times *more* resistant to turning cancerous than our own. Could we perhaps learn something about cancer resistance from studying these cells?" he has written.

"Maybe the individual could live forever."

So far, Austad himself isn't working with elephants. Instead he's looking at parakeets. "They live up to 20-plus years," he says admiringly. "That's seven times as long as a mouse, and they're the same size. They have unbelievable resistance to oxidative damage . . . if we could somehow mimic that in humans . . ."

So, downside or no, Austad also thinks findings from the Human Genome project will help us increase human longevity. "We already know that there are some genes that are associated with longer life in animals. I think we'll find the [corresponding] genes in humans that have a small but measurable effect on how long we live. And it won't be too many years before we have gene therapy for all kinds of things. It hasn't worked too well yet, but that's just a technical problem."

Is there any theoretical limit that would keep increased longevity from becoming immortality? Warner says "There's no theoretical limit. There's a balance between constant damage and repair. It's like a car. Theoretically you should be able to keep a car going forever—not yours, maybe, and not mine—but if you keep replacing the parts the car could last forever. Maybe the individual could live forever."

"The only limit is that there is no such thing such as immortality because accidents still happen," says Austad. "The theoretical limit is human behavior, not human physiology. If teenagers didn't drive cars like crazy people, that would probably have more effect on life expectancy than curing cancer."

Dr. Leonard Hayflick takes a darker view of longevity research than many scientists do. Hayflick's view of significantly increased longevity is, basically, that it won't happen, it can't happen, and if it did happen it would be a bad thing.

Hayflick, a professor of anatomy at the University of California at San Francisco's school of medicine, is the author of *How and Why We Age,* and has been thinking about longevity for 30 years, ever since he discovered what's now called the Hayflick Limit. Until his research, it was thought that animal cells growing in tissue culture were immortal and could divide forever. In a series of meticulous experiments, Hayflick showed that normal cells in culture have life spans: They flourish and divide for a while, but after a certain number of generations, divide no longer and eventually die. The cell lines that do go on forever are cancer cells.

People fail to distinguish between curing disease and ending aging, Hayflick says. If all the diseases currently written on death certificates in developed countries were resolved, you could add perhaps at the most 15 years to human life expectancy. "And that's it. Period."

Aging itself will not be affected. "Aging is an inexorable process that begins at about the age of 30 in humans and continues indefinitely. If you resolve disease you then expose or reveal the underlying real cause of that vulnerability, and hence death."

Hayflick doesn't believe that we will be able to go beyond resolving disease to slowing or stopping the process of aging. You can replace parts all you want he says, but what will you do when you have to replace your brain?

It's true that people object to aging as well as to death. Long life, while much admired, isn't sought after so much as long healthy life, or perhaps long youth. We want to be 100 years old *and* dewy fresh.

Dr. Pier Paolo Pandolfo, one of the scientists who studied the mice that live 30 percent longer, told the *New York Times* that a drug to block the self-destruct protein p66shc (the one the mice were engineered not to have) could be applied in the form of a cream to reverse wrinkling and blemishes on aging skin.

Can we have both long life and long youth? "I would say that there's no question about that," says Austad. "Most people would say that if you can't have better function there's no sense in keeping people alive."

It's increasingly easy to imagine replacing our parts, renewing our tissues, and rewriting our DNA. We would also need to fix our memories. They can hold a great deal, but never needed to hold an infinite amount of experience. Yet there are various ways we might deal with that, such as adding memory chips to our brains. Or perhaps we'll even figure out how to get rid of unneeded, unpleasant old memories and provide room for delightful new memories. It'll be doable, eventually.

Is this really possible? I believe it is, though I'm not fool enough to suggest a timetable. To those who say it'll never happen, I say: Don't confuse "a hell of a long time" with never. I think rather highly of human ingenuity and biological science. I see no reason why we won't eventually learn how to live forever and to live forever young.

I think less highly of collective human common sense. (As Kay tells Jay in that brilliant philosophical work, *Men in Black,* "A *person* is smart. People are dumb . . .") And so there's no reason to suppose we will handle this knowledge wisely.

Why aren't we immortal already? If it's so easy to turn on a gene here and turn off a gene there, why do we wear out and die? It's all about reproduction, of course. Once we've produced the next generation and gotten them on their feet, what happens to us is of no relevance to the future. People who have two children and live to be 100 are less successful from an evolutionary standpoint than people who have three children and keel over in their 50s.

So the impressive genes that allow people to reach 100 on a diet of bacon and beer are not favored by natural selection. (Although if the centenarians spend all their time calling up their great-grandchildren and asking when they're going to have babies and the great-grandchildren cave in and produce more children than they otherwise would have, that might favor those genes a bit.)

Still, it seems a little odd that there are no immortal species around. Quahogs live to be 200, but they probably feel that's not nearly long enough. Perhaps species of immortal animals would always be outcompeted by species of mortal animals, since mortal species evolve and acquire exciting new bells and whistles to repel insect pests, protect against disease, and fool dinosaurs into thinking you wouldn't dream of eating their eggs.

If we stop dying will our species stop evolving? Not if we keep reproducing. Not everyone thinks we need to keep evolving. Many of us feel that we are already the pinnacle of perfection and that all our species needs to do is stay as sweet as we are. Others disagree.

If we stop dying will our species stop evolving?

My friend Cynthia Heimel says she does not feel we are nearly finished evolving, and she is eagerly looking forward to an era when we have progressed to having just four toes on each foot. She says it is because little toes are no use and catch on the bed corner, but I believe she just wants to wear pointier shoes.

In the choice between living long and having kids, natural selection has always favored having kids. Now that choice will be up to us. Obviously if we choose to do both, the world will fill up with people to such an extent that we'll have to look for new planets.

We will ourselves become natural selection—unnatural selection if you prefer. Instead of allowing the ceaseless cherry-picking of the generations to get rid of our back problems, our impetuous driving habits, and that pesky fifth toe, we will do it all at once with gene therapy.

Will everyone get to live forever, or will we make decisions about how long people get to live and when they have to stop?

This is one of the reasons Hayflick thinks increasing longevity is a dreadful idea. "I defy anyone to describe a scenario in which it would be a good thing," he says.

Hayflick told the *Savannah Morning News,* "If indeed we had a way of extending human longevity the probability is very high that therapy would be available to the rich and powerful. I don't know how you feel about the rich and powerful, but I can think of lots of them that I would not like to see live forever." For example, he notes, "I don't think that having Adolf Hitler around for the next 500 years makes much sense."

You know Fidel Castro isn't ready to die. And while I am under the impression that I have accepted my own mortality, I must admit that I don't accept the mortality of my loved ones. It's not that I want them to be immortal, it's just that I don't want them ever to die.

The fact that we spend such a huge proportion of our health budget in the last few months of our lives is testimony to this. (As my father remarks, "You can't tell what truly expensive way of living a little longer will be discovered.")

Spending money on gene therapy will undoubtedly be more popular than the feeble unappealing ways we have now of extending life span a little. You know, boring stuff like eating right, keeping fit, signalling your lane changes.

The world will fill up a lot faster if nobody dies.

There are some things people won't do to live longer, after all. Yes, we'll slam down melatonin, DHEA, and random antioxidants by the fistful just in case they slow aging. But almost nobody has leapt on the caloric restriction bandwagon (which holds that since rats on meager diets live longer, maybe we would too, so let's not eat anything at all every other day), because it's so unpleasant.

I have also heard men complain about how unfair it is that women live longer on the average. (Some of them will glare at a lady as if she'd been sprinkling free radicals on their salads.) Yet although it has long been known that castration can extend a man's life span by an average of 14 years, guys consistently pass on the chance to even the score.

Is it any more unnatural to use gene therapy to become more or less immortal, than it is to prolong life in other ways? After all, during most of human history most children died as infants, women couldn't effectively limit how many children they gave birth to (and were far more apt to die in childbirth), and very few of them reached old age—yet hardly anybody objects to medical care to fight these causes of death.

But what all these changes amount to for our species is simply a movement along the spectrum from the kinds of species that have brief risky lives in which they produce as many progeny as possible—like mice—to the kinds of species that have longer lives during which they have fewer progeny, in whom they invest more parental care—like elephants. These life strategies are called r selection and K selection, and there's nothing so unusual about a species becoming more or less K-selected.

But among all the variously r- and K-selected creatures in the world, one thing seems constant: Everybody dies eventually. Immortality is something different.

Then there's the matter of addressing ethical conflicts before we proceed. The track record on this is not so great. Conferences are held and panels meet and people go right ahead and do what they want. And people really really want to live. "If it becomes possible, people will do it," says Steven Austad.

There are people worrying now about the way better health care is producing an unprecedentedly large population of older people, and the effects this has on medical spending, education spending, Social Security, and the GNP. Oh, and the ballot box.

Well, they haven't seen anything yet. The world will fill up a lot faster if nobody dies.

Maybe we'll make people choose between living forever and having kids. If you're going to bring more people into the world, you'll have to be willing to leave it yourself on a reasonable schedule. Conversely, if you refuse to leave the party, you can't bring crashers. Of course, this would create an interesting two-tiered world full of crabby child-haters who think they know so much because they've seen it all and breeders speaking smugly about how they're being not only natural but also more evolved.

What about natural selection? It got us this far, didn't it? If immortality is a bad idea, won't nature take care of it? It might do just that, but not in a way we'll enjoy. Since natural selection is mindless and purposeless, it has no objection to dead ends and short-term successes. Eventually some species could come along which has all our excellences, plus the advantages of mortality, and it will eliminate us. Not if we can stop them first, of course, but eventually (and this is a very long run indeed) we will be out-competed. Will the new Lords of the Earth then turn to making themselves immortal? Very likely, but it won't be our problem. Mother Nature doesn't care, ahistorical, short-sighted fool that she is.

Perhaps in the far reaches of time, as one mortal species after another crushes species that have succumbed to the temptation of eternal life, a species will arise that will remain mortal, and will allow itself to change. Perhaps they will never be overthrown by another species. Perhaps they'll have a zoo, and we'll be in it, and will learn the full reality of a life sentence.

▶ Analyzing the Text

1. Based on your notes, what are the main arguments presented in this essay about the benefits and limitations of pursuing longevity, and ultimately immortality, as a scientific goal?

2. **Interrogating Assumptions.** How does McCarthy's essay challenge the third assumption in this chapter's introduction, that "nature cannot be improved upon" (see p. 471)? According to this essay, what cultural attitudes or assumptions are behind the desire to live longer?

3. One theme of this essay is that, in nature, there are always trade-offs. For example, the zoologist Austad notes that to live longer some animals become less able to produce young. In general, how does this theme about trade-offs in nature drive McCarthy's discussion?

4. Among the researchers McCarthy quotes in this essay, there are geneticists, zoologists, biologists, and medical doctors. What assumptions or attitudes about the relationship of science to nature are revealed by the way these specialists present their arguments? How would McCarthy's essay be different if she had sought out opinions of philosophers or spiritual leaders, for example?

Writing about Cultural Practices

5. How have science fiction writers explored the human drive to prevent aging? Identify a science fiction movie that explores themes of aging or immortality. Some possibilities include *The Island, Cocoon, Gattica, AI,* and *Blade Runner.* Then write a critical analysis of the movie's themes. As you write, consider the following questions.

   - What themes about aging or immortality does the movie present? What is the underlying message of the film regarding humankind's desire to live forever?

   - How is the idea of aging presented in the film? What assumptions are behind the film's portrayal of aging?

   - How does the film's underlying argument compare to either McCarthy's in "On Immortality" or Lewis Thomas's in "On Cloning a Human Being" (p. 532)?

Eric Schlosser, Why McDonald's Fries Taste So Good

Award-winning journalist Eric Schlosser has written for the *Atlantic Monthly* and has contributed to the *New Yorker* and *Rolling Stone*. He published his first book, *Fast Food Nation: The Dark Side of the All American Meal*, in 2002; it was a national best seller for over a year. Excerpts from his second book, *Reefer Madness: Sex, Drugs, and Cheap Labor in the American Black Market* (2003), received the National Magazine Award. In *Fast Food Nation*, Schlosser observes that "what we eat has changed more in the last 40 years than in the last 40,000," yet the average consumer knows very little about how that food is made, where, by whom, and at what cost. In this essay, Schlosser explains the workings of one crucial segment of the food industry—the flavor-makers.

> ### Mapping Your Reading
>
> "The human craving for flavor," writes Schlosser, "has been a largely unacknowledged and unexamined force in history." In the following essay, Schlosser aims at making readers conscious of the impact of the flavor industry on the food we eat. What is the relationship between the "flavor industry" and fast foods? What is the difference between "natural flavor" and "artificial flavor"? And why *do* McDonald's fries taste so good?

The french fry was "almost sacrosanct for me," Ray Kroc, one of the founders of McDonald's, wrote in his autobiography, "its preparation a ritual to be followed religiously." During the chain's early years french fries were made from scratch every day. Russet Burbank potatoes were peeled, cut into shoestrings, and fried in McDonald's kitchens. As the chain expanded nationwide, in the mid-1960s, it sought to cut labor costs, reduce the number of suppliers, and ensure that its fries tasted the same at every restaurant. McDonald's began switching to frozen french fries in 1966—and few customers noticed the difference. Nevertheless, the change had a profound effect on the nation's agriculture and diet. A familiar food had been transformed into a highly processed industrial commodity. McDonald's fries now come from huge manufacturing plants that can peel, slice, cook, and freeze 2 million pounds of potatoes a day. The rapid expansion of McDonald's and the popularity of its low-cost, mass-produced fries changed the way Americans eat. In 1960 Americans consumed an average of about 81 pounds of fresh potatoes and 4 pounds of frozen french fries. In 2000 they consumed an average of about 50 pounds of fresh potatoes and 30 pounds of frozen fries. Today McDonald's is the largest buyer of potatoes in the United States.

The taste of McDonald's french fries played a crucial role in the chain's success—fries are much more profitable than hamburgers—and was long praised by customers, competitors, and even food critics. James Beard loved McDonald's fries. Their distinctive taste does not stem from the kind of potatoes that McDonald's buys, the technology that processes them, or the restaurant equipment that fries them: Other chains use Russet Burbanks, buy their french fries from the same large processing companies, and have similar fryers in their restaurant kitchens. The taste of a french fry is largely determined by the cooking oil. For decades McDonald's cooked its french fries in a mixture of about 7 percent cottonseed oil and 93 percent beef tallow. The mixture gave the fries their unique flavor—and more saturated beef fat per ounce than a McDonald's hamburger.

In 1990, amid a barrage of criticism over the amount of cholesterol in its fries, McDonald's switched to pure vegetable oil. This presented the company with a challenge: how to make fries that subtly taste like beef without cooking them in beef tallow. A look at the ingredients in McDonald's french fries suggests how the problem was solved. Toward the end of the list is a seemingly innocuous yet oddly mysterious phrase: "natural flavor." That ingredient helps to explain not only why the fries taste so good but also why most fast food—indeed, most of the food Americans eat today—tastes the way it does.

Open your refrigerator, your freezer, your kitchen cupboards, and look at the labels on your food. You'll find "natural flavor" or "artificial flavor" in just about every list of ingredients. The similarities between these two broad categories are far more significant than the differences. Both are man-made additives that give most processed food most of its taste. People usually buy a food item the first time because of its packaging or appearance. Taste usually determines whether they buy it again. About 90 percent of the money that Americans now spend on food goes to buy processed food. The canning, freezing, and dehydrating techniques used in processing destroy most of food's flavor—and so a vast industry has arisen in the United States to make processed food palatable. Without this flavor industry today's fast food would not exist. The names of the leading American fast-food chains and their best-selling menu items have become embedded in our popular culture and famous worldwide. But few people can name the companies that manufacture fast food's taste.

> **Without the flavor industry today's fast food would not exist.**

The flavor industry is highly secretive. Its leading companies will not divulge the precise formulas of flavor compounds or the identities of clients. The secrecy is deemed essential for protecting the reputations of beloved brands. The fast-food chains, understandably, would like the public to believe that the flavors of the food they sell somehow originate in their restaurant kitchens, not in distant factories run by other firms. A

McDonald's french fry is one of countless foods whose flavor is just a component in a complex manufacturing process. The look and the taste of what we eat now are frequently deceiving—by design.

The New Jersey Turnpike runs through the heart of the flavor industry, an industrial corridor dotted with refineries and chemical plants. International Flavors & Fragrances (IFF), the world's largest flavor company, has a manufacturing facility off Exit 8A in Dayton, New Jersey; Givaudan, the world's second-largest flavor company, has a plant in East Hanover. Haarmann & Reimer, the largest German flavor company, has a plant in Teterboro, as does Takasago, the largest Japanese flavor company. Flavor Dynamics has a plant in South Plainfield; Frutarom is in North Bergen; Elan Chemical is in Newark. Dozens of companies manufacture flavors in the corridor between Teaneck and South Brunswick. Altogether the area produces about two-thirds of the flavor additives sold in the United States.

The IFF plant in Dayton is a huge pale-blue building with a modern office complex attached to the front. It sits in an industrial park, not far from a BASF plastics factory, a Jolly French Toast factory, and a plant that manufactures Liz Claiborne cosmetics. Dozens of tractor-trailers were parked at the IFF loading dock the afternoon I visited, and a thin cloud of steam floated from a roof vent. Before entering the plant, I signed a nondisclosure form, promising not to reveal the brand names of foods that contain IFF flavors. The place reminded me of Willy Wonka's chocolate factory. Wonderful smells drifted through the hallways, men and women in neat white lab coats cheerfully went about their work, and hundreds of little glass bottles sat on laboratory tables and shelves. The bottles contained powerful but fragile flavor chemicals, shielded from light by brown glass and round white caps shut tight. The long chemical names on the little white labels were as mystifying to me as medieval Latin. These odd-sounding things would be mixed and poured and turned into new substances, like magic potions.

I was not invited into the manufacturing areas of the IFF plant, where, it was thought, I might discover trade secrets. Instead I toured various laboratories and pilot kitchens, where the flavors of well-established brands are tested or adjusted, and where whole new flavors are created. IFF's snack-and-savory lab is responsible for the flavors of potato chips, corn chips, breads, crackers, breakfast cereals, and pet food. The confectionery lab devises flavors for ice cream, cookies, candies, toothpastes, mouthwashes, and antacids. Everywhere I looked, I saw famous, widely advertised products sitting on laboratory desks and tables. The beverage lab was full of brightly colored liquids in clear bottles. It comes up with flavors for popular soft drinks, sports drinks, bottled teas, and wine coolers, for all-natural juice drinks, organic soy drinks, beers, and malt liquors. In one pilot kitchen I saw a dapper food technologist, a middle-aged man with an elegant tie beneath his crisp lab coat, carefully preparing a batch of cookies with white frosting and pink-and-white sprinkles. In another pilot kitchen I saw a pizza oven, a grill, a milk-shake machine, and a french fryer identical to those I'd seen at innumerable fast-food restaurants.

In addition to being the world's largest flavor company, IFF manufactures the smells of six of the ten best-selling fine perfumes in the United States, including Estée Lauder's Beautiful, Clinique's Happy, Lancôme's Trésor, and Calvin Klein's Eternity. It also makes the smells of household products such as deodorant, dishwashing detergent, bath soap, shampoo, furniture polish, and floor wax. All these aromas are made through essentially the same process: the manipulation of volatile chemicals. The basic science behind the scent of your shaving cream is the same as that governing the flavor of your TV dinner.

> The science behind the scent of your shaving cream is the same as that governing the flavor of your TV dinner.

Scientists now believe that human beings acquired the sense of taste as a way to avoid being poisoned. Edible plants generally taste sweet, harmful ones bitter. The taste buds on our tongues can detect the presence of half a dozen or so basic tastes, including sweet, sour, bitter, salty, astringent, and umami, a taste discovered by Japanese researchers—a rich and full sense of deliciousness triggered by amino acids in foods such as meat, shellfish, mushrooms, potatoes, and seaweed. Taste buds offer a limited means of detection, however, compared with the human olfactory system, which can perceive thousands of different chemical aromas. Indeed, "flavor" is primarily the smell of gases being released by the chemicals you've just put in your mouth. The aroma of a food can be responsible for as much as 90 percent of its taste.

The act of drinking, sucking, or chewing a substance releases its volatile gases. They flow out of your mouth and up your nostrils, or up the passageway in the back of your mouth, to a thin layer of nerve cells called the olfactory epithelium, located at the base of your nose, right between your eyes. Your brain combines the complex smell signals from your olfactory epithelium with the simple taste signals from your tongue, assigns a flavor to what's in your mouth, and decides if it's something you want to eat.

A person's food preferences, like his or her personality, are formed during the first few years of life, through a process of socialization. Babies innately prefer sweet tastes and reject bitter ones; toddlers can learn to enjoy hot and spicy food, bland health food, or fast food, depending on what the people around them eat. The human sense of smell is still not fully understood. It is greatly affected by psychological factors and expectations. The mind focuses intently on some of the aromas that surround us and filters out the overwhelming majority. People can grow accustomed to bad smells or good smells; they stop noticing what once seemed overpowering. Aroma and memory are somehow inextricably linked. A smell can suddenly evoke a long-forgotten moment. The flavors of childhood foods seem to leave an indelible mark, and adults often return to them, without always knowing why. These "comfort foods" become a source of pleasure and reassurance—a fact that fast-food chains use to their advantage. Childhood memories of Happy Meals, which come with french fries, can translate into frequent adult visits to McDonald's. On average, Americans now eat about four servings of french fries every week.

Quick frozen—for quick serving

An old-fashioned fried chicken dinner

with fluffy mashed potatoes

Remember how Mom used to get up early every Sunday to fix a scrumptious chicken dinner? We do ... so we've patterned our newest TV Dinner after that good, old-fashioned feast. However, *our* complete chicken dinners are all cooked and ready to pop into the oven on their own individual serving trays. No thawing.

In 25 minutes, you'll be enjoying this irresistible well-balanced meal: Plenty of extra-meaty, extra-tender, golden-fried Swanson Chicken ... garden-fresh vegetables ... and fluffy mashed potatoes whipped in milk.

You never cooked so well, so fast before. Do get Swanson TV Chicken Dinners for your family right away. Now available at frozen food counters.

Swanson TV. Dinners

Made by the makers of Campbell's Soups

C. A. SWANSON & SONS • OMAHA 8, NEBRASKA

A 1950s ad promoting a highly processed version of a "good, old-fashioned feast."

The human craving for flavor has been a largely unacknowledged and unexamined force in history. For millennia royal empires have been built, unexplored lands traversed, and great religions and philosophies forever changed by the spice trade. In 1492 Christopher Columbus set sail to find seasoning. Today the influence of flavor in the world marketplace is no less decisive. The rise and fall of corporate empires—of soft-drink companies, snack-food companies, and fast-food chains—is often determined by how their products taste.

The flavor industry emerged in the mid-nineteenth century, as processed foods began to be manufactured on a large scale. Recognizing the need for flavor additives, early food processors turned to perfume companies that had long experience working with essential oils and volatile aromas. The great perfume houses of England, France, and the Netherlands produced many of the first flavor compounds. In the early part of the twentieth century Germany took the technological lead in flavor production, owing to its powerful chemical industry. Legend has it that a German scientist discovered methyl anthranilate, one of the first artificial flavors, by accident while mixing chemicals in his laboratory. Suddenly the lab was filled with the sweet smell of grapes. Methyl anthranilate later became the chief flavor compound in grape Kool-Aid. After World War II much of the perfume industry shifted from Europe to the United States, settling in New York City near the garment district and the fashion houses. The flavor industry came with it, later moving to New Jersey for greater plant capacity. Man-made flavor additives were used mostly in baked goods, candies, and sodas until the 1950s, when sales of processed food began to soar. The invention of gas chromatographs and mass spectrometers—machines capable of detecting volatile gases at low levels—vastly increased the number of flavors that could be synthesized. By the mid-1960s flavor companies were churning out compounds to supply the taste of Pop Tarts, Bac-Os, Tab, Tang, Filet-O-Fish sandwiches, and literally thousands of other new foods.

> In 1492 Christopher Columbus set sail to find seasoning.

The American flavor industry now has annual revenues of about $1.4 billion. Approximately 10,000 new processed-food products are introduced every year in the United States. Almost all of them require flavor additives. And about 9 out of 10 of these products fail. The latest flavor innovations and corporate realignments are heralded in publications such as *Chemical Market Reporter, Food Chemical News, Food Engineering,* and *Food Product Design.* The progress of IFF has mirrored that of the flavor industry as a whole. IFF was formed in 1958, through the merger of two small companies. Its annual revenues have grown almost fifteenfold since the early 1970s, and it currently has manufacturing facilities in 20 countries.

Today's sophisticated spectrometers, gas chromatographs, and headspace-vapor analyzers provide a detailed map of a food's flavor components, detecting chemical aromas present in amounts as low as one part per billion. The human nose, however, is even more sensitive. A nose can detect aromas present in quantities of a few parts per trillion—an amount equivalent to about 0.000000000003 percent. Complex aromas, such as those of coffee and roasted meat, are composed of volatile gases from nearly a thousand different chemicals. The smell of a strawberry arises from the interaction of about 350 chemicals that are present in minute amounts. The quality that people seek most of all in a food—flavor—is usually present in a quantity too infinitesimal to be measured in traditional culinary terms such as ounces or teaspoons. The chemical that provides the dominant flavor of bell pepper can be tasted in amounts as low as 0.02 parts per billion; one drop is sufficient to add flavor to five average-size swimming pools. The flavor additive usually comes next to last in a processed food's list of ingredients and often costs less than its packaging. Soft drinks contain a larger proportion of flavor additives than most products. The flavor in a 12-ounce can of Coke costs about half a cent.

The color additives in processed foods are usually present in even smaller amounts than the flavor compounds. Many of New Jersey's flavor companies also manufacture these color additives, which are used to make processed foods look fresh and appealing. Food coloring serves many of the same decorative purposes as lipstick, eye shadow, mascara—and is often made from the same pigments. Titanium dioxide, for example, has proved to be an especially versatile mineral. It gives many processed candies, frostings, and icings their bright white color; it is a common ingredient in women's cosmetics; and it is the pigment used in many white oil paints and house paints. At Burger King, Wendy's, and McDonald's coloring agents have been added to many of the soft drinks, salad dressings, cookies, condiments, chicken dishes, and sandwich buns.

Studies have found that the color of a food can greatly affect how its taste is perceived. Brightly colored foods frequently seem to taste better than bland-looking foods, even when the flavor compounds are identical. Foods that somehow look off-color often seem to have off tastes. For thousands of years human beings have relied on visual cues to help determine what is edible. The color of fruit suggests whether it is ripe, the color of meat whether it is rancid. Flavor researchers sometimes use colored lights to modify the influence of visual cues during taste tests. During one experiment in the early 1970s people were served an oddly tinted meal of steak and french fries that appeared normal beneath colored lights. Everyone thought the meal tasted fine until the lighting was changed. Once it became apparent that the steak was actually blue and the fries were green, some people became ill.

The federal Food and Drug Administration does not require companies to disclose the ingredients of their color or flavor additives so long as all the chemicals in them are considered by the agency to be GRAS ("generally recognized as safe"). This enables companies to maintain the secrecy of their formulas. It also hides the fact that flavor compounds often contain more ingredients than the foods to which they give taste. The phrase "artificial strawberry flavor" gives little hint of the chemical wizardry and manufacturing skill that can make a highly processed food taste like strawberries.

A typical artificial strawberry flavor, like the kind found in a Burger King strawberry milk shake, contains the following ingredients: amyl acetate, amyl butyrate, amyl valerate, anethol, anisyl formate, benzyl acetate, benzyl isobutyrate, butyric acid, cinnamyl isobutyrate, cinnamyl valerate, cognac essential oil, diacetyl, dipropyl ketone, ethyl acetate, ethyl amyl ketone, ethyl butyrate, ethyl cinnamate, ethyl heptanoate, ethyl heptylate, ethyl lactate, ethyl methylphenylglycidate, ethyl nitrate, ethyl propionate, ethyl valerate, heliotropin, hydroxyphenyl-2-butanone (10 percent solution in alcohol), α-ionone, isobutyl anthranilate,

FOUND

from mcdonalds.com

McDONALD'S FRENCH FRIES: LIST OF INGREDIENTS

French fries

Potatoes

Partially hydrogenated soybean oil

Natural flavor (beef source)

Dextrose

Sodium acid pyrophosphate (to preserve natural color)

Cooked in partially hydrogenated oils (may contain partially hydrogenated soybean oil and/or partially hydrogenated corn oil and/or partially hydrogenated canola oil and/or cottonseed oil and/or sunflower oil and/or corn oil)

Ketchup packet

Tomato concentrate from red ripe tomatoes

Distilled vinegar

High fructose corn syrup

Corn syrup

Water

Salt

Natural flavors (vegetable source)

Salt packet

Table salt

McDonald's attempts to provide nutrition and ingredient information regarding its products that is as complete as possible. Some menu items may not be available at all restaurants; test products, test formulations, or regional items have not been included. While the ingredient information is based on standard product formulations, variations may occur depending on the local supplier, the region of the country, and the season of the year. Further, product formulations change periodically. Serving sizes may vary from quantity upon which the analysis was conducted. Serving size designation for beverages refers to total cup capacity; the actual amounts of beverage (and ice) may vary. No products are certified as vegetarian; all products may contain trace amounts of ingredients derived from animals. If you wish further information or have special sensitivities or dietary concerns regarding specific ingredients in specific menu items please call us at the number below. This listing is continuously updated in an attempt to reflect the current status of our products and may vary from printed materials.

McDonald's Quality & Nutrition Information, McDonald's Corporation, 2111 McDonald's Drive, Oak Brook, IL 60523, 1-877-MCD-FOOD isobutyl butyrate, lemon essential oil, maltol, 4-methylacetophenone, methyl anthranilate, methyl benzoate, methyl cinnamate, methyl heptine carbonate, methyl naphthyl ketone, methyl salicylate, mint essential oil, neroli essential oil, nerolin, neryl isobutyrate, orris butter, phenethyl alcohol, rose, rum ether, γ-undecalactone, vanillin, and solvent.

Although flavors usually arise from a mixture of many different volatile chemicals, often a single compound supplies the dominant aroma. Smelled alone, that chemical provides an unmistakable sense of the food. Ethyl-2-methyl butyrate, for example, smells just like an apple. Many of today's highly processed foods offer a blank palette: Whatever chemicals are added to them will give them specific tastes. Adding methyl-2-pyridyl ketone makes something taste like popcorn. Adding ethyl-3-hydroxy butanoate makes it taste like marshmallow. The possibilities are now almost limitless. Without affecting appearance or nutritional value, processed foods could be made with aroma chemicals such as hexanal (the smell of freshly cut grass) or 3-methyl butanoic acid (the smell of body odor).

The 1960s were the heyday of artificial flavors in the United States. The synthetic versions of flavor compounds were not subtle, but they did not have to be, given the nature of most processed food. For the past 20 years food processors have tried hard to use only "natural flavors" in their products. According to the FDA, these must be derived entirely from natural sources—from herbs, spices, fruits, vegetables, beef, chicken, yeast, bark, roots, and so forth. Consumers prefer to see natural flavors on a label, out of a belief that they are more healthful. Distinctions between artificial and natural flavors can be arbitrary and somewhat absurd, based more on how the flavor has been made than on what it actually contains.

"A natural flavor," says Terry Acree, a professor of food science at Cornell University, "is a flavor that's been derived with an out-of-date technology." Natural flavors and artificial flavors sometimes contain exactly the same chemicals, produced through different methods. Amyl acetate, for example, provides the dominant note of banana flavor. When it is distilled from bananas with a solvent, amyl acetate is a natural flavor. When it is produced by mixing vinegar with amyl alcohol and adding sulfuric acid as a catalyst, amyl acetate is an artificial flavor. Either way it smells and tastes the same. "Natural flavor" is now listed among the ingredients of everything from Health Valley Blueberry Granola Bars to Taco Bell Hot Taco Sauce.

A natural flavor is not necessarily more healthful or purer than an artificial one. When almond flavor—benzaldehyde—is derived from natural sources, such as peach and apricot pits, it contains traces of hydrogen cyanide, a deadly poison. Benzaldehyde derived by mixing oil of clove and amyl acetate does not contain any cyanide. Nevertheless, it is legally considered an artificial flavor and sells at a much lower price. Natural and artificial flavors are now manufactured at the same chemical plants, places that few people would associate with Mother Nature.

The small and elite group of scientists who create most of the flavor in most of the food now consumed in the United States are called "flavorists." They draw on a number of disciplines in their work: biology, psychology, physiology, and organic chemistry. A flavorist is a chemist with a trained nose and a poetic sensibility. Flavors are created by blending scores of different chemicals in tiny amounts—a process governed by scientific principles but demanding a fair amount of art. In an age when delicate aromas and microwave ovens do not easily coexist, the job of the flavorist is to conjure illusions about processed food and, in the words of one flavor company's literature, to ensure "consumer likeability." The flavorists with whom I spoke were discreet, in keeping with the dictates of their trade. They were also charming, cosmopolitan, and ironic. They not only enjoyed fine wine but could identify the chemicals that give each grape its unique aroma. One flavorist compared his work to composing music. A well-made flavor compound will have a "top note" that is often followed by a "dry-down" and a "leveling-off," with different chemicals responsible for each stage. The taste of a food can be radically altered by minute changes in the flavoring combination. "A little odor goes a long way," one flavorist told me.

> A flavorist is a chemist with a trained nose and a poetic sensibility.

In order to give a processed food a taste that consumers will find appealing, a flavorist must always consider the food's "mouthfeel"—the unique combination of textures and chemical interactions that affect how the flavor is perceived. Mouthfeel can be adjusted through the use of various fats, gums, starches, emulsifiers, and stabilizers. The aroma chemicals in a food can be precisely analyzed, but the elements that make up mouthfeel are much harder to measure. How does one quantify a pretzel's hardness, a french fry's crispness? Food technologists are now conducting basic research in rheology, the branch of physics that examines the flow and deformation of materials. A number of companies sell sophisticated devices that attempt to measure mouthfeel. The TA.XT2i Texture Analyzer, produced by the Texture Technologies Corporation, of Scarsdale, New York, performs calculations based on data derived from as many as 250 separate probes. It is essentially a mechanical mouth. It gauges the most important rheological properties of a food—bounce, creep, breaking point, density, crunchiness, chewiness, gumminess, lumpiness, rubberiness, springiness, slipperiness, smoothness, softness, wetness, juiciness, spreadability, springback, and tackiness.

Some of the most important advances in flavor manufacturing are now occurring in the field of biotechnology. Complex flavors are being made using enzyme reactions, fermentation, and fungal and tissue cultures. All the flavors created by these methods—including the ones being synthesized by fungi—are considered natural flavors by the FDA. The new enzyme-based processes are responsible for extremely true-to-life dairy flavors. One company now offers not just butter flavor but also fresh creamy butter, cheesy butter, milky butter, savory melted butter, and super-concentrated butter flavor, in liquid or powder form. The development of new fermentation techniques, along with new techniques for heating mixtures of sugar and amino acids, have led to the creation of much more realistic meat flavors.

The McDonald's Corporation most likely drew on these advances when it eliminated beef tallow from its french fries. The company will not reveal the exact origin of the natural flavor added to its fries. In response to inquiries from *Vegetarian Journal,* however. McDonald's did acknowledge that its fries derive some of their characteristic flavor from "an animal source." Beef is the probable source, although other meats cannot be ruled out. In France, for example, fries are sometimes cooked in duck fat or horse tallow.

Other popular fast foods derive their flavor from unexpected ingredients. McDonald's Chicken McNuggets contain beef extracts, as does Wendy's Grilled Chicken Sandwich. Burger King's BK Broiler Chicken Breast Patty contains "natural smoke flavor." A firm called Red Arrow Products specializes in smoke flavor, which is added to barbecue sauces, snack foods, and processed meats. Red Arrow manufactures natural smoke flavor by charring sawdust and capturing the aroma chemicals released into the air. The smoke is captured in water and then bottled, so that other companies can sell food that seems to have been cooked over a fire.

The Vegetarian Legal Action Network recently petitioned the FDA to issue new labeling requirements for foods that contain natural flavors. The group wants food processors to list the basic origins of their flavors on their labels. At the moment vegetarians often have no way of knowing whether a flavor additive contains beef, pork, poultry, or shellfish. One of the most widely used color additives—whose presence is often hidden by the phrase "color added"—violates a number of religious dietary restrictions, may cause allergic reactions in susceptible people, and comes from an unusual source. Cochineal extract (also known as carmine or carminic acid) is made from the desiccated bodies of female *Dactylopius coccus Costa,* a small insect harvested mainly in Peru and the Canary Islands. The bug feeds on red cactus berries, and color from the berries accumulates in the females and their unhatched larvae. The insects are collected, dried, and ground into a pigment. It takes about seventy thousand of them to produce a pound of carmine, which is used to make processed foods look pink, red, or purple. Dannon strawberry yogurt gets its color from carmine, and so do many frozen fruit bars, candies, and fruit fillings, and Ocean Spray pink-grapefruit juice drink.

In a meeting room at IFF, Brian Grainger let me sample some of the company's flavors. It was an unusual taste test—there was no food to taste. Grainger is a senior flavorist at IFF, a soft-spoken chemist with graying hair, an English accent, and a fondness for understatement. He could easily be mistaken for a British diplomat or the owner of a West End brasserie with two Michelin stars. Like many in the flavor industry, he has an Old World, old-fashioned sensibility. When I suggested that IFF's policy of secrecy and discretion was out of step with our mass-marketing, brand-conscious, self-promoting age, and that the company should put its own logo on the countless products that bear its flavors, instead of allowing other companies to enjoy the consumer loyalty and affection inspired by those flavors, Grainger politely disagreed, assuring me that such a thing would never be done. In the absence of public credit or acclaim, the small and secretive fraternity of flavor chemists praise one another's work. By analyzing the flavor formula of a product, Grainger can often tell which of his counterparts at a rival firm devised it. Whenever he walks down a supermarket aisle, he takes a quiet pleasure in seeing the well-known foods that contain his flavors.

Grainger had brought a dozen small glass bottles from the lab. After he opened each bottle, I dipped a fragrance-testing filter into it—a long white strip of paper designed to absorb aroma chemicals without producing off notes. Before placing each strip of paper in front of my nose, I closed my eyes. Then I inhaled deeply, and one food after another was conjured from the glass bottles. I smelled fresh cherries, black olives, sautéed onions, and shrimp. Grainger's most remarkable creation took me by surprise. After closing my eyes, I suddenly smelled a grilled hamburger. The aroma was uncanny, almost miraculous—as if someone in the room were flipping burgers on a hot grill. But when I opened my eyes, I saw just a narrow strip of white paper and a flavorist with a grin.

▶ **Analyzing the Text**

1. According to Schlosser, what is the role of "flavorists"? How do flavorists impact the food we buy today?

2. **Interrogating Assumptions.** How have changing attitudes about what's "natural" changed the ingredients and taste of food in recent decades? How does Schlosser's essay challenge the third assumption in this chapter introduction that "nature cannot be improved upon" (see p. 471)?

3. Why does Schlosser contend that the similarities between "natural flavor" and "artificial flavor" are more interesting than their differences? Before you read this essay, how would you have explained the difference between "natural flavor" and "artificial flavor"? How has this essay changed your perspective?

4. According to Schlosser, why do McDonald's fries taste so good? In general, what makes food taste good?

▶ **Writing about Cultural Practices**

5. Of the money Americans spend on food, about 90 percent is spent on processed foods. But what's in them? As Schlosser discovered in his research of the flavor industry, many processed foods contain unexpected ingredients. For example, many snack foods, sauces, processed meats, and fast-food sandwiches contain "natural smoke flavor," which is, as Schlosser points out, manufactured by "capturing the aroma chemicals" of charred sawdust. For this assignment, investigate your favorite processed foods by discovering their actual ingredients. To begin, collect the labels of two to three foods you or someone you know eats regularly. Write a critical analysis of these labels that takes a clear position on whether the packaging gives you enough information to make a responsible choice about whether to eat the product (include copies of the labels). As you draft, consider the following questions.

   • Do you usually pay attention to the ingredients of the foods you eat? Why or why not?

- What ingredients are included in the foods you've chosen? Can you tell by reading the labels? That is, can you identify each ingredient? Does the food include chemicals? Do the labels include enough information? If not, what information would you want to know that is not provided?

- Are you surprised by any of the ingredients? Why or why not? Do these ingredients affect whether you want to eat the food?

- Are the foods labeled "natural" or "artificial" or with some other indicator? Does it matter whether the foods you eat are "natural" or "artificial" or "organic" or "farm-raised," etc.? Why or why not?

- What do the labels and ingredient lists you've gathered suggest about our cultural attitudes toward processed foods? About the choices we do or do not have as consumers?

Annie Dillard, **Living Like Weasels**

Annie Dillard is a critically acclaimed writer who also teaches creative writing at Wesleyan University, Connecticut. Dillard, whose writing deals with the themes of nature, religion, philosophy, and the sciences, was awarded a Pulitzer Prize for nonfiction for *Pilgrim at Tinker Creek* (1974). In addition to writing for publications like *Harper's*, the *Christian Science Monitor*, and *Cosmopolitan*, Dillard has published poetry in *Ticket for a Prayer Wheel* (1975) and *Mornings Like This: Found Poems* (1995); an autobiography, *An American Childhood* (1988); and a textbook, *The Writing Life* (1990). This essay originally appeared in *Teaching a Stone to Talk* (1982). As is the case with this essay, Dillard's writing often starts with an observation from nature, followed by scientific explanation, and ending in a reflection on how this all fits together. In "Living Like Weasels," Dillard looks to the natural world to attempt to find a better way of living.

 Mapping Your Reading

Dillard writes, "I would like to learn, or remember, how to live." As you read, make notes in the margins wherever Dillard calls on people to live differently. How should we live? What role can the natural world have in teaching us?

A weasel is wild. Who knows what he thinks? He sleeps in his underground den, his tail draped over his nose. Sometimes he lives in his den for two days without leaving. Outside, he stalks rabbits, mice, muskrats, and birds, killing more bodies than he can eat warm, and often dragging the carcasses home. Obedient to instinct, he bites his prey at the neck, either splitting the jugular vein at the throat or crunching the brain at the base of the skull, and he does not let go. One naturalist refused to kill a weasel who was socketed into his hand deeply as a rattlesnake. The man could in no way pry the tiny weasel off, and he had to walk half a mile to water, the weasel dangling from his palm, and soak him off like a stubborn label.

And once, says Ernest Thompson Seton°—once, a man shot an eagle out of the sky. He examined the eagle and found the dry skull of a weasel fixed by the jaws to his throat. The supposition is that the eagle had pounced on the weasel and the weasel swiveled and bit as instinct taught him, tooth to neck, and nearly won. I would like to have seen that eagle from the air a few weeks or months before he

---

Ernest Thompson Seton (1860–1946), American author and naturalist.

A long-tail weasel, native to North and Central America.

was shot. Was the whole weasel still attached to his feathered throat, a fur pendant? Or did the eagle eat what he could reach, gutting the living weasel with his talons before his breast, bending his beak, cleaning the beautiful airborne bones?

I have been reading about weasels because I saw one last week. I startled a weasel who startled me, and we exchanged a long glance.

Near my house in Virginia is a pond—Hollins Pond. It covers two acres of bottomland near Tinker Creek with 6 inches of water and 6,000 lily pads. There is a 55 mph highway at one end of the pond, and a nesting pair of wood ducks at the other. Under every bush is a muskrat hole or a beer can. The far end is an alternating series of fields and woods, fields and woods, threaded everywhere with motorcycle tracks—in whose bare clay wild turtles lay eggs.

One evening last week at sunset, I walked to the pond and sat on a downed log near the shore. I was watching the lily pads at my feet tremble and part over the thrusting path of a carp. A yellow warbler appeared to my right and flew behind me. It caught my eye; I swiveled around— and the next instant, inexplicably, I was looking down at a weasel, who was looking up at me.

Weasel! I'd never seen one wild before. He was 10 inches long, thin as a curve, a muscled ribbon, brown as fruitwood, soft-furred, alert. His face was fierce, small and pointed as a lizard's; he would have made a good arrowhead. There was just a dot of chin, maybe two brown hairs' worth, and then the pure white fur began that spread down his underside. He had two black eyes I didn't see, any more than you see a window.

The weasel was stunned into stillness as he was emerging from beneath an enormous shaggy wild rose bush 4 feet away. I was stunned into stillness twisted backward on the tree trunk. Our eyes locked, and someone threw away the key.

Our look was as if two lovers, or deadly enemies, met unexpectedly on an overgrown path when each had been thinking of something else: a clearing blow to the gut. It was also a bright blow to the brain, or a sudden beating of brains, with all the charge and intimate grate of rubbed balloons. It emptied our lungs. It felled the forest, moved the fields, and drained the pond; the world dismantled and tumbled into that black hole of eyes. If you and I looked at each other that way, our skulls would split and drop to our shoulders. But we don't. We keep our skulls.

He disappeared. This was only last week, and already I don't remember what shattered the enchantment. I think I blinked, I think I retrieved my brain from the weasel's brain, and tried to memorize what I was seeing, and the weasel felt the yank of separation, the careening splashdown into real life and the urgent current of instinct. He vanished under the wild rose. I waited motionless, my mind suddenly full of data and my spirit with pleadings, but he didn't return.

A weasel is wild. Who knows what he thinks?

Please do not tell me about "approach-avoidance conflicts." I tell you I've been in that weasel's brain for 60 seconds, and he was in mine. Brains are private places, muttering through unique and secret tapes— but the weasel and I both plugged into another tape simultaneously, for a sweet and shocking time. Can I help it if it was a blank?

What goes on in his brain the rest of the time? What does a weasel think about? He won't say. His journal is tracks in clay, a spray of feathers, mouse blood and bone: uncollected, unconnected, loose-leaf, and blown.

I would like to learn, or remember, how to live. I come to Hollins Pond not so much to learn how to live as, frankly, to forget about it. That is, I don't think I can learn from a wild animal how to live in particular—shall I suck warm blood, hold my tail high, walk with my footprints precisely over the prints of my hands?—but I might learn something of mind-lessness, something of purity of living in the physical senses and the dignity of living without bias or motive. The weasel lives in necessity and we live in choice, hating necessity and dying at the last ignobly in its talons. I would like to live as I should, as the weasel lives as he should. And I suspect that for me the way is like the weasel's: open to time and death painlessly, noticing everything, remembering nothing, choosing the given with a fierce and pointed will.

I missed my chance. I should have gone for the throat. I should have lunged for that streak of white under the weasel's chin and held on, held on through mud and into the wild rose, held on for a dearer life. We could live under the wild rose wild as weasels, mute and uncomprehending. I could very calmly go wild. I could live two days in the den, curled, leaning on mouse fur, sniffing bird bones, blinking, licking, breathing musk, my hair tangled in the roots of grasses. Down is a good place to go, where the mind is single. Down is out, out of your ever-loving mind and back to your careless senses. I remember muteness as a pro-longed and giddy fast, where every moment is a feast of ut-terance received. Time and events are merely poured, unre-marked, and ingested directly, like blood pulsed into my gut through a jugular vein. Could two live that way? Could two live under the wild rose, and explore by the pond, so that the smooth mind of each is as everywhere present to the other, and as received and as unchallenged, as falling snow?

We could, you know. We can live any way we want. People take vows of poverty, chastity, and obedience—even of silence—by choice. The thing is to stalk your calling in a certain skilled and supple way, to locate the most tender and live spot and plug into that pulse. This is yielding, not fighting. A weasel doesn't "attack" anything; a weasel lives as he's meant to, yielding at every moment to the perfect freedom of single necessity.

I think it would be well, and proper, and obedient, and pure, to grasp your one necessity and not let it go, to dangle from it limp wherever it takes you. Then even death, where you're going no matter how you live, cannot you part. Seize it and let it seize you up aloft even, till your eyes burn out and drop; let your musky flesh fall off in shreds, and let your very bones unhinge and scatter, loosened over fields, over fields and woods, lightly, thoughtless, from any height at all, from as high as eagles.

▶ Analyzing the Text

1. Dillard begins her essay with two stories about weasels. What characteristics of weasels do these two stories introduce? How do these stories establish the theme of the essay?

2. Dillard describes in vivid detail her encounter with a weasel in the wild. How does she use this experience to construct an argument for the type of relationship people should have with the natural world?

3. The title of this essay is "Living Like Weasels." What is it about how weasels live that Dillard wants us to imitate? How would the impact of her essay change if she had used a different, perhaps more docile, animal?

4. **Interrogating Assumptions.** Identify passages in the essay where Dillard uses the word "wild." How does she characterize the wild? What assumptions about nature are revealed by her use of this word?

▶ Writing about Cultural Practices

5. Dillard's chance encounter with a weasel was the impetus for further research and the writing of "Living Like Weasels." How do you experience the natural world around you? Have you had an encounter like Dillard's? Recall an encounter, if you've had one—or take a walk (even if you live in a city) to encounter nature— and then write a descriptive analysis of your impressions about a specific live creature (or creatures). You may also want to conduct research, as Dillard did, to enrich your paper. To begin, recall your encounter, or, as you take your walk, pay attention to any birds, squirrels, insects, etc., that cross your path, and take notes. What do you notice about the behavior of the creatures? What, if anything, can be learned from these creatures? As you draft, consider the following questions.

   • What aspects of the creatures' behavior or habits most impressed you? Why? What connections, if any, can you make to the behavior and habits of humans?

   • Would you describe the creatures as wild? Why or why not?

   • Did your encounter challenge any assumptions you may have had about the creatures or the natural world? If so, how?

   • What, if anything, did your encounter reveal to you about the similarities or differences in the lives of animals vs. humans? Do you agree with Dillard that animals live "in necessity" and humans live "in choice"? Why or why not?

SPACIOUS SKIES

AMBER WAVES OF GRAIN

PURPLE MOUNTAINS

FRUITED PLAIN

LEO'S DINER

s.harris

Mixing Words and Images

PICTURING NATURE

Several of the readings in this chapter consider representations of nature and cultural assumptions about the natural world. Some of the images in this chapter reflect a cultural tendency to idealize nature—to present it as a paradise unoccupied and unspoiled by humans.

For this assignment, you will create a calendar, poster, or cartoon that works against a typical romanticized view of nature—one that reflects a different, perhaps more realistic, or more "unnatural," or satirical view of nature in contemporary America. Your finished work should incorporate carefully chosen text and image(s) that make a specific argument about nature, one that you can later articulate in writing.

Designing Your Calendar, Poster, Postcard, or Cartoon

- You may want to first find a classic romanticized example of the kind of image you'd like to respond against. For example, you may want to counter Audubon or National Geographic calendars or other similar images.

- Consider the assumptions built into the romanticized example. How do you want to handle or counter those assumptions in your design? What statement about nature do *you* want to make?

- What images and text do you want to include in your piece? What is the best way to present them to make your argument?

- Visualize your audience. What do you want your viewers or readers to think, feel, or do when they encounter your work?

Writing about Your Calendar, Poster, Postcard, or Cartoon

Once you have created your design, draft an analysis to accompany it. First, provide a rationale for your design and text decisions; second, explain the cultural messages it conveys about nature in modern American life. These questions may help you draft.

- What themes or assumptions about the natural world are you trying to counter or convey with your design, and why?

- What details in your design help communicate your message? That is, what makes your design successful? What would you change about it to improve it?

Connecting to Culture Suggestions for Writing

1. Constructing Nature: Evaluating Representations of Nature in Art

Several readings in this chapter, including "The American Geographies" (p. 486) and "We Are All Part of Nature" (p. 498), investigate how the natural world is presented in popular culture. Write a critical analysis of how the natural world is represented in a piece of music or in an image from art, photography, or film. As you draft, consider the following questions.

- What audience is the work aimed at? What artist's statement might the creator of this work make about the piece and how it presents or relates to nature?

- How does this work construct a particular view of the natural world? What assumptions about nature or what is "natural" does this work rely on?

- What does this artistic representation of nature suggest about our relationship to—and desires about—nature?

ON THE WEB
For help with these assignments, go to Chapter 6, bedfordstmartins.com/remix

2. What Makes Tomatoes Juicy? Investigating the Food Industry

Several chapter readings—"American Bioscience Meets the American Dream" (p. 508), "You—Only Better" (p. 517), and "Why McDonald's Fries Taste So Good" (p. 552)—question the label "natural" and how we use it. For this assignment, identify a food from your local grocery store and research its origins and how it was produced and prepared for sale. Choose a type of food that is generally considered "natural," such as one from the produce, dairy, or meat section. When conducting this primary research, seek answers to the following questions.

- Who supplied the product to your store?

- Where it was grown, manufactured, or produced??

- How or in what ways has this food been altered or enhanced?

Next, conduct library research to learn how the food industry produces this product for national distribution.

- What methods are commonly used in the food industry to grow or raise this product?

- How or in what ways has this food been genetically modified, altered, or enhanced?

Once you have collected your research, draft a critical analysis, reporting what you have learned about how natural foods are prepared for market.

3. How to Connect to Nature: Proposing a Nature Trail

Working collaboratively, propose the building of a nature trail or greenway that connects your college campus to a local park or green space. If your campus is located in a completely developed area, locate the closest green space that students might visit. Use the following steps to develop your proposal.

- Identify a workable site for your trail and determine its length and the materials required to build it.
- Research and identify funding sources both on campus and in the local community to fund your project.
- Research and identify any governing bodies that will need to approve this project, such as the college administration, neighborhood associations, and local municipalities.

When you have completed this research, you may work in groups or individually to draft a proposal to one of the decision-making organizations that would be involved in approving your nature trail. As you draft, consider the following questions.

- What are the details of your proposed trail? Where will it be located? What materials will be needed? Who will build it? What will it cost? What will be the benefits?

- What constraints—of money, time, and geography—will have to be taken into account?
- What kinds of information will your chosen organization want before giving its approval for the project? What questions will it need answered?

4. Interrogating Assumptions: What's So Natural about Nature?

The introduction of this chapter explains three commonly held assumptions that dominate our understanding of nature and the term "natural" in contemporary culture.

Nature is a spiritual and nurturing force.

Nature is a person's essential character.

Nature cannot be improved upon.

Each of the readings in this chapter question one or more of these assumptions, asking "What does it mean to call something 'natural'?" and "How does popular culture 'construct' our understanding of the natural world?" Develop a critical analysis of how two or three chapter readings interrogate one of these assumptions.

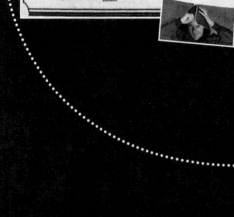

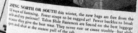

7 Technology

Examining the Everyday
Technology and Zippers

When most people hear the word "technology," they typically think of computers, cell phones, or cars. Yet an object does not have to contain a motor or a computer chip to qualify as a technology. We often take for granted many of the technologies that we use every day. Consider, for example, the zipper.

Before zippers came along, clothes and footwear were either laced up or held together by hooks and eyelets. According to *Advertising in America* (1990) by

Charles Goodrum and Helen Dalrymple, what we know as the "zipper" was invented in 1893 by Whitcomb L. Judson. His design arranged hooks and eyes so that a slider could, with some difficulty, open and close them. With businessman Lewis Walker, Whitcomb formed the Universal Fastener Company and hired a young Swedish engineer, Gideon Sundback, to improve Whitcomb's original "clasp locker" design. In 1913, Sundback came up with a reliable zipper that he named the "hookless

ON THE WEB
For additional resources for this
assignment, go to Chapter 7,
bedfordstmartins.com/remix

fastener." Hookless fasteners gained popularity only after 1923, when the navy installed them on its flight suits and the B. F. Goodrich Company, which coined the term "zipper," began using them in boots.

The two advertisements on page 574—from 1926 and 1930 respectively—show that, nearly 30 years after the introduction of its invention, the manufacturer was still trying to explain the usefulness of its product to the public. Today, however, we take zippers for granted.

To begin investigating the impact of technology on our culture, we need to first become aware of the ordinary technologies that exist all around us and have been created to meet human needs. Beginning to see these technologies will help you respond to one of the key questions of this chapter: How do technologies shape or define human activity? That is, how do technologies impact human life? Although we may not think much about the zipper, it is an innovation that has influenced the design and use of many products.

For this initial assignment, identify one everyday technology and analyze how it affects your daily life. Because one goal of this exercise is to help you begin to notice technologies that we usually take for granted, the object you choose *must be nonelectric and nonelectronic.* To begin, spend one to two hours keeping a running list of every technology you use during that time period. If you keep this list while you are getting ready to leave your house in the morning, you might include items like a hairbrush, shoelaces, or vitamins. If you keep this list while you are at work, you might include items like sticky notes or pencils. Review your list and choose one object that perhaps surprises you the most. Write a one-page profile of this object in which you answer the following questions.

- What makes this object a technology?

- How does it impact your daily life?

- Why is it surprising to think of it as a technology?

Finally, add an additional paragraph that answers these questions.

- How does this everyday object affect how you define a technology?

- What makes something a technology?

Technology, as the opening assignment demonstrates, is all around us, even in the most everyday objects. If we expand our understanding of what counts as technology beyond electronic devices, we also begin to expand our ability to investigate the significance of technology—of all kinds—on modern life.

The questions that will drive this investigation include: How do technologies help shape or define human activity? In what ways do technologies reflect and reinforce cultural values? How do technologies contribute to cultural change, both positive and negative?

Consider first two common assumptions about technology that tend to dominate discussions about technology. On one side is the view that technology always represents progress; on the other side is the view that technology is perilous to humans or the cause of the breakdown of society. Although there is, arguably, some validity to both of these claims, the reality is that neither of these stark arguments helps us truly develop a critical understanding of the complex ways technology impacts culture. In *Critical Theory of Technology* (1991), Andrew Feenberg offers another, more useful, view on technology: "Technology is not a destiny but a scene of struggle. It is a social battlefield, or perhaps a better metaphor would be a *parliament of things* on which civilizational alternatives are debated and decided" (14). Viewing technology as a scene of debate recognizes that technologies are part of culture. As such, they are not simply tools serving our needs; rather, they are imbued with cultural values and assumptions.

The readings in this chapter will challenge you to reflect on the cultural attitudes and assumptions built into how we define technology and how technologies influence or shape daily life. Following is a brief overview of some popular assumptions about technology to keep in mind as you work through this chapter.

introduction

Assumption 1

Technologies are machines.

Ask people to name as many technologies as they can in 20 seconds, and no doubt they will list a variety of tools, instruments, machines, appliances, and gadgets. A common assumption is that all technologies have power switches and moving parts. They move us from place to place, serve us in our workplace, keep us warm in the winter and cool in the summer, and generally make our lives better. Consider pencils, hammers, and ID cards, however. None contain moving parts, but all are extremely important examples of technologies.

What, then, counts as a technology? In 2002, the National Academy of Engineering (NAE) and the Committee on Technological Literacy published a report titled *Technically Speaking: Why All Americans Need to Know More about Technology*. The report defines technology as "the process by which humans modify nature to meet their needs and wants." Such a definition includes a great many objects or artifacts: cell phones, MP3 players, computers and software, coffee makers, pocket knives, thermometers, microwave ovens, pesticides, water-treatment plants, and aspirin, to name a few. But technology is more than these tangible objects. In his book *Autonomous Technology* (1973), Langdon Winner, one of the authors included in this chapter, developed a three-part description to explain the wide range of things that he considers to be technologies. According to Winner, tangible objects fall in the category of apparatuses. Apparatuses include all manner of human-made objects and devices.

Winner's second category includes technical activities that fall under the description of skills or techniques that people engage in to accomplish tasks. These skills—or methods, procedures, and routines—are all techniques we employ systematically to achieve specific purposes. As Winner points out, the root of the word "technique" is the Greek word "techne" which means "art," "craft," or "skill." For example, cell phones are technologies, but technology also includes all of the skills necessary for the design, manufacture, and support of cell phones. In other words, the people who develop and maintain telecommunications systems employ many technical skills, and these skills are themselves a form of technology. Language—which is a human invention that is used systematically—is also a form of technology, as argued by Neil Postman on page 623 of this chapter. As these examples illustrate, this second category opens up a wider range of what counts as a technology.

Winner's third category includes social organizations as types of technologies. Social organizations include any institutions and networks that support and enable the use of apparatuses and techniques. Schools, governments, medical centers, armies, and factories are all examples of this third form of technology, as are the networks that make cell phones work. The design, manufacture, and support of the cell phone takes place within a range of organizations that link its various technologies—from corporate headquarters and engineering schools that train the designers to manufacturing plants and satellite maintenance facilities to the cell phone sales kiosks at your local mall.

Langdon Winner and the NAE both offer broad definitions of technology. According to the NAE, because human cultures use a range of objects, skills, and organizations to "modify nature to meet their needs and wants," then skills and organizations can be considered technologies too.

What questions can you ask to uncover the benefits and limitations of the assumption that technologies are machines?

- How do skills or abilities that we take for granted represent forms of technology?
- What stories can technological objects tell us about the social forces that helped them come into being?
- How do social institutions and networks support and enable the use of particular technologies? In what ways do they constrain or limit the use of them?

Assumption 2

Technologies bring progress or peril.

As mentioned previously, this assumption offers opposing views on the impact of technology in our lives. On the one hand is the perspective that technologies always improve our lives. Particularly in American culture, "new" is better than "old." For example, at regular intervals new models of consumer products are rolled out, each of them hailed as the "next best thing." Whether they are computers, MP3 players, cars, stereos, running

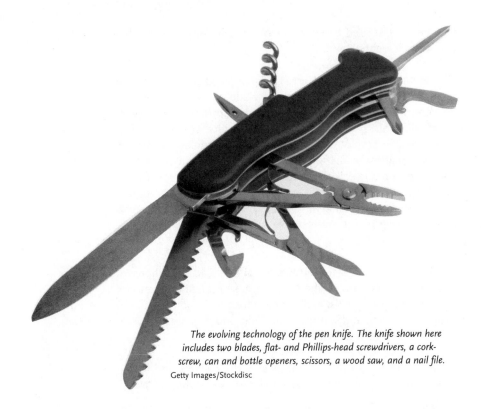

The evolving technology of the pen knife. The knife shown here includes two blades, flat- and Phillips-head screwdrivers, a cork-screw, can and bottle openers, scissors, a wood saw, and a nail file.
Getty Images/Stockdisc

shoes, sports drinks, or toothpastes, there is always a new version about to be released, one that offers more features, runs faster, or tastes better than the previous model. The same is true in the fields of science and medicine. Newspaper headlines frequently report a new scientific breakthrough or announce that a new miracle drug, one that is predicted to ease the lives of millions, has been approved for use.

On the other hand is the perspective that warns of the perils of technologies. For instance, almost as often as the Internet is described in glowing terms as the "Information Superhighway," it is also portrayed as a locus for dangers including identity theft and computer viruses, and as a haven for stalkers and child molesters. Similarly, the potential medical benefits of bioengineering, for example, can be overshadowed by wild and sinister images of cloned humans—images spawned by a generalized fear that science will inevitably spin out of control and do us harm.

These two perspectives are flip sides of the romanticized view that technology is all-powerful. They are grounded in the opposing ideas that technology can save us or can destroy us. These assumptions are so powerful because there is some truth to them. You could argue, for example, that the Internet benefits humans by giving us access to unlimited information; you could also argue that it is a tool used by stalkers. You could argue that bioengineering has the potential to cure disease; you could also argue that it is potentially hazardous in terms of the development and spread of new diseases.

Sometimes technologies have unexpected consequences. Consider the household products introduced to middle America in the postwar 1950s. Prepared or "instant" foods like boxed pudding, bread, and cake mixes were meant to save women from spending all day in the kitchen. Also, a new wave of cleaning products and appliances—dishwashers, washers, and dryers—were marketed as time-savers and were meant to free women from the drudgery of household labors. While it is true that these innovations did relieve women from the time-consuming work of washing clothes by hand or preparing meals "from scratch," sociolinguist Victoria Leto suggests that this progress came at a cost. In an essay titled "'Washing, Seems It's All We Do': Washing Technology and Women's Communication," Leto contends that while the washing machine made washing easier, it also broke up the washing circles that women formed among their families and neighbors. These social networks—which helped women support and connect with one another—gradually dissolved. This unexpected consequence was coupled with another: Leto points out that traditional attitudes about the gendered division of labor in the home did not "progress" or change with the advent of the washing machine. Women were still expected to cook and clean.

As this example illustrates, technologies almost always impact human experience in unintended or unexpected ways. Many technology critics argue that, like Faust—the alchemist of German legend who sells his soul to the devil in exchange for power and knowledge—we make a bargain to enjoy the progress that technologies provide: For every gain, there is a loss.

What questions can you ask to uncover the benefits and limitations of the assumption that technologies represent progress or peril?

- What are the arguments surrounding how people discuss the positive or negative impacts of technology in our culture?

- How does the view of technology-as-progress help or expand how people think about technology's role or purpose? What about the view that technology represents peril or danger? In what ways do these views constrain or limit our thinking?

- What are some of the trade-offs associated with the technologies you use?

Godzilla, the famous sci-fi monster of a 1954 Japanese film (released in the United States in 1956), was an unexpected by-product of hydrogen bomb testing. The creature Godzilla, imagined in the wake of the bombings of Hiroshima and Nagasaki, can be seen as a symbol of the massive devastation by the era's new weapons technology.

Assumption 3

Technologies are neutral.

According to this view, a technology is a neutral tool, simply waiting to be put to use. The impact of a technology—positive, negative, or otherwise—is the responsibility of the people who use it. For example, as Langdon Winner writes in "Technological Somnambulism" (p. 594), "Tools can be 'used well or poorly' and for 'good or bad purposes'; I can use my knife to slice a loaf of bread or to stab the next person [who] walks by." In either case, as Winner explains, we may judge the values of the user of the knife, not the knife itself. When it comes to moral standing, technologies are themselves thought to be neutral. However, this assumption overlooks a crucial point: Because technologies are human-made artifacts, practices, or organizations forged within a culture, they always embody the values and assumptions of their designers. This is not a flaw, but an inevitable by-product of a postindustrial culture.

This illustration from a 1950 issue of Popular Mechanics *projects a view of the world in the year 2000 in which "miraculous" plastic furnishings simplify everyday life for housewives.*

Because everything in her home is waterproof, the housewife of 2000 can do her daily cleaning with a hose

How do cultural values impact the design of technology? In an interview[1] for Gotomedia.com (2004), cultural anthropologist Genevieve Bell observes that Americans commonly assume that the United States is the technological "center of the world" and that other cultures are simply trying to keep pace with American practices. Such a misperception can make engineers and designers blind to their own biases. Her research—conducted for Intel—demonstrates how American concepts of "home," "family," and "individual" are inextricably woven into the design of technologies, which then do not always translate well in other cultures. For instance, in some Asian cultures people are more likely to define themselves as members of a family or household than as self-sufficient individuals, and as Bell explains, such cultural assumptions impact "the notion of technology ownership." In Indonesia, she observed that some families share all their cell phones. Phones, thus, create connections between social networks, not individuals, and people assume when they call a number that someone in the family will respond. In this cultural context, specific phone numbers do not necessarily correspond to specific individuals. This practice contrasts dramatically with American attitudes about efficiency and individualism.

Cultural anthropologists like Bell remind us that, on some level, technologies reflect the biases or values of those designing them. In some cases, technologies have a bias that the mainstream accepts. Consider how the designs of many everyday technologies assume that the user is right-handed. From scissors and classroom desks to musical instruments and stick shifts in cars, left-handed people are forced to use many technologies that have been designed with a right-handed bias. As these examples show, the bias of a technology is often unintended. However, this is not always the case. In "A Wicked Cheat" (p. 617), Gustav Peebles critiques the widely accepted practice of charging fees to use ATM machines. Such fees, he suggests, make it "dramatically more expensive for poor people to use cash." Moreover, he links these fees to other practices in the banking industry that regularly disadvantage poor people. As Peebles makes clear, the banking system, with its power to regulate the use and flow of money, reveals a bias that is highly problematic.

---

[1] Kelly Goto and Subha Subramanian, "Culture Matters: An Interview with Genevieve Bell," http://www.gotomedia.com/gotoreport/november2004/news _1104_bell.html, accessed August 4, 2005.

Cultural anthropologists like Genevieve Bell point out that, while Americans prize technologies that promote efficiency and create progress and change, other cultures think very differently about technology. In Malaysia, the phone is a religious and spiritual tool that connects people to long-standing religious practices. The Malaysian woman pictured here shows the words "Bismi Allahi Alrrahmani Alrraheemi," meaning "In the Name of Allah, the Most Beneficent, the Most Merciful," on a cell phone. Cellular communications companies such as LG Electronics have designed phones for these cultures that provide free call-to-prayer (Salat) alerts five times a day and contain built-in compasses that point users toward Mecca, Saudi Arabia. (Muslims pray facing Mecca.)

Whether intentionally or unintentionally, technologies are anything but neutral. As part of a culture, they embody the values and biases of their designers.

What questions can you ask to uncover the benefits and limitations of the assumption that technologies are neutral?

- Have you noticed any unintended consequences of using technologies?

- Have you ever used technologies in ways that were not intended by their designers?

- What do technologies reveal about the biases of those who created them? What do they reveal about your own cultural contexts?

Questioning These Assumptions

All too often we think of technology as something we need to learn, rather than as something we should critique. Throughout this chapter, you will be asked to examine the impact of cultural assumptions about technology and to answer questions such as: How do technologies represent the cultural values of a society? How do they shape human activity?

Ellen DeGeneres, **This Is How We Live**

Ellen DeGeneres is a comedian, an actress, and a producer and the host of the talk show *The Ellen DeGeneres Show,* which began airing in 2003. In 1997, she made history when her *Ellen* character became the first openly gay leading character on television. DeGeneres has toured the United States performing stand-up comedy and doing promotional tours for her best-selling books *My Point . . . And I Do Have One* (1995) and *The Funny Thing Is . . .* (2003). During a 2003 interview, DeGeneres said of her career, "I've worked for 20 years to get where I am. I'm a writer and a performer and I love making people laugh. This I what I'm meant to do." The following excerpt is from her book *The Funny Thing Is . . .* and chronicles DeGeneres's concerns about technological advances ranging from automated toilet flushing to the hands-free cell phone.

> ▶ **Mapping Your Reading**
>
> "Frankly, I think modern technology is hurting us. I really do," writes DeGeneres. In the following essay, she describes her frustrations with everyday technologies and pokes fun at the ways technology makes people lazy. As you read, put checks in the margins next to passages where DeGeneres takes her observations about human behavior in this more serious direction. Why is it that each new technology seems to demand a whole new set of other technologies to support it? Do technologies reflect human laziness?

E veryone likes to talk about how advancements in technology will change the way we live forever. Frankly, I think modern technology is hurting us. I really do.

If you want to know the truth, I blame the microwave for most of our problems. Anything that gets food that hot without fire is from the devil. If you don't believe me, put a Hot Pocket in your microwave for three or four minutes, then pop that thing in your mouth. If that's not Hell, my friend, I don't know what is.

Modern life requires hardly any physical activity. We just push a button and stand there. Take the car window. Someone decided that having to crank the window down yourself was too hard. "I don't want to churn butter, I just want fresh air!" So we got a button to do it.

We're just so lazy. We used to have breath mints. Now we have breath strips that just dissolve on our tongue. Can we not *suck* anymore?

Yes, we're lazy. Yet we also can't seem to sit still. So we've started making things like GO-GURT. That's yogurt for people on the go. Let me ask you, was there a big mobility problem with yogurt before? How time-consuming was it, really?

"Hello? . . . Oh, hi, Tom . . . Oh, I've been *dying* to see that movie . . . Umm, no . . . I just opened up some yogurt . . . Yeah, I'm in for the night . . . No, not even later—it's the kind with fruit on the bottom. Well, have fun. Thanks anyway."

Was there a big mobility problem with yogurt before?

And people are eating power bars all the time. Power bars were made for mountain-climbing expeditions and hiking, not really made to be eaten in the car on the way to the mall. Is it really that much faster and more convenient? It takes longer to chew one bite of those things than it takes to make an entire sandwich. I don't know what they're made from, but you could insulate a house with that stuff.

There are certain things that they're coming up with that I just don't think we need. Top of the list is that moving sidewalk you find in airports. It's like a little ride in the middle of nowhere, but I don't know what function it really serves. I mean, it's fun because it moves, so if you walk while you're on it you're almost like the Bionic Woman, just flying past the people trudging beside you on the ground. But you know how hard it is to adjust to walking again once you get off that thing? And what about those people who get on there and just stand? I guess we have to thank God they found the moving sidewalk. Without it, I don't know how they'd get anywhere.

You'd think with all these innovations that are speeding things up for us and moving us along, people would be early—or at least on time—when they're going places. But somehow, everybody's still always late. And people always say the same thing when they finally show up after you've been waiting for them. "Oh, sorry. Traffic." "Really? How do you think I got here? Helicoptered in? I *allow* for it."

How else does technology torture us? Well, try opening up a brand-new CD. What has happened to the packaging of CDs? These are angry, angry people, these CD packagers. "Open here," it says. Is that sarcasm? Are they mocking me? The plastic they use is so thick, it's like government plastic—civilians can't buy this stuff. And you can't get through it without slashing it with a knife or scissors or something. In fact, I find you need a sharp pair of scissors to get into just about anything these days. Have you tried to open a package of scissors lately? You need *scissors* to get into scissors. And what if you're buying scissors for the first time? I mean, how can you possibly get in there? Talk about a catch-22.

Batteries are also packaged as though the manufacturers never want you to get to them. What could possibly happen to batteries that they need to be packaged like that? On the other hand, take a good look at a package of lightbulbs. Thin, thin, thin cardboard that's open on both ends. What are *those* packagers thinking? "Oh, the lightbulbs? They'll be fine."

It's hard to get into anything, even toilet paper. What has happened to toilet paper in public bathrooms? It's not even one-ply anymore, is it? It's a sheer suggestion of toilet paper. It's an *innuendo*. It's like prosciutto, it's so thin. And if you're in a public bathroom and it's a brand-new roll that hasn't gotten started yet, just try to find the start of that toilet paper roll. First you turn it slowly. You think, *surely I've gone around once or twice by now*. Then you go fast. Maybe the wind will open up the first flap. Then you turn it the other way, thinking maybe you're going in the wrong direction. And back to the slow again. And then you find it, and it's glued down. So then you try to pull it apart but only a quarter of an inch separates and the rest stays glued. So you're pulling and pulling and soon you've got a five-foot-long quarter-of-an-inch strip. I don't want a streamer, I want toilet paper! So now one side is fully intact and you've got a groove cut out on the other side. Then you use your finger to try to even it out, but you never get it exactly even, so then you finally just claw at it like a wild animal. "Jesus, I just want toilet paper!"

On the other hand, some things that don't need to be made easier are being made easier. They're making these automated toilets that flush entirely on their own schedule. Sometimes they just go off randomly. You're still sitting down and suddenly it just flushes. "How *dare* you! I'll decide when I'm done!" And then other times it won't go off when you want it to. You stand up and stare at the toilet. Sometimes you have to fake it out. You sit back down . . . stand up! Sit down . . . stand up! Then you try tiptoeing away as if you're leaving. Nothing works.

Then, when you go to wash your hands, you don't have any control of that either. The faucet has to see your hands first so it can decide how much water it's going to give you. It gives out only a certain amount of water. You don't know how much you're getting, so you're like a little raccoon under there, rubbing your little paws together. It gives you some, then it decides *that's enough*, and it's not. So you have to pull out and pretend like you are a new set of hands going back in again. Same thing happens with the dryer—you don't have any control. You have to put your hands under the vent to get the air to come out. It's all to avoid germs, which is great, fantastic. Good for the health of the world. Then you walk over to that disease-ridden door handle, open it up, and head to the bowl of mixed nuts you're sharing at the bar.

Technology has done one beautiful thing for us. It's called the cell phone. There is now not one place in the world where a cell phone is not going off. And every cell phone now has its own little song! Good thing we got rid of those obnoxious rings, isn't it?

When you're on a cell phone, you can't ever have a full conversation. Usually the reception is terrible, and somehow it's only bad on your side. The person talking to you has no idea that you have bad reception. They're rambling on and on and you've got your finger jammed in your ear. You're shushing people on the street, ducking behind a Dumpster, putting your head between your knees, just so you can hear about your friend's new haircut. "What about the bangs? Are they shorter? Are the bangs shorter? THE BANGS!!"

THE WORLD IS A
NOISY PLACE.
YOU AREN'T
HELPING THINGS.

SHHH! | Society for HandHeld Hushing

DEAR CELL PHONE USER

We are aware that your ongoing conversation

about,

your husband's vasectomy

is very important to you, but we thought you'd like to know
that it *doesn't interest us in the least.* In fact, your babbling
disregard for others is more than a little annoying.

This message brought to you
by a concerned member of:

SHHH! | Society for HandHeld Hushing

www.coudal.com

*A sampling of the message
cards created by the Society
for HandHeld Hushing
(aka SHHH!), available
at www.cloudal.com. According to SHHH!, "It's time
to fight back" against annoying cell phone users.*

SHHH! SHHH! SHHH!
SHHH! SHHH! SHHH!
SHHH! SHHH! SHHH!
SHHH! SHHH! SHHH!

SHHH! | Society for HandHeld Hushing

— Sincerely, The Rest of Us

At least if there's static you have some clue that you may get cut off. There's nothing worse than when you have crystal-clear reception and you've been rambling on for who knows how long, only to find out that the connection cut out who knows how long ago. Then you get paranoid. You're scared to talk too long ever again. Next time you're on the phone you become obsessed with checking. "So we were going to go to the cheese shop. . . . *Hello? Okay* . . . And we knew we were having white wine. . . . *Still there?* All right. And I thought, what kind of cheese would go with . . . ? *Did I lose you?* Okay . . . And I like Muenster. . . ."

Even if you're on a regular phone at home, you'll be interrupted somehow. You'll be interrupted by call-waiting most likely. Call-waiting was invented as a convenience, but let's face it—it's really turned into a mini People's Choice awards. You find out right away who wins or loses. You're having a pleasant conversation with someone you think is a good friend, and you hear the click, and you're confident that they're going to come back to you. Then they come back and say, "I've got to take this other call." And you know what that means. They just said to the other person, "Let me get rid of this other call." That's what you just became: a call to get rid of. Then you learn to trick them the next time, when they say they've got to check on the other call. "Hey, when you come back, remind me to tell you something that somebody said about you! . . . *Hello?*"

Of course, you don't have to pick up call-waiting. You can get voice mail. Voice mail will pick it up for you. My favorite voice mail is the one where you insert your name into a robotic message, and you end up sounding more like a robot than the robot itself. "Your call has been forwarded to an automatic voice message system. El-len is not available." Is that how I say my name? Like HAL from *2001:A Space Odyssey*? "Yeah, I'd like to make reservations for dinner tonight, there's four of us, and the name is El-len."

Phones have gone through such an evolution. Now we have this wireless technology that lets us talk to anybody, anywhere, anytime. Think about how far phones have come. You'll remember there was a time when there was one phone in the house, when cord was just being invented. There was a shortage of cord back then. Maybe you had a foot or two from the wall to the phone. Back then, when you said you were on the phone, you were *on the phone*.

> **Back then, when you were on the phone, you were on the phone.**

Then the kitchen wall phone came along, usually a lovely mustard or an avocado green. It had a 90-foot-long cord that allowed you to walk all around the house, clearing tables, wrapping around dogs, so that by the time you hung up the phone, it had become this tangled wire of cord confusion. But what was fun about it was that every once in a while you would hold the phone upside down by the cord and let that thing spin and spin, around and around, till it found its center. Good times.

One surefire sign that things are going the wrong way? Now we have the hands-free phone so you can concentrate on the thing you're really supposed to be doing. My thought is this: Chances are, if you need both of your hands to do something, your brain should be in on it too.

Analyzing the Text

1. DeGeneres questions the value of technologies, observing that developments like drinkable yogurt and moving sidewalks have made people lazy. To what extent have other technologies made people lazy? Can you think of more examples that support this argument?

2. Elsewhere, DeGeneres cites examples of how technologies like packaging have created another layer of work for us or have changed our social relationships in fundamental ways, as with the "call-waiting" and "voice mail" function of phones. What is DeGeneres's main argument about these technologies? How do you respond to her view?

3. How does the humorous tone of this essay help DeGeneres convey her argument? How would the impact of the argument change if the tone were serious?

4. **Interrogating Assumptions.** How does DeGeneres's essay challenge the second assumption in this chapter's introduction that "technologies bring progress or peril" (p. 579)? How do you respond to DeGeneres's point that most technological advancements come at a cost?

Writing about Cultural Practices

5. DeGeneres's essay calls into question some of the irritating side effects of technology. However, sometimes frustration with a technological object, device, or practice can be a cue for asking the kinds of questions that DeGeneres asks in her essay. Identify a particular technology or technological practice that has frustrated you. Write a critical narrative that describes your encounter with this object or practice and reflect on it. As you write, consider the following questions.

   - What is the technological object, device, or practice that caused your frustration? When, where, and how did you encounter it?

   - Was your frustration caused by an intended or unintended consequence of the design of this technology? Are there specific assumptions or biases built into the design or any other aspect of the technology?

   - How would you improve this technology or technological practice?

   - How does this technology or technological practice reflect or reinforce specific cultural values or biases?

Langdon Winner, **Technological Somnambulism**

Langdon Winner is a political theorist and professor at Rensselaer Polytechnic Institute who writes about a range of social and political issues that surround technological change. In addition to numerous published essays, he has written two books, *Autonomous Technology* (1978) and *The Whale and the Reactor: A Search for Limits in the Age of High Technology* (1986), which have become central texts to modern-day technology analysts. He has been praised by the *Wall Street Journal* as "[t]he leading academic on the politics of technology." As Winner has argued, "I regularly praise technologies that reflect reasonable practices of democracy, justice, ecological sustainability, and human dignity. Unfortunately, a great many of the technical devices and systems that surround us are designed, built, and deployed in flagrant disregard of humane principles." This essay, published in *The Whale and the Reactor*, introduces two prevailing theories or viewpoints about technology: technological determinism and technological somnambulism (sleepwalking).

▶ **Mapping Your Reading**

In the following essay, Winner describes the most common assumptions people have about technology and argues that there are specific questions we should ask when we investigate the impact of technology on everyday life. As you read, pay attention to Winner's use of concrete examples to explain and support his argument, and underline those that are most compelling. Why does Winner think it is important for people to overcome the assumption that technologies exist simply because they are useful? What are the moral negotiations that accompany technological change?

W hy is it that the philosophy of technology has never really gotten under way? Why has a culture so firmly based upon countless sophisticated instruments, techniques, and systems remained so steadfast in its reluctance to examine its own foundations? Much of the answer can be found in the astonishing hold the idea of "progress" has exercised on social thought during the industrial age. It is usually taken for granted that the only reliable sources for improving the human condition stem from new machines, techniques, and chemicals. Even the recurring environmental and social ills that have accompanied technological advancement have rarely dented this faith. It is still a prerequisite that the person running for public office swear his or her unflinching confidence in a positive link between technical development and human well-being and affirm that the next wave of innovations will surely be our salvation.

There is, however, another reason why the philosophy of technology has never gathered much steam. According to conventional views, the human relationship to technical things is too obvious to merit serious reflection: The deceptively reasonable notion that we have inherited from much earlier and less complicated times divides the range of possible concerns about technology into two basic categories: *making* and *use.* In the first of these our attention is drawn to the matter of "how things work" and of "making things work." We tend to think that this is a fascination of certain people in certain occupations, but not for anyone else. "How things work" is the domain of inventors, technicians, engineers, repairmen, and the like who prepare artificial aids to human activity and keep them in good working order. Those not directly involved in the various spheres of "making" are thought to have little interest in or need to know about the materials, principles, or procedures found in those spheres.

What the others do care about, however, are tools and uses. This is understood to be a straightforward matter. Once things have been made, we interact with them on occasion to achieve specific purposes. One picks up a tool, uses it, and puts it down. One picks up a telephone, talks on it, and then does not use it for a time. A person gets on an airplane, flies from point A to point B, and then gets off. The proper interpretation of the meaning of technology in the mode of use seems to be nothing more complicated than an occasional, limited, and nonproblematic interaction.

The language of the notion of "use" also includes standard terms that enable us to interpret technologies in a range of moral contexts. Tools can be "used well or poorly" and for "good or bad purposes"; I can use my knife to slice a loaf of bread or to stab the next person [who] walks by. Because technological objects and processes have a promiscuous utility, they are taken to be fundamentally neutral as regards their moral standing.

The conventional idea of what technology is and what it means, an idea powerfully reinforced by familiar terms used in everyday language, needs to be overcome if a critical philosophy of technology is to move ahead. The crucial weakness of the conventional idea is that it disregards the many ways in which technologies provide structure for human activity. Since, according to accepted wisdom, patterns that take shape in the sphere of "making" are of interest to practitioners alone, and since the very essence of "use" is its occasional, innocuous, nonstructuring occurrence, any further questioning seems irrelevant.

If the experience of modern society shows us anything, however, it is that technologies are not merely aids to human activity, but also powerful forces acting to reshape that activity and its meaning. The introduction of a robot to an industrial workplace not only increases productivity, but often radically changes

> The next wave of innovations will surely be our salvation.

> Technologies are not merely aides to human activity, but also powerful forces acting to reshape that activity.

the process of production, redefining what "work" means in that setting. When a sophisticated new technique or instrument is adopted in medical practice, it transforms not only what doctors do, but also the ways people think about health, sickness, and medical care. Widespread alterations of this kind in techniques of communication, transportation, manufacturing, agriculture, and the like are largely what distinguishes our times from early periods of human history. The kinds of things we are apt to see as "mere" technological entities become much more interesting and problematic if we begin to observe how broadly they are involved in conditions of social and moral life.

It is true that recurring patterns of life's activity (whatever their origins) tend to become unconscious processes taken for granted. Thus, we do not pause to reflect upon how we speak a language as we are doing so or the motions we go through in taking a shower. There is, however, one point at which we may become aware of a pattern taking shape—the very first time we encounter it. An opportunity of that sort occurred several years ago at the conclusion of a class I was teaching. A student came to my office on the day term papers were due and told me his essay would be late. "It crashed this morning," he explained. I immediately interpreted this as a "crash" of the conceptual variety, a flimsy array of arguments and observations that eventually collapses under the weight of its own ponderous absurdity. Indeed, some of my own papers have "crashed" in exactly that manner. But this was not the kind of mishap that had befallen this particular fellow. He went on to explain that his paper had been composed on a computer terminal and that it had been stored in a time-sharing minicomputer. It sometimes happens that the machine "goes down" or "crashes," making everything that happens in and around it stop until the computer can be "brought up," that is, restored to full functioning.

As I listened to the student's explanation, I realized that he was telling me about the facts of a particular form of activity in modern life in which he and others similarly situated were already involved and that I had better get ready for. I remembered J. L. Austin's little essay "A Plea for Excuses" and noticed that the student and I were negotiating one of the boundaries of contemporary moral life—where and how one gives and accepts an excuse in a particular technology-mediated situation. He was, in effect, asking me to recognize a new world of parts and pieces and to acknowledge appropriate practices and expectations that hold in that world. From then on, a knowledge of this situation would be included in my understanding of not only "how things work" in that generation of computers, but also how we do things as a consequence, including which rules to follow when the machines break down. Shortly thereafter I got used to computers crashing, disrupting hotel reservations, banking, and other everyday transactions; eventually, my own papers began crashing in this new way.

Some of the moral negotiations that accompany technological change become matters of law.

Some of the moral negotiations that accompany technological change eventually become matters of law. In recent times, for example, a number of activities that employ computers as their operating medium have been legally defined as "crimes." Is unauthorized access to a computerized data base a criminal offense? Given the fact that electronic information is in the strictest sense intangible, under what conditions is it "property" subject to theft? The law has had to stretch and reorient its traditional categories to encompass such problems, creating whole new classes of offenses and offenders.

The ways in which technical devices tend to engender distinctive worlds of their own can be seen in a more familiar case. Picture two men traveling in the same direction along a street on a peaceful, sunny day, one of them afoot and the other driving an automobile. The pedestrian has a certain flexibility of movement: he can pause to look in a shop window, speak to passersby, and reach out to pick a flower from a sidewalk garden. The driver, although he has the potential to move much faster, is constrained by the enclosed space of the automobile, the physical dimensions of the highway, and the rules of the road. His realm is spatially structured by his intended destination, by a periphery of more-or-less irrelevant objects (scenes for occasional side glances), and by more important objects of various kinds—moving and parked cars, bicycles, pedestrians, street signs, etc., that stand in his way. Since the first rule of good driving is to avoid hitting things, the immediate environment of the motorist becomes a field of obstacles.

Imagine a situation in which the two persons are next-door neighbors. The man in the automobile observes his friend strolling along the street and wishes to say hello. He slows down, honks his horn, rolls down the window, sticks out his head, and shouts across the street. More likely than not the pedestrian will be startled or annoyed by the sound of the horn. He looks around to see what's the matter and tries to recognize who can be yelling at him across the way. "Can you come to dinner Saturday night?" the driver calls out over the street noise. "What?" the pedestrian replies, straining to understand. At that moment another car to the rear begins honking to break up the temporary traffic jam. Unable to say anything more, the driver moves on.

What we see here is an automobile collision of sorts, although not one that causes bodily injury. It is a collision between the *world* of the driver and that of the pedestrian. The attempt to extend a greeting and invitation, ordinarily a simple gesture, is complicated by the presence of a technological device and its standard operating conditions. The communication between the two men is shaped by an incompatibility of the form of locomotion known as walking and a much newer one, automobile driving. In cities such as Los Angeles, where the physical landscape and prevailing social habits assume everyone drives a car, the simple act of walking can be cause for alarm. The U.S. Supreme Court decided one case involving a young man who enjoyed taking long walks late at night through the streets of San Diego and was repeatedly arrested by police as a suspicious character. The Court decided in favor of the pedestrian, noting that he had not been engaged in burglary or any other illegal act. Merely traveling by foot is not yet a crime.

Knowing how automobiles are made, how they operate, and how they are used and knowing about traffic laws and urban transportation policies does little to help us understand how automobiles affect the texture of modern life. In such cases a strictly instrumental/functional understanding fails us badly. What is needed is an interpretation of the ways, both obvious and subtle, in which every-day life is transformed by the mediating role of technical devices. In hindsight the situation is clear to everyone. Individual habits, perceptions, concepts of self, ideas of space and time, social relationships, and moral and political boundaries have all been powerfully restructured in the course of modern technological de-velopment. What is fascinating about this process is that societies involved in it have quickly altered some of the fundamental terms of human life without ap-pearing to do so. Vast transformations in the structure of our common world have been undertaken with little attention to what those alterations mean. Judgments about technology have been made on narrow grounds, paying attention to such matters as whether a new device serves a particular need, performs more effi-ciently than its predecessor, makes a profit, or provides a convenient service. Only later does the broader significance of the choice become clear, typically as a series of surprising "side effects" or "secondary consequences." But it seems character-istic of our culture's involvement with technology that we are seldom inclined to examine, discuss, or judge pending innovations with broad, keen awareness of what those changes mean. In the technical realm we repeatedly enter into a series of social contracts, the terms of which are revealed only after the signing.

It may seem that the view I am suggesting is that of technological deter-minism: the idea that technological innovation is the basic cause of changes in society and that human beings have little choice other than to sit back and watch this ineluctable process unfold. But the concept of determinism is much too strong, far too sweeping in its implications to provide an adequate theory. It does little justice to the genuine choices that arise, in both principle and practice, in the course of technical and social transformation. Being saddled with it is like at-tempting to describe all instances of sexual intercourse based only on the concept of rape. A more revealing notion, in my view, is that of technological somnam-bulism. For the interesting puzzle in our times is that we so willingly sleepwalk through the process of reconstituting the conditions of human existence.

▶ **Analyzing the Text**

1. **Interrogating Assumptions.**   As Winner sees it, what common attitudes get in the way of attempts to understand the impact of technologies on everyday life? How does Winner address the assumption that technologies are neutral (see this chapter's introduction, p. 583)?

2. According to Winner, why is it a problem that people are sleepwalking as "the conditions of human existence" are increasingly transformed by technologies?

3. What distinguishes "technological determinism" from "technological somnam-bulism"? Both try to explain how technologies redefine human activity and be-havior. Although the theory of technological determinism may make people uncomfortable, it is not difficult to identify examples—as Winner and other authors in this chapter do—that support the view that technologies have rede-fined a range of human activities in ways beyond our control. What examples can you think of?

4. **Connecting to Another Reading.** To what extent are the behaviors that Ellen DeGeneres pokes fun at in "This Is How We Live" (p. 588) examples of technological determinism? In other words, to what extent is she pointing out how human behavior is directly affected (determined) by everyday technologies?

▶ **Writing about Cultural Practices**

5. Perhaps no other technology is surrounded by more grand claims about its promise than the computer. For example, the mere presence of computers in schools is often taken as a sign of educational success. For this assignment, follow Winner's example by deconstructing the myths surrounding popular representations of computers in the media. To begin, collect examples of the portrayal of the computer in television commercials, television shows, or movies. Pay attention to how computers or a particular type of software is represented. Choose an example you find most interesting and draft a critical analysis. As you draft, consider the following questions.

   • How are computers presented in your example? How are the computers meant to be used? By whom? What is the computer's relationship to the other objects or people that surround it in this example?

   • Who is the intended audience for your example? What do the producers seem to assume about this audience?

   • How does this presentation of computers reflect or reinforce specific cultural assumptions or attitudes about technology?

   • In his essay, Winner describes some of the moral negotiations that accompany the use of computers (see his discussion of computer crashes and computer crime). What kinds of moral negotiations accompany the use of computers in your media example? How are they resolved?

Sampling the Old and the New

Defining Women's Work: The "Western Washer" vs. The Modern Kenmore

In the nineteenth century, household work—considered women's work—was burdensome, inefficient, and stifling. In 1874, William Blackstone, a Bluffton, Indiana, merchant and manufacturer of corn planters, invented a washing machine as a birthday present for his wife. Within five years his invention became big business, but, Blackstone's thoughtfulness notwithstanding, the Industrial Revolution, which had succeeded in transforming the workplace, was the real impetus for transforming domestic work, the home itself, and women's roles through the introduction of household appliances, like the washing machine depicted above. Appliances helped liberate women from the isolation of the home, and it was believed these time- and labor-saving devices could provide women with greater access to the larger world.

However, household labor largely remains women's work today. According to a 2004 survey published by the U.S. Department of Labor, on an average day 20 percent of men reported doing housework compared to 55 percent of women. Thus, the belief that appliances can play the role of liberator of women is still used today to sell household devices, as the ad at right demonstrates. Such messages reinforce cultural attitudes that bind domesticity to women's identities. These messages simultaneously direct women to achieve liberation from certain onerous household tasks but also to take pride in others, such as cooking, cleaning, and child care.

600

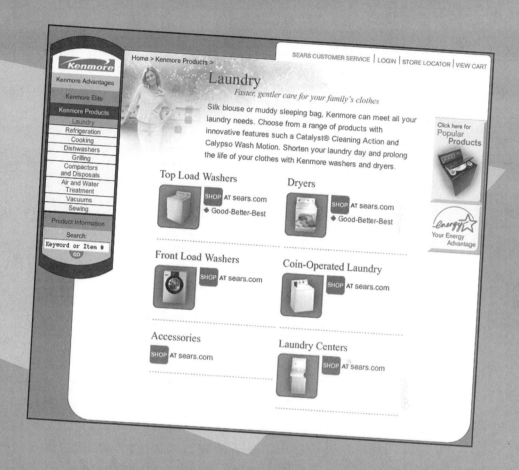

1. What do these images suggest about how domestic technologies are interconnected with cultural assumptions about women's and men's roles in the home? What do they convey about cultural attitudes toward technology as a source of liberation?

2. How interdependent are our assumptions about domesticity and womanhood? Many cultural critics believe the formula for defining womanhood in many women's magazines depends on validating housework through the consumption of goods. Test this argument by studying several homemaking magazines such as *Ladies' Home Journal, Good Housekeeping,* and *Martha Stewart Living.* How do the ads and content of these magazines connect certain domestic technologies to women's identities?

3. As Thomas Hine points out in "Looking Alive" (see p. 602), smart technologies are the future in home automation. Domotics, the application of robot and remote control technologies to domestic appliances, has already taken off. Some examples include robotic vacuum cleaners, "smart" garden sprinklers, programmable indoor climate and lighting controls, and centralized remote control home entertainment systems. What assumptions about household chores and gender roles do these smart technologies create or reinforce?

Thomas Hine, **Looking Alive**

Praised in the *New Yorker* by John Updike for his "mischievously alert sensibility," Thomas Hine brings this sensibility to his writing on history, culture, and design. He has written five books, *Populuxe* being the first in 1986. Hine has taught at the University of Pennsylvania and Temple University and frequently contributes to *Philadelphia Magazine, Martha Stewart Living, Architectural Record,* and *Atlantic Monthly.* This essay, originally published in 2001 in *Atlantic Monthly,* observes that the prevailing metaphors about biology and technology have been reversed. "Rather than thinking about our bodies in terms of mechanics," Hine writes, "we are now encouraged to think about technology as if it were a form of biology."

▶ **Mapping Your Reading**

In "Looking Alive," Hine explores the directions contemporary design takes as technologies become more lifelike. As you read, highlight passages in which Hine demonstrates his skepticism about the so-called smart designs of the future. What promises have designers made about the increasingly blurry line dividing humans and technologies? How does it reflect our sense of ourselves? How does it impact the way we live?

L ike many members of the Baby Boom generation, I grew up thinking about the human body in mechanistic terms. In elementary school I sat through repeated showings of a film in the Bell Science series, *Hemo the Magnificent,* which depicted the body as a factory staffed by little men who were constantly turning valves on and off, or running from cell to cell like milkmen, delivering oxygen. Even at age nine I knew this wasn't how things really worked. Still, metaphors matter. Those cute little animated workers may not be manning my aorta, but they have stuck in my mind ever since.

In recent years, though, our culture's metaphors about biology and technology have been reversed. Rather than thinking about our bodies in terms of mechanics, we are now encouraged to think about technology as if it were a form of biology. Computer viruses are a good example. IBM made front-page news when it announced plans to develop "self-healing" computers, which will analyze their own malfunctions, repair them, and keep working while doing so. Whereas we once thought steel strong and flesh weak, now the steam drill is learning from John Henry.

When metaphors change, it usually means that reality has done so already. And in fact our bodies are filling up with machinery. Pacemakers, knee and hip replacements, eye implants, artificial skin, and even man-made organs are becoming so commonplace that cyborgs—hybrids of human being and machine—are already living in our midst. But they don't look like Arnold Schwarzenegger in *Terminator*. They aren't supermen; they're only us.

Then, too, there's the Speedo Fastskin wet suit, which was worn by a majority of the top swimmers in the 2000 Olympics. This second skin enhances swimmers' performance not by making their bodies smooth—the traditional swimmer's strategy. Rather, the fabric of the suit replicates structures found on the skin of a shark, which act like tiny hydrofoils and redirect the flow of water over the animal's body. Although the suit is a high-tech product, its sophistication relies entirely on mimicking biological forms. Swimmers wear the suit because it helps them go faster. The fact that it makes its wearers look as if they just stepped out of a Marvel comic doesn't hurt. With a change of costume a mere human being becomes a shark-skinned superswimmer.

It's almost impossible to separate the engineering features that make the Fastskin work from its "design"—those qualities of form, texture, and color that make a thing memorable and meaningful.

An X-ray showing a pacemaker.

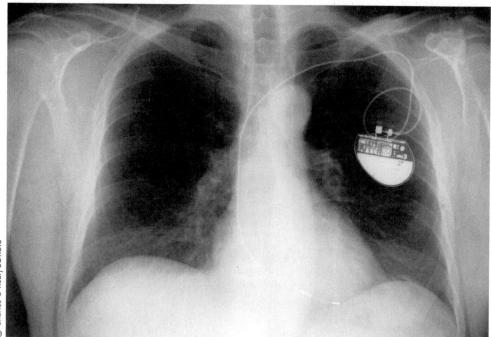

The Fastskin comes close to the ideal that form should follow function. However, most of the time function needs a little help. It falls to designers to make people feel comfortable with technology. Throughout the twentieth century they generally did so by dramatizing an object's benefits—speed, power, and efficiency, for instance—while hiding the things that made the object work. They took the early automobile, for example, in which each functional part was visible, and fashioned a steel shell that hid the machinery and gave the car a personality. In so doing they turned a contraption into a convenience.

Sometimes function has little to do with it. There was no practical reason for a 1930s refrigerator to be streamlined, but its new profile turned the erstwhile icebox into an embodiment of modernity and progress. The objects in which form follows not function but fantasy are often the most revealing ones.

During much of the past century designers' principal aim was to encourage people to welcome technology into their homes and their lives. This battle has long since been won. Now, at the beginning of the twenty-first century, we are accustomed to carrying powerful electronic devices in our pockets. Soon many of us will be wearing them, and before long they may be part of us.

The age of inanimate objects may be coming to a close. Some of the most sought-after pieces of contemporary personal technology, such as the titanium-clad Macintosh PowerBook and the aluminum-clad Palm V, hark back to twentieth-century notions of hard-shelled competence. But as distinctions between technology and biology blur, glossy, sculptural steel-age objects are being supplanted by forms that are supple, ambiguous, subtly sexy, and even a little bit creepy. The age of inanimate objects—at least those that look and act inanimate—may be coming to a close.

Ellen Lupton, a design curator at the Cooper-Hewitt National Design Museum, in New York City, believes that some new designs stand in for living beings, others celebrate the artificial augmentation of the body, and still others reflect anxieties about what may be a hostile merger of human being and machine. She has a computer hard drive full of images of furniture, buildings, clothing, and other products to show what she means. When I visited her recently, at her home in Baltimore, she called up, for instance, a photograph of a robot face that has been engineered to signal compassion to those in need of an electronic friend. There was also a very funny drawing of a pair of baggy shorts whose seat inflates to become a stool, and an unsettling image of a chair that seems to support itself on crutches.

"At many times in the past designers have looked to biological or organic forms for inspiration," Lupton told me. "What's different now is that the thinking is less humanist, more cyborg. It's not about creating forms that are comfortable for the body, or of celebrating the natural. . . . Many women and men nowadays give at least some thought to cosmetic surgery. The idea is to be natural, only better."

The creator of one particularly arresting item recorded in Lupton's files—and of many arresting objects elsewhere—is Karim Rashid, a prolific young de-

Industrial designer Karim Rashid at home.

signer of furniture, lighting, and other products, who lives and works in New York. Rashid's designs are both respected by his peers and wildly popular. You've probably seen his colorful plastic Garbo wastebasket, but he has also been commissioned by various high-end companies to design everything from champagne glasses to clothing to store interiors. Rashid's Chromazone Table, which caught Lupton's attention, exists only in prototype now, but Totem, a New York gallery, plans to produce and sell it in limited numbers. The table has a high-tech laminate surface, a sort of artistically sensitive Formica top. When you place your hand on it, the heat of your body creates a visible, subtly shaded corona on the

FOUND

from pbs.org

A 1950s VIEW OF THE FUTURE

- Atomic-powered cars will travel five million miles on one tank of fuel.
- There will be no more wars because we will be able to produce so much that everyone will have what they need.
- The cans that food comes in will be edible too.
- People will live to be 115 years old.
- We will watch television on a flat screen that hangs on the wall.
- With a flip of a switch our cars will automatically follow a route on an electronic highway.
- Doctors will perform operations with the help of other doctors from all over the world by watching them on TV.
- Clothes will be made from chemical fibers. They will not tear or get dirty.
- Every garage will have a helicopter in it.
- Robots will pick up our clothes, make our beds, vacuum our floors, do our laundry, and cook our food.

tabletop. If you place a steaming mug of coffee on the table, it will generate all the colors in the rainbow. Rashid does not plan to have the table be able to scream if something that threatens permanent damage is placed on it, but no doubt this could be engineered. Even in its silent form, this is a table that lets you know how it is feeling.

Rashid is convinced that almost everything in our lives will soon be "smart," and he is working to make that vision come true, developing designs for a world in which we won't know where the body ends and the machine begins. He designed the table, he told me recently, in order to enable a real-world object to compete with the seductions of the digital world, which he believes have decreased people's sensitivity to what they experience directly. As if to prove his point, our conversation took place by e-mail.

Rashid's table is primitive in responsiveness compared with another project of his that he mentioned: clothing that will react to its wearer's moods, while incorporating temperature controls, databases, and telecommunications capabilities. Much of the technology for such "smart" clothing already exists. As part of a Navy project to create computer-driven body armor, engineers at Georgia Tech have found a way to knit a flexible computer into the fabric of a shirt. The version of this Smart Shirt that has been licensed for production uses its computer power to monitor its wearer's health and location, and it is being marketed primarily to police and fire departments for officers on duty.

We won't know where the body ends and the machine begins.

Its information-storage and data-processing capacities could potentially be used to make people into walking libraries, with vast amounts of information even closer than their fingertips. Already about a thousand technicians who work for Bell Canada, Federal Express, and other companies are wearing sophisticated computers designed as vests, complete with tiny head-mounted display screens positioned a few inches in front of their eyes. It seems inevitable that such devices will become less bulky, more powerful, less expensive, and more stylish. The introduction in Europe by Philips and Levi Strauss of a line of wearable electronics—essentially sportswear with wires integrated in the design and special pockets for Philips telephones, digital audio players, and other gadgets that can be operated from a single remote control—suggests that this once visionary idea is moving toward the marketplace.

But perhaps a technologically enhanced second skin will prove to be only a transitional stage. Rashid, for one, believes that the next step after smart clothing will be even more amazing: smart people. "I see technology being embedded in our bodies so that we become digital within ourselves," he said. "We can interface by touching our skins, almost like having keyboards and chips planted under our skin—or by neural-triggered synapses where our minds control the technology and devices." Implants are, after all, the ultimate portables.

The mind boggles. The body shudders. The stomach turns. The next time I upgrade my computer, I wonder, will it involve surgery?

But since I'm old enough to remember *Hemo the Magnificent*, I'm old enough to remember those who predicted that I would be running to the supermarket in a helicopter and that my front porch would be equipped with a ray that could kill any germs that threatened to cross the doorstep. There is a long tradition of overselling the future, and those who call themselves visionaries—designers prominent among them—rarely envision that anything will go wrong. A pessimist by nature, I am certain that sooner or later the brilliant mind of the Smart Shirt will start to unravel, the self-healing computer will contract a flu it can't shake, and the color-changing table will turn an ugly shade and stay that way.

Designers can't guarantee that the brave new world will work. Indeed, making things work isn't really their job. What they do is make us feel, help us understand, allow us to sense how things can be useful. Even Rashid, who makes ambitious claims for the role of design in culture, says that designers will be little involved with what he terms "the banalities of problem-solving." Certainly this was true for earlier generations of design visionaries. Their role was not to make the future function but to show where we were going, and to make us feel good about it when we got there.

▶ **Analyzing the Text**

1. One undercurrent in this essay is that, through their design, technologies reveal the hopes and dreams of a culture. What examples in Hine's essay illustrate this? Do you agree with this idea? Why or why not?

2. Hine explains that the "look" of technological objects is changing. He writes, "[G]lossy, sculptural steel-age objects are being supplanted by forms that are supple, ambiguous, subtly sexy, and even a little bit creepy." What are the implications of this shift toward a more seamlessly integrated design, one in which the line between the animate and inanimate is blurred? What does this new design sensibility reveal about changing attitudes toward our relationship to technology?

3. "Smart" design involves the seamless integration of technological objects onto and, in some cases, into the human body. What is the intent of labeling this design "smart"?

4. Hine points out, "There is a long tradition of overselling the future, and those who call themselves visionaries . . . rarely envision that anything will go wrong." How do you respond to Hine's skepticism about the claims of "smart" design?

5. **Connecting to Another Reading.**   To what extent do proponents of smart design like Karim Rashid rely on the concept of technological determinism that Langdon Winner critiques in "Technological Somnambulism" (p. 594)?

▶ **Writing about Cultural Practices**

6. There are many examples from the twentieth century of new inventions that were hailed with grand claims about how they would revolutionize people's lives. Hine refers to this as a "tradition of overselling the future." For this assignment, research one innovation or invention that came along in the second half of the twentieth century. Your task is to identify the claims that surrounded it during the time it was introduced. You may consider inventions such as the Internet, the television, the compact disc (CD), or the laptop computer. Find three articles published when this invention was first introduced, specifically, articles that identify promising claims for the new technology. Write a critical analysis of how the claims made about your chosen technological innovation compare to the claims made in "Looking Alive" about how "smart" design will transform our lives. As you draft your analysis, consider the following questions.

   - When and how was this invention originally introduced? Who were the intended consumers or users of this invention?

   - What was "new" or innovative about this invention at the time? What problem(s) did its inventors claim this product would resolve? What new abilities was it supposed to give the user or consumer?

   - What were the main claims made at the time about how this new invention would change or reshape human activity?

   - Considering how this invention is (and isn't) used in our present time, to what extent were the initial claims "overselling the future"? In other words, do these claims rely too narrowly on the view of technology-as-progress (see this chapter's introduction, p. 579)?

   - In your experience with this product today, what are some of the trade-offs associated with it? What have consumers gained and what have they lost by using this technology?

Malcolm Gladwell, Smaller: The Disposable Diaper and the Meaning of Progress

Best-selling author Malcolm Gladwell has also been a staff writer for the *New Yorker* since 1996. Gladwell has authored two books, *The Tipping Point: How Little Things Can Make a Big Difference* (2002) and *Blink: The Power of Thinking Without Thinking* (2005). In interviews, he has explained how he approaches subjects in his surroundings as well as his writing: "I like looking at things that we take for granted. . . . I'm not interested in the exotic." This essay originally appeared in the *New Yorker* in 2001. In it, Gladwell writes, "For years, . . . we have considered the microchip the embodiment of the technological age. But if the diaper is also a perfect innovation, doesn't it deserve a place beside the chip?"

> ▶ **Mapping Your Reading**
>
> In this essay, Gladwell uses the technological innovations surrounding disposable diapers and other everyday objects to examine the meaning of progress. As you read, pay attention to how he draws out the social and economic implications of innovations surrounding the diaper. How do smaller diapers represent progress? How have they come to represent how dependent people have become on certain technologies?

The best way to explore the mystery of the Huggies Ultratrim disposable diaper is to unfold it and then cut it in half, widthwise, across what is known as the diaper's chassis. At Kimberly-Clark's Lakeview plant, in Neenah, Wisconsin, where virtually all the Huggies in the Midwest are made, there is a quality-control specialist who does this all day long, culling diapers from the production line, pinning them up against a lightboard, and carefully dismembering them with a pair of scissors. There is someone else who does a "visual cull," randomly picking out Huggies and turning them over to check for flaws. But a surface examination tells you little. A diaper is not like a computer that makes satisfying burbling noises from time to time, hinting at great inner complexity. It feels like papery underwear wrapped around a thin roll of Cottonelle. But peel away the soft fabric on the top side of the diaper, the liner, which receives what those in the trade delicately refer to as the "insult." You'll find a layer of what's called polyfilm, which is thinner than

---

For another reading on everyday objects, see Peebles, p. 617.—EDS.

a strip of Scotch tape. This layer is one of the reasons the garment stays dry: It has pores that are large enough to let air flow in, so the diaper can breathe, but small enough to keep water from flowing out, so the diaper doesn't leak.

Or run your hands along that liner. It feels like cloth. In fact, the people at Kimberly-Clark make the liner out of a special form of plastic, a polyresin. But they don't melt the plastic into a sheet, as one would for a plastic bag. They spin the resin into individual fibers, and then use the fibers to create a kind of microscopic funnel, channeling the insult toward the long, thick rectangular pad that runs down the center of the chassis, known as the absorbent core. A typical insult arrives at a rate of 7 millilitres a second, and might total 70 millilitres of fluid. The liner can clear that insult in less than 20 seconds. The core can hold three or more of those insults, with a chance of leakage in the single digits. The baby's skin will remain almost perfectly dry, and that is critical, because prolonged contact between the baby and the insult (in particular, ammonium hydroxide, a breakdown product of urine) is what causes diaper rash. And all this will be accomplished by a throwaway garment measuring, in the newborn size, just 7 by 13 inches. This is the mystery of the modern disposable diaper: How does something so small do so much?

Thirty-seven years ago, the Silicon Valley pioneer Gordon Moore made a famous prediction. The number of transistors that engineers could fit onto a microchip, he said, would double every two years. It seemed like a foolhardy claim: It was not clear that you could keep making transistors smaller and smaller indefinitely. It also wasn't clear that it would make sense to do so. Most of the time when we make things smaller, after all, we pay a price. A smaller car is cheaper and more fuel-efficient, and easier to park and maneuver, but it will never be as safe as a larger car. In the 1950s and '60s, the transistor radio was all the rage; it could fit inside your pocket and run on a handful of batteries. But, because it was so small, the sound was terrible, and virtually all the other mini-electronics turn out to be similarly imperfect. Tiny cell phones are hard to dial. Tiny televisions are hard to watch. In making an object smaller, we typically compromise its performance. The remarkable thing about chips, though, was that there was no drawback: If you could fit more and more transistors onto a microchip, then instead of using 10 or 20 or 100 microchips for a task you could use just one. This meant, in turn, that you could fit microchips in all kinds of places (such as cellular phones and laptops) that you couldn't before, and, because you were using one chip and not 100, computer power could be had at a fraction of the price, and because chips were now everywhere and in such demand they became even cheaper to make—and so on and so on. Moore's Law, as it came to be called, describes that rare case in which there is no trade-off between size and performance. Microchips are what might be termed a perfect innovation.

Most of the time when we make things smaller, we pay a price.

In the past 20 years, diapers have got smaller and smaller, too. In the early '80s, they were three times bulkier than they are now, thicker and substantially wider in the crotch. But in the mid-'80s Huggies and Procter & Gamble's Pampers were reduced in bulk by 50 percent; in the mid-'90s they shrank by a third or so; and in the next few years they may shrink still more. It seems reasonable that there should have been a downside to this, just as there was to the shrinking of cars and radios: How could you reduce the amount of padding in a diaper and not, in some way, compromise its ability to handle an insult? Yet, as diapers got smaller, they got better, and that fact elevates the diaper above nearly all the thousands of other products on the supermarket shelf.

Kimberly-Clark's Lakeview plant is a huge facility, just down the freeway from Green Bay. Inside, it is as immaculate as a hospital operating room. The walls and floors have been scrubbed white. The stainless-steel machinery gleams. The employees are dressed in dark-blue pants, starched light-blue button-down shirts, and tissue-paper caps. There are rows of machines in the plant, each costing more than $15 million—a dizzying combination of conveyor belts and whirling gears and chutes stretching as long as a city block and creating such a din that everyone on the factory floor wears headsets and communicates by radio. Computers monitor a million data points along the way, insuring that each of those components is precisely cut and attached according to principles and processes and materials protected, on the Huggies Ultratrim alone, by hundreds of patents. At the end of the line, the Huggies come gliding out of the machine, stacked upright, one after another in an endless row, looking like exquisitely formed slices of white bread in a toast rack. For years, because of Moore's Law, we have considered the microchip the embodiment of the technological age. But if the diaper is also a perfect innovation, doesn't it deserve a place beside the chip?

The modern disposable diaper was invented twice, first by Victor Mills and then by Carlyle Harmon and Billy Gene Harper. Mills worked for Procter & Gamble, and he was a legend. Ivory soap used to be made in an expensive and time-consuming batch-by-batch method. Mills figured out a simpler, continuous process. Duncan Hines cake mixes used to have a problem blending flour, sugar, and shortening in a consistent mixture. Mills introduced the machines used for milling soap, which ground the ingredients much more finely than before, and the result was New, Improved Duncan Hines cake mix. Ever wonder why Pringles, unlike other potato chips, are all exactly the same shape? Because they are made like soap: The potato is ground into a slurry, then pressed, baked, and wrapped—and that was Victor Mills's idea, too.

> Moore's Law describes that rare case in which there is no trade-off between size and performance.

In 1957, Procter & Gamble bought the Charmin Paper Company, of Green Bay, Wisconsin, and Mills was told to think of new products for the paper business. Since he was a grandfather—and had always hated washing diapers—he thought of a disposable diaper. "One of the early researchers told me that among the first things they did was go out to a toy store and buy one of those Betsy Wetsy-type dolls, where you put water in the mouth and it comes out the other end," Ed Rider, the head of the archives department at Procter & Gamble, says. "They brought it back to the lab, hooked up its legs on a treadmill to make it walk, and tested diapers on it." The end result was Pampers, which were launched in Peoria, in 1961. The diaper had a simple rectangular shape. Its liner, which lay against the baby's skin, was made of rayon. The outside material was plastic. In between were multiple layers of crêped tissue. The diaper was attached with pins and featured what was known as a Z fold, meaning that the edges of the inner side were pleated, to provide a better fit around the legs.

In 1968, Kimberly-Clark brought out Kimbies, which took the rectangular diaper and shaped it to more closely fit a baby's body. In 1976, Procter & Gamble brought out Luvs, which elasticized the leg openings to prevent leakage. But diapers still adhered to the basic Millsian notion of an absorbent core made out of paper—and that was a problem. When paper gets wet, the fluid soaks right through, which makes diaper rash worse. And if you put any kind of pressure on paper—if you squeeze it, or sit on it—it will surrender some of the water it has absorbed, which creates further difficulties, because a baby, in the usual course of squirming and crawling and walking, might place as much as five kilopascals of pressure on the absorbent core of a diaper. Diaper-makers tried to address this shortcoming by moving from crêped tissue to what they called fluff, which was basically finely shredded cellulose. Then they began to compensate for paper's failing by adding more and more of it, until diapers became huge. But they now had Moore's Law in reverse: In order to get better, they had to get bigger—and bigger still wasn't very good.

Carlyle Harmon worked for Johnson & Johnson and Billy Gene Harper worked for Dow Chemical, and they had a solution. In 1966, each filed separate but virtually identical patent applications, proposing that the best way to solve the diaper puzzle was with a peculiar polymer that came in the form of little pepperlike flakes and had the remarkable ability to absorb up to 300 times its weight in water.

In the Dow patent, Harper and his team described how they sprinkled two grams of the superabsorbent polymer between two 20-inch-square sheets of nylon broadcloth, and then quilted the nylon layers together. The makeshift diaper was "thereafter put into use in personal management of a baby of approximately 6 months age." After four hours, the diaper was removed. It now weighed a 120 grams, meaning the flakes had soaked up 60 times their weight in urine.

Harper and Harmon argued that it was quite unnecessary to solve the paper problem by stuffing the core of the diaper with thicker and thicker rolls of shredded pulp. Just a handful of superabsorbent polymer would do the job. Thus was the modern diaper born. Since the mid-'80s, Kimberly-Clark and Procter & Gamble have made diapers the Harper and Harmon way, pulling out paper and replacing it with superabsorbent polymer. The old, paper-filled diaper could hold, at most, 275 millilitres of fluid, or a little more than a cup. Today, a diaper full of superabsorbent polymer can handle as much as 500 millilitres, almost twice that. The chief characteristic of the Mills diaper was its simplicity: The insult fell directly into the core. But the presence of the polymer has made the diaper far more complex. It takes longer for the polymer than it does paper to fully absorb an insult, for instance. So another component was added, the acquisition layer, between the liner and the core. The acquisition layer acts like blotting paper, holding the insult while the core slowly does its work, and distributing the fluid over its full length.

Diaper researchers sometimes perform what is called a re-wet test, where they pour 100 millilitres of fluid onto the surface of a diaper and then apply a piece of filter paper to the diaper liner with 5 kilopascals of pressure—the average load a baby would apply to a diaper during ordinary use. In a contemporary superabsorbent diaper, like a Huggies or a Pampers, the filter paper will come away untouched after one insult. After two insults, there might be 0.1 millilitres of fluid on the paper. After three insults, the diaper will surrender, at most, only 2 millilitres of moisture—which is to say that, with the aid of superabsorbents, a pair of Huggies or Pampers can effortlessly hold, even under pressure, a baby's entire night's work.

The heir to the legacy of Billy Gene Harper at Dow Chemical is Fredric Buchholz, who works in Midland, Michigan, a small town two hours northwest of Detroit, where Dow has its headquarters. His laboratory is in the middle of the sprawling chemical works, a mile or two away from corporate headquarters, in a low, unassuming brick building. "We still don't understand perfectly how these polymers work," Buchholz said on a recent fall afternoon. What we do know, he said, is that superabsorbent polymers appear, on a microscopic level, to be like a tightly bundled fisherman's net. In the presence of water, that net doesn't break apart into thousands of pieces and dissolve, like sugar. Rather, it just unravels, the way a net would open up if you shook it out, and as it does the water gets stuck in the webbing. That ability to hold huge amounts of water, he said, could make superabsorbent polymers useful in fire fighting or irrigation, because slightly gelled water is more likely to stay where it's needed. There are superabsorbents mixed in with the sealant on the walls of the Chunnel between England and France, so if water leaks in the polymer will absorb the water and plug the hole.

Right now, one of the major challenges facing diaper technology, Buchholz said, is that urine is salty, and salt impairs the unraveling of the netting: Superabsorbents can handle only a tenth as much salt water as fresh water. "One idea is to remove the salt from urine. Maybe you could have a purifying screen," he said. If the molecular structure of the superabsorbent were optimized, he went on, its absorptive capacity could increase by another 500 percent. "Superabsorbents could go from absorbing 300 times their weight to absorbing 500 times their weight. We could have just one perfect particle of superabsorbent in a diaper. If you are going to dream, why not make the diaper as thin as a pair of underwear?"

Buchholz was in his laboratory, and he held up a small plastic cup filled with a few tablespoons of superabsorbent flakes, each not much larger than a grain of salt. "It's just a granular material, totally nontoxic," he said. "This is about 2 grams." He walked over to the sink and filled a large beaker with tap water, and poured the contents of the beaker into the jar of superabsorbent. At first, nothing happened. The amounts were so disproportionate that it looked as if the water would simply engulf the flakes. But, slowly and steadily, the water began to thicken. "Look," Buchholz said. "It's becoming soupy." Sure enough, little beads of gel were forming. Nothing else was happening: There was no gas given off, no burbling or sizzling as the chemical process took place. The superabsorbent polymer was simply swallowing up the water, and within minutes the contents of the cup had thickened into what looked like slightly lumpy, spongy pudding. Buchholz picked up the jar and tilted it, to show that nothing at all was coming out. He pushed and prodded the mass with his finger. The water had disappeared. To soak up that much liquid, the Victor Mills diaper would have needed a thick bundle of paper toweling. Buchholz had used a few tablespoons of superabsorbent flakes. Superabsorbent was not merely better; it was *smaller.*

Why does it matter that the diaper got so small? It seems a trivial thing, chiefly a matter of convenience to the parent taking a bag of diapers home from the supermarket. But it turns out that size matters a great deal. There's a reason that there are now "new, improved concentrated" versions of laundry detergent, and that some cereals now come in smaller boxes. Smallness is one of those changes that send ripples through the whole economy. The old disposable diapers, for example, created a transportation problem. Tractor-trailers are prohibited by law from weighing more than 80,000 pounds when loaded. That's why a truck carrying something heavy and compact like bottled water or Campbell's soup is "full," when the truck itself is still half empty. But the diaper of the '80s was what is known as a "high cube" item. It was bulky and not very heavy, meaning that a diaper truck was full before it reached its weight limit. By cutting the size of a diaper in half, companies could fit twice as many diapers on a truck, and cut transportation expenses in half. They could also cut the amount of warehouse space and labor they needed in half. And companies could begin to rethink their manufacturing operations. "Distribution costs used to force you to have plants in lots of places," Dudley Lehman, who heads the Kimberly-Clark diaper business, says. "As that becomes less and less of an issue, you say, 'Do I really need all my plants?' In the United States, it used to take eight. Now it takes five." (Kimberly-Clark didn't close any plants. But other manufacturers did, and here, perhaps, is a partial explanation for the great wave of corporate restructuring that swept across America in the late '80s and early '90s: Firms could downsize their workforce because they had downsized their products.) And, because using five plants to make diapers is more efficient than using eight, it became possible to improve diapers without raising diaper prices—which is important, because the sheer number of diapers parents have to buy makes it a price-sensitive product. Until recently, diapers were fastened with little pieces of tape, and if the person changing the diapers got lotion or powder on her fingers the tape wouldn't work. A hook-and-loop, Velcro-like fastener doesn't have this problem. But it was years before the hook-and-loop fastener was incorporated into the diaper chassis: Until overall manufacturing costs were reduced, it was just too expensive.

> Smallness is one of those changes that sends ripples through the whole economy.

Most important, though, is how size affects the way diapers are sold. The shelves along the aisles of a supermarket are divided into increments of 4 feet, and the space devoted to a given product category is almost always a multiple of that. Diapers, for example, might be presented as a 20-foot set. But when diapers were at their bulkiest the space reserved for them was never enough. "You could only get a limited number on the shelf," says Sue Klug, the president of Catalina Marketing Solutions and a former executive for Albertson's and Safeway. "Say you only had six bags. Someone comes in and buys a few, and then someone else comes in and buys a few more. Now you're out of stock until someone reworks the shelf, which in some supermarkets might be a day or two." Out-of-stock rates are already a huge problem in the retail business. At any given time, only about 92 percent of the products that a store is supposed to be carrying are actually on the shelf—which, if you consider that the average supermarket has 35,000 items, works out to 2,800 products that are simply not there. (For a highly efficient retailer like Wal-Mart, in-stock rates might be as high as 99 percent; for a struggling firm, they might be in the low 80s.) But, for a fast-moving, bulky item like diapers, the problem of restocking was much worse. Supermarkets could have allocated more shelf space to diapers, of course, but diapers aren't a particularly profitable category for retailers—profit margins are about half what they are for the grocery department. So retailers would much rather give more shelf space to a growing and lucrative category like bottled water. "It's all a trade-off," Klug says. "If you expand diapers 4 feet, you've got to give up 4 feet of something else." The only way diaper-makers could insure that their products would actually be on the shelves was to make the products smaller, so they could fit 12 bags into the space of 6. And if you can fit 12 bags on a shelf, you can introduce different kinds of diapers. You can add pull-ups and premium diapers and low-cost private-label diapers, all of which give parents more options.

"We cut the cost of trucking in half," says Ralph Drayer, who was in charge of logistics for Procter & Gamble for many years and now runs his own supply-chain consultancy in Cincinnati. "We cut the cost of storage in half. We cut handling in half, and we cut the cost of the store shelf in half, which is probably the most expensive space in the whole chain." Everything in the diaper world, from plant closings and trucking routes to product improvements and consumer choice and convenience, turns, in the end, on the fact that Harmon and Harper's absorbent core was smaller than Victor Mills's.

The shame of it, though, is that Harmon and Harper have never been properly celebrated for their accomplishment. Victor Mills is the famous one. When he died, he was given a *Times* obituary, in which he was called "the father of disposable diapers." When Carlyle Harmon died, seven months earlier, he got 400 words in Utah's *Deseret News*, stressing his contributions to the Mormon Church. We tend to credit those who create an idea, not those who perfect it, forgetting that it is often only in the perfection of an idea that true progress occurs. Putting 64 transistors on a chip allowed people to dream of the future. Putting 4 million transistors on a chip actually gave them the future. The diaper is no different. The paper diaper changed parenting. But a diaper that could hold four insults without leakage, keep a baby's skin dry, clear an insult in 20 seconds flat, and would nearly always be in stock, even if you arrived at the supermarket at eight o'clock in the evening—and that would keep getting better at all those things, year in and year out—was another thing altogether. This was more than a good idea. This was something like perfection.

▶ **Analyzing the Text**

1. **Interrogating Assumptions.** According to Gladwell, why does the diaper represent a perfect innovation? How does the diaper illustrate the assumption that technologies represent progress? How does Gladwell's discussion challenge the second assumption in this chapter's introduction that "technologies bring progress or peril" (see p. 579)?

2. How has smallness come to signify the cutting edge of technology and of modern life? Do you think this represents a shift in the values of our culture? If so, how?

3. In *The Question Concerning Technology* (1977), philosopher Martin Heidegger argues that seeing technologies as tools for solving problems leads people to understand and experience the world as a series of problems amenable to technological fixes. The danger of this, for Heidegger, is that it encourages a mindset that the natural world is a kind of "standing reserve" of resources, waiting to be used to create still more technologies. To what extent are the stories Gladwell shares in this essay about the development of diapers, microchips, soap, and potato chips illustrations of the view Heidegger critiques? What are the drawbacks to presenting progress narratives about technology in the way Gladwell does?

▶ **Writing about Cultural Practices**

4. Gladwell describes the disposable diaper as a technology that got smaller over time. What other everyday technologies have altered in size over time, and why? Choose a technology, such as a type of car, household item, furniture, or fashion, that has changed in size and style over a period of years. As you write a critical analysis of this item, consider the following questions.

   - Describe the object you've chosen. What is its history? Its original purpose and its purpose today? Its main audience or user group?

   - Why has the object changed in size over time? How does its changed size reflect changing cultural or political values?

   - In general, what objects do we value for being small? Which ones for being large? What does this say about us and our culture?

Gustav Peebles, **A Wicked Cheat**

A postdoctoral fellow in anthropology at Columbia University, Gustav Peebles studies history and the involvement of the state and government in credit and debt issues. He researches currency control, the process of exchanging goods and services, and the practices of dealing with personal indebtedness. As a system, banking is a service that we tend to take for granted, like the U.S. mail or mass transportation. We are not accustomed to thinking of banking as a political process that treats people unevenly based on wealth. In this annotation, published in *Harper's* in 2004, Peebles contends that bank fees represent one measure of how the banking industry does, in fact, operate in this way.

 Mapping Your Reading

In the following essay, Peebles both looks back in time, comparing modern-day fees with money-handling practices of the Middle Ages, and looks ahead, stating his concerns about where these practices are leading us. Highlight passages in which Peebles states his argument most persuasively. What do ATM slips tell us about the practices of banking today? How does the ATM receipt reflect the values and goals of the free market economy? To what extent is our currency becoming a two-tiered system—cash-based and credit-based?

For another reading on everyday objects, see Gladwell, p. 609.—EDS.

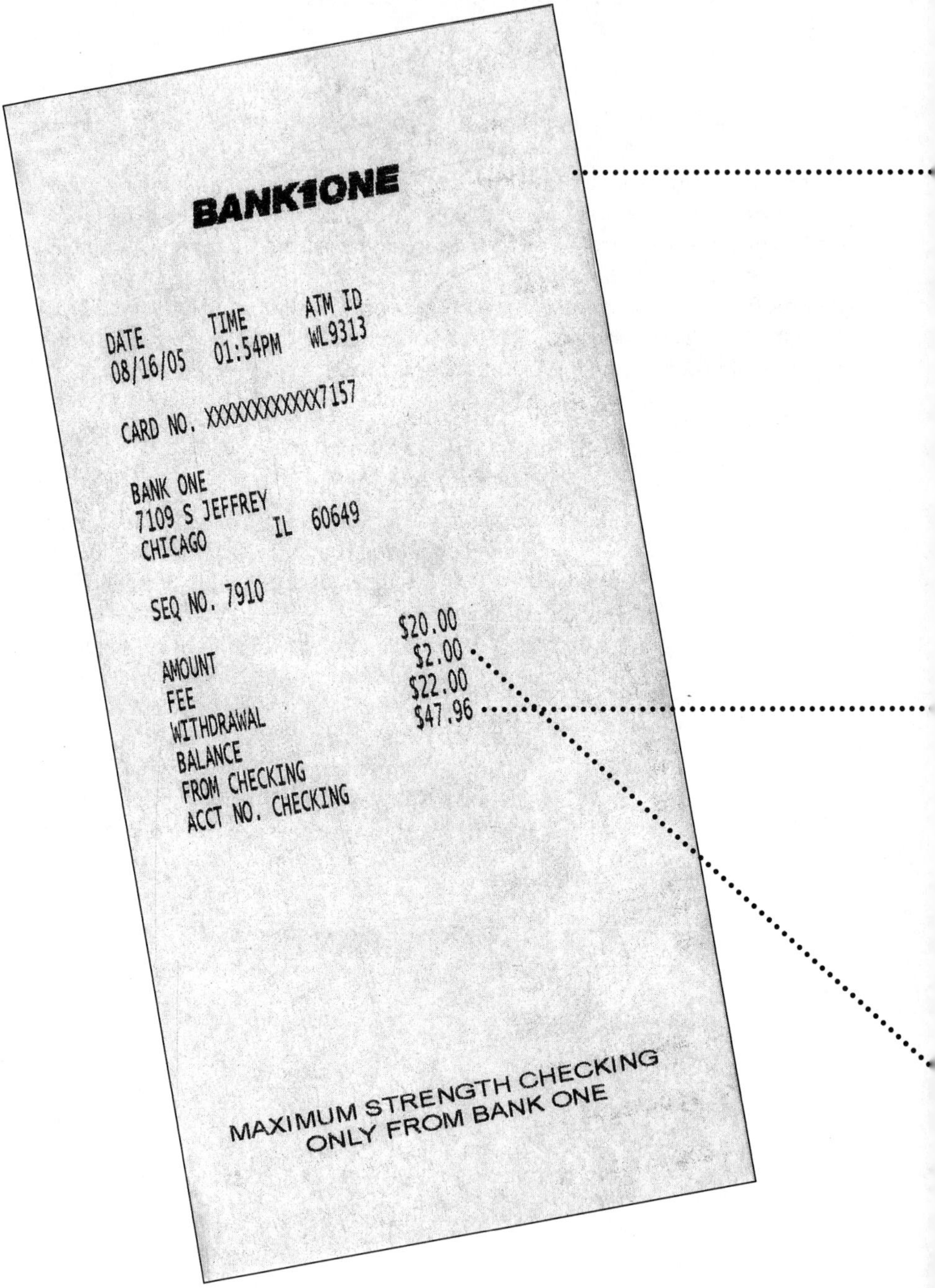

BANK1ONE

DATE   TIME   ATM ID
08/16/05   01:54PM   WL9313

CARD NO. XXXXXXXXXXXX7157

BANK ONE
7109 S JEFFREY
CHICAGO   IL 60649

SEQ NO. 7910

                              $20.00
AMOUNT $2.00
FEE $22.00
WITHDRAWAL $47.96
BALANCE
FROM CHECKING
ACCT NO. CHECKING

MAXIMUM STRENGTH CHECKING
ONLY FROM BANK ONE

In the garbage can beside the Automated Teller Machine at 7109 South Jeffrey Boulevard on Chicago's South Side, one will find a preponderance of receipts like this one, recording a $20 withdrawal—the minimum allowed—at a $2 fee, i.e., a rate of 10 percent. For a resident in wealthy Lincoln Park, 14 miles north, who withdraws $200 from an ATM with the same fee, the rate drops to a far more palatable 1 percent. This disparity is universally known but seldom discussed; we Americans seem to have accepted that it is dramatically more expensive for poor people to use cash. Although one might imagine that the disbursement of currency would be a matter of public policy, today our nation has left it, as with so many other vital functions, to the whim of the marketplace. And yet the ATM fee, seemingly an exponent of twenty-first-century technology and commerce, in fact has given our monetary system a decidedly archaic turn.

"$" connotes, for us, a single currency, backed by the full force of our government. But we should remember that only since the beginning of the modern era has the task and expense of producing and circulating currency fallen solely to nation-states. Prior to this in Europe, getting cash was often a private affair. At "feudal mints" in the Middle Ages and later at locally "patented" mints, citizens were charged a percentage fee, called "seigniorage," for the assaying and imprinting of gold and silver. But eventually, private seigniorage was outlawed as an encumbrance on the economy. Denounced as "robbers' dens" in official proclamations, private mints were recognized as effectively being a private tax on cash transactions. Jonathan Swift, writing of an Irish private currency in 1724, called it "A WICKED CHEAT" and argued, on economic grounds, for its rejection.

The corner ATM is, in effect, a reincarnation of the private mint; the "owner fee" is the seigniorage charged for stamping one's virtual gold into the circulating medium of the physical world. Such fees burden the economy of the twenty-first century just as they did that of the sixteenth, except today they are far more widespread. In 1996, America had 140,000 ATMs, only a third of which charged fees to anyone. Today that number has grown to 371,000—or nearly five times the number of bank offices—with 89 percent charging fees to at least some users. Even worse, faced with ATM fees, plus the minimum-balance surcharges and overdraft penalties associated with having a bank account to begin with, many poor Americans have chosen instead to pay seigniorage to another type of private mint: the nation's check-cashing agencies, which generally extract fees of $5 per paycheck, or up to 1 to 6 percent of a check's face value.

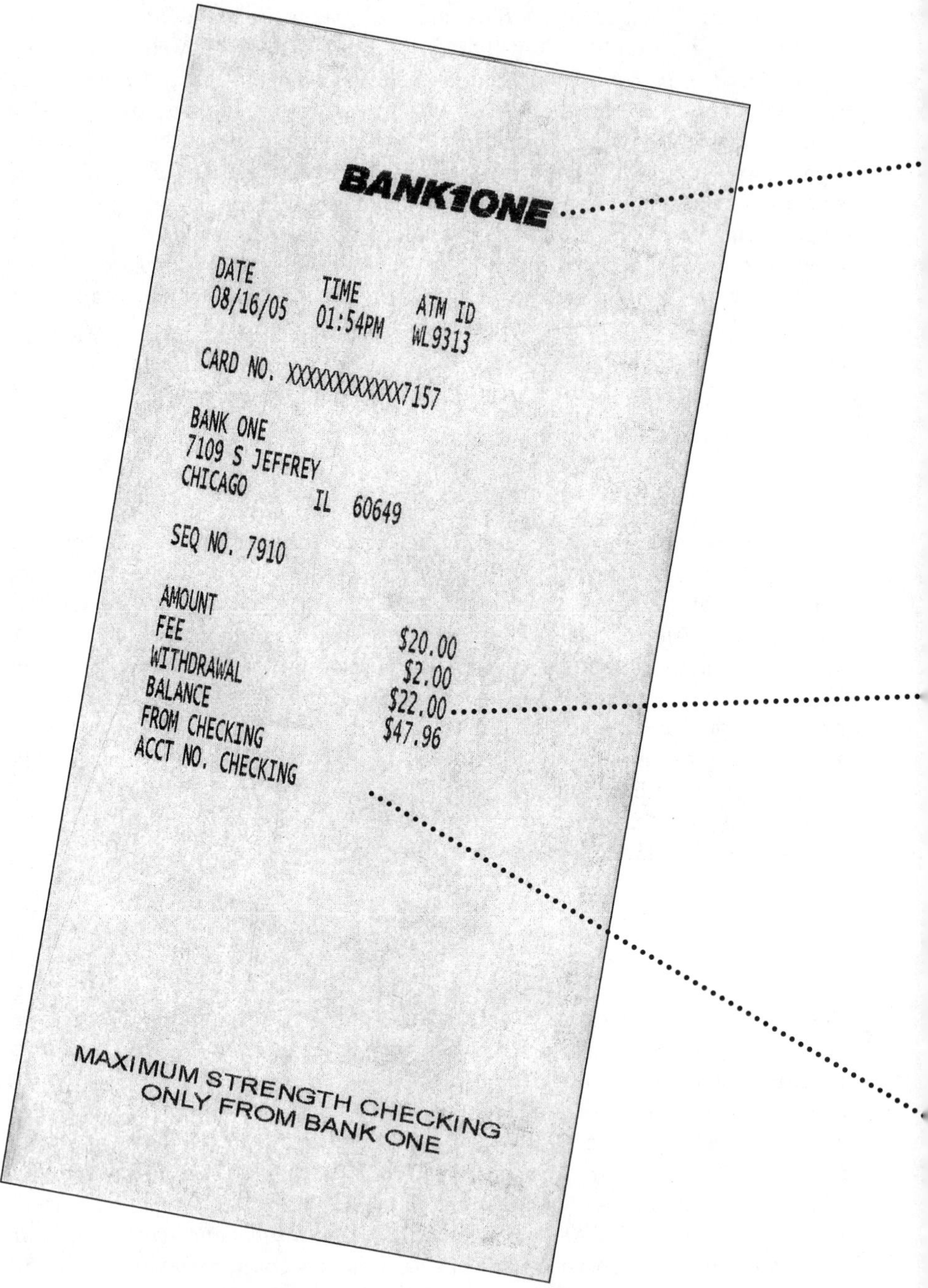

BANK1ONE

DATE   TIME   ATM ID
08/16/05   01:54PM   WL9313

CARD NO. XXXXXXXXXXXX7157

BANK ONE
7109 S JEFFREY
CHICAGO   IL   60649

SEQ NO. 7910

AMOUNT
FEE $20.00
WITHDRAWAL $2.00
BALANCE $22.00
FROM CHECKING $47.96
ACCT NO. CHECKING

MAXIMUM STRENGTH CHECKING
ONLY FROM BANK ONE

As well-off customers, seeking to avoid ATM fees, flee to more prevalent networks—such as Bank One's, the fifth largest in the country—the nation's community banks, which tend to charge far less in account fees and thereby allow poorer customers to bank there, are fast disappearing. Today some 12 million U.S. families cannot afford even a simple checking account, which, for those who cannot maintain a minimum balance, costs on average $228 dollars per year. In the nineteenth century, bankers and governments convinced the people to "draw the money out of the mattresses" (where it had been hidden for much of human history) and into the banks with a promise that the money would grow, or at least keep pace with inflation. This win-win covenant was a virtuous circle that helped to build the capitalist system. Now this covenant has, for many, been perverted, in that it is more expensive to keep their money in the bank than out of it.

Slowly, the cash withdrawal is becoming less preferred as a prelude to purchasing; today almost a third of transactions are made with credit or debit cards, up from 19 percent in 1990. Credit and debit cards, because they are neither accepted by all merchants nor available to all consumers, are in a sense a separate currency, pegged to cash but distinct from it. Anthropologists who have studied societies with multiple currencies almost always have found that one becomes privileged, with some people never gaining access to it. Someday, perhaps, our high-end restaurants will refuse cash—as, for example, many FedEx locations already do—thus assuring a more exclusive, credit-toting clientele. At the very least, it is not far-fetched to imagine that the number of ATMs may begin to decline, in a pattern that mimics the rise and fall of pay phones: Initially available only in rich neighborhoods, ATMs may soon be found only in poor ones, as only people without access to credit bother with the tawdry greenback.

The ATM fee, frankly, should be dispensed with, for it is not a necessary component of a healthy economy. A visit to Europe can attest to this: It is cheaper to use an American ATM card in England or Denmark than to use that same card at most ATMs in the United States itself. Access to cash is not a market-organized choice but is, for poorer Americans, at least, a daily necessity. The unequal burden of ATM fees represents a retreat—one of many, in recent decades—from the modern ideal of social equality, which developed, it should be noted, at the same time we abandoned private mints in the first place. Today's legislators should see such extortionate systems of currency circulation just as critics of a previous era saw them: as embarrassing indices of a feudalist economy, which thrives on the unsubtle and unjust transfer of wealth from the poorer to the wealthier classes.

Analyzing the Text

1. According to Peebles, how does the ATM fee help support an unjust financial system that increasingly takes advantage of poor people? How does Peebles connect the modern-day ATM, with its fees, to the banking practices of the Middle Ages?

2. How does the ATM slip, which is an individual record of a personal transaction, connect people to a larger system of technological practices?

3. What is the significance of the difference between using cash as a primary means to pay for goods and services and using credit or debit cards, in Peebles's view? Is cash fast becoming the currency of the young and the poor? If so, what are the implications of this?

4. By organizing this essay as a series of annotations of a standard ATM receipt, Peebles constructs his argument in a very unusual and yet powerful way. What is the impact of this organizational structure on his argument? How does each separate annotation make its own point while also forming a more unified argument?

Writing about Cultural Practices

5. One issue that Peebles does not directly address is how the banking industry treats young people who are financial novices. Financial companies often appear on college campuses to entice students into opening credit card accounts. Slogans like "Apply for a credit card, get a free t-shirt" paper student centers at many colleges and universities, and many young people from ages 16 to 21 find their mailboxes stuffed with credit card applications on a weekly basis. For this assignment, develop a critical analysis of how the banking industry, particularly credit card companies, treats young people. To begin, collect two or three examples of marketing campaigns from banks or credit card companies such as flyers, letters, emails, or websites that specifically target young people. As you write your analysis, consider the following questions.

   - What tactics do banks or credit card companies use to target young people?

   - What assumptions do the designers of these documents make regarding young people? What details in the text and visual design lead you to your analysis?

   - How would you compare the marketing text used to attract readers' attention to the information provided in fine print in these documents?

   - What kinds of financial products or services are most typically directed at young people? How might these products or services shape young people's understanding of banking and finance?

Neil Postman, **Invisible Technologies**

A media critic who was a professor of media ecology at New York University, Neil Postman devoted his career to studying the effects of new media and technology on children, schools, and learning. He authored 18 books and published over 100 articles before he died in 2003. In his book *Technopoly: The Surrender of Culture to Technology* (1993), Postman examines the ideological implications of technology, particularly technologies that influence our thinking without our knowledge. In that book, Postman argues that both language and mathematics are "invisible technologies" with cultural significance. "I don't suppose," he writes, "there is a clearer example of a technology that doesn't look like one than the mathematical sign known as zero." The following essay, excerpted from *Technopoly*, focuses on language as both a technology and an ideology.

> ▶ **Mapping Your Reading**
>
> In the following essay, Postman argues that we need to become more conscious of the ways in which certain "invisible technologies" shape human activity and function in important ways in culture. As you read, pay attention to how Postman supports his argument. Why should we think of language as a technology? What "ideological agendas" are behind the words we choose?

If we define ideology as a set of assumptions of which we are barely conscious but which nonetheless directs our efforts to give shape and coherence to the world, then our most powerful ideological instrument is the technology of language itself. Language is pure ideology. It instructs us not only in the names of things but, more important, in what things can be named. It divides the world into subjects and objects. It denotes what events shall be regarded as processes, and what events, things. It instructs us about time, space, and number, and forms our ideas of how we stand in relation to nature and to each other. In English grammar, for example, there are always subjects who act, and verbs which are their actions, and objects which are acted upon. It is a rather aggressive grammar, which makes it difficult for those of us who must use it to think of the world as benign. We are obliged to know the world as made up of things pushing against, and often attacking, one another.

> **Our most powerful ideological instrument is the technology of language itself.**

Of course, most of us, most of the time, are unaware of how language does its work. We live deep within the boundaries of our linguistic assumptions and have little sense of how the world looks to those who speak a vastly different tongue. We tend to assume that everyone sees the world in the same way, irrespective of differences in language. Only occasionally is this illusion challenged, as when the differences between linguistic ideologies become noticeable by one who has command over two languages that differ greatly in their structure and history. For example, several years ago, Susumu Tonegawa, winner of the 1987 Nobel Prize in Medicine, was quoted in the newspaper *Yomiuri* as saying that the Japanese language does not foster clarity or effective understanding in scientific research. Addressing his countrymen from his post as a professor at MIT in Cambridge, Massachusetts, he said, "We should consider changing our thinking process in the field of science by trying to reason in English." It should be noted that he was not saying that English is better than Japanese; only that English is better than Japanese for the purposes of scientific research, which is a way of saying that English (and other Western languages) have a particular ideological bias that Japanese does not. We call that ideological bias "the scientific outlook." If the scientific outlook seems natural to you, as it does to me, it is because our language makes it appear so. What we think of as reasoning is determined by the character of our language. To reason in Japanese is apparently not the same thing as to reason in English or Italian or German.

To put it simply, like any important piece of machinery—television or the computer, for example—language has an ideological agenda that is apt to be hidden from view. In the case of language, that agenda is so deeply integrated into our personalities and world-view that a special effort and, often, special training are required to detect its presence. Unlike television or the computer, language appears to be not an extension of our powers but simply a natural expression of who and what we are. This is the great secret of language: Because it comes from inside us, we believe it to be a direct, unedited, unbiased, apolitical expression of how the world really is. A machine, on the other hand, is outside of us, clearly created by us, modifiable by us, even discardable by us; it is easier to see how a machine re-creates the world in its own image. But in many respects, a sentence functions very much like a machine, and this is nowhere more obvious than in the sentences we call questions.

> **We have little sense of how the world looks to those who speak a different language.**

As an example of what I mean, let us take a "fill-in" question, which I shall require you to answer exactly if you wish full credit:

Thomas Jefferson died in the year _____.

Suppose we now rephrase the question in multiple-choice form:

Thomas Jefferson died in the year (a) 1788 (b) 1826 (c) 1926 (d) 1809.

Which of these two questions is easier to answer? I assume you will agree with me that the second question is easier unless you happen to know precisely the year of Jefferson's death, in which case neither question is difficult. However, for most of us who know only roughly when Jefferson lived, Question Two has arranged matters so that our chances of "knowing" the answer are greatly increased. Students will always be "smarter" when answering a multiple-choice test than when answering a "fill-in" test, even when the subject matter is the same. A question, even of the simplest kind, is not and can never be unbiased. I am not, in this context, referring to the common accusation that a particular test is "culturally biased." Of course questions can be culturally biased. (Why, for example, should anyone be asked about Thomas Jefferson at all, let alone when he died?) My purpose is to say that the structure of any question is as devoid of neutrality as is its content. The form of a question may ease our way or pose obstacles. Or, when even slightly altered, it may generate antithetical answers, as in the case of the two priests who, being unsure if it was permissible to smoke and pray at the same time, wrote to the Pope for a definitive answer. One priest phrased the question "Is it permissible to smoke while praying?" and was told it is not, since prayer should be the focus of one's whole attention; the other priest asked if it is permissible to pray while smoking and was told that it is, since it is always appropriate to pray. The form of a question may even block us from seeing solutions to problems that become visible through a different question. Consider the following story, whose authenticity is questionable but not, I think, its point:

Once upon a time, in a village in what is now Lithuania, there arose an unusual problem. A curious disease afflicted many of the townspeople. It was mostly fatal (though not always), and its onset was signaled by the victim's lapsing into a deathlike coma. Medical science not being quite so advanced as it is now, there was no definite way of knowing if the victim was actually dead when burial appeared seemly. As a result, the townspeople feared that several of their relatives had already been buried alive and that a similar fate might await them. How to overcome this uncertainty was their dilemma.

One group of people suggested that the coffins be well stocked with water and food and that a small air vent be drilled into them, just in case one of the "dead" happened to be alive. This was expensive to do but seemed more than worth the trouble. A second group, however, came up with a less expensive and more efficient idea. Each coffin would have a twelve-inch stake affixed to the inside of the coffin lid, exactly at the level of the heart. Then, when the coffin was closed, all uncertainty would cease.

The story does not indicate which solution was chosen, but for my purposes the choice is irrelevant. What is important to note is that different solutions were generated by different questions. The first solution was an answer to the question, How can we make sure that we do not bury people who are still alive? The second was an answer to the question, How can we make sure that everyone we bury is dead?

Questions, then, are like computers or television or stethoscopes or lie detectors, in that they are mechanisms that give direction to our thoughts, generate new ideas, venerate old ones, expose facts, or hide them.

Analyzing the Text

1. What is the message Postman wants readers to grasp through his analysis of language?

2. **Interrogating Assumptions.** Postman defines language as "pure ideology." What are the implications of this claim? How is Postman challenging the third assumption in this chapter's introduction that "technologies are neutral" (see p. 583)?

3. Postman describes the effect or power of questions—how their wording influences the type of answers that become possible—to demonstrate that language, as a form of technology, can never be unbiased. How have you used these or similar question-asking techniques or had others use them on you in an attempt to control the answers? Why does Postman want readers to make the biases or ideologies of language more visible?

4. According to Postman, why do most people think language is unbiased? Do you agree? Why or why not?

Writing about Cultural Practices

5. Postman writes, "A question, even of the simplest kind, is not and can never be unbiased. . . . The form of a question may ease our way or pose obstacles . . . it may even block us from seeing solutions to problems that become visible through a different question." For this assignment, test Postman's argument by evaluating a questionnaire. How does the form of a question shape its possible answers? How does the way a question is written "give direction to our thoughts, generate new ideas, venerate old ones, expose facts, or hide them"? To begin, gather print and online questionnaires. Possible sources may be print questionnaires from credit card companies, the government, or your school; online sources include any website that asks you to register or asks for feedback in questionnaire format. Choose one questionnaire to evaluate. As you write your critical analysis, consider the following questions.

   • What is the purpose and who is the audience for the questionnaire? What assumptions are built into the way the questions are written? What details in the text lead you to your analysis?

   • How does the form of the questions shape the answers they will generate? Do the questions "give direction" to the respondents' thoughts? Do they allow for new ideas? What do they expose? What do they hide? Provide examples.

   • How might you revise the questions? What became "visible" to you as you evaluated the questionnaire? How is language a technology that we can control for different purposes?

Jill Walker, **Weblog: A Definition**
Bonnie A. Nardi, Diane J. Schiano, Michelle Gumbrecht, and Luke Swartz, **Why We Blog**

Jill Walker is an associate professor at the University of Bergen, Norway. She teaches and writes about various forms of networked fiction, including electronic literature and art, weblogs, and web hoaxes. "Weblog" reprinted here from Walker's blog, also appeared as an entry in the *Routledge Encyclopedia of Narrative Theory* in 2005.

The essay "Why We Blog" originally appeared in a professional journal, *Communications of the ACM*, in 2004. Bonnie A. Nardi is an associate professor in the School of Information and Computer Science at the University of California, Irvine. She is an anthropologist who specializes in the study of technology. Her recent research has focused on e-democracy, including an ethnographic study of how presidential candidates used the Internet in the 2004 campaign. Diane J. Schiano is a freelance consultant and a visiting professor at the Center for Study of Language and Information at Stanford University. Michelle Gumbrecht is a graduate student working on her PhD in cognitive psychology at Stanford University. Luke Swartz has a masters degree in computer science from Stanford University.

Weblogs, or blogs, have existed in various forms since the beginning of the Web; however, their popularity has increased dramatically since 2002. Put simply, a blog is a frequently updated website consisting primarily of short posts by the blog host and sometimes by visitors. To many blogging fans, cultural analysts, and researchers, blogs represent a new and still unfolding form of communication and community-building. The following readings and sample blogs offer descriptions of blogs and explanations of why people create and read them.

> ### Mapping Your Reading
>
> Weblogs offer opportunities for reflecting critically on the impact of the Internet on the ways we communicate. As you read the following, underline passages in which the authors explain what motivates people to create and maintain blogs. How are weblogs different from other types of sites on the Web? What motivates people to maintain their own blogs? How do blogs help people forge a sense of community on the Internet?

jill/txt

this season on jill/ txt

Jill's a lot calmer two and a half months into her sudden leadership of her department. Her web design by blogging students are working on their projects, her daughter's doing great and she's going to spend all summer with her lover. She's even found time to do some research! Read on to keep the story rolling!

You can send me email too, at jill.walker@uib.no. I'm especially keen on emails that involve paid flights to interesting places. I'm a really enthusiastic speaker! (Damn, that feels really embarrassing to write. But I'm sick of women not asking. Hm.)

[FEEDBURNER]

Search

[Search]

quick links

Åsane Bygg & Eiendom AS – The guys who are renovating my flat.
What are you going to do with that English degree? – Commencement address.
HÄKKI? – Vissa har det, andra inte... – Interestingly different kind of a web shop.
UiB: eksempel på hvordan lange semestre ikke trenger innebære større undervisningsbyrde (og andre ting)
50 Fun Things To Do With Your iPod (kottke.org)

[what's this?]

28/6/2003

[final version of weblog definition]

This is the definition of "weblog" I've written for the Routledge Encyclopedia of Narrative Theory, which is forthcoming in 2005. It's limited in size and scope: I had to keep to a maximum of 500 words, including the references, and I wrote it for an encyclopedia of *narrative*. The asterixes indicate cross references to other entries in the encyclopedia.

UPDATE 22/8: I received some useful feedback from the editors and have revised the definition accordingly. Since there are a lot of links to this post, I'm putting the final, final version here at the top of the post, and the draft I sent the editors in June is still here after the horisontal rule.

Weblog

A weblog, or *blog, is a frequently updated website consisting of dated entries arranged in reverse chronological order so the most recent post appears first (see temporal ordering). Typically, weblogs are published by individuals and their style is personal and informal. Weblogs first appeared in the mid–1990s, becoming popular as simple and free publishing tools became available towards the turn of the century. Since anybody with a net connection can publish their own weblog, there is great variety in the quality, content, and ambition of weblogs, and a weblog may have anywhere from a handful to tens of thousands of daily readers.

Examples of the *genre exist on a continuum from *confessional, online *diaries to logs tracking specific topics or activities through links and commentary. Though weblogs are primarily textual, experimentation with sound, *images, and videos has resulted in related genres such as photoblogs, videoblogs, and audioblogs (see intermediality; media and narrative).

Most weblogs use links generously, allowing readers to follow conversations between weblogs by following links between entries on related topics. Readers may start at any point of a weblog, seeing the most recent entry first, or arriving at an older post via a search engine or a link from another site, often another weblog. Once at a weblog, readers can read on in various orders: chronologically, thematically, by following links between entries or by searching for keywords. Weblogs also generally include a blogroll, which is a list of links to other weblogs the author recommends. Many weblogs allow readers to enter their own comments to individual posts.

Weblogs are serial and cumulative, and readers tend to read small amounts at a time, returning hours, days, or weeks later to read entries written since their last visit. This serial or episodic structure is similar to that found in *epistolary novels or *diaries, but unlike these a weblog is open–ended, finishing only when the writer tires of writing (see narrative structure).

Many weblog entries are shaped as brief, independent narratives, and some are explicitly or implicitly fictional, though the standard genre expectation is non–fiction. Some weblogs create a larger frame for the micro–narratives of individual posts by using a consistent rule to constrain their structure or themes (see Oulipo), thus, Francis Strand connects his stories of life in Sweden by ending each with a Swedish word and its translation. Other weblogs connect frequent but dissimilar entries by making a larger narrative explicit: Flight Risk is about an heiress's escape from her family, The Date Project documents a young man's search for a girlfriend, and Julie Powell narrates her life as she works her way through Julia Child's cookbook.

Courtesy of Jill Walker and *Routledge Encyclopedia of Narrative Theory*, David Herman, Manfred Jahn, and Marie-Laure Ryan, eds. (London; New York: Routledge, 2005).

B logging is sometimes viewed as a new, grassroots form of journalism and a way to shape democracy outside the mass media and conventional party politics.[1] Blog sites devoted to politics and punditry, as well as to sharing technical developments (such as www.slashdot.org), receive thousands of hits a day. But the vast majority of blogs are written by ordinary people for much smaller audiences. Here, we report the results of an ethnographic investigation of blogging in a sample of ordinary bloggers. We investigated blogging as a form of personal communication and expression, with a specific interest in uncovering the range of motivations driving individuals to create and maintain blogs.

Blogs combine the immediacy of up-to-the-minute posts, latest first, with a strong sense of the author's personality, passions, and point of view. We investigated blogging practice to help determine why people blog, finding that bloggers have many varied reasons for letting the world in on what they think.

We conducted in-depth interviews with bloggers primarily in and around Stanford University, audiotaping in-person and phone interviews from April to June 2003. The interviews were conversational in style but covered a fixed set of questions about the informants' blogs, blogging habits, thoughts on blogging, and use of other communication media as compared to blogs. We interviewed most of them at least twice, with follow-up sessions in person or by phone, email, or instant messaging. We read their blogs throughout the time we were writing this article. To identify motivations for blogging, we analyzed the content of the blogs and the interview data. Interview follow-ups helped us clarify puzzling questions and gain additional understanding of the reasons for blogging.

We interviewed 23 people altogether, 16 men and 7 women, aged 19 to 60. All lived in California or New York and were well-educated, middle-class adults in school or employed in knowledge work or artistic pursuits. We developed the sample by searching Google's Stanford portal (www.google.com/univ/stanford/) for "blog" and for "Weblog," creating an initial list of Stanford-hosted blogs. We also contacted several bloggers we knew personally. We then snowballed the sample, asking informants for the names of other bloggers to contact. We used pseudonyms when discussing specific informants and obtained permission for all quotes and images.

Blogging Practices

The informants typically found blogs through other blogs they were reading, through friends or colleagues, and through inclusion of the blog link in an instant

---

[1] Gillmor, D. Making the news. *E-Journal: News, Views, and a Silicon Valley Diary* (Apr. 11, 2003); Weblog.siliconvalley.com/column/dangillmor/archives/000924.shtml.

message profile or homepage. Most blog pages reserve space for linking to other blogs.

Some bloggers post multiple times a day, others as infrequently as once a month. Bloggers sometimes poured out their feelings or ideas and sometimes struggled to find something to say. One informant stopped blogging when he inadvertently hurt the feelings of a friend he had mentioned. He took down his blog and later put up another, this time without advertising the URL in his instant messenger profile. Other bloggers experienced blog burnout and stopped blogging from time to time.

> **We found tremendous diversity in blog content.**

We found tremendous diversity in blog content, even in our limited sample. On the serious side, Evan, a graduate student in genetics, posted commentaries on science and health, covering such topics as AIDS, heart disease, science education, and health care policy. On the other end of the scale—blog-as-personal-revelation—Lara, an undergraduate, wrote: "I've come to realize rather recently that I can't regret that I didn't form any romantic attachments [my phrases for such things are always overly formal to the point of stupidity, and I don't know why or what to use instead, but bear with me] because, at the end of the day, a boyfriend would have taken away from all the awesome things that happened with people in the dorm, and all the great friendships that I formed and that will hopefully continue after this year (if you're reading this blog, you're most likely one of those people). Thinking back to the last couple of years, it's pretty obvious that I was really stifled by my insular, extremely time-consuming group of friends, and part of my discontent stemmed from a relative dearth of fun, casual relationships with interesting people. My friends are great, but they are also tightly knit to the point of being incestuous, and when I hang out with them it is difficult to maintain the time and energy necessary to play with other people."

This post encouraged a future connection to friends while Lara worked through her emotional issues.

Most bloggers are acutely aware of their readers, even in confessional blogs, calibrating what they should and should not reveal. Although Lara's post appears highly personal, she also kept a separate paper diary. Many bloggers have personal codes of ethics dictating what goes into their blogs (such as never criticize friends or express political opinions that are openly inflammatory). Not that bloggers eschew controversy—quite the opposite—but they express themselves in light of their audience. One blogger of liberal political opinions sometimes wrote posts she knew would irritate her Republican uncle. She was tactful enough to keep lines of communication open. Another blogger kept his writing suitable for a family audience: "Yeah . . . My mom mentioned something that was in [my blog] . . . my grandma reads it, too; she just got the Internet . . . It means that I kind of have to censor—less cursing and stuff."

> **Most bloggers are acutely aware of their readers.**

Blogging thus provides scope for an enormous variety of expression within a simple, restricted format.

Motivations

Previous survey research[2] examined some reasons people blog but without the rich data of in-depth interviews. In our sample, we discovered five major motivations for blogging: documenting one's life; providing commentary and opinions; expressing deeply felt emotions; articulating ideas through writing; and forming and maintaining community forums. This list is not exhaustive, covering all bloggers, but does describe our sample. These motivations are by no means mutually exclusive and might come into play simultaneously.

Blogs to "document my life." Many informants blogged to record activities and events. Harriet, a Stanford graduate student, blogged to "document my life" for her family and friends in Iceland, as well as for her fellow students. Blogs were used by many as a record to inform and update others of their activities and whereabouts, often including photos. Depending on the audience and content, a blog could be a public journal, a photo album, or a travelogue.

A blog could be a public journal, a photo album, or a travelogue.

Don, a technology consultant, called blogs "belogs" because he felt blogging is used to "log your being." This took a serious turn for him when his wife became gravely ill. He took over her blog to document the progress of her illness and treatment through text and photos. Blogging was an important way for him to communicate during this time: "[Blogging is helpful] when people's lives are compromised in some way . . . when [my wife] was sick, [I] was going through [the] hospital with the lens of how can I share this with others?"

Keeping family and friends abreast of life events is a key use of blogging. Katie, a graduate student, said she blogged to relate her life to others by telling her own personal story in close to real time. Even Evan, whose blog was primarily about scientific subjects, let his friends know of his whereabouts and sometimes to report a cold or other minor disturbance in his life. Arthur, a Stanford professor, and several others, found blogging a superior alternative to mass email: "[I started blogging] to communicate with friends and family, as well as [for] professional connections. It's easier than sending lots of email. I'll just put it on my blog."

Why use blogs instead of just sending email? Arthur felt blogging involves less overhead (such as addressing) than email, with added scope for other communication, including "rants" and speculation. Several bloggers emphasized the broadcast nature of blogging; they put out information, and no one need respond unless they wished to. Blogs are not intrusive. No one is "forced to pay attention," observed Lara, as they are with email. Reading is voluntary, when convenient.

---

[2] Efimova, L. Blogs: The stickiness factor. Presented at Blog Talk: A European Conference on Weblogs (Vienna, May 23, 2003); Herring, S., Scheidt, L., Bonus, S., and Wright, E. Bridging the gap: A genre analysis of Weblogs. In *Proceedings 37th Annual* Hawaii International Conference on System Sciences (Big Island, HI, Jan. 5–8, 2004).

Why not Web pages? A blog is a kind of Web page. What drew writers and readers alike to blogs is the rhythm of frequent, usually brief posts, with the immediacy of reverse chronological order. Writers could put up something short and sweet, expecting their audience would check in regularly. Readers knew they would be likely to get fresh news of friends, family, and colleagues in the convenient format of the blog, with no work-related email or the distractions often found on a homepage. Several informants saw homepages as more "static" than blogs, more formal and carefully considered, and somewhat less authentic. Jack, a poet and avid blogger, said, "[With a Web page] you don't hear their voice in the same way."

Blogs as commentary. Our bloggers found their voices by using blogs to express their opinions. While blogs are often portrayed as a breakthrough form of democratic self-expression, the darker side of the stereotype casts blogs as indulgent chatter of little interest to anyone but the blogger. Many of our informants were sensitive about this characterization and emphasized they blogged to comment on topics they found pertinent and important. A blog, said one, can be "a point of view, not just chatter."

Sam, a technology consultant, was knowledgeable about information technology and politics in developing countries. He started blogging to comment on a conference he attended but then decided to devote his blog to technology in developing countries: "[My blog started as] . . . a critique on [a] . . . conference called World Summit on the Information Society, which was a project that began a few years ago by the International Telecommunications Union . . . I was kind of interested in the way people reacted to it, putting a lot of resources into this conference, so I started tracking that, and I got very discouraged with . . . what was going on. So I just switched to . . . information technology in developing countries as a theme [for my blog], so that's really about all I'll . . . write about, looking at it . . . from a critical standpoint."

Part of the allure of blogs is the easy way they move between the personal and the profound.

Part of the allure of blogs is the easy way they move between the personal and the profound. Alan, a historian of science, started a post by documenting his life, describing an incident in which his daughter wanted to watch a *Sesame Street* video clip. He added commentary on how "DVDs make it very easy to treat movies not as whole works, but as collections of scenes." He ended the post with a discussion of John Locke's worries about the way numbering biblical verses would change people's perceptions of the Bible (with a link to further discussion on Locke). Alan's post integrated comments on popular trends, works by other authors, relevant links, and personal experience.

Arthur, a humanities professor, explained why he blogged, saying: "I guess I'm an amateur rock and cultural critic. I also comment on things that I'd be embarrassed to email to others. I mean [they would think], 'Why do I care?' On the blog, you can be an amateur rock critic."

misbehaving.net
"Well-behaved women seldom make history." --Laurel Thatcher Ulrich

« different takes on gender and blogs | Main | One small step »

November 22, 2003

musings on diverse presentations of self

During the early days of cyberculture research, many folks argued for a utopian reading of the digital domain. People could be whomever they wanted. Race, sex, sexuality - it would no longer matter. But, through The Turing Game, Amy Bruckman and gang found that people are not actually able to construct entirely different presentations of self.. much of who they are physically seeps through into their digital presentation. In Sexing the Internet, i argued that coarse profiles are problematic because we interpolate the information we're given to derive a much more detailed (but often inaccurate) image of the other person.

Together, this creates an interesting dilemma for digital presentations of self. Many of us would love to live in a world where issues of difference were to be celebrated, not loathed. But simply wishing for that world doesn't create it. Identity issues play a significant role in how we interact with others and, even when it is not immediately obvious online, it plays into how we present ourselves.

Furthermore, our readings of others' presentations are hugely dependent on our own experiences and our own expectations. The readers of this blog know that we are women and couch all of our statements in this identity. But, in some places in the blogosphere, you might not know the complex identities that come into play when someone posts something. Yet, you still envision the person on the other end. What do they look like? How often do you assume them to be like you?

I often wonder if non-radical blog voices get homogenized not by the presenters, but by the readers. Identity places such a critical role in how we read others and in how we interact with them. While we can often figure out identity features of speakers, it is not written on the blog in the way that it is written on the body. Yet, are folks aware of who they are reading?

Communities with diverse backgrounds coming together to talk about something is often critical. But what does it mean if you cannot discern whether or not there is a diverse crowd participating? What does it mean when the majority of people in the blogosphere are reading and lurking, but not posting?

I don't have any wonderful answers on this, but i'd love to know if anyone out there is thinking about issues of diversity and blogging, not just whether or not diverse groups are blogging, but whether or not they're seen and acknowledged for their diversity.

Btw: if issues of identity presentation (offline and online) are new to you, you might want to pick up Erving Goffman's "The Presentation of Self in Everyday Life" or feel free to read my thesis "Faceted Id/entity: Managing Representation in a Digital World"

Posted by zephoria at 07:33 AM in Academia | Permalink

Misbehaving.net offers women in technology fields an opportunity to critique cyber culture and other topics of interest to their readers.

 SIMMONS
BOSTON, MASSACHUSETTS

Carmel's
student blog

« Our Daily Lives | Home | Pumpkins »

I Watched The Debate Last Night! Did You?
October 06, 2004

I watched Vice President Dick Cheney and Senator John Edwards debate last night. I thought that it was an intense debate. In my opinion, both candidates voiced their opinions in a strong and eloquent way. Also, with all the slander and arguing that has been present throughout the campaigns, it was heartwarming to see the candidates sharing a little respect for each other. I think that is something we need nowadays. Besides the debate, I went to my first meeting of the Simmons Community Outreach club. It was very interesting. I am looking forward to doing the Serve-A-Thon. I did it last year in Boston and it was one of the best experiences of my senior year. We got these amazing t-shirts.

This a small update, but I'll be back soon! By the way, I am watching the next presidential debate, are you?

carmel | 04:58 PM

« Our Daily Lives | Home | Pumpkins »

Interests:

Books
The Autobiography of Malcolm X
The Color of Water
1984

Movies
Crouching Tiger Hidden Dragon
Catch Me If You Can
Menace 2 Society

Music
The Black Eyed Peas
Alicia Keys
The Roots

Others:

Student Blogs
Shelley
Justine
» Carmel
Kristin
Katherine

Archive:

Recent
Pumpkins
I Watched The Debate Last Night! Did You?
Our Daily Lives

Simmons College student Carmel updates her readers on her activities and plans. The sidebar hints at some of her cultural interests and links to other blogs.

Blogging provided an outlet for expressing a point of view on topics the authors considered much more than just chatter.

Blogs as catharsis. Several of our informants viewed blogging as an outlet for thoughts and feelings. Their content was sometimes patently emotional. Lara described hers as "me working out my own issues." Undercurrents of more subtle but deeply felt emotions fueled other blogs. Jack started blogging around the time of the start of the Iraq war in March 2003, because, despite attending demonstrations and supporting anti-war politicians, he felt "futile" and that "no one was listening." Vivian, an attorney, called her blog "Shout," writing about such topics as the misapplication of the death penalty in the U.S. justice system.

Blogs helped explore issues the authors felt "obsessive" or "passionate" about. Blogs gave people a place to "shout," or express themselves by writing to an audience of sometimes total strangers, sometimes their best friends and colleagues and family members.

The format of frequent posts, diary-style, was both outlet and stimulus for working through personal issues. A blog often serves as a relief valve, a place to "get closure out of writing," as Lara said of a post on the death of her grandfather. Another claimed, "I just needed to, like, get it out there." Others needed to "let off steam."

Blog as muse. Still others found they could "get it out there" in a more constructive manner through what previous research termed "thinking with computers."[3] Evan liked blogging because for him it was "thinking by writing." He wanted to see if he really had anything to say about what he had been reading in the news and in scholarly journals. Blogging let him test his ideas by writing them down for an audience. Alan said, "I am one of those people for whom writing and thinking are basically synonymous." His blog "forced" him to keep writing, a discipline he deemed important for his work. Jack noted that as a graduate student, "nobody wants to hear from me yet." For the moment, blogging gave him a small audience and a chance to "prove to myself that I can do it," that is, write.

Jack, Evan, Alan, and Vivian observed that some of their posts might have a future life in magazine articles, scholarly research, or other conventional publications. Alan said scholars generate a tremendous amount of material that usually stays private but could actually be a public good if released and shared with a general-interest audience. Vivian saw her posts as "good fodder for . . . political arguments later on." Jack archived his posts himself because he wasn't sure how long they would last on the www.blogger.com Web site and felt that some of them would "continue to be interesting to me."

For those who think by writing, blogging provides two main benefits: an audience to shape the writing and an archive of potentially reusable posts. Most

---

[3]Mortensen, T. and Walker, J. Blogging thoughts: Personal publication as an online research tool. In *Researching ICTs in Context*, A. Morrison, Ed. InterMedia Report, Oslo, Norway, 2002.

bloggers reported they had regular readers. They could direct their writing at them, solving the key problem of knowing for whom they were writing. Having readers helped keep the writing moving along, as bloggers knew their readers expected new posts.

Blogs as community forum. Some of our informants expressed their views to one another in community settings. One blog supported a community of poets. Two supported educational communities. Another was devoted to a "collective" of people who exchanged political opinions. We also learned of workplace blogs supporting workgroups we could not investigate directly because they were proprietary. Workplace blogs are a form of communication we expect to see much more of soon, as people become more familiar with reading and writing blogs.

Rob, who taught a class called dorm.net/residential-rhetorics, focused the class blog on locating the "intersection of residence community and all electronic communication tools," noting: "We'll try to take advantage of the general nature of Weblogs as 'public journals' in using them for personal reflection, in the context of a learning community, on issues that arise in the course, both rhetorical and content-related."

He required students to conduct field studies, post weekly blogs on assigned topics, and read and comment on one another's. He hoped to "facilitate the building of the learning community by getting [students] in conversation with each other electronically." Students found that blogging created a sense of community that would be less likely to emerge in a conventional classroom setting.

Colleen, an academic technology specialist, created a blog for an undergraduate archaeology course. The professor posted periodic reports on a class project involving the cataloging of artifacts from a nineteenth century San Jose Chinatown site. This blog succeeded as a Web site but failed to generate a sense of community among the students. The professor and teaching assistants made most of the comments, the students almost none. The students were either not moved to comment or decided not to, given the lack of a course requirement. As with other electronic media, blogs in themselves are not sufficient for building a community.

> **Blogs in themselves are not sufficient for building a community.**

The most authentic, grassroots blogging community we investigated was that of a group of poetry bloggers. Comments on blog posts flew back and forth on the blogs, in email, and in person. Jack belonged to a poetry community and kept a set of links to others' poetry blogs that "map[ped] a community," as he described it. The community generated "peer pressure" to post regularly because people regularly checked the blogs for new posts. Jack said there was "a kind of reciprocity expected because I read others' blogs, so I have to make my contribution."

This community changed over time. During the study, several poetry bloggers began to post original poems, although at first many considered it "egotistical." Jack changed his mind on the issue, and the community became his muse; his poems developed as a "conversation" between himself and other bloggers. Jack began posting poems about halfway through the study, though he had initially told us the blog was not a proper forum for poems. Later he said: "I . . .

discovered that allowing myself to post poems was helping me write poems, since I could think of it as material for the blog to be immediately posted, as opposed to being stowed in a drawer somewhere."

Here, thinking by writing intersected with blogging as community forum.

Blogs can be characterized as having limited interactivity.[4] The modal number of comments in individually authored blogs has been found to be zero.[5] Many of our informants liked the interaction-at-one-remove provided by blogs. Max said: "I feel like I can say something in the blog and then have it be sort of like my safety net. Whereas like in a more immediate and personal like form of impersonal digital communication . . . I would sort of have to face their reaction. Metaphorically speaking, anyway . . . two bad things that blogging does for me, anyway, endorses [are] laziness and cowardice."

Blogs combine information and modulated interactivity. Bloggers value that they can post and share their thoughts without the intensive feedback associated with other forms of communication.

Conclusion

In our sample, we found a range of motivations for blogging. Blog content was equally diverse, ranging from journals of daily activities to serious commentaries on important issues. Blogging is an unusually versatile medium, employed for everything from spontaneous release of emotion to archivable support of group collaboration and community. Our investigation is an early look at blogging as a mainstream use of the Internet. Much work must still be done in examining this flourishing phenomenon as it grows and changes.

 Analyzing the Text

1. On the surface, there are certain similarities between weblogs and conventional diaries. Having read this essay and studied the samples on pages 633–34, what are these similarities? What are the key differences between diaries and weblogs?

2. In "Why We Blog," the authors observe that weblogs appear to be a "new, grassroots form of journalism." How does comparing blogs to journalistic forms of writing influence your reactions to them? What metaphors or analogies does Walker use to describe blogs in her encyclopedia entry?

---

[4]Gumbrecht, M. Blogs as "protected space." Presented at the Workshop on the Weblogging Ecosystem: Aggregation, Analysis, and Dynamics (New York, May 17–22). ACM Press, New York, 2004. Herring, S., Scheidt, L., Bonus, S., and Wright, E. Bridging the gap: A genre analysis of Weblogs. In *Proceedings 37th Annual* Hawaii International Conference on System Sciences (Big Island, HI, Jan. 5–8, 2004).

[5]Herring, S., Scheidt, L., Bonus, S., and Wright, E. Bridging the gap: A genre analysis of Weblogs. In *Proceedings 37th Annual* Hawaii International Conference on System Sciences (Big Island, HI, Jan. 5–8, 2004).

3. Based on their study of bloggers, the authors of "Why We Blog" observe that there are five reasons that motivate people to keep a blog. What does each of these reasons reveal about the nature of blogging? If you are already familiar with blogging, which of these reasons seem to be the most common? Which is the least common?

4. Blogs clearly are not isolated texts. Perhaps more so than any other type of writing, they rely heavily and explicitly on a social network of other writers and readers. Can you trace the interconnections within the sample weblogs on pages 633–34? What do these interconnections reveal about how people's concept of written communication is changing?

▶ **Writing about Cultural Practices**

5. Analyze the structure, content, and interconnectedness of one weblog. To find examples, find a website that hosts weblogs, such as www.blogger.com, and search the lists of blogs on that site for one that interests you. After you have selected a blog, familiarize yourself with it by reading several posts and following any links that are provided. After studying this blog, write a descriptive analysis essay about it that answers the following questions.

- Who reads this blog? How is the presence of readers made apparent at the site? Are they referred to by the writer? Is there a discussion section that readers participate in?

- What characterizes a typical post on this blog? What topics are addressed? How long is a typical post?

- Does the blog have a history? Does it include an archive that makes older posts available?

- What is the writer's goal or purpose for this blog? Which of the five reasons for blogging from "Why We Blog" would you say best describes the motivation of the writer of this blog?

- If the blog includes images, how do they connect or relate to the written posts? What message(s) do they convey?

- What types of links are provided in the posts or on the home page of this blog? How would you characterize the typography of interconnections on this blog? Does it, for instance, make regular use of definitional links? Elaboration links? Biographical links?

- In what respects is the writer participating in a larger conversation? Does the writer belong to a larger weblog community? What is the nature of this community? What conversations or interests hold this community together?

- How does this blog differ from other blogs? In general, how does it differ from other sites on the Web?

- How would you compare blogs to other forms of communication such as diaries, letters, email, newspapers, magazines, radio or television shows, novels, and the like?

Ellen Ullman, **The Museum of Me**

Essayist and memoirist Ellen Ullman has worked as a software engineer since 1978. A central theme in her writing is technology's alienating effect. She is the author of the memoir *Close to the Machine: Technophilia and Its Discontents* (1997) and *The Bug* (2003), a novel about a programmer's battle with an elusive electronic bug. Her essays, reviews, and opinion pieces have appeared in *Harper's, Salon, Wired,* the *Washington Post,* and the *New York Times,* and she has been a regular commentator on National Public Radio's *All Things Considered.* This essay originally appeared in *Harper's* in 2000. In it, Ullman expresses her concern that, rather than connecting people and building communities, the Internet promotes the "glorification of the self, at home, alone."

> ▶ **Mapping Your Reading**
>
> Ullman's chief criticism of the Internet is that it "represents a retreat not only from political life but also from culture." As you read, notice how Ullman supports her point by presenting her experiences and observations as an industry insider. Use the margins to make notes, tracing the connection between her observations. To what extent does the Internet promote asocial behavior? Is 24/7 Internet access good for us?

Years ago, before the Internet as we know it had come into existence—I think it was around Christmas, in 1990—I was at a friend's house, where her nine-year-old son and his friend were playing the video game that was the state of the art at the time, Sonic the Hedgehog. They jumped around in front of the TV and gave off the sort of rude noises boys tend to make when they're shooting at things in a video game, and after about half an hour they stopped and tried to talk about what they'd just been doing. The dialogue went something like this:

"I wiped out at that part with the ladders."

"Ladders? What ladders?"

"You know, after the rooms."

"Oh, you mean the stairs?"

"No, I think they were ladders. I remember, because I died there twice."

"I never killed you around any ladders. I killed you where you jump down off this wall."

"Wall? You mean by the gates of the city?"

"Are there gates around the city? I always called it the castle."

The boys muddled along for several more minutes, making themselves more confused as they went. Finally they gave up trying to talk about their time with Sonic the Hedgehog. They just looked at each other and shrugged.

I didn't think about the two boys and Sonic again until I watched my clients try out the World Wide Web. By then it was 1995, the Internet as we know it was beginning to exist, but the two women who worked for my client, whom I'd just helped get online, had never before connected to the Internet or surfed the Web. They took to it instantly, each disappearing into nearly an hour of obsessive clicking, after which they tried to talk about it:

"It was great! I clicked that thing and went to this place. I don't remember its name."

"Yeah. It was a link. I clicked here and went there."

"Oh, I'm not sure it was a link. The thing I clicked was a picture of the library."

"Was it the library? I thought it was a picture of City Hall."

"Oh, no. I'm sure it was the library."

"No, City Hall. I'm sure because of the dome."

"Dome? Was there a dome?"

Right then I remembered Sonic and the two boys; my clients, like the two boys, had experienced something pleasurable and engaging, and they very much wanted to talk about it—talking being one of the primary ways human beings augment their pleasure. But what had happened to them, each in her own electronic world, resisted description. Like the boys, the two women fell into verbal confusion. How could they speak coherently about a world full of little wordless pictograms, about trails that led off in all directions, of idle visits to virtual places chosen on a whim-click?

Following hyperlinks on the Web is like the synaptic drift of dreams, a loosening of intention, the mind associating freely, an experience that can be compelling or baffling or unsettling, or all of those things at once. And like dreams, the experience of the Web is intensely private, charged with immanent meaning for the person inside the experience, but often confusing or irrelevant to someone else.

Following hyperlinks is like the synaptic drift of dreams.

At the time, I had my reservations about the Web, but not so much about the private, dreamlike state it offered. Web surfing seemed to me not so much antisocial as asocial, an adventure like a video game or pinball, entertaining, sometimes interesting, sometimes a trivial waste of time; but in a social sense it seemed harmless, since only the person engaged in the activity was affected.

Something changed, however, not in me but in the Internet and the Web and in the world, and the change was written out in person-high letters on a billboard on the corner of Howard and New Montgomery Streets in San Francisco. It was the fall of 1998. I was walking toward Market Street one afternoon when I saw it, a background of brilliant sky blue, with writing on it in airy white letters, which said: *Now the world really does revolve around you.* The letters were lowercase, soft-edged, spaced irregularly, as if they'd been skywritten over a hot August beach and were already drifting off into the air. The message they left behind was a child's secret wish, the ultimate baby-world narcissism we are all supposed to abandon when we grow up: The world really does revolve around me.

What was this billboard advertising? Perfume? A resort? There was nothing else on it but the airy, white letters, and I had to walk right up to it to see a URL written at the bottom; it was the name of a company that makes semiconductor equipment, machinery used by companies like Intel and AMD to manufacture integrated circuits. Oh, chips, I thought. Computers. Of course. What other subject produces such hyperbole? Who else but someone in the computer industry could make such a shameless appeal to individualism?

The billboard loomed over the corner for the next couple of weeks. Every time I passed it, its message irritated me more. It bothered me the way the "My Computer" icon bothers me on the Windows desktop, baby names like "My Yahoo" and "My Snap"; my, my, my; two-year-old talk; infantilizing and condescending.

But there was something more disturbing about this billboard, and I tried to figure out why, since it simply was doing what every other piece of advertising does: whispering in your ear that there is no one like you in the entire world, and what we are offering is for you, special you, and you alone. What came to me was this: Toyota, for example, sells the idea of a special, individual buyer ("It's not for everyone, just for you"), but chip makers, through the medium of the Internet and the World Wide Web, are creating the actual infrastructure of an individualized marketplace.

What had happened between 1995, when I could still think of the Internet as a private dream, and the appearance of that billboard in 1998 was the near-complete commercialization of the Web. And that commercialization had proceeded in a very particular and single-minded way: by attempting to isolate the individual within a sea of economic activity. Through a process known as "disintermediation," producers have worked to remove the expert intermediaries, agents, brokers, middlemen, who until now have influenced our interactions with the commercial world. What bothered me about the billboard, then, was that its message was not merely hype but the reflection of a process that was already under way: an attempt to convince the individual that a change currently being visited upon him or her is a good thing, the purest form of self, the equivalent of freedom. The world really does revolve around you.

In Silicon Valley, in Redmond, Washington, the home of Microsoft, and in the smaller silicon alleys of San Francisco and New York, "disintermediation" is a word so common that people shrug when you try to talk to them about it. Oh, disintermediation, that old thing. Everyone already knows about that. It has become accepted wisdom, a process considered inevitable, irrefutable, good.

I've long believed that the ideas embedded in technology have a way of percolating up and outward into the nontechnical world at large, and that technology is made by people with intentions and, as such, is not neutral. In the case of disintermediation, an explicit and purposeful change is being visited upon the structure of the global marketplace. And in a world so dominated by markets, I

"I can't explain it—it's just a funny feeling that I'm being Googled."

don't think I go too far in saying that this will affect the very structure of reality, for the Net is no longer simply a zone of personal freedoms, a pleasant diversion from what we used to call "real life"; it has become an actual marketplace that is changing the nature of real life itself.

Removal of the intermediary. All those who stand in the middle of a transaction, whether financial or intellectual: out! Brokers and agents and middlemen of every description: good-bye! Travel agents, real-estate agents, insurance agents, stockbrokers, mortgage brokers, consolidators, and jobbers, all the scrappy percentniks who troll the bywaters of capitalist exchange—who needs you? All those hard-striving immigrants climbing their way into the lower middle class through the penny-ante deals of capitalism, the transfer points too small for the big guys to worry about—find yourself some other way to make a living. Small retailers and store clerks, salespeople of every kind—a hindrance, idiots, not to be trusted. Even the professional handlers of intellectual goods, anyone who sifts through information, books, paintings, knowledge, selecting and summing up: librarians, book reviewers, curators, disc jockeys, teachers, editors, analysts—why trust anyone but yourself to make judgments about what is more or less interesting, valuable, authentic, or worthy of your attention? No one, no professional interloper, is supposed to come between you and your desires, which, according to this idea, are nuanced, difficult to communicate, irreducible, unique.

The Web did not cause disintermediation, but it is what we call an "enabling technology": a technical breakthrough that takes a difficult task and makes it suddenly doable, easy; it opens the door to change, which then comes in an unconsidered, breathless rush.

We are living through an amazing experiment: an attempt to construct a capitalism without salespeople, to take a system founded upon the need to sell ever greater numbers of goods to ever growing numbers of people, and to do this without the aid of professional distribution channels—without buildings, side-walks, shops, luncheonettes, street vendors, buses, trams, taxis, other women in the fitting room to tell you how you look in something and to help you make up your mind, without street people panhandling. Santas ringing bells at Christmas, shop women with their perfect makeup and elegant clothes, fashionable men and women strolling by to show you the latest look—in short, an attempt to do away with the city in all its messy stimulation, to abandon the agora for home and hearth, where it is safe and everything can be controlled.

The first task in this newly structured capitalism is to convince consumers that the services formerly performed by myriad intermediaries are useless or worse, that those commissioned brokers and agents are incompetent, out for themselves, dishonest. And the next task is to glorify the notion of self-service. Where companies once vied for your business by telling you about their courteous people and how well they would serve you—"Avis, We Try Harder"— their job now is to make you believe that only you can take care of yourself. The lure of personal service that was dangled before the middle classes, momentarily making us all feel almost as lucky as the rich, is being withdrawn. In the Internet age, under the pressure of globalized capitalism and its slimmed-down profit margins, only the very wealthy will be served by actual human beings. The rest of us must make do with Web pages, and feel happy about it.

Technology is made by people with intentions, and, as such, is not neutral.

One evening while I was watching television, I looked up to see a commercial that seemed to me to be the most explicit statement of the ideas implicit in the disintermediated universe. I gaped at it, because usually such ideas are kept implicit, hidden behind symbols. But this commercial was like the sky-blue billboard: a shameless and naked expression of the Web world, a glorification of the self, at home, alone.

It begins with a drone, a footstep in a puddle, then a ragged band pulling a dead car through the mud—road warriors with bandanas around their foreheads carrying braziers. Now we see rafts of survivors floating before the ruins of a city, the sky dark, red-tinged, as if fires were burning all around us, just over the horizon. Next we are outside the dead city's library, where stone lions, now coated in gold and come to life, rear up in despair. Inside the library, redcoated Fascist guards encircle the readers at the table. A young girl turns a page, loudly, and the guards say, "Shush!" in time to their march-step. We see the title of the book the girl is reading: *Paradise Lost*. The bank, too, is a scene of ruin. A long line snakes outside it in a dreary rain. Inside, the teller is a man with a white, spectral face, who gazes upon the black spider that is slowly crawling up his window. A young woman's face ages right before us, and in response, in ridicule, the bank guard laughs. The camera now takes us up over the roofs of this post-apocalyptic city. Lightning crashes in the dark, red-tinged sky. On a telephone pole, where the insulators should be, are skulls.

Cut to a cartoon of emerald-green grass, hills, a Victorian house with a white picket fence and no neighbors. A butterfly flaps above it. What a relief this house is after the dreary, dangerous, ruined city. The door to this charming house opens, and we go in to see a chair before a computer screen. Yes, we want to go sit in that chair, in that room with candy-orange walls. On the computer screen, running by in teasing succession, are pleasant virtual reflections of the world outside: written text, a bank check, a telephone pole, which now signifies our connection to the world. The camera pans back to show a window, a curtain swinging in the breeze, and our sense of calm is complete. We hear the Intel-Inside jingle, which sounds almost like chimes. Cut to the legend: Packard Bell. Wouldn't you rather be at home?

In 60 seconds, this commercial communicates a worldview that reflects the ultimate suburbanization of existence: a retreat from the friction of the social space to the supposed idyll of private ease. It is a view that depends on the idea that desire is not social, not stimulated by what others want, but generated internally, and that the satisfaction of desires is not dependent upon other persons, organizations, structures, or governments. It is a profoundly libertarian vision, and it is the message that underlies all the mythologizing about the Web: the idea that the civic space is dead, useless, dangerous. The only place of pleasure and satisfaction is your home. You, home, family; and beyond that, the world. From the intensely private to the global, with little in between but an Intel processor and a search engine.

In this sense, the ideal of the Internet represents the very opposite of democracy, which is a method for resolving differences in a relatively orderly manner through the mediation of unavoidable civil associations. Yet there can be no notion of resolving differences in a world where each person is entitled to get exactly what he or she wants. Here all needs and desires are equally valid and equally powerful. I'll get mine and you'll get yours; there is no need for compromise and discussion. I don't have to tolerate you, and you don't have to tolerate me. No need for messy debate and the whole rigmarole of government with all its creaky, bothersome structures. There's no need for any of this, because now that we have the World Wide Web the problem of the pursuit of happiness has been solved! We'll each click for our individual joys, and our only dispute may come if something doesn't get delivered on time. Wouldn't you really rather be at home?

But who can afford to stay at home? Only the very wealthy or a certain class of knowledge worker can stay home and click. On the other side of this ideal of work-anywhere freedom (if indeed it is freedom never to be away from work) is the reality that somebody had to make the thing you ordered with a click. Somebody had to put it in a box, do the paperwork, carry it to you. The reality is a world divided not only between the haves and have-nots but between the ones who get to stay home and everyone else, the ones who deliver the goods to them.

The Net ideal represents a retreat not only from political life but also from culture—from that tumultuous conversation in which we try to talk to one another about our shared experiences. As members of a culture, we see the same movie, read the same book, hear the same string quartet. Although it is difficult for us to agree on what we might have seen, read, or heard, it is out of that difficult conversation that real culture arises. Whether or not we come to an agreement or understanding, even if some decide that understanding and meaning are impossible, we are still sitting around the same campfire.

But the Web as it has evolved is based on the idea that we do not even want a shared experience. The director of San Francisco's Museum of Modern Art once told an audience that we no longer need a building to house works of art; we don't need to get dressed, go downtown, walk from room to room among crowds of other people. Now that we have the Web, we can look at anything we want whenever we want, and we no longer need him or his curators. "You don't have to walk through *my* idea of what's interesting to look at," he said to a questioner in the audience named Bill. "On the Web," said the director, "you can create the museum of Bill."

And so, by implication, there can be the museums of George and Mary and Helene. What then will this group have to say to one another about art? Let's say the museum of Bill is featuring early Dutch masters, the museum of Mary is playing video art, and the museum of Helene is displaying French tapestries. In this privatized world, what sort of "cultural" conversation can there be? What can one of us possibly say to another about our experience except, "Today I visited the museum of me, and I liked it."

Analyzing the Text

1. Why does the billboard slogan "now the world really does revolve around you" worry Ullman? What does it represent for her?

2. According to Ullman, how has online shopping changed the way in which people conduct business? What is the meaning and the implication of the concept "disintermediation"? What other areas of public life are affected (negatively, in Ullman's view) by the promise of direct access to goods and services on the Internet?

3. To illustrate her argument, Ullman describes a Packard Bell commercial in detail, stating that it "communicates a worldview that reflects the ultimate suburbanization of existence: a retreat from the friction of the social space to the supposed idyll of private ease." According to Ullman, what is the danger of the assumptions underlying this worldview? Can you think of other examples of commercials that use this assumption?

4. In your opinion, to what extent has the Internet become an asocial space in people's lives? What is the Internet's role in contributing to the further distancing of people from a sense of a community or shared experience?

Writing about Cultural Practices

5. Ullman's essay offers a counterargument for the typically positive claims about the Internet that we encounter through advertising and the popular press. The trap that both sides of this debate fall into is they make universalizing claims: From one side, the Internet promises to make our lives better, and from the other side, the Internet represents the ultimate peril. How can we develop a

more deliberative approach to thinking about the Internet's impact? For this assignment, conduct your own study of how the Internet impacts people's lives. To do this, observe and interview three to five people to learn how and why they use the Internet. With their permission, spend one hour observing each person as they use the Internet. At the end of the hour, interview each person and review the history trail of websites he or she visited. As you conduct your research; consider the following questions.

- Why do the people you observed use the Internet? What personal needs or wants drive their use of the Internet? Are they seeking entertainment, or are they trying to solve a problem or complete a task? Do their needs overlap? If so, how?

- What expectations do they have about the Internet? Does their experience online meet their expectations? What, if anything, do they find surprising or unexpected about the Internet?

Following your interviews, write a descriptive analysis that paints a more complex picture of the ways people use the Internet. Address these questions in your essay.

- Why do the people you observed use the Internet? What problems or needs are they using the Internet to resolve?

- How does the Internet mediate these people's work or social relationships?

- What are some intended and unintended consequences of their Internet use?

- What are some of the trade-offs associated with their Internet use? What are the benefits and limitations marking these people's Internet use?

The Onion, New Technological Breakthrough to Fix Problems of Previous Breakthrough

The creation of two students in Madison, Wisconsin, the *Onion* has become a journalistic phenomenon. Called "satire at its finest" by *Wired* magazine, the *Onion* is a humorous news and entertainment publication that has inspired six books and hailed ten Webby Awards, and attracts more than three million readers every week. The following article was published on onion.com and highlights the often unconsidered repercussions of scientific research and technology.

▶ **Mapping Your Reading**

Through this mock news story, writers at the *Onion* critique the popular attitude that science improves our lives and that technology always leads to progress. As you read, pay attention to how closely these writers follow the typical organization and style of newspaper reporting to poke fun at our obsession with scientific breakthroughs.

the ONION®

| VOLUME 37 ISSUE 17 | AMERICA'S FINEST NEWS SOURCE™ | 10–16 MAY 2001 |

New Technological Breakthrough To Fix Problems Of Previous Breakthrough

COLLEGE STATION, TX—Agricultural scientists around the world are hailing what is being called "the biggest breakthrough in biotechnology since the breakthrough it fixes."

On Monday, Texas A&M chemists unveiled Zovirex-10, a revolutionary new fungicide capable of halting the spread of a fungus unexpectedly spawned by a July 2000 breakthrough, an advanced soy hybrid that grows 10 times better in soil over-saturated with chemical herbicides.

The fungus, which, if left unchecked, would likely have destroyed 98 percent of Earth's soy crop and wrought untold environmental havoc, made the latest scientific advance possible.

"It's an extraordinary development," said Dr. Nathan Oberst, project coordinator and the man responsible for both breakthroughs. "At the time, we thought the soy hybrid was a fantastic thing. When the resultant fungus started wiping out other soybean plants at an alarming rate, we thought we might have blundered, but now it's clear that this potential global disaster was just the precondition we needed for a major leap forward."

Oberst dismissed charges that the development of new biotechnological advances to counteract unexpected side effects of prior biotechnological advances constitutes a dangerous Moebius loop.

"It may seem dangerous to tinker with nature without knowing the long-term effects," he said. "But without the threat of environmental disaster caused by the short-sighted unbalancing of natural forces, how are we to bring about positive change in the world around us?"

Oberst downplayed claims that if Zovirex-10 were to seep into the groundwater, it would kill off 70 percent of fish and aquatic plant life, poison 35 percent of the human population, and raise the temperature of the sea by seven degrees.

"If this is true, it shouldn't be thought of as a disaster," he said. "Modern science has a long, proven track record of correcting the mistakes it inadvertently unleashes on the world. I'm confident that if the worst ever came to pass, science would find some way to fix it. That's what science does."

According to Oberst, flawed and dangerous technological advances have helped broaden understanding in all fields of science.

"Just think about the hydrogen bomb," Oberst said. "Not only was it a tremendous breakthrough in physics, it broadened our knowledge of everything from radiation containment to bomb-shelter construction to hair loss. Science has been coming up with breakthrough after breakthrough to fix the problems that the H-bomb has created. Without the H-bomb, we would know significantly less about the potential problems associated with the H-bomb."

"People shouldn't see man-made global disasters as a bad thing," Oberst added. "They should see them as scientific breakthroughs waiting to happen." Ø

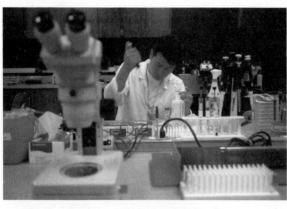

Above: A Texas A&M chemist works on the breakthrough.

Analyzing the Text

1. What assumptions about science and technology are these writers aiming their criticism at? How do the *Onion* writers use the fictional character of Dr. Nathan Oberst as the voice of the scientific community? What quotes are particularly effective in conveying Oberst's attitudes?

2. How does the circular logic of this story increase its humor? For instance, the final lines of the story are a quote from Oberst: "People shouldn't see man-made global disasters as a bad thing. They should see them as scientific breakthroughs waiting to happen."

3. What other characteristics of this story are clearly intended to have a humorous yet thought-provoking impact?

4. **Connecting to Other Readings.**   Using their brand of biting humor, the writers for the *Onion* critique the faith our culture has in science and technology. What are the connections between this humor piece and Langdon Winner's "Technological Somnambulism" (p. 594) or Daniel Harris's "Cleanness" (p. 661)? How do these readings reflect on technological determinism—that is, our tendency to embrace uncritically the conditions and consequences brought on by technological change?

Writing about Cultural Practices

5. The *Onion* article is a spoof on the kinds of news stories and commentaries that announce new scientific discoveries uncritically. In the *Onion* piece, objections to the new technology are addressed by the confident scientist, Oberst, who believes that "modern science has a long, proven track record of correcting the mistakes it inadvertently unleashes on the world." He downplays claims that "Zovirex-10" would pretty much poison the environment and kill about a third of the population.

   But how do objections to scientific "advancements" get addressed in the popular, or even scientific, press? For this assignment, collect articles and editorials (print or online) on a specific proposed technological advancement. The articles and commentaries might be on a proposed project such as a new power plant, a plan for offshore windmills, or a new potentially hazardous medical research lab, for example. Working with the article that interests you most, write a critical analysis that addresses the following questions.

   • How rigorously does the article challenge the proposed project? Are the potential risks addressed fairly? Is there evidence that the author or publisher of the piece is biased in any way regarding the project?

   • How are the different voices in the debate represented—for example, the science community, business community, and any groups that might be critical of the project? Do some voices seem to be privileged over others? Is "progress" and money favored over health and safety?

   • Does the article provide enough information for the reader to think critically about the proposed project and its impact on humans and the environment? If not, how could it have done a better job? How has reading the article shaped your opinion on the topic?

Clarence Page, **Should We Still Be Involved in Space Exploration?**

Pulitzer Prize–winner Clarence Page has been a member of the *Chicago Tribune* editorial board since 1984. Serving as a correspondent, an investigative reporter, and a columnist, Page traveled around the world, became a foreign correspondent in Africa in 1976, and earned a place in the Chicago Journalism Hall of Fame in 1992. As a freelance writer, he has been published in *Washington Monthly*, *New Republic*, the *Wall Street Journal*, and *New York Newsday*. His first book, *Showing My Color: Impolite Essays on Race and Identity*, was published in 1996. Page also contributes to *News Hour with Jim Lehrer* and *The McLaughlin Group* and writes an op-ed column for the *Chicago Tribune*. This article was originally published in the *Tribune* on February 5, 2003. Perhaps more than any other common national undertaking, space travel represents the promise of technology and reveals the extent to which technology is bound to a culture's values. As Page writes, "Space travel binds us together as a nation and touches our secret hope that there is something better waiting for us out there in the unknown."

 Mapping Your Reading

In the wake of the crash of the *Columbia* space shuttle, Page suggests that the country needs to return to the question, "Why pursue space exploration?" As you read, pay attention to Page's explanation of how reasons for exploring space have changed. What originally drove America to space exploration? Should we continue exploring space?

I t's hard to imagine an America that has stopped putting humans into space, but let's try.

The *Columbia* tragedy serves to remind even the biggest boosters of space travel, as I have been in the past, of how much the space shuttle program is a relic of Cold War politics and technology.

Most of the national debate that the *Columbia* disaster ignited in the media and among politicians has been polarized between two alternatives: scrap manned missions or resume the space shuttle and International Space Station once the National Aeronautics and Space Administration fixes what went wrong this time.

Here's a better alternative: Let's start over. Let's rethink why we want to go into space and, not just whether, but precisely how and when the risks of send-

An astronaut from the Apollo 15 *salutes as he stands next to the American flag on the moon in August of 1971.*

ing manned flights into space are worth the rewards of what we want to accomplish there.

Most Americans seem to be quite keen on resuming the space shuttle program, not just because of its technological promise but also because of the inspirational uplift space exploration gives to our national spirits.

Tang, Teflon, and other great astronaut-era scientific advances do not, by themselves, begin to explain why the Air and Space Museum in Washington, D.C., is the nation's most visited museum, even on Christmas and Thanksgiving Day.

Space travel binds us together as a nation and touches our secret hope that there is something better waiting for us out there in the unknown.

Conventional wisdom holds that the public and, therefore, politicians, are not nearly as captivated by unmanned missions. Yet the Mars *Pathfinder* mission in 1997 drew record numbers of hits by those eager to see the spectacular video it sent back from the surface of Mars.

And although NASA's Hubble Space Telescope required repairs by space-walking astronauts, its robotic mechanism does a better job of sending back breathtaking images from deep space without the shakiness of human hands to guide it.

The space shuttle, by comparison, is basically a holdover from the Cold War when we were still racing people into space to outdo the Russians.

"The shuttle's main engines, first tested in the late 1970s, use hundreds more moving parts than do new rocket-motor designs," writes shuttle-critic Gregg Easterbrook, a senior editor of the *New Republic* and a visiting fellow at the Brookings Institution, in the February 10 edition of *Time*.

"The fragile heat-dissipating tiles were designed before breakthroughs in materials science. Until recently, the flight-deck computers on the space shuttle used old 8086 chips from the early 1980s, the sort of pre-Pentium electronics no self-respecting teenager would dream of using for a video game."

The space shuttle program is a relic of Cold War politics and technology.

Easterbrook's view is sobering because it updates his call to scrap the shuttle that first was published in an April 1980 cover story in the *Washington Monthly*. At the time, NASA officials responded with a defensive eight-page memo. When *Challenger* blew up six years later, Easterbrook looked like a prophet.

He's not alone. It is time to listen with new ears to the shuttle program's many critics. Hovering over the post-*Columbia* controversies are the unanswered questions about what precisely we want to do in space, now that we no longer have to prove anything to the Russians or, for that matter, to ourselves.

Space experts from industry and academia need to huddle with Congress and NASA officials to decide the future direction of our country's mission in space. Ultimately President Bush will have to decide where we go from here, at least in the short term, in much the way President John F. Kennedy set the moon as America's goal by the end of the 1960s.

Significantly, new White House tapes released by the John F. Kennedy Library and Museum reveal that JFK privately told then-NASA administrator James Webb in 1962 that the space race was "important for political reasons" and that "everything we do should be tied into getting onto the moon ahead of the Russians."

"Otherwise we shouldn't be spending this kind of money," he said, "because I am not that interested in space."

With that in mind, the best way for us Americans to honor those who died in *Challenger* and *Columbia* is to ask ourselves why we are still interested in space. After we have figured out what we are trying to do there, then we can determine whether and when astronauts will provide the best way for us to do it.

▶ **Analyzing the Text**

1. **Interrogating Assumptions.** Page asks readers to reconsider the popular assumption that technology equals progress. What does he suggest space exploration represents to the wider culture?

2. Page points out that the original reasons behind space travel no longer seem relevant. What does he think the next steps should be regarding the space program? Should we explore outer space?

3. How effective are the arguments of critics of the space shuttle program? What seem to be their main concerns or criticisms? Do you think their arguments are valid? Why or why not?

Writing about Cultural Practices

4. Why is space exploration so deeply embedded in the popular imagination of America? Answer this question by developing a reflective analysis of popular representations of space exploration. To begin, your class may choose one or two popular television shows or movies in which space travel is an important theme. After watching and discussing these shows or movies, draft your own critical analysis of one of them. As you draft your essay, consider the following questions.

- What is the context or reason given within this program or movie for space travel?

- How do the producers of this program or movie use space exploration as a theme? What other themes, if any, are attached to it?

- What cultural values or assumptions surround space exploration in the program or movie? What details lead you to this observation?

Atul Gawande, **The Learning Curve**

Atul Gawande is a Harvard Medical School graduate, best-selling author, and has been called "[a] rock n' roll loving surgeon who writes for the *New Yorker*." His first collection of essays, *Complications: A Surgeon's Notes on an Imperfect Science*, was nominated for a 2002 National Book Award. When asked about his writing, Gawande explains, "I don't write out of inspiration. . . . I write because it's my way of finding cool ideas, thinking through hard problems and things I don't understand, and getting better at something. I was never born to write. I was taught to write. And I am still being taught to write." This sense of humility is apparent in his essay, "The Learning Curve," originally published in the *New Yorker* and included in *The Best American Essays 2003*. In this piece, Gawande discusses how surgeons learn to treat patients. He explains, "We practice on people."

▶ **Mapping Your Reading**

In this essay, Gawande explores the difficulties of learning surgical practices with often unswerving honesty. As you read, pay attention to his descriptions and how he communicates. How does one learn a profession? How does one learn the language, skills, routines, and decision-making abilities that a profession demands? What if that profession involves matters of life and death? Do cultural assumptions about the authority of the surgeon get in the way of honest discussion about medical practices?

The patient needed a central line. "Here's your chance," S., the chief resident, said. I had never done one before. "Get set up and then page me when you're ready to start."

It was my fourth week in surgical training. The pockets of my short white coat bulged with patient printouts, laminated cards with instructions for doing CPR and reading EKGs and using the dictation system, two surgical handbooks, a stethoscope, wound-dressing supplies, meal tickets, a penlight, scissors, and about a dollar in loose change. As I headed up the stairs to the patient's floor, I rattled.

This will be good, I tried to tell myself: my first real procedure. The patient— fiftyish, stout, taciturn—was recovering from abdominal surgery he'd had about a week earlier. His bowel function hadn't yet returned, and he was unable to eat.

I explained to him that he needed intravenous nutrition and that this required a "special line" that would go into his chest. I said that I would put the line in him while he was in his bed, and that it would involve my numbing a spot on his chest with a local anesthetic, and then threading the line in. I did not say that the line was eight inches long and would go into his vena cava, the main blood vessel to his heart. Nor did I say how tricky the procedure could be. There were "slight risks" involved, I said, such as bleeding and lung collapse; in experienced hands, complications of this sort occur in fewer than one case in a hundred.

But, of course, mine were not experienced hands. And the disasters I knew about weighed on my mind: the woman who had died within minutes from massive bleeding when a resident lacerated her vena cava; the man whose chest had to be opened because a resident lost hold of a wire inside the line, which then floated down to the patient's heart; the man who had a cardiac arrest when the procedure put him into ventricular fibrillation. I said nothing of such things, naturally, when I asked the patient's permission to do his line. He said, "OK."

> Mine were not experienced hands. And the disasters I knew about weighed on my mind.

I had seen S. do two central lines; one was the day before, and I'd attended to every step. I watched how she set out her instruments and laid her patient down and put a rolled towel between his shoulder blades to make his chest arch out. I watched how she swabbed his chest with antiseptic, injected lidocaine, which is a local anesthetic, and then, in full sterile garb, punctured his chest near his clavicle with a fat three-inch needle on a syringe. The patient hadn't even flinched. She told me how to avoid hitting the lung ("Go in at a steep angle," she'd said. "Stay *right* under the clavicle"), and how to find the subclavian vein, a branch to the vena cava lying atop the lung near its apex ("Go in at a steep angle. Stay *right* under the clavicle"). She pushed the needle in almost all the way. She drew back on the syringe. And she was in. You knew because the syringe filled with maroon blood. ("If it's bright red, you've hit an artery," she said. "That's not good.") Once you have the tip of this needle poking in the vein, you somehow have to widen the hole in the vein wall, fit the catheter in, and snake it in the right direction—down to the heart, rather than up to the brain—all without tearing through vessels, lung, or anything else.

To do this, S. explained, you start by getting a guide wire in place. She pulled the syringe off, leaving the needle in. Blood flowed out. She picked up a two-foot-long twenty-gauge wire that looked like the steel D string of an electric guitar, and passed nearly its full length through the needle's bore, into the vein, and onward toward the vena cava. "Never force it in," she warned, "and never, ever let go of it." A string of rapid heartbeats fired off on the cardiac monitor, and she quickly pulled the wire back an inch. It had poked into the heart, causing momentary fibrillation. "Guess we're in the right place," she said to me quietly. Then to the patient: "You're doing great. Only a few minutes now." She pulled the needle out over the wire and replaced it with a bullet of thick, stiff plastic, which she pushed in tight to widen the vein opening. She then removed this dilator and threaded the central line—a spaghetti-thick, flexible yellow plastic tube—over the wire until it was all the way in. Now she could remove the wire. She flushed the line with a heparin solution and sutured it to the patient's chest. And that was it.

Today, it was my turn to try. First, I had to gather supplies—a central-line kit, gloves, gown, cap, mask, lidocaine—which took me forever. When I finally had the stuff together, I stopped for a minute outside the patient's door, trying to recall the steps. They remained frustratingly hazy. But I couldn't put it off any longer. I had a page-long list of other things to get done: Mrs. A needed to be discharged; Mr. B needed an abdominal ultrasound arranged; Mrs. C needed her skin staples removed. And every 15 minutes or so I was getting paged with more tasks: Mr. X was nauseated and needed to be seen; Miss Y's family was here and needed "someone" to talk to them; Mr. Z needed a laxative. I took a deep breath, put on my best don't-worry-I-know-what-I'm-doing look, and went in.

I took a deep breath, put on my best don't-worry-I-know-what-I'm-doing look, and went in.

I placed the supplies on a bedside table, untied the patient's gown, and laid him down flat on the mattress, with his chest bare and his arms at his sides. I flipped on a fluorescent overhead light and raised his bed to my height. I paged S. I put on my gown and gloves and, on a sterile tray, laid out the central line, the guide wire, and other materials from the kit. I drew up five cc's of lidocaine in a syringe, soaked two sponge sticks in the yellow-brown Betadine, and opened up the suture packaging.

S. arrived. "What's his platelet count?"

My stomach knotted. I hadn't checked. That was bad: too low and he could have a serious bleed from the procedure. She went to check a computer. The count was acceptable.

Chastened, I started swabbing his chest with the sponge sticks. Got the shoulder roll underneath him?" S. asked. Well, no, I had forgotten that, too. The patient gave me a look. S., saying nothing, got a towel, rolled it up, and slipped it under his back for me. I finished applying the antiseptic and then draped him so that only his right upper chest was exposed. He squirmed a bit beneath the drapes. S. now inspected my tray. I girded myself.

"Where's the extra syringe for flushing the line when it's in?" Damn. She went out and got it.

I felt for my landmarks. *Here?* I asked with my eyes, not wanting to undermine the patient's confidence any further. She nodded. I numbed the spot with lidocaine. ("You'll feel a stick and a burn now, sir.") Next, I took the three-inch needle in hand and poked it through the skin. I advanced it slowly and uncertainly, a few millimeters at a time. This is a big goddamn needle, I kept thinking. I couldn't believe I was sticking it into someone's chest. I concentrated on maintaining a steep angle of entry, but kept spearing his clavicle instead of slipping beneath it.

"Ow!" he shouted.

"Sorry," I said. S. signaled with a kind of surfing hand gesture to go underneath the clavicle. This time, it went in. I drew back on the syringe. Nothing. She pointed deeper. I went in deeper. Nothing. I withdrew the needle, flushed out some bits of tissue clogging it, and tried again.

"Ow!"

Too steep again. I found my way underneath the clavicle once more. I drew the syringe back. Still nothing. He's too obese, I thought. S. slipped on gloves and a gown. "How about I have a look?" she said. I handed her the needle and stepped aside. She plunged the needle in, drew back on the syringe, and, just like that, she was in. "We'll be done shortly," she told the patient.

She let me continue with the next steps, which I bumbled through. I didn't realize how long and floppy the guide wire was until I pulled the coil out of its plastic sleeve, and, putting one end of it into the patient, I very nearly contaminated the other. I forgot about the dilating step until she reminded me. Then, when I put in the dilator, I didn't push quite hard enough, and it was really S. who pushed it all the way in. Finally, we got the line in, flushed it, and sutured it in place.

Outside the room, S. said that I could be less tentative the next time, but that I shouldn't worry too much about how things had gone. "You'll get it," she said. "It just takes practice." I wasn't so sure. The procedure remained wholly mysterious to me. And I could not get over the idea of jabbing a needle into someone's chest so deeply and so blindly. I awaited the X-ray afterward with trepidation. But it came back fine: I had not injured the lung and the line was in the right place.

Not everyone appreciates the attractions of surgery. When you are a medical student in the operating room for the first time, and you see the surgeon press the scalpel to someone's body and open it like a piece of fruit, you either shudder in horror or gape in awe. I gaped. It was not just the blood and guts that enthralled me. It was also the idea that a person, a mere mortal, would have the confidence to wield that scalpel in the first place.

There is a saying about surgeons. "Sometimes wrong; never in doubt." This is meant as a reproof, but to me it seemed their strength. Every day, surgeons are faced with uncertainties. Information is inadequate; the science is ambiguous; one's knowledge and abilities are never perfect. Even with the simplest operation, it cannot be taken for granted that a patient will come through better off—or even alive. Standing at the operating table, I wondered how the surgeon knew that all the steps would go as planned, that bleeding would be controlled and infection would not set in and organs would not be injured. He didn't, of course. But he cut anyway.

> There is a saying about surgeons. "Sometimes wrong; never in doubt."

Later, while still a student, I was allowed to make an incision myself. The surgeon drew a six-inch dotted line with a marking pen across an anesthetized patient's abdomen and then, to my surprise, had the nurse hand me the knife. It was still warm from the autoclave. The surgeon had me stretch the skin taut with the thumb and forefinger of my free hand. He told me to make one smooth slice down to the fat. I put the belly of the blade to the skin and cut. The experience was odd and addictive, mixing exhilaration from the calculated violence of the act, anxiety about getting it right, and a righteous faith that it was somehow for the person's good. There was also the slightly nauseating feeling of finding that it took more force than I'd realized.

STEVE MARTIN
. . . on Medical Progress

(as Theodoric of York, a medieval barber): "You know, medicine is not an exact science, but we're learning all the time. Why, just 50 years ago we would've thought your daughter's illness was caused by demonic possession or witchcraft. But nowadays, we know that Isabelle is suffering from an imbalance of bodily humors. Perhaps caused by a toad or a small dwarf living in her stomach."

–From *Saturday Night Live: The Best of Steve Martin,* 1997

(Skin is thick and springy, and on my first pass I did not go nearly deep enough; I had to cut twice to get through.) The moment made me want to be a surgeon—not an amateur handed the knife for a brief moment but someone with the confidence and ability to proceed as if it were routine.

A resident begins, however, with none of this air of mastery—only an overpowering instinct against doing anything like pressing a knife against flesh or jabbing a needle into someone's chest. On my first day as a surgical resident, I was assigned to the emergency room. Among my first patients was a skinny, dark-haired woman in her late 20s who hobbled in, teeth gritted, with a two-foot-long wooden chair leg somehow nailed to the bottom of her foot. She explained that a kitchen chair had collapsed under her and, as she leaped up to keep from falling, her bare foot had stomped down on a three-inch screw sticking out of one of the chair legs. I tried very hard to look like someone who had not got his medical diploma just the week before. Instead, I was determined to be nonchalant, the kind of guy who had seen this sort of thing a hundred times before. I inspected her foot, and could see that the screw was embedded in the bone at the base of her big toe. There was no bleeding and, as far as I could feel, no fracture.

"Wow, that must hurt," I blurted out idiotically.

The obvious thing to do was give her a tetanus shot and pull out the screw. I ordered the tetanus shot, but I began to have doubts about pulling out the screw. Suppose she bled? Or suppose I fractured her foot? Or something worse? I excused myself and tracked down Dr. W., the senior surgeon on duty. I found him tending to a car-crash victim. The patient was a mess, and the floor was covered with blood. People were shouting. It was not a good time to ask questions.

I ordered an X-ray. I figured it would buy time and let me check my amateur impression that she didn't have a fracture. Sure enough, getting the X-ray took about an hour, and it showed no fracture—just a common screw embedded, the radiologist said, "in the head of the first metatarsal." I showed the patient the X-ray. "You see, the screw's embedded in the head of the first metatarsal," I said. And the plan? she wanted to know. Ah, yes, the plan.

I went to find Dr. W. He was still busy with the crash victim, but I was able to interrupt to show him the X-ray. He chuckled at the sight of it and asked me what I wanted to do. "Pull the screw out?" I ventured. "Yes," he said, by which he meant "Duh." He made sure I'd given the patient a tetanus shot and then shooed me away.

Back in the examining room, I told her that I would pull the screw out, prepared for her to say something like "You?" Instead she said, "OK, Doctor." At first, I had her sitting on the exam table, dangling her leg off the side. But that didn't look as if it would work. Eventually, I had her lie with her foot jutting off the table end, the board poking out into the air. With every move, her pain increased. I injected a local anesthetic where the screw had gone in and that helped a little. Now I grabbed her foot in one hand, the board in the other, and for a moment I froze. Could I really do this? Who was I to presume?

Finally, I gave her a one-two-three and pulled, gingerly at first and then hard. She groaned. The screw wasn't budging. I twisted, and abruptly it came free. There was no bleeding. I washed the wound out, and she found she could walk. I warned her of the risks of infection and the signs to look for. Her gratitude was immense and flattering, like the lion's for the mouse—and that night I went home elated.

In surgery, as in anything else, skill, judgment, and confidence are learned through experience, haltingly and humiliatingly. Like the tennis player and the oboist and the guy who fixes hard drives, we need practice to get good at what we do. There is one difference in medicine, though: we practice on people.

Analyzing the Text

1. How does Gawande use his process of learning to perform a medical procedure to demonstrate a larger point about how people learn?

2. What are the technological practices, routines, and decision-making skills that Gawande struggles to learn? What are the challenges and risks of doing so?

3. Gawande uses vivid detail to recall his experiences as a surgical resident. What is the impact of this technique of writing? What effect does he create in the way his narrative almost positions readers just over his shoulder as he performs various procedures on patients?

4. **Interrogating Assumptions.** How does Gawande's discussion about the training of surgeons challenge the first assumption in this chapter's introduction that "technologies are machines" (p. 578)?

5. **Connecting to Another Reading.** How would you relate Gawande's essay to "Invisible Technologies" (p. 623) by Neil Postman? To what extent are learning processes in the medical profession invisible technologies? And what does the public's need for "perfection without practice," which Gawande describes as "the uncomfortable truth about teaching," reveal about the biases or value systems of this learning process?

Writing about Cultural Practices

6. Gawande's essay examines the process of learning the new skills, language, and routines of being a doctor. Write a critical narrative in which you describe a time

when you were new to a particular environment and needed to learn new skills, ways of talking, and routines. For example, have you ever joined a club, team, or other organization? Have you ever taken a new job or moved to a new school and had to learn "the system" of that particular environment? Use a personal experience from your past such as these to write about your process of learning the skills, ways of talking, and routines involved in this community. Follow the example Gawande provides and focus on how you learned one particular skill or routine. As you write, consider the following questions.

- When have you been the "new" person? What was the setting or context? Who were the people in this environment? How were you expected to interact with them?

- By what direct and indirect methods did you begin to learn the skills, ways of talking, and routines necessary for getting along in this new setting or environment? Did someone act as a guide for you? Were there actual written procedures or rules that you had to study? What were the unwritten rules that people seemed to abide by? What role did observing how others interacted play in helping you learn the ropes?

- Looking back, how did your experience of learning the system of this new environment affect your sense of identity at the time? Of how you thought about who you were?

Daniel Harris, **Cleanness**

With a biting wit, Daniel Harris writes about pop culture and consumerism. In addition to being a regular contributor to *Harper's, Salmagundi,* and the *Nation,* Harris has written two books, *The Rise and Fall of Gay Culture* (1997) and *Cute, Quaint, Hungry, and Romantic: The Aesthetics of Consumerism* (2001). This most recent book is best described in Harris's own words: "I attempt to recover the repressed aesthetic data of our lives; to make this vast archive of subliminal images accessible to conscious analysis; and to remove the mental obstructions, the inveterate habits of inattentiveness, that prevent us from seeing how carefully even the most insignificant of our possessions have been designed." This excerpt, taken from one chapter of the book, examines the American obsession with obliterating dirt.

▶ **Mapping Your Reading**

In the following essay, Harris argues that cleanness is a moral aesthetic that is marketed to us. As you read, pay attention to the many examples of mass-marketed cleaning products that Harris uses to support his claims. How are attitudes about cleanness the result of the marketing of cleaning products? What are the implications that accompany these kinds of marketing messages about cleanness?

Dirtiness has physical characteristics but cleanness does not. When something is dirty we see dusty smudges, we feel the grimy patina of grease mixed with soot, and we smell the odors wafting up from garbage cans overflowing with scraps of meat or from vegetables liquefying in our crisper drawers. Cleanness, however, is simply an absence of qualities, an absence of stains, tacky to the touch, an absence of the pungent aromas that assault us when we open a quart of curdled milk, unfold a mildewed rag, or pry too deeply into the debris moldering in the dank regions beneath our kitchen sinks.

Manufacturers of cleaning products, however, would have us believe otherwise, that washing something brings out its sensual properties rather than simply eliminates them, that Mr. Clean makes your toilet bowl smell like "a field of wildflowers blowing in the wind," that Tide imbues your clothes with the "scent of crisp mountain air," and that Colgate "leaves your teeth sparkling white," while Gain creates "whites that wow." In this sense, the rhetoric of cleanness is strikingly similar to the rhetoric of deliciousness. In the case of the aesthetic of food, advertisers circumvent the difficulties of representing such an elusive experience as taste by talking dirty to the consumer and exaggerating the act of chewing, swallowing, and ingesting, providing television audiences, salivating on their sofas, with a vicarious tongue. In the case of representing something as imperceptible as cleanness, manufacturers don't engage in dirty talk, but, more appropriately, in its sanitized equivalent, in clean talk, a way of endowing an invisible state with a marketable set of properties, whether it be the lurid color of a bathroom bowl deodorizer that "blues with each flush, so you know it's cleaning" or the cloying perfumes in soaps that "smell good enough to eat" and toilet paper dispensers rigged with a potent fumigating device that gives off "an extra burst of freshness with every spin."

The problems involved in selling something that cannot be detected with the senses have profound aesthetic consequences for advertising. Faced with the unglamorous task of persuading people to buy products whose function is purely negative, namely, to get rid of dirt, companies have devised an imaginary, exhibitionistic type of cleanliness that we can see and smell, a glittering mirage that makes an emphatic impression on our bodies and seduces us with its lustrous sheen and mirror-like polish, thus reassuring us that we have indeed gotten something for our money.

Companies have devised an imaginary, exhibitionistic type of cleanliness that we can see and smell.

Cleanness has, for instance, transformed the nose into the primary sensory organ for detecting sterility, the exquisitely sensitive instrument with which vigilant housekeepers sniff anxiously about their kitchens like bloodhounds. In an effort to make a freshly laundered blouse or a well-mopped kitchen appeal to our imaginations as vividly as a fetid pile of rags or a scuffed linoleum floor, advertisers promote the fiction that the essentially odorless state of cleanness has a distinct smell, that tidiness is as aromatic as dirtiness is malodorous, a fiction they construct by doctoring their detergents with over-powering fragrances that are "country fresh," "rain fresh," "pine fresh," "baby-powder fresh," "rose-petal fresh," and "fresh, like a cool mountain stream." Moreover, according to the false sensuality of the immaculate, we can not only smell cleanness but hear it (hair is described as "squeaky clean," sheets as "crisp and crackling") and, what's more, feel it (as in the case of such an irresistibly squeezable product as Charmin Toilet Paper or Ultra Snuggle Laundry Detergent, whose mascot is a fuzzy teddy bear that promises to make our clothing as downy soft as a plush animal). The fruit names of air fresheners ("Tropical Nectar," "Citrus Sunrise," "Green Apple") also suggest that cleanness appeals to the consumer's taste buds—a grotesque idea because even the most fastidious housewives refrain from licking their bathtubs and commodes after they have swabbed them out with lemon-scented Lysol or cherry Blossom Bowl cleaner. Consumerism has dramatically expanded the way we react to cleanness, making something as inconspicuous and unappealing as the antiseptic an all-encompassing sensual experience that triggers a barrage of vivid stimuli. By filling their bottles with potentially toxic additives that elicit tactile responses, manufacturers have complicated and therefore heightened our awareness of cleanness, which we no longer define as the mere absence of grime but as the *presence* of heady perfumes, garish dyes, and fabric softeners, the superfluous new prerequisites of hygiene. Such cosmetic features have lowered our tolerance for dirt and raised our standards of sanitation, spoiling our senses and enslaving us to products that have created entirely new ways of perceiving dust mops, wet sponges, and pails of soapy water, the banal munitions of housework.

> Heady perfumes, garish dyes, and fabric softeners have lowered our tolerance for dirt, spoiling our senses and enslaving us to products.

Among the prominent aesthetic features of cleanness are suds, a thick lather of foam that, while playing an insignificant role in the actual process of laundering clothes or washing dishes, plays a major psychological role in reminding the consumer that, beneath a detergent's frothy effervescence, a purifying chemical reaction is indeed occurring. In the first half of the century, billowing clouds of pink bubbles were essential to products like Super Suds, which gave "you suds in a flash" or Chipso Quick Suds, which produced, "not thin listless suds, [but] *lasting* suds," unlike their competitors' detergents which, rather than boiling over in torrents of sweet-smelling fizz, sank to the bottom of stagnant sinks full of cloudy water covered in an iridescent slick of oil. As ecology has made us more conscious of the destructive effects of phosphates on the environment, however, the whole aesthetic of cleanness has been revolutionized and soap bubbles are now inextricably linked in the consumer's mind with sinister culverts disgorging spates of industrial waste into dead lakes and rivers that catch fire. As a result, the once-buoyant image of the happy housewife plunged elbow-deep in suds has acquired such uncongenial undertones that advertisers have been forced to develop a more ecologically sensitive way of depicting the invisible process of cleaning: the old-fashioned soap bubble, which was pink, viscous, and semi-opaque, has given way to the new modern bubble, which is transparent and colorless. Moreover, old-fashioned suds were invariably depicted in a fleecy cloud that erupted out of sinks and washing machines, whereas contemporary bubbles travel alone, are relatively sparse, and, when represented at all, are often suspended in a wholesome-looking green fluid, replete with nurturing agricultural associations. In an ecologically correct age like our own, the soap itself has been laundered, reconstrued as an invigorating form of carbonation rather than as septic lather, thus severing subliminal connections of detergents with illegal spigots gushing effluents into aquifers.

While the aesthetic of cleanness usually operates by inventing sensual qualities for a state that has none, it also deliberately plays upon the imperceptibility of something it prefers us to imagine and intuit rather than to see: bacteria. The spurious sensuality of the aesthetic is thus complemented by its strategic use of the nonsensual, the invisible, the spectral threat that pervades the harmless-looking kitchen counter, which is in fact a petri dish swarming with staphylococcus and spirochetes, as in an ad for Lysol that presents a wide-eyed toddler reaching for a doorknob booby-trapped with pathogens: "One of the most dangerous things in your kitchen," the advertisement tells us, "may be something you can't even see." Similarly, Bounty, the Quilted Quicker Picker-Upper, shows a curious cherub standing before a counter on tippy toes about to snatch up a scouring pad marked with a warning as ominous as a skull and crossbones: "Pick up Bounty before somebody picks up a sponge full of germs." Cleanness is often a ghost story that instills alarm about an unspecified microbial menace, not by representing the threat but by toying with the elusiveness of the infinitesimal and thereby intensifying our fears of dangerous contaminants, much as tall tales told around campfires play upon the suggestiveness of empty rooms, showing us curtains that move, not who moved them, doors that slam, not who slammed them. The aesthetic of cleanness thus works in two contradictory ways: It endows nonphysical states with a superabundance of sensual qualities and it dwells upon the invisibility of things that are indeed real, conjuring up putatively normal kitchens that are actually death traps ready to ambush our offspring, who sicken and waste away from unseen hazards breeding on the knobs of our Kenmores and Hotpoints.

If bubbles have become cleaner and bacteria more threatening, skin has become more vulnerable. It is now described according to a new aesthetic that functions as a bizarre sort of meat tenderizer for a paperthin pelt that is constantly wrinkling, scarring, spotting, cracking, and breaking out into patches of acne. Early in the twentieth century, it was still possible to find advertisements for lye soap that could be used for either cleaning one's clothing or washing one's face, or for Zonite, a "nontoxic," "non-caustic," "non-burning" mouthwash that was so versatile that it could be used both for gargling and for scrubbing bathroom sinks, for shampooing hair and de-grouting shower stalls. In the nineteenth century, the distinction between organic and inorganic surfaces was far less categorical than it is in an age in which the face is portrayed as such a fragile ornament that only the most advanced techniques of dermatological conservation will keep it from shriveling up like a prune or developing double chins and pendulous jowls. Through the rhetoric of the cosmetics industry, consumerism grafts onto our bodies a second skin, a hypothetical membrane so soft, so easily damaged, that plain old soap has become altogether taboo, replaced by scientifically engineered "sanitizing systems" that "cleanse" rather than "clean," that protect, soothe, and mollify rather than corrode and cauterize, such as Dove's Sensitive Skin Moisturizing Body Wash, which "is not a soap" but "a soap-free formula." The portrayal of skin as a permeable substance has led to the false specialization of cleaning products and the extinction of such unthinkably adaptable commodities as Zonite, which emerged from a culture still capable of seeing the body as just another inert object, subject to the same slow descent into rusty dilapidation as our stoves and wringer washers. As the distinction between the organic and the inorganic became absolute in the course of the twentieth century and a separate aesthetic of morbid vulnerability was invented for skin, soap suddenly went upscale and was diversified into a plethora of "cleansing" formulae and "spa concepts" that "hydrate," "anti-oxidize," and "nourish," acting as taxidermic agents on an artificially sickly

> Zonite mouthwash was so versatile it could be used for shampooing hair and degrouting shower stalls.

This Duz detergent ad from 1950 sells an aesthetic that depends on suds and whiteness.

substance that seems to serve no protective function whatsoever but is as easily bruised and perforated as the delicate tissues inside of our bodies.

This same hypochondriacal aesthetic of the disintegrating human pelt, whose "moisture-retaining lipid barrier" can be protected only by rubbing it with "extra-strength emollients and humectants," is now even being extended to porcelain and enamel fixtures, which must contend not only with the ravages of ring-around-the-tub and "waxy yellow build-up" but also with the damage of scouring pads and carbolic acids that scrape, scratch, and erode "today's beautiful surfaces," unlike Soft Scrub, which "kill[s] bacteria without killing your tub." The neo-natal delicacy of the models featured in advertisements for Estee

Lauder's Multi-Action Complex or ReJuveness, which cures "hypertrophic and keloid scars," has been transferred to our sinks and floors, which are described as organisms whose "complexions" will become "sallow" unless they receive "the modern 'beauty treatment' for today's brilliant baths." The adaptability of cleaning products has been compromised, first by creating two separate and irreconcilable realms of the organic and the inorganic and then by paradoxically conflating the two, transforming the bathtub into a beleaguered odalisque who, like our "sleek new silky soft" hands and faces, must be "caressed" and "pampered" by a homemaker who functions less as a janitor than as a masseuse. Consumerism extends the metaphor of flesh to plastic, Lucite, Teflon, and tile and then creates new commodities that will be "gentle," "kind," "careful," and "whisper-soft" to cupboards and countertops that now demand from the housewife a fictional new level of diligence and caution to prevent dermatological disasters on sensitive toilet seats and nonstick skillets.

The new metaphors of cleanness work both ways, for if linoleum has become flesh, flesh has become linoleum. Manufacturers of antiperspirants in particular concoct a skin-substitute that mimics other synthetic household substances, whose dryness, durability, and stainlessness we have come to depend on. Advertisements for products like Ban, Mum, and Lady's Speed Stick create a sci-fi image of a plastic armpit, a type of prosthetic hinge that neither sweats nor smells but offers all of the water-repellent features of Formica. At the same time that consumerism conjures up images of artificially soft skin, it also fabricates a fantastic vision of an unnaturally hard body, a Teflon mannequin that embodies a dream of futuristic efficiency, as easily sprayed, wiped, and cleaned as a toaster or a microwave. This inorganic cyborg finds one of its most immodest expressions in commercials in which models obscenely bare their naked, depilated pits, defiantly holding them up to the camera for inspection in a way that is only slightly less exhibitionistic than the vixens who sprawl spread-eagled in pornographic magazines. The "underarm," to use the expression advertisers still bashfully prefer over the more uncouth "armpit," was the first taboo part of a woman's body to be represented in advertising, as in the case of Dew Deodorant, which throughout the 1920s featured on its bottle a simple line drawing of a figure in a sleeveless negligee exposing to us an area so forbidden that it was once euphemistically known as "the curve beneath a woman's arm." Far from being sexual in appeal, these seemingly salacious images of women lolling about bewitchingly, their arms thrown up over their heads, inviting the photographer to poke his nose into their bald, sapless pits, are in fact utterly sexless. They depict a consumer who has been liberated from her own excretions and achieved an ideal state of inhuman desiccation, proudly triumphing over her own messy physiology to become a kitchen counter in a dress, a large, unperforated surface with no pores and no orifices.

> These images depict a consumer who has been liberated from her own excretions.

Our confused and contradictory obsession with surfaces has been intensified by the radical changes that have occurred in the appearance of our houses in the course of the last hundred years. Virtually every object we own is now potentially a mirror, from our stainless steel convection ovens and our polished floors to our dinner plates ("I can see myself") and our flatware (a tiny image of an ecstatic bride and groom is reflected on the knife blade featured in one advertisement). Before the twentieth century, we lived in a world of unreflective surfaces, of flagstone floors and dark armoires that absorbed rather than transmitted the intermittent light cast by kerosene lamps that created at best small pools of incandescence hemmed in by shadows. The blazing hall of mirrors in which we now live has dramatically changed the way we perceive dirt, producing an omnipresent shine whose radiance is easily dulled by rust, abrasions, and patches of grime. When our eyes pass over a reflective surface, a lackluster smudge leaps out at us, whereas it tended to merge with its surroundings when most things were made out of wood or stone, materials now gilded with synthetic laminates that make everything as smooth as a billiard ball. This punitive new patina conscripts housewives in an endless war against the forces that tarnish the shellacked surfaces of rooms in which even the slightest diminishment of their bright, coercive luster triggers our instinct to clean. The pictorial convention in advertisements of the flashing star, the burst of celestial light that bounces like a streak of lightning off the mop in a commercial for linoleum floors or detonates on the crystal goblet drawn on the label of a dish detergent, is the fascist symbol of the new religion of shininess, whose disciples expend untold hours burnishing their acquisitions, coating them with polyurethane, rubbing them with Johnson's Wax, and polishing them with Lemon Pledge and Endust. New nonporous surfaces like enamel and plastic may be easy to clean, being free of crevices that catch dust, but they also must be cleaned more often to preserve easily dulled glazes that do not hide dirt but advertise it, making every spill, every stain, every spot painfully conspicuous.

> The pictorial convention in advertisements is the fascist symbol of the new religion of shininess.

Throughout the twentieth century, the aesthetic of cleanness has been simultaneously militaristic and ladylike. The rhetoric of germ warfare infuses descriptions of cleaning products, which depict housewives as soldiers on the front lines, "killing dirt," "cutting through stains," or "getting brutal with soiled clothing," as in an advertisement for Gain detergent that shows a laundress in a boxing glove clutching a pair of men's underwear ("Give your boxers some punch"); or in Procter & Gamble's classic advertisements for the "grime fighter" Mr. Clean, a muscle-bound pirate who, like a policeman, "arrests your dirt problem," knocking out grease with one fist and leaving a shine with the other. This saber-rattling of broomsticks and dust mops introduces narrative excitement into the drudgery of housework, transforming janitorial duties into an epic battle between an evil empire and a warrior princess, a virago who annihilates such foes as ring-around-the-collar and "those stubborn stains" that require "the added muscle" of Comet cleanser to make your house "company clean." Such hawkishness becomes more integral to the aesthetic of cleanness as housework becomes simpler and less time-consuming and women's confidence about the value of their domestic activities begins to wane. Consumerism compensates psychologically for the diminishment of women's historic custodial roles by reassuring them that, far from being mere squeezers of spray nozzles, pushers of self-cleaning oven buttons, and flickers of switches on garbage disposals, they are crackshot marksmen wielding potentially toxic, high-tech smart bombs. This martial aesthetic emerges only as women's roles begin to evolve beyond that of the nineteenth-century washerwoman, who had an unchallengeable sense of her own value and who therefore didn't need to be told that she was a commando in a hygienic crusade, a jihad against "greasy build-ups" and "those creepy odor-causing germs."

This lank-haired charwoman, her hands covered with calluses and chilblains, is the subtext of most cleaning advertisements from the first half of the twentieth century, which portray housewives as exemplars of daintiness and good taste, aristocrats who sought to dissociate themselves from the chores of the scullery maid. Manufacturers emphasized that their products would enable these women to save precious time for social engagements and, moreover, would spare them the disfiguring effects of house cleaning on skin unaccustomed to the indignities of labor. Companies created props for a Little Lady fantasy about imaginary duchesses who seldom crawled around on all fours, their heads stuck in toilet bowls, but maintained their feminine dignity as useless ornaments who affected a pose of patrician uninvolvement from such tasks as washing windows and scouring pots and pans. Over time, manufacturers invented ways of keeping the cleaner clean, of sparing her the ordeal of wallowing in grime, thus enabling her to remain immaculate even in the midst of sordid jobs in which, in maga-zine advertisements, she is shown in all of her manicured, well-coifed splendor, darting about the room joyfully flicking her feather duster over her family pho-tographs and porcelain figurines. The whole experience of cleaning has been re-designed in the course of the twentieth century so that we ourselves don't be-come dirty, the result in part of developments in cleaning products, most of which are disposable and do not themselves need to be cleaned, from "comfy-soft" paper towels and Sure & Natural Maxishields to Kleenex ColdCare tissues ("the yuck stops here") and Pampers that "clean perfect little tushies perfectly."

▶ **Analyzing the Text**

1. **Interrogating Assumptions.** What attitudes and assumptions make up what Harris refers to as the rhetoric or aesthetic of cleanness? Which of his examples supports his argument most powerfully? How does Harris's analysis of the rhetoric of cleanness challenge the third assumption in this chapter's introduc-tion that "technologies are neutral" (see p. 583)?

2. Harris observes that in the marketing of cleanness, the human body is increas-ingly objectified, while household objects are increasingly personified—de-scribed as having "skin" and other lifelike attributes. What are the larger impli-cations of this blurring of humans and technological objects?

3. How does Harris use examples to support his claim that, in the modern era, "The aesthetic of cleanness has been simultaneously militaristic and lady-like"? What are we to make of these two radically different value systems being used to create a unified message to consumers?

4. According to Harris, in what ways have the packaging and marketing of household cleaning products reinforced a gendered division of labor in household work?

Writing about Cultural Practices

5. Harris points out that we are sold cultural messages about "cleanness" through the use of specific language, metaphors, and stereotypes. Analyze the rhetoric used to sell one specific product over time. To begin, choose a product that has existed for at least 20 years and locate ads, packaging, or other marketing materials for the product from both the past and present. Write a critical analysis that compares the language, metaphors, and stereotypes from examples from the past with that of the present. As you draft, consider the following questions.

- How do the messages of the examples—past and present—compare? And what persuasive tactics does each example employ? Explain, drawing on details from your examples.

- What analogies or metaphors are used to portray and sell cleanness? How do the contemporary analogies or metaphors compare to those of the past? (For example, is the product marketed as a technological innovation? Is it imbued with human qualities?)

- What assumptions are built into these examples? For example, do they use stereotypes of women or other groups to sell the product? Do they convey particular messages about social class? How do these examples reflect the social attitudes of their time(s)?

ON THE WEB
For links to advertising archives, go to Chapter 7, bedfordstmartins.com/remix

Mixing Words and Images

ANNOTATING A TECHNOLOGICAL OBJECT

As the readings in this chapter point out, one of the challenges of investigating the impact or influence of technologies on our everyday lives is that technologies themselves often resist close examination. As the essays by Langdon Winner, Neil Postman, Malcolm Gladwell, and Daniel Harris, among others, suggest, most everyday technologies are designed to remain in the background—to be used like a tool and then set down when we are finished with them. However, these same essays demonstrate that, whether intentionally or unintentionally, technologies are anything but neutral.

But how do we examine the cultural dimensions of an everyday technology? Gustav Peebles provides one approach in his essay, "A Wicked Cheat" (see p. 617). Peebles constructs a visual essay by critically annotating an ATM receipt. An annotation is an explanatory or critical comment that is meant to deepen a reader's understanding about an object, book, or concept.

Following Peebles's example, identify a particular everyday technology and create an annotated visual essay. The purpose of this assignment is to investigate the cultural and political dimensions of your chosen technological object or device.

Researching Your Chosen Technology

- Begin by identifying several everyday technologies, including objects like bank slips or keyboards, that people either take for granted or do not tend to think of as technologies.

- Conduct research to learn the history of your chosen technology. What circumstances surround its creation? How does its design accommodate cultural contexts?

Annotating Your Chosen Technology

As you conduct your research, begin to draft annotations to accompany the image of your technology.

- When was this technology originally introduced? Who is its creator? Who are the intended consumers or users of this technology?

- What problem is this technology supposed to resolve? Or, what abilities is it supposed to give the consumer?

- How has this technology changed over time, and why? How do the cultural values and biases of the designers affect the ongoing use of this product?

- What are some unintended consequences—both positive and negative—of this technology? How does it affect the people who use it? How is it thought of by its users?

ON THE WEB
For help with these assignments, go to Chapter 7, **bedfordstmartins.com/remix**

Connecting to Culture Suggestions for Writing

1. Why Context Matters: Investigating Technology Use

Investigate how the contexts within which technologies are found or used impact human activity by becoming a kind of social anthropologist, studying one group's dynamics. To begin, identify one community group to which you belong. Groups might include a work environment, club, team, neighborhood group, or school.

After gaining the group's permission, you'll become a field observer, studying how the group uses technology. Pay attention to how the space where this group meets, the people, and the technology interact and influence each other. Take notes on the layout of the space, seating arrangements, discussion and interaction patterns among group members, lighting, noise levels, and the like. Draw a map of the space. Write a descriptive analysis of your observations that addresses the following questions.

- What are the issues, interests, and expectations of this group, and what roles do technological objects or practices play for them?
- How does context shape their technology use?
- How do the interests, values, and biases of the group influence their use of and attitudes toward technologies?

2. Interrogating Assumptions: Blogging as a Form of Critical Analysis

Create a weblog that is connected to a class weblog set up by your instructor. In your blog, respond to how the chapter readings question one or more of the assumptions described in the chapter introduction. They are

Technologies are machines.

Technologies bring progress or peril.

Technologies are neutral.

The goal is for you to develop your own series of principles for living with technology. Follow these guidelines for keeping a blog.

- Select a name for your blog and a visual design theme. (Options for themes are usually available on blog-hosting sites.) Before doing so, consider how the blog's name and design will affect your audience's responses to it.

- Write daily entries over a two-week period. These entries should respond to the chapter readings, exploring connections among them and allowing you to develop your own position(s) about the impact of technologies and technological practices on everyday life.

- Incorporate links in these entries. Consider linking to a classmate's blog entry or to a web page that provides an example that supports your point, defines a concept, or offers biographical information.
- In a private journal, record your thoughts about blogging. What's fun about it? What's difficult?

After two weeks, draft a critical analysis about the experience.

- How would you compare blogging to other kinds of writing? What is challenging about it? What is surprising? How will it affect the way you write in other contexts?
- How has blogging helped you think about how people read texts? How they write them? How texts function for different audiences?
- How has blogging enabled you to respond to claims from the chapter readings?

3. Tracing the Internet: Using the Wayback Machine

Analyze how one powerful form of technology—the Internet—has evolved over time. Choose one website and examine what the text and visual design reveal about its changing purposes, expectations, and audiences. To trace the history of a particular website, use the Wayback Machine (archive.org) to access archived versions of stored websites.

Choose a website that has existed for several years such as your school's website; a government agency's site; a major online publication, like a news organization; or a major web browser's site. To access the Wayback Machine's archive, type in your chosen URL and study the search results. After completing your research, write a critical analysis that considers these questions.

- How do the text and design of past and present versions of this website compare?
- What messages did the original design convey about the site's purpose? As the design changed, how has that message evolved?
- What assumptions do the designers make about the site's users? How have their assumptions changed over time?
- What details in the content and design of this site give you clues about the cultural assumptions or values of its designers? Of its users? How have they evolved?

Acknowledgments (continued from page iv)

Natalie Guice Adams and Pamela J. Bettis. "Cheerleader! An American Icon." From *Cheerleader! An American Icon* by Natalie Guice Adams and Pamela J. Bettis. Copyright © 2003 by Natalie Guice Adams and Pamela J. Bettis. Reprinted with permission of Palgrave Macmillan.

Gloria Anzaldúa. "How to Tame a Wild Tongue." From *Borderlands/La Frontera: The New Mestiza*. Copyright © 1987, 1999 by Gloria Anzaldúa. Reprinted by permission of Aunt Lute Books.

Kevin Arnovitz. "Virtual Dictionary." From *Slate.com*, Sept. 14, 2004. Reprinted by permission.

David Berreby. "It Takes A Tribe." From the *New York Times*, August 1, 2004. Copyright © 2004 by The New York Times Company. Reprinted by permission.

Charles Bowden. "Come and Get It: Last Meals and the People Who Eat Them." Originally appeared in *Aperture* 172 (Fall 2003). Copyright © 2003 *Aperture*. Reprinted by permission.

David Brooks. "Our Sprawling, Supersize Utopia." From *On Paradise Drive: How We Live Now (and Always Have) in the Future Tense* by David Brooks. Copyright © 2004 by David Brooks. Reprinted by permission of the author.

Ayana D. Byrd and Lori L. Tharps. "The Rituals of Black Hair Culture." Excerpt from *Hair Story: Untangling the Roots of Black Hair in America* by Ayana D. Byrd and Lori L. Tharps. Copyright © 2001 by Ayana D. Byrd and Lori L. Tharps. Reprinted by permission.

Sasha Cagen. "People Like Us: The Quirkyalones." From *The Quirkyalone: Loners Are the Last True Romantics* by Sasha Cagen. Copyright © 2000. Originally published in *Utne Reader*, October 2000. Reprinted by permission of the author.

Benedict Carey. "The Brain in Love." Published in the *Los Angeles Times*, December 16, 2002. Copyright © 2002 *The Los Angeles Times*. Reprinted by permission of TMS Reprints.

George Carlin. "On Where He Lives." Excerpt from *Brain Droppings* by George Carlin. Copyright © 1997 by Comedy Concepts, Inc. Reprinted by permission of Time Warner Book Group. All rights reserved.

Ana Castillo. "Bowing Out." First published in *Salon.com*, April 12, 1999. Copyright © 1999 by Ana Castillo. Reprinted by permission of Susan Bergholz Literary Services, New York. All rights reserved.

Samantha Daniels. "20 Simple Tips for the Perfect Date." From www.menshealth.com.

Alain de Botton. "Comedy." From *Status Anxiety* by Alain de Botton. Copyright © 2004 by Alain de Botton. Used by permission of Pantheon Books, a division of Random House, Inc.

Ellen DeGeneres. "On Celebrity." Excerpt from *My Point . . . and I Do Have One* by Ellen DeGeneres. Used by permission of Bantam Books, a division of Random House, Inc. "This Is How We Live." From *The Funny Thing Is . . .* by Ellen DeGeneres. Copyright © 1995 by Crazy Monkey, Inc. Reprinted with the permission of Simon & Schuster Adult Publishing Group. All rights reserved.

Annie Dillard. "Living Like Weasels." From *Teaching a Stone to Talk: Expeditions and Encounters* by Annie Dillard. Copyright © 1982 by Annie Dillard. Reprinted by permission of HarperCollins Publishers.

Bill Donahue and Peter Granser. "The Land of the Setting Sun." From *Mother Jones*, November/December 2002. Copyright © 2002 Bill Donahue.

Firoozeh Dumas. "The 'F Word.'" From *Funny in Farsi* by Firoozeh Dumas. Copyright © 2003 by Firoozeh Dumas. Used by permission of Villard Books, a division of Random House, Inc.

Jennifer Egan. "Love in the Time of No Time." From the *New York Times Magazine*, November 23, 2003. Copyright © 2003 Jennifer Egan. Reprinted by permission.

Carl Elliott. "American Bioscience Meets the American Dream." From *Better Than Well: American Medicine Meets the American Dream* by Carl Elliott. Copyright 2003 by Carl Elliott. Reprinted by permission.

Ellen Fein and Sherrie Schneider. "Don't Talk to a Man First." From *The Rules* by Ellen Fein and Sherrie Schneider. Copyright © 1995 by Ellen Fein and Sherrie Schneider. By permission of Warner Books, Inc.

Jennifer Bishop Fulwiler. "An Ode to Friendster." Posted on www.buttafly.com, October 27, 2003. © 2003 www.buttafly.com. Reprinted by permission of the author.

Janeane Garofalo. "On Her Teenage Years." Excerpt from *Feel This Book: An Essential Guide to Self-Empowerment, Spiritual Supremacy, and Sexual Satisfaction* by Ben Stiller and Janeane Garofalo. Copyright © 1999 by Smooth Daddy, Inc., and I Hate Myself Productions, Inc. Reprinted by permission of The Ballantine Publishing Group, a division of Random House, Inc.

Henry Louis Gates Jr. Excerpts from *America Behind the Color Line* by Henry Gates. Copyright © 2004 by Henry Louis Gates Jr. By permission of Warner Books, Inc.

Atul Gawande. "The Learning Curve." Excerpt from "Education of a Knife" in *Complications: A Surgeon's Notes on an Imperfect Science* by Atul Gawande. Copyright © 2002 by Atul Gawande. This essay first appeared in the *New Yorker* under the title "The Learning Curve." Reprinted by permission of Henry Holt and Company, LLC.

Malcolm Gladwell. "Smaller: The Disposable Diaper and the Meaning of Progress." First published in the *New Yorker*, November 2001. Copyright © 2001. Reprinted by permission of the author.

Ira Glass. "Howard and Me." From the *New York Times*, May 9, 2004. Copyright © 2004 Ira Glass. Reprinted by permission.

Lucy Grealy. "Masks." From *Autobiography of a Face* by Lucy Grealy. Copyright © 1994 by Lucy Grealy. Reprinted by permission of Houghton Mifflin Company. All rights reserved.

Daniel Harris. "Cleanness." From *Cute, Quaint, Hungry and Romantic: The Aesthetics of Consumerism* by Daniel Harris. Copyright © 2000 by Daniel Harris. Reprinted by permission of Basic Books, a member of Perseus Books, LLC.

Jason Hill. "Save Lives! Defy Nature!" First published on *Salon.com*, July 10, 2001. Copyright © 2001 Jason Hill. Reprinted by permission of the author.

Thomas Hine. "Looking Alive: The Objects Around Us." Posted on *Atlantic Monthly Online*, November 2001. © 2001. Reprinted by permission of the author. Thomas Hine, a writer on design, culture, and history, is the author of four books, including *Populuxe: The Look and Life of America in the 1950s and 1960s* and *I Want That! How We All Became Shoppers*.

bell hooks. "Baba and Daddy Gus." Originally titled "Inspired Eccentricity." From *Family* by Sharon Sloane Fiffer and Steve Fiffer, editors. Copyright © 1996 by bell hooks. Copyright © 1996 by Sharon Sloane Fiffer and Steve Fiffer. Reprinted by permission of Pantheon Books, a division of Random House, Inc.

John A. Hostetler. "The Amish Chapter." From *Amish Society*, pp. 47–52, 58–66. © 1968. Reprinted with permission of The Johns Hopkins University Press.

Hemal Jhaveri. "Queer Eye: Searching for a Real Gay Man." Posted on www.poppolitics.com. Copyright © 2003. Reprinted by permission of the author.

Jon Katz. "Petophilia." From *Slate.com*. April 8, 2004. © Slate, Inc. Reprinted by permission of United Media, Inc.

Garrison Keillor. "A Wobegon Holiday Dinner." Published in and by the *Washington Post (The Best of American Humor)*. Copyright © 1990 by Garrison Keillor. Reprinted by permission of Garrison Keillor/Prairie Home Productions.

Laura Kipnis. "Against Love." From *Against Love: A Polemic* by Laura Kipnis. Copyright © 2003 by Laura Kipnis. Used by permission of Pantheon Books, a division of Random House, Inc.

Michelle Lee. "The Fashion Victim's Ten Commandments." From *Fashion Victim: Our Love-Hate Relationship with Dressing, Shopping, and the Cost of Style* by Michelle Lee. Copyright © 2003 by Michelle Lee. Used by permission of Broadway Books, a division of Random House, Inc.

Caitlin Leffel. "The Look of Love: Wedding Announcements." Originally published in *Annabelle Magazine*, www.annabellemagazine.com. © 2004. Reprinted by permission of the author.

Andrew Leonard. "You Are Who You Know." This article first appeared in *Salon.com* at www.salon.com, June 15, 2004. Copyright © 2004. An online version remains in the *Salon* archives. Reprinted with permission.

Barry Lopez. "The American Geographies." From *About This Life: Journeys on the Threshold of Memory* by Barry Lopez. Copyright © 1998 by Barry Lopez. Reprinted by permission of Random House, Inc.

Wangari Maathai. "Trees for Democracy." From her Nobel lecture, 2004. Reprinted by permission.

Susan McCarthy. "On Immortality." First appeared in *Salon.com* at www.salon.com, March 30, 2000. Copyright © 2000 Salon.com. An online version remains in the *Salon* archives. Reprinted by permission.

Tom Magliozzi and Ray Magliozzi. "On Caging Wild Animals." Excerpt from *In Our Humble Opinion* by Tom Magliozzi and Ray Magliozzi. Copyright © 2000 by Tom Magliozzi and Ray Magliozzi. Used by permission of Perigee Books, an imprint of Penguin Group (USA) Inc.

John Margolies. "Amazing! Incredible! The Roadside Attraction." From *Fun Along the Road* by John Margolies. Copyright © 1998 by John Margolies. By permission of Little, Brown and Company, Inc.

Rosario Morales and Aurora Levins Morales. "Ending Poem." From *Getting Home Alive* by Aurora Levins Morales and Rosario Morales. Copyright © 1986 by Aurora Levins Morales and Rosario Morales. Reprinted by permission of Firebrand Books, Ann Arbor, Michigan.

Bonnie A. Nardi, Diane J. Schiano, Michelle Gumbrecht, and Luke Swartz. "Why We Blog." From *Communications of the ACM* 47.12 (December 2004). Copyright © 2004. Reprinted by permission.

David Nasaw. "The Pernicious 'Moving Picture' Abomination." Copyright © David Nasaw. Reprinted by permission of The Wylie Agency, on behalf of the author.

"New Technological Breakthrough to Fix Problems of Previous Breakthrough." From www.theonion.com. Copyright © 2001 by Onion, Inc. Reprinted with permission.

Kathleen Norris. "Can You Tell the Truth in a Small Town?" From *Dakota: A Spiritual Geography* by Kathleen Norris. Copyright © 1993 by Kathleen Norris. Reprinted by permission of Houghton Mifflin Company. All rights reserved.

Susan Orlean. "Lifelike." Originally published in the *New Yorker*, June 9, 2003. Copyright © 2003 by Susan Orlean. Reprinted by permission of the author.

Gamaliel Padilla. "Moshing Etiquette." First published in *Dig*, the monthly California State University magazine (Long Beach).

Clarence Page. "Should We Still Be Involved in Space Exploration?" From the *Chicago Tribune*, February 5, 2003. Copyright © 2003. Reprinted by permission.

Gustav Peebles. "A Wicked Cheat." Copyright © 2004 by *Harper's Magazine*. All rights reserved. Reproduced from the June issue by special permission.

Richard Pillsbury. "Thoroughly Modern Dining: A Look at America's Changing Celebration Dinner." From *Phi Kappa Phi Forum* 82.3 (Summer 2002). Copyright © by Richard Pillsbury. By permission of the publishers.

Steven Pinker. "Against Nature." First published in *Discover* magazine, October 1997. Copyright © 1997. Reprinted by permission of the author.

Neil Postman. "Invisible Technologies." From *Technology* by Neil Postman. Copyright © 1992 by Neil Postman. Used by permission of Alfred A. Knopf, a division of Random House, Inc.

Jennifer Pozner. "The Unreal World." First published in *Ms.*, 2004. Copyright © 2004. Reprinted by permission of the author.

Laura Randall. "Things You Only Do in College." From the *New York Times*, August 1, 2004. Copyright © 2004 by The New York Times Company. Reprinted by permission.

Chris Rock. "On Marriage." Excerpts published online from *Cosmopolitan* 223 (October 1997), n4 pl 62(2), and blackfilm.com.

Richard Rodriguez. "'Blaxicans' and Other Reinvented Americans." Copyright © 2003 by Richard Rodriguez. Reprinted by permission of Georges Borchardt, Inc., Literary Agency.

Katie Roiphe. "Profiles Encouraged." From *Brill's Content*, December 2000/January 2001. Copyright © 2000 by Katie Roiphe. Reprinted by permission of William Morris Agency, LLC, on behalf of the author.

Pete Rojas. "Bootleg Culture." This article first appeared in *Salon.com* at www.salon.com, August 1, 2002. Copyright © 2002. An online version remains in the *Salon* archives. Reprinted with permission.

Christine Rosen. "You—Only Better." First published in the *New Atlantis* 5 (Spring 2004), pp. 19–35. Copyright © 2004. Reprinted by permission.

Scott Russell Sanders. "Looking at Women." Originally appeared in the *Georgia Review*, 1989. Reprinted by permission of Virginia Kidd Literary Agency.

Eric Schlosser. "Why McDonald's Fries Taste So Good." From *Fast Food Nation: The Dark Side of the All-American Meal* by Eric Schlosser. Copyright © 2001 by Eric Schlosser. Excerpted and reprinted by permission of Houghton Mifflin Company. All rights reserved. First published in the *Atlantic Monthly*, January 2001.

David Sedaris. "The End of the Affair." From *Dress Your Family in Corduroy and Denim* by David Sedaris. Copyright © 2004 by David Sedaris. "On Being a Macy's Christmas Elf." Excerpt from "Santaland Diaries" from *Holidays on Ice* by David Sedaris. Copyright © 1997 by David Sedaris. By permission of Little, Brown and Company, Inc.

Celia A. Shapiro. "Last Suppers." Reprinted by permission.

Jenn Shreve. "A Fitting Memorial: The Commemorative T-Shirt." First published on *Slate.com*, 2003. Copyright © 2003 Jenn Shreve. Reprinted by permission of the author.

Dave Singleton. Excerpt from *The MANdates: 25 Real Rules for Successful Gay Dating* by Dave Singleton. Copyright © 2004 by Dave Singleton. Used by permission of Three Rivers Press, a division of Random House, Inc.

Brent Staples. "The Star-Spangled Hard Hat." From the *New York Times*, November 9, 2001. Copyright © 2001 by The New York Times Company. Reprinted by permission.

Adam Sternbergh. "Britney Spears: The Pop Tart in Winter." First published on *Slate.com*, October 28, 2004. Copyright © 2004 by Adam Sternbergh. Reprinted by permission.

David Sterritt. "Face of An Angel." First published in the *Christian Science Monitor*, July 11, 2003 www.csmonitor.com. © 2003 The Christian Science Monitor. Reproduced with permission. All rights reserved.

Jon Stewart. "Commencement Address." Reprinted by permission of William and Mary College.

Andrew Sullivan. "The 'He' Hormone." First appeared in the *New York Times*. Copyright © 2000 by Andrew Sullivan. Reprinted with the permission of the Wylie Agency Inc.

Lewis Thomas. "On Cloning a Human Being." From *The Medusa and the Snail* by Lewis Thomas. Copyright © 1974, 1975, 1976, 1977, 1978, 1979 by Lewis Thomas. Used by permission of Viking Penguin, a division of Penguin Group (USA) Inc.

Russell Thornton. "What the Census Doesn't Count." First published in the *New York Times*, March 23, 2001. Copyright © 2001 by The New York Times Company. Reprinted by permission.

Mim Udovitch. "A Secret Society of the Starving." Originally published in the *New York Times Magazine*, September 8, 2002. Copyright © 2002 by The New York Times Company. Reprinted by permission.

Ellen Ullman. "The Museum of Me." First published in *Harper's Magazine*, May 2000. © 2000 by Ellen Ullman. Reprinted by permission of the author.

Sarah Vowell. "Pop-A-Shot." From *The Partly Cloudy Patriot* by Sarah Vowell. Copyright © 2002 by Sarah Vowell. Reprinted with the permission of Simon & Schuster Adult Publishing Group. All rights reserved.

Jill Walker. "Weblog: A Definition." Entry in *Routledge Encyclopedia of Narrative Theory*, 2005. Reprinted by permission.

Emily White. "High School's Secret Life." From *Fast Girls: Teenage Tribes and the Myth of the Slut* by Emily White. Copyright © 2002 by Emily White. Reprinted with the permission of Scribner, an imprint of Simon & Schuster Adult Publishing Group.

Kathy Wilson. "Dude Looks Like a Lady." From *Your Negro Tour Guide* by Kathy Wilson. Copyright © 2004 Kathy Y. Wilson. Reprinted by permission of Emmis Books.

Langdon Winner. "Technological Somnambulism." First published in *The Whale and the Reactor* by Langdon Winner. Reprinted by permission of The University of Chicago Press.

Additional Art Credits

Page 2: Photo courtesy of Casimiro Naranjo/*Corpus Christi Caller-Times.*

Page 17: Mean Girls poster used by permission of Paramount Pictures/Kobal Collection.

Page 18: Janeane Garofalo photo © Getty Images/Evan Agostini.

Pages 40–41: Vintage photobooth photos from the collection of Babbette Hines; modern photobooth photos courtesy of Andrea Scher/www.superherodesigns.com.

Page 84: Nike billboard photo © Leasa Burton.

Pages 118–19: Greek vase photo © Getty Images/Hutton Archive; Greek women's track team photo used with permission of IOC Information Management Department/Images Section.

Page 144: George Carlin photo courtesy of Getty Images/Kevin Winter.

Page 172: Candied apples © Royalty-Free/Corbis.

Page 229: David Sedaris photo © Getty Images/Ralph Orlowski.

Page 230: Dyngus Day stamp courtesy of the Polish Post Philatelic Center.

Pages 246–47: Vietnam Veterans Memorial photo © Getty Images/Spencer Platt; WTC Tribute in Light photo © Getty Images/Don Murray.

Page 273: P. Diddy photo courtesy of Getty Images/Frank Micelotta.

Page 290: Vintage valentine courtesy of Hillstock LLC.

Page 315: Chris Rock photo courtesy of Getty Images/Sean Gallup.

Page 374: Ellen DeGeneres photo courtesy of Getty Images/Vince Bucci.

Page 393: Laura Bush photo courtesy of Getty Images/Shah Marai.

Pages 436–37: The Partridge Family and the Osbournes photos courtesy of the Everett Collection, Inc.

Page 462: Ivory soap photo courtesy of Rachel Epstein/The Image Works.

Page 483: Two-headed chick photo courtesy of Sarina Brewer/www.CustomCreatureTaxidermy.com.

Page 526: Jonathan Swift © Bettmann/Corbis.

Pages 530–31: Phrenology chart © Mary Evans Picture Library/The Image Works; MRI © Royalty-Free/Corbis.

Page 568: Tom Magliozzi photo © Getty Images/Richard Howard.

Page 574: Zipper ads photographed by Jonathan Wallen, from *Advertising in America: The First 200 Years* (Harry N. Abrams, Inc., 1990).

Pages 600–1: Nineteenth-century washing machine ad © Bettmann/Corbis; Sears/Kenmore webscreen © 2005 Sears Brands, LLC.

Page 628: Jill Walker's definition of "weblog" reproduced with permission of Jill Walker and *Routledge Encyclopedia of Narrative Theory,* 2005.

Page 658: Steve Martin photo courtesy of Greg Gorman Photography.

Page 670: Typewriter photo © Jason Reblando.

Index of Authors and Titles